L = quantity of land (Chapter 6)
L = real money demand function
M = money supply
$MC(I)$ = marginal cost of investment
$MB(I)$ = marginal benefit of investment
MPC = marginal propensity to consume
MP_K = marginal product of capital
MP_N = marginal product of labor
$MRS_{x,y}$ = marginal rate of substitution of x for y
$MRT_{x,y}$ = marginal rate of transformation of x for y
MU_c = marginal utility of consumption
N = employment
NFP = net factor payments
NL = number not in the labor force
NX = net exports
P = price level
P^* = foreign price level
PPF = production possibilities frontier
R = nominal interest rate
S = aggregate savings
S^p = private savings
S^g = government savings
T = current taxes
$TOT_{a,b}$ = terms of trade or world price of a in terms of b
TR = aggregate transfers from the government
U = utility function (Chapters 4 and 15)
U = unemployment (Chapter 16)
V = present value of profits (Chapter 9)
V = velocity of money (Chapter 10)
$V_e(w)$ = welfare of a worker with a job paying real wage w
V_u = welfare of an unemployed worker
W = nominal wage
Y = aggregate real income
Y^d = disposable income
Y^T = trend level of output
π = profits

Notes

- Primes denote future variables, for example C' denotes the future level of aggregate consumption.
- A superscript $-$ denotes variables for the previous period, for example B^- are bonds acquired in the previous period in Chapter 10.
- A superscript d denotes demand, for example N^d is labor demand.
- A superscript s denotes supply, for example N^s is labor supply.
- In Chapters 6 and 7, lower case letters are variables in per-worker terms.

CONGRATULATIONS!

As a student purchasing Williamson's *Macroeconomics*, Second Edition, you are entitled to a prepaid subscription to premium services on our Companion Website at **www.aw-bc.com/williamson**.

The duration of your subscription is 6 months.

To activate your prepaid subscription:

1. Launch your Web browser and go to **www.aw-bc.com/williamson**

2. When you select a protected section of the Web site, you will be asked to log in.

3. Follow the instructions on the screen to register yourself as a new user. Your pre-assigned Access Code is located underneath the scratch-off area below:

Access Code:

4. During registration, you will choose a personal Login Name and Password for use in logging into the Web site.

5. Once your personal Login Name and Password are confirmed, you can begin using the Web site.

IMPORTANT

The Access Code on this page can only be used to establish a subscription to the *Macroeconomics*, Second Edition Companion Website. The subscription is valid for six months upon activation, and is not transferable. If this Access Code has already been scratched off, it may no longer be valid. If this is the case, you can purchase a subscription by going to **http://www.aw-bc.com/williamson**.

MACROECONOMICS

second edition

Stephen D. Williamson
University of Iowa

PEARSON

Addison
Wesley

Boston San Francisco New York
London Toronto Sydney Tokyo Singapore Madrid
Mexico City Munich Paris Cape Town Hong Kong Montreal

Editor-in-Chief: Denise Clinton
Acquisitions Editor: Adrienne D'Ambrosio
Senior Project Manager: Mary Clare McEwing
Managing Editor: Jim Rigney
Senior Production Supervisor: Katherine Watson
Design Manager: Regina Hagen Kolenda
Cover Designer: Regina Hagen Kolenda
Digital Assets Manager: Jason Miranda
Marketing Manager: Deb Meredith
Manufacturing Manager: Hugh Crawford
Project Coordination, Composition and Illustration: Nesbitt Graphics, Inc.
Cover Photo: © Masterfile

Library of Congress Cataloging-in-Publication Data
    Williamson, Stephen D.
        Macroeconomics / Stephen D. Williamson.--2nd ed.
            p. cm.
        ISBN 0-321-24093-6
        1. Macroeconomics.   I. Title.

    HB172.5 .W55 2005
    339--dc22   2004003023

For information on obtaining permission for the use of material from this work, please submit a written request to Pearson Education, Inc., 75 Arlington St., Suite 300, Boston, MA 02116 or fax your request to (617) 848-7047.

ISBN: 0-321-24093-6

1 2 3 4 5 6 7 8 9 10—CRW—08 07 06 05 04

BRIEF CONTENTS

CONTENTS

PART II   A One-Period Model of
the Macroeconomy   89

PART III   Economic Growth   165

Chapter 6   Economic Growth: Malthus and Solow   167

Chapter 9   A Real Intertemporal Model with Investment   293

PART V   Money and Business Cycles   347

Chapter 10   A Monetary Intertemporal Model: The Neutrality of Money   349

PART VI International Macroeconomics   463

Chapter 13   International Trade in Goods and Assets   465

Chapter 14   Money in the Open Economy   499

PART VII   Money, Banking, Unemployment, and Inflation   533

Chapter 15   Money, Inflation, and Banking   535

Chapter 16   Unemployment: Search and Efficiency Wages   569

PREFACE

This book follows a modern approach to macroeconomics by building macroeconomic models from microeconomic principles. As such, it is consistent with the way that macroeconomic research is conducted today.

This approach has three advantages. First, it allows deeper insights into economic growth processes and business cycles, the key topics in macroeconomics. Second, an emphasis on microeconomic foundations better integrates the study of macroeconomics with approaches that students learn in courses in microeconomics and in field courses in economics. Learning in macroeconomics and microeconomics thus becomes mutually reinforcing, and students learn more. Third, in following an approach to macroeconomics that is consistent with current macroeconomic research, students will be better prepared for advanced study in economics.

Structure

The text begins in Part I with an introduction and study of measurement issues. Chapter 1 describes the approach taken in the book and the key ideas that students should take away. It previews the important issues that will be addressed throughout the book, along with some recent issues in macroeconomics, and the highlights of how these will be studied. Measurement is discussed in Chapters 2 and 3, first with regard to gross domestic product, prices, savings, and wealth, and then with regard to business cycles. In Chapter 3, we develop a set of key business cycle facts that will be used throughout the book, particularly in Chapters 11 and 12 where we investigate how alternative business cycle theories fit the facts.

Our study of macroeconomic theory begins in Part II. In Chapter 4, we study the behavior of consumers and firms in detail. In the one-period model developed in Chapter 5, we use the approach of capturing the behavior of all consumers and all firms in the economy with a single representative consumer and a single representative firm. The one-period model is used to show how changes in government spending and total factor productivity affect aggregate output, employment, consumption, and the real wage.

With a basic knowledge of static macroeconomic theory from Part II, we proceed in Part III to the study of economic growth. In Chapter 6 we discuss a set of economic growth facts which are then used to organize our thinking in the context of models of economic growth. The first growth model we examine is a Malthusian growth model, consistent with the late-18th century ideas of Thomas Malthus. The Malthusian model predicts well the features of economic growth in the world before the Industrial

Revolution, but it does not predict the sustained growth in per capita incomes that occurred in advanced countries after 1800. The Solow growth model, which we examine next, does a good job of explaining some important observations concerning modern economic growth. Finally, Chapter 6 explains growth accounting, which is an approach to disentangling the sources of growth. In Chapter 7 we discuss income disparities across countries in light of the predictions of the Solow model, and introduce a model of endogenous growth.

In Part IV, we first use the theory of consumer and firm behavior developed in Part II to construct (in Chapter 8) a two-period model that can be used to study consumption–savings decisions and the effects of government deficits on the economy. The two-period model is then extended to include investment behavior in the real intertemporal model of Chapter 9. This model will then serve as the basis for much of what is done in the remainder of the book.

In Part V, we include monetary phenomena in the real intertemporal model of Chapter 9, so as to construct a monetary intertemporal model. This model is used in Chapter 10 to examine the effects of changes in the money supply on the economy. Then, in Chapters 11 and 12, we study equilibrium theories of the business cycles as well as traditional Keynesian business cycle theory. These theories are compared and contrasted, and we examine how alternative business cycle theories fit the data and how they help us to understand recent business cycle behavior in the United States.

Part VI is devoted to international macroeconomics. In Chapter 13, the models of Chapters 5 and 9 are used to show what benefits accrue from international trade, how changes in the relative prices of imports and exports affect the economy, and what determines the current account surplus. Then, in Chapter 14, we show how exchange rates are determined, and we investigate the roles of fiscal and monetary policy in an open economy that trades goods and assets with the rest of the world.

Finally, Part VII examines some important topics in macroeconomics. In Chapter 15, we study in more depth the role of money in the economy, the effects of money growth on inflation and aggregate economic activity, banking, and deposit insurance. Then, in Chapter 16, we study the determinants of unemployment and two models of unemployment: the search model and the efficiency wage model. In Chapter 17, we see how central banks can cause inflation, either because they do not correctly understand the relationship between real macroeconomic activity and inflation, or because they cannot commit themselves to a low-inflation policy. We also demonstrate in this chapter how inflation has been reduced over the last twenty years in the United States, New Zealand, and Hong Kong.

Features

Several key features enhance the learning process and illuminate critical ideas for the student. The intent is to make macroeconomic theory transparent, accessible, and relevant.

Real-World Applications.   Applications to current and historical problems are emphasized throughout in two running features. The first is a set of "Theory Confronts the Data" sections, which show how macroeconomic theory comes to life in matching (or sometimes falling short of matching) the characteristics of real-world economic data. A sampling of some of these sections includes the effects of the increase in government spending during World War II, the impact of the tax-withholding reductions implemented by President Bush in 1992, the macroeconomic impact of increases in energy prices, and the macroeconomic effects of the events of September 11, 2001. The second running feature is a series of "Macroeconomics in Action" boxes. These real-world applications relating directly to the theory encapsulate ideas from front-line research in macroeconomics and the history of economic thought, and they aid students in understanding the core material. For example, some of the subjects examined in these boxes are the pitfalls of macroeconomic forecasting, Henry Ford and technological change, East Asian growth miracles, and the financing of social security.

Art Program.   Graphs and charts are plentiful in this book, as visual representations of macroeconomic models that can be manipulated to derive important results, and for showing the key features of important macro data in applications. To aid the student, graphs and charts use a consistent two-color system that encodes the meaning of particular elements in graphs and of shifts in curves.

End-of-Chapter Summary and List of Key Terms.   Each chapter wraps up with a bullet-point summary of the key ideas contained in the chapter, followed by a glossary of the chapter's key terms. The key terms are listed in the order in which they appear in the chapter, and they are highlighted in bold typeface where they first appear.

Questions for Review.   These questions are intended as self-tests for students after they have finished reading the chapter material. The questions relate directly to ideas and facts covered in the chapter, and answering them will be straightforward if the student has read and comprehended the chapter material.

Problems.   The end-of-chapter problems will help the student in learning the material and applying the macroeconomic models developed in the chapter. These problems are intended to be challenging and thought-provoking.

"Working with the Data" Problems.   These problems guide the student in making use of the database that can be accessed on-line from the web site accompanying this text at www.aw-bc.com/williamson. The database is a comprehensive set of macroeconomic data, which can be used to understand the chapter material and to gain a deeper knowledge of macroeconomic data and phenomena.

Notation.   For easy reference, definitions of all variables used in the text are contained on the end papers.

Mathematics and Mathematical Appendix.   In the body of the text, the analysis is mainly graphical, with some knowledge of basic algebra required; calculus is not used. However, for students and instructors who desire a more rigorous treatment of the material in the text, a mathematical appendix develops the key models and results more formally, assuming a basic knowledge of calculus and the fundamentals of mathematical economics. The Mathematical Appendix also contains problems on this more advanced material.

Flexibility

This book was written to be user-friendly for instructors with different preferences and with different time allocations. The core material that is recommended for all instructors is the following:

Chapter 1. Introduction
Chapter 2. Measurement
Chapter 3. Business Cycle Measurement
Chapter 4. Consumer and Firm Behavior: The Work–Leisure Decision and Profit Maximization
Chapter 5. A Closed-Economy One-Period Macroeconomic Model
Chapter 8. A Two-Period Model: The Consumption–Savings Decision and Ricardian Equivalence
Chapter 9. A Real Intertemporal Model with Investment

Some instructors find measurement issues uninteresting, and may choose to omit parts of Chapter 2, though at the minimum instructors should cover the key national income accounting identities. Parts of Chapter 3 can be omitted if the instructor chooses not to emphasize business cycles, but there are some important concepts introduced here that are generally useful in later chapters, such as the meaning of correlation and how to read scatter plots and time series plots.

Chapters 6 and 7 introduce economic growth at an early stage, in line with a modern emphasis in macreconomics on growth over business cycles. However, Chapters 6 and 7 are essentially self-contained, and nothing is lost from leaving growth until later in the sequence—for example, after the business cycle material in Chapters 11 and 12. Though the text has an emphasis on microfoundations, Keynesian analysis receives a balanced treatment. For example, we study a Keynesian sticky wage business cycle model in Chapter 10, and also examine a Keynesian coordination failure model in Chapter 11. Chapter 15 also looks at the efficiency wage model. Those instructors who choose to ignore Keynesian analysis can do so without any difficulty. Instructors can choose to emphasize economic growth or business cycle analysis, or they can give their course an international focus. As well, it is possible to deemphasize monetary factors. As a guide, the text can be adapted as follows:

Focus on Equilibrium Models.   Omit Chapter 12 (Keynesian Business Cycle Theory: The Sticky Wage Model).

Focus on Economic Growth.   Include Chapters 6 and 7, and consider dropping Chapters 11 and 12, depending on time available.

Focus on Business Cycles.   Drop Chapter 6 and 7, and include Chapters 10, 11, and 12.

International Focus.   Chapters 13 and 14 can be moved up in the sequence. Chapter 13 can follow Chapter 9, and Chapter 14 can follow Chapter 10.

Advanced Mathematical Treatment.   Add material as desired from the Mathematical Appendix.

What's New in the Second Edition

The first edition of *Macreconomics* had an excellent reception in the market. In the second edition, I build on the strengths of the first while modifying the sequencing of chapters, streamlining some topics, and adding material, in line with the interests of students and instructors. As well, applications have been added to help students understand macroeconomic events that have occurred since the first edition was written, and the end-of-chapter problems have been expanded. In more detail, here are the highlights of the revision.

- There are now two chapters on economic growth–Chapters 6 and 7. Growth is now treated earlier in the sequence than is the case in most intermediate macroeconomics texts. Our sequencing conforms to the modern emphasis in macroeconomics on growth relative to business cycles, and allows the instructor to engage the students early in topics that they will find exciting. Chapter 6 opens with a discussion of the important facts concerning economic growth, which are used to frame the study of economic growth models and their predictions. Chapter 6 then moves on to a treatment of a Malthusian growth model, which to my knowledge is unique in the intermediate macro textbook market. The Malthusian model is an important step in the history of economic thought, and it fits well with world growth experience before the Industrial Revolution. Further, it provides a good warmup in dynamic macroeconomics before students see the more complicated Solow model, the primary workhorse of modern macroeconomic growth theory. Chapter 7 is devoted to the study of income disparity among countries and modern endogenous growth theory.

- The discussion of the Ricardian equivalence theorem in Chapter 8 has been streamlined, and a broader discussion of fiscal policy issues has been added. In particular, the financing of social security is studied in detail.

- The treatment of monetary issues has been streamlined and improved. Chapter 10 contains a more straightforward exposition of the monetary intertemporal model, with more advanced material on the role of money, money growth, banking, banking panics, and deposit insurance in Chapter 15.

- New features help the student understand how to apply macroeconomics to events that have occurred since the first edition was published. New "Theory Confronts the Data" features include "The New Economy Becomes Old Again," and "9/11 As a Sectoral Shock," and new "Macroeconomics in Action" boxes include "The Transition from Pay-As-You-Go to Fully-Funded Social Security" and "Bank Failures and Banking Panics in the United States and Canada."

- New end-of-chapter problems have been added, and there are now problems in the Mathematical Appendix.
- "Working with the Data" sections at the end of each chapter allow students to work with our comprehensive online database. By working through these problems, students will learn more about economic data and how to use them, and will deepen their knowledge of macroeconomic theory and issues.

Supplements

The following materials that accompany the main text will enrich the intermediate macroeconomics course for instructors and students alike.

Instructor's Manual/Test Bank. Written by Stephen McCafferty of Ohio State University, the Instructor's Manual/Test Bank provides strong instructor support. The Instructor's Manual portion contains sections on Teaching Goals, which give an aerial view of the chapters; classroom discussion topics, which explore lecture-launching ideas and questions; chapter outlines; and solutions to all Questions for Review and Problems found in the text. The Test Bank portion contains multiple-choice questions and answers. The Test Bank is also available in Test Generator Software (TestGen-EQ with QuizMaster-EQ). Fully networkable, this software is available for Windows and Macintosh. Test-Gen-EQ's friendly graphical interface enables instructors to easily view, edit, and add questions; export questions to create tests; and print tests in a variety of fonts and forms. Search and sort features let the instructor quickly locate questions and arrange them in a preferred order. QuizMaster-EQ automatically grades the exams, stores results on a disk, and allows the instructor to view or print a variety of reports. The Instructor's Manual and Test Bank can be found on the instructor's portion of the Web site accompanying this book at www.aw-be.com/williamson.

Study Guide. Prepared by John Stinespring of Colorado College and Paul Zak of Claremont Graduate University, the Study Guide contains true/false questions, short-answer questions, and multiple-choice questions, with complete answers—many presented as worked solutions. The Study Guide can be found on the Web site accompanying this text at www.aw-be.com/williamson.

Instructor's Resource Disk. The Instructor's Resource Disk includes Microsoft Power-Point files of key figures from the text, the Computerized Test Bank files, the Instructor's Manual, and the Test Bank Microsoft Word files.

Acknowledgments

Special thanks go to Denise Clinton, Adrienne D'Ambrosio, Mary Clare McEwing, Katherine Watson, Deborah Meredith, Regina Hagen Kolenda, and all the people at Addison Wesley who provided so much help and encouragement. I am also indebted to Dave Andolfatto, Scott Baier, Ken Beauchemin, Edward Kutsoati, Kuhong Kim, Young Sik Kim, Mike Loewy, B. Ravikumar, Ping Wang, and Bradley Wilson, who used early versions of the manuscript in their classes. Key critical input was also provided by the following reviewers, who helped immensely in improving the manuscript:

Terry Alexander, Iowa State University; Alaa AlShawa, University of Western Ontario; David Aschauer, Bates College; Irasema Alonso, University of Rochester; David Andolfatto, Simon Fraser University; Scott Baier, Clemson University; Ken Beauchemin, State University of New York at Albany; Joydeep Bhattacharya, Iowa State University; Michael Binder, University of Maryland; Marco Cagetti, University of Virginia; Mustafa Caglayan, University of Liverpool; Gabriele Camera, Purdue University; Leo Chan, University of Kansas; Troy Davig, College of William and Mary; Matthias Doepke, UCLA; Ayse Y. Evrensel, Portland State University; Timothy Fuerst, Bowling Green State University; Lisa Geib-Gundersen, University of Maryland; John Graham, Rutgers University; Yu Hsing, Southeastern Louisiana University; Petur O. Jonsson, Fayetteville State University; Bryce Kanago, University of Northern Iowa; George Karras, University of Illinois; John Knowles, University of Pennsylvania; Hsien-Feng Lee, Taiwan University; Michael Loewy, University of South Florida; Kathryn Marshall, Ohio State University; Steve McCafferty, Ohio State University; Oliver Morand, University of Connecticut; Douglas Morgan, University of California, Santa Barbara; Giuseppe Moscarini, Yale University; Daniel Mulino, doctoral candidate, Yale University; Liwa Rachel Ngai, London School of Economics; Christopher Otrok, University of Virginia; Stephen Parente, University of Illinois at Urbana-Champaign; Prosper Raynold, Miami University; Kevin Reffett, Arizona State University; Robert J. Rossana, Wayne State University; Thomas Tallarini, Carnegie Mellon University; Paul Wachtel, Stern School of Business, New York University; Ping Wang, Vanderbilt University; Bradley Wilson, University of Alabama; Paul Zak, Claremont Graduate University; and Christian Zimmermann, University of Connecticut.

I also wish to thank the economists who worked on the supplements that accompany this text and who did such a fine job: Stephen McCafferty of Ohio State University (Instructor's Manual/Test Bank author), John Stinespring of Colorado College (Study Guide co-author), and Paul Zak of Claremont Graduate University (Study Guide co-author). Finally, I wish to thank those economists who specifically reviewed material on economic growth for this edition: Kenneth Beauchemin, State University of New York at Albany; William Blankenau, Kansas State University; Matthias Doepke, UCLA; Igor Livshits, University of Western Ontario; Christopher Otrok, University of Virginia; and Stephen Parente, University of Illinois at Urbana-Champaign.

Stephen D. Williamson

To

my mother and father

About the Author

Stephen Williamson is the Chester A. Phillips Professor of Financial Economics in the Department of Economics, Tippie College of Business, University of Iowa, and is a Visiting Scholar at the Federal Reserve Bank of Richmond. He received a B.Sc. in Mathematics and an M.A. in Economics from Queen's University in Kingston, Canada, and his Ph.D. from the University of Wisconsin–Madison. He has held academic positions at Queen's University and the University of Western Ontario, and has worked as an economist at the Federal Reserve Bank of Minneapolis and the Bank of Canada. Professor Williamson has been an academic visitor at the Federal Reserve Banks of Atlanta, Cleveland, Kansas City, Minneapolis, and the Board of Governors of the Federal Reserve System. He has also been a long-term visitor at the London School of Economics; the University of Edinburgh; Tilburg University, the Netherlands; and Victoria University of Wellington, New Zealand. Professor Williamson has published scholarly articles in the *American Economic Review,* the *Journal of Political Economy,* the *Quarterly Journal of Economics,* the *Review of Economic Studies,* the *Journal of Economic Theory,* and the *Journal of Monetary Economics,* among other prestigious economics journals.

The Addison-Wesley Series in Economics

Introduction and Measurement Issues

Part I contains an introduction to macroeconomic analysis and a description of the approach in this text of building useful macroeconomic models based on microeconomic principles. We discuss the key ideas that are analyzed and some current issues that the macroeconomic theory developed in Parts II to VII help us to understand. Then, to lay a foundation for what is done later, we explore how the key variables relating to macroeconomic theory are measured in practice. Finally, we analyze the key empirical facts concerning business cycles. These facts prove useful in Parts II to VII in showing the successes and shortcomings of macroeconomic theory in explaining real-world phenomena.

CHAPTER 1

Introduction

This chapter frames the approach to macroeconomics that we take in this book, and it foreshadows the basic macroeconomic ideas and issues that we develop in later chapters. We first discuss what macroeconomics is, and we then go on to look at the two phenomena that are of primary interest to macroeconomists, economic growth and business cycles, in terms of post-1900 U.S. economic history. Then, we explain the approach this book takes—building macroeconomic models with microeconomic principles as a foundation—and discuss the issue of disagreement in macroeconomics. Finally, we explore the key lessons that we learn from macroeconomic theory, and we discuss how macroeconomics helps us understand recent and current issues.

WHAT IS MACROECONOMICS?

Macroeconomists are motivated by large questions and by issues that affect many people and many nations of the world. Why are some countries exceedingly rich while others are exceedingly poor? Why are most Americans so much better off than their parents and grandparents? Why are there fluctuations in aggregate economic activity? What causes inflation? Why is there unemployment?

Macroeconomics is the study of the behavior of large collections of economic agents. It focuses on the aggregate behavior of consumers and firms, the behavior of governments, the overall level of economic activity in individual countries, the economic interactions among nations, and the effects of fiscal and monetary policy. Macroeconomics is distinct from microeconomics in that it deals with the overall effects on economies of the choices that all economic agents make, rather than on the choices of individual consumers or firms. Since the 1970s, however, the distinction between microeconomics and macroeconomics has blurred in that microeconomists and macroeconomists now use much the same kinds of tools. That is, the **economic models** that macroeconomists use, consisting of descriptions of consumers and firms, their objectives and constraints, and how they interact, are built up from microeconomic principles, and these models are typically analyzed and fit to data using methods similar to those used by microeconomists. What continues to make macroeconomics distinct, though, is the issues it focuses on, particularly **long-run growth** and **business cycles.** Long-run growth refers to the increase in a nation's productive capacity and average standard of living that occurs over a long period of time, whereas business cycles are the short-run ups and downs, or booms and recessions, in aggregate economic activity.

The approach in this book is consistently to build up macroeconomic analysis from microeconomic principles. There is some effort required in taking this type of approach, but the effort is well worth it. The result is that you will understand better how the economy works and how to improve it.

GROSS NATIONAL PRODUCT, ECONOMIC GROWTH, AND BUSINESS CYCLES

To begin our study of macroeconomic phenomena, we must first understand what facts we are trying to explain. The most basic set of facts in macroeconomics has to do with the behavior of aggregate economic activity over time. One measure of aggregate economic activity is **gross national product (GNP)**,[1] which is the quantity of goods and services produced by a country's residents during some specified period of time. GNP also represents the aggregate quantity of income earned by a country's residents. In Figure 1.1 we show real GNP per capita for the United States for the period 1900–2002. This is a measure of aggregate output that adjusts for inflation and population growth, and the unit of measure is thousands of 1996 dollars per person.

The first observation we can make concerning Figure 1.1 is that there has been sustained growth in per capita GNP during the period 1900–2002. In 1900, the average income for an American was $4,055 (1996 dollars), and this grew to $32,713 (1996 dollars) in 2002. Thus, the average American became about eight times richer in real terms over the course of 102 years, which is quite remarkable! The second important observation from Figure 1.1 is that, while growth in per capita real GNP was sustained over long periods of time in the United States during the period 1900–2002, this growth was certainly not steady. Growth was higher at some times than at others, and there were periods over which per capita real GNP declined. These fluctuations in economic growth are business cycles.

Two key, though unusual, business cycle events in U.S. economic history that show up in Figure 1.1 are the Great Depression and World War II, and these events dwarf any other twentieth-century business cycle events in the United States in terms of the magnitude of the short-run change in economic growth. During the Great Depression, real GNP per capita dropped from a peak of $6,807 (1996 dollars) per person in 1929 to a low of $4,828 (1996 dollars) per person in 1933, a decline of about 29%. At the peak of war production in 1944, GNP had risen to $12,419 (1996 dollars) per person, an increase of 157% from 1933. These wild gyrations in aggregate economic activity over a 15-year period are as phenomenal, and certainly every bit as interesting, as the long-run sustained growth in per capita GNP that occurred from 1900 to 2002. In addition to the Great Depression and World War II, Figure 1.1 shows other business cycle upturns and downturns in the growth of per capita real GNP in the United States that, though less dramatic than the Great Depression or World War II, represent important macroeconomic events in U.S. history.

---

[1] In Chapter 2, the standard measure of aggregate economic activity we use is gross domestic product (GDP). Gross national product is used here because historical data on GDP were not available; furthermore, in the United States there is little difference between GDP and GNP.

FIGURE 1.1   **Per Capita Real GNP (in 1996 dollars) for the United States, 1900–2002**

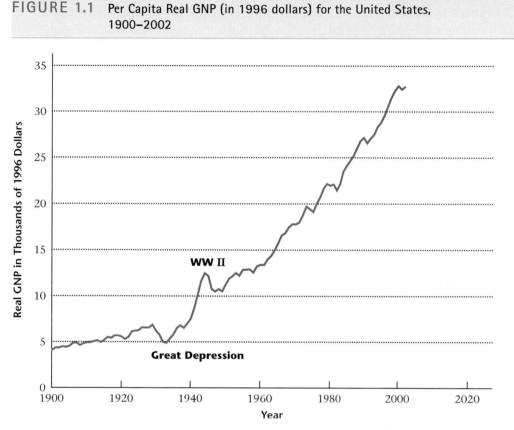

Per capita real GNP is a measure of the average level of income for a U.S. resident. Two unusual, though key, events in the figure are the Great Depression, when there was a large reduction in living standards for the average American, and World War II, when per capita output increased greatly.

Figure 1.1, thus, raises the following fundamental macroeconomic questions, which motivate much of the material in this book:

1. What causes sustained economic growth?
2. Could economic growth continue indefinitely, or is there some limit to growth?
3. Is there anything that governments can or should do to alter the rate of economic growth?
4. What causes business cycles?
5. Could the dramatic decreases and increases in economic growth that occurred during the Great Depression and World War II be repeated?
6. Should governments act to smooth business cycles?

In analyzing economic data to study economic growth and business cycles, it often proves useful to transform the data in various ways, so as to obtain sharper insights. For economic time series that exhibit growth, such as per capita real GNP in Figure 1.1, a useful transformation is to take the natural logarithm of the time series. To show why this is useful, suppose that y_t is an observation on an economic time series in period t; for example, y_t could represent per capita real GNP in year t, where $t = 1900, 1901, 1902$, etc. Then, the growth rate from period $t-1$ to period t in y_t can be denoted by g_t, where

$$g_t = \frac{y_t}{y_{t-1}} - 1.$$

Now, if x is a small number, then $\ln(1+x) \approx x$, that is, the natural logarithm of $1+x$ is approximately equal to x. Therefore, if g_t is small,

$$\ln(1+g_t) \approx g_t,$$

or

$$\ln\left(\frac{y_t}{y_{t-1}}\right) \approx g_t,$$

or

$$\ln y_t - \ln y_{t-1} \approx g_t.$$

Because $\ln y_t - \ln y_{t-1}$ is the slope of the graph of the natural logarithm of y_t between periods $t-1$ and t, then the slope of the graph of the natural logarithm of a time series y_t is a good approximation to the growth rate of y_t when the growth rate is small.

In Figure 1.2 we graph the natural logarithm of real per capita GNP in the United States for the period 1900–2002. As explained above, the slope of the graph is a good approximation to the growth rate of real per capita GNP, so that changes in the slope (e.g., when there is a slight increase in the slope of the graph in the 1950s and 1960s) represent changes in the growth rate of real per capita GNP. It is striking that in Figure 1.2, except for the Great Depression and World War II, a straight line would fit the graph quite well. That is, over the period 1900–2002 (again, except for the Great Depression and World War II), growth in per capita real GNP has been "roughly" constant at about 2.1% per year.

A second useful transformation to carry out on an economic time series is to separate the series into two components: the growth or **trend** component, and the business cycle component. For example, the business cycle component of real per capita GNP can be captured as the deviations of real per capita GNP from a smooth trend fit to the data. In Figure 1.3 we show the trend in the natural log of real per capita GNP as a colored line,[2] while the natural log of actual real per capita GNP is the black line. We then define the business cycle component of the natural log of real per capita GNP to be the difference between the black line and the colored line in Figure 1.3. The logic behind this decomposition of real per capita GNP into trend and business cycle components is that it is often simpler and more productive to consider separately the theory that

---

[2] Trend GDP was computed using a Hodrick–Prescott filter, as in E. Prescott, 1986. "Theory Ahead of Business Cycle Measurement," *Federal Reserve Bank of Minneapolis Quarterly Review,* Fall.

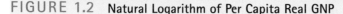

FIGURE 1.2   Natural Logarithm of Per Capita Real GNP

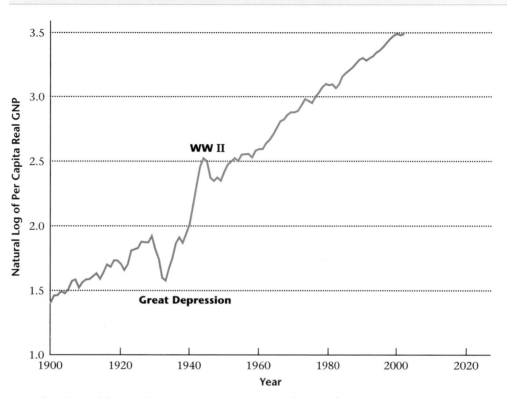

Here, the slope of the graph is approximately equal to the growth rate of per capita real GNP. Excluding the Great Depression and World War II, the growth rate of per capita real GNP is remarkably close to being constant for the period 1900–2002. That is, a straight line would fit the graph fairly well.

explains trend growth and the theory that explains business cycles, which are the deviations from trend.

In Figure 1.4 we show only the percentage deviations from trend in real per capita GNP. The Great Depression and World War II represent enormous deviations from trend in real per capita GNP relative to anything else during the time period in the figure. During the Great Depression the percentage deviation from trend in real per capita GNP was close to −20%, whereas the percentage deviation from trend was about 20% during World War II. In the period after World War II, which is the focus of most business cycle analysis, the deviations from trend in real per capita GNP are at most about ±5%.[3]

---

[3]The extremely large deviation from trend in real per capita GNP in the late 1920s is principally a statistical artifact of the particular detrending procedure used here, which is akin to drawing a smooth curve through the time series. The presence of the Great Depression forces the growth rate in the trend to decrease long before the Great Depression actually occurs.

FIGURE 1.3   Natural Logarithm of Per Capita Real GNP and Trend

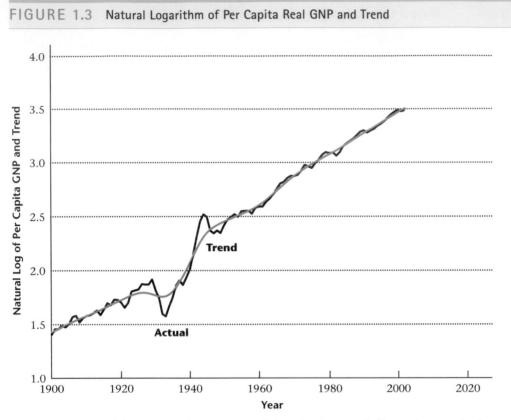

Sometimes it is useful to separate long-run growth from business cycle fluctuations. In the figure, the black line is the natural log of per capita real GNP, while the colored line denotes a smooth growth trend fit to the data. The deviations from the smooth trend then represent business cycles.

MACROECONOMIC MODELS

Economics is a scientific pursuit involving the formulation and refinement of theories that can help us better understand how economies work and how they can be improved. In some sciences, such as chemistry and physics, theories are tested through laboratory experimentation. In economics, experimentation is a new and growing activity, but for most economic theories experimental verification is simply impossible. For example, suppose an economist constructs a theory that implies that U.S. output would drop by half if there were no banks in the United States. To evaluate this theory, we could shut down all U.S. banks for a year to see what would happen. Of course, we know in advance that banks play a very important role in helping the U.S. economy function efficiently, and that shutting them down for a year would likely cause significant irreparable damage. It is extremely unlikely, therefore, that the experiment would be carried out. In macroeconomics, most experiments that could be informative are simply too costly to

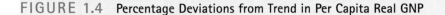

FIGURE 1.4 **Percentage Deviations from Trend in Per Capita Real GNP**

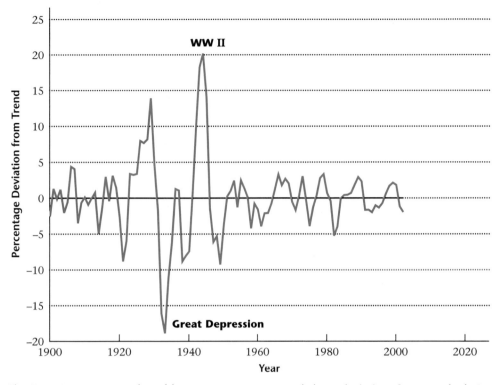

The Great Depression and World War II represent extremely large deviations from trend relative to post–World War II business cycle activity and business cycles before the Great Depression.

carry out, and in this respect macroeconomics is much like meteorology or astronomy. In predicting the weather or how planets move in space, meteorologists and astronomers rely on **models,** which are artificial devices that can replicate the behavior of real weather systems or planetary systems, as the case may be.

Just like researchers in meteorology or astronomy, macroeconomists use models, which in our case are organized structures to explain long-run economic growth, why there are business cycles, and what role economic policy should play in the macroeconomy. All economic models are abstractions. They are not completely accurate descriptions of the world, nor are they intended to be. The purpose of an economic model is to capture the essential features of the world needed for analyzing a particular economic problem. To be useful then, a model must be simple, and simplicity requires that we leave out some "realistic" features of actual economies. For example, a roadmap is a model of a part of the earth's surface, and it is constructed with a particular purpose in mind, to help motorists guide themselves through the road system from one point to another. A roadmap is hardly a realistic depiction of the earth's surface, as it does not capture the curvature of the earth, and it does not typically include a great deal of information on topography, climate, and vegetation. However, this does not limit the map's usefulness; a roadmap serves the purpose for which it was constructed, and it does so without a lot of extraneous information.

To be specific, the basic structure of a macroeconomic model is a description of the following features:

1. The consumers and firms that interact in the economy
2. The set of goods that consumers wish to consume
3. Consumers' preferences over goods
4. The technology available to firms for producing goods
5. The resources available

In this book, the descriptions of the above five features of any particular macroeconomic model are provided in mathematical and graphical terms.

Once we have a description of the main economic actors in a model economy (the consumers and firms), the goods consumers want, and the technology available to firms for producing goods from available resources, we want to then use the model to make predictions. This step requires that we specify two additional features of the model. First, we need to know what the goals of the consumers and firms in the model are. How do consumers and firms behave given the environment they live in? In all the models we use in this book, we assume that consumers and firms **optimize**, that is, they do the best they can given the constraints they face. Second, we must specify how consistency is achieved in terms of the actions of consumers and firms. In economic models, this means that the economy must be in **equilibrium.** Several different concepts of equilibrium are used in economic models, but the one that we use almost universally in this book is **competitive equilibrium.** In a competitive equilibrium, we assume that goods are bought and sold on markets in which consumers and firms are price-takers; they behave as if their actions have no effect on market prices. The economy is in equilibrium when market prices are such that the quantity of each good offered for sale (quantity supplied) is equal to the quantity that economic agents want to buy (quantity demanded) in each market.

Once we have a working economic model, with a specification of the economic environment, optimizing firms and consumers, and a notion of equilibrium, we can then begin to ask the model questions.[4] One way to think of this process is that the economic model is an experimental apparatus, and we want to attempt to run experiments using this apparatus. Typically, we begin by running experiments for which we know the answers. For example, suppose that we build an economic model so that we can study economic growth. The first experiment we might like to run is to determine, by working through the mathematics of the model, using graphical analysis, or running the model on a computer, whether in fact the model economy will grow. Further, will it grow in a

---

[4]The following description of macroeconomic science is similar to that provided by Robert Lucas in "Methods and Problems in Business Cycle Theory," reprinted in *Studies in Business Cycle Theory,* 1981, MIT Press, pp. 271–296.

manner that comes close to matching the data? If it does not, then we want to ask why and to determine whether it would be a good idea to refine the model in some way or to abandon it altogether and start over.

Ultimately, once we are satisfied that a model reasonably and accurately captures the economic phenomenon in which we are interested, we can start running experiments on the model for which we do not know the answers. An experiment we might want to conduct with the economic growth model is to ask, for example, how historical growth performance would have differed in the United States had the level of government spending been higher. Would aggregate economic activity have grown at a higher or a lower rate? How would this have affected the consumption of goods? Would economic welfare have been higher or lower?

In keeping with the principle that models should be simple and designed specifically for the problem at hand, we do not stick to a single all-purpose model in this book. Instead, we use an array of different models for different purposes, though these models share a common approach and some of the same principal building blocks. For example, sometimes it proves useful to build models that do not include international trade, macroeconomic growth, or the use of money in economic exchange, whereas at other times it is crucially important for the issue at hand that we explicitly model one, two, or perhaps all of these features.

Generally, macroeconomic research is a process whereby we continually attempt to develop better models, along with better methods for analyzing those models. Economic models continue to evolve in a way that helps us better understand the economic forces that shape the world in which we live, so that we can promote economic policies that make society better off.

MICROECONOMIC PRINCIPLES

This book emphasizes building macroeconomic models on sound microeconomic principles. Because the macroeconomy consists of many consumers and firms, each making decisions at the micro level, macroeconomic behavior is the sum of many microeconomic decisions. It is not immediately obvious, however, that the best way to construct a macroeconomic model is to work our way up from decision making at the microeconomic level. In physics, for example, there is often no loss in ignoring micro behavior. If I throw a brick from the top of a five-story building, and if I know the force that I exert on the brick and the force of gravity on the brick, then Newtonian physics does a very accurate job of predicting when and where the brick lands. However, Newtonian physics ignores micro behavior, which in this case is the behavior of the molecules in the brick.

Why is it that there may be no loss in ignoring the behavior of molecules in a brick, but that ignoring the microeconomic behavior of consumers and firms when doing macroeconomics could be devastating? Throwing a brick from a building does not affect the behavior of the molecules within the brick in any way that would significantly change the trajectory of the brick. Changes in government policy, however, generally alter the behavior of consumers and firms in ways that significantly affect the behavior of the economy as a whole. Any change in government policy effectively alters the features of the economic environment in which consumers and firms must make their decisions.

To confidently predict the effects of a policy change in terms of aggregate behavior, we must analyze how the change in policy affects individual consumers and firms. For example, if the federal government changes the income tax rate, and we are interested in the macroeconomic effects of this policy change, the most productive approach is first to use microeconomic principles to determine how a change in the tax rate affects an individual consumer's labor supply and consumption decisions, based on optimizing behavior. Then, we can aggregate these decisions to arrive at a conclusion that is consistent with how the individuals in the economy behave.

Macroeconomists were not always sympathetic to the notion that macro models should be microeconomically sound. Indeed, before the **rational expectations revolution** in the 1970s, which generally introduced more microeconomics into macroeconomics, most macroeconomists worked with models that did not have solid microeconomic foundations, though there were some exceptions.[5] The argument that macroeconomic policy analysis could be done in a sensible way only if microeconomic behavior is taken seriously was persuasively expressed by Robert E. Lucas, Jr. in a journal article published in 1976.[6] This argument is often referred to as the **Lucas critique.**

DISAGREEMENT IN MACROECONOMICS

There is little disagreement in macroeconomics concerning the general approach to be taken to construct models of economic growth. The Solow growth model,[7] studied in Chapters 6 and 7, is a widely accepted framework for understanding the economic growth process, and newer **endogenous growth models,** which model the economic mechanism determining the rate of economic growth and are covered in Chapter 7, have been well received by most macroeconomists. This is not to say that disagreement has been absent from discussions of economic growth in macroeconomics, only that the disagreement has not generally been over basic approaches to modeling growth.

The study of business cycles in macroeconomics, however, is another story. As it turns out, there is much controversy among macroeconomists concerning business cycle theory and the role of the government in smoothing business cycles over time. In Chapters 11 and 12 we study four competing theories of the business cycle.

The first theory is the **money surprise theory** of Milton Friedman[8] and Robert Lucas[9] developed in the late 1960s and early 1970s. In the money surprise theory, monetary factors are the primary cause of business cycles, but the government should not play an active role in smoothing out cycles, as this only make matters worse. The second approach is **real business cycle theory,** initiated by Edward Prescott and

---

[5]See M. Friedman, 1968. "The Role of Monetary Policy," *American Economic Review* 58, 1–17.

[6]See R.E. Lucas, 1976. "Econometric Policy Evaluation: A Critique," *Carnegie-Rochester Conference Series on Public Policy* 1, 19–46.

[7]See R. Solow, 1956. "A Contribution to the Theory of Economic Growth," *Quarterly Journal of Economics* 70, 65–94.

[8]See M. Friedman, 1968. "The Role of Monetary Policy," *American Economic Review* 58, 1–17.

[9]See R. Lucas, 1972. "Expectations and the Neutrality of Money," *Journal of Economic Theory* 4, 103–124.

Finn Kydland in the early 1980s.[10] Real business cycle theory is similar to the money surprise theory in that it implies that government policy aimed at smoothing business cycles is at best ineffective and at worst detrimental to the economy's performance. However, real business cycle theorists argue that business cycles are caused primarily by shocks to the economy's technological ability to produce goods and services. The third business cycle theory we study is the **Keynesian coordination failure theory,** which is a modern approach to **Keynesian** ideas. Keynesian macroeconomists are influenced by a line of work dating back to J. M. Keynes's *General Theory of Employment, Interest, and Money* published in 1936. Keynesians argue that the government can and should play an active role in smoothing out business cycles. In the coordination failure approach, business cycles can be caused by waves of self-fulfilling optimism and pessimism, and government policy may be effective in smoothing out business cycles.

All three of the aforementioned business cycle theories, covered in Chapter 11, are equilibrium models, that is, all prices and wages are perfectly flexible and move so that the quantity supplied equals the quantity demanded in each market. In the fourth theory we study, in Chapter 12, business cycles arise because wages are sufficiently inflexible that supply is not always equal to demand in the labor market. This is a traditional Keynesian sticky wage model, and it is consistent with the original ideas of Keynes in his *General Theory.*

This book seeks to take an objective view of all these competing theories of the business cycle. In Chapters 11 and 12, we study the key features of each of the above four theories of the business cycle, and we evaluate the theories in terms of how their predictions match the data.

What Do We Learn from Macroeconomic Analysis?

At this stage, it is useful to map out some of the basic insights that can be learned from macroeconomic analysis and which we develop in the remainder of this book. These are the following:

1. *What is produced and consumed in the economy is determined jointly by the economy's productive capacity and the preferences of consumers.* In Chapters 4 and 5, we develop a one-period model of the economy, which specifies the technology for producing goods from available resources, the preferences of consumers over goods, and how optimizing consumers and firms come together in competitive markets to determine what is produced and consumed.

2. *In free market economies, there are strong forces that tend to produce socially efficient economic outcomes.* Social inefficiencies can arise, but they should be considered unusual. The notion that an unregulated economy peopled by selfish individuals could result in a socially efficient state of affairs is surprising, and this idea goes back at least as far as Adam Smith's *Wealth of Nations,* written in the eighteenth century. In Chapter 5, we show this result in our one-period model, and we explain the circumstances under which social inefficiencies can arise in practice.

---

[10] F. Kydland and E. Prescott, 1982. "Time to Build and Aggregate Fluctuations," *Econometrica* 50, 1345–1370.

3. *Improvements in a country's standard of living are brought about in the long run by technological progress.* In Chapters 6 and 7, we study the Solow growth model (along with the Malthusian model of economic growth and an endogenous growth model), which gives us a framework for understanding the forces that account for growth. This model shows that growth in aggregate output can be produced by growth in a country's capital stock, growth in the labor force, and technological progress. In the long run, however, growth in the standard of living of the average person comes to a stop unless there are continuous technological improvements. Thus, economic well-being ultimately cannot be improved simply by constructing more machines and buildings; economic progress depends on continuing advances in knowledge.

4. *A tax cut is not a free lunch.* When the government reduces taxes, this increases current incomes in the private sector, and it may seem that this implies that people are wealthier and may want to spend more. However, if the government reduces taxes and holds its spending constant, it must borrow more, and the government will have to increase taxes in the future to pay off this higher debt. Thus, future incomes in the private sector must fall. In Chapter 8, we show that there are circumstances in which a current tax cut has no effects whatsoever; the private sector is no wealthier, and there is no change in aggregate economic activity.

5. *What consumers and firms anticipate for the future has an important bearing on current macroeconomic events.* In Chapters 8 and 9, we consider two-period models in which consumers and firms make dynamic decisions; consumers save for future consumption needs, and firms invest in plant and equipment so as to produce more in the future. If consumers anticipate, for example, that their future incomes will be high, they want to save less in the present and consume more, and this has important implications for current aggregate production, employment, and interest rates. If firms anticipate that a new technological innovation will come on line in the future, this makes them more inclined to invest today in new plant and equipment, and this in turn also affects aggregate production, employment, and interest rates. Consumers and firms are forward-looking in ways that matter for current aggregate economic activity and for government policy.

6. *Money takes many forms, and having it is much better than not having it. Once we have it, however, changing its quantity ultimately does not matter.* What differentiates money from other assets is its value as a medium of exchange, and having a medium of exchange makes economic transactions much easier in developed economies. Currently in the United States, there are several assets that act as a medium of exchange, including U.S. Federal Reserve notes, transactions deposits at banks, and travelers' checks. In Chapters 10 and 15, we explore the role of money and banking in the economy. One important result in Chapter 10 is that a one-time increase in the money supply, brought about by the central bank, has no long-run effect on any real economic magnitudes in the economy; it only increases all prices in the same proportion.

7. *Business cycles are similar, but they can have many causes.* In Chapter 3, we show that there are strong regularities in how aggregate macroeconomic variables fluctuate

over the business cycle. In Chapters 11 and 12, we also study several theories that can potentially explain business cycles. The fact that there are several business cycle theories to choose from does not mean that only one can be right and all the others are wrong, though some may be more right than others. Potentially, all of these theories shed some light on why we have business cycles and what can be done about them.

8. *Countries gain from trading goods and assets with each other, but trade is also a source of shocks to the domestic economy.* Economists tend to support the lifting of trade restrictions, as free trade allows a country to exploit its comparative advantage in production and, thus, make its citizens better off. However, the integration of world financial and goods markets implies that events in other countries can cause domestic business cycles. In Chapters 13 and 14, we explore how changes in goods prices and interest rates on world markets affect the domestic economy.

9. *In the long run, inflation is caused by growth in the money supply.* **Inflation,** the rate of growth in the average level of prices, can vary over the short run for many reasons. Over the long run, however, the rate at which the central bank (the **Federal Reserve System** in the United States) causes the stock of money to grow determines what the inflation rate is. We study this process in Chapter 15.

10. *Unemployment is painful for individuals, but it is a necessary evil in modern economies.* There will always be unemployment in a well-functioning economy. Unemployment is measured as the number of people who are not employed and are actively seeking work. Because all of these people are looking for something they do not have, unemployment might seem undesirable, but the time unemployed people spend searching for jobs is typically well spent from a social point of view. It is economically efficient for workers to be well matched with jobs, in terms of their skills, and if an individual spends a longer time searching for work, this increases the chances of a good match. In Chapter 16, we explore the determinants of the aggregate unemployment rate, in terms of two theories of unemployment, **search theory** and **efficiency wage theory.** Search theory explains unemployment in terms of the costs and benefits of searching for job offers, while efficiency wage theory posits that workers are unemployed because of an excess supply of labor brought about when firms pay high wages to induce their workers not to shirk.

11. *There may be a significant short-run trade-off between aggregate output and inflation, but aside from the inefficiencies caused by long-run inflation, there is no long-run trade-off.* In some countries and for some historical periods, a positive relationship appears to exist between the deviation of aggregate output from trend and the inflation rate. This relationship is called the **Phillips curve,** and in general the Phillips curve appears to be a quite unstable empirical relationship. The Friedman–Lucas money surprise model, discussed in Chapter 11, provides an explanation for the observed Phillips curve relationship. It also explains why the Phillips curve is unstable and does not represent a long-run trade-off between output and inflation that can be exploited by government policymakers. In Chapter 17, we explore the importance of commitment on the part of central bank policymakers in explaining recent inflation experience in the United States.

UNDERSTANDING RECENT AND CURRENT MACROECONOMIC EVENTS

Part of the excitement of studying macroeconomics is that it can make sense of recent and currently unfolding economic events. In this section, we give an overview of some recent and current issues and how we can understand them better using macroeconomic tools.

Aggregate Productivity

A measure of productivity in the aggregate economy is **average labor productivity,** $\frac{Y}{N}$, where Y denotes aggregate output and N denotes employment. That is, we can measure aggregate productivity as the total quantity of output produced per worker. Aggregate productivity is important, as economic growth theory tells us that growth in aggregate productivity is what determines growth in living standards in the long run. In Figure 1.5 we plot the log of average labor productivity for the United States, measured as the log of real **gross domestic product (GDP)** (the quantity of goods and services produced within U.S. borders) per worker. Here, we show the log of average labor productivity (the blue line), because then the slope of the graph denotes the growth rate in average labor productivity. The key features of Figure 1.5 are that average labor productivity grew at a high rate during the 1950s and most of the 1960s, growth slowed down from the late 1960s until the early 1980s, and then productivity growth increased beginning in the mid-1980s and remained high through the 1990s and into the early twenty-first century. The period from the late 1960s until the early 1980s is referred to as the **productivity slowdown.**

What caused the productivity slowdown, and what led to the resurgence in productivity growth after 1980? If we can understand this recent behavior of aggregate productivity, we might be able to avoid productivity slowdowns in the future and to bring about larger future increases in our standard of living. One potential explanation for the productivity slowdown is that it simply reflects a measurement problem. Estimates of economic growth during the productivity slowdown period could have been biased downward for various reasons, which would also cause productivity growth to be biased downward. This explanation seems quite unexciting, but economic measurement generally is imperfect. Economists have to be very careful in tempering their conclusions with a thorough knowledge of the data they are studying. A more exciting potential explanation for the productivity slowdown, and the subsequent increase in productivity growth, is that this is symptomatic of the adoption of new technology. Modern information technology began to be introduced in the late 1960s with the wide use of high-speed computers. In learning to use computer technology, there was a temporary adjustment period, which could have slowed down productivity growth from the late 1960s to the early 1980s. By the early 1980s, however, according to this story, people discovered how to embody new information technology in personal computers, and the 1990s saw further uses for computer technology via the Internet. Thus, the productivity slowdown could have been caused by the costs of adjusting to new technology, with productivity growth rebounding as information technology became widely diffused through the economy. We explore these issues further in Chapters 6 and 7.

FIGURE 1.5   Natural Logarithm of Average Labor Productivity

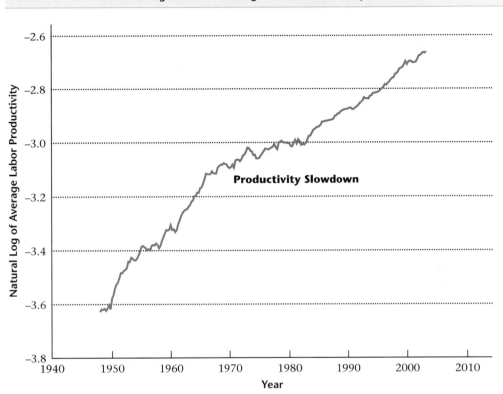

Average labor productivity is the quantity of aggregate output produced per worker. Because the graph is of the log of average labor productivity (the blue line), the slope of the graph is approximately the growth rate in average labor productivity. A key feature in the figure is the productivity slowdown, which we see as a decrease in the slope of the graph beginning in the late 1960s and continuing into the early 1980s.

Taxes, Government Spending, and the Government Deficit

In Figure 1.6 we show total taxes (the black line) and government spending (the colored line) by all levels of government (federal, state, and local) in the United States from 1947 to 2003, as percentages of total gross domestic product. Note the broad upward trend in both taxes and spending. Total taxes were about 24% of GDP in 1947, and they increased to more than 30% of GDP in 2000, while total spending rose from about 20% of GDP in 1947 to a high of more than 32% of GDP in the early 1990s. These trends generally reflect an increase in the size of government in the United States relative to the aggregate economy over this period.

What ramifications does a larger government have for the economy as a whole? How does higher government spending and taxation affect private economic activity?

FIGURE 1.6   Total Taxes (black line) and Total Government Spending (colored line)
in the United States, as Percentages of GDP

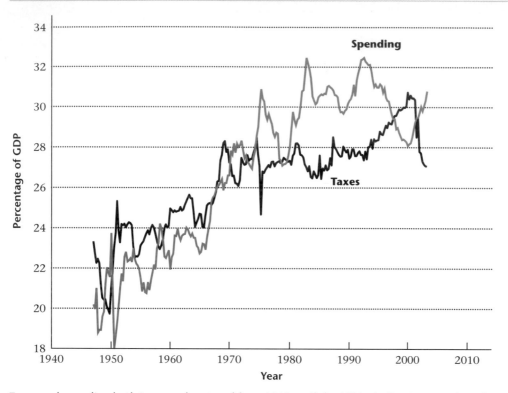

Taxes and spending both increased on trend from 1947 until the 1990s, indicating growth in the size of
government in the United States.

We show in Chapters 5 and 9 that increased government activity in general causes
a **crowding out** of private economic activity. That is, the government competes for
resources with the rest of the economy. If the size of the government increases, then
through several economic mechanisms there is a reduction in the quantity of spending
by private firms on new plant and equipment, and there is a reduction in private
consumption expenditures.

An interesting feature of Figure 1.6 is that governments in the United States sometimes spent more than they received in the form of taxes, and sometimes the reverse
was true. Just as is the case for private consumers, the government can in principle
spend more than it earns by borrowing and accumulating debt, and it can earn more
than it spends and save the difference, thus, reducing its debt. Figure 1.7 shows the total **government surplus** or total **government saving**, which is the difference between
taxes and spending. From Figure 1.7, the government surplus was positive for most

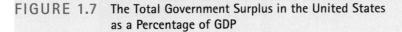

FIGURE 1.7   The Total Government Surplus in the United States
as a Percentage of GDP

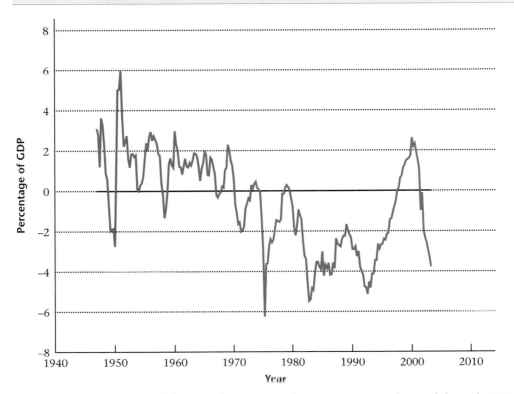

Of particular note is the trend decrease that occurs in the government surplus until the early 1990s, with the government surplus being negative for most of the period from the late 1960s until the late 1990s. The government surplus increases through most of the 1990s and becomes positive in the late 1990s, before decreasing sharply beginning in 2000.

of the period from 1948 until 1970, but from 1970 until the late 1990s the surplus was usually negative. When there is a negative government surplus, we say that the government is running a deficit; the **government deficit** is the negative of the government surplus. The largest government deficit over this period was more than 6% of GDP, in 1975. It was not until the late 1990s that there was again a positive government surplus; in 1999, the government surplus had reached more than 2% of GDP. However, the surplus declined dramatically after 1999, reaching −4% of GDP in 2003.

What are the consequences of government deficits? We might think, in a manner similar to popular conceptions of household finance, that accumulating debt (running a deficit) is bad, whereas reducing debt (running a surplus) is good, but at the aggregate level the issue is not so simple. One principal difference between an individual and the government is that when the government accumulates debt by borrowing from its citizens, then this is debt that we as a nation owe to ourselves. Then, it turns out that the effects of a government deficit depend on what the source of the deficit is. Is the government running a deficit because taxes have decreased or because government spending has increased? If the deficit is the result of a decrease in taxes, then the government debt that is issued to finance the deficit will have to be paid off ultimately by higher future taxes. Thus, running a deficit in this case implies that there is a redistribution of the tax burden from one group to another; one group has its current taxes reduced while another has its future taxes increased. Under some circumstances, these two groups might essentially be the same, in which case there would be no consequences of having the government run a deficit. This idea, that government deficits do not matter under some conditions, is called the **Ricardian equivalence theorem,** and we study it in Chapter 8. In the case of a government deficit resulting from higher government spending, then there are always implications for aggregate economic activity, as discussed earlier in terms of the crowding out of private spending. We examine the effects of government spending in Chapters 5 and 9.

Interest Rates

Interest rates are important, as they affect many private economic decisions, particularly the decisions of consumers as to how much they borrow and lend, and the decisions of firms concerning how much to invest in new plant and equipment. Further, movements in interest rates are an important element in the economic mechanism by which monetary policy affects real magnitudes in the short run. In Figure 1.8 we show the behavior of the short-term **nominal interest rate** (the blue line) in the United States over the period 1950–2003. This is the interest rate in money terms on 91-day U.S. Treasury bills, which are essentially riskless short-term government securities. In 1950, the short-term nominal interest rate was about 1%, but it rose on trend through the 1950s, 1960s, and 1970s, reaching a high of more than 15% early in 1980. Since then, the nominal interest rate has declined on trend, and it was below 1% in late 2003.

What explains the level of the nominal interest rate? In the figure we have plotted the inflation rate as the black line, which is measured here by the rate of increase in the consumer price index. The consumer price index is a measure of the price level, the average level of prices across goods in the economy. In the figure the inflation rate tracks the nominal interest rate reasonably closely. Also, several of the peaks in inflation, around 1970, in the mid-1970s, around 1980, around 1990, and in 2001, are coupled with peaks in the nominal interest rate. Thus, the nominal interest rate tends to rise and fall with the inflation rate. Why is this? Economic decisions are based on real rather than nominal interest rates. The **real interest rate,** roughly speaking, is the nominal interest rate minus the expected rate of inflation. That is, the real interest rate is the rate that a borrower expects to have to repay, adjusting for the inflation that is expected to occur over the period of time until the borrower's debt is repaid. If Allen obtains a one-year car loan at an interest rate of 9%, and he expects the inflation rate to be 3% over the next year, then he faces a real interest rate on the car loan of 6%. Now, because economic decisions are based on real interest rates rather than nominal

FIGURE 1.8   The Nominal Interest Rate and the Inflation Rate

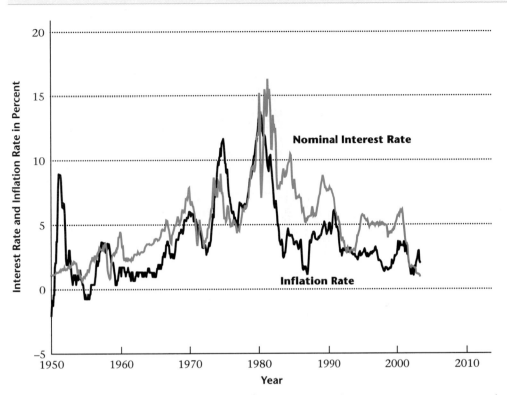

Macroeconomic theory tells us that the nominal interest rate and the inflation rate are positively related. The nominal interest rate, which is the 91-day Treasury bill rate (a short-term interest rate on federal government securities) tends to track the ups and downs in the inflation rate.

interest rates, market forces tend to determine the real interest rate. Therefore, as the inflation rate rises, the nominal interest rate tends to rise along with it. In Chapters 7 and 9, we study the determination of real and nominal interest rates in the long run, and the relationship between real and nominal rates.

In Figure 1.9 we plot an estimate of the real interest rate, which is the nominal interest rate minus the actual rate of inflation. Thus, this would be the actual real interest rate if consumers and firms could correctly anticipate inflation, so that actual inflation is equal to expected inflation. Consumers and firms cannot correctly anticipate the actual inflation rate. However, given that inflation does not change too much from quarter to quarter, their forecasts are fairly accurate, and our estimate of the real interest rate has a reasonably small measurement error. The real interest rate fluctuates a great deal over time. The real rate has sometimes been negative, falling to almost −8% early in the 1950s, and to −6% in 1980. For most of the period since the early 1980s, the real interest rate has been positive, but it fell below zero early in the 1990s and in 2003.

FIGURE 1.9   **Real Interest Rate**

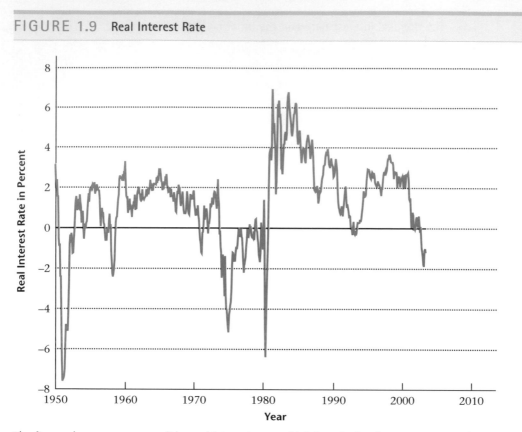

The figure shows a measure of the real interest rate, which here is the short-term nominal interest rate minus the actual rate of inflation. Monetary policy can have a short-run effect on the real interest rate; for example, the high real interest rates in the early 1980s and the low real interest rates during 1990–91 and 2001 recessions are often attributed to monetary policy actions.

In the short run, the real interest rate is affected by monetary policy, though there is some disagreement among macroeconomists concerning why the central bank can control the real interest rate, and for how long it can do so. We can give the following interpretation to the path of the real interest rate from the mid-1970s to 2003 in Figure 1.9. First, the real interest rate was low in the mid to late 1970s because the Federal Reserve (the Fed) was causing the money supply to grow at a high rate, that is, monetary policy was expansionary and accommodating. As a result of the high inflation caused by this high money growth, the Fed embarked on a contractionary course in the early 1980s, reducing money supply growth and causing the real interest rate to rise. Since the mid-1980s, the Fed has remained seriously concerned about the possibility that high inflation could reemerge, and it has for the most part maintained a nonaccommodating monetary policy stance, which has caused the real interest rate to be historically high. During the business cycle downturn in the early 1990s, the Fed temporarily relaxed, causing the real interest rate to dip below 1%. Then, in 2001, the Fed acted to reduce the real interest rate again, in response to a slowdown in aggregate economic activity. As there appeared to be no threat of serious inflation and economic activity had not picked up significantly, the real interest rate continued to fall through late 2003. In Chapters 11 and 12, we study some theories of the business cycle that explain how the central bank can influence the real interest rate in the short run. While the rate of money growth may affect real interest rates in the long run, monetary policy is aimed not at setting the long-run real interest rate but at determining long-run inflation while staying in tune with the short-run effects of monetary policy.

Business Cycles in the United States

As was mentioned above, individual business cycle events may have many causes, and the causes that are important in one business cycle event may be very unimportant in others. For example, a particular recession might be attributed to monetary policy actions, while another recession may have been caused primarily by a downturn in aggregate productivity.

As above, we define business cycles to be the deviations from trend in aggregate economic activity. In Figure 1.10, we show the percentage deviations from trend in GDP for the period 1947–2003. Recessions in the figure are negative deviations from trend, and the significant recent recessions in the United States were those of 1974–75, 1981–82, 1990–91, and 2001. What were the causes of these recessions?

Before the 1974–75 recession, there was a particularly sharp rise in the price of energy on world markets, caused by a restriction of oil output by the Organization of Petroleum Exporting Countries (OPEC). In Chapters 4, 5, and 9, we explain how an increase in the price of energy acts to reduce productivity and leads to a decrease in aggregate output, which occurred in 1974–75 as we see in Figure 1.10. Other features of the 1974–75 recession, including a reduction in measured productivity, a fall in employment, and a decrease in consumption and investment expenditures, are all consistent with this recession having been caused by the increase in the price of energy.

The recession of 1981–82, like the recession of 1974–75, was preceded by a large increase in the price of energy, which in this case occurred in 1979–80. For this second recession, the energy price increase perhaps happened too soon before the recession to have been its principal cause. As well, other evidence seems to point to monetary policy as the primary cause of the 1981–82 recession. As we see later in this section, inflation had become relatively high in the 1970s in the United States, and by the early 1980s the Federal Reserve System (the Fed), under then-Chairman Paul Volcker, took dramatic steps to reduce inflation by restricting growth in the supply of money and driving up interest rates. This produced the side effect of a recession. While there is much controversy among macroeconomists concerning the short run effects of monetary policy, and the role of money in the business cycle, most macroeconomists are inclined to view the 1981–82 recession as being caused primarily by monetary policy.

The 1991–92 recession was mild compared to the previous two major recessions (the negative deviation from trend in Figure 1.10 is smaller), and it was the only

FIGURE 1.10   Percentage Deviations from Trend in GDP, 1947–2003

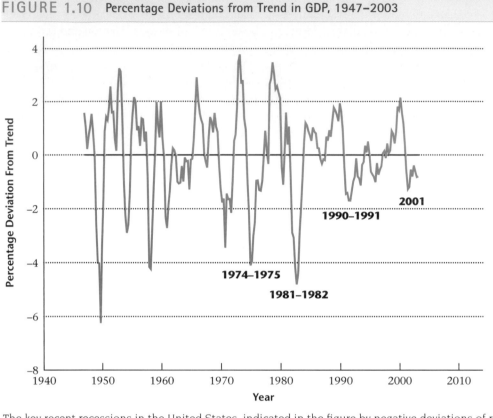

The key recent recessions in the United States, indicated in the figure by negative deviations of real GDP from trend, occurred in 1973–75, 1981–82, 1990–91, and 2001.

interruption in sustained economic growth over a roughly 19-year period from 1982 to 2001 in the United States. For this recession, it is difficult to pinpoint a single cause. Possibly an increase in energy prices during the Persian Gulf War was an important contributing factor, though this price increase was temporary.

The most recent recession of 2001, though even milder than the 1991–92 recession (see Figure 1.10), appears to have been the result of a collapse in optimism in the United States. During the 1990s, there was a boom in investment expenditures—spending on new plants, equipment, and housing—fed in part by great optimism concerning the revolution in information technology and its implications for future productivity. This optimism was also reflected in a large increase in the average price of stocks in the 1990s. In about 2000, optimism faded rapidly, investment expenditures and the stock market crashed, and the result was the recession of 2001. Also contributing to the 2001 recession were the terrorist attacks of September 2001, which acted to reduce aggregate output through several mechanisms that we study in Chapter 9.

The Current Account Surplus and the Government Surplus

As the technology for transporting goods and information across countries has advanced and government-imposed impediments to trade have been reduced in the post–World War II period, the United States has become a more open economy. That is, trade in goods and in assets between the United States and the rest of the world has increased. The change in the flow of goods and services between the United States and the rest of the world is shown in Figure 1.11, where we plot U.S. exports (the black line) and imports (the colored line) as percentages of GDP from 1947 to 2003. U.S. exports increased from somewhat less than 6% of GDP in 1947 to about 12% of GDP in 2000, while imports increased from somewhat more than 3% in 1947 to about 16% in 2003. As mentioned in the previous section, more trade has a positive effect on general economic welfare, as it allows countries to specialize in production and exploit

FIGURE 1.11   Exports and Imports of Goods and Services for the United States as Percentages of GDP

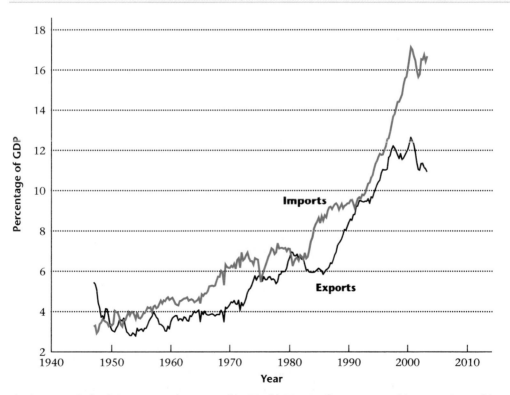

The increase in both imports and exports after World War II reflects a general increase in world trade. Exports have been lower than imports for most of this period.

their comparative advantages. However, more trade could also expose a given country to the transmission of business cycle fluctuations from abroad, though this need not necessarily be the case.

While the level of trade with the outside world is important in terms of aggregate economic activity and how it fluctuates, the balance of trade also plays an important role in macroeconomic activity and macroeconomic policymaking. One measure of the balance of trade is the **current account surplus**, which is **net exports** of goods and services (exports minus imports) plus **net factor payments** (net income from abroad). In Figure 1.12 we have graphed the current account surplus for the period 1960 to 2003. In the figure the current account surplus was positive for most of the period 1960–1985, and it has been negative for most of the period 1985–2003.

Why is the current account surplus important? When the current account surplus in the United States is negative, there is a **current account deficit,** and the quantity of

---

FIGURE 1.12   The Current Account Surplus and the Government Surplus, 1960–2003

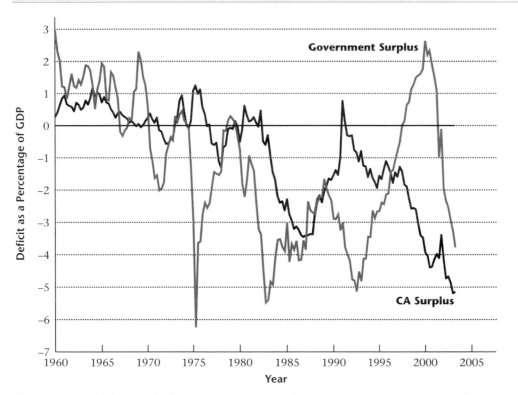

There was a trend decrease in the current account surplus from 1960 until 2003. During the 1980s, the current account surplus and the government surplus tended to move in the same direction, but they moved in opposite directions during the 1990s.

goods and services purchased abroad by domestic residents is smaller than the quantity of domestic goods and services purchased by foreigners. To finance this current account deficit, residents of the United States and/or the U.S. government must be borrowing abroad. Is it a bad idea for a country to run a current account deficit? This need not be the case, for two reasons. First, just as it may make sense for an individual to borrow so as to smooth his or her flow of consumption over time, it may also be beneficial for a country to borrow in the short run by running a current account deficit so as to smooth aggregate consumption over time. Second, persistent current account deficits may make sense if the associated foreign borrowing is used to finance additions to the nation's productive capacity that will allow for higher future living standards.

What accounts for movements over time in the current account surplus? One important influence on the current account surplus is government spending. When the government increases its spending, holding taxes constant, this increases the government deficit, which needs to be financed by increased government borrowing. If the private sector does not save more, so as to increase its lending to the government, then the increased government borrowing is done abroad, and it shows up as an increase in the current account deficit. Thus, an increase in the government deficit can be coupled with an increase in the current account deficit. This is exactly what appears to have occurred in the United States in the mid-to-late 1980s. In Figure 1.12, we see a sharp decrease during this period in the current account surplus. As well, we have shown the government surplus in the figure, and this also decreases sharply in the 1980s (though the decline in the government surplus precedes the decline in the current account surplus). This phenomenon is referred to as the **twin deficits.**

The government surplus need not always be the primary influence on the current account surplus. For example, from the early 1990s until 2000, the current account surplus was decreasing while the government surplus was increasing, which is inconsistent with the twin deficits phenomenon, where the two surpluses moved in the same direction. During the 1990s, the current account surplus was primarily influenced by a boom in U.S. investment spending that was essentially financed through borrowing from the rest of the world, which caused a large current account deficit.

We study international trade, the determinants of the current account surplus, and other issues associated with international business cycles and international financial relations in Chapters 13 and 14.

Inflation

Inflation, as mentioned earlier, is the rate of change in the average level of prices. The average level of prices is referred to as the price level. In Figure 1.13 we show the inflation rate, the black line in the figure, as the percentage rate of increase in the consumer price index over the period 1960–2003. The inflation rate was quite low in the early 1960s and then began climbing in the late 1960s, reaching peaks of about 12% per year in 1975 and about 14% per year in 1980. The inflation rate then declined steadily, reaching rates of 2% and below in the late 1990s.

Inflation is economically costly, but the low recent rates of inflation we are experiencing are certainly not viewed by the public or by policymakers as being worthy of

FIGURE 1.13 The Inflation Rate and the Money Growth Rate

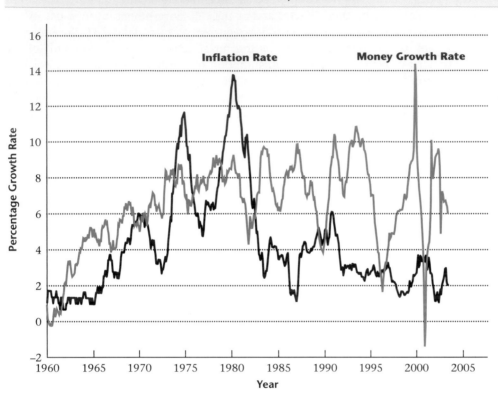

Money growth and inflation show a trend increase from 1960 until the 1980s, and then the inflation rate falls on trend. After 1980, the money growth rate is quite erratic and the relationship between money growth and inflation is loose.

much attention. However, it is certainly useful to understand the causes of inflation, its costs, and why and how inflation was reduced in the United States. There are good reasons to think that the inflation experience of the 1970s and early 1980s, or worse, could be repeated. The inflation rate is explained in the long run by the rate of growth in the supply of money. Without money supply growth, prices cannot continue to increase, and higher money supply growth implies that there is more and more money chasing a given quantity of goods. This will ultimately cause prices to be bid up at a higher rate. In Figure 1.13 we show the rate of money growth (measured as the percentage rate of growth in M0, a narrow monetary aggregate) as the colored line. Here, it is clear that the short-run relationship between the rate of inflation and the rate of money growth is not a tight one; there are many short-run ups and downs in the rate of money growth that are not reflected in similar movements in the inflation rate and vice versa. Thus, there must be other factors that explain short-run movements in the rate of inflation in addition to changes in the money growth rate. However, the broad trends in money growth in Figure 1.13 match the broad trends in the inflation rate. Money growth increases, on trend, until the 1980s, and then falls, as does the inflation rate, though money growth behavior is quite erratic from the mid-1980s on. We study the short-run effects of nonmonetary factors on the price level in Chapters 10, 11, and 12, and in Chapter 15 the long-run effects of money growth on inflation are explored.

Long-run inflation is costly, in that it tends to reduce employment, output, and consumption, as we show in Chapter 15. However, because inflation is caused in the long run by money growth, the central bank determines the long run inflation rate through its control of the rate at which the money supply grows. Why would the central bank want to generate inflation if it is costly? In Chapter 17, we explore the answer to this question, with recent experience in the United States as a backdrop. Surprise increases in the rate of inflation can cause short-run increases in employment and output, and the central bank might be tempted to generate these short-run surprises, either because it has not learned the consequences of long-run inflation, or because there is a failure of the central bank to commit itself to long-run actions. In Chapter 17, we study the importance of central bank learning and commitment for the behavior of inflation.

Unemployment

In the previous section we explained how the phenomenon of unemployment need not represent a problem, because unemployment is in general a socially useful search activity that is necessary, though painful to the individuals involved. As macroeconomists, we are interested in what explains the level of unemployment and what the reasons are for fluctuations in unemployment over time. If we can understand these features, we can then go on to determine how macroeconomic policy can be formulated so that labor markets work as efficiently as possible.

In Figure 1.14 we show the unemployment rate in the United States for the period 1948–2003. There are three important features that can be observed in Figure 1.15. First, the average unemployment rate in the period after 1970 is much higher than the average unemployment rate before 1970. Second, the unemployment rate fluctuates significantly; it is not unusual for it to move up or down by four or five percentage points within a year or two. Third, since 1970 there was a trend increase in the unemployment rate until about the mid-1980s and then a trend decrease; in 1999 the unemployment rate was lower than it had been at any point since 1970. What explains these features of the data?

There are four factors affecting unemployment that can explain essentially all of the observed behavior of the unemployment rate in Figure 1.14. These four factors are aggregate economic activity, the structure of the population, government intervention, and sectoral shifts. First, in general the unemployment rate fluctuates inversely along with aggregate economic activity; when aggregate output is above trend, then the unemployment rate tends to be low. Second, the population structure affects the unemployment rate, as workers in different age cohorts tend to behave differently in the labor market. For example, younger workers have a weaker attachment to jobs than older workers, and they tend to experience more frequent episodes of unemployment

FIGURE 1.14   **The Unemployment Rate in the United States, 1948–2003**

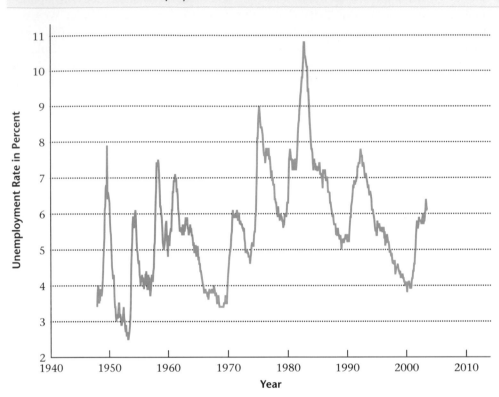

The unemployment rate is affected by aggregate economic activity, the structure of the population, government intervention, and sectoral shifts.

as they change jobs early in their careers. Third, government intervention affects the unemployment rate, particularly through the unemployment insurance system. For example, more generous unemployment compensation implies that the cost of searching for a job is reduced, and unemployed workers then tend to search longer, increasing the unemployment rate. Fourth, sectoral shifts are long-run changes that occur in the sectoral structure of production. For example, in the United States there has been a shift from the manufacturing sector of the economy to the services sector. This kind of sectoral shift tends to displace workers from the declining sector, and they need to acquire new skills and to spend time searching to find jobs in the expanding sector of the economy. Therefore, the greater the extent of sectoral shifts occurring in the economy, the higher the unemployment rate is.

The fact that the unemployment rate is on average higher after 1970 than before, as observed in Figure 1.14, is probably mainly the result of changes in the population structure. The postwar baby boom generation entered the labor force mostly between

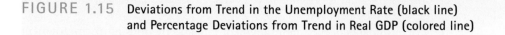

FIGURE 1.15   Deviations from Trend in the Unemployment Rate (black line)
and Percentage Deviations from Trend in Real GDP (colored line)

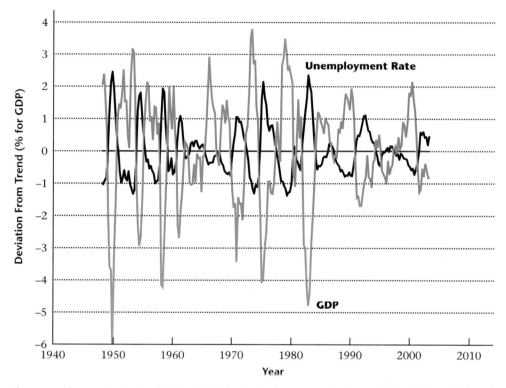

The unemployment rate tends to be high (low) relative to trend when real GDP is low (high) relative to trend.

the late 1960s and 1980, so that the working age population became more youthful through the 1970s, which would tend to push the unemployment rate up. Sectoral shifts may have also played a role in pushing up the unemployment rate after 1970. The unemployment rate fluctuated from 1948 to 2003 mainly because of fluctuations in aggregate economic activity. In Figure 1.15 we show deviations from trend in real GDP (in percentage terms) as the colored line and deviations from trend in the unemployment rate (in percentage points) as the black line. Clearly, when GDP is above (below) trend, the unemployment rate tends to be below (above) trend. Finally, the pattern in the unemployment rate since 1970 can be explained in part by the population structure and in part by the influence of aggregate economic activity. As the postwar baby boom generation began to age in the 1980s and 1990s, the unemployment rate fell as this large group of workers entered a phase in their careers when unemployment spells were less frequent. Also, the sustained growth in the U.S. economy since the early 1980s, interrupted only by the mild recessions in the early 1990s and 2001, contributed to a decrease in the unemployment rate.

We study determinants of the unemployment rate and theories of unemployment in Chapter 16.

CHAPTER SUMMARY

- Modern macroeconomics analyzes issues associated with long-run growth and business cycles, using models that are built up from microeconomic principles.

- During the twentieth century, the United States experienced long-run sustained growth in per capita gross national product; we also observed that gross national product exhibits business cycle fluctuations about a smooth long-run trend.

- Two unusual but important events in twentieth-century U.S. economic history were the Great Depression and World War II.

- The primary questions of interest to macroeconomists involve the causes of long-run growth and business cycles and the appropriate role for government policy in influencing the performance of the economy.

- Macroeconomists rely mainly on abstract models to draw conclusions about how the world works, because it is usually very costly or impossible to experiment with the real economy. A good macroeconomic model is simple, while retaining all of the features essential for addressing the macroeconomic issue for which the model was intended.

- The models we construct and use in this book are ones in which price-taking consumers and firms optimize given the constraints they face and in which the actions of consumers and firms are consistent in a competitive equilibrium.

- Building models from microeconomic principles is important, because this will more often give us the correct answers to questions regarding the effects of changes in economic policy.

- There is relatively little disagreement among macroeconomists concerning approaches to modeling growth, but there are contentious issues in business cycle modeling, between Keynesian macroeconomists and those who argue for non-Keynesian alternative explanations for business cycles.

- The issues discussed in this chapter, to be addressed later in the book, are: the productivity slowdown; taxes, government spending, and the government deficit; interest rates; business cycles in the United States; the current account surplus and the government surplus; inflation; and unemployment.

KEY TERMS

Economic model: A description of consumers and firms, their objectives and constraints, and how they interact.

Long-run growth: The increase in a nation's productive capacity and average standard of living that occurs over a long period of time.

Business cycles: Short-run ups and downs, or booms and recessions, in aggregate economic activity.

Gross national product (GNP): The quantity of goods and services produced by a country's residents during some specified period of time.

Trend: The smooth growth path around which an economic variable cycles.

Models: Artificial devices that can replicate the behavior of real systems.

Optimize: The process by which economic agents (firms and consumers) do the best they can given the constraints they face.

Equilibrium: The situation in an economy when the actions of all the consumers and firms are consistent.

Competitive equilibrium: Equilibrium in which firms and households are assumed to be price-takers, and market prices are such that the quantity supplied equals the quantity demanded in each market in the economy.

Rational expectations revolution: Macroeconomics movement that occurred in the 1970s, introducing more microeconomics into macroeconomics.

Lucas critique: The idea that macroeconomic policy analysis can be done in a sensible way only if microeconomic behavior is taken seriously.

Endogenous growth models: Models that describe the economic mechanism determining the rate of economic growth.

Money surprise theory: In this theory, developed by Milton Friedman and Robert Lucas, monetary factors are the primary cause of business cycles, and the government should not be active in smoothing cycles.

Real business cycle theory: Initiated by Finn Kydland and Edward Prescott, this theory implies that business cycles are caused primarily by shocks to technology and that the government should play a passive role over the business cycle.

Keynesian coordination failure theory: A modern incarnation of Keynesian business cycle theory positing that business cycles are caused by self-fulfilling waves of optimism and pessimism, which may be countered with government policy.

Keynesian: Describes macroeconomists who are followers of J. M. Keynes and who see an active role for government in smoothing business cycles.

Inflation: The rate of change in the average level of prices over time.

Federal Reserve System (Fed): The central bank of the United States.

Search theory: Theory that explains unemployment in terms of the costs and benefits of searching for job offers.

Efficiency wage theory: Theory positing that workers are unemployed because of an excess supply of labor brought about when firms pay high wages to induce their workers not to shirk.

Phillips curve: A positive relationship between the deviation of aggregate output from trend and the inflation rate.

Average labor productivity: The quantity of aggregate output produced per worker.

Gross domestic product: The quantity of goods and services produced within a country's borders over a specified period of time.

Productivity slowdown: The period of low productivity growth occurring from the late 1960s until the early 1980s.

Crowding out: The process by which government spending reduces private sector expenditures on investment and consumption.

Government surplus: The difference between taxes and government spending.

Government saving: Identical to the government surplus.

Government deficit: The negative of the government surplus.

Ricardian equivalence theorem: Theory asserting that a change in taxation by the government has no effect.

Nominal interest rate: The interest rate in money terms.

Real interest rate: Approximately equal to the nominal interest rate minus the expected rate of inflation.

Current account surplus: Exports minus imports plus net factor payments to domestic residents from abroad.

Net exports: Exports of goods and services minus imports of goods and services.

Net factor payments: These are the payments received by domestic factors of production from abroad minus the payments to foreign factors of production from domestic sources.

Current account deficit: Situation in which the current account surplus is negative.

Twin deficits: The phenomenon during the late 1980s when the U.S. government was running a deficit at the same time that the United States was running a current account deficit.

QUESTIONS FOR REVIEW

1. What are the primary defining characteristics of macroeconomics?

2. What makes macroeconomics different from microeconomics? What do they have in common?

3. How much richer was the average American in 2002 than in 1900?

4. What are two striking business cycle events in the United States during the last 103 years?

5. List six fundamental macroeconomic questions.

6. In a graph of the natural logarithm of an economic time series, what does the slope of the graph represent?

7. What is the difference between the trend and the business cycle component of an economic time series?

8. Explain why experimentation is difficult in macroeconomics.

9. Why should a macroeconomic model be simple?

10. Should a macroeconomic model be an exact description of the world? Explain why or why not.

11. What are the five elements that make up the basic structure of a macroeconomic model?

12. Why can macroeconomic models be useful? How do we determine whether or not they are useful?

13. Explain why a macroeconomic model should be built from microeconomic principles.

14. What are the four theories of the business cycle that we study?

15. What are two possible causes of the productivity slowdown?

16. What is the principal effect of an increase in government spending?

17. Why might a decrease in taxes have no effect?

18. What is the cause of inflation in the long run?

19. Explain the difference between the nominal interest rate and the real interest rate.

20. When did the four most recent recessions occur in the United States?

21. How are the government surplus and the current account surplus connected?

22. What are four factors that determine the quantity of unemployment?

PROBLEMS

1. Consider the following data on real GDP per capita in the United States:

Year	U.S. Real GDP per Capita (1996 Dollars)
1950	$11,205
1960	$13,339
1970	$17,718
1980	$21,904
1990	$27,100
1995	$28,747
1996	$29,520
1997	$30,519
1998	$31,478
1999	$32,238
2000	$32,748
2001	$32,375
2002	$32,713

(a) Calculate the percentage growth rates in real GDP per capita in each of the years 1996 through 2002, from the previous year.
(b) Now, instead of calculating the annual percentage growth rates in the years 1996 through 2002 directly, use as an approximation $100 \times (\ln y_t - \ln y_{t-1})$, where y_t is real per capita GNP in year t. How close does this approximation come to the actual growth rates you calculated in part (a)?
(c) Repeat parts (a) and (b), but now calculate the percentage rates of growth in real per capita GDP from 1950 to 1960, from 1960 to 1970, from 1970 to 1980, 1980 to 1990, and 1990 to 2000. In this case, how large an error do you make by approximating the growth rate by the change in the natural log? Why is there a difference here relative to parts (a) and (b)?
(d) During what decade from 1950 to 2000 was growth in real per capita GDP the highest? When was it the lowest?

2. Suppose that you had the special power to travel in time and to carry out any experiment you wanted on the economy. If you could turn back the clock to the time of the Great Depression, what experiment would you like to run on the U.S. economy? Why?

3. Give an example of a model that is used in some area other than economics, other than the roadmap example explained in this chapter. What is unrealistic about this model? How well does the model perform its intended function?

4. Why do you think taxes would fall during a recession, as happened in the mid-1970s (see Figure 1.6)?

5. Explain why the total government surplus became positive in the United States in the late 1990s, in terms of the behavior of taxes and government spending.

6. Does Figure 1.13 make you suspicious of the claim that a high rate of inflation is caused by a higher rate of money growth? Why or why not?

7. Why do you think the real interest rate was low during the recession in the mid-1970s?

8. How do the behavior of imports and exports help to explain the decrease in the current account surplus beginning in the early 1990s?

9. Why do you think the unemployment rate in the United States was very low at the end of the 1960s?

WORKING WITH THE DATA

1. Graph gross domestic product (GDP) and gross national product (GNP) in 1996 dollars for 1947 and thereafter. Is there much difference in these two measures of aggregate economic activity for the United States?

2. Total government expenditures consist of expenditures by the federal government and by state and local governments. Calculate and graph the ratio of federal government expenditures to total government expenditures. Has the federal government become larger or smaller relative to state and local governments over time?

3. Using the consumer price index as a measure of the price level, calculate and graph the annual inflation rate for 1960 to 2003. Calculate this as the percentage increase in the CPI from December to December (the annual inflation rate for 1999 would be the percentage increase in the CPI from December 1998 to December 1999). In addition, calculate and graph on the same chart the percentage annual increase in M2 (a measure of the money supply) for the same years. How does your picture differ from Figure 1.13?

CHAPTER 2

Measurement

Economics is built on the twin pillars of measurement and theory. Measurements of the performance of the economy motivate macroeconomists to build simple models that can organize our thinking about how the economy works. For example, surveys of consumer prices done every year can tell us something about how prices change over time and, coupled with observations on other economic variables, can help us to develop theories that explain why prices change over time. Meanwhile, economic theory can better inform us about the most efficient ways to carry out economic measurement. For example, theories of consumer behavior can tell us something about the appropriate way to use the prices of consumer goods to derive a price index that is a good measure of the price level.

Our goal in this chapter is to understand the basic issues concerning how key macroeconomic variables are measured. These key macroeconomic variables play the most important roles in the economic models that we construct and study in the remainder of this book. In particular, in the rest of this chapter we examine the measurement of GDP and its components, and the measurement of prices, savings, wealth, capital, and labor market variables.

MEASURING GDP: THE NATIONAL INCOME AND PRODUCT ACCOUNTS

The chief aim of national income accounting is to obtain a measure of the total quantity of goods and services produced for the market in a given country over a given period of time. For many issues in macroeconomics (though by no means for all), the measure of aggregate economic activity we are interested in is **gross domestic product (GDP)**, which is the dollar value of final output produced during a given period of time within the borders of the United States. GDP is published on a quarterly basis as part of the **National Income and Product Accounts (NIPA)**, one source for which is the Survey of Current Business, published by the U.S. Department of Commerce.

There are three approaches to measuring GDP, each of which is incorporated in some way in NIPA. All three approaches give exactly the same measure of GDP, provided there are no errors of measurement in using any of these approaches. The three approaches are the **product approach,** the **expenditure approach,** and the **income approach.** We discuss each in turn, using an example.

In our running example, we consider a simple fictional economy that captures the essentials of national income accounting. This is an island economy where there is a coconut producer, a restaurant, consumers, and a government. The coconut producer owns all of the coconut trees on the island, harvests the coconuts that grow on the trees, and in the current year produces 10 million coconuts, which are sold for $2.00 each, yielding total revenue of $20 million. The coconut producer pays wages of $5 million to its workers (who are some of the consumers in this economy), $0.5 million in interest on a loan to some consumers, and $1.5 million in taxes to the government. The relevant data for the coconut producer are shown in Table 2.1.

Table 2.1 **Coconut Producer**	
Total Revenue	$20 million
Wages	$5 million
Interest on Loan	$0.5 million
Taxes	$1.5 million

Of the 10 million coconuts produced, 6 million go to the restaurant, which specializes in innovative ways of serving coconuts—for example "shredded coconut in its own milk," "coconut soup," and "coconut in the half-shell." The remaining 4 million coconuts are bought by the consumers. Again, all coconuts are $2 each. Coconuts serve two roles in this economy. First, a coconut is an **intermediate good,** a good that is produced and then used as an input to another production process—here, the production of restaurant food. Second, it is a final consumption good, in that coconuts are purchased by consumers. The restaurant sells $30 million in restaurant meals during the year (this is a rather large restaurant). The total cost of coconuts for the restaurant is $12 million, and the restaurant pays its workers $4 million in wages and the government $3 million in taxes. Data for the restaurant are provided in Table 2.2.

Table 2.2 **Restaurant**	
Total Revenue	$30 million
Cost of Coconuts	$12 million
Wages	$4 million
Taxes	$3 million

Next, we need to calculate after-tax profits for each of the producers (the coconut producer and the restaurant). After-tax profits in this example are simply

$$\text{After-tax profits} = \text{Total Revenue} - \text{Wages} - \text{Interest} - \text{Cost of intermediate inputs} - \text{Taxes}$$

Therefore, from Tables 2.1 and 2.2 above, we calculate after-tax profits in Table 2.3.

Table 2.3 **After-Tax Profits**	
Coconut Producer	$13 million
Restaurant	$11 million

The government's role in this economy is to provide protection from attacks from other islands. In the past, foreign invaders have destroyed coconut trees and made off with coconuts. The government collects taxes to provide national defense. That is, it uses all of its tax revenue to pay wages to the army. Total taxes collected are $5.5 million ($4.5 million from producers and $1 million from consumers), and so the data for the government are as shown in Table 2.4.

Table 2.4 **Government**

Tax Revenue	$5.5 million
Wages	$5.5 million

Consumers work for the producers and for the government, earning total wages of $14.5 million. They receive $0.5 million in interest from the coconut producer, pay $1 million in taxes to the government, and receive after-tax profits of $24 million from the producers, because some of the consumers own the coconut firm and the restaurant. Data for the consumers are shown in Table 2.5.

Table 2.5 **Consumers**

Wage Income	$14.5	million
Interest Income	$0.5	million
Taxes	$1	million
Profits Distributed by Producers	$24	million

Now, given the abovementioned data for this simple economy, we examine how GDP would be calculated using the three different national income accounting approaches.

The Product Approach to Measuring GDP

The product approach to NIPA is also called the **value-added** approach. This is because the main principle in the product approach is that GDP is calculated as the sum of value added to goods and services in production across all productive units in the economy. To calculate GDP using the product approach, we add the value of all goods and services produced in the economy and then subtract the value of all intermediate goods used in production to obtain total value added. If we did not subtract the value of intermediate goods used in production, we would be double-counting. In our example, we do not want to count the value of the coconuts used in the production of restaurant services as part of GDP.

In the example, the coconut producer does not use any intermediate goods in production, so value added in producing coconuts, which is the coconut producer's total revenue, is $20 million. For the restaurant, however, valued added is total revenue minus the value of the coconuts used in production; thus, total value added for the restaurant is $18 million. For government production, we have a problem, because the national defense services provided by the government are not sold at market prices. Standard practice here is to value national defense services at the cost of the inputs to production. Here, the only input to production was labor, so the total value added for the government is $5.5 million. Total value added, or GDP, therefore, is $43.5 million. The GDP calculation using the product approach is summarized in Table 2.6.

Table 2.6 **GDP Using the Product Approach**	
Value added—coconuts	$20 million
Value added—restaurant food	$18 million
Value added—government	$5.5 million
GDP	$43.5 million

The Expenditure Approach

In the expenditure approach, we calculate GDP as *total spending on all final goods and services production in the economy*. Note again that we do not count spending on intermediate goods. In the NIPA, total expenditure is calculated as

$$\text{Total expenditure} = C + I + G + NX,$$

where C denotes expenditures on consumption, I is investment expenditure, G is government expenditure, and NX is net exports—that is, total exports of U.S. goods and services minus total imports into the United States. We add exports because this includes goods and services produced within the United States. Imports are subtracted because, in general, each of C, I, and G includes some goods and services that were produced abroad, and we do not want to include these in U.S. GDP.

In our example, there is no investment, no exports, and no imports, so that $I = NX = 0$. Consumers spend $8 million on coconuts and $30 million at the restaurant, so that $C = \$38$ million. For government expenditures, again we count the $5.5 million in wages spent by the government as if national defense services had been purchased as a final good at $5.5 million, and so $G = \$5.5$ million. Therefore, calculating GDP using the expenditure approach, we get

$$GDP = C + I + G + NX = \$43.5 \text{ million.}$$

The GDP calculation using the expenditure approach is shown in Table 2.7. Note that we obtain the same answer calculating GDP this way as using the product approach, as we should.

Table 2.7 **GDP Using the Expenditure Approach**	
Consumption	$38 million
Investment	0
Government Expenditures	$5.5 million
Net Exports	0
GDP	$43.5 million

The Income Approach

To calculate GDP using the income approach, we *add up all incomes received by economic agents contributing to production*. Incomes include the profits made by firms. In the NIPA, incomes include compensation of employees (wages, salaries, and benefits), proprietors' income (self-employed firm owners), rental income, corporate profits, net interest, indirect business taxes (sales and excise taxes paid by businesses), and depreciation (consumption of fixed capital). Depreciation represents the value of productive capital (plant and equipment) that wears out during the period we are considering. Depreciation is taken out when we calculate profits, and so it needs to be added in again when we compute GDP.

In the example, we need to include the wage income of consumers, $14.5 million, as a component of GDP. In addition, we need to count the profits of producers. If we do this on an after-tax basis, total profits for the two producers are $24 million. Next, we add the interest income of consumers (this is net interest), which is $0.5 million. Finally, we need to add the taxes paid by producers to the government, which are essentially government income. This amount is $4.5 million. Total GDP is then $43.5 million, which of course is the same answer that we obtained for the other two approaches. The calculation of GDP using the income approach is summarized in Table 2.8.

Table 2.8 **GDP Using the Income Approach**

Wage income	$14.5 million
After-tax profits	$24 million
Interest income	$0.5 million
Taxes	$4.5 million
GDP	$43.5 million

Why do the product approach, the expenditure approach, and the income approach yield the same GDP measure? It is because the total quantity of output, or value added, in the economy is ultimately sold, thus showing up as expenditure, and what is spent on all output produced is income, in some form or other, for someone in the economy. If we let Y denote total GDP in the economy, then Y is total aggregate output, and it is also aggregate income. Further, it is also true as an identity that aggregate income equals aggregate expenditure, or

$$Y = C + I + G + NX.$$

This relationship is sometimes referred to as the **income–expenditure identity,** as the quantity on the left-hand side of the identity is aggregate income, and the right-hand side is the sum of the components of aggregate expenditure.

An Example with Inventory Investment

One component of investment expenditures is inventory investment, which consists of any goods that are produced during the current period but are not consumed. Stocks of inventories consist of inventories of finished goods (for example, automobiles that are stored on the lot), goods in process (for example, automobiles still on the assembly line), and raw materials.

Suppose in our running example that everything is identical to the above, except that the coconut producer produces 13 million coconuts instead of 10 million, and that the extra 3 million coconuts are not sold but are stored as inventory. In terms of the value-added approach, GDP is the total value of coconuts produced, which is now $26 million, plus the value of restaurant food produced, $30 million, minus the value of intermediate goods used up in the production of restaurant food, $12 million, plus value added by the government, $5.5 million, for total GDP of $49.5 million. Note that we value the coconut inventory at the market price of coconuts in the example. In practice, this need not be the case; sometimes the book value of inventories carried by firms is not the same as market value, though sound economics says it should be.

Now, for the expenditure approach, $C = \$38$ million, $NX = 0$, and $G = \$5.5$ million as before, but now $I = \$6$ million, so GDP $= C + I + G + NX = \$49.5$ million. It may seem odd that the inventory investment of $6 million is counted as expenditure, because this does not appear to be expenditure on a final good or service. The convention, however, is to treat the inventory investment here as if the coconut producer bought $6 million in coconuts from itself.

Finally, in terms of the income approach, wage income to consumers is $14.5 million, interest income to consumers is $0.5 million, taxes are $4.5 million, as before, and total profits after taxes for the two producers are now $30 million, for total GDP of $49.5 million. Here, we add the $6 million in inventories to the coconut producer's profits, because this is an addition to the firm's assets.

An Example with International Trade

To show what can happen when international trade in goods comes into the picture, we take our original example and alter it slightly. Suppose that the restaurant imports 2 million coconuts from other islands at $2 each, in addition to the coconuts purchased from the domestic coconut producer, and that all of these coconuts are used in the restaurant. The restaurant still sells $30 million in restaurant food to domestic consumers.

Here, following the value-added approach, the value added by the domestic coconut producer is $20 million as before. For the restaurant, value added is the value of food produced, $30 million, minus the value of intermediate inputs, which is $16 million, including the cost of imported coconuts. As before, total value added for the government is $5.5 million. Therefore, GDP is total value added for the two producers and the government, or $39.5 million.

Next, using the expenditure approach, consumption of coconuts by consumers is $8 million and restaurant service consumption is $30 million, so that $C = \$38$ million. Government expenditures are the same as in the initial example, with $G = \$5.5$ million, and we have $I = 0$. Total exports are 0, while imports (of coconuts) are $4 million, so that net exports are $NX = -\$4$ million. We then have GDP $= C + I + G + NX = \$39.5$ million.

Finally, following the income approach, the wage income of consumers is $14.5 million, interest income of consumers is $0.5 million, and taxes are $4.5 million, as in the initial example. The after-tax profits of the coconut producer are $13 million, also as before. The change here is in the after-tax profits of the restaurant, which are reduced by $4 million, the value of the imported coconuts, so that after-tax restaurant profits are $7 million. Total GDP is then $39.5 million.

Gross National Product

At one time, **gross national product (GNP)** was used in the United States as the official measure of aggregate production. In line with international practice, however, the official measure is now GDP. In practice, there is little difference between GDP and

GNP in the United States, but in principle the difference could matter significantly. GNP measures the value of output produced by domestic factors of production, whether or not the production takes place (as is the case for GDP) inside U.S. borders. For example, if a Nike plant in Southeast Asia is owned and managed by American residents, then the incomes accruing to U.S. factors of production include the managerial income and profits of this plant, and this is included in U.S. GNP, but not in U.S. GDP. Similarly, if a Honda plant in Ohio has Japanese owners, the profits of the plant would not be included in GNP, as these profits are not income for American residents, but the profits would be included in GDP.

Gross national product is the sum of GDP and net factor payments (NFP) from abroad to domestic residents or

$$GNP = GDP + NFP,$$

where *NFP* denotes net factor payments from abroad. For 2002, GDP for the United States was $10,446.2 billion, and GNP was $10,436.7 billion, so NFP was −$9.5 billion. Thus, for this typical year, the difference between GDP and GNP for the United States was 0.091% of GDP, which is very small. For some countries, however, there is a significant difference between GDP and GNP, particularly for those countries where a large fraction of national productive capacity is foreign-owned, in which case NFPs from abroad are significant.

What Does GDP Leave Out?

GDP is intended simply as a measure of the quantity of output produced and exchanged in the economy as a whole. Sometimes GDP, or GDP per person, however, is used as a measure of aggregate economic welfare. There are at least two problems with this approach. The first is that aggregate GDP does not take into account how income is distributed across the individuals in the population. At the extreme, if one person in the economy has all the income and the rest of the people have no income, the average level of economic welfare in the economy would be very low. Second, GDP leaves out all nonmarket activity, with work in the home being an example. If people eat restaurant meals rather than eating at home, then GDP rises, because there are now more services produced in the market than before. People should be better off as a result, because they had the option of eating at home but chose to go out. However, the increase in GDP exaggerates the increase in economic welfare, as GDP does not measure the value added when food is cooked at home.

GDP may be an inaccurate measure of welfare, but there are also some problems with GDP as a measure of aggregate output, and two of these problems are the following. First, economic activities in the so-called **underground economy** are, by definition, not counted in GDP. The underground economy includes any unreported economic activity. A high-profile example of underground activity is trade in illegal drugs; a low-profile example is the exchange of baby-sitting services for cash. Economic activity goes underground so as to avoid legal penalties and taxation, and underground activity often involves cash transactions. The size of the underground economy may indeed be significant in the United States, as evidenced by the fact that the quantity of U.S.

currency held per U.S. resident was approximately $2,200 in April 2003.[1] Clearly, most individuals engaged in standard market transactions do not hold this much currency. This large quantity of currency in circulation can in part be explained by the large amount of U.S. currency held outside the country, but it still reflects the fact that the underground economy matters for the measurement of GDP in the United States.

A second problem in measuring GDP, which we encountered in our example, involves how government expenditures are counted. Most of what the government produces is not sold at market prices. For example, how are we to value roads, bridges, and national defense services? The solution in the NIPA, as in our example, is to value government expenditures at cost, that is, the payments to all of the factors of production that went into producing the good or service. In some cases this could overvalue what is produced; for example, if the government produced something that nobody wanted, such as a highway to nowhere. In other cases, government production could be undervalued; for example, we may be willing to pay much more for national defense than what it costs in terms of wages, salaries, materials, and so forth.

The Components of Aggregate Expenditure

Typically, particularly in constructing economic models to understand how the economy works, we are interested mainly in the expenditure side of the NIPA. Here, we consider each of the expenditure components in more detail. Table 2.9 gives the GDP components for 2002.

Table 2.9 **Gross Domestic Product for 2002**

Component of GDP	$ Billions	% of GDP
GDP	10,446.2	100
Consumption	7,307.7	70.0
Durables	871.9	8.3
Nondurables	2,115.0	20.2
Services	4,316.8	41.3
Investment	1,593.2	15.3
Fixed investment	1,589.3	15.2
Nonresidential	1,117.4	10.7
Residential	471.9	4.5
Inventory investment	3.9	0.0
Net exports	−423.6	−4.1
Exports	1,014.9	9.7
Imports	−1,438.5	−13.8
Government expenditures	1,972.9	18.9
Federal defense	447.4	4.3
Federal nondefense	246.3	2.4
State and local	1,279.2	12.2

[1] *Source:* U.S. Department of Commerce and Board of Governors of the Federal Reserve System.

Consumption   Consumption expenditures are the largest expenditure component of GDP, accounting for 70.0% of GDP in 2002 (see Table 2.9). **Consumption** is expenditure on consumer goods and services during the current period, and the components of consumption are durable goods, nondurable goods, and services. Durable goods include items like new automobiles, appliances, and furniture. Nondurables include food and clothing. Services are nontangible items like haircuts and hotel stays. Clearly, the division between durables and nondurables is somewhat imprecise because, for example, shoes (a nondurable) could be viewed as being as durable as washing machines (a durable). Further, some items included in consumption are clearly not consumed within the period. For example, if the period is one year, an automobile may provide services to the buyer for ten years or more, and is, therefore, not a consumption good but might economically be more appropriately considered an investment expenditure when it is bought. The purchase of a used car or other used durable good is not included in GDP, but the services provided (for example, by a dealer) in selling a used car would be included.

Investment   In Table 2.9, investment expenditures were 15.3% of GDP in 2002. **Investment** is expenditure on goods that are produced but not consumed during the current period. There are two types of investment. **Fixed investment** is production of capital, such as plant, equipment, and housing, and **inventory investment** consists of goods that are essentially put into storage. The components of fixed investment are nonresidential investment and residential investment. Nonresidential investment adds to the plant, equipment, and software that make up the capital stock for producing goods and services. Residential investment—housing—is also productive, in that it produces housing services.

Though investment is a much smaller fraction of GDP than is consumption, investment plays a very important role in business cycles. Investment is much more variable than GDP or consumption, and some components of investment also tend to lead the business cycle. For example, an upward or downward blip in housing investment tends to precede an upward or downward blip in GDP. We study this phenomenon further in Chapter 3.

Net Exports   As exports were less than imports in 2002, the United States ran a trade deficit in goods and services with the rest of the world—that is, **net exports** were negative (see Table 2.9)—though this deficit was small relative to GDP. However, exports were 9.7% of GDP in 2002 while imports were 13.8% of GDP. Trade with the rest of the world in goods and services, therefore, is quite important to the U.S. economy, as we noted in Chapter 1.

Government Expenditures   **Government expenditures,** which consists of expenditures by federal, state, and local governments on final goods and services, were 18.9% of GDP in 2002, as seen in Table 2.9. The main components of government expenditures are federal defense spending (4.3% of GDP in 2002), federal nondefense spending (2.4% of GDP in 2002), and state and local spending (12.2% of GDP in 2002).

The NIPA also make the important distinction between government consumption and government gross investment, just as we distinguish between private consumption and private investment. An important point is that the government spending included in the NIPA is only the expenditures on final goods and services. This does not include **transfers,** which are very important in the government budget. These outlays essentially transfer purchasing power from one group of economic agents to another, and they include such items as Social Security payments and unemployment insurance payments. Transfers are not included in GDP, as they are simply money transfers from one group of people to another, or income redistribution rather than income creation.

NOMINAL AND REAL GDP AND PRICE INDICES

While the components of GDP for any specific time period give us the total dollar value of goods and services produced in the economy during that period, for many purposes we would like to make comparisons between GDP data in different time periods. This might tell us something about growth in the productive capacity of the economy over time and about growth in our standard of living. A problem, however, is that the average level of prices changes over time, so that generally part of the increase in GDP that we observe is the result of inflation. In this section, we show how to adjust for this effect of inflation on the growth in GDP and, in so doing, arrive at a measure of the price level and the inflation rate.

A **price index** is a weighted average of the prices of a set of the goods and services produced in the economy over a period of time. If the price index includes prices of all goods and services, then that price index is a measure of the general **price level,** or the average level of prices across goods and services. We use price indices to measure the **inflation rate,** which is the rate of change in the price level from one period of time to another. If we can measure the inflation rate, we can also determine how much of a change in GDP from one period to another is purely **nominal** and how much is **real.** A nominal change in GDP is a change in GDP that occurred only because the price level changed, whereas a real change in GDP is an increase in the physical quantity of output.

Real GDP

To see how real GDP is calculated in the NIPA, it helps to consider an example. Imagine an economy in which the only goods produced are apples and oranges. In year 1, 50 apples and 100 oranges are produced, and the prices of apples and oranges are $1.00 and $0.80, respectively. In year 2, 80 apples and 120 oranges are produced, and the prices of apples and oranges are $1.25 and $1.60, respectively. These data are displayed in Table 2.10. For convenience in expressing the formulas for real GDP calculations, we let the quantities of apples and oranges, respectively, in year 1 be denoted by Q_1^a and Q_1^o with respective prices denoted by P_1^a and P_1^o. Quantities and prices in year 2 are represented similarly (see Table 2.10).

Table 2.10 **Data for Real GDP Example**

	Apples	Oranges
Quantity in year 1	$Q_1^a = 50$	$Q_1^o = 100$
Price in year 1	$P_1^a = \$1.00$	$P_1^o = \$0.80$
Quantity in year 2	$Q_2^a = 80$	$Q_2^o = 120$
Price in year 2	$P_2^a = \$1.25$	$P_2^o = \$1.60$

The calculation of nominal GDP in each year is straightforward here, as there are no intermediate goods. Year 1 nominal GDP is

$$GDP_1 = P_1^a Q_1^a + P_1^o Q_1^o = (\$1.00 \times 50) + (\$0.80 \times 100) = \$130.$$

Similarly, year 2 nominal GDP is

$$GDP_2 = P_2^a Q_2^a + P_2^o Q_2^o = (\$1.25 \times 80) + (\$1.60 \times 120) = \$292,$$

so the percentage increase in nominal GDP from year 1 to year 2 is equal to

$$\left(\frac{GDP_2}{GDP_1} - 1 \right) \times 100\% = \left(\frac{292}{130} - 1 \right) \times 100\% = 225\%.$$

That is, nominal GDP more than doubled from year 1 to year 2.

Now, the question is, how much of this increase in nominal GDP is accounted for by inflation, and how much by an increase in the real quantity of aggregate output produced? Until 1996, the practice in the U.S. NIPA was first to choose a base year and then to calculate real GDP using these base year prices. That is, rather than multiplying the quantities produced in a given year by current year prices (which is what we do when calculating nominal GDP), we multiply by base year prices to obtain real GDP. In the example, suppose that we use year 1 as the base year, and let $RGDP_1^1$ and $RGDP_2^1$ denote real GDP in years 1 and 2, respectively, calculated using year 1 as the base year. Then, real GDP in year 1 is the same as nominal GDP for that year, because year 1 is the base year, so we have

$$RGDP_1^1 = GDP_1 = \$130$$

Now, for year 2 real GDP, we use year 2 quantities and year 1 prices to obtain

$$RGDP_2^1 = P_1^a Q_2^a + P_1^o Q_2^o = (\$1.00 \times 80) + (\$0.80 \times 120) = \$176.$$

Therefore, the ratio of real GDP in year 2 to real GDP in year 1, using year 1 as the base year is

$$g_1 = \frac{RGDP_2^1}{RGDP_1^1} = \frac{176}{130} = 1.354,$$

so the percentage increase in real GDP using this approach is $(1.354 - 1) \times 100\% = 35.4\%$. Alternatively, suppose that we use year 2 as the base year and let $RGDP_1^2$ and $RGDP_2^2$ denote real GDP in years 1 and 2, respectively, calculated using this approach.

Then, year 2 real GDP is the same as year 2 nominal GDP, that is

$$RGDP_2^2 = GDP_2 = \$292$$

Year 1 GDP, using year 1 quantities and year 2 prices, is

$$RGDP_1^2 = P_2^a Q_1^a + P_2^o Q_1^o = (\$1.25 \times 50) + (\$1.60 \times 100) = \$222.50.$$

Then, the ratio of real GDP in year 2 to real GDP in year 1, using year 2 as the base year, is

$$g_2 = \frac{RGDP_2^2}{RGDP_1^2} = \frac{292}{222.5} = 1.312,$$

and the percentage increase in GDP from year 1 to year 2 is $(1.312 - 1) \times 100\% = 31.2\%$.

A key message from the example is that the choice of the base year matters for the calculation of GDP. If year 1 is used as the base year, then the increase in real GDP is 35.4%, and if year 2 is the base year, real GDP is calculated to increase by 31.2%. The reason the choice of the base year matters in the example, and in reality, is that the relative prices of goods change over time. That is, the relative price of apples to oranges is $\frac{\$1.00}{\$0.80} = 1.25$ in year 1, and this relative price is $\frac{\$1.25}{\$1.60} = 0.78$ in year 2. Therefore, apples became cheaper relative to oranges from year 1 to year 2. If relative prices had remained the same between year 1 and year 2, then the choice of the base year would not matter. In calculating real GDP, the problem of changing relative prices would not be too great in calculating GDP close to the base year (say, 2002 or 2003 relative to a base year in 2001), because relative prices would typically not change much over a short period of time. Over many years, however, the problem could be severe, for example, in calculating real GDP in 2003 relative to a base year in 1982. The solution to this problem, adopted in the NIPA, is to use a **chain-weighting** scheme for calculating real GDP.

With the chain-weighting approach, a "Fisher index" is used, and the approach is essentially like using a rolling base period. The chain-weighted ratio of real GDP in year 2 to real GDP in year 1 is

$$g_c = \sqrt{g_1 \times g_2} = \sqrt{1.354 \times 1.312} = 1.333,$$

so that the chain-weighted ratio of real GDP in the two years is a geometric average of the ratios calculated using each of years 1 and 2 as base years.[2] In the example, we calculate the percentage growth rate in real GDP from year 1 to year 2 using the chain-weighting method to be $(1.333 - 1) \times 100\% = 33.3\%$. The growth rate in this case falls between the growth rates we calculated using the other two approaches, which is of course what we should get given that chain-weighting effectively averages (geometrically) the growth rates using years 1 and 2 as base years.

Now, once we have the chain-weighted ratio of real GDP in one year relative to another (g_c in this case), we can calculate real GDP in terms of the dollars of any year

---

[2]For more detail on the calculation of real GDP using the chain-weighting method, see *A Guide to the NIPA's*, available from the Bureau of Economic Analysis at http://www.bea.doc.gov/bea/an/nipaguid.htm.

we choose. For example, in our example, if we want real GDP in year 1 dollars, then real GDP in year 1 is the same as nominal GDP or $GDP_1 = \$130$, and real GDP in year 2 is equal to $GDP_1 \times g_c = \$130 \times 1.333 = \$173.29$. Alternatively, if we want real GDP in year 2 dollars, then real GDP in year 2 is $GDP_2 = \$292$, and real GDP in year 1 is $\frac{GDP_2}{g_c} = \frac{\$292}{1.333} = \$219.05$.

In practice, the growth rates in real GDP in adjacent years are calculated just as we have done it here, and then real GDP is "chained" together from one year to the next. Chain-weighting should in principle give a more accurate measure of the year-to-year, or quarter-to-quarter, changes in real GDP. In Figure 2.1 we show nominal GDP and real GDP, calculated using the chain-weighting approach, for the United States over the period 1947–2003. Real GDP is measured here in 1996 dollars, so that real GDP is

---

FIGURE 2.1 Nominal GDP (black line) and Chain-Weighted Real GDP (colored line) for the Period 1947–2003.

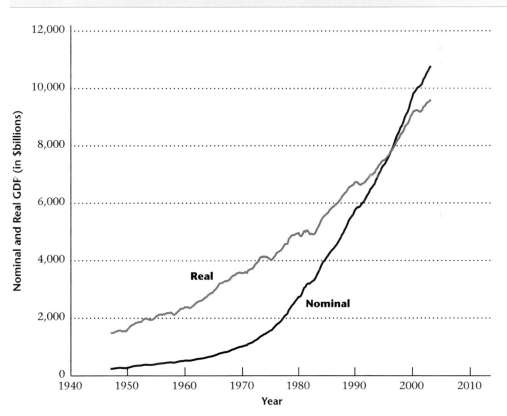

Note that the two time series cross in 1996 because real GDP is measured in 1996 dollars. The growth rate in real GDP is smaller than the growth rate for nominal GDP because of positive inflation over this period.

Source: U.S. Department of Commerce, Bureau of Economic Analysis.

equal to nominal GDP in 1996. Because the inflation rate was generally positive over the period 1947–2003, and was particularly high in the 1970s, real GDP grows in Figure 2.1 at a lower rate than does nominal GDP.

Measures of the Price Level

There are two commonly used measures of the price level. The first is the **implicit GDP price deflator,** and the second is the **consumer price index (CPI).** The implicit GDP price deflator is measured as

$$\text{Implicit GDP price deflator} = \frac{\text{Nominal GDP}}{\text{Real GDP}} \times 100.$$

Here, multiplying by 100 just normalizes the price deflator to 100 in the year we are choosing nominal GDP to be equal to real GDP. For the example above, the price deflator we calculate would depend on whether we use year 1 or year 2 as a base year, or compute chain-weighted real GDP. We give the results in Table 2.11, and arbitrarily choose chain-weighted real GDP to be in year 1 dollars. Note in Table 2.11 that the answers we get for the percentage rate of inflation between year 1 and year 2 depend critically on how we measure real GDP.

Table 2.11 **Implicit GDP Price Deflators, Example**

	Year 1	Year 2	% Increase
Year 1 = base year	100	165.9	65.9%
Year 2 = base year	58.4	100	71.2
Chain-weighting	100	168.5	68.5

The alternative measure of the price level, the CPI, is not as broadly based as the implicit GDP price deflator, because it includes only goods and services that are purchased by consumers. Further, the CPI is a fixed-weight price index, which takes the quantities in some base year as being the typical goods bought by the average consumer during that base year, and then uses those quantities as weights to calculate the index in each year. Thus, the CPI in the current year would be

$$\text{Current year CPI} = \frac{\text{Cost of base year quantities at current prices}}{\text{Cost of base year quantities at base year prices}} \times 100$$

In the example, if we take year 1 as the base year, then the year 1 (base year) CPI is 100, and the year 2 CPI is $\frac{222.5}{130} \times 100 = 171.2$, so that the percentage increase in the CPI from year 1 to year 2 is 71.2%.

In practice, there can be substantial differences between the inflation rates calculated using the implicit GDP price deflator and those calculated using the CPI. Figure 2.2 shows the GDP deflator inflation rate (the black line) and CPI inflation rate (the blue line), calculated quarter by quarter, for the United States over the period 1947–2003. The two measures of the inflation rate track each other broadly, but the CPI inflation rate tends to be more volatile than the GDP deflator inflation rate. At times, there can be substantial differences between the two measures. For example, in late 1979, the CPI

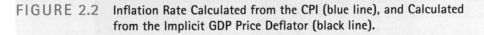

FIGURE 2.2   Inflation Rate Calculated from the CPI (blue line), and Calculated from the Implicit GDP Price Deflator (black line).

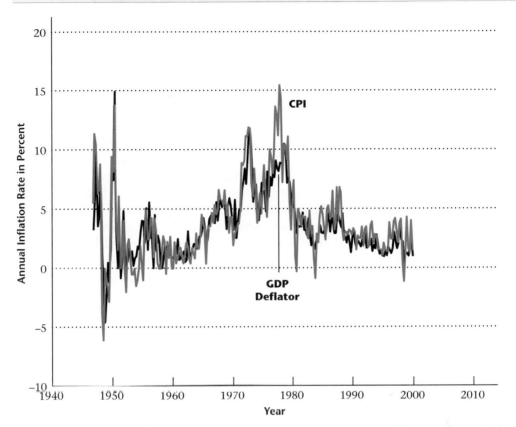

These measures are broadly similar, but at times there can be substantial differences. In particular, note the spikes in the CPI inflation rate occurring in the late 1970s, the 1980s, and the early 1990s, which are not replicated in the GDP deflator inflation rate series.

Source: U.S. Department of Commerce, Bureau of Economic Analysis, and Bureau of Labor Statistics.

inflation rate exceeded 15%, while the GDP deflator inflation rate was about 8%. These differences in inflation rate measures could matter greatly for contracts (for example, labor contracts) that are geared to the inflation rate or for the formulation of monetary policy, where close attention is paid to inflation performance.

Problems with Measuring Real GDP and the Price Level

As we saw above, particularly in how the implicit GDP price deflator is derived, the measurement of real GDP and the measurement of the price level are intimately related. If a particular measure of real GDP underestimates growth in real GDP, then the rate of inflation is overestimated. In practice, there are three important problems with measuring real GDP and the price level.

The first problem was mentioned above, which is that relative prices change over time. We showed how chain-weighting corrects for this problem in the measurement of real GDP and, therefore, corrects for the bias relative price changes would introduce in the measurement of inflation using the implicit GDP price deflator. Changes in relative prices can also introduce severe bias in how the CPI measures inflation. When there is a relative price change, consumers typically purchase less of the goods that have become more expensive and more of those that have become relatively cheap. In the previous example, apples became cheaper relative to oranges in year 2, and the ratio of apples consumed to oranges consumed increased. In computing the CPI, the implicit assumption is that consumers do not change their buying habits when relative price changes occur, which is clearly false. As a result, goods that become relatively more expensive receive a higher weight than they should in the CPI, and, therefore, the CPI-based measure of the rate of inflation is biased upward. This is, in fact, a serious policy issue (see the box on the Boskin Commission), because some federal transfer payments, including Social Security, are indexed to the CPI, and, therefore, an upward bias in CPI inflation would also commit the federal government to higher transfer payments, which in turn would increase the size of the federal government budget deficit. Also, federal income tax brackets are geared to CPI inflation. Upward bias in CPI inflation causes tax revenues to fall, increasing the government deficit. Rather than the rate of increase in the CPI, a more accurate measure of the rate of inflation in consumer goods is the implicit consumption price deflator, which is the price deflator associated with chain-weighted real consumption expenditures.

A second problem in measuring real GDP is changes in the quality of goods over time. Consider the case of 2003 vintage cars versus 1953 vintage cars. Clearly, the price of a new car in 2003 was much higher than the price of a new car in 1953, but the 2003 car is very different from the 1953 car. In 2003, most cars sold in the United States had computerized devices to monitor engine performance, automatic transmissions, power windows, air bags, seat belts, and CD players, none of which were standard equipment (or in some cases even invented) in 1953. In a sense, the 2003 car is "more car," because its quality is higher; therefore, some of the increase in price from 1953–2003 simply represents the fact that the buyer is receiving more in exchange for his or her money. To the extent that NIPA does not compensate for changes in quality over time, growth in real GDP is biased downward and inflation is biased upward.

A third problem is how measured GDP takes account of new goods. For example, personal computers were introduced in the early 1980s, and they did not exist in the NIPA before then. Clearly, we cannot make a straightforward calculation of real GDP growth from the 1970s to the 1980s, as there were no prices existing for personal computers in the 1970s. If the NIPA does not correctly take account of the fact that the new personal computers that were introduced (initially at very high prices) were a huge quality advance over old-fashioned calculators and slide rules, then this could bias downward the measure of real GDP growth and bias upward the measure of the inflation rate.

MACROECONOMICS IN ACTION

The Boskin Commission and the Consumer Price Index

The Boskin Commission, or more formally, the Advisory Commission to Study the Consumer Price Index, was appointed by the Senate Finance Committee in June 1995 to review CPI measurement and come up with recommendations for improvement. The Commission's report, authored by a group of well-known economists and published in 1996,[1] came to some perhaps startling conclusions. Given the biases in the inflation rate computed from the CPI, as discussed in the text, the Commission estimated that the upward bias in the CPI inflation rate was a substantial 1.1 percentage points per year. It was estimated that this upward bias in CPI inflation would contribute an extra $202 billion to government spending and $1.07 trillion to the government debt by 2008, primarily as a result of the indexing of Social Security benefits and federal income taxes. Government spending as a result of the CPI inflation bias would then be the fourth largest component of federal spending, behind Social Security, health care, and defense!

The Boskin Commission recommended that the Bureau of Labor Statistics refine its measurement procedures so as to reduce or eliminate the CPI inflation bias, but not everyone greeted the Commission's recommendations with adulation. Given that the elimination of the CPI inflation bias would reduce substantially the future income of senior citizens from Social Security, lobby groups representing seniors put considerable effort into casting doubt on the Commission's findings. Many of the Boskin Commission's recommendations, however, were implemented by the Bureau of Labor Statistics, and Robert Gordon estimated that these changes had eliminated about half of the CPI inflation bias.[2]

[1] M. Boskin, E. Deulberger, R. Gordon, Z. Griliches, and D. Jorgensen, 1996, "Toward a More Accurate Measure of the Cost of Living," in *Final Report of the Senate Finance Committee.*

[2] See R. Gordon, "The Boskin Commission Report and Its Aftermath," in *Monetary and Economic Studies*, Bank of Japan, December 1999; also available on the web at http://www.imes.boj.or.jp/japanese/all99/abst/me17-3-2.html.

SAVINGS, WEALTH, AND CAPITAL

While the components of GDP in the NIPA measure aggregate activity that takes place within the current period, another key aspect of the economy that is of interest to macroeconomists is aggregate productive capacity, and how aggregate savings adds to this productive capacity. In this section we explore, by way of several accounting identities, the relationships among savings, wealth, and capital.

An important distinction in economics is between **flows** and **stocks.** A flow is a rate per unit time, while a stock is the quantity in existence of some object at a point in time. In the NIPA, GDP, consumption, investment, government spending, and net exports are all flows. For example, GDP is measured in dollars spent per period. In contrast, the quantity of housing in existence in the United States at the end of a given year is a stock. In the following, we see that national saving is a flow, while the nation's wealth is a stock. In this case, national saving is the flow that is added to the stock of the nation's wealth in each year. A classic analogy is the example of water flowing into a bathtub, where the quantity of water coming out of the faucet per minute is a flow, while the quantity of water in the bathtub at any point in time is a stock.

Savings can mean very different things, depending on whether we are referring to the private (nongovernment) sector, the government, or the nation as a whole. For the private sector, to determine savings we first need to start with what the private sector has available to spend, which is **private disposable income**, denoted Y^d. We have

$$Y^d = Y + NFP + TR + INT - T,$$

where Y is GDP, NFP is net factor payments from abroad to U.S. residents, TR is transfers from the government to the private sector, INT is interest on the government debt, and T is taxes. Recall that GNP is $Y + NFP$. What the private sector saves is simply what it has available to spend minus what it consumes, and so letting S^p denote **private sector saving**, we have

$$S^p = Y^d - C = Y + NFP + TR + INT - T - C.$$

What the government has available to spend is its tax revenue, T, minus TR, minus INT, and what it consumes is government expenditures, G. Thus, **government saving** S^g is given by

$$S^g = T - TR - INT - G.$$

Government saving is simply the **government surplus**, and the government surplus is the negative of the **government deficit**, denoted D, or

$$D = -S^g = -T + TR + INT + G,$$

which is just government outlays minus government receipts. If we add private saving and government saving, we obtain **national saving**,

$$S = S^p + S^g = Y + NFP - C - G,$$

which is GNP minus private consumption, minus government consumption. Because the income–expenditure identity gives $Y = C + I + G + NX$, we can substitute for Y in the previous equation to obtain

$$S = Y + NFP - C - G$$
$$= C + I + G + NX + NFP - C - G$$
$$= I + NX + NFP.$$

Thus, national saving must equal investment plus net exports plus net factor payments from abroad. The quantity $NX + NFP$ is the **current account surplus** with the rest of the world, which we denote CA; thus, we have

$$S = I + CA.$$

The current account surplus is a measure of the balance of trade in goods with the rest of the world. The above identity reflects the fact that any domestic savings not absorbed by domestic investment must be shipped outside the country in the form of goods and services.

As a flow, national saving represents additions to the nation's wealth. Because $S = I + CA$, wealth is accumulated in two ways. First, wealth is accumulated through investment, I, which is additions to the nation's **capital stock.** The capital stock is the quantity of plants, equipment, housing, and inventories in existence in an economy at a point in time. Second, wealth is accumulated through current account surpluses, CA, because a current account surplus implies that U.S. residents are accumulating claims on foreigners. The current account surplus, CA, represents increases in claims on foreigners because if goods are flowing from the United States to other countries, then these goods must be paid for with a transfer of wealth from outside the United States to U.S. residents. The current account surplus is then a flow, while the quantity of claims on foreigners in existence in the United States is a stock.

LABOR MARKET MEASUREMENT

The labor market variables we focus on here are those measured in the monthly household survey, carried out by the Bureau of Labor Statistics. In this survey, people are divided into three groups: the **employed**—those who worked part-time or full-time during the past week; the **unemployed**—those who were not employed during the past week but actively searched for work at some time during the last four weeks; and **not in the labor force**—those who are neither employed or unemployed. Thus, the labor force is the employed plus the unemployed.

Of key interest in analyzing the results of the household survey are the **unemployment rate,** measured as

$$\text{Unemployment rate} = \frac{\text{Number unemployed}}{\text{Labor force}},$$

and the **participation rate,** measured as

$$\text{Participation rate} = \frac{\text{Labor force}}{\text{Total working age population}}.$$

The unemployment rate is potentially useful as a measure of **labor market tightness,** which is the degree of difficulty firms face in hiring workers. However, there are two ways in which the unemployment rate might mismeasure labor market tightness (see Macroeconomics in Action: Measuring Unemployment and Labor Force Attachment). First, some people, referred to as **discouraged workers,** are not counted in the labor force and have stopped searching for work but actually wish to be employed. Thus, during a long recession, when the level of aggregate economic activity is depressed for an extended duration, the unemployment rate possibly might fall only because some unemployed people have become discouraged and stopped looking for work. In this circumstance, labor market tightness would not really have increased with the decrease in the unemployment rate, but we might be fooled into thinking so.

The second factor that could cause the unemployment rate to be a bad measure of labor market tightness is that the unemployment rate does not adjust for how intensively the unemployed are searching for work. When the unemployment rate is high, the unemployed might not search very hard for work—for example, each worker might spend one or two hours per day trying to find work. When the unemployment rate is low, however, the unemployed might all be searching very hard—for example, they might each search eight or ten hours per day. If this were the case, we might actually think of a high unemployment rate as being associated with high labor market tightness and a low unemployment rate as being associated with low labor market tightness. This would be because, for a firm looking for workers, it is more difficult to find workers if the unemployed are not looking hard for work.

Partly because of problems in interpreting what movements in the unemployment rate mean, macroeconomists often focus attention on the level and growth rate of employment when they analyze the implications of labor market activity. Indeed, many of the models we analyze in this book do not explain the behavior of unemployment; however, we study some explanations for unemployment in Chapters 12 and 15.

So far, we have learned how aggregate economic activity is measured in the NIPA, how nominal GDP can be decomposed to obtain measures of real GDP and the price level, what the relationships are among savings, wealth, and capital, and what the key measurement issues in the labor market are. Before we begin our study of macroeconomic theory in Chapter 4, in Chapter 3 we deal with business cycle measurement, deriving a set of key business cycle facts that focus our theoretical discussion in the following chapters.

MACROECONOMICS IN ACTION

Measuring Unemployment and Labor Force Attachment

The traditional approach to labor market measurement is to divide the working age population into three groups, the employed (E), the unemployed (U), and those not in the labor force (N). This approach is useful, as the economic behavior of the three groups is in principle distinct. Those in group E are engaged in the production of goods and services for the market, those in group U are engaged in search activity with the goal of joining group E, and those in group N are engaged in home production (child care and home maintenance for example) and leisure. Once labor market measurement is done in this way, we can then use the data in conjunction with economic theory to understand better why people choose to be in each of the three groups and to understand the implications for government policy.

Some recent research casts doubt on the traditional approach to labor market measurement. Leaving aside the issue of who should be counted as employed (rules about how many hours of work constitute employment are clearly arbitrary), there are varying degrees of search activity and

(continued)

separation from the labor force in the groups U and N, respectively. Stephen Jones and Craig Riddell[1] find that these differences among people in groups U and N appear to matter sufficiently that we should change how people are categorized in the labor force survey.

The first issue addressed by Jones and Riddell is related to the behavior of discouraged workers, or what they call the "marginally attached." This group of people expresses a desire to be employed, but they are not engaged in any of the activities constituting search behavior. A possibility is that the marginally attached are just engaged in wishful thinking and that they are appropriately included in N. However, Jones and Riddell's statistical analysis shows that the behavior of the marginally attached is distinct from the remainder of the people in group N, as well as from those included in U. Further, the marginally attached constitute a significant fraction of the population. This finding points to the need for distinguishing the marginally attached from U and N in the labor force survey.

A second issue studied by Jones and Riddell is the behavior of the subgroup of marginally attached people who are "waiting." This group is not actively searching for work but is waiting for a recall from a layoff period, waiting for replies from potential employers, etc. Jones and Riddell find that it would be appropriate to categorize the waiting as U rather than N. In fact, the waiting are more likely to be employed in the future than are those in group U.

Finally, Jones and Riddell examine the differing behavior of those who are currently classified as U. There is some question as to whether those who simply look at job postings in newspapers, for example, should be classified as U rather than N, as such persons may be uninterested in actually contacting potential employers. However, the general behavior of those engaged in low-level search activity shares more with the remainder of the U group than with the N group.

Ultimately, the primary recommendation coming from the work of Jones and Riddell is that labor market measurement and research should be conducted based on the notion of four distinct groups. Adding a group of discouraged workers (the marginally attached) to the three traditional labor market groups appears to be a sound approach.

---

[1]See S.R.G. Jones and W.C. Riddell, 1999, "The Measurement of Unemployment: An Empirical Approach," *Econometrica* 67, 147–162.

CHAPTER SUMMARY

- Gross Domestic Product (GDP) is measured in the National Income and Product Accounts (NIPA) of the United States. GDP can be measured via the product approach, the expenditure approach, or the income approach, which each yield the same quantity of GDP in a given period if there is no measurement error.

- GDP must be used carefully as a measure of aggregate welfare, because it leaves out home production. Further, there are problems with GDP as a measure of aggregate output, because of the existence of the underground economy and because government output is difficult to measure.

- It is useful to take account of how much of nominal GDP growth is accounted for by inflation and how much is growth in real GDP. Two approaches to measuring real GDP are choosing a base year and chain-weighting. The latter is the current method used in the NIPA. Chain-weighting corrects for the bias that arises in real GDP calculations when a base year is used and there are changes in relative prices over time. Problems with real GDP measurement arise because it is difficult to account for changes in the quality of goods over time and because new goods are introduced and others become obsolete.

- Private saving is private disposable income minus consumption, while government saving is government receipts minus government spending and transfers. The government surplus is equal to government saving. National saving is the sum of private and government saving and is equal to investment expenditures plus the current account surplus. National saving is just the accumulation of national wealth, which comes in the form of additions to the capital stock (investment) and additions to domestic claims on foreigners (the current account surplus).

- The labor market variables we focus on are those measured in the household survey of the Bureau of Labor Statistics. The working age population consists of the employed, the unemployed (those searching for work), and those not in the labor force. Two key labor market variables are the unemployment rate and the participation rate. The unemployment rate is sometimes used as a measure of labor market tightness, but care must be taken in how the unemployment rate is interpreted in this respect.

KEY TERMS

Gross domestic product (GDP): The dollar value of final output produced during a given period of time within a country's borders.

National Income and Product Accounts (NIPA): The official U.S. accounts of aggregate economic activity, which include GDP measurements.

Product approach: The approach to GDP measurement that determines GDP as the sum of value added to goods and services in production across all productive units in the economy.

Expenditure approach: The approach to GDP measurement that determines GDP as total spending on all final goods and services production in the economy.

Income approach: The approach to GDP measurement that determines GDP as the sum of all incomes received by economic agents contributing to production.

Intermediate good: A good that is produced and then used as an input in another production process.

Value added: The value of goods produced minus the value of intermediate goods used in production.

Income–expenditure identity: $Y = C + I + G + NX$, where Y is aggregate income (output), C is consumption expenditures, I is investment expenditures, G is government expenditures, and NX is net exports.

Gross national product (GNP): $GNP = GDP +$ net factor payments to U.S. residents from abroad.

Underground economy: All unreported economic activity.

Consumption: Goods and services produced and consumed during the current period.

Investment: Goods produced in the current period but not consumed in the current period.

Fixed Investment: Investment in plant, equipment, and housing.

Inventory investment: Goods produced in the current period that are set aside for future periods.

Net exports: Expenditures on domestically produced goods and services by foreigners (exports) minus expenditures on foreign-produced goods and services by domestic residents (imports).

Government expenditures: Expenditures by federal, state, and local governments on final goods and services.

Transfers: Government outlays that are transfers of purchasing power from one group of private economic agents to another.

Price index: A weighted average of prices of some set of goods produced in the economy during a particular period.

Price level: The average level of prices across all goods and services in the economy.

Inflation rate: The rate of change in the price level from one period to another.

Nominal change: The change in the dollar value of a good, service, or asset.

Real change: The change in the quantity of a good, service, or asset.

Chain-weighting: An approach to calculating real GDP that uses a rolling base year.

Implicit GDP price deflator: Nominal GDP divided by real GDP, all multiplied by 100.

Consumer price index (CPI): Expenditures on base year quantities at current year prices divided by total expenditures on base year quantities at base year prices, all multiplied by 100.

Flow: A rate per unit time.

Stock: Quantity in existence of some object at a point in time.

Private disposable income: GDP plus net factor payments, plus transfers from the government, plus interest on the government debt, minus taxes.

Private sector saving: Private disposable income minus consumption expenditures.

Government saving: Taxes minus transfers, minus interest on the government debt, minus government expenditures.

Government surplus: Identical to government saving.

Government deficit: The negative of the government surplus.

National saving: Private sector saving plus government saving.

Current account surplus: Net exports plus net factor payments from abroad.

Capital stock: The quantity of plant, equipment, housing, and inventories in existence in an economy at a point in time.

Employed: In the Bureau of Labor Statistics household survey, those who worked part-time or full-time during the past week.

Unemployed: In the Bureau of Labor Statistics household survey, those who were not employed during the past week but actively searched for work at some time during the last four weeks.

Not in the labor force: In the Bureau of Labor Statistics household survey, those who are neither employed or unemployed.

Unemployment rate: The number of unemployed divided by the number in the labor force.

Participation rate: the number in the labor force divided by the working age population.

Labor market tightness: The degree of difficulty firms face in hiring workers.

Discouraged workers: Those who are not counted in the labor force and have stopped searching for work but actually wish to be employed.

QUESTIONS FOR REVIEW

1. What are the three approaches to measuring GDP?
2. Explain the concept of value added.
3. Why is the income–expenditure identity important?
4. What is the difference between GDP and GNP?
5. Is GDP a good measure of economic welfare? Why or why not?

6. What are two difficulties in the measurement of aggregate output using GDP?

7. What is the largest expenditure component of GDP?

8. What is investment?

9. Is national defense a large fraction of government spending?

10. Why does the base year matter in calculating real GDP?

11. Explain what chain-weighting is.

12. Explain three problems in the measurement of real GDP.

13. What are the differences and similarities among private sector saving, government saving, and national saving?

14. What are the two ways in which national wealth is accumulated?

15. Give two reasons that the unemployment rate may mismeasure the degree of labor market tightness.

PROBLEMS

1. Assume an economy where there are two producers: a wheat producer and a bread producer. In a given year, the wheat producer grows 30 million bushels of wheat of which 25 million bushels are sold to the bread producer at $3 per bushel, and 5 million bushels are stored by the wheat producer to use as seed for next year's crop. The bread producer produces and sells 100 million loaves of bread to consumers for $3.50 per loaf. Determine GDP in this economy during this year using the product and expenditure approaches.

2. Assume an economy with a coal producer, a steel producer, and some consumers (there is no government). In a given year, the coal producer produces 15 million tons of coal and sells it for $5 per ton. The coal producer pays $50 million in wages to consumers. The steel producer uses 25 million tons of coal as an input into steel production, all purchased at $5 per ton. Of this, 15 million tons of coal comes from the domestic coal producer and 10 million tons is imported. The steel producer produces 10 million tons of steel and sells it for $20 per ton. Domestic consumers buy 8 million tons of steel, and 2 million tons are exported. The steel producer pays consumers $40 million in wages. All profits made by domestic producers are distributed to domestic consumers.
   (a) Determine GDP using (i) the product approach, (ii) the expenditure approach, and (iii) the income approach.
   (b) Determine the current account surplus.
   (c) What is GNP in this economy? Determine GNP and GDP in the case where the coal producer is owned by foreigners, so that the profits of the domestic coal producer go to foreigners and are not distributed to domestic consumers.

3. Assume an economy with two firms. Firm A produces wheat and firm B produces bread. In a given year, firm A produces 50,000 bushels of wheat, sells 20,000 bushels of wheat to firm B at $3 per bushel, exports 25,000 bushels of wheat at $3 per bushel, and stores 5,000 bushels as inventory. Firm A pays $50,000 in wages to consumers. Firm B produces 50,000 loaves of bread, and sells all of it to domestic consumers at $2 per loaf. Firm B pays consumers $20,000 in wages. In addition to the 50,000 loaves of bread consumers buy from firm B, consumers import and consume 15,000 loaves of bread, and they pay $1 per loaf for this imported bread. Calculate gross domestic product for the year using (a) the product approach, (b) the expenditure approach, and (c) the income approach.

4. In year 1 and year 2, there are two products produced in a given economy, computers and bread. Suppose that there are no intermediate goods. In year 1, 20 computers are produced and sold at $1,000 each, and in year 2, 25 computers are sold at $1,500 each. In year 1, 10,000 loaves of bread are sold for $1.00 each, and in year 2, 12,000 loaves of bread are sold for $1.10 each.
   (a) Calculate nominal GDP in each year.
   (b) Calculate real GDP in each year, and the percentage increase in real GDP from year 1 to year 2 using year 1 as the base year. Next, do the same calculations using the chain-weighting method
   (c) Calculate the implicit GDP price deflator and the percentage inflation rate from year 1 to year 2 using year 1 as the base year. Next, do the same calculations using the chain-weighting method.
   (d) Suppose that computers in year 2 are twice as productive as computers in year 1. How does this change your calculations in parts (a) to (c)? Explain any differences.

5. Assume an economy in which only broccoli and cauliflower are produced. In year 1, 500 million pounds of broccoli are produced and consumed and its price is $0.50 per pound, while 300 million pounds of cauliflower are produced and consumed and its price is $0.80 per pound. In year 2, 400 million pounds of broccoli are produced and consumed and its price is $0.60 per pound, while 350 million pounds of cauliflower are produced and consumed and its price is $0.85 per pound.
   (a) Using year 1 as the base year, calculate the GDP price deflator in years 1 and 2, and calculate the rate of inflation between years 1 and 2 from the GDP price deflator.
   (b) Using year 1 as the base year, calculate the CPI in years 1 and 2, and calculate the CPI rate of inflation. Explain any differences in your results between parts (a) and (b).

6. Consider an economy with a corn producer, some consumers, and a government. In a given year, the corn producer grows 30 million bushels of corn and the market price for corn is $5 per bushel. Of the 30 million bushels produced, 20 million bushels are sold to consumers, 5 million are stored in inventory, and 5 million are sold to the government to feed the army. The corn producer pays $60 million in wages to consumers and $20 million in taxes to the government. Consumers pay $10 million in taxes to the government, receive $10 million in interest on the government debt, and receive $5 million in Social Security payments from the government. The profits of the corn producer are distributed to consumers.
   (a) Calculate GDP using (i) the product approach, (ii) the expenditure approach, and (iii) the income approach.
   (b) Calculate private disposable income, private sector saving, government saving, national saving, and the government deficit. Is the government budget in deficit or surplus?

7. In some countries, price controls exist on some goods, which set maximum prices at which these goods can be sold. Indeed, the United States experienced a period of wage and price controls when the Nixon administration introduced wage and price controls in 1971. Sometimes the existence of price controls leads to the growth of black markets, where goods are exchanged at prices above the legal maximums. Carefully explain how price controls present a problem for measuring GDP and for measuring the price level and inflation.

8. Consider the identity

$$S^{p} - I = CA + D,$$

where S^{p} is private sector saving, I is investment, CA is the current account surplus, and D is the government deficit.

(a) Show that the above identity holds.

(b) Explain what the above identity means.

9. Suppose that the government deficit is 10, interest on the government debt is 5, taxes are 40, government expenditures are 30, consumption expenditures are 80, net factor payments are 10, the current account surplus is −5, and national saving is 20. Calculate the following (not necessarily in the order given):

(a) Private disposable income

(b) Transfers from the government to the private sector

(c) Gross national product

(d) Gross domestic product

(e) The government surplus

(f) Net exports

(g) Investment expenditures

WORKING WITH THE DATA

1. Calculate consumption of durables, consumption of nondurables, and consumption of services as percentages of total consumption, and plot these time series. Comment on the changes that have taken place over time in the consumption of services relative to durables and nondurables.

2. Macroeconomists sometimes study the behavior of the consumer price index, leaving out food and energy prices. Calculate the year-to-year inflation rate (December to December), in percentage terms, using the consumer price index (all items) and using the consumer price index less food and energy. Plot the two inflation rates, and comment on the differences. Why would we want to neglect food and energy in our calculation of the CPI? Why would we not want to neglect these items?

3. Plot the stocks of capital, private nonresidential capital, private residential capital, government capital, and consumer durable goods over time. Comment on the movements in these time series and the proportion that each component of capital takes up in the total.

CHAPTER 3

Business Cycle Measurement

Before we go on to build models of aggregate economic activity that can explain why business cycles exist and what, if anything, should be done about them, we must understand the key features that we observe in economic data that define a business cycle. In this chapter, we move beyond the study of the measurement of gross domestic product (GDP), the price level, savings, and wealth, which we covered in Chapter 2, to an examination of the regularities in the relationships among aggregate economic variables as they fluctuate over time.

We show that business cycles are quite irregular, in that they are unpredictable; macroeconomic forecasters often have a difficult time predicting the timing of a business cycle upturn or downturn. Business cycles are quite regular, however, in terms of comovements, which is to say that macroeconomic variables move together in highly predictable ways. We focus separately on the components of real GDP, nominal variables, and labor market variables.

This chapter describes a set of key business cycle facts concerning comovements in U.S. macroeconomic data. In Chapters 4, 5, 8 and 9, we use these facts to show how our models can make sense of what we observe in the data. Then, in Chapters 11 and 12, we use the key business cycle facts to help us evaluate alternative theories of the business cycle.

REGULARITIES IN GDP FLUCTUATIONS

The primary defining feature of **business cycles** is that they are *fluctuations about trend in real GDP.* Recall from Chapter 1 that we represent the trend in real GDP with a smooth curve that closely fits actual real GDP, with the trend representing that part of real GDP that can be explained by long-run growth factors. What is left over, the deviations from trend, we take to represent business cycle activity.

In Figure 3.1 we show idealized business cycle activity in real GDP, with fluctuations about a long-run trend. In the figure, real GDP is represented by the black line, while the trend is represented by the colored line. There are **peaks** and **troughs** in real GDP, a peak being a relatively large positive deviation from trend, and a trough a relatively large negative deviation from trend. Peaks and troughs in the deviations from trend in real GDP are referred to as **turning points.** In a manner analogous to wave motion in the physical sciences, we can think of the maximum deviation from trend in Figure 3.1 as the **amplitude** of the business cycle, and the number of peaks in real GDP that occur per year as the **frequency** of the business cycle.

Next, in Figure 3.2 we show the actual percentage deviations from trend in real GDP for the United States over the period 1947–2003. A series of positive deviations from

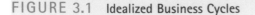

FIGURE 3.1   Idealized Business Cycles

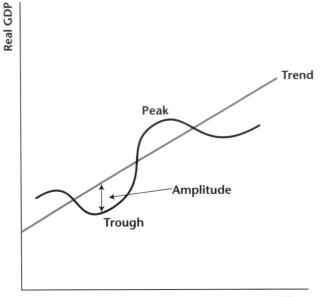

The black curve is an idealized path for real GDP over time, while the colored line is the growth trend in real GDP. Real GDP cycles around the trend over time, with the maximum negative deviation from trend being a trough and the maximum positive deviation from trend being a peak. The amplitude is the size of the maximum deviation from trend, and the frequency is the number of peaks that occur within a year's time.

trend culminating in a peak represents a **boom,** whereas a series of negative deviations from trend culminating in a trough represents a **recession.** In Figure 3.2, we have marked four important recessions, which occurred in 1973–75, 1981–82, 1990–91, and 2001. The first two of these recessions were quite significant, with the deviation from trend in real GDP exceeding 4%, whereas the last two were relatively mild, with deviations from trend of between 1% and 2%. In fact, since the 1981–82 recession real GDP has been remarkably stable in the United States, in that it has stayed much closer to trend than in the period from World War II to 1982.

An examination of Figure 3.2 indicates a striking regularity, which is that the deviations from trend in real GDP are **persistent.** That is, when real GDP is above trend, it tends to stay above trend, and when it is below trend, it tends to stay below trend. This feature is quite important in terms of economic forecasting over the short run; persistence implies that we can fairly confidently predict that if real GDP is currently below (above) trend, then it will be below (above) trend several months from now.

FIGURE 3.2   **Percentage Deviations from Trend in Real GDP from 1947–2003**

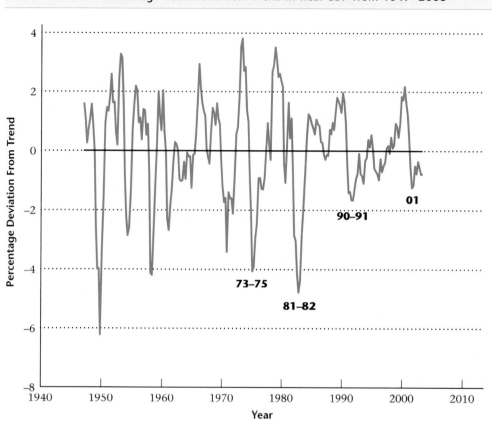

Of particular note are the four most recent recessions, in 1973–1975, 1981–1982, 1990–1991, and 2001. Since the 1981–1982 recession, real GDP has stayed quite close to trend, relative to the entire post–World War II history.

Source: U.S. Department of Commerce.

Other than being persistent, however, the deviations from trend in real GDP are actually quite irregular. There are three other features to note in Figure 3.2:

1. The time series of deviations from trend in real GDP is quite choppy.
2. There is no regularity in the amplitude of fluctuations in real GDP about trend. Some of the peaks and troughs represent large deviations from trend, whereas other peaks and troughs represent small deviations from trend.
3. There is no regularity in the frequency of fluctuations in real GDP about trend. The length of time between peaks and troughs in real GDP varies considerably.

Though deviations from trend in real GDP are persistent, which makes short-term forecasting relatively easy, the above three features imply that longer-term forecasting is difficult. The choppiness of fluctuations in real GDP make these fluctuations difficult to predict, while the lack of regularity in the amplitude and frequency of fluctuations implies that it is difficult to predict the severity and length of recessions and booms. Therefore, predicting future fluctuations in real GDP by looking only at past real GDP is much like attempting to forecast the weather by looking out the window. If it is sunny today, it is likely that it will be sunny tomorrow (weather is persistent), but the fact that it is sunny today may give us very little information on whether it will be sunny one week from today.

MACROECONOMICS IN ACTION

The Pitfalls of Macroeconomic Forecasting

In the United States, macroeconomic forecasting is done by government agencies such as the Congressional Budget Office and the Federal Reserve System and by private firms such as the Conference Board that sell forecasts to government and businesses. There are essentially three approaches to macroeconomic forecasting: judgmental forecasting, model forecasting, and statistical forecasting.

Judgmental forecasters gather various kinds of information and data from official and unofficial sources, and then they forecast future macroeconomic activity based on their own informal judgment about how the economy works. A judgmental forecaster does not use sophisticated statistical methods or macroeconomic theory in a rigorous way but instead relies on his or her "gut feelings" about where the economy is headed.

Model forecasting is done using an explicit macroeconomic model that is constructed using macroeconomic theory. The types of models used vary considerably, but those developed in the 1960s and 1970s,

some of which are still in use at central banks, in governments, and at private forecasting firms, consist of several hundred equations that capture the relationships among several hundred macroeconomic variables. A forecast using one of these models can involve work by a team of people who fine-tune the model before the forecast, and then generate a forecast that is a computer simulation of the model's predictions for future macroeconomic activity.

Statistical forecasting is a reaction to model forecasting, in that some macroeconomists argue that forecasting models had simply got out of hand. These macroeconomists argue that typical macroeconomic forecasting models are so large and complicated that no one actually understands how they work. Further, as they argue, a forecasting exercise with a large team of forecasters typically degenerates into an exercise where members of the team supply "add factors" to the model to make the forecast results conform to their own judgment concerning how the forecast should look.

(continued)

At worst then, the model is not allowed to make predictions but is simply a device for enforcing national income accounting identities (like the income–expenditure identity). As critics argued, the forecast is then judgmental and not a model forecast at all.

An example of a statistical model is the Bayesian Vector Autoregression (or BVAR) model developed at the Federal Reserve Bank of Minneapolis in the 1970s and 1980s. This is a model that is quite small and simple, and, once up and running, it can generate a forecast using the time of one person who need not be a trained economist.

No matter what the forecasting method used, macroeconomic forecasters can often be wrong, particularly in predicting turning points and in making predictions over a long horizon. A case in point occurred during the 2001 recession. In January 2001, the Congressional Budget Office (CBO) forecast that there would be a mild slowdown in real GDP growth from 3.8% in 2000 to 2.4% in 2001, with a recovery to robust growth of 3.4% in real GDP in 2002.[1] This forecast turned out to be exceedingly optimistic, particularly for 2001, as real GDP ultimately grew by 0.3% in 2001 and 2.4% in 2002. The CBO failed to predict the 2001 recession, which included negative growth

in real GDP in the first, second, and third quarters of 2001. Perhaps surprisingly, the events of September 11, 2001 cannot receive much of the blame for the large forecast error for 2001, as real GDP actually grew by 2.7% in the fourth quarter of 2001 at a time when the airlines and the travel industry were suffering from the negative effects of the terrorist attacks.

Were the economists at the CBO in January 2001 an especially bad group of forecasters? Apparently not, as the Blue Chip consensus forecast (an average of 50 private-sector forecasts) in January 2001 was if anything slightly more optimistic than the CBO forecast, predicting growth in real GDP of 2.6% and 3.4% for 2001 and 2002, respectively.[2] The evidence would seem to indicate that the large error in the CBO forecast was not because of incompetence. This is simply an example illustrating that macroeconomic forecasters are often wrong because forecasting the course of the macroeconomy can be extremely difficult.

[1] See "The Budget and Economic Outlook: Fiscal Years 2002–2011, January 2001," at http://www.cbo.gov/showdoc.cfm?index=2727&sequence=3.

[2] See "The Budget and Economic Outlook: Fiscal Years 2002–2011, January 2001," at http://www.cbo.gov/showdoc.cfm?index=2727&sequence=3.

COMOVEMENT

While real GDP fluctuates in irregular patterns, macroeconomic variables fluctuate together in patterns that exhibit strong regularities. We refer to these patterns in fluctuations as **comovement.** Robert Lucas once remarked that "with respect to qualitative behavior of comovements among [economic time] series, business cycles are all alike."[1]

Macroeconomic variables are measured as **time series;** for example, real GDP is measured in a series of quarterly observations over time. When we examine

[1] See R. Lucas, "Understanding Business Cycles," in *Studies in Business Cycle Theory,* MIT Press, p. 218.

FIGURE 3.3   Time Series Plots of x and y

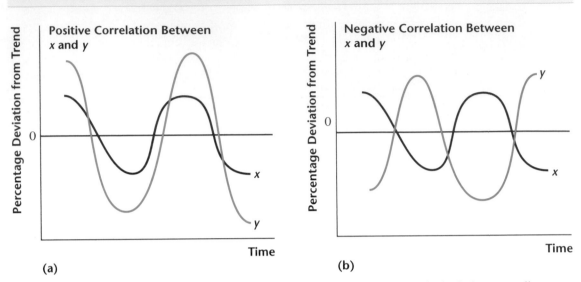

(a) Two time series that are positively correlated. When x is high (low), y tends to be high (low) as well.

(b) Two time series that are negatively correlated. In this case, when x is high (low), y tends to be low (high).

comovements in macroeconomic time series, typically we look at these time series two at a time, and a good starting point is to plot the data. Suppose, for example, that we have two macroeconomic time series and we would like to study their comovement. We first transform these two time series by removing trends, and we let x and y denote the percentage deviations from trend in the two time series. One way to plot x and y is in time series form, as in Figure 3.3. What we want to look for first in the time series plot is a pattern of **positive correlation** or **negative correlation** in x and y. In Figure 3.3(a), there is positive correlation between x and y: x is high when y is high, and x is low when y is low. That is, one economic time series tends to be above (below) trend when the other economic time series is above (below) trend. In Figure 3.3(b) x and y are negatively correlated: x is high (low) when y is low (high).

Another way to plot the data is as a **scatter plot,** with x on the horizontal axis and y on the vertical axis. In Figure 3.4, each point in the scatter plot is an observation on x and y for a particular time period. Here, whether x and y are positively or negatively correlated is determined by the slope of a straight line that best fits the points in the scatter plot. The top panel of Figure 3.4 shows a positive correlation between x and y, the middle panel a negative correlation, and the bottom panel a zero correlation. For example, in the U.S. population, if we plotted cigarettes smoked per year against the incidence of lung cancer, we would observe a positive correlation, and if we plotted the level of good cholesterol in the blood against the incidence of heart disease, we would observe a negative correlation in the scatter plot.

FIGURE 3.4   Correlations Between Variables y and x

(a) A scatter plot of two variables, x and y, that are positively correlated. (b) x and y are negatively correlated. (c) x and y are uncorrelated.

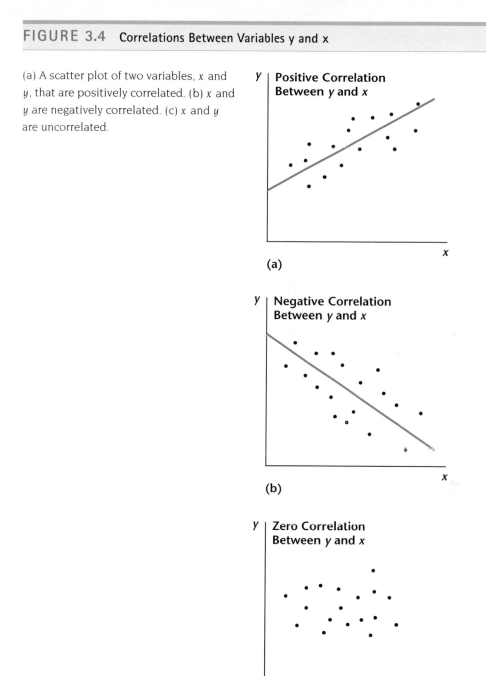

(a)

(b)

(c)

FIGURE 3.5   Imports and GDP

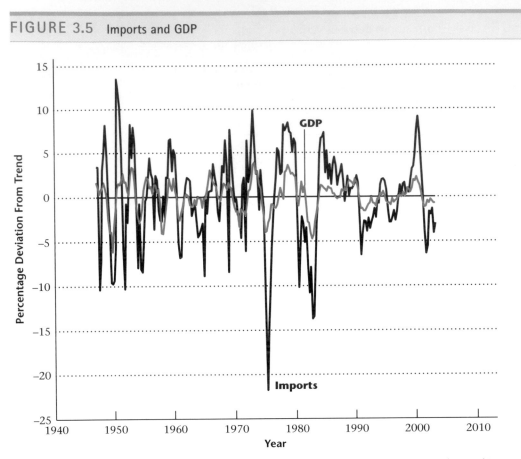

This figure, as an example, shows the time series of percentage deviations from trend in real imports (black line) and real GDP (colored line) for the United States for the period 1947–2003. Imports and GDP are clearly positively correlated, so imports are procyclical.

Source: U.S. Department of Commerce, Bureau of Economic Analysis.

Macroeconomists are often primarily interested in how an individual macroeconomic variable comoves with real GDP. An economic variable is said to be **procyclical** if its deviations from trend are positively correlated with the deviations from trend in real GDP, **countercyclical** if its deviations from trend are negatively correlated with the deviations from trend in real GDP, and **acyclical** if it is neither procyclical nor countercyclical. As an example of comovement between two macroeconomic time series, we consider real GDP and real imports for the United States over the period 1947–2003. In Figure 3.5 we plot the percentage deviations from trend in real GDP (the colored line) and real imports (the black line) in time series form. There is a distinct pattern of positive correlation in Figure 3.5; when GDP is high (low) relative to trend, imports

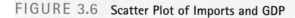

FIGURE 3.6   Scatter Plot of Imports and GDP

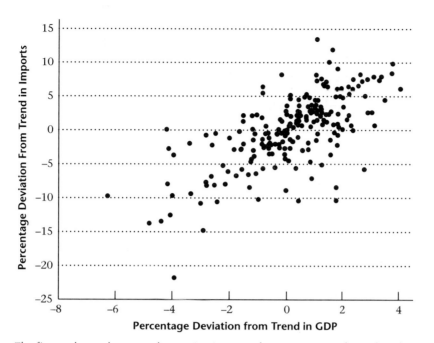

The figure shows the same data as in Figure 3.5 but in a scatter plot rather than in time series form. Here, we again observe the positive correlation between imports and GDP, as a positively sloped straight line would best fit the scatter plot. Again, imports are procyclical.

Source: U.S. Department of Commerce, Bureau of Economic Analysis.

tend to be high (low) relative to trend. This positive correlation also shows up in the scatter plot in Figure 3.6, where we show a graph of observations of percentage deviations from trend in imports versus percentage deviations from trend in GDP. Note that a straight line fit to the points in Figure 3.6 would have a positive slope.

A measure of the degree of correlation between two variables is the **correlation coefficient.** The correlation coefficient between two variables, x and y, takes on values between -1 and 1. If the correlation coefficient is 1, then x and y are **perfectly positively correlated** and a scatter plot of observations on x and y falls on a positively sloped straight line. If the correlation coefficient is -1, then x and y are **perfectly negatively correlated** and a scatter plot would consist of points on a negatively sloped straight line. If the correlation coefficient is 0, then x and y are uncorrelated. In the example above, the percentage deviations from trend in real GDP and real imports have a correlation coefficient of 0.67, indicating positive correlation.

An important element of comovement is the leading and lagging relationships that exist in macroeconomic data. If a macroeconomic variable tends to aid in predicting the

FIGURE 3.7   Leading and Lagging Variables

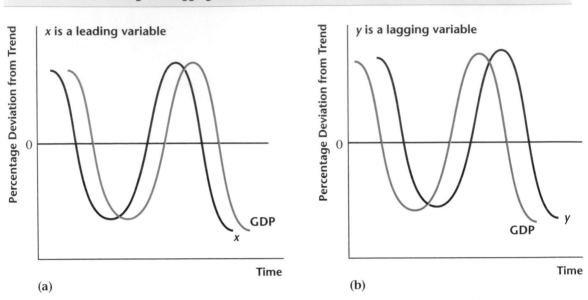

In (a), x is a leading variable, as its peaks and troughs tend to precede those of real GDP. In (b), y is a lagging variable, as the peaks and troughs in real GDP tend to lead those in y.

future path of real GDP, we say that it is a **leading variable,** whereas if real GDP helps to predict the future path of a particular macroeconomic variable, then that variable is said to be a **lagging variable.** In Figure 3.7 we show idealized time series plots of the percentage deviations from trend in real GDP and two variables, x and y. In Figure 3.7(a), variable x is a leading variable, whereas variable y is a lagging variable in Figure 3.7(b). A **coincident variable** is one which neither leads nor lags real GDP.

If it is known that some set of macroeconomic variables all tend to be leading variables, this information can be very useful in macroeconomic forecasting, as timely information on leading variables can then be used to forecast real GDP. One way to use this information is to construct a macroeconomic model, grounded in economic theory, that incorporates the relationships between leading variables and real GDP, and which can then be used for forecasting. Some economists, however, argue that forecasting can be done simply by exploiting past statistical relationships among macroeconomic variables to project into the future. A very simple form of this approach is the construction and use of the Conference Board's **index of leading economic indicators.** This index is a weighted average of macroeconomic variables that has been found to do a good job of predicting future real GDP. Watching the index of leading economic indicators can sometimes provide useful information for forecasters, particularly with respect to the turning points in aggregate economic activity. In Figure 3.8 we show a

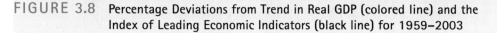

FIGURE 3.8 **Percentage Deviations from Trend in Real GDP (colored line) and the Index of Leading Economic Indicators (black line) for 1959–2003**

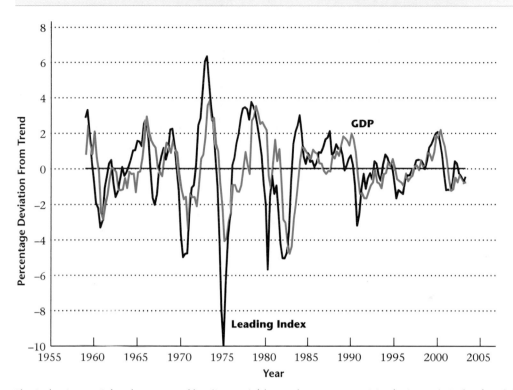

The index is a weighted average of leading variables and so, not surprisingly, it tends to lead real GDP

plot of the percentage deviations from trend in real GDP (the colored line) and in the index of leading economic indicators (the black line). The index of leading economic indicators tends to track real GDP fairly closely but with a lead. In particular, turning points in the index of leading economic indicators in Figure 3.8 tend to fall before turning points in real GDP.

Finally, there are key regularities in terms of the variability of economic variables over the business cycle. As we will see, some macroeconomic variables are highly volatile, while others behave in a very smooth way relative to trend. These patterns in variability are an important part of business cycle behavior that we would like to understand. A measure of cyclical variability is the **standard deviation** of the percentage deviations from trend. For example, in Figure 3.5, imports are much more variable than GDP. The standard deviation of the percentage deviations from trend in imports is more than twice that for GDP.

Next we examine some key macroeconomic variables, and we evaluate for each whether they are (1) procyclical or countercyclical, (2) leading or lagging, and (3) more or less variable relative to real GDP. These facts then make up the set of important business cycle regularities that we explain using macroeconomic theory.

THE COMPONENTS OF GDP

In Figure 3.9 we show the percentage deviations from trend in real aggregate consumption (the black line) and real GDP (the colored line). Clearly, the deviations from trend in consumption and in GDP are highly positively correlated, in that consumption tends to be above (below) trend when GDP is above (below) trend; these two time series move very closely together. The correlation coefficient between the percentage deviation from trend in real consumption and the percentage deviation from trend in real GDP is 0.76, which is greater than zero, so consumption is procyclical. There appears

FIGURE 3.9   Percentage Deviations from Trend in Real Consumption (black line) and Real GDP (colored line)

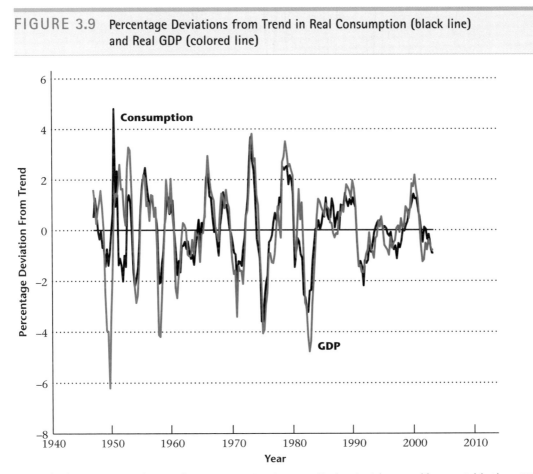

From the figure, we can observe that consumption is procyclical, coincident, and less variable than GDP.

Source: U.S. Department of Commerce, Bureau of Economic Analysis.

to be no discernible lead lag relationship between real consumption and real GDP in Figure 3.9—the turning points in consumption do not appear to lead or lag the turning points in real GDP. Consumption, therefore, is a coincident variable.

From Figure 3.9, note that consumption is less variable than GDP, in that the deviations from trend in consumption tend to be smaller than those in GDP. In Chapter 8 we study the theory of consumption decisions over time, and this theory explains why consumption tends to be smoother than GDP. For the data displayed in Figure 3.9, the standard deviation of the percentage deviations in real consumption is 75.6% of that for real GDP. This is a more precise measure of what our eyes tell us about Figure 3.9, which is that consumption is smoother than GDP.

The percentage deviations from trend in real investment (the black line) and real GDP (the colored line) are plotted in Figure 3.10. As with consumption, investment

FIGURE 3.10   Percentage Deviations from Trend in Real Investment (black line) and Real GDP (colored line)

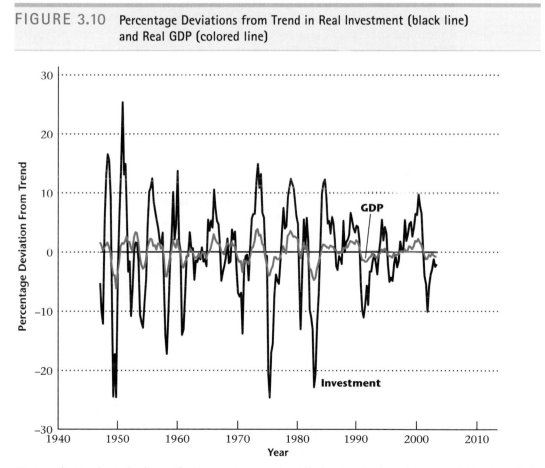

We can observe from the figure that investment is procyclical, coincident, and more variable than GDP.

Source: U.S. Department of Commerce, Bureau of Economic Analysis.

is procyclical, because it tends to be above (below) trend when GDP is above (below) trend. The correlation coefficient between the percentage deviations from trend in investment and those in GDP is 0.83. There is no tendency for investment to lead or lag GDP from Figure 3.10, and so investment is a coincident variable. However, some components of investment, in particular residential investment and inventory investment, tend to lead the business cycle. In contrast to consumption, investment is much more volatile than is GDP. This is indicated in Figure 3.10, where the deviations from trend in investment tend to be much larger than those for GDP. The standard deviation of the percentage deviations from trend in investment is 469.2% of what it is for GDP. Given that some components of investment lead GDP and that it is highly volatile, investment can play a very important role over the business cycle.

NOMINAL VARIABLES

The correlation between money prices and aggregate economic activity has long been of interest to macroeconomists. In the 1950s, A. W. Phillips observed that there was a negative relationship between the rate of change in money wages and the unemployment rate in the United Kingdom, a relationship that came to be known as the **Phillips curve.**[2] If we take the unemployment rate to be a measure of aggregate economic activity (as we see in Chapter 16, the unemployment rate is a strongly countercyclical variable; when real GDP is above trend, the unemployment rate is low), then the Phillips curve captures a positive relationship between the rate of change in a money price (the money wage) and the level of aggregate economic activity. Since Phillips made his initial observation, "Phillips curve" has come to be applied to any positive relationship between the rate of change in money prices or wages, or the deviation from trend in money prices or wages, and the deviation from trend in aggregate economic activity. As we see in Chapter 16, observed Phillips curves are notoriously unstable—that is, they tend to shift over time—and there are sound theories to explain this instability. However, a regularity in the 1947–2003 period in the United States is the negative correlation between deviations of the price level from trend and deviations of GDP from trend, observed in the scatter plot in Figure 3.11. We might think of this as a **reverse Phillips curve,** as there is a negative rather than a positive correlation between the price level and real GDP, with the correlation coefficient for the data in Figure 3.11 being −0.26. Over the period 1947–2003, therefore, the price level is a countercyclical variable.

In Figure 3.12 the price level (black line) is quite smooth relative to real GDP (colored line); the standard deviation of the percentage deviations from trend in the price level is 57.6% of that for GDP. The price level tends to be much smoother than most asset prices. For example, the average price of shares traded on the stock market is highly variable relative to the money prices of goods and services. In Figure 3.12 there appears to be no tendency for the price level to lead or lag real GDP, so that the price level appears to be coincident.

---

[2] See A. Phillips, 1958, "The Relationship Between Unemployment and the Rate of Change of Money Wages in the United Kingdom, 1861–1957," *Econometrica* 25, 283–299.

FIGURE 3.11   Scatter Plot for the Percentage Deviations from Trend in the Price Level (the Implicit GDP Price Deflator) and Real GDP

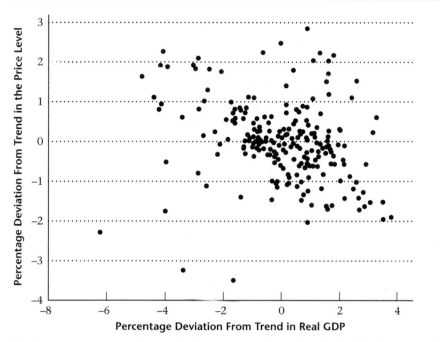

The figure shows a negative correlation between the two for 1947–2003; therefore, the price level is countercyclical for this period. The figure captures a reverse Phillips curve relationship.

Source: U.S. Department of Commerce, Bureau of Economic Analysis.

Whether the price level is procyclical or countercyclical, and whether it is a leading or a lagging variable, can play an important role in resolving debates concerning the causes of business cycles, as we see in Chapters 11 and 12. In contrast to the 1947–2003 U.S. data examined previously, it appears that the price level was a procyclical variable over some periods of history in some countries, for example, during the period between the World Wars in the United States. An alternative interpretation of Figure 3.12 is that the price level is a procyclical and lagging variable. That is, when real GDP is above (below) trend, the price level tends to be above (below) trend about two years later. Without other evidence to guide us, however, we stick to the interpretation that the price level is a countercyclical coincident variable in the post–World War II U.S. data.

In addition to Phillips curve relationships and reverse Phillips curve relationships, a key element of the comovement between nominal variables and aggregate economic activity is the positive correlation between deviations from trend in the nominal money supply and deviations from trend in real GDP. The money supply is a measure of the nominal quantity of assets used in making transactions in the economy. In the United

FIGURE 3.12   **Price Level and GDP**

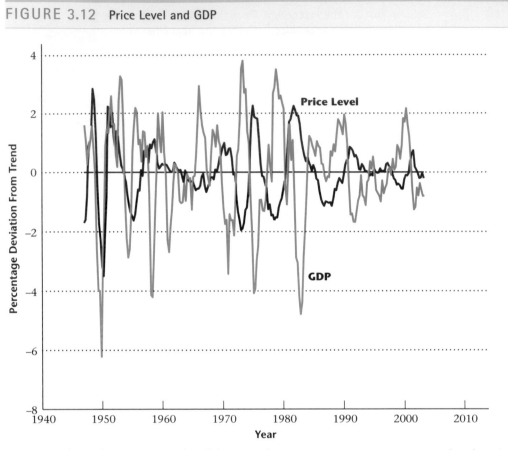

This figure shows the time series plot of the same data as in Figure 3.11. Here, we see that the price level (black line) is countercyclical, coincident, and less variable than real GDP (colored line).

Source: U.S. Department of Commerce, Bureau of Economic Analysis.

States, the money supply includes U.S. currency and checking accounts at banks and other depository institutions. In Figure 3.13 we show the percentage deviations from trend in a measure of the money supply (black line) and in real GDP (colored line) over the period 1959–2003.[3] The procyclical nature of the money supply is quite pronounced until about 1980, after which the link between the money supply and real GDP weakens. The correlation coefficient for the data in Figure 3.13 is 0.38. Another important observation concerning the nominal money supply and real GDP is that money tends to be a leading variable, which we observe as a tendency for turning

[3]The money supply measure used here is M2. In Chapters 9 and 15, we discuss the measurement of the money supply in more detail.

FIGURE 3.13   **Percentage Deviations from Trend in the Money Supply (black line) and Real GDP (colored line) for the Period 1959–2003**

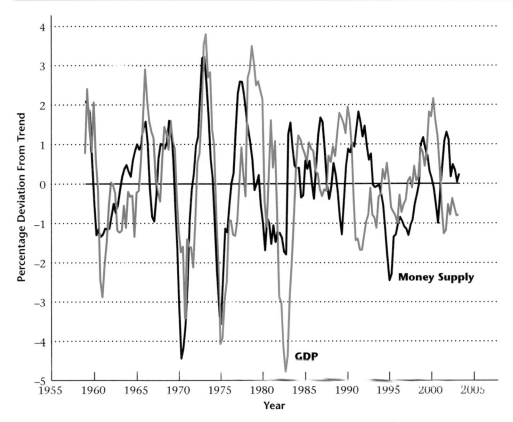

Money is a procyclical and leading variable, and it is less variable than real GDP.

Source: U.S. Department of Commerce, Bureau of Economic Analysis, and Board of Governors of the Federal Reserve System.

points in the money supply to lead turning points in GDP in Figure 3.13. This observation was emphasized by Milton Friedman and Anna Schwartz,[4] who studied the behavior of the money supply and real GDP in the United States over the period 1867–1960 (see Macroeconomics in Action: The Money Supply and Aggregate Economic Activity).

The money supply is somewhat smoother than GDP, with the standard deviation of the percentage deviations from trend in the money supply being 77.9% of what it is for GDP. This can also be observed in Figure 3.13.

---

[4]See M. Friedman and A. Schwartz, 1963, *A Monetary History of the United States: 1867–1960*, Princeton University Press, Princeton, NJ.

MACROECONOMICS IN ACTION

The Money Supply and Aggregate Economic Activity

Among the most influential works in economics is *A Monetary History of the United States, 1867–1960* by Milton Friedman and Anna Schwartz.[1] This research was intended as a body of empirical work and historical anecdotes that would document the role of monetary factors in aggregate economic activity in the United States over a period of almost a century. Part of the agenda of Friedman and Schwartz was to convince macroeconomists that fluctuations in the money supply played an important role in business cycles and that appropriate monetary policy was key to good macroeconomic performance.

An important contribution of Friedman and Schwartz was in economic measurement. They constructed what had not existed to that date: consistent measures of the money supply and other financial variables from 1867. This data, along with other historical evidence, was used by Friedman and Schwartz to show that large movements in real GDP were typically preceded by large movements in the nominal money supply in the same direction. That is, the money supply is procyclical and is a leading variable. As Friedman and Schwartz were well aware (and as we discuss further in Chapter 11), the fact that money leads output does not allow us to conclude that fluctuations in money cause fluctuations in output. In the words of Friedman and Schwartz,

"The monetary changes might be dancing to the tune called by independently originating changes in the other economic variables; the changes in income ... might be dancing to the tune called by independently originating monetary changes; ... or both might be dancing to the common tune of still a third set of influences."[2]

Friedman and Schwartz took care to find instances where they could argue that large monetary changes occurred independently and to find a causal link between movements in money and movements in output in these instances. In making their point that money was important for aggregate economic activity, this added weight to the statistical fact that money leads output.

The relationship between money and output has been extensively studied since Friedman and Schwartz's book was published. For example, an important piece of empirical work by Christopher Sims using sophisticated statistical techniques supported the conclusion of Friedman and Schwartz that increases (decreases) in money precede increases (decreases) in output.[3] While controversy remains concerning the interpretation of the statistical facts, as we discuss in Chapter 11, *A Monetary History of the United States* remains a key reference for macroeconomists.

---

[1] See M. Friedman and A. Schwartz, 1963, *A Monetary History of the United States: 1867–1960,* Princeton University Press, Princeton, NJ.

[2] M. Friedman and A. Schwartz, 1963, *A Monetary History of the United States: 1867–1960,* Princeton University Press, Princeton, NJ, page 686.

[3] See C. Sims, 1972. "Money, Income, and Causality," *American Economic Review* 52, 540–552.

LABOR MARKET VARIABLES

The last business cycle regularities we examine are those in labor markets, relating to the variables we determine in the business cycle models in Chapters 9–12. First, in Figure 3.14 we show percentage deviations from trend in employment (black line) and in real GDP (colored line) for the period 1948–2003. Clearly, the deviations from trend in employment closely track those in real GDP, and so employment is a procyclical variable. The correlation coefficient for the data in Figure 3.14 is 0.81. In terms of lead/lag relationships, we can observe a tendency in Figure 3.14 for turning points in employment to lag turning points in GDP, and so employment is a lagging variable. Employment is less variable than GDP, with the standard deviation of the

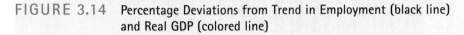

FIGURE 3.14   **Percentage Deviations from Trend in Employment (black line) and Real GDP (colored line)**

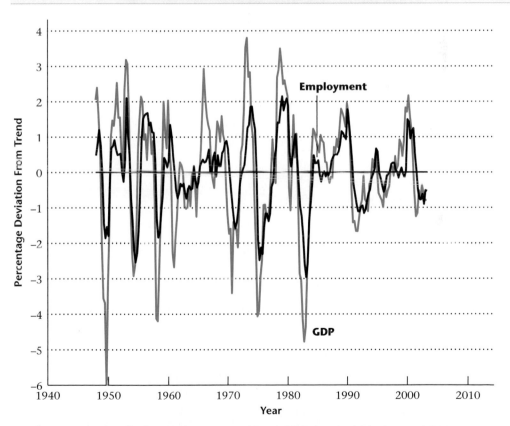

Employment is procyclical, it is a lagging variable, and it is less variable than real GDP.

Source: U.S. Department of Commerce, Bureau of Economic Analysis, and Bureau of Labor Statistics.

FIGURE 3.15   Percentage Deviations from Trend in Average Labor Productivity (black line) and Real GDP (colored line) for 1948–2003

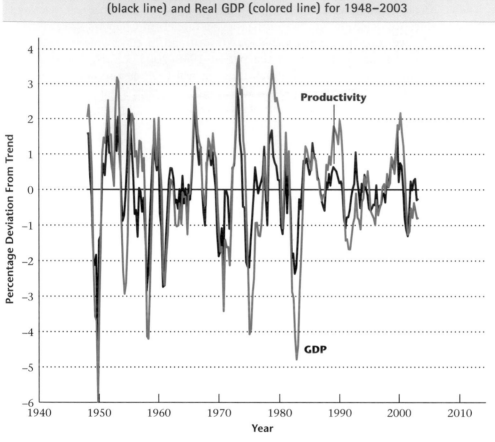

Average labor productivity is procyclical and coincident, and it is less variable than is real GDP.

Source: U.S. Department of Commerce, Bureau of Economic Analysis, and Bureau of Labor Statistics.

percentage deviation from trend for employment being 59.3% of that for real GDP in Figure 3.14.

In the macroeconomic models we analyze, a key variable is the market **real wage**, which is the purchasing power of the wage earned per hour worked. This is measured from the data as the average money wage for all workers, divided by the price level. The cyclical behavior of the real wage proves to be crucial in helping us discriminate among different theories of the business cycle in Chapters 11 and 12. The weight of empirical evidence indicates that the real wage is procyclical.[5] We do not show data on the

---

[5]See G. Solon, R. Barsky, and J. Parker, 1994, "Measuring the Cyclicality of Real Wages: How Important Is Composition Bias?" *Quarterly Journal of Economics*, February, 1–25.

aggregate real wage, as it is difficult to measure the relationship between real wages and real GDP by examining aggregate data. The key problem is that the composition of the labor force tends to change over the business cycle, which tends to bias the correlation between the real wage and real GDP. There is no strong evidence on whether the real wage is a leading or a lagging variable.

Productivity plays a key role in the economy, as was mentioned in Chapter 1, and in later chapters productivity is an important element in our study of business cycles and economic growth. One measure of productivity is **average labor productivity,** $\frac{Y}{N}$, where Y is aggregate output and N is total labor input. For our purposes Y is GDP and N is total employment, so we are measuring average labor productivity as output per worker. In Figure 3.15 we show the percentage deviations from trend in real GDP (colored line) and average labor productivity (black line). From the figure, average labor productivity is clearly a procyclical variable. The correlation coefficient for percentage deviations from trend in real GDP and average labor productivity is 0.83. Average labor productivity is less volatile than GDP; the standard deviation of the percentage deviations from trend in average labor productivity is 62.8% of that for real GDP. Further, there is no apparent tendency for average labor productivity to lead or lag real GDP in Figure 3.15, so average labor productivity is a coincident variable. In Chapters 11 and 12, the predictions of different business cycle theories for the comovements between average labor productivity and real GDP are important in helping us to evaluate and compare these theories.

COMOVEMENT SUMMARY

To summarize the business cycle facts discussed above, we present Tables 3.1 and 3.2. These two tables, particularly Table 3.2, prove very useful, particularly when we discuss the predictions of different theories of the business cycle in Chapters 11 and 12. A first test of the usefulness of macroeconomic theories is their ability to match what we see in macroeconomic data.

We have concluded our study of measurement issues, in that we now know the basics of national income accounting, basic macroeconomic accounting identities, price measurement, labor market facts, and business cycle facts. In the next chapters, we

Table 3.1 **Correlation Coefficients and Variability of Percentage Deviations from Trend**

	Correlation Coefficient	Standard Deviation (% of S.D. of GDP)
Consumption	0.76	75.6%
Investment	0.83	469.2
Price Level	−0.26	57.6
Money Supply	0.38	77.9
Employment	0.81	59.3
Average Labor Productivity	0.83	62.8

Table 3.2 **Summary of Business Cycle Facts**

	Cyclicality	Lead/Lag	Variability Relative to GDP
Consumption	Procyclical	Coincident	Smaller
Investment	Procyclical	Coincident	Larger
Price Level	Countercyclical	Coincident	Smaller
Money Supply	Procyclical	Leading	Smaller
Employment	Procyclical	Lagging	Smaller
Real Wage	Procyclical	?	?
Average Labor Productivity	Procyclical	Coincident	Smaller

proceed to build useful macroeconomic models, starting with some basic microeconomic principles concerning the behavior of consumers and firms.

CHAPTER SUMMARY

- The key business cycle facts relate to the deviations of important macroeconomic variables from their trends and the comovements in these deviations from trend.

- The most important business cycle fact is that real GDP fluctuates about trend in an irregular fashion. Though deviations from trend in real GDP are persistent, there is no observed regularity in the amplitude or frequency of fluctuations in real GDP about trend.

- Business cycles are similar mainly in terms of the comovements among macroeconomic time series. Comovement can be discerned by plotting the percentage deviations from trend in two economic variables in a time series or in a scatter plot or by calculating the correlation coefficient between the percentage deviations from trend.

- We are interested principally in how a particular variable moves about trend relative to real GDP (whether it is procyclical, countercyclical, or acyclical), whether it is a leading, lagging or coincident variable (relative to real GDP), and how variable it is relative to real GDP.

- Consumption is procyclical, coincident, and less variable than real GDP.

- Investment is procyclical, coincident, and more variable than real GDP.

- In the data set we examined here, the price level is a countercyclical variable (there is a reverse Phillips curve), it is coincident, and it is less variable than GDP.

- The money supply is procyclical, leading, and about as variable as real GDP. The fact that the money supply tends to lead real GDP was assigned much importance by Milton Friedman.

- In the labor market, employment is procyclical, lagging, and less variable than real GDP. The real wage, too, is procyclical. There is, however, no consensus among macroeconomists on whether the real wage is a leading or lagging variable. Average labor productivity is procyclical, coincident, and less variable than real GDP.

KEY TERMS

Business cycles: Fluctuations about trend in real GDP.
Peak: A relatively large positive deviation from trend in real GDP.
Trough: A relatively large negative deviation from trend in real GDP.

Turning points: Peaks and troughs in real GDP.

Amplitude: The maximum deviation from trend in an economic time series.

Frequency: The number of peaks in an economic time series that occur per year.

Boom: A series of positive deviations from trend in real GDP, culminating in a peak.

Recession: A series of negative deviations from trend in real GDP, culminating in a trough.

Persistent: Describes an economic time series that tends to stay above (below) trend when it has been above (below) trend during the recent past.

Comovement: How aggregate economic variables move together over the business cycle.

Time series: Sequential measurements of an economic variable over time.

Positive correlation: Relationship between two economic time series when a straight line fit to a scatter plot of the two variables has a positive slope.

Negative correlation: Relationship between two economic time series when a straight line fit to a scatter plot of the two variables has a negative slope.

Scatter plot: A plot of two variables, x and y, with x measured on the horizontal axis and y measured on the vertical axis.

Procyclical: Describes an economic variable that tends to be above (below) trend when real GDP is above (below) trend.

Countercyclical: Describes an economic variable that tends to be below (above) trend when real GDP is above (below) trend.

Acyclical: Describes an economic variable that is neither procyclical nor countercyclical.

Correlation coefficient: A measure of the degree of correlation between two variables.

Perfectly positively correlated: Describes two variables that have a correlation coefficient of 1.

Perfectly negatively correlated: Describes two variables that have a correlation coefficient of -1.

Leading variable: An economic variable that helps to predict future real GDP.

Lagging variable: An economic variable that past real GDP helps to predict.

Coincident variable: An economic variable that neither leads nor lags real GDP.

Index of leading economic indicators: A weighted average of leading macroeconomic variables, which is sometimes used to forecast the deviations of real GDP from trend.

Standard deviation: A measure of variability. The cyclical variability in an economic time series can be measured by the standard deviation of the percentage deviations from trend.

Phillips curve: A positive correlation between a money price or the rate of change in a money price and a measure of aggregate economic activity.

Reverse Phillips curve: A negative correlation between a money price or the rate of change in a money price and a measure of aggregate economic activity.

Real wage: The purchasing power of the wage earned per hour worked.

Average labor productivity: Equal to $\frac{Y}{N}$, where Y is aggregate output and N is total labor input.

QUESTIONS FOR REVIEW

1. What is the primary defining feature of business cycles?
2. Besides persistence, what are three important features of the deviations from trend in GDP?
3. Explain why forecasting GDP over the long term is difficult.
4. Why are the comovements in aggregate economic variables important?
5. What did Robert Lucas say about the comovements among economic variables?

6. How can we discern positive and negative correlation in a time series plot? In a scatter plot?

7. Give a noneconomic example of two variables that are positively correlated and an example of two variables that are negatively correlated.

8. Why is the index of leading economic indicators useful for forecasting GDP?

9. What are the three features of comovement that macroeconomists are interested in?

10. Describe the key business cycle regularities in consumption and investment expenditures.

11. What are the key business cycle regularities with respect to the price level and the money supply?

12. Does a Phillips curve relationship exist in the data set that was studied in this chapter?

13. What are the key business cycle regularities in the labor market?

PROBLEMS

1. Consider the following data, which are observations on x and y over several periods of time.

Period	x	y
1	100	500
2	200	500
3	200	1000
4	100	1000
5	50	500
6	50	250
7	100	250

(a) Construct a scatter plot of y against x. Are y and x positively correlated, negatively correlated, or uncorrelated? Explain your answer.

(b) Now, construct a time series of y and x. Is y a leading, lagging, or coincident variable with respect to x? Explain your answer.

(c) Do x and y exhibit persistence? Explain.

2. From Figure 3.2, determine how many booms and recessions occurred from 1947–1974, and from 1975–2003, and calculate the average strength of booms and the average severity of recessions from 1947–74 and from 1975–93. To do this, count as peaks and troughs only those deviations from trend that exceed ±2%. As a measure of the strength of a boom or the severity of a recession, use the percentage deviation from trend of real GDP at the peak of trough, respectively.

(a) When were booms more frequent, from 1947–74 or from 1975–2003?

(b) When were recessions more frequent, from 1947–74 or from 1975–2003?

(c) When were booms stronger, from 1947–74 or from 1975–2003?

(d) When were recessions more severe, from 1947–74 or from 1975–2003?

3. For each of the following sets of two variables, determine whether there is a positive or negative correlation, and explain your answer.

(a) Volume of auto traffic and the auto accident rate

(b) Average level of training of air traffic controllers and airplane crashes

(c) Seat belt use and deaths on the road

   (d) Use of pesticides and crop yields

   (e) Success as a politician and I.Q.

4. For each of the following sets of two variables, determine whether the second variable leads or lags the first, and explain your answer.
    (a) (i) Strictness of environmental protection laws; (ii) cleanliness of rivers
    (b) (i) Average height of the population; (ii) average nutrition level of the population
    (c) (i) Depth of the Mississippi at St. Louis; (ii) depth of the Mississippi at Minneapolis
    (d) (i) Prison population; (ii) length of prison sentences mandated by law
    (e) (i) Hours spent doing homework; (ii) GPA

5. From Figure 3.5, we determined that real imports and real GDP were positively correlated. Suggest a reason for this, and discuss.

6. From Figure 3.8, is the index of leading indicators infallible? That is, do peaks and troughs in the index always predict peaks and troughs in real GDP? Explain.

7. We have measured average labor productivity in this chapter as $\frac{Y}{N}$, where Y is real GDP and N is employment. The business cycle facts concerning employment relate to how the denominator (N) comoves with the numerator (Y), and those concerning average labor productivity relate to how $\frac{Y}{N}$ comoves with Y. Explain how the business cycle facts concerning employment and average labor productivity in Tables 3.1 and 3.2 are consistent.

8. Consumption of durables is more variable relative to trend than is consumption of non-durables, and consumption of nondurables is more variable relative to trend than is consumption of services. Speculate on why we observe these phenomena, and relate this to the key business cycle facts in Tables 3.1 and 3.2.

WORKING WITH THE DATA

1. Calculate the year-to-year (December-to-December) percentage increase in the consumer price index (CPI), and then do a scatter plot of this against the unemployment rate (match the December 1996 unemployment rate with the percentage change in the CPI from December 1995 to December 1996, for example). Do you observe a positive correlation, a negative correlation, or a correlation that is essentially zero? Is there a Phillips curve relationship here or a reverse Phillips curve?

2. The index of industrial production is an output measure that is not as comprehensive as GDP, but it is available on a more timely basis (monthly rather than quarterly). Calculate the percentage year-to-year (December-to-December) growth rates in the index of industrial production and the percentage year-to-year growth rates in the money supply (M2). Graph the growth in industrial production and in the money supply using a time series plot and using a scatter plot.
    (a) Are growth in industrial production and in the money supply positively correlated or negatively correlated?
    (b) Does one time series lead the other, or are they coincident?
    (c) Are your answers to (a) and (b) consistent with what we observed in Figure 3.13? Explain.

3. Plot: (i) detrended GDP and detrended consumption of durables; (ii) detrended GDP and detrended consumption of nondurables; (iii) detrended GDP and detrended consumption of services.

    (a) What do you notice in these plots compared to Figure 3.9 for GDP and total consumption and Figure 3.10 for GDP and investment?

    (b) Provide an explanation for the your observations in part (a).

4. Plot detrended GDP along with each of detrended residential investment, detrended non-residential investment, and inventory investment.

    (a) Which of the components of investment shows the most (least) variability relative to GDP?

    (b) What lead/lag patterns do you detect in the plots?

    (c) Provide possible explanations for the patterns you detected in parts (a) and (b).

PART II

A One-Period Model of the Macroeconomy

The goal of Part II is to construct a working model of the macroeconomy that can be used to analyze some key macroeconomic issues. The basic building blocks of this model are the microeconomic behavior of consumers and firms. We, therefore, start in Chapter 4 by analyzing the behavior of a representative consumer and a representative firm, with each making decisions over one period. The representative consumer's fundamental choice in this environment concerns how to allocate time between work and leisure, making himself or herself as well off as possible while obeying his or her budget constraint. The representative firm chooses how much labor it should hire so as to maximize profits. In Chapter 5, we build consumer behavior and firm behavior into a one-period macroeconomic model, in which there is a government that can spend and tax. This model is then used to show that, under ideal conditions, free market outcomes can be socially efficient, that government spending crowds out private consumption while increasing aggregate output, and that increases in productivity increase welfare, consumption, and aggregate output.

CHAPTER 4

Consumer and Firm Behavior: The Work-Leisure Decision and Profit Maximization

Chapters 2 and 3 focused on how we measure variables of macroeconomic interest. We now turn to the construction and analysis of a particular macroeconomic model. Recall that, in Chapter 1, we saw how a macroeconomic model is built from a description of consumers and their preferences over goods and of firms and the technology available to produce goods from available resources. In this chapter, we focus on the behavior of consumers and firms in a simple model environment with only one time period. One-period decision making for consumers and firms limits the kinds of macroeconomic issues we can address with the resulting model. This simplification, however, makes it easier to understand the basic microeconomic principles of consumer and firm optimization on which we build in the rest of this book. Given that there is only one time period, consumers and firms make **static,** as opposed to **dynamic,** decisions. Dynamic decision making involves planning over more than one period, as, for example, when individuals make decisions concerning how much to spend today and how much to save for the future. Dynamic decisions are analyzed in Parts III and IV.

With regard to consumer behavior, we focus on how a consumer makes choices concerning the trade-off between consuming and working. For the consumer, consuming more goods comes at a cost: the consumer must work harder and will enjoy less leisure time. Primarily, we are interested in how a consumer's work–leisure choice is affected by his or her preferences and by the constraints he or she faces. For example, we want to know how a change in the market wage rate and in the consumer's nonwage income affects his or her choices concerning how much to work, how much to consume, and how much leisure time to take. For the firm, we focus on how the available technology for producing goods and the market environment influence the firm's decision concerning how much labor to hire during the period.

As we discussed in Chapter 1, a fundamental principle that we adhere to here is that consumers and firms optimize. That is, a consumer wishes to make himself or herself as well off as possible given the constraints he or she faces. Likewise, a firm acts to maximize profits, given market prices and the available technology. The optimization principle is a very powerful and useful tool in economics, and it helps in sharpening the predictions of economic models. Given optimizing behavior by consumers and firms, we can then analyze how these economic agents respond to changes in the environment in which they live. For example, we show how consumers and firms change their labor supply and labor demand, respectively, in response to a change in the market wage rate, and how consumers respond to a change in taxes. The knowledge we build up in this chapter concerning these optimal responses is critical in the next chapter, where we study what happens in the economy as a whole when there is an important shock to the system, for example, a large increase in government spending or a major new invention.

THE REPRESENTATIVE CONSUMER

To begin, we consider the behavior of a single representative consumer, who acts as a stand-in for all of the consumers in the economy. We show how to represent a consumer's preferences over the available goods in the economy and how to represent the consumer's budget constraint, which tells us what goods it is feasible for the consumer to purchase given market prices. We then put preferences together with the budget constraint to determine how the consumer behaves given market prices, and how he or she responds to a change in nonwage income and to a change in the market wage rate.

The Representative Consumer's Preferences

It proves simplest to analyze consumer choice and is adequate for the issues we want to address in this chapter and the next, to suppose that there are two goods that consumers desire. The first is a physical good, which we can think of as an aggregation of all consumer goods in the economy, or measured aggregate consumption. We call this the **consumption good.** The second good is **leisure,** which is any time spent not working in the market. In terms of our definition, therefore, leisure could include recreational activities, sleep, and work at home (cooking, yardwork, housecleaning).

For macroeconomic purposes, it proves convenient to suppose that all consumers in the economy are identical. In reality, of course, consumers are not identical, but for many macroeconomic issues diversity among consumers is not essential to addressing the economics of the problem at hand, and considering it only clouds our thinking. Identical consumers, in general, behave in identical ways, and so we need only analyze the behavior of one of these consumers. Further, if all consumers are identical, the economy behaves as if there were only one consumer, and it is, therefore, convenient to write down the model as having only a single **representative consumer.** We must recognize, however, that the representative consumer in our macroeconomic model plays the role of a stand-in for all consumers in the economy.

A key step in determining how the representative consumer makes choices is to show how we can capture the preferences of the representative consumer over leisure and consumption goods by a **utility function,** written as

$$U(C, l),$$

where U is the utility function, C is the quantity of consumption, and l is the quantity of leisure. We refer to a particular combination of consumption and leisure—for example, (C_1, l_1), where C_1 is a particular consumption quantity and l_1 is a particular quantity of leisure—as a **consumption bundle.** The utility function represents how the consumer ranks different consumption bundles. That is, suppose that there are two different consumption bundles, representing different quantities of consumption and leisure, denoted (C_1, l_1) and (C_2, l_2). We say that (C_1, l_1) is strictly preferred by the consumer to (C_2, l_2) if

$$U(C_1, l_1) > U(C_2, l_2);$$

(C_2, l_2) is strictly preferred to (C_1, l_1) if

$$U(C_1, l_1) < U(C_2, l_2);$$

and the consumer is indifferent between the two consumption bundles if

$$U(C_1, l_1) = U(C_2, l_2).$$

It is useful to think of $U(C, l)$ as giving the level of happiness, or utility, that the consumer receives from consuming the bundle (C, l). The actual level of utility, however, is irrelevant; all that matters for the consumer is what the level of utility is from a given consumption bundle *relative* to another one.

To use our representation of the consumer's preferences for analyzing macroeconomic issues, we must make some assumptions concerning the form that preferences take. These assumptions are useful for making the analysis work, and they are also consistent with how consumers actually behave. We assume that the representative consumer's preferences have three properties: more is preferred to less; the consumer likes diversity in his or her consumption bundle; and consumption and leisure are normal goods. We discuss each of these in turn.

1. *More is always preferred to less.* A consumer always prefers a consumption bundle that contains more consumption, more leisure, or both. This may appear unnatural, because it seems that we can get too much of a good thing. For example, consuming too much of one good may sometimes make one worse off, as when we overeat. In terms of general consumption goods, however, the average consumer in the United States today consumes far more than the average consumer 200 years ago would have dreamed possible, and it certainly seems that the average consumer today in the United States would like to consume more if it were feasible. Indeed, even the extremely wealthy appear to desire more than they have.

2. *The consumer likes diversity in his or her consumption bundle.* To see that this is a natural property of consumer preferences, consider a consumer who, instead of consuming consumption goods and leisure, is making a decision about where to eat lunch during the week. Lynn can go to one of two restaurants to eat lunch, one of which serves only hamburgers, while the other serves only tuna sandwiches. One choice open to Lynn is to eat a hamburger for lunch on each day of the week, and another choice is to eat tuna sandwiches all week. Suppose that Lynn is indifferent between these two choices. If, however, she has a preference for diversity, Lynn would prefer to alternate between restaurants during the week rather than eat at one place every day. In the case of our representative consumer, who is choosing among consumption bundles with different combinations of consumption goods and leisure, a preference for diversity means that, if the consumer

is indifferent between two consumption bundles, then some mixture of the two consumption bundles is preferable to either one. At the extreme, suppose that the consumer is indifferent between a consumption bundle that has 6 units of consumption and no leisure and another bundle that has no consumption goods and 8 units of leisure. Then, a preference for diversity implies that the consumer would prefer a third consumption bundle, consisting of half of each of the other bundles, to having either of the other consumption bundles. This preferable third consumption bundle would have 3 units of consumption goods and 4 units of leisure.

3. *Consumption and leisure are normal goods*. A good is **normal** for a consumer if the quantity of the good that he or she purchases increases when income increases. For example, meals at high-quality restaurants are a normal good for most people; if our income increases, we tend to eat out more in good places. In contrast, a good is **inferior** for a consumer if he or she purchases less of that good when income increases. An example of an inferior good is food from Bob Evans; most people would tend to eat less at Bob Evans as their income increases. In our model, then, given that consumption and leisure are normal goods, the representative consumer purchases more consumption goods and increases his or her leisure time when income increases. This seems intuitively appealing; if, for example, you received a windfall increase in your income, perhaps through an inheritance, you would probably want to consume more goods as well as taking more vacation time (leisure). In practice, the behavior of consumers is consistent with consumption and leisure being normal goods.

While we postpone discussion of property (3) of the representative consumer's preferences until we have more machinery to analyze how the consumer behaves, our next step is to show how we represent properties (1) and (2) graphically. It is helpful to consider the representative consumer's preferences using a graphical representation of the utility function, called the **indifference map.** The indifference map is a family of **indifference curves.**

DEFINITION
An **indifference curve** *connects a set of points, with these points representing consumption bundles among which the consumer is indifferent.*

Figure 4.1 shows two indifference curves. In the figure, I_1 is an indifference curve, and two points on the indifference curve are (C_1, l_1) (point B) and (C_2, l_2) (point D). Because these two consumption bundles lie on the same indifference curve, we must have $U(C_1, l_1) = U(C_2, l_2)$. That is, being indifferent implies that the consumer obtains the same level of happiness from each consumption bundle. Another indifference curve is I_2. Because indifference curve I_2 lies above indifference curve I_1, and we know more is preferred to less, consumption bundles on I_2 are strictly preferred to consumption bundles on I_1. For example, consider point A, which represents a consumption bundle with the same quantity of leisure as at point B, but with a higher quantity

---

FIGURE 4.1   Indifference Curves

The figure shows two indifference curves for the consumer. Each indifference curve represents a set of consumption bundles among which the consumer is indifferent. Higher indifference curves represent higher welfare for the consumer.

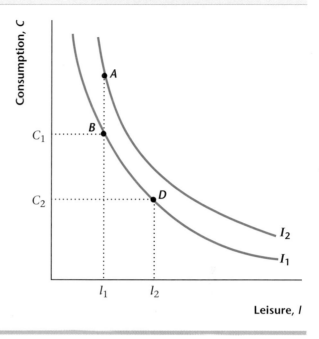

---

of the consumption good. Because more is preferred to less, A is strictly preferred to B.

An indifference curve has two key properties:

1. An indifference curve slopes downward.
2. An indifference curve is convex, that is bowed-in toward the origin.

Because the indifference map is just the graphical representation of preferences, it should not be surprising that the properties of the indifference curve are related to the properties of preferences, (1) and (2), described above. In fact, property (1) of an indifference curve follows from property (1) of preferences (more is always preferred to less), and property (2) of an indifference curve follows from property (2) of preferences (the consumer likes diversity in his or her consumption bundles).

To see why the fact that indifference curves slope downward follows from the fact that more is preferred to less, consider Figure 4.2. At point A, consumption is C_1 and leisure is l_1. Suppose that we now consider holding the quantity of leisure constant for the consumer at l_1 and reduce the consumer's quantity of consumption to C_2, so that the consumer now has the consumption bundle represented by point D. Because more is preferred to less, point D must be on a lower indifference curve (indifference curve I_2) than is point A (on indifference curve I_1). Now we can ask how much leisure we would have to add to l_1, holding consumption constant at C_2, to obtain a consumption bundle B such that the consumer is indifferent between A and B. Point B must lie

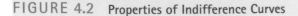

FIGURE 4.2   Properties of Indifference Curves

Indifference curves are downward-sloping because more is preferred to less. A preference for diversity implies that indifference curves are convex (bowed-in toward the origin). The slope of an indifference curve is the negative of the marginal rate of substitution.

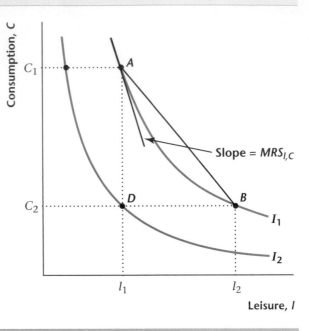

below and to the right of point A because, if we are taking consumption goods away from the consumer, we need to give him or her more leisure. Thus, the indifference curve I_1 is downward-sloping because more is preferred to less.

To understand why the convexity of the indifference curve follows from the preference of the representative consumer for diversity, we introduce the following concept.

> ### DEFINITION
> The **marginal rate of substitution** *of leisure for consumption, denoted* $MRS_{l,C}$, *is the rate at which the consumer is just willing to substitute leisure for consumption goods.*

We have

$$MRS_{l,C} = -[\text{the slope of the indifference curve passing through } (C, l)].$$

To see why the marginal rate of substitution is minus the slope of the indifference curve, consider consumption bundles A and B in Figure 4.2. There, the rate at which the consumer is willing to substitute leisure for consumption in moving from A to B is the ratio $\frac{C_1 - C_2}{l_2 - l_1}$, or minus the slope of the line segment AB. Minus the slope of AB tells us how much consumption we need to take away for each unit of leisure added as we move from A to B, with the consumer being just indifferent between A and B.

If we imagine choosing a point like point B on the indifference curve I_1 below point A but closer and closer to A, then as the distance between that point and A becomes small, the rate at which the consumer is willing to substitute leisure for consumption between A and the chosen point is the marginal rate of substitution, which is minus the slope of the indifference curve at point A (or minus the slope of a tangent to the indifference curve at A).

Suppose, for example, that Marla can choose how many weeks of vacation to take each year, and that she currently works 50 weeks in the year and takes 2 weeks of vacation, so that her leisure time is 2 weeks. To keep things simple, suppose Marla consumes only coconuts, so that we can measure her consumption in coconuts. Currently, she eats 500 coconuts per year. If Marla were to take one more week of vacation per year, she would be just as happy as she is now if she were to give up 50 coconuts per year. This implies that Marla's marginal rate of substitution of leisure for consumption, given her current consumption bundle of 500 coconuts of consumption and 2 weeks of leisure, is 50 coconuts per week.

Stating that an indifference curve is convex [property (2) of the indifference curve] is identical to stating that the marginal rate of substitution is diminishing. That is, note that the indifference curve in Figure 4.2 becomes flatter as we move down the indifference curve from left to right, that is, as the consumer receives more leisure and less of the consumption good. Thus, minus the slope of the indifference curve becomes smaller as leisure increases and consumption decreases. In other words, the marginal rate of substitution is diminishing. This is because, as we increase the quantity of leisure and reduce the quantity of consumption, the consumer needs to be compensated more and more in terms of leisure time to give up another unit of consumption. The consumer requires this extra compensation because of a preference for diversity.

To give a concrete example of a preference for diversity in terms of a consumption–leisure choice, suppose that Allen sleeps 8 hours in every 24-hour period. He, therefore, has 112 hours per week to split between work and leisure. Consider two situations. In the first, Allen takes 10 hours of leisure per week and works 102 hours, and in the second he takes 102 hours of leisure per week and works 10 hours. In the first circumstance, Allen is willing to give up much more consumption expenditure in exchange for one extra hour of leisure than in the second case.

The Representative Consumer's Budget Constraint

Now that we know something about the representative consumer's preferences, we must also specify his or her constraints and objectives to predict what he or she will do. We assume that the representative consumer behaves competitively. Here, **competitive behavior** means that the consumer is a price-taker; that is, he or she treats market prices as being given and acts as if his or her actions have no effect on those prices. This is certainly an accurate description of reality if the consumer is small relative to the market, but of course this is not literally true if there is only one consumer. Recall, however, that the single representative consumer is a stand-in for all the consumers in the economy. Even though it is obvious that real economies do not have only one consumer, a real economy can still behave as if there were a single representative consumer.

An important assumption that we make at this stage is that there is no money in this economy. That is, there is no government-supplied currency to be used in exchange, and no banks through which people can conduct transactions, for example, through checking accounts. For some macroeconomic issues, the complication of introducing money does not add anything to our analysis and is best left out. Later, however, in Chapters 9 to 11, we begin to analyze the role that money plays in the macroeconomy, so that we can address issues such as the effects of inflation and the conduct of monetary policy.

An economy without monetary exchange is a **barter** economy. In a barter economy, all trade involves exchanges of goods for goods. There are only two goods here: consumption goods and time. When time is used at home, we call it leisure time, and when time is exchanged in the market, we call it work—more explicitly, labor time. Any trades in this economy must involve exchanges of labor time for consumption goods, or vice versa. The consumer is assumed to have h hours of time available, which can be allocated between leisure time, l, and time spent working (or labor supply), denoted by N^s. The **time constraint** for the consumer is then

$$l + N^s = h, \tag{4.1}$$

which states that leisure time plus time spent working must sum to total time available.

The Consumer's Real Disposable Income   Having specified how the representative consumer allocates time between work and leisure, we can describe the consumer's real disposable income, which is wage income plus dividend income minus taxes.

Labor time is sold by the consumer in the labor market at a price w in terms of consumption goods. That is, one unit of labor time exchanges for w units of consumption goods. Therefore, w is the **real wage,** or the wage rate of the consumer in units of purchasing power. Throughout, the consumption good plays the role of **numeraire,** or the good in which all prices and quantities are denominated. In actual economies, money is the numeraire, but in our barter economy model, the choice of numeraire is arbitrary. We choose the consumption good as numeraire, as this is a common convention.

If the consumer works N^s hours, then his or her real wage income is wN^s, which is expressed in units of the consumption good. The second source of income for the consumer is profits distributed as dividends from firms. We let π be the quantity of profits, in real terms, that the consumer receives. In our model, firms have to be owned by someone, and this someone must be the representative consumer. Any profits earned by firms, therefore, must be distributed to the representative consumer as income, which we can think of as dividends. We refer to π as real **dividend income.**

Finally, the consumer pays taxes to the government. We assume that the real quantity of taxes is a lump-sum amount T. A **lump-sum tax** is a tax that does not depend in any way on the actions of the economic agent who is being taxed. In practice, no taxes are lump sum; for example, the quantity of sales taxes we pay depends on the quantity of taxable goods that we buy, and our income taxes depend on how much we work. Taxes that are not lump sum have important effects on the effective prices that consumers face in the market. For example, an increase in the sales tax on gasoline increases the effective price of gasoline for consumers relative to other goods. This change in the effective relative price of gasoline in turn affects the demand for gasoline and for other goods. These distorting effects of taxation are important, but we confine attention to lump-sum taxation for now, as this is simpler.

Real wage income plus real dividend income minus taxes is the consumer's real disposable income, and this is what the consumer has available to spend on consumption goods.

The Budget Constraint   Now that we know how the representative consumer can allocate time between work and leisure and what his or her real disposable income is, we can derive the consumer's budget constraint algebraically and show it graphically.

We can view the representative consumer as receiving his or her real disposable income and spending it in the market for consumption goods. What actually happens, however, is that the consumer receives income and pays taxes in terms of consumption goods, and then he or she decides how much to consume out of this disposable income. Because this is a one-period economy, which implies that the consumer has no motive to save, and because the consumer prefers more to less, all disposable income is consumed, so that we have

$$C = wN^s + \pi - T, \tag{4.2}$$

or, total real consumption equals real disposable income. Equation (4.2) is the consumer's **budget constraint.** Now, substituting for N^s in (4.2) using Equation (4.1), we get

$$C = w(h - l) + \pi - T. \tag{4.3}$$

The interpretation of Equation (4.3) is that the right-hand side is real disposable income, while the left-hand side is expenditure on consumption goods, so that total market expenditure is equal to disposable income.

Alternatively if we add wl to both sides of (4.3), we get

$$C + wl = wh + \pi - T. \tag{4.4}$$

An interpretation of Equation (4.4) is that the right-hand side is the implicit quantity of real disposable income the consumer has, and the left-hand side is implicit expenditure on the two goods, consumption and leisure. On the right-hand side of (4), because the consumer has h units of time, with each unit of time valued in real terms according to the market real wage w, and $\pi - T$ is real dividend income minus taxes, the total quantity of implicit real disposable income is $wh + \pi - T$. On the left-hand side of (4.4), C is what is spent on consumption goods, while wl is what is implicitly "spent" on leisure. That is, w is the market price of leisure time, because each unit of leisure is forgone labor, and labor time is priced at the real wage w. Thus, $C + wl$ is implicit real expenditure on consumption goods and leisure.

To graph the consumer's budget constraint, it is convenient to write Equation (4.4), in slope–intercept form, with C as the dependent variable, to get

$$C = -wl + wh + \pi - T, \tag{4.5}$$

so that the slope of the budget constraint is $-w$, and the vertical intercept is $wh + \pi - T$. In Figure 4.3 we graph the budget constraint, Equation (4.5), as the line AB. Here,

FIGURE 4.3   **Representative Consumer's Budget Constraint ($T > \pi$)**

The figure shows the consumer's budget constraint for the case in which taxes are greater than the consumer's dividend income. The slope of the budget constraint is $-w$, and the constraint shifts with the quantity of nonwage real disposable income, $\pi - T$. All points in the shaded area and on the budget constraint can be purchased by the consumer.

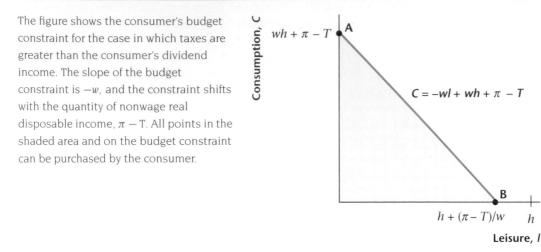

we have drawn the budget constraint for the case where $T > \pi$, so that dividend income minus taxes, $\pi - T$, is negative. Further, by setting $C = 0$ in Equation (4.5) and solving for l, we can get the horizontal intercept, $h + \frac{\pi - T}{w}$. The vertical intercept is the maximum quantity of consumption attainable for the consumer, which is what is achieved if the consumer works h hours and consumes no leisure. The horizontal intercept is the maximum number of hours of leisure that the consumer can take and still be able to pay the lump-sum tax.

Figure 4.4 shows what the consumer's budget constraint looks like in the case where $T < \pi$, in which case dividend income minus taxes, $\pi - T$, is positive. Here, the budget constraint is somewhat unusual, as it is kinked; the slope of the budget constraint is $-w$ over its upper portion, and the constraint is vertical over its lower portion. There is a kink in the budget constraint because the consumer cannot consume more than h hours of leisure. Thus, at point B we have $l = h$, which implies that the number of hours worked by the consumer is zero. Points along BD all involve the consumer working zero hours and consuming some amount $C \le \pi - T$—that is, the consumer always has the option of throwing away some of his or her dividend income. Even though the consumer does not work at point B, we have $C = \pi - T > 0$, as dividend income exceeds taxes. In what follows, we always consider the case where $\pi - T > 0$, as this is the more complicated case (because of the kink in the consumer's budget constraint), and because ultimately it does not make any difference for our analysis whether we look only at the case $\pi - T > 0$ or $\pi - T < 0$.

The representative consumer's budget constraint tells us what consumption bundles are feasible for him or her to consume given the market real wage, dividend income, and taxes. In Figure 4.4, consumption bundles in the shaded region inside and on the budget constraint are feasible; all other consumption bundles are infeasible.

FIGURE 4.4   **Representative Consumer's Budget Constraint ($T < \pi$)**

The figure shows the consumer's budget constraint when taxes are less than dividend income. This implies that the budget constraint is kinked. The examples we study always deal with this case, rather than the one in which taxes are greater than dividend income. Consumption bundles in the shaded region and on the budget constraint are feasible for the consumer; all other consumption bundles are not feasible.

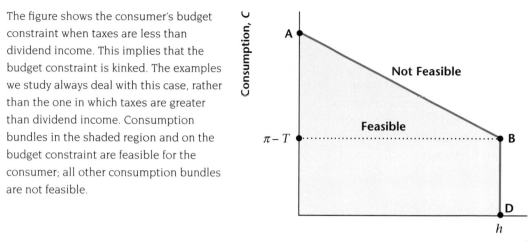

Consumer Optimization

We have now described the representative consumer's preferences over consumption and leisure, and determined the budget constraint that tells us what combinations of consumption and leisure are feasible. Our next step is to put preferences together with the budget constraint so as to analyze how the representative consumer behaves.

To determine what choice of consumption and leisure the consumer makes, we assume that the consumer is **rational.** Rationality in this context means that the representative consumer knows his or her own preferences and budget constraint and can evaluate which feasible consumption bundle is best for him or her. Basically, we are assuming that the consumer can make an informed optimization decision.

DEFINITION   *The* **optimal consumption bundle** *is the point representing a consumption–leisure pair that is on the highest possible indifference curve and is on or inside the consumer's budget constraint.*

Consider Figure 4.5, and note that we are considering only the case where $T < \pi$, because ignoring the case where $T > \pi$ does not matter. We want to demonstrate why point H, where indifference curve I_1 is just tangent to the budget constraint ABD, is the optimal consumption bundle for the consumer. First, the consumer would never choose a consumption bundle inside the budget constraint. This is because the consumer prefers more to less. For example, consider a point like J in Figure 4.5, which

FIGURE 4.5   Consumer Optimization

The consumption bundle represented by point H, where an indifference curve is tangent to the budget constraint, is the optimal consumption bundle for the consumer. Points inside the budget constraint, such as J, cannot be optimal (more is preferred to less), and points such as E and F, where an indifference curve cuts the budget constraint, also cannot be optimal.

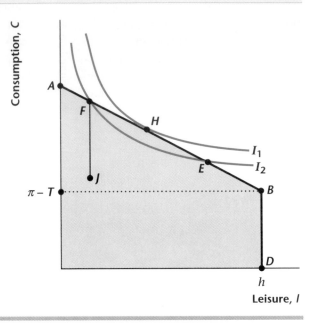

lies inside the budget constraint. Clearly, point F, which is on the budget constraint, is strictly preferred by the consumer to J because the consumer gets more consumption at point F than at J, while receiving the same quantity of leisure. Further, the consumer would not choose any points along BD other than B; B is preferred to any point on BD because more consumption goods are preferred to fewer consumption goods.

In considering the consumer's optimization problem, given our reasoning thus far we can restrict attention solely to points on the line segment AB in Figure 4.5. Which of these points does the consumer choose? Given the assumptions we have made about the representative consumer's preferences, we are guaranteed that there is a single consumption bundle on AB that is optimal for the consumer: the point at which an indifference curve is tangent to AB. Why is this the best the consumer can do? Again, consider Figure 4.5. At a point like F, minus the slope of the indifference curve passing through F, or $MRS_{l,C}$, is greater than minus the slope of the budget constraint at F, which is equal to w. Alternatively, at F the rate at which the consumer is willing to trade leisure for consumption is greater than the rate at which the consumer can trade leisure for consumption in the market, or $MRS_{l,C} > w$. The consumer would be better off, therefore, if he or she sacrificed consumption for more leisure by moving from point F in the direction of H. In so doing, the consumer moves to successively higher indifference curves, which is another indication that he or she is becoming better off. Similarly, at point E in Figure 4.5, the indifference curve is flatter than the budget constraint, so that $MRS_{l,C} < w$. Thus, moving from point E toward point H implies that the consumer substitutes consumption for leisure and moves to higher indifference curves, becoming better off as a result. At point H, where an indifference curve is just tangent to the budget constraint, the rate at which the consumer is willing to trade leisure for consumption is equal to the rate at which leisure trades for consumption in the market, and, thus, the consumer is at his or her optimum. In other words, when the representative consumer is optimizing, we have

$$MRS_{l,C} = w, \tag{4.6}$$

or the marginal rate of substitution of leisure for consumption is equal to the real wage. In Equation (4.6), this optimizing, or marginal, condition, takes the following form: marginal rate of substitution of leisure for consumption equals the **relative price** of leisure in terms of consumption goods. In general, the relative price of a good x in terms of a good y is the number of units of y that trade for a unit of x. It is generally true that consumer optimization in competitive markets implies that the consumer sets the marginal rate of substitution of any good x for any other good y equal to the relative price of x in terms of y. We use this fact in later chapters.

Given the way we have drawn the budget constraint in Figure 4.5, there seems no obvious reason that the highest indifference curve could not be reached at point B, in which case the consumer would choose to consume all of his or her time as leisure, as in Figure 4.6. However, this could not happen when we take account of the interaction of consumers and firms—it would imply that the representative consumer would not work, in which case nothing would be produced, and, therefore, the consumer would

---

FIGURE 4.6   **The Representative Consumer Chooses Not to Work**

The consumer's optimal consumption bundle is at the kink in the budget constraint, at B, so that the consumer does not work ($l = h$). This is a situation that cannot happen, taking into account consistency between the actions of the consumer and of firms.

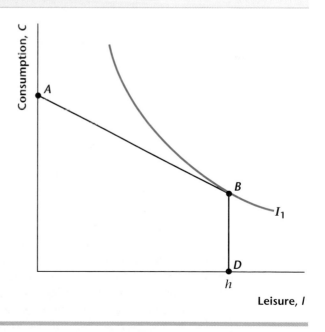

not have anything to consume. The assumption that the consumer always wishes to consume some of both goods (the consumption good and leisure) prevents the consumer from choosing either point A or point B in Figure 4.5.

The assumption that the representative consumer behaves optimally subject to his or her constraints is very powerful in giving us predictions about what the consumer does when his or her budget constraint changes, or when his or her preferences change. Is it plausible to assume that a consumer makes optimizing decisions? In our own lives, we can generally think of many occasions on which we did not make optimal decisions. For example, suppose Jennifer is self-employed and can choose how much vacation to take every year. Suppose that, for ten years, Jennifer takes two weeks of vacation every summer. One year, by chance, she takes three weeks of vacation and finds that she is much happier than before. We might imagine this happening not because Jennifer's preferences or budget constraint changed, but because she does not really know her own preferences without experimenting with different consumption–leisure combinations. This would violate the assumption of rationality that we have made for the representative consumer, who always knows exactly what his or her preferences are. The defense for using optimizing behavior for consumers as a fundamental principle in our models is that mistakes by consumers are not likely to persist for a long time. Eventually, people learn how to behave optimally, and what is important, particularly in terms of macroeconomic models, is that people on average behave optimally, not that each individual in the economy always does so. Further, if we were to abandon optimization behavior, there would be many possible alternatives, and it would be extremely difficult to get our models to make any predictions at all. While there is typically only one way to behave optimally, there are many ways in which individuals can be stupid!

How Does the Representative Consumer Respond to a Change in Real Dividends or Taxes?
Recall from Chapter 1 that a macroeconomic model, once constructed, can be used to conduct "experiments," somewhat like the experiments conducted by a chemist or a physicist using a laboratory apparatus. Now that we have shown how the representative consumer makes choices about consumption and leisure, we are interested as economists in how the consumer responds to changes in the economic environment he or she faces. We carry out two experiments on the representative consumer. The first is to change his or her real dividend income minus taxes, $\pi - T$, and the second is to change the market real wage w that he or she faces. In each case, we are interested in how these experiments affect the quantities of consumption and leisure chosen by the representative consumer.

We first look at a change in real dividend income minus taxes, or $\pi - T$, which is the component of real disposable income that does not depend on the real wage w. In changing $\pi - T$, we hold w constant. A change in $\pi - T$ could be caused either by a change in π or a change in T, or both. For example, an increase in π could be caused by an increase in the productivity of firms, which in turn results in an increase in the dividends that are paid to the consumer. Similarly, if T decreases, this represents a tax cut for the consumer, and disposable income increases. In any case, we think of the increase in $\pi - T$ as producing a **pure income effect** on the consumer's choices, because prices remain the same (w remains constant) while disposable income increases.

For the case where $\pi > T$, we consider an increase in $\pi - T$ (recall that the $\pi < T$ case is not fundamentally different). In Figure 4.7 suppose that initially $\pi = \pi_1$ and $T = T_1$, and then there are changes in π and T so that $\pi = \pi_2$ and $T = T_2$ with $\pi_2 - T_2 > \pi_1 - T_1$. Recall that the vertical intercept of the budget constraint is $wh + \pi - T$, so that initially the budget constraint of the consumer is ABD and, with the increase in $\pi - T$, the constraint shifts out to FJD. FJ is parallel to AB, because the real wage has not changed, leaving the slope of the budget constraint ($-w$) identical to what it was initially. Now suppose that initially the consumer chooses point H, where the highest indifference curve I_1 is reached on the initial budget constraint, and we have $l = l_1$ and $C = C_1$. When $\pi - T$ increases, which consumption bundle does the consumer choose? We have the consumer choosing point K, where the indifference curve I_2 is tangent to the new budget constraint. At point K, we have $l = l_2$ and $C = C_2$, so that consumption and leisure are both higher. Why would this necessarily be the case? Indeed, we could draw indifference curves that are consistent with more being preferred to less and a preference for diversity—which could have consumption falling or leisure falling—when income increases. Recall, however, that we assumed earlier in this chapter that consumption and leisure are normal goods. This means that, if we hold the real wage constant, then an increase in income implies that the representative consumer chooses more consumption and more leisure, as is the case in Figure 4.7.

To see why it is natural to assume that consumption and leisure are both normal goods, consider a consumer, Paula, who receives a windfall increase in her income from winning a lottery. It seems likely that, as a result, Paula spends more on consumption goods and takes more vacation time, thus working less and increasing leisure time. This would happen only if Paula's preferences have the property that consumption and leisure are normal goods.

The assumption that consumption and leisure are both normal implies that higher nonwage disposable income increases consumption and reduces labor supply. Thus, for example, given lower real taxes, consumers spend more and work less. The increase in income is given in Figure 4.7 by the distance AF, but the increase in consumption, $C_2 - C_1$, is less than AF. This is because, though nonwage income increases, wage income falls because the consumer is working less. The reduction in income from the decrease in wage income does not completely offset the increase in nonwage income, as consumption has to increase because it is a normal good.

The Representative Consumer and Changes in the Real Wage: Income and Substitution Effects   The second experiment we conduct is to change the real wage faced by the representative consumer, holding everything else constant. In studying how consumer behavior changes when the market real wage changes, we have some interest in how the consumer's quantity of consumption is affected, but we are perhaps most concerned with what happens to leisure and labor supply. In elementary economics, we typically treat supply curves as being upward-sloping, in that the quantity of a good supplied increases with the market price of the good, holding everything else constant.

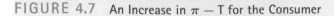

FIGURE 4.7   **An Increase in $\pi - T$ for the Consumer**

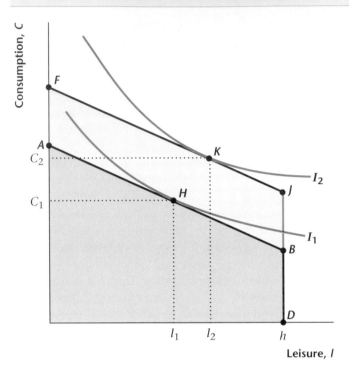

Initially the consumer chooses H, and when $\pi - T$ rises this shifts the budget constraint out in a parallel fashion (the real wage, which determines the slope of the budget constraint, stays constant). Consumption and leisure both increase, as both are normal goods.

Labor supply, however, is different. Although it is straightforward to show that the quantity of consumption goods chosen by the consumer increases when the real wage increases, labor supply, N^s, may rise or fall when the real wage rises. Part of this section focuses on why this is the case.

In considering how the behavior of the consumer changes in response to a change in the real wage w, we hold constant real dividends π and real taxes T. We do the experiment in this way to remove the pure income effect on consumer behavior that we studied in the previous subsection. Consider Figure 4.8, where initially the budget constraint is *ABD*, and an increase in the real wage w causes the budget constraint to shift out to *EBD*. Here, *EB* is steeper than *AB* because the real wage has increased, but the kink in the budget constraint remains fixed at B, as nonwage disposable income, $\pi - T$, is unchanged. Initially, the consumer chooses point F, where indifference curve I_1 is tangent to the initial budget constraint. Here, $l = l_1$ and $C = C_1$. When the real wage increases, the consumer might choose a point like H, where indifference curve I_2 is tangent to the new budget constraint. As Figure 4.8 is drawn, leisure remains

FIGURE 4.8   **Increase in the Real Wage Rate—Income and Substitution Effects**

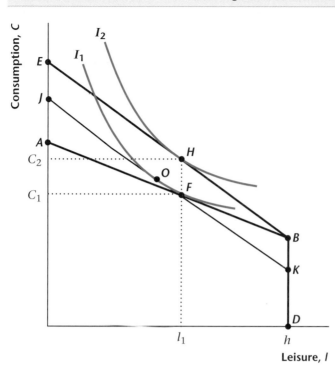

An increase in the real wage shifts the budget constraint from ABD to EBD. The kink in the constraint remains fixed, and the budget constraint becomes steeper. Consumption must increase, but leisure may rise or fall, because of opposing substitution and income effects. The substitution effect is the movement from F to O; the income effect is the movement from O to H.

unchanged at l_1, and consumption increases from C_1 to C_2. What we want to show is that, given that consumption and leisure are normal goods, consumption must increase but leisure may increase or decrease in response to an increase in the real wage. To understand why this is the case, we need to introduce the concepts of *income effect* and *substitution effect.*

The effects of an increase in the real wage on the consumer's optimal choice of consumption and leisure can be broken down into an income effect and a substitution effect as follows. First, given the new higher real wage, suppose that we take away dividend income from the consumer or increase taxes until he or she chooses a consumption bundle O that is on the initial indifference curve I_1. Thus, given the increase in the real wage, we have taken real disposable income away from the consumer so that he or she is just indifferent between the consumption bundle chosen (point O) and the initial consumption bundle (F). It is as if the consumer now faces the budget constraint JKD. The movement from F to O is a pure **substitution effect** in that it just captures the movement along the indifference curve in response to the increase in the real wage. The real wage increases, so that leisure has become more expensive relative to consumption goods, and the consumer substitutes away from the good that has become more expensive (leisure) to the one that has become relatively cheaper (consumption). Therefore, the substitution effect of the real wage increase is for consumption to increase and for leisure to decrease, and so the substitution effect is for labor supply, $N^s = h - l$, to increase.

Now, the movement from O to H is then a pure **income effect,** as the real wage stays the same as the budget constraint shifts out from JKD to EBD, and nonwage income increases. Because both goods are normal, consumption increases and leisure increases in moving from O to H. Thus, when the real wage increases, the consumer can consume more consumption goods and more leisure, because the budget constraint has shifted out. On net, then, consumption must increase, because the substitution and income effects both act to increase consumption. There are opposing substitution and income effects on leisure, however, so that it is ultimately unclear whether leisure rises or falls. Therefore, an increase in the real wage could lead to an increase or a decrease in labor supply N^s.

To understand the intuition behind this result, assume Alex is working 40 hours per week and earning $15.00 per hour, so that his weekly wage income is $600.00. Now suppose that Alex's wage rate increases to $20.00 per hour and that he is free to set his hours of work. On the one hand, because his wage rate is now higher, the cost of taking leisure has increased, and Alex may choose to work more (the substitution effect). On the other hand, he could now work 30 hours per week, still receive $600.00 in wage income per week, and enjoy 10 more hours of free time (the income effect), so that Alex may choose to reduce his hours of work.

While some of the analysis we do, particularly in Chapter 5, involves work with indifference curves, it is sometimes useful to summarize consumer behavior with supply and demand relationships. In Chapter 9 and in later chapters, it often proves useful to work at the level of supply and demand curves in different markets. Then, an important relationship is the **labor supply curve,** which tells us how much labor the representative consumer wishes to supply given any real wage. To construct the labor supply curve, one could imagine presenting the representative consumer with different real wage rates and asking what quantity of labor the consumer would choose to supply at each wage rate. That is, suppose $l(w)$ is a function that tells us how much leisure the consumer wishes to consume, given the real wage w. Then, the labor supply curve is given by

$$N^s(w) = h - l(w).$$

Now, because the effect of a wage increase on the consumer's leisure choice is ambiguous, we do not know whether labor supply is increasing or decreasing in the real wage. Assuming that the substitution effect is larger than the income effect of a change in the real wage, labor supply increases with an increase in the real wage, and the labor supply schedule is upward-sloping as in Figure 4.9. Furthermore, we know that, because the quantity of leisure increases when nonwage disposable income increases, an increase in nonwage disposable income shifts the labor supply curve to the left, that is, from N^s to N_1^s as shown in Figure 4.10. In analysis where we work with supply and demand relationships, we typically assume that the substitution effect of an increase in the real

FIGURE 4.9 **Labor Supply Curve**

The labor supply curve tells us how much labor the consumer wishes to supply for each possible value for the real wage. Here, the labor supply curve is upward-sloping, which implies that the substitution effect of an increase in the real wage is larger than the income effect for the consumer.

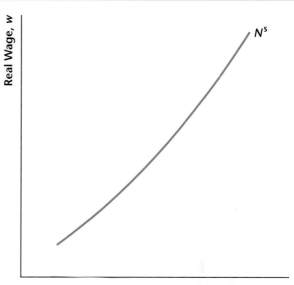

FIGURE 4.10 **Effect of an Increase in Dividend Income or a Decrease in Taxes**

The labor supply curve shifts to the left when dividend income increases or taxes fall, as a result of a positive income effect on leisure for the consumer.

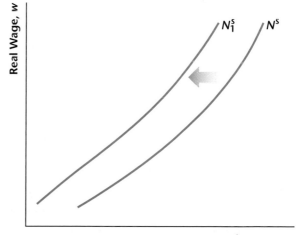

wage dominates the income effect, so that the labor supply curve is upward-sloping, as in Figure 4.9.

An Example: Consumption and Leisure are Perfect Complements   An example of consumer optimization that we can work out in a straightforward way, both algebraically and graphically, is the case in which the representative consumer's preferences have the **perfect complements** property. Goods are perfect complements for the consumer if he or she always wishes to consume these goods in fixed proportions. In practice, there are many cases of goods that are perfect complements. For example, right shoes are almost always consumed one-to-one with left shoes, in that a right shoe is typically not much good without the left shoe. Also, cars and tires are usually consumed in fixed proportions of one to four (ignoring the spare tire, of course).

If consumption and leisure are perfect complements, then the consumer always wishes to have $\frac{C}{l}$ equal to some constant, or

$$C = al, \tag{4.7}$$

where $a > 0$ is a constant. With perfect complements, the indifference curves of the consumer are L-shaped, as in Figure 4.11, with the right angles of the indifference curves falling along the line $C = al$. At a point such as E on indifference curve I_2, adding more consumption while holding leisure constant simply makes the consumer indifferent, as does adding more leisure while holding consumption constant. The consumer can be

---

FIGURE 4.11   Perfect Complements

When consumption and leisure are perfect complements for the consumer, indifference curves are L-shaped with right angles along the line $C = al$, where a is a constant. The budget constraint is ABD, and the optimal consumption bundle is always on the line $C = al$.

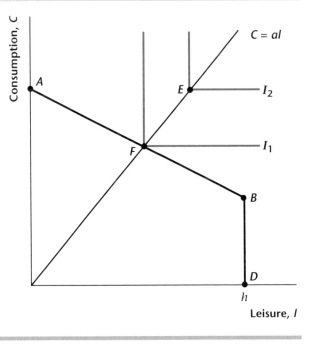

better off only if he or she receives more of both goods. Note that perfect complements preferences do not satisfy all the properties for preferences that we assumed in general. More is not always preferred to less, as the consumer is not better off with more of one good unless he or she has more of the other good as well. However, the consumer does have a preference for diversity, but of a very dramatic sort. That is, as we move downward along the indifference curve, the slope does not become flatter in a smooth way but goes instantly from vertical to horizontal.

The optimal consumption bundle for the consumer is always along the line $C = al$, as in Figure 4.11, where the budget constraint is ABD and the consumer optimizes by choosing a point that is on the budget constraint and on the highest indifference curve, which is point F. Algebraically, the quantities of consumption and leisure must solve (4.7) and must also satisfy the budget constraint

$$C = w(h - l) + \pi - T. \tag{4.8}$$

Now, Equations (4.7) and (4.8) are two equations in the two unknowns, C and l, with a, w, h, π, and T given. We can solve these two equations for the two unknowns by substitution to get

$$l = \frac{wh + \pi - T}{a + w},$$

$$C = \frac{a(wh + \pi - T)}{a + w}.$$

From the above solution, note that leisure and consumption increase with nonwage disposable income $\pi - T$, and we can also show that consumption and leisure both increase when the real wage w increases. With perfect complements there are no substitution effects. Further, if a increases, so that the consumer prefers more consumption relative to leisure, then it is obvious that the consumer chooses more of C and less of l at the optimum.

We use perfect complements preferences in examples in Chapter 8. Another simple example that is dealt with in the problems at the end of this chapter is the case where preferences have the **perfect substitutes** property. In that case, the marginal rate of substitution is constant and the indifference curves are downward-sloping straight lines.

INCOME AND SUBSTITUTION EFFECTS AND LABOR SUPPLY IN THE UNITED STATES, 1980–2003

THEORY confronts the DATA

In Figures 4.12 and 4.13 we examine some empirical evidence on the behavior of the real wage rate and hours worked per week in the United States for the period 1980–2003. The real wage rate is measured as an employment cost index divided by the consumer price index, and it corresponds to the real wage rate w in our model. Likewise, average hours worked per week corresponds to $N^s = h - l$ in the model. To use the theory of the representative consumer in this chapter to address what we see in Figures 4.12 and 4.13, we need to

FIGURE 4.12   **Real Wage in the United States, 1980–2003**

An upward trend in real wages over this period corresponds to a downward trend in average weekly hours over the same period shown in Figure 4.13. This can be explained by a tendency over this period for the income effect to outweigh the substitution effect.

Source: Bureau of Labor Statistics.

assume that the main factor affecting labor supply for the average worker in this sample over this period was changes in the real wage. This may not be a bad assumption for the sample of workers covered here, and neglecting changes in taxation probably is not too harmful.

In Figure 4.12 we observe an increase in the real wage from 1980–2003 of about 9% (note that we have normalized so that the real wage at the beginning of the sample is 100). Figure 4.13 shows that, from 1980 until the late 2003, average hours worked per week decreased from close to 35.4 hours per week to about 33.7 hours per week. If our model of labor supply is an upward-sloping curve, these observations might be puzzling. In the data the quantity of labor supplied per worker per week decreases when the real wage increases. What gives?

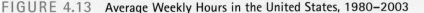

FIGURE 4.13   **Average Weekly Hours in the United States, 1980–2003**

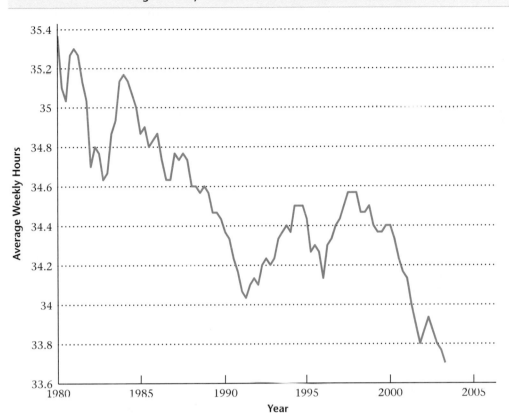

Average hours show a trend decrease over this period, corresponding to an upward trend in the real wage rate over the same period, shown in Figure 4.12.

The data in Figures 4.12 and 4.13 is not puzzling if we interpret it in terms of the income and substitution effects of changes in the real wage on labor supply. If the income effect exceeded the substitution effect for the average worker over the period 1980 to 2003, then an increase in the real wage would lead to a fall in hours worked per person, as we see in the data.

Given the deeper knowledge of labor supply that comes from an analysis of income and substitution effects, the observations in Figures 4.12 and 4.13 are not puzzling at all. This is not to say that we can explain anything in terms of labor market observations by appealing to opposing income and substitution effects. A careful analysis of the data would require that our explanations for what we see in Figures 4.12 and 4.13 be quantitatively consistent, and consistent with other kinds of evidence about labor market behavior.

The Representative Firm

In our model economy, consumers and firms come together to exchange labor for consumption goods. While the representative consumer supplies labor and demands consumption goods, we turn now to the behavior of firms, which demand labor and supply consumption goods. The choices of the firms are determined by the available technology and by profit maximization. As with consumer behavior, we ultimately focus here on the choices of a single, representative firm.

The firms in this economy own productive capital (plant and equipment), and they hire labor to produce consumption goods. We can describe the production technology available to each firm by a **production function,** which describes the technological possibilities for converting factor inputs into outputs. We can express this relationship in algebraic terms as

$$Y = zF(K, N^d), \tag{4.9}$$

where z is total factor productivity, Y is output of consumption goods, K is the quantity of capital input in the production process, N^d is the quantity of labor input measured as total hours worked by employees of the firm, and F is a function. Because this is a one-period or static (as opposed to dynamic) model, we treat K as being a fixed input to production, and N^d as a variable factor of production. That is, in the short run, firms cannot vary the quantity of plant and equipment (K) they have, but they have flexibility in hiring and laying off workers (N^d). **Total factor productivity** z captures the degree of sophistication of the production process. That is, an increase in z makes both factors of production, K and N^d, more productive, in that, given factor inputs, higher z implies that more output can be produced.

For example, suppose that the above production function represents the technology available to a bakery. The quantity of capital, K, includes the building in which the bakery operates, ovens for baking bread, a computer for doing the bakery accounts, and other miscellaneous equipment. The quantity of labor, N^d, is total hours worked by all the bakery employees, including the manager, the bakers who operate the ovens, and the employees who work selling the bakery's products to customers. The variable z, total factor productivity, can be affected by the techniques used for organizing production. For example, bread could be produced either by having each baker operate an individual oven, using this oven to produce different kinds of bread, or each baker could specialize in making a particular kind of bread and use the oven that happens to be available when an oven is needed. If the latter production method produces more bread per day using the same inputs of capital and labor, then that production process implies a higher value of z than does the first process.

For our analysis, we need to discuss several important properties of the production function. Before doing this, we need the following definition.

D E F I N I T I O N

The **marginal product** *of a factor of production is the additional output that can be produced with one additional unit of that factor input, holding constant the quantities of the other factor inputs.*

FIGURE 4.14   **Production Function, Fixing the Quantity of Capital and Varying the Quantity of Labor**

The marginal product of labor is the slope of the production function at a given point. Note that the marginal product of labor declines with the quantity of labor.

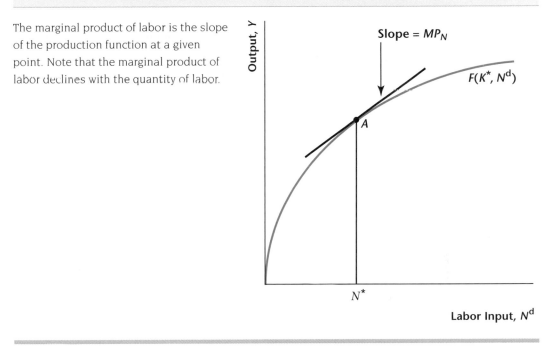

In the production function of Equation (4.9), there are two factor inputs, labor and capital. Figure 4.14 shows a graph of the production function, fixing the quantity of capital at some arbitrary value, K^*, and allowing the labor input, N^d, to vary. Some of the properties of this graph require further explanation. In the figure, the marginal product of labor, given the quantity of labor N^*, is the slope of the production function at point A; this is because the slope of the production function is the additional output produced from an additional unit of the labor input when the quantity of labor is N^* and the quantity of capital is K^*. We let MP_N denote the marginal product of labor.

Next, in Figure 4.15 we graph the production function again, but this time we fix the quantity of labor at N^* and allow the quantity of capital to vary. In Figure 4.15, the marginal product of capital, denoted MP_K, given the quantity of capital K^*, is the slope of the production function at point A.

The production function has five key properties, which we will discuss in turn.

1. *The production function exhibits constant returns to scale.* **Constant returns to scale** means that, given any constant $x > 0$, the following relationship holds:

$$zF(xK, xN^d) = xzF(K, N^d).$$

That is, if all factor inputs are changed by a factor x, then output changes by the same factor x. For example, if all factor inputs double ($x = 2$), then output also

FIGURE 4.15   **Production Function, Fixing the Quantity of Labor and Varying the Quantity of Capital**

The slope of the production function is the marginal product of capital, and the marginal product of capital declines with the quantity of capital.

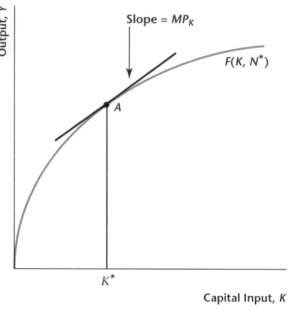

doubles. The alternatives to constant returns to scale in production are **increasing returns to scale** and **decreasing returns to scale.** Increasing returns to scale implies that large firms (firms producing a large quantity of output) are more efficient than small firms, whereas decreasing returns to scale implies that small firms are more efficient than large firms. With constant returns to scale, a small firm is just as efficient as a large firm. Indeed, constant returns to scale means that a very large firm simply replicates how a very small firm produces many times over. Given a constant-returns-to-scale production function, the economy behaves in exactly the same way if there were many small firms producing consumption goods as it would if there were a few large firms, provided that all firms behave competitively (they are price-takers in product and factor markets). Given this, it is most convenient to suppose that there is only one firm in the economy, the **representative firm.** Just as with the representative consumer, it is helpful to think of the representative firm as a convenient stand-in for many firms, which all have the same constant-returns-to-scale production function. In practice, it is clear that in some industries decreasing returns to scale are important. For example, high-quality restaurant food seems to be produced most efficiently on a small scale. Alternatively, increasing returns to scale are important in the automobile industry, where essentially all production occurs in very large scale firms, such as General

Motors. This does not mean, however, that it is harmful to assume that there exists constant returns to scale in production at the aggregate level, as is the case in our model. This is because even the largest firm in the U.S. economy produces a small amount of output relative to U.S. GDP, and the aggregate economy can exhibit constant returns to scale in aggregate production, even if this is not literally true for each firm in the economy.

2. *The production function has the property that output increases when either the capital input or the labor input increases.* In other words, the marginal products of labor and capital are both positive: $MP_N > 0$ and $MP_K > 0$. In Figures 4.14 and 4.15, these properties of the production function are exhibited by the upward slope of the production function. Recall that the slope of the production function in Figure 4.14 is the marginal product of labor and the slope in Figure 4.15 is the marginal product of capital. Positive marginal products are quite natural properties of the production function, as this states simply that more inputs yield more output. In the bakery example discussed previously, if the bakery hires more workers given the same capital equipment, it will produce more bread, and if it installs more ovens given the same quantity of workers, it will also produce more bread.

3. *The marginal product of labor decreases as the quantity of labor increases.* In Figure 4.14 the declining marginal product of labor is reflected in the concavity of the production function. That is, the slope of the production function in Figure 4.14, which is equal to MP_N, decreases as N^d increases. The following example helps to illustrate why the marginal product of labor should fall as the quantity of labor input increases: Suppose accountants work in an office building that has one photocopy machine, and suppose that they work with pencils and paper but at random intervals need to use the photocopy machine. The first accountant added to the production process, Sara, is very productive—that is, she has a high marginal product—as she can use the photocopy machine whenever she wants. However, when the second accountant, Paul, is added, Sara on occasion wants to use the machine and she gets up from her desk, walks to the machine, and finds that Paul is using it. Thus, some time is wasted that could otherwise be spent working. Paul and Sara produce more than Sara alone, but what Paul adds to production (his marginal product) is lower than the marginal product of Sara. Similarly, adding a third accountant, Julia, makes for even more congestion around the photocopy machine, and Julia's marginal product is lower than Paul's marginal product, which is lower than Sara's. Figure 4.16 shows the representative firm's marginal product of labor schedule. This is a graph of the firm's marginal product, given a fixed quantity of capital, as a function of the labor input. That is, this is the graph of the slope of the production function in Figure 4.14. The marginal product schedule is always positive, and it slopes downward.

4. *The marginal product of capital decreases as the quantity of capital increases.* This property of the production function is very similar to the previous one, and it is illustrated in Figure 4.15 by the decreasing slope, or concavity, of the production

FIGURE 4.16   **Marginal Product of Labor Schedule for the Representative Firm**

The marginal product of labor declines as the quantity of labor used in the production process increases.

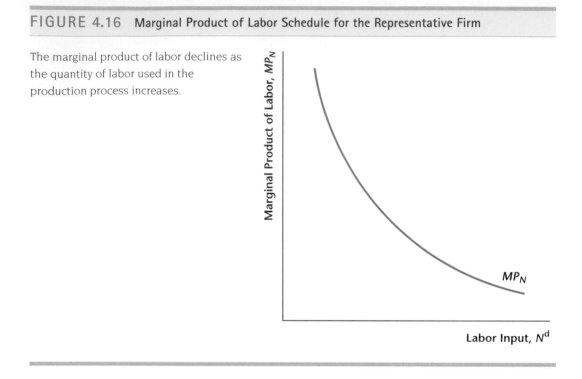

function. In terms of the example above, if we suppose that Sara, Paul, and Julia are the accountants working in the office and imagine what happens as we add photocopy machines, we can gain some intuition as to why the decreasing-marginal-product-of-capital property is natural. Adding the first photocopy machine adds a great deal to total output, as Sara, Paul, and Julia now can duplicate documents that formerly had to be copied by hand. With three accountants in the office, however, there is congestion around the machine. This congestion is relieved with the addition of a second machine, so that the second machine increases output, but the marginal product of the second machine is smaller than the marginal product of the first machine, and so on.

5. *The marginal product of labor increases as the quantity of the capital input increases.* To provide some intuition for this property of the production function, let's once again return to the example of the accounting firm. Suppose that Sara, Paul, and Julia initially have one photocopy machine to work with. Adding another photocopy machine amounts to adding capital equipment, and this relieves congestion around the copy machine and makes each of Sara, Paul, and Julia more productive, including Julia, who was the last accountant added to the workforce at the firm. Therefore, adding more capital increases the marginal product of labor, for each quantity of labor. In Figure 4.17 an increase in the quantity of capital from K_1 to K_2 shifts the marginal product of labor schedule to the right, from MP_N^1 to MP_N^2.

FIGURE 4.17   Adding Capital Increases the Marginal Product of Labor

For each quantity of the labor input, the marginal product of labor increases when the quantity of capital used in production increases.

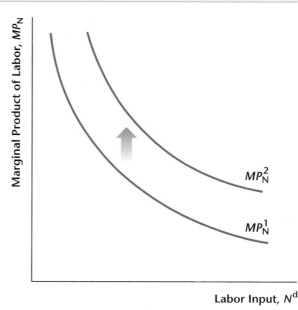

The Effect of a Change in Total Factor Productivity on the Production Function

Changes in total factor productivity, z, are critical to our understanding of the causes of economic growth and business cycles, and so we must understand how a change in z alters the production technology. An increase in total factor productivity z has two important effects. First, because more output can be produced given capital and labor inputs when z increases, this shifts the production function up. In Figure 4.18, with the quantity of capital fixed at K^*, there is an upward shift in the production function when z increases from z_1 to z_2. Second, the marginal product of labor increases when z increases. This is reflected in the fact that the slope of the production function when $z = z_2$ in Figure 4.18 is higher than the slope given $z = z_1$, for any given quantity of the labor input, N^d. In Figure 4.19 the marginal product of labor schedule shifts to the right from MP_N^1 to MP_N^2 when z increases. An increase in z has a similar effect on the marginal product of labor schedule to an increase in the capital stock (see Figure 4.17).

What could cause a change in total factor productivity? In general, an increase in z arises from anything that permits more output to be produced for given inputs. In the macroeconomy, there are many factors that can cause z to increase. One of these factors is technological innovation. The best examples of technological innovations that increase total factor productivity are changes in the organization of production or in management techniques. For example, the assembly line, introduced to automobile manufacturing by Henry Ford (see Macroeconomics in Action: Henry Ford and Total

FIGURE 4.18   Total Factor Productivity Increases

An increase in total factor productivity has two effects: More output is produced given each quantity of the labor input, and the marginal product of labor increases for each quantity of the labor input.

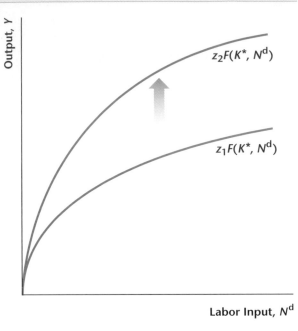

Factor Productivity) brought about a huge increase in the quantity of Model T Fords that could be produced using the same quantities of capital equipment and workers. Some of the most important inventions of the twentieth century—for example, the personal computer—might more appropriately be considered to involve increases in the capital stock rather than increases in z, because the new technology is embodied in capital equipment. A second factor that acts to increase z is good weather. Weather is very important for production in the agricultural and construction sectors, in particular. For example, crop yields are higher, given factor inputs, if rainfall is higher (as long as it is not too high), and construction projects proceed more quickly if rainfall is lower. A third factor affecting z is government regulations. For example, if the government imposes regulations requiring that firms install pollution abatement equipment, this may be good for the welfare of the population, but it results in a decrease in z. This happens because pollution abatement equipment increases the quantity of the capital input in the production process but contributes nothing to measured output. Finally, an increase in the relative price of energy is often interpreted as a decrease in z. When the relative price of energy increases, firms use less energy in production, and this reduces the productivity of both capital and labor, thus causing a decrease in z. Major increases in the price of energy occurred in the United States in 1973–1974 and in 1979, 1990, and 2000, and these energy price increases had important macroeconomic consequences, which we study in Chapters 5, 9, and 11.

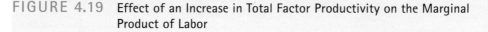

FIGURE 4.19   Effect of an Increase in Total Factor Productivity on the Marginal
Product of Labor

When total factor productivity increases,
the marginal product of labor schedule
shifts to the right.

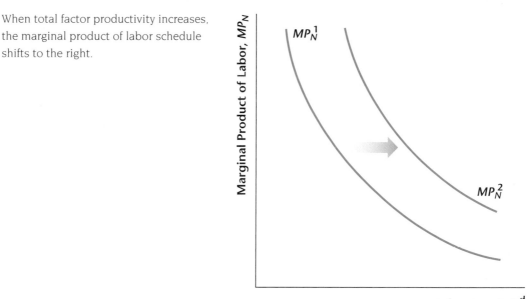

MACROECONOMICS IN ACTION

Henry Ford and Total Factor Productivity

The Ford Motor Company was founded in
1903 by Henry Ford and a financial backer,
but Ford achieved only modest success until the introduction to the market of the
Model T Ford in 1908. This car proved to
be extremely popular, because it was light,
strong, simple, and relatively easy to drive.
Given the high demand for Model T cars,
Henry Ford decided to increase output, but
he did this not by simply replicating his existing production process through the construction of identical plants; rather, he increased total factor productivity, while also
augmenting the capital and labor inputs

in production. A key element of the total
factor productivity increase was the introduction of the assembly line to automobile manufacturing. Henry Ford borrowed
this idea from assembly lines used in the
Chicago meat-packing industry. However,
the general principle at work in the assembly line was known much earlier, for example by Adam Smith, the father of modern economics. In the *Wealth of Nations*,
Smith discusses how production was organized in a pin factory, as an illustration
of what he called the "division of labor":
(*continued*)

One man draws out the wire, another straightens it, a third cuts it . . . the important business of making a pin is, in this manner, divided into about eighteen distinct operations. . . .[1]

Smith was impressed by how the specialization of tasks led to increased productivity in the manufacture of pins. More than a century later, Henry Ford's assembly line replaced an arrangement where automobiles were assembled by teams that each accumulated parts and completed a single automobile in a single location in the plant. Just as in the pin factory, Ford was able to exploit the gains from specialization that the assembly line permitted, where each worker performed only one specialized task, and, therefore, automobiles could be completed at a much higher rate.

The increase in total factor productivity at the Ford Motor Company was reflected in the fact that, in 1914, 13,000 workers produced 260,720 cars at Ford, while in the rest of the U.S. automobile industry 66,350 workers produced 286,770 cars. Thus, output per worker at Ford was almost five times that in the rest of the U.S. auto industry! We do not have measures of the size of the capital stock at Ford and elsewhere in the auto industry, so that there is a slim chance that the higher quantity of output per worker at Ford could have been due simply to higher capital per worker. However, it seems safe to say that total factor productivity at Ford Motor Company increased by a remarkable amount because of the innovations of Henry Ford, and these innovations were quickly imitated in the rest of the auto industry.[2]

---

[1] See Adam Smith, *An Enquiry into the Nature and Causes of the Wealth of Nations*, Liberty Fund, Indianapolis, reprinted 1981, p. 15.

[2] See H. Ford, 1926, *My Life and Work*, Doubleday, Page and Co., New York; A. Nevins, 1954, *Ford: The Times, the Man, the Company*, Charles Scribner's and Sons, New York.

TOTAL FACTOR PRODUCTIVITY AND THE U.S. AGGREGATE PRODUCTION FUNCTION

THEORY confronts the DATA

So far we have assumed that the production function for the representative firm takes the form $Y = zF(K, N^d)$, where the function F has some very general properties (constant returns to scale, diminishing marginal products, etc.). When macroeconomists work with data to test theories, or when they want to simulate a macroeconomic model on the computer to study some quantitative aspects of a theory, they need to be much more specific about the form the production function takes. A very common production function used in theory and empirical work is the **Cobb–Douglas production function.** This function takes the form

$$Y = zK^a(N^d)^{1-a},$$

where a is a parameter, with $0 < a < 1$. The exponents on K and N^d in the function sum to 1 ($a + 1 - a = 1$), which reflects constant returns to scale. If there are profit-maximizing, price-taking firms and constant returns to scale, then a Cobb–Douglas production function implies that a will be the share that capital receives of national income (in our model, the profits of firms), and $1-a$ the share that labor receives (wage income before taxes) in equilibrium. What is remarkable is that, from the National Income and Product Accounts (NIPA) of the United States, the capital and labor shares of national income have been roughly constant in the United States, which is consistent with the Cobb–Douglas production function. Given this, an empirical estimate of a is the average share of capital in national income, which from the data is about 0.36,[1] or 36%, so a good approximation to the actual U.S. aggregate production function is

$$Y = zK^{0.36}(N^d)^{0.64}. \tag{4.10}$$

In Equation (4.10), the quantities Y, K, and N^d can all be measured. For example, Y can be measured as real GDP from the NIPA, K can be measured as the total quantity of capital in existence, built up from expenditures on capital goods in the NIPA, and N^d can be measured as total employment, in the Current Population Survey done by the Bureau of Labor Statistics. But how is total factor productivity z measured? Total factor productivity cannot be measured directly, but it can be measured indirectly, as a residual. That is, from Equation (4.10), if we can measure Y, K, and N^d, then a measure of z is the **Solow residual,** which is calculated as

$$z = \frac{Y}{K^{0.36}(N^d)^{0.64}}. \tag{4.11}$$

This measure of total factor productivity is named after Robert Solow.[2] In Figure 4.20 we graph the Solow residual for the United States for the period 1948–2001, calculated using Equation (4.11) and measurements of Y, K, and N^d as described above. Measured total factor productivity grows over time, and it fluctuates about trend. In Chapters 6, 7, and 11, we see how growth and fluctuations in total factor productivity can cause growth and fluctuations in real GDP.

The Profit Maximization Problem of the Representative Firm

Now that we have studied the properties of the representative firm's production technology, we can examine the determinants of the firm's demand for labor. Like the representative consumer, the representative firm behaves competitively, in that it takes as given the real wage, which is the price at which labor trades for consumption goods. The goal of the firm is to maximize its profits, given by $Y - wN^d$, where Y is the total revenue that the firm receives from selling its output, in units of the consumption good, and wN^d is the total real cost of the labor input, or total real variable costs. Then, substituting for Y using the production function $Y = zF(K, N^d)$, the firm's problem is to choose N^d to maximize

$$\pi = zF(K, N^d) - wN^d,$$

[1] See E. Prescott, 1986, "Theory Ahead of Business Cycle Measurement," *Federal Reserve Bank of Minneapolis Quarterly Review,* Fall, 9–22.

[2] See R. Solow, 1957, "Technical Change and the Aggregate Production Function," *Review of Economic Statistics* 39, 312–320.

FIGURE 4.20   The Solow Residual for the United States

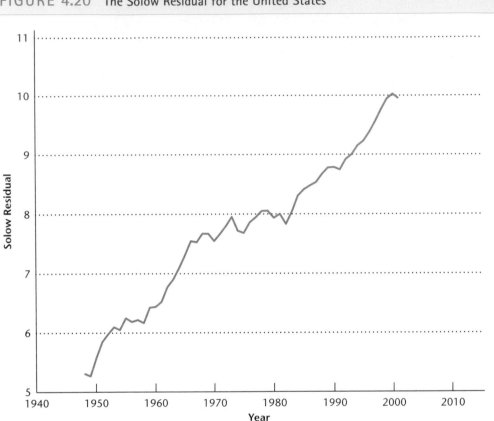

The Solow residual is a measure of total factor productivity, and it is calculated here using a Cobb–Douglas production function. Measured total factor productivity has increased over time, and it also fluctuates about trend, as shown for the period 1948–2001.

where K is fixed. Here, π is real profit. In Figure 4.21 we graph the revenue function, $zF(K, N^d)$, and the variable cost function, wN^d. Profit is then the difference between total revenue and total variable cost. Here, to maximize profits, the firm chooses $N^d = N^*$ in Figure 4.21. The maximized quantity of profits, π^*, is the distance AB in Figure 4.21. For future reference, π^* is the distance ED, where AE is a line drawn parallel to the variable cost function. Thus, AE has slope w. At the profit-maximizing quantity of labor, N^*, the slope of the total revenue function is equal to the slope of the total variable cost function. The slope of the total revenue function, however, is just the slope of the production function, or the marginal product of labor, and the slope of the total variable cost function is the real wage w. Thus, the firm maximizes profits by setting

$$MP_N = w. \tag{4.12}$$

FIGURE 4.21   Revenue, Variable Costs, and Profit Maximization

$Y = zF(K, N^d)$ is the firm's revenue, while wN^d is the firm's variable cost. Profits are the difference between the former and the latter. The firm maximizes profits at the point where marginal revenue equals marginal cost, or $MP_N = w$. Maximized profits are the distance AB, or the distance ED.

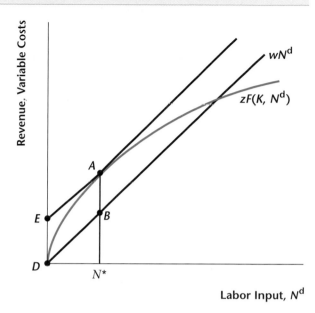

To understand the intuition behind Equation (4.12), note that the contribution to the firm's profits of having employees work an extra hour is the extra output produced minus what the extra input costs—that is, $MP_N - w$. Given a fixed quantity of capital, the marginal product of labor is very high for the first hour worked by employees, and the way we have drawn the production function in Figure 4.17, MP_N is very large for $N^d - 0$, so that $MP_N - w > 0$ for $N^d = 0$, and it is worthwhile for the firm to hire the first unit of labor, as this implies positive profits. As the firm hires more labor, MP_N falls, so that each additional unit of labor is contributing less to revenue, but contributing the same amount, w, to costs. Eventually, at $N^d = N^*$, the firm has hired enough labor so that hiring an additional unit implies $MP_N - w < 0$, which in turn means that hiring an additional unit of labor only causes profits to go down, and this cannot be optimal. Therefore, the profit-maximizing firm chooses its labor input according to Equation (4.12).

In our earlier example of the accounting firm, suppose that there is one photocopy machine at the firm, and output for the firm can be measured in terms of the clients the firm has. Each client pays $20,000 per year to the firm, and the wage rate for an accountant is $50,000 per year. Therefore, the real wage is $\frac{50,000}{20,000} = 2.5$ clients. If the firm has 1 accountant, it can handle 5 clients per year, if it has 2 accountants it can handle 9 clients per year, and if it has 3 accountants it can handle 11 clients per year. What is the profit-maximizing number of accountants for the firm to hire? If the firm hires Sara, her marginal product is 5 clients per year, which exceeds the real wage of

FIGURE 4.22   **The Marginal Product of Labor Curve Is the Labor Demand Curve of the Profit-Maximizing Firm**

This is true because the firm hires labor up to the point where $MP_N = w$.

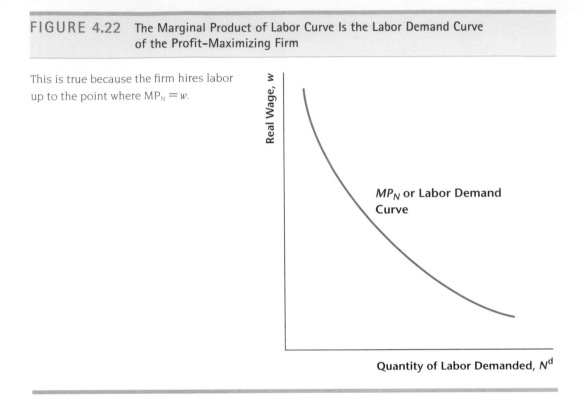

2.5 clients, and so it would be worthwhile for the firm to hire Sara. If the firm hires Sara and Paul, then Paul's marginal product is 4 clients per year, which also exceeds the market real wage, and so it would also be worthwhile to hire Paul. If the firm hires Sara, Paul, and Julia, then Julia's marginal product is 2 clients per year, which is less than the market real wage of 2.5 clients. Therefore, it would be optimal in this case for the firm to hire 2 accountants, Sara and Paul.

Our analysis tells us that the representative firm's marginal product of labor schedule, as shown in Figure 4.22, is the firm's demand curve for labor. This is because the firm maximizes profits for the quantity of labor input that implies $MP_N = w$. Therefore, given a real wage w, the marginal product of labor schedule tells us how much labor the firm needs to hire such that $MP_N = w$, and so the marginal product of labor schedule and the firm's demand curve for labor are the same thing.

In this chapter, we have determined the important elements of the microeconomic behavior of a representative consumer and a representative firm. In the next chapter, we put this behavior together in a macroeconomic model that can be used to address some important macroeconomic issues. In this model, the consumer and the firm interact in markets, where the consumer supplies labor and demands consumption goods, and the firm demands labor and supplies consumption goods.

CHAPTER SUMMARY

- In this chapter, we studied the behavior of the representative consumer and the representative firm in a one-period, or static, environment. This behavior is the basis for constructing a macroeconomic model that we can work with in Chapter 5.

- The representative consumer stands in for the large number of consumers that exist in the economy as a whole, and the representative firm stands in for a large number of firms.

- The representative consumer's goal is to choose consumption and leisure to make himself or herself as well off as possible while respecting his or her budget constraint.

- The consumer's preferences have the properties that more is always preferred to less and that there is preference for diversity in consumption and leisure. The consumer is a price-taker in that he or she treats the market real wage as given, and his or her real disposable income is real wage income plus real dividend income, minus real taxes.

- Graphically, the representative consumer optimizes by choosing the consumption bundle where an indifference curve is tangent to the budget constraint or, what is the same thing, the marginal rate of substitution of leisure for consumption is equal to the real wage.

- Under the assumption that consumption and leisure are normal goods, an increase in the representative consumer's income leads to an increase in consumption and an increase in leisure, implying that labor supply goes down.

- An increase in the real wage leads to an increase in consumption, but it may cause leisure to rise or fall, because there are opposing income and substitution effects. The consumer's labor supply, therefore, may increase or decrease when the real wage increases.

- The representative firm chooses the quantity of labor to hire so as to maximize profits, with the quantity of capital fixed in this one-period environment.

- The firm's production technology is captured by the production function, which has constant returns to scale, a diminishing marginal product of labor, and a diminishing marginal product of capital. Further, the marginal products of labor and capital are positive, and the marginal product of labor increases with the quantity of capital.

- An increase in total factor productivity increases the quantity of output that can be produced with any quantities of labor and capital, and it increases the marginal product of labor.

- When the firm optimizes, it sets the marginal product of labor equal to the real wage. This implies that the firm's marginal product of labor schedule is its demand curve for labor.

KEY TERMS

Static decision: A decision made by a consumer or firm for only one time period.

Dynamic decision: A decision made by a consumer or firm for more than one time period.

Consumption good: A single good that represents an aggregation of all consumer goods in the economy.

Leisure: Time spent not working in the market.

Representative consumer: A stand-in for all consumers in the economy.

Utility function: A function that captures a consumer's preferences over goods.

Consumption bundle: A given consumption–leisure combination.

Normal good: A good for which consumption increases as income increases.

Inferior good: A good for which consumption decreases as income increases.

Indifference map: A set of indifference curves representing a consumer's preferences over goods; has the same information as the utility function.

Indifference curve: A set of points that represents consumption bundles among which a consumer is indifferent.

Marginal rate of substitution: Minus the slope of an indifference curve, or the rate at which the consumer is just willing to trade one good for another.

Competitive behaviour: Actions taken by a consumer or firm if market prices are outside its control.

Barter: An exchange of goods for goods.

Time constraint: Condition that hours worked plus leisure time sum to total time available to the consumer.

Real wage: The wage rate in units of the consumption good.

Numeraire: The good in which prices are denominated.

Dividend income: Profits of firms that are distributed to the consumer, who owns the firms.

Lump-sum tax: A tax that is unaffected by the actions of the consumer or firm being taxed.

Budget constraint: Condition that consumption equals wage income plus nonwage income minus taxes.

Rational: Describes a consumer who can make an informed optimizing decision.

Optimal consumption bundle: The consumption bundle for which the consumer is as well off as possible while satisfying the budget constraint.

Relative price: The price of a good in units of another good.

Pure income effect: The effect on the consumer's optimal consumption bundle due to a change in real disposable income, holding prices constant.

Substitution effect: The effect on the quantity consumed of a good of a price change, holding the consumer's welfare constant.

Income effect: The effect on the quantity consumed of a good of a price change, as a result of having an effectively different income.

Labor supply curve: A relationship describing the quantity of labor supplied for each level of the real wage.

Perfect complements: Two goods that are always consumed in fixed proportions.

Perfect substitutes: Two goods with a constant marginal rate of substitution between them.

Production function: A function describing the technological possibilities for converting factor inputs into output.

Total factor productivity: A variable in the production function that makes all factors of production more productive if it increases.

Marginal product: The additional output produced when another unit of a factor of production is added to the production process.

Constant returns to scale: A property of the production technology whereby if the firm increases all inputs by a factor x, this increases output by the same factor x.

Increasing returns to scale: A property of the production technology whereby if the firm increases all inputs by a factor x, this increases output by more than the factor x.

Decreasing returns to scale: A property of the production technology whereby if the firm increases all inputs by a factor x, this increases output by less than the factor x.

Representative firm: A stand-in for all firms in the economy.

Cobb–Douglas production function: A particular mathematical form for the production function that fits U.S. aggregate data well.

Solow residual: A measure of total factor productivity obtained as a residual from the production function, given measures of aggregate output, labor input, and capital input.

QUESTIONS FOR REVIEW

All questions refer to the elements of the macroecomic model developed in this chapter.

1. What goods do consumers consume in this model?
2. How are a consumer's preferences over goods represented?
3. What three properties do the preferences of the representative consumer have? Explain the importance of each.
4. What two properties do indifference curves have? How are these properties associated with the properties of the consumer's preferences?
5. What is the representative consumer's goal?
6. When the consumer chooses his or her optimal consumption bundle while respecting his or her budget constraint, what condition is satisfied?
7. How is the representative consumer's behavior affected by an increase in real dividend income?
8. How is the representative consumer's behavior affected by an increase in real taxes?
9. Why might hours worked by the representative consumer decrease when the real wage increases?
10. What is the representative firm's goal?
11. Why is the marginal product of labor diminishing?
12. What are the effects on the production function of an increase in total factor productivity?
13. Explain why the marginal product of labor curve is the firm's labor demand curve.

PROBLEMS

1. Using a diagram show that, if the consumer prefers more to less, then indifference curves cannot cross.
2. In this chapter, we showed an example in which the consumer has preferences for consumption with the perfect complements property. Suppose, alternatively, that leisure and consumption goods are perfect substitutes. In this case, an indifference curve is described by the equation

$$u = al + bC,$$

where a and b are positive constants, and u is the level of utility. That is, a given indifference curve has a particular value for u, with higher indifference curves having higher values for u.

(a) Show what the consumer's indifference curves look like when consumption and leisure are perfect substitutes, and determine graphically and algebraically what consumption bundle the consumer chooses. Show that the consumption bundle the consumer chooses depends on the relationship between $\frac{a}{b}$ and w, and explain why.
(b) Do you think it likely that any consumer would treat consumption goods and leisure as perfect substitutes?
(c) Given perfect substitutes, is more preferred to less? Do preferences satisfy the diminishing marginal rate of substitution property?

3. Suppose that the government imposes a proportional income tax on the representative consumer's wage income. That is, the consumer's wage income is $w(1-t)(h-l)$, where t is the tax rate. What effect does the income tax have on consumption and labor supply? Explain your results in terms of income and substitution effects.

4. Suppose that the representative consumer's dividend income increases, and his or her wage rate falls at the same time. Determine the effects on consumption and labor supply, and explain your results in terms of income and substitution effects.

5. Suppose that a consumer can earn a higher wage rate for working "overtime." That is, for the first q hours the consumer works, he or she receives a real wage rate of w_1, and for hours worked more than q he or she receives w_2, where $w_2 > w_1$. Suppose that the consumer pays no taxes and receives no nonwage income, and he or she is free to choose hours of work.
   (a) Draw the consumer's budget constraint, and show his or her optimal choice of consumption and leisure.
   (b) Show that the consumer would never work q hours, or anything very close to q hours. Explain the intuition behind this.
   (c) Determine what happens if the overtime wage rate w_2 increases. Explain your results in terms of income and substitution effects. You must consider the case of a worker who initially works overtime, and a worker who initially does not work overtime.

6. Show that the consumer is better off with a lump-sum tax rather than a proportional tax on wage income (as in question 3) given that either tax yields the same revenue for the government. You must use a diagram to show this. *Hint:* The consumption bundle the consumer chooses under the proportional tax must be just affordable given the lump-sum tax.

7. Suppose that the government imposes a producer tax. That is, the firm pays t units of consumption goods to the government for each unit of output it produces. Determine the effect of this tax on the firm's demand for labor.

8. Suppose that the government subsidizes employment. That is, the government pays the firm s units of consumption goods for each unit of labor that the firm hires. Determine the effect of the subsidy on the firm's demand for labor.

9. Suppose that the firm has a minimum quantity of employment, N^*, that is the firm can produce no output unless the labor input is greater than or equal to N^*. Otherwise, the firm produces output according to the same production function as specified in this chapter. Given these circumstances, determine the effects of an increase in the real wage on the firm's choice of labor input. Construct the firm's demand curve for labor.

10. Supposing that a single consumer works for a firm, the quantity of labor input for the firm, N, is identical to the quantity of hours worked by the consumer, $h - l$. Graph the relationship between output produced, Y, on the vertical axis and leisure hours of the consumer, l, on the horizontal axis, which is implied by the production function of the firm. (In Chapter 5, we refer to this relationship as the production possibilities frontier.) What is the slope of the curve you have graphed?

11. Suppose a firm has a production function given by $Y = zK^{0.3}N^{0.7}$.
   (a) If $z = 1$ and $K = 1$, graph the production function. Is the marginal product of labor positive and diminishing?
   (b) Now, graph the production function when $z = 2$ and $K = 1$. Explain how the production function changed from part (a).
   (c) Next, graph the production function when $z = 1$ and $K = 2$. What happened now?

(d) Given this production function, the marginal product of labor is given by $MP_N = 0.7zK^{0.3}N^{-0.3}$. Graph the marginal product of labor for $(z, K) = (1, 1), (2, 1), (1, 2)$, and explain what you get.

WORKING WITH THE DATA

1. The ratio of employment to the total labor force might be taken to be a measure of the fraction of time spent working by the average working age person in the population. This measure might correspond to the concept of employment, N, in our model
   (a) Calculate and plot the ratio of employment to the total labor force for the years 1980 through 2003.
   (b) Comment on the movements over time in this ratio, with particular reference to the real wage data in Figure 4.12.
   (c) How would you tell a story about the income and substitution effects in labor supply decisions that would be consistent with this data?
   (d) Do you think that the ratio of employment to the total labor force is a good measure of average hours worked per person in the economy? Explain why or why not.

2. Using annual data on real gross domestic product, employment, and the total capital stock, calculate the Solow residual using a Cobb–Douglas production function for the years 1948 through 2001.
   (a) Calculate the percentage growth rate in the Solow residual for each of the years 1949 through 2001.
   (b) Calculate the percentage growth rate in real GDP for the years 1949 through 2001.
   (c) Plot the percentage growth rates in parts (a) and (b), and comment on the relationship between the two. What might explain this relationship?

3. An alternative measure of productivity to total factor productivity is average labor productivity, which is calculated as Y/N, where Y is aggregate output and N is employment. Calculate average labor productivity from annual data for 1948–2001, and compare this to your plot of the Solow residual for the same years as calculated in problem 2. Comment on what you see in the two plots, and explain.

CHAPTER 5

A Closed-Economy One-Period Macroeconomic Model

In Chapter 4, we studied the microeconomic behavior of a representative consumer and a representative firm. In this chapter, our first goal is to take this microeconomic behavior and build it into a working model of the macroeconomy. Then, we use this model to illustrate how unconstrained markets can produce economic outcomes that are socially efficient. This social efficiency proves to be useful in how we use our model to analyze some important macroeconomic issues. We show how increases in government spending increase aggregate output and crowd out private consumption expenditures and how increases in productivity lead to increases in aggregate output and the standard of living.

We want to start our approach to macroeconomic modeling in this chapter by analyzing how consumers and firms interact in markets in a **closed economy.** This is a model of a single country that has no interaction with the rest of the world—it does not trade with other countries. It is easier to first understand how a closed economy works, and much of the economic intuition we build up for the closed-economy case carries over to an **open economy,** where international trade is allowed. Further, for many economic questions, particularly the ones addressed in this chapter, the answers are not fundamentally different if we allow the economy to be open.

There are three different actors in this economy, the representative consumer who stands in for the many consumers in the economy that sell labor and buy goods, the representative firm that stands in for the many firms in the economy that buy labor and sell goods, and the government. We have already described the behavior of the representative consumer and representative firm in detail in Chapter 4, and we only need to explain what the government does.

GOVERNMENT

The behavior of the government here is quite simple. It wishes to purchase a given quantity of consumption goods, G, and finances these purchases by taxing the representative consumer. In practice, governments provide many different goods and services, including roads and bridges, national defense, air traffic control, and education. Which goods and services the government should provide is subject to both political and economic debate, but economists generally agree that the government has a special role to play in providing **public goods,** such as national defense, which are difficult or impossible for the private sector to provide. National defense is a good example of a public good, because it is difficult to get an individual to pay for national defense in a private market according to how much of it he or she uses.

To keep things as simple as possible, for now we are not specific about the public goods nature of government expenditure. What we want to capture here is that government spending uses up resources, and we model this by assuming that government spending simply involves taking goods from the private sector. Output is produced, and the government purchases an **exogenous** amount G of this output, with the remainder consumed by the representative consumer. An exogenous variable is determined outside the model, while an **endogenous** variable is determined by the model itself. Government spending is exogenous in our model, as we are assuming that government spending is independent of what happens in the rest of the economy. The government must abide by the **government budget constraint,** which we write as

$$G = T,$$

or government purchases equal taxes, in real terms.

Introducing the government in this way allows us to study some basic effects of **fiscal policy.** In general, fiscal policy refers to the government's choices over its expenditures, taxes, transfers, and borrowing. Recall from Chapter 2 that government expenditures are purchases of final goods and services, while transfers are simply reallocations of purchasing power from one set of individuals to another. Because this is a one-period economic environment, the government's choices are very limited, as described by the above government budget constraint. The government cannot borrow to finance government expenditures, because there is no future in which to repay its debt, and the government does not tax more than it spends, as this would imply that the government would foolishly throw goods away. The government budget deficit, which is $G - T$ here, is always zero. Thus, the only elements of fiscal policy we study in this chapter are the setting of government purchases, G, and the macroeconomic effects of changing G. In Chapter 8, we explore what happens when the government can run deficits and surpluses.

COMPETITIVE EQUILIBRIUM

Now that we have looked at the behavior of the representative consumer, the representative firm, and the government, what remains in constructing our model is to show how consistency is obtained in the actions of all these economic agents. Once we have done this, we can use this model to make predictions about how the whole economy behaves in response to changes in the economic environment.

Mathematically, a macroeconomic model takes the exogenous variables, which for the purposes of the problem at hand are determined outside the system we are modeling, and determines values for the endogenous variables, as outlined in Figure 5.1. In the model we are working with here, the exogenous variables are G, z, and K—that is, government spending, total factor productivity, and the economy's capital stock, respectively. The endogenous variables are C, N^s, N^d, T, Y, and w—that is, consumption, labor supply, labor demand, taxes, aggregate output, and the market real wage, respectively. Making use of the model is a process of running experiments to determine how changes in the exogenous variables change the endogenous variables. By running these

FIGURE 5.1   A Model Takes Exogenous Variables and Determines Endogenous Variables

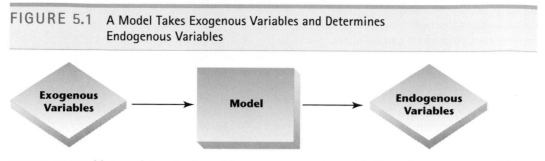

Exogenous variables are determined outside a macroeconomic model. Given the exogenous variables, the model determines the endogenous variables. In experiments, we are interested in how the endogenous variables change when there are changes in exogenous variables.

experiments, we hope to understand real-world macroeconomic events and to say something about macroeconomic policy. For example, one of the experiments we run on our model in this chapter is to change exogenous government spending and then determine the effects on consumption, employment, aggregate output, and the real wage. This helps us to understand, for example, the events that occurred in the U.S. economy during World War II, when there was a large increase in government spending.

By consistency we mean that, given market prices, demand is equal to supply in each market in the economy. Such a state of affairs is called a **competitive equilibrium.** Here, competitive refers to the fact that all consumers and firms are price-takers, and the economy is in equilibrium when the actions of all consumers and firms are consistent. When demand equals supply in all markets, we say that markets **clear.** In our model economy, there is only one price, which is the real wage w. We can also think of the economy as having only one market, on which labor time is exchanged for consumption goods. In this labor market, the representative consumer supplies labor and the representative firm demands labor. A competitive equilibrium is achieved when, given the exogenous variables G, z, and K, the real wage w is such that, at that wage, *the quantity of labor the consumer wishes to supply is equal to the quantity of labor the firm wishes to hire.* The consumer's supply of labor is in part determined by taxes T and dividend income π. In a competitive equilibrium, T must satisfy the government budget constraint, and π must be equal to the profits generated by the firm.

A competitive equilibrium is a set of endogenous quantities, C (consumption), N^s (labor supply), N^d (labor demand), T (taxes), and Y (aggregate output), and an endogenous real wage w, such that, given the exogenous variables G (government spending), z (total factor productivity), and K (capital stock), the following are satisfied:

1. The representative consumer chooses C (consumption) and N^s (labor supply) to make himself or herself as well off as possible subject to his or her budget constraint, given w (the real wage), T (taxes), and π (dividend income). That is, the representative consumer optimizes given his or her budget constraint, which is determined by the real wage, taxes, and the profits that the consumer receives from the firm as dividend income.

2. The representative firm chooses N^d (quantity of labor demand) to maximize profits, with maximized output $Y = zF(K, N^d)$, and maximized profits $\pi = Y - wN^d$. The firm treats z (total factor productivity), K (the capital stock), and w (the real wage) as given. That is, the representative firm optimizes given total factor productivity, its capital stock, and the market real wage. In equilibrium, the profits that the representative firm earns must be equal to the dividend income that is received by the consumer.

3. The market for labor clears, that is, $N^d = N^s$. The quantity of labor that the representative firm wants to hire is equal to the quantity of labor the representative consumer wants to supply.

4. The government budget constraint is satisfied, that is, $G = T$. The taxes paid by consumers are equal to the exogenous quantity of government spending.

An important property of a competitive equilibrium is that

$$Y = C + G, \tag{5.1}$$

which is the income–expenditure identity. Recall from Chapter 2 that we generally state the income–expenditure identity as $Y = C + I + G + NX$, where I is investment and NX is net exports. In this economy, there is no investment expenditure, as there is only one period, and net exports are zero, as the economy is closed, so that $I = 0$ and $NX = 0$.

To show why the income–expenditure identity holds in equilibrium, we start with the representative consumer's budget constraint,

$$C = wN^s + \pi - T, \tag{5.2}$$

or consumption expenditures equal real wage income plus real dividend income minus taxes. In equilibrium, dividend income is equal to the firm's maximized profits, or $\pi = Y - wN^d$, and the government budget constraint is satisfied, so that $T = G$. If we then substitute in Equation (5.2) for π and T, we get

$$C = wN^s + Y - wN^d - G. \tag{5.3}$$

In equilibrium, labor supply is equal to labor demand, or $N^s = N^d$, which then gives us, substituting for N^s in Equation (5.3) and rearranging, the identity in Equation (5.1).

There are many ways to work with macroeconomic models. Modern macroeconomic researchers sometimes work with an algebraic representation of a model, sometimes with a formulation of a model that can be put on a computer and simulated, and sometimes with a model in graphical form. We use the last approach most often in this book. In doing graphical analysis, sometimes the simplest approach is to work with a model in the form of supply and demand curves, with one supply curve and one demand curve for each market under consideration. As the number of markets in the model increases, this approach becomes most practical, and in Chapters 8 to 12 and some later chapters, we work mainly with models in the form of supply and demand curves. These supply and demand curves are derived from the microeconomic behavior of consumers and firms, as was the case when we examined labor supply and labor demand curves in Chapter 4, but the underlying microeconomic behavior is not explicit. For our analysis here, however, where exchange takes place between the representative consumer and the representative firm in only one market, it is relatively straightforward to be entirely explicit about microeconomic principles. The approach we follow in this chapter is to study competitive equilibrium in our model by examining the consumer's and the firm's decisions in the same diagram, so that we can determine how aggregate consistency is achieved in competitive equilibrium.

We want to start first with the production technology operated by the representative firm. In a competitive equilibrium, $N^d = N^s = N$—that is, labor demand equals labor supply—and we refer to N as employment. Then, as in Chapter 4, from the production function, output is given by

$$Y = zF(K, N), \tag{5.4}$$

and we graph the production function in Figure 5.2(a), for a given capital stock K. Because the representative consumer has a maximum of h hours to spend working, N can be no larger than h, which implies that the most output that could be produced in this economy is Y^* in Figure 5.2(a).

Another way to graph the production function, which proves very useful for integrating the firm's production behavior with the consumer's behavior, is to use the fact that, in equilibrium, we have $N = h - l$. Substituting for N in the production function (5.4), we get

$$Y = zF(K, h - l), \tag{5.5}$$

which is a relationship between output Y and leisure l, given the exogenous variables z and K. If we graph this relationship, as Figure 5.2(b), with leisure on the horizontal axis and Y on the vertical axis, then we get a mirror image of the production function in Figure 5.2(a). That is, the point $(l, Y) = (h, 0)$ in panel (b) of the figure corresponds to the point $(N, Y) = (0, 0)$ in panel (a). When the consumer takes all of his or her time as leisure, then employment is zero and nothing gets produced. As leisure falls in (b) from h, employment increases in (a) from zero and output increases. In (b), when $l = 0$, the consumer is using all of his or her time for work and consuming no leisure and the maximum quantity of output, Y^*, is produced. Because the slope of the production function in panel (a) of the figure is MP_N, the marginal product of labor, the slope of the relationship in panel (b) is $-MP_N$, because this relationship is just the mirror image of the production function.

Now, because in equilibrium $C = Y - G$, from the income–expenditure identity, given (5.5) we get

$$C = zF(K, h - l) - G,$$

which is a relationship between C and l, given the exogenous variables z, K, and G. This relationship is graphed in Figure 5.2(c), and it is just the relationship in (b) shifted down by the amount G, because consumption is output minus government spending in equilibrium. The relationship in Figure 5.2(c) is called a **production possibilities frontier** (PPF), and it describes what the technological possibilities are for the economy as a whole, in terms of the production of consumption goods and leisure. Though leisure is not literally produced, all of the points in the shaded area inside the PPF and on the PPF in Figure 5.2(c) are technologically possible in this economy. The PPF

FIGURE 5.2   The Production Function and the Production Possibilities Frontier

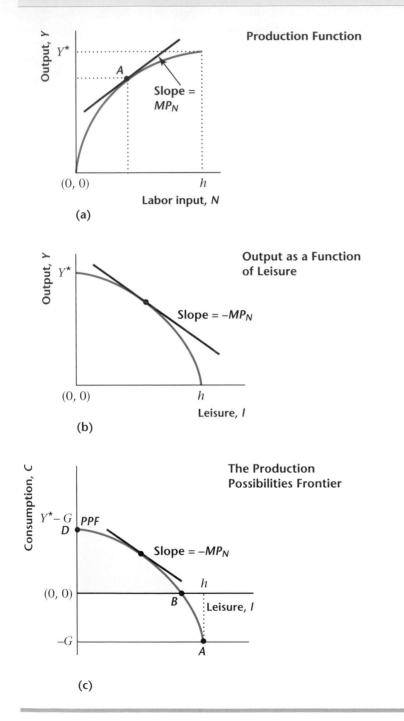

(a)

(b)

(c)

captures the trade-off between leisure and consumption that the available production technology makes available to the representative consumer in the economy. The points on the *PPF* on *AB* are not feasible for this economy, as consumption is negative. Only the points on the *PPF* on *DB* are feasible, because here enough consumption goods are produced so that the government can take some of these goods and still leave something for private consumption.

As in Figure 5.2(b), the slope of the *PPF* in (c) is $-MP_N$. Another name for the negative of the slope of the *PPF* is the **marginal rate of transformation.** The marginal rate of transformation is the rate at which one good can be converted technologically into another; in this case, the marginal rate of transformation is the rate at which leisure can be converted in the economy into consumption goods through work. We let $MRT_{l,C}$ denote the marginal rate of transformation of leisure into consumption. Then, we have

$$MRT_{l,C} = MP_N = -(\text{the slope of the } PPF).$$

Our next step is to put the *PPF* together with the consumer's indifference curves, and to show how we can analyze a competitive equilibrium in a single diagram in Figure 5.3. In the figure, the *PPF* is given by the curve *HF*. From the relationship between the production function and the *PPF* in Figure 5.2, and given what we know about the profit-maximizing decision of the firm from Chapter 4, we can determine the production point on the *PPF* chosen by the firm, given the equilibrium real wage *w*. Namely, the representative firm chooses the labor input to maximize profits in equilibrium by setting $MP_N = w$, and so in equilibrium minus the slope of the *PPF* must be equal to *w*, because $MRT_{l,C} = MP_N = w$ in equilibrium. Therefore, if *w* is an equilibrium real wage rate, we can draw a line *AD* in Figure 5.3 that has slope $-w$ and that is tangent to the *PPF* at point *J*, where $MP_N = w$. Then, the firm chooses labor demand equal to $h - l^*$ and produces $Y^* = zF(K, h - l^*)$, from the production function. Maximized profits for the firm are $\pi^* = zF(K, h - l^*) - w(h - l^*)$ (total revenue minus the cost of hiring labor), or the distance *DH* in Figure 5.3 (recall this from Chapter 4). Now, *DB* in Figure 5.3 is equal to $\pi^* - G = \pi^* - T$, from the government budget constraint $G = T$.

One must recognize that *ADB* in the figure is the budget constraint that the consumer faces in equilibrium, because the slope of *AD* is $-w$ and the length of *DB* is the consumer's dividend income minus taxes, where dividend income is the profits that the firm earns and distributes to the consumer. Because *J* represents the competitive equilibrium production point, where C^* is the quantity of consumption goods produced by the firm and $h - l^*$ is the quantity of labor hired by the firm, then it must be the case (as is required for aggregate consistency) that C^* is also the quantity of consumption goods that the representative consumer desires and l^* is the quantity of leisure the consumer desires.

Panel (a) shows the production function of the representative firm, while panel (b) shows the equilibrium relationship between the quantity of leisure consumed by the representative consumer and aggregate output. The relationship in (b) is the mirror image of the production function in (a). In (c), we show the production possibilities frontier (PPF), which is the technological relationship between C and l, determined by shifting the relationship in (b) down by the amount G. The shaded region in (c) represents consumption bundles that are technologically feasible to produce in this economy.

FIGURE 5.3   Competitive Equilibrium

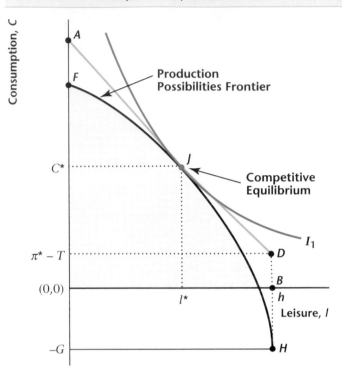

This figure brings together the representative consumer's preferences and the representative firm's production technology to determine a competitive equilibrium. Point J represents the equilibrium consumption bundle. ADB is the budget constraint faced by the consumer in equilibrium, with the slope of AD equal to minus the real wage and the distance DB equal to dividend income minus taxes.

This implies that an indifference curve (curve I_1 in Figure 5.3) must be tangent to AD (the budget constraint) at point J in Figure 5.3. Given this, in equilibrium at point J we have $MRS_{l,C} = w$—that is, the marginal rate of substitution of leisure for consumption for the consumer is equal to the real wage. Because $MRT_{l,C} = MP_N = w$ in equilibrium, we have, at point J in Figure 5.3,

$$MRS_{l,C} = MRT_{l,C} = MP_N, \tag{5.6}$$

or the marginal rate of substitution of leisure for consumption is equal to the marginal rate of transformation, which is equal to the marginal product of labor. That is, because the consumer and the firm face the same market real wage in equilibrium, the rate at which the consumer is just willing to trade leisure for consumption is the same as the rate at which leisure can be converted into consumption goods using the production technology.

The condition expressed in Equation (5.6) is important in the next subsection in establishing the economic efficiency of a competitive equilibrium. The connection between market outcomes and economic efficiency is critical in making the analysis of macroeconomic issues with this model simple.

OPTIMALITY

Now that we know what the characteristics of a competitive equilibrium are from Figure 5.3, we can analyze the connection between a competitive equilibrium and economic efficiency. This connection is important for two reasons. First, this illustrates how free markets can produce socially optimal outcomes. Second, it proves to be much easier to analyze a social optimum than a competitive equilibrium in this model, and so our analysis in this section allows us to use our model efficiently.

An important part of economics is analyzing how markets act to arrange production and consumption activities and asking how this arrangement compares with some ideal or efficient arrangement. Typically, the efficiency criterion that economists use in evaluating market outcomes is **Pareto optimality.** (Pareto, a 19th-century Italian economist, is famous for, among other things, his application of mathematics to economic analysis and introducing the concept of indifference curves.)

DEFINITION
A *competitive equilibrium* is **Pareto optimal** *if there is no way to rearrange production or to reallocate goods so that someone is made better off without making someone else worse off.*

For this model, we would like to ask whether the competitive equilibrium is Pareto optimal, but our job is relatively easy because there is only one representative consumer, so that we do not have to consider how goods are allocated across people. In our model, we can focus solely on how production is arranged to make the representative consumer as well off as possible. To construct the Pareto optimum here, we introduce the device of a fictitious social planner. This device is commonly used to determine efficiency in economic models. The social planner does not have to deal with markets, and he or she can simply order the representative firm to hire a given quantity of labor and produce a given quantity of consumption goods. The planner also has the power to coerce the consumer into supplying the required amount of labor. Produced consumption goods are taken by the planner, G is given to the government, and the remainder is allocated to the consumer. The social planner is benevolent, and he or she chooses quantities so as to make the representative consumer as well off as possible. In this way, the choices of the social planner tell us what, in the best possible circumstances, could be achieved in our model economy.

The social planner's problem is to choose C and l, given the technology for converting l into C, to make the representative consumer as well off as possible. That is, the social planner chooses a consumption bundle that is on or within the production

FIGURE 5.4   **Pareto Optimality**

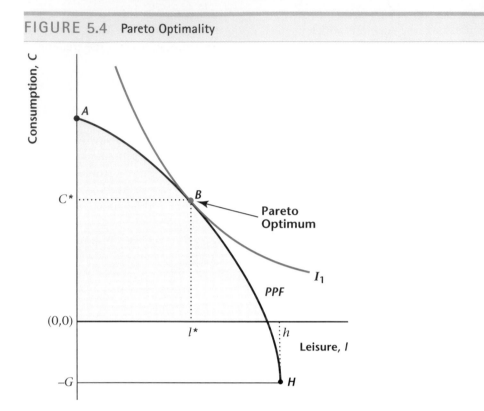

The Pareto optimum is the point that a social planner would choose where the representative consumer is as well off as possible given the technology for producing consumption goods using labor as an input. Here the Pareto optimum is B, where an indifference curve is tangent to the PPF.

possibilities frontier (*PPF*), and that is on the highest possible indifference curve for the consumer. In Figure 5.4 the Pareto optimum is located at point B, where an indifference curve is just tangent to the *PPF*—curve *AH*. The social planner's problem is very similar to the representative consumer's problem of making himself or herself as well off as possible given his or her budget constraint. The only difference is that the budget constraint of the consumer is a straight line, while the *PPF* is bowed-out from the origin (i.e., it is concave).

From Figure 5.4, because the slope of the indifference curve is minus the marginal rate of substitution, $-MRS_{l,C}$, and the slope of the *PPF* is minus the marginal rate of transformation, $-MRT_{l,C}$, or minus the marginal product of labor, $-MPN$, the Pareto optimum has the property that

$$MRS_{l,C} = MRT_{l,C} = MP_N.$$

This is the same property that a competitive equilibrium has, or Equation (5.6). Comparing Figures 5.3 and 5.4, we easily see that the Pareto optimum and the competitive equilibrium are the same thing, because a competitive equilibrium is the point where an indifference curve is tangent to the *PPF* in Figure 5.3, and the same is true of the Pareto optimum in Figure 5.4. A key result of this chapter is that, for this model, the competitive equilibrium is identical to the Pareto optimum.

There are two fundamental principles in economics that apply here, and these are the following:

DEFINITION
The **first fundamental theorem of welfare economics** *states that, under certain conditions, a competitive equilibrium is Pareto optimal.*

DEFINITION
The **second fundamental theorem of welfare economics** *states that, under certain conditions, a Pareto optimum is a competitive equilibrium.*

These two theorems are often referred to as the "first welfare theorem" and the "second welfare theorem." In our model, one can clearly see, from Figures 5.3 and 5.4, that the first and second welfare theorems hold, because there is one competitive equilibrium and one Pareto optimum, and they are clearly the same thing. In other kinds of economic models, however, showing whether or not the first and second welfare theorems hold can be hard work.

The idea behind the first welfare theorem goes back at least as far as Adam Smith's *Wealth of Nations*. Smith argued that an unfettered market economy composed of self-interested consumers and firms could achieve an allocation of resources and goods that was socially efficient, in that an unrestricted market economy would behave as if an "invisible hand" were guiding the actions of individuals toward a state of affairs that was beneficial for all. The model we have constructed here has the property that a competitive equilibrium, or unfettered market outcome, is the same outcome that would be chosen by the invisible hand of the fictitious social planner.

The first welfare theorem is quite remarkable, because it appears to be inconsistent with the training we receive early in life, when we are typically encouraged to have empathy for others and to share our belongings. Most people value generosity and compassion, and so it certainly seems surprising that individuals motivated only by greed and profit maximization could achieve some kind of social utopia. If we consider, however, economies with many consumers instead of a single representative consumer, then a Pareto optimum might have the property that some people are very poor and some are very rich. That is, we may not be able to make the poor better off without making the rich worse off. At the extreme, a state of affairs where one person has all of society's wealth may be Pareto optimal, but few would argue that this is a sensible way to arrange an economy. Pareto optimality is a very narrow concept of social optimality. In some instances, society is interested in equity as well as efficiency, and there may be a trade-off between the two.

MACROECONOMICS IN ACTION

The Invisible Hand, Capitalism, Socialism, and the Former Soviet Union

In discussing the idea that private market forces could lead to socially efficient outcomes, Adam Smith argued in the *Wealth of Nations* that the owner of a private business

> by directing that industry in such a manner as its produce may be of the greatest value, he intends only his own gain, and he is in this, as in many other cases, led by an invisible hand to promote an end which was no part of his intention. Nor is it always the worse for the society that it was no part of it. By pursuing his own interest he frequently promotes that of the society more effectually than when he really intends to promote it. I have never known much good done by those who affected to trade for the public good. It is an affectation, indeed, not very common among merchants, and very few words need be employed in dissuading them from it.[1]

This statement of Smith's concerning the benefits to be had from a free market economy is even stronger than saying that a society of self-interested individuals can produce a socially efficient outcome. Smith appears to argue that, even if a group of individuals were given the power to decide what is in the public good, they would actually do worse in terms of general social welfare than would private markets. That is, it appeared to have been clear to Smith that socialism is less efficient than a market-based economy.

The controversy about the relative efficiency of socialist economies and market economies was taken up by economists beginning in the late 19th century in the so-called "socialist calculation debate.[2]" On the one hand Abba Lerner, for example, argued that a socialist economy could be no less efficient than a market economy. He argued that a central planner in a socialist economy could play the role of social planner, finding the appropriate market-clearing prices. Lerner also argued that a central planner had the advantage of being able to determine the distribution of wealth in the population in a more equitable way than would be the case in a market economy. On the other hand, Friedrich von Hayek, among others, countered that the quantity of information required to make a socialist economy run efficiently is staggering.

Von Hayek's argument was essentially the following. In a market economy, no one needs to acquire detailed information on production technologies and consumer preferences. The economy generally operates efficiently if each producer and each consumer pay attention only to the signals that come from market prices. When the price of a particular good, oranges for example, is high, this high price reflects a scarcity of oranges. A central planner might react to a scarcity of oranges by directing that more oranges be produced and by perhaps discouraging some consumers from eating oranges and encouraging them to eat apples instead. In a market economy, the high price of oranges would result in higher profits for the producers of oranges, which would make the production of oranges attractive for other would-be producers, and the supply of oranges would tend to increase.

(continued)

Higher prices of oranges would also cause consumers to substitute away form oranges, perhaps to apples. A market economy can generally react much faster to the shortage of a good and with the correct result. Market prices are a highly efficient device for effectively transmitting all of the relevant information to the producers and consumers in an economy.

As with many debates in economics, empirical evidence was critical in deciding the socialist calculation debate in favor of market over socialist economies. As of the beginning of the 21st century, socialist economies have fared poorly relative to market economies, with the former Soviet Union being a key example of a socialist economy that was widely judged to have been extremely inefficient.

In the former Soviet Union, much economic activity was managed by way of central planning. That is, a group of planners in the Soviet government would make detailed decisions about the quantities of output that would be produced at different plants, where investment in new plant and equipment would take place, who would be employed where and in what capacity, and so on. The key problem with the Soviet system, however, was that the Soviet central planners knew much less about the economy

than does the social planner we invented to determine what was socially efficient in our model. For a planner to efficiently determine how production and consumption should take place in the economy, he or she would need to know all the details about the available technologies for producing different goods, what resources are available, and the preferences of all consumers for all goods in existence. Collecting all of this information would clearly be impossible, and so it is not surprising that there were problems in the Soviet Union in running the economy efficiently. Examples of the types of problems that arose were that consumers had to wait in queues for goods that were short in supply, and firms did not always receive supplies of intermediate goods or raw materials in a timely way, so that production was interrupted.

The conclusion is that Adam Smith's instincts seem to have been correct. Often, trying to substitute organizational planning for market mechanisms can be a recipe for disaster.

---

[1] A. Smith, reprinted 1981, *An Enquiry into the Nature and Causes of the Wealth of Nations,* Liberty Fund, Indianapolis, p. 456.

[2] See http://cepa.newschool.edu/het/essays/paretian/social.htm.

Sources of Social Inefficiencies

What could cause a competitive equilibrium to fail to be Pareto optimal? In practice, many factors can result in inefficiency in a market economy.

First, a competitive equilibrium may not be Pareto optimal because of **externalities.** An externality is any activity for which an individual firm or consumer does not take account of all associated costs and benefits; externalities can be positive or negative. For example, pollution is a common example of a negative externality. Suppose that Disgusting Chemical Corporation (DCC) produces and sells chemicals, and in the production process generates a by-product that is released as a gas into the atmosphere.

This by-product stinks and is hazardous, and there are people who live close to DCC who are worse off as the result of the air pollution that DCC produces; however, the negative externality that is produced in the form of pollution costs to the neighbors of DCC is not reflected in any way in DCC's profits. DCC, therefore, does not take the pollution externality into account in deciding how much labor to hire and the quantity of chemicals to produce. As a result, DCC tends to produce more of these pollution-causing chemicals than is socially optimal. The key problem is that there is not a market on which pollution (or the rights to pollute) is traded. If such a market existed, then private markets would not fail to produce a socially optimal outcome. This is because the people who bear the costs of pollution could sell the rights to pollute to DCC, and there would then be a cost to DCC for polluting, which DCC would take into account in making production decisions. Of course, such markets in pollution rights do not exist in practice as it is hard to measure and monitor pollution and very difficult to verify who bears the costs of pollution. In practice, the typical method used to correct a negative externality is regulation, for example, through the Environmental Protection Agency (EPA) in the United States.

A positive externality is a benefit that other people receive for which an individual is not compensated. For example, suppose that DCC has an attractive head office designed by a high-profile architect in a major city. This building yields a benefit to people who can walk by the building on a public street and admire the fine architecture. These people do not compensate the firm for this positive externality, as it would be very costly or impossible to set up a fee structure for the public viewing of the building. As a result, DCC tends to underinvest in its head office. Likely, the building that DCC would construct would be less attractive than if the firm took account of the positive externality. Positive externalities, therefore, lead to social inefficiencies, just as negative externalities do, and the root cause of an externality is a market failure; it is too costly or impossible to set up a market to buy and sell the benefits or costs associated with the externality.

A second reason that a competitive equilibrium may not be Pareto optimal is that there are **distorting taxes.** In Chapter 4 we discussed the difference between a lump-sum tax, which does not depend on the actions of the person being taxed, and a distorting tax, which does. An example of a distorting tax in our model would be if government purchases were financed by a proportional wage income tax rather than by a lump-sum tax. That is, for each unit of real wage income earned, the representative consumer pays t units of consumption goods to the government, so that t is the tax rate. Then, wage income is $w(1-t)(h-l)$, and the effective wage for the consumer is $w(1-t)$. Then, when the consumer optimizes, he or she sets $MRS_{l,C} = w(1-t)$, while the firm optimizes by setting $MP_N = w$. Therefore, in a competitive equilibrium

$$MRS_{l,C} < MPN = MRT_{l,C},$$

so that the tax drives a "wedge" between the marginal rate of substitution and the marginal product of labor. Equation (5.6), therefore, does not hold, as required for a Pareto optimum, so that the competitive equilibrium is not Pareto optimal and the first welfare theorem does not hold. In a competitive equilibrium, a proportional wage income tax tends to discourage work (so long as the substitution effect of a change in the wage is larger than the income effect), and there tends to be too much leisure consumed relative to consumption goods. In practice, all taxes, including sales taxes, the income tax, and property taxes, cause distortions. Lump-sum taxes are, in fact, infeasible to implement in practice,[1] though this does not mean that having lump-sum taxes in our model is nonsense. The assumption of lump-sum taxation in our model is a convenient simplification, in that for most of the macroeconomic issues we address with this model, the effects of more realistic distorting taxation are unimportant.

A third reason market economies do not achieve efficiency is that firms may not be price-takers. If a firm is large relative to the market, it can use its monopoly power to restrict output, raise prices, and increase profits. Monopoly power tends to lead to underproduction relative to what is socially optimal. There are many examples of monopoly power in the United States. For example, the market in computer operating systems is dominated by a few producers, as is the automobile industry in the United States.

Because there are good reasons to believe that the three inefficiencies discussed above—externalities, tax distortions, and monopoly power—are important in modern economies, two questions arise. First, why should we analyze an economy that is efficient in the sense that a competitive equilibrium for this economy is Pareto optimal? The reason is that in studying most macroeconomic issues, an economic model with inefficiencies behaves much like an economic model without inefficiencies. However, actually modeling all of these inefficiencies would add clutter to our model and make it more difficult to work with, and it is often best to leave out these extraneous details. The equivalence of the competitive equilibrium and the Pareto optimum in our model proves to be quite powerful in terms of analyzing a competitive equilibrium. This is because determining the competitive equilibrium need only involve solving the social planner's problem and not the more complicated problem of determining prices and quantities in a competitive equilibrium.

A second question that arises concerning real-world social inefficiencies is whether Adam Smith was completely off track in emphasizing the tendency of unrestricted markets to produce socially efficient outcomes. It might appear that the existence of externalities, tax distortions, and monopoly power should lead us to press for various government regulations to offset the negative effects of these inefficiencies. However, the tendency of unregulated markets to produce efficient outcomes is a powerful one, and sometimes the cost of government regulations, in terms of added waste, outweighs the gains, in terms of correcting private market failures. The cure can often be worse than the disease.

How to Use the Model

The key to using our model is the equivalence between the competitive equilibrium and the Pareto optimum. We need only draw a picture as in Figure 5.5, where we are essentially considering the solution to the social planner's problem. Here, the *PPF* is

---

[1]This is because any lump-sum tax is large enough that someone cannot pay it. Therefore, some people must be exempt from the tax; but, if this is so, then people will alter their behavior so as to be exempt from the tax, so that the tax will, therefore, distort private decisions.

FIGURE 5.5   **Using the Second Welfare Theorem to Determine a Competitive Equilibrium**

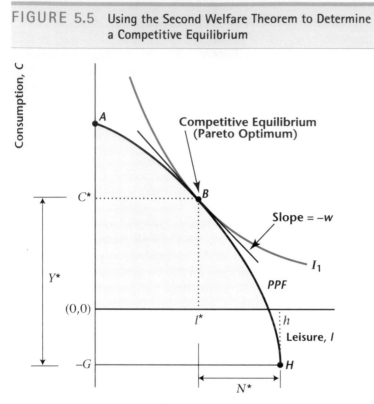

Because the competitive equilibrium and the Pareto optimum are the same thing, we can analyze a competitive equilibrium by working out the Pareto optimum, which is point B in the figure. At the Pareto optimum, an indifference curve is tangent to the PPF, and the equilibrium real wage is equal to minus the slope of the PPF and minus the slope of the indifference curve at B.

curve AH, and the competitive equilibrium (or Pareto optimum) is at point B, where an indifference curve, I_1, is tangent to the *PPF.* The equilibrium quantity of consumption is then C^*, and the equilibrium quantity of leisure is l^*. The quantity of employment is $N^* = h - l^*$, as shown in Figure 5.5, and the quantity of output is $Y^* = C^* + G$, as also shown in the figure. The real wage w is determined by minus the slope of the *PPF*, or minus the slope of the indifference curve I_1 at point B. The real wage is determined in this way because we know that, in equilibrium, the firm optimizes by setting the marginal product of labor equal to the real wage, and the consumer optimizes by setting the marginal rate of substitution equal to the real wage.

What we are primarily interested in now is how a change in an exogenous variable affects the key endogenous variables C, Y, N, and w. The exogenous variables G, z, and K, which are government spending, total factor productivity, and the capital stock, respectively, all alter the endogenous variables by shifting the *PPF* in particular ways. We examine these effects and their interpretation in the next sections.

Figure 5.5 illustrates a key concept of this chapter in the clearest possible way. What is produced and consumed in the economy is determined entirely by the interaction of consumer preferences with the technology available to firms. Though economic activity involves a complicated array of transactions among many economic actors, fundamentally aggregate economic activity boils down to the preferences of consumers, as captured by the representative consumer's indifference curves, and the technology of firms, as captured by the *PPF*. Both consumer preferences and the firm's technology are important for determining aggregate output, aggregate consumption, employment, and the real wage. A change either in indifference curves or the *PPF* affects what is produced and consumed.

WORKING WITH THE MODEL: THE EFFECTS OF A CHANGE IN GOVERNMENT PURCHASES

Recall from Chapter 1 that working with a macroeconomic model involves carrying out experiments. The first experiment we conduct here is to change government spending G, and ask what this does to aggregate output, consumption, employment, and the real wage. In Figure 5.6 an increase in G from G_1 to G_2 shifts the *PPF* from PPF_1 to PPF_2, where the shift down is by the same amount, $G_2 - G_1$, for each quantity of leisure, l. This shift leaves the slope of the *PPF* constant for each l. The effect of shifting the *PPF* downward by a constant amount is very similar to shifting the budget constraint for the consumer through a reduction in his or her nonwage disposable income, as we did in Chapter 4. Indeed, because $G = T$, an increase in government spending must necessarily increase taxes by the same amount, which reduces the consumer's disposable income. It should not be surprising, then, that the effects of an increase in government spending essentially involve a negative income effect on consumption and leisure.

In Figure 5.6 the initial equilibrium is at point A, where indifference curve I_1 is tangent to PPF_1, the initial *PPF*. Here, equilibrium consumption is C_1, while the equilibrium quantity of leisure is l_1, and so equilibrium employment is $N_1 = h - l_1$. The initial equilibrium real wage is minus the slope of the indifference curve (or PPF_1) at point A. Now, when government spending increases, the *PPF* shifts to PPF_2, and the equilibrium point is at B, where consumption and leisure are both lower, at C_2 and l_2, respectively. Why do consumption and leisure decrease? This is because consumption and leisure are normal goods. Given the normal goods assumption, a negative income effect from the downward shift in the *PPF* must reduce consumption and leisure. Because leisure falls, then employment, which is $N_2 = h - l_2$, must rise. Further, because employment increases, the quantity of output must rise. We know this because the quantity of capital is fixed in the experiment, while employment has increased, and so the production function tells us that output must increase.

Now, the income–expenditure identity tells us that $Y = C + G$; therefore, $C = Y - G$, and so

$$\Delta C = \Delta Y - \Delta G,$$

where Δ denotes "the change in." Thus, because $\Delta Y > 0$, we have that $\Delta C > -\Delta G$, so that private consumption is **crowded out** by government purchases, but it is not

FIGURE 5.6   Equilibrium Effects of an Increase in Government Spending

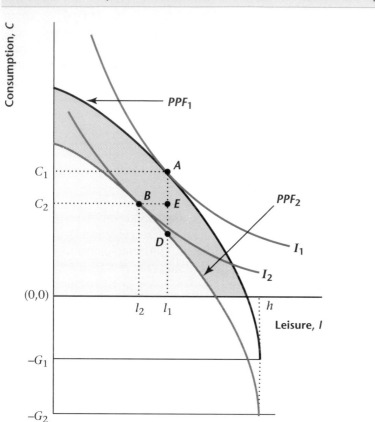

An increase in government spending shifts the PPF down by the amount of the increase in G. There are negative income effects on consumption and leisure, so that both C and l fall, and employment rises, while output (equal to C + G) increases.

completely crowded out as a result of the increase in output. In Figure 5.6 ΔG is the distance AD, and ΔC is the distance AE. While a larger government, reflected in increased government spending, results in more output being produced, because there is a negative income effect on leisure and, therefore, a positive effect on labor supply, a larger government reduces private consumption, through a negative income effect produced by the higher taxes required to finance higher government spending. As the representative consumer pays higher taxes, his or her disposable income falls, and in equilibrium he or she spends less on consumption goods, and works harder to support a larger government.

What happens to the real wage when G increases? In Figure 5.6 the slope of PPF_2 is identical to the slope of PPF_1 for each quantity of leisure, l. Therefore, because the PPF

becomes steeper as l increases (the marginal product of labor increases as employment decreases), PPF_2 at point B is less steep than is PPF_1 at point A. Thus, because minus the slope of the PPF at the equilibrium point is equal to the equilibrium real wage, the real wage falls as a result of the increase in government spending. The real wage must fall, as we know that equilibrium employment rises, and the representative firm would hire more labor only in response to a reduction in the market real wage.

Now, a question we might like to ask is whether or not fluctuations in government spending are a likely cause of business cycles. Recall that in Chapter 3 we developed a set of key business cycle facts. If fluctuations in government spending are important in causing business cycles, then it should be the case that our model can replicate these key business cycle facts in response to a change in G. The model predicts that, when government spending increases, aggregate output and employment increase, and consumption and the real wage decrease. One of our key business cycle facts is that employment is procyclical. This fact is consistent with government spending shocks causing business cycles, because employment always moves in the same direction as aggregate output in response to a change in G. Additional business cycle facts are that consumption and the real wage are procyclical, but the model predicts that consumption and the real wage are countercyclical in response to government spending shocks. This is because, when G changes, consumption and the real wage always move in the direction opposite to the resulting change in Y. Therefore, government spending shocks do not appear to be a good candidate as a cause of business cycles. Whatever the primary cause of business cycles, it is unlikely to be the fact that governments change their spending plans from time to time. We explore this idea further in Chapters 11 and 12.

GOVERNMENT SPENDING IN WORLD WAR II

THEORY confronts the DATA

Wars typically involve huge increases in government expenditure, and they, therefore, represent interesting "natural experiments" that we can examine as an informal empirical test of the predictions of our model. An interesting example involves the effects of increased government spending in the United States during World War II. Shortly after the beginning of U.S. involvement in World War II in late 1941, aggregate output was channeled from private consumption to military uses, and there was a sharp increase in total real GDP. Figure 5.7 shows the natural logarithms of real GDP, real consumption expenditures, and real government expenditures for the period 1929–2002. Of particular note is the extremely large increase in government expenditures that occurred during World War II, which clearly swamps the small fluctuations in G about trend that happened before and after World War II. Clearly, GDP also increases above trend in the figure during World War II, and consumption dips somewhat below trend. Thus, these observations on the behavior of consumption and output during World War II are consistent with our model, in that private consumption is crowded out somewhat and output increases.

FIGURE 5.7   GDP, Consumption, and Government Expenditures

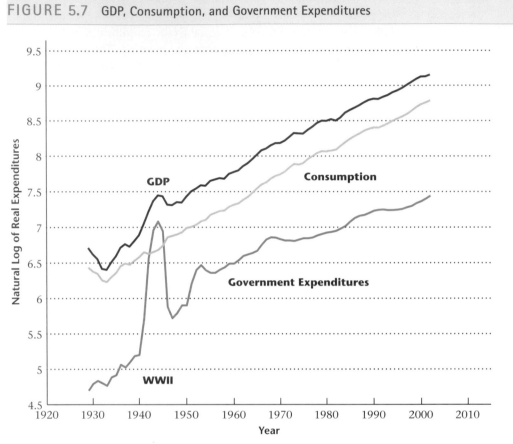

During World War II, an increase in government spending is associated with an increase in aggregate output and a slight decrease in consumption, as is consistent with our model.

Source: Department of Commerce, Bureau of Economic Analysis.

WORKING WITH THE MODEL: A CHANGE IN TOTAL FACTOR PRODUCTIVITY

An increase in total factor productivity involves a better technology for converting factor inputs into aggregate output. As we see in this section, increases in total factor productivity increase consumption and aggregate output, but there is an ambiguous effect on employment. This ambiguity is the result of opposing income and substitution effects on labor supply. While an increase in government spending essentially produces only an income effect on consumer behavior, an increase in total factor productivity generates both an income effect and a substitution effect.

Suppose that total factor productivity z increases. As mentioned previously, the interpretation of an increase in z is as a technological innovation (a new invention

FIGURE 5.8   **Increase in Total Factor Productivity**

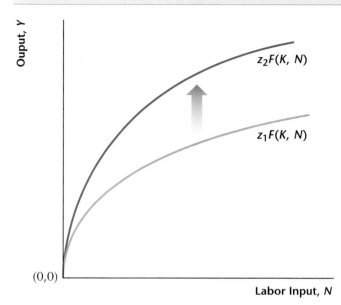

An increase in total factor productivity shifts the production function up and increases the marginal product of labor for each quantity of the labor input.

or an advance in management techniques), a spell of good weather, a relaxation in government regulations, or a decrease in the price of energy. The interpretation of the increase in z and the resulting effects depend on what we take one period in the model to represent relative to time in the real world. One period could be many years—in which case, we interpret the results from the model as capturing what happens over the long run—or one period could be a month, a quarter, or a year—in which case, we are studying short-run effects. After we examine what the model tells us, we provide interpretations in terms of the **short-run** and **long-run** economic implications. In general, the short run in macroeconomics typically refers to effects that occur within a year's time, whereas the long run refers to effects occurring beyond a year's time. However, what is taken to be the boundary between the short run and the long run can vary considerably in different contexts.

The effect of an increase in z is to shift the production function up, as in Figure 5.8. An increase in z not only permits more output to be produced given the quantity of labor input, but it increases the marginal product of labor for each quantity of labor input; that is, the slope of the production function increases for each N. In Figure 5.8, z increases from z_1 to z_2. We can show exactly the same shift in the production function as a shift outward in the PPF in Figure 5.9 from AB to AD. Here, more consumption is attainable given the better technology, for any quantity of leisure consumed. Further, the trade-off between consumption and leisure has improved, in that the new PPF is

FIGURE 5.9   **Competitive Equilibrium Effects of an Increase in Total Factor Productivity**

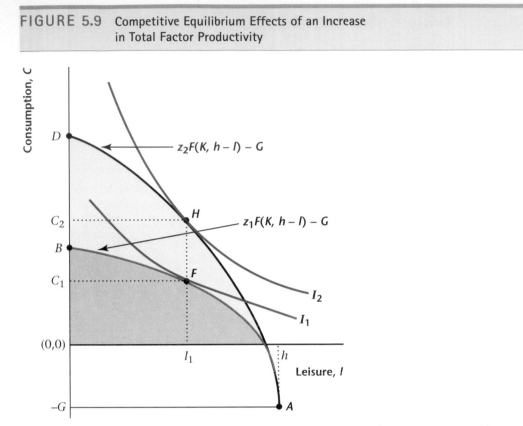

An increase in total factor productivity shifts the PPF from AB to AD. The competitive equilibrium changes from F to H as a result. Output and consumption increase, the real wage increases, and leisure may rise or fall. Because employment is $N = h - l$, employment may rise or fall.

steeper for any given quantity of leisure. That is, because MP_N increases and the slope of the PPF is $-MP_N$, the PPF is steeper when z increases.

Figure 5.9 allows us to determine all the equilibrium effects of an increase in z. Here, indifference curve I_1 is tangent to the initial PPF at point F. After the shift in the PPF, the economy is at a point such as H, where there is a tangency between the new PPF and indifference curve I_2. What must be the case is that consumption increases in moving from F to H, in this case increasing from C_1 to C_2. Leisure, however, may increase or decrease, and here we have shown the case where it remains the same at l_1. Because $Y = C + G$ in equilibrium and because G remains constant and C increases, there is an increase in aggregate output, and because $N = h - l$, employment is unchanged (but employment could have increased or decreased). The equilibrium real wage is minus the slope of the PPF at point H (i.e., $w = MP_N$). When we separate the income and substitution effects of the increase in z, we show that the real wage must increase in equilibrium. In Figure 5.9 the PPF clearly is steeper at H than at F,

FIGURE 5.10 Income and Substitution Effects of an Increase in Total Factor Productivity

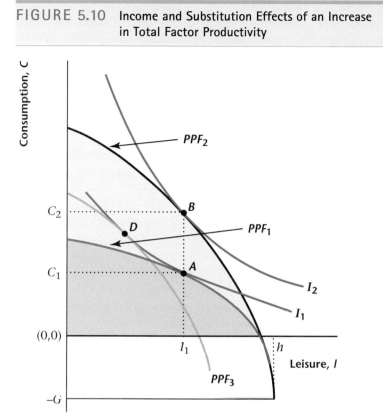

Here, the effects of an increase in total factor productivity are separated into substitution and income effects. The increase in total factor productivity involves a shift form PPF_1 to PPF_2. The curve PPF_3 is an artificial PPF, and it is PPF_2 with the income effect of the increase in z taken out. The substitution effect is the movement from A to D, and the income effect is the movement from D to B.

so that the real wage is higher in equilibrium, but we show how this must be true in general, even when the quantities of leisure and employment change.

To see why consumption has to increase and why the change in leisure is ambiguous, we separate the shift in the *PPF* into an income effect and a substitution effect. In Figure 5.10, PPF_1 is the original *PPF*, and it shifts to PPF_2 when z increases from z_1 to z_2. The initial equilibrium is at point A, and the final equilibrium is at point B after z increases. The equation for PPF_2 is given by

$$C = z_2 F(K, h - l) - G.$$

Now, consider constructing an artificial *PPF*, called PPF_3, which is obtained by shifting PPF_2 downward by a constant amount. That is, the equation for PPF_3 is given by

$$C = z_2 F(K, h - l) - G - C_0.$$

Here C_0 is a constant that is large enough so that PPF_3 is just tangent to the initial indifference curve I_1. What we are doing here is taking consumption (i.e., "income") away from the representative consumer to obtain the pure substitution effect of an increase in z. In Figure 5.10 the substitution effect is then the movement from A to D, and the income effect is the movement from D to B. Much the same as when we considered income and substitution effects for a consumer facing an increase in his or her wage rate, here the substitution effect is for consumption to increase and leisure to decrease, so that hours worked increase. Also, the income effect is for both consumption and leisure to increase. As before, consumption must increase as both goods are normal, but leisure may increase or decrease because of opposing income and substitution effects.

Now, why must the real wage increase in moving from A to B, even if the quantities of leisure and employment rise or fall? First, the substitution effect involves an increase in $MRS_{l,C}$ (the indifference curve gets steeper) in moving along the indifference curve from A to D. Second, because PPF_2 is just PPF_3 shifted up by a fixed amount, the slope of PPF_2 is the same as the slope of PPF_3 for each quantity of leisure. As the quantity of leisure is higher at point B than at point D, the PPF is steeper at B than at D, and so $MRS_{l,C}$ also increases in moving from B to D. Thus, the real wage, which is equal to the marginal rate of substitution in equilibrium, must be higher in equilibrium when z is higher.

The increase in total factor productivity causes an increase in the marginal productivity of labor, which increases the demand for labor by firms, driving up the real wage. Workers now have more income given the number of hours worked, and they spend the increased income on consumption goods. Because there are offsetting income and substitution effects on labor supply, however, hours worked may increase or decrease. An important feature of the increase in total factor productivity is that the welfare of the representative consumer must increase. That is, the representative consumer must consume on a higher indifference curve when z increases. Therefore, increases in total factor productivity unambiguously increase the aggregate standard of living.

Interpretation of the Model's Predictions

Figure 5.9 tells a story about the long-term economic effects of long-run improvements in technology, such as those that have occurred in the United States since World War II. There have been many important technological innovations since World War II, particularly in electronics and information technology. Also, some key observations from post–World War II U.S. data are that aggregate output has increased steadily, consumption has increased, the real wage has increased, and hours worked per employed person have remained roughly constant. Figure 5.9 matches these observations in that it predicts that a technological advance leads to increased output, increased consumption, a higher real wage, and ambiguous effects on hours worked. Thus, if income and substitution effects roughly cancel over the long run, then the model is consistent with the fact that hours worked per person have remained roughly constant over the post–World War II period in the United States. There may have been many other factors in addition to technological change affecting output, consumption, the real wage, and hours worked over this period in U.S. history. Our model, however, tells us that empirical observations for this period are consistent with technological innovations having been an important contributing factor to changes in these key macroeconomic variables.

A second interpretation of Figure 5.9 is in terms of short-run aggregate fluctuations in macroeconomic variables. Could fluctuations in total factor productivity be an important cause of business cycles? Recall from Chapter 3 that three key business cycle facts are that consumption is procyclical, employment is procyclical, and the real wage is procyclical. From Figure 5.9, our model predicts that, in response to an increase in z, aggregate output increases, consumption increases, employment may increase or decrease, and the real wage increases. Therefore, the model is consistent with procyclical consumption and real wages, as consumption and the real wage always move in the same direction as output when z changes. Employment, however, may be procyclical or countercyclical, depending on the strength of opposing income and substitution effects. For the model to be consistent with the data requires that the substitution effect dominate the income effect, so that the consumer wants to increase labor supply in response to an increase in the market real wage. Thus, it is certainly possible that total factor productivity shocks could be a primary cause of business cycles, but to be consistent with the data requires that workers increase and decrease labor supply in response to increases and decreases in total factor productivity over the business cycle.

Some macroeconomists, the advocates of **real business cycle theory,** view total factor productivity shocks as the most important cause of business cycles. This view may seem to be contradicted by the long-run evidence that the income and substitution effects on labor supply of real wage increases appear to roughly cancel in the post–World War II period. Real business cycle theorists, however, argue that much of the short-run variation in labor supply is the result of **intertemporal substitution of labor,** which is the substitution of labor over time in response to real wage movements. For example, a worker may choose to work harder in the present if he or she views his or her wage as being temporarily high, while planning to take more vacation in the future. The worker basically "makes hay while the sun shines." In this way, even though income and substitution effects may cancel in the long run, in the short run the substitution effect of an increase in the real wage could outweigh the income effect. We explore intertemporal substitution further in Chapters 8 to 12.

THEORY
confronts the
DATA

TOTAL FACTOR PRODUCTIVITY, REAL GDP, AND ENERGY PRICES

Shocks to total factor productivity appear to play a key role in business cycles. As evidence of this, Figure 5.11 shows the percentage deviations from trend in real GDP and in the Solow residual for the period 1948–2001. Recall from Chapter 4 that the Solow residual is a measure of total factor productivity, calculated as the quantity of real output that cannot be accounted for by capital and labor inputs. Clearly, the figure shows that the Solow residual and real GDP move together closely. This observation is part of the motivation for real business cycle theory, which we study in detail in Chapter 11. Real business cycle theorists argue that shocks to total factor productivity are the primary source of business cycles, and that seems hard to deny given Figure 5.11, if we accept that the Solow residual is a good measure of total factor productivity (there are some doubts

FIGURE 5.11   Deviations from Trend in Real GDP and the Solow Residual

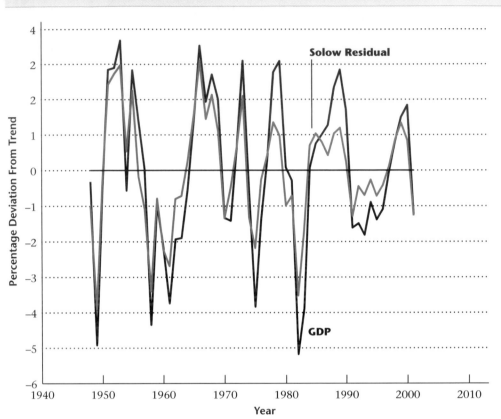

Deviations from trend in the Solow residual closely track deviations from trend in real GDP, as is consistent with real business cycle theory.

about this, as we discuss in Chapter 11). Other data fit the predictions of our model closely. In particular, the fluctuations in real GDP and the Solow residual in Figure 5.11 are tracked closely by fluctuations about trend in consumption and employment (see Chapter 3), as the theory predicts (so long as the substitution effect on labor supply of an increase in total factor productivity outweighs the income effect).

Though Figure 5.11 shows a strong link between fluctuations about trend in total factor productivity and real GDP, the figure is not informative about the underlying shocks that are causing total factor productivity to fluctuate. In Chapter 4, we discussed how changes in total factor productivity can arise because of technological innovation, changes in the weather, changes in government regulations, and changes in the relative price of energy, among other things. Since the 1970s, large changes in the relative price of energy appear to have been a key influence on total factor productivity and have played an important role in post-1970 recessions.

FIGURE 5.12 **The Relative Price of Energy**

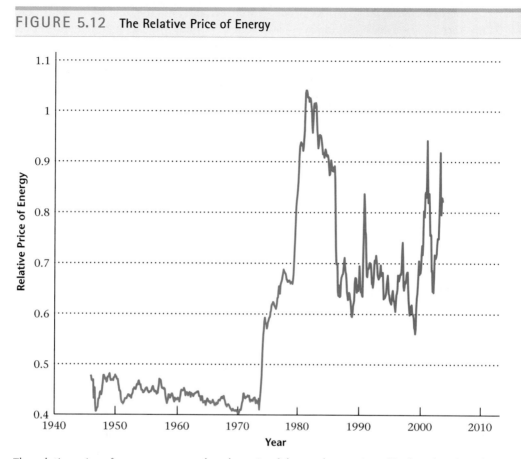

The relative price of energy, measured as the ratio of the producer price of fuels, related products, and power to the producer price of all commodities, exhibits large increases in 1973–1974, 1979–1980, 1990, and 2000, just before the four most recent major recessions.

Source: Bureau of Labor Statistics.

In Figure 5.12, we show the relative price of energy in the United States, for the period 1946–2003, measured as the ratio of the producer price index for fuels, related products, and power, to the producer price index for all commodities. As can be seen in Figures 5.11 and 5.12, several large increases in the relative price of energy were followed closely by sharp decreases below trend in the Solow residual and real GDP. In particular, the Organization of Petroleum Exporting Countries (OPEC) sharply reduced output of crude oil in 1973 and in 1979, leading to large increases in the relative price of energy in 1973–1974 and 1979–1980 (see Figure 5.12). These two events were followed closely by recessions in 1974–1975 and 1981–1982. Similarly, the increases in the relative price of energy during the Persian Gulf War (1990) and in 2000 were followed, respectively, by the recessions of 1990–1991 and 2001.

Increases in the relative price of energy were certainly not the only factor contributing to post-1970 recessions. In particular, monetary policy appears to have contributed significantly to the 1981–1982 recession, and the events of 9/11/01 and an investment collapse driven by pessimism were also important causes of the 2001 recession. It seems clear, however, that large movements in the relative price of energy were of key importance in post-1970 U.S. business cycles and will continue to be important for macroeconomic events in the United States in the future.

Now that we have gained some knowledge from a one-period model concerning how the macroeconomy functions, we can move on in Part III to study the causes and consequences of economic growth.

CHAPTER SUMMARY

- In this chapter, we took the consumer behavior and firm behavior developed in Chapter 4, added government behavior, and constructed a complete one-period macroeconomic model.

- In a competitive equilibrium, the actions of the representative consumer, the representative firm, and the government must be mutually consistent, which implies that the market on which labor is exchanged for goods must clear, and the government budget constraint must hold.

- In a competitive equilibrium, aggregate output, consumption, employment, taxes, and the real wage (the endogenous variables) are determined given the capital stock, total factor productivity, and government spending (the exogenous variables).

- A competitive equilibrium can be represented in a single diagram, and this diagram was used to illustrate the equivalence between the competitive equilibrium and the Pareto optimum, which is an economically efficient state of affairs.

- The model shows how an increase in government spending has a pure negative income effect on the representative consumer, so that employment increases and consumption decreases. Government spending thus crowds out private consumption, but not completely, as there is an increase in aggregate output.

- An increase in total factor productivity, which may arise from improved technology, leads to an increase in output, consumption, and the real wage, but employment may increase or decrease due to opposing income and substitution effects.

KEY TERMS

Closed economy: An economy that does not trade with the rest of the world.

Open economy: An economy that engages in trade with the rest of the world.

Public goods: Goods that are difficult or impossible for the private sector to provide, for example, national defense.

Exogenous variable: A variable determined outside the model.

Endogenous variable: A variable that the model determines.

Government budget constraint: An equation describing the sources and uses of government revenues.

Fiscal policy: The government's choices over government expenditures, taxes, transfers, and government borrowing.

Competitive equilibrium: A state of the economy where prices and quantities are such that the behavior of price-taking consumers and firms is consistent.

Market clearing: When supply equals demand in a particular market or markets.

Production possibilities frontier (PPF): The boundary of a set that describes what consumption bundles are technologically feasible to produce.

Marginal rate of transformation: Minus the slope of the PPF, or the rate at which one good in the economy can be technologically exchanged for another.

Pareto optimality: A state of the economy that cannot be improved on by making one consumer better off without making another worse off.

First fundamental theorem of welfare economics (or first welfare theorem): Result stating that, under certain conditions, a competitive equilibrium is Pareto optimal.

Second fundamental theorem of welfare economics (or second welfare theorem): Result stating that, under certain conditions, a Pareto optimum is a competitive equilibrium.

Externality: The effect an action taken by an economic agent has on another economic agent or agents, where the agent performing the action does not take into account this effect on others.

Distorting tax: A tax, such as an income tax, that creates a difference between the effective prices faced by buyers and sellers of some good.

Crowding out: The displacement of private expenditures by government purchases.

Short run: Typically describes macroeconomic effects that occur within a year's time.

Long run: Typically describes macroeconomic effects that occur beyond a year's time.

Real business cycle theory: A theory postulating that the primary cause of aggregate fluctuations is fluctuations in total factor productivity.

Intertemporal substitution of labor: The substitution of labor over time by a worker in response to movements in real wages.

QUESTIONS FOR REVIEW

All questions refer to the macroeconomic model developed in this chapter.

1. Why is it useful to study a closed-economy model?
2. What is the role of the government in the one-period, closed-economy model?
3. Can the government run a deficit in the one-period model? Why or why not?
4. What are the endogenous variables in the model?
5. What are the exogenous variables in the model?
6. What are the four conditions that a competitive equilibrium must satisfy for this model?
7. What is the economic significance of the slope of the production possibilities frontier?
8. Why is the competitive equilibrium in this model Pareto optimal?
9. Explain the difference between the first and second welfare theorems. Why is each useful?
10. Give three reasons that an equilibrium might not be Pareto optimal.
11. What are the effects of an increase in government purchases?

12. Why does government spending crowd out government purchases?

13. What are the equilibrium effects of an increase in total factor productivity?

14. Explain why employment may rise or fall in response to an increase in total factor productivity.

PROBLEMS

1. Many negative externalities exist in cities. For example, a high concentration of automobile traffic in cities generates pollution and causes congestion, and both pollution and congestion are negative externalities. When a particular person decides to drive a car in a city on a given day, he or she does not take into account the negative effects that driving his or her car has in terms of pollution and deterring other drivers from reaching their destinations (congestion). Although negative externalities (including pollution and congestion) appear to abound in cities, people still prefer to live in cities (otherwise, they would not exist). In economic terms, discuss the forces that cause people to prefer life in the city. How do these forces relate to whether or not market outcomes are economically efficient?

2. Suppose that the government decides to reduce taxes. In the model used in this chapter, determine the effects this has on aggregate output, consumption, employment, and the real wage, and explain your results.

3. Suppose that there is a natural disaster that destroys part of the nation's capital stock.
   (a) Determine the effects on aggregate output, consumption, employment, and the real wage, with reference to income and substitution effects, and explain your results.
   (b) Do you think that changes in the capital stock are a likely cause of business cycles? Explain, with reference to your answer to part (a) and the key business cycle facts described in Chapter 3.

4. Suppose that the government treats government expenditures G as a policy instrument, and suppose that the policy goal of the government is to stabilize consumption for the representative consumer. That is, whenever z changes in the economy, the government observes this, and changes G in such a way that C is the same before and after the change in z. Now, suppose that z falls.
   (a) In what direction does the government need to change G to stabilize C when z falls?
   (b) If the government stabilizes C when z falls, show that employment and aggregate output must fall and that the representative consumer must be better off than before the decrease in z. Explain your results. You must show the income and substitution effects involved to solve the problem.

5. Suppose that the government's goal is to make GDP as large as possible and that it sets out to accomplish this goal by manipulating the quantity of government purchases. Show using a diagram that this type of government policy gives a very poor result for the economy as a whole, and discuss.

6. Suppose that total factor productivity, z, affects the productivity of government production just as it affects private production. That is, suppose that when the government collects taxes, that it acquires goods that are then turned into government-produced goods according to $G = zT$, so that z units of government goods are produced for each unit of taxes collected. With the government setting G, an increase in z implies that a smaller quantity of taxes are required to finance the given quantity of government purchases G. Under

these circumstances, using a diagram determine the effects of an increase in z on output, consumption, employment, and the real wage, treating G as given. Explain your results.

7. Suppose that the representative consumer's preferences change, in that his or her marginal rate of substitution of leisure for consumption increases for any quantities of consumption and leisure.
   (a) Explain what this change in preferences means in more intuitive language.
   (b) What effects does this have on the equilibrium real wage, hours worked, output, and consumption?
   (c) Do you think that preference shifts like this might explain why economies experience recessions (periods when output is low)? Explain why or why not, with reference to the key business cycle facts in Chapter 3.

8. Suppose that government spending makes private firms more productive; for example, government spending on roads and bridges lowers the cost of transportation. This means that there are now two effects of government spending, the first being the effects discussed in this chapter of an increase in G, and the second being similar to the effects of an increase in the nation's capital stock K.
   (a) Show that an increase in government spending that is productive in this fashion could increase welfare for the representative consumer.
   (b) Show that the equilibrium effects on consumption and hours worked of an increase in government spending of this type are ambiguous but that output increases. You must consider income and substitution effects to show this.

WORKING WITH THE DATA

1. Calculate and plot the annual percentage growth rates in real GDP and in total real government purchases from 1948 to 2002. Calculate these growth rates from quarterly data, as percentage growth rates from four previous quarters.
   (a) Does there appear to be any relationship between the growth rates in GDP and in government purchases?
   (b) What does your answer to part (a) tell you about the role in business cycles of fluctuations in government purchases?

2. Calculate the real wage as the employment cost index divided by the consumer price index. With reference to Figure 5.11, do fluctuations in the real wage about trend appear to be consistent with the notion that shocks to total factor productivity are the primary cause of business cycles?

3. One reason that increases in the relative price of energy have a negative impact on U.S. GDP is that a large fraction of energy products used in the United States are imported. Calculate net exports of energy products for the United States (exports minus imports) as a fraction of GDP. Comment on how this quantity has evolved over time compared to the relative price of energy in Figure 5.12.

PART III

Economic Growth

In this part, we study the primary facts of economic growth and the key macroeconomic models that economists have used to understand these facts. In Chapter 6, we first examine the Malthusian model of economic growth, in which population growth increases with the standard of living. Any improvements in the technology for producing goods leads to more population growth, and in the long run there is no improvement in the standard of living. The Malthusian model does a good job of explaining economic growth in the world prior to the Industrial Revolution in the 19th century, but it cannot explain growth experience after 1800. What Malthus did not envision was the role of capital accumulation in economic growth. Capital accumulation plays an important role in the Solow model of economic growth, which is the preeminent framework used in modern economic growth theory. The Solow growth model predicts that long-run improvements in the standard of living are generated by technological progress, that countries with high (low) savings rates tend to have high (low) levels of per-capita income, and that countries with high (low) rates of population growth tend to have low (high) levels of per capita income. The Solow growth model is much more optimistic than the Malthusian model about the prospects for improvements in the standard of living. Finally, in Chapter 6 we study growth accounting, an approach to attributing economic growth to growth in factors of production and in productivity.

In Chapter 7, we first study the predictions of the Solow growth model for convergence in standards of living across countries. In the data, there is a tendency for convergence in per-capita incomes among the richest countries in the world, but apparently no tendency for convergence among all countries. The Solow model is consistent with this if we allow for differences in the adoption of technology across countries. Next in Chapter 7, we examine an endogenous growth model, which helps us in analyzing the determinants of the rate of economic growth. This endogenous growth model has the property that differences in standards of living persist across countries, and that education is an important factor in determining the rate of economic growth.

CHAPTER 6

Economic Growth: Malthus and Solow

The two primary phenomena that macroeconomists study are business cycles and economic growth. Though much macroeconomic research focuses on business cycles, the study of economic growth has also received a good deal of attention, especially since the late 1980s. Robert Lucas[1] has argued that the potential social gains from a greater understanding of business cycles are dwarfed by the gains from understanding growth. This is because, even if (most optimistically) business cycles could be completely eliminated, the worst events we would be able to avoid would be reductions of real GDP below trend on the order of 5%, based on post–World War II U.S. data. However, if changes in economic policy could cause the growth rate of real GDP to increase by 1% per year for 100 years, then GDP would be 2.7 times higher after 100 years than it would otherwise have been.

The effects of economic growth have been phenomenal. Per-capita U.S. income in 2002 was $36,362,[2] but before the Industrial Revolution in the early nineteenth century, per-capita U.S. income was only several hundred 2002 dollars. In fact, before 1800 the standard of living differed little over time and across countries. Since the Industrial Revolution, however, economic growth has not been uniform across countries, and there are currently wide disparities in standards of living among the countries of the world. In 1995, income per worker in Mexico was 37.4% of what it was in the United States, in Egypt it was 22.0% of that in the United States, and in Burundi it was about 2.4% of the U.S. figure. Currently, there also exist large differences in rates of growth across countries. Between 1960 and 1995, while income per worker was growing at an average rate of 1.77% in the United States, the comparable figure for Angola was −1.90%, for the Congo it was −3.37%, for Hong Kong it was 6.44%, and for Taiwan it was 6.41%.[3]

In this chapter we first discuss some basic economic growth facts, and this provides a useful context in which to organize our thinking using some standard models of growth. The first model we study formalizes the ideas of Thomas Malthus, who wrote in the late eighteenth century. This Malthusian model has the property that any improvements in the technology for producing goods lead to increased population growth, so that in the long run there is no improvement in the standard of living. The population

---

[1] See R. Lucas, 1987, *Models of Business Cycles*, Basil Blackwell, Oxford, UK.

[2] Source: Bureau of Economic Analysis, Department of Commerce.

[3] The income-per-worker statistics come for A. Heston, R. Summers, and B. Aten, *Penn World Table Version 6.1*, Center for International Comparisons at the University of Pennsylvania (CICUP), October 18, 2002, available at pwt.econ.upenn.edu.

is sufficiently higher that there is no increase in per-capita consumption and per-capita output. Consistent with the conclusions of Malthus, the model predicts that the only means for improving the standard of living is population control.

The Malthusian model yields quite pessimistic predictions concerning the prospects for long-run growth in per-capita incomes. Of course, the predictions of Malthus were wrong, as he did not foresee the Industrial Revolution. After the Industrial Revolution, economic growth was in part driven by growth in the stock of capital over time and was not limited by fixed factors of production (such as land), as in the Malthusian model.

Next, we study the Solow growth model, which is the most widely used model of economic growth, developed by Robert Solow in the 1950s.[4] The Solow growth model makes important predictions concerning the effects of savings rates, population growth, and changes in total factor productivity on a nation's standard of living and growth rate of GDP. We show that these predictions match economic data quite well.

A key implication of the Solow growth model is that a country's standard of living cannot continue to improve in the long run in the absence of continuing increases in total factor productivity. In the short run, the standard of living can improve if a country's residents save and invest more, thus accumulating more capital. However, the Solow growth model tells us that building more productive capacity will not improve long-run living standards unless the production technology becomes more efficient. The Solow model is thus more optimistic about the prospects for long-run improvement in the standard of living than is the Malthusian model, but only to a point. The Solow model tells us that improvements in knowledge and technical ability are necessary to sustain growth.

The Solow growth model is an **exogenous growth** model, in that growth is caused in the model by forces that are not explained by the model itself. To gain a deeper understanding of economic growth, it is useful to examine the economic factors that cause growth, and this is done in **endogenous growth** models, one of which we examine in Chapter 7.

Finally, in this chapter we study growth accounting, which is an approach to attributing the growth in GDP to growth in factor inputs and in total factor productivity. Growth accounting can highlight interesting features of the data, such as the slowdown in productivity growth that occurred in the United States from the late 1960s to the early 1980s.

ECONOMIC GROWTH FACTS

Before proceeding to construct and analyze models of economic growth, we summarize the key empirical regularities relating to growth within and across countries. This gives us a framework for evaluating our models and helps in organizing our thinking about growth. The important growth facts are the following:

1. *Before the Industrial Revolution in about 1800, standards of living differed little over time and across countries.* There appeared to have been essentially no improvement in standards of living for a long period of time prior to 1800. Though population

---

[4]See R. Solow, 1956, "A Contribution to the Theory of Economic Growth," *Quarterly Journal of Economics* 70, 65–94.

FIGURE 6.1   **Natural Log of Real per Capita Income in the United States, 1869–2002**

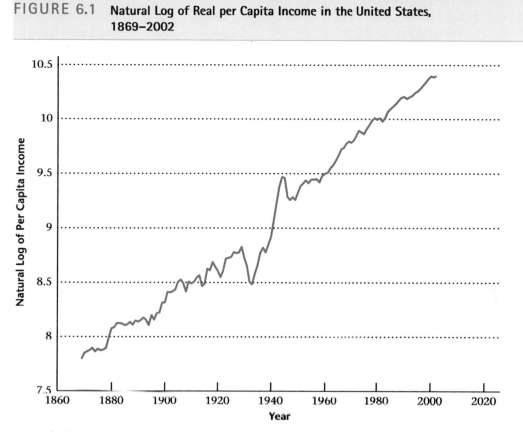

A straight line provides a good fit. Growth in per capita income in the United States has not strayed far from 2% per year for this period.

Source: Bureau of Economic Analysis, Department of Commerce and Romer, C. 1989. "The Prewar Business Cycle Reconsidered: New Estimates of Gross National Product, 1869–1908," *Journal of Political Economy* 97, 1–37.

and aggregate income grew, with growth sometimes interrupted by disease and wars, population growth kept up with growth in aggregate income, so that there was little change in per capita income. Living standards did not vary much across the countries of the world. In particular, Western Europe and Asia had similar standards of living.[5]

2. *Since the Industrial Revolution, per capita income growth has been sustained in the richest countries. In the United States, average annual growth in per capita income has been about 2% since 1869.* The Industrial Revolution began about 1800 in the United Kingdom, and the United States eventually surpassed the United Kingdom as the world industrial leader. Figure 6.1 shows the natural logarithm of per capita income

---

[5]See S. Parente and E. Prescott, 2000. *Barriers to Riches*, MIT Press, Cambridge, MA.

in the United States for the years 1869–2002. Recall from Chapter 1 that the slope of the natural log of a time series is approximately equal to the growth rate. What is remarkable about the figure is that a straight line would be a fairly good fit to the natural log of per capita income in the United States over this period of 134 years. That is, average per capita income growth in the United States has not strayed far from an average growth rate of about 2% per year for the whole period, except for major interruptions like the Great Depression (1929–1939) and World War II (1941–1945) and the minor variability introduced by business cycles.

3. *There is a positive correlation between the rate of investment and output per worker across countries.* In Figure 6.2 we show a scatter plot of output per worker (as a

FIGURE 6.2   Output per Worker vs. Investment Rate

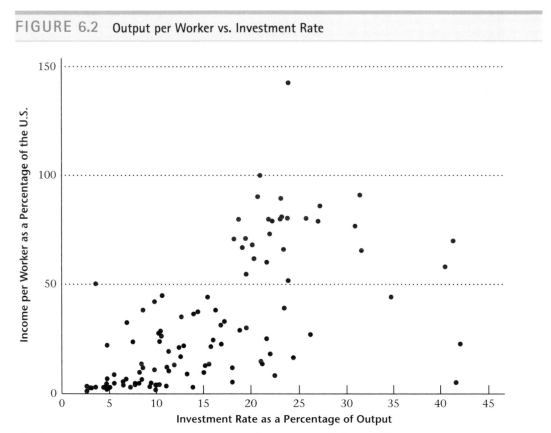

The figure shows a positive correlation across the countries of the world between output per worker and the investment rate.

Source: A. Heston, R. Summers, and B. Aten, *Penn World Table Version 6.1*, Center for International Comparisons at the University of Pennsylvania (CICUP), October 18, 2002, available at pwt.econ.upenn.edu.

percentage of output per worker in the United States) versus the rate of investment (as a percentage of aggregate output) in the countries of the world in 1995. Clearly, a straight line fit to these points would have a positive slope, so the two variables are positively correlated. Thus, countries in which a relatively large (small) fraction of output is channeled into investment tend to have a relatively high (low) standard of living. This fact is particularly important in checking the predictions of the Solow growth model against the data.

4. *There is a negative correlation between the population growth rate and output per worker across countries.* Figure 6.3 shows a scatter plot of output per worker (as a percentage of output per worker in the United States) versus the average annual population growth rate for 1960–1995 for the countries of the world. Here, a

FIGURE 6.3   **Output per Worker vs. the Population Growth Rate**

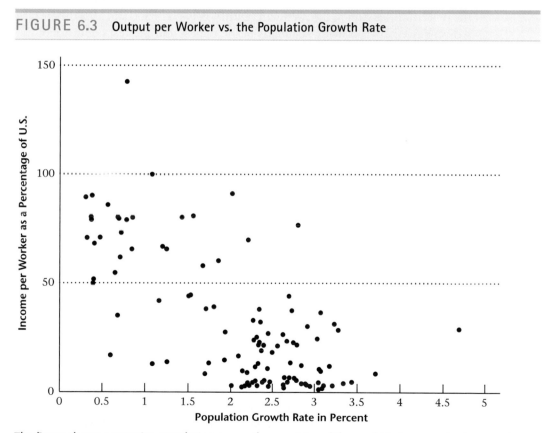

The figure shows a negative correlation across the countries of the world between output per worker and the population growth rate.

Source: A. Heston, R. Summers, and B. Aten, *Penn World Table Version 6.1*, Center for International Comparisons at the University of Pennsylvania (CICUP), October 18, 2002, available at pwt.econ.upenn.edu.

straight line fit to the points in the figure would have a negative slope, so the two variables are negatively correlated. Countries with high (low) population growth rates tend to have low (high) standards of living. As with the previous fact, this one is important in matching the predictions of the Solow growth model with the data.

5. *Differences in per capita incomes increased dramatically among countries of the world between 1800 and 1950, with the gap widening between the countries of Western Europe, the United States, Canada, Australia, and New Zealand, as a group, and the rest of the world.* A question that interests us in this chapter and the next is whether standards of living are converging across countries of the world. The Industrial Revolution spread in the early 19th century from the United Kingdom to Western Europe and the United States, then to the new countries of Canada, Australia, and New Zealand. The countries of Africa, Asia, and South America were mainly left behind, with some Asian (and to some extent South American) countries closing the gap with the rich countries later in the twentieth century. Between 1800 and 1950, there was a divergence between living standards in the richest and poorest countries of the world.[6]

6. *There is essentially no correlation across countries between the level of output per worker in 1960 and the average rate of growth in output per worker for the years 1960–1995.* Standards of living would be converging across countries if income (output) per worker were converging to a common value. For this to happen, it would have to be the case that poor countries (those with low levels of income per worker) are growing at a higher rate than are rich countries (those with high levels of income per worker). Thus, if convergence in incomes per worker is occurring, we should observe a negative correlation between the growth rate in income per worker and the level of income per worker across countries. Figure 6.4 looks at data for 1960–1995, the period for which good data exists for most of the countries in the world. The figure shows the average rate of growth in output per worker for the period 1960 to 1995, versus the level of output per worker (as a percentage of output per worker in the United States) in 1960 for a set of 108 countries. There is essentially no correlation shown in the figure, which indicates that, for all countries of the world, convergence is not detectable for this period.

7. *Among the richest countries, there is a negative correlation between the level of output per worker in 1960 and the average rate of growth in output per worker for the years 1960–1995.* Figure 6.5 shows the same data as for fact (6) but restricts attention to only the countries that were richest in 1960, that is, the countries with incomes per worker in 1960 of at least 50% of that in the United States (20 of the original set of 108 countries). Here, we observe a clear negative correlation, so that convergence appears to be occurring for the richest countries in the world for this period.

---

[6]See S. Parente and E. Prescott, 2000. *Barriers to Riches*, MIT Press, Cambridge, MA.

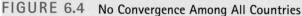

FIGURE 6.4   No Convergence Among All Countries

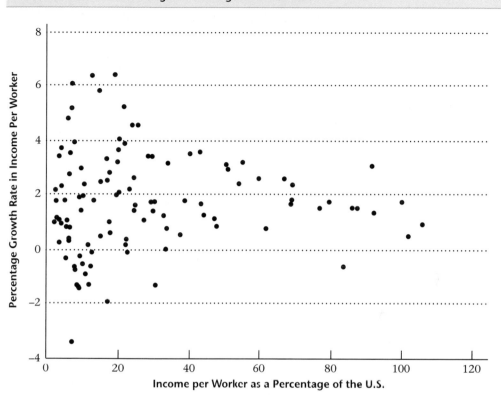

There is essentially no correlation between the level of output per worker and the growth rate in output per worker across all countries in the world.

Source: A. Heston, R. Summers, and B. Aten, *Penn World Table Version* 6.1, Center for International Comparisons at the University of Pennsylvania (CICUP), October 18, 2002, available at pwt.econ.upenn.edu.

8. *Among the poorest countries, there is essentially no correlation between the level of output per worker in 1960 and the average rate of growth in output per worker for the years 1960–1995.* In Figure 6.6, we consider the same data set as for fact (6) but include only those countries with output per worker that was 20% or less of that in the United States in 1960. Here, we observe no correlation, so that there is no evidence of convergence among the poorest countries of the world for this period.

In this chapter and Chapter 7, we use growth facts 1 to 8 to motivate the structure of our models and as checks on the predictions of those models.

FIGURE 6.5 Convergence Among the Richest Countries

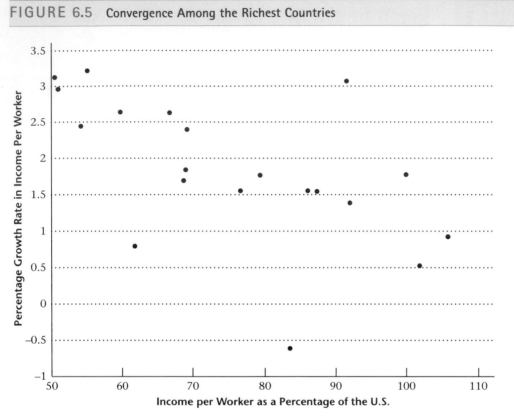

There is a negative correlation between the level of output per worker and the growth rate in output per worker among the richest countries.

Source: A. Heston, R. Summers, and B. Aten, *Penn World Table Version* 6.1, Center for International Comparisons at the University of Pennsylvania (CICUP), October 18, 2002, available at pwt.econ.upenn.edu.

THE MALTHUSIAN MODEL OF ECONOMIC GROWTH

In 1798, Thomas Malthus, a political economist in England, wrote the highly influential *An Essay on the Principle of Population*.[7] Malthus did not construct a formal economic model of the type that we would use in modern economic arguments, but his ideas are clearly stated and coherent and can be easily translated into a structure that is easy to understand.

Malthus argued that any advances in the technology for producing food would inevitably lead to further population growth, with the higher population ultimately

---

[7]See Malthus, T. 1798. "An Essay on the Principle of Population," St. Paul's Church-Yard, London, available at http://www.ac.wwu.edu/~stephan/malthus/malthus.0.html.

FIGURE 6.6   No Convergence Among the Poorest Countries

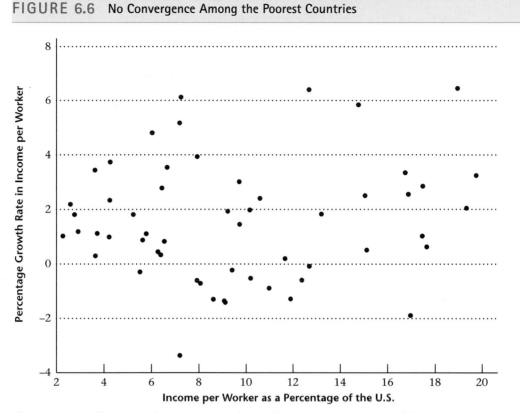

There is essentially no correlation between the level of output per worker and the growth rate in output per worker among the poorest countries.

Source: A. Heston, R. Summers, and B. Aten, *Penn World Table Version* 6.1, Center for International Comparisons at the University of Pennsylvania (CICUP), October 18, 2002, available at pwt.econ.upenn.edu.

reducing the average person to the subsistence level of consumption they had before the advance in technology. The population and level of aggregate consumption could grow over time, but in the long run there would be no increase in the standard of living unless there were some limits on population growth. Malthusian theory is, therefore, very pessimistic about the prospects for increases in the standard of living, with collective intervention in the form of forced family planning required to bring about gains in per capita income.

The following model formalizes Malthusian theory. The model is a dynamic one with many periods, though for most of the analysis we confine attention to what happens in the *current period* and the *future period* (the period following the current period). We start with an aggregate production function that specifies how current aggregate output,

Y, is produced using current inputs of land, L, and current labor, N, that is

$$Y = zF(L, N), \qquad (6.1)$$

where z is total factor productivity, and F is a function having the same properties, including constant returns to scale, that we specified in Chapter 4, except here land replaces capital in the production function. It helps to think of Y as being food, which is perishable from period to period. In this economy there is no investment (and, therefore, no saving—recall from Chapter 2 that savings equals investment in a closed economy) as we assume there is no way to store food from one period to the next and no technology for converting food into capital. For simplicity, there is assumed to be no government spending. Land, L, is in fixed supply. That is, as was the case in Western Europe in 1798, essentially all of the land that could potentially be used for agriculture is under cultivation. Assume that each person in this economy is willing to work at any wage and has one unit of labor to supply (a normalization), so that N in Equation (6.1) is both the population and the labor input.

Next, suppose that population growth depends on the quantity of consumption per worker, or

$$\frac{N'}{N} = g\left(\frac{C}{N}\right), \qquad (6.2)$$

where N' denotes the population in the future (next) period, g is an increasing function, and C is aggregate consumption, so that $\frac{C}{N}$ is current consumption per worker. We show the relationship described by Equation (6.2) in Figure 6.7. In Equation (6.2), the ratio of future population to current population depends positively on consumption per worker mainly due to the fact that higher food consumption per worker reduces death rates through better nutrition. With poor nutrition, infants have a low probability of surviving childbirth, and children and adults are highly succeptible to disease.

In equilibrium, all goods produced are consumed, so $C = Y$, which is the income-expenditure identity for this economy (because $I = G = NX = 0$ here; see Chapter 2). Therefore, substituting C for Y in Equation (6.2), in equilibrium we have

$$C = zF(L, N). \qquad (6.3)$$

We can then use Equation (6.3) to substitute for C in Equation (6.2) to get

$$\frac{N'}{N} = g\left(\frac{zF(L, N)}{N}\right). \qquad (6.4)$$

Now, recall from Chapter 4 that the constant-returns-to-scale property of the production function implies that

$$xzF(L, N) = zF(xL, xN)$$

for any $x > 0$, so if $x = \frac{1}{N}$ in the above equation, then

$$\frac{zF(L, N)}{N} = zF\left(\frac{L}{N}, 1\right)$$

As a result, we can rewrite Equation (6.4), after multiplying each side by N, as

$$N' = g\left(zF\left(\frac{L}{N}, 1\right)\right)N. \qquad (6.5)$$

FIGURE 6.7   **Population Growth Depends on Consumption per Worker
in the Malthusian Model**

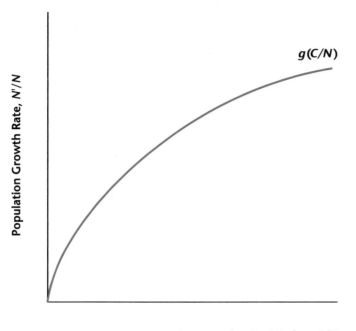

Here, Equation (6.5) tells us how the population evolves over time in equilibrium, as it gives the future population as a function of the current population. We assume that the relationship described in Equation (6.5) can be depicted as in Figure 6.8.[8] In the figure N^* is a rest point or **steady state** for the population, determined by the point where the curve intersects the 45° line. If the current population is N^* then the future population is N^*, and the population is N^* forever after. In the figure, if $N < N^*$ then $N' > N$ and the population increases, whereas if $N > N^*$ then $N' < N$ and the population decreases. Thus, whatever the population is currently, it eventually comes to rest at N^* in the long run. That is, the steady state N^* is the long-run equilibrium for the population. The reason that population converges to a steady state is the following. Suppose, on the one hand, that the population is currently below its steady state value. Then there will be a relatively large quantity of consumption per worker, and this will imply that the population growth rate is relatively large and positive, and the population will increase. On the other hand, suppose that the population is above its steady state value. Then there will be a small quantity of consumption per worker, and the population growth rate will be relatively low and negative, so that the population will decrease.

---

[8]For example, if $F(L, N) = L^\alpha N^{1-\alpha}$ and $g\left(\frac{C}{N}\right) = \left(\frac{C}{N}\right)^\gamma$, with $0 < \alpha < 1$ and $0 < \gamma < 1$, we get these properties.

FIGURE 6.8   **Determination of the Population in the Steady State**

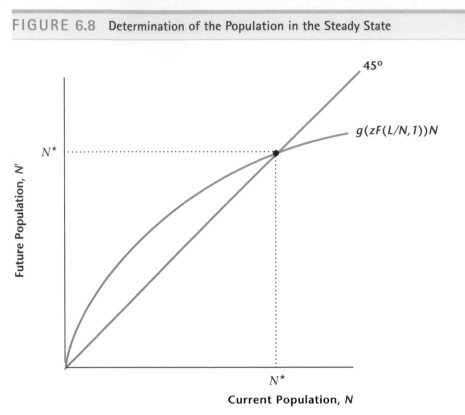

In the figure, N^* is the steady state population, determined by the intersection of the curve and the 45° line. If $N > N^*$ then $N' < N$ and the population falls over time, and if $N < N^*$ then $N' > N$ and the population rises over time.

Because the quantity of land is fixed, when the population converges to the long-run equilibrium N^*, aggregate consumption (equal to aggregate output here) converges, from Equation (6.3), to

$$C^* = zF(L, N^*).$$

Analysis of the Steady State in the Malthusian Model

Because the Malthusian economy converges to a long-run steady state equilibrium with constant population and constant aggregate consumption, it is useful to analyze this steady state to determine what features of the environment affect steady state variables. In this subsection, we show how this type of analysis is done.

Given that the production function F has the constant returns to scale property, if we divide the left-hand and right-hand sides of Equation (6.1) by N and rearrange, we get

$$\frac{Y}{N} = zF\left(\frac{L}{N}, 1\right).$$

FIGURE 6.9   The Per–Worker Production Function

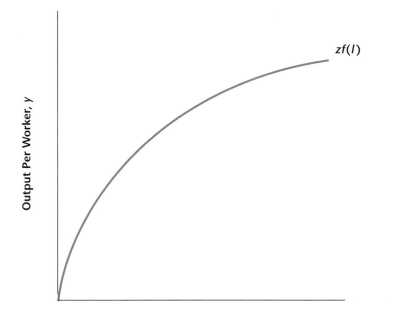

This describes the relationship between output per worker and land per worker in the Malthusian model, assuming constant returns to scale.

Then letting lower-case letters denote per-worker quantities, that is $y \equiv \frac{Y}{N}$ (output per worker), $l = \frac{L}{N}$ (land per worker), and $c \equiv \frac{C}{N}$ (consumption per worker), we have

$$y = zf(l), \qquad (6.6)$$

where $zf(l)$ is the **per-worker production function**, which describes the quantity of output per worker y that can be produced for each quantity of land per worker l, with the function f defined by $f(l) \equiv F(l, 1)$. The per-worker production function is displayed in Figure 6.9. Then, as $c = y$ in equilibrium, from Equation (6.6) we have

$$c = zf(l) \qquad (6.7)$$

We can also rewrite Equation (6.2) as

$$\frac{N'}{N} = g(c). \qquad (6.8)$$

Now, we can display Equations (6.7) and (6.8) in Figure 6.10. In the steady state, $N' = N = N^*$, so $\frac{N'}{N} = 1$, and in panel (b) of the figure this determines c^*, the steady state quantity of consumption per worker. Then, in panel (a) of the figure, c^* determines the steady state quantity of land per worker, l^*. Because the quantity of land is fixed

FIGURE 6.10   Determination of the Steady State in the Malthusian Model

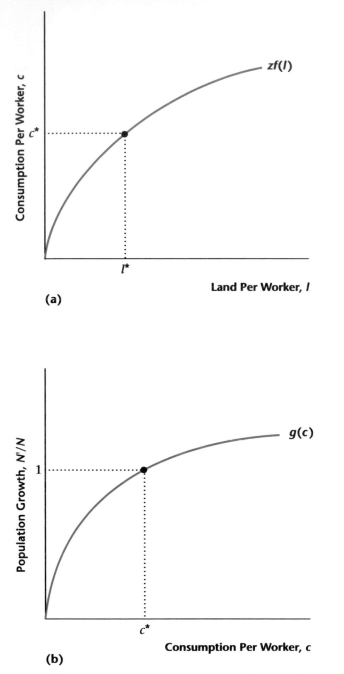

(a)

(b)

In panel (b), steady state consumption per worker c^* is determined as the level of consumption per worker that implies no population growth. Given c^*, the quantity of land per worker in the steady state l^* is determined from the per-worker production function in panel (a).

at L, we can then determine the steady state population as $N^* = \frac{L}{l^*}$. In the model, we can take the standard of living as being given by steady state consumption per worker, c^*. Therefore, the long-run standard of living is determined entirely by the function g, which captures the effect of the standard of living on population growth. The key property of the model is that nothing in panel (a) of Figure 6.10 affects c^*, so that improvements in the production technology or increases in the quantity of land have no effect on the long-run standard of living.

The Effects of an Increase in z on the Steady State   We now consider an experiment in which total factor productivity increases, which we can interpret as an improvement in agricultural techniques. That is, suppose that the economy is initially in a steady state, with a given level of total factor productivity z_1, which then increases once and for all time to z_2. The steady state effects are shown in Figure 6.11. In panel (a) of the figure, the per-worker production function shifts up from $z_1 f(l)$ to $z_2 f(l)$. This has no effect on steady state consumption per worker c^*, which is determined in panel (b) of the figure. In the new steady state, in panel (a) the quantity of land per worker falls from l_1^* to l_2^*. This implies that the steady state population increases from $N_1^* = \frac{L}{l_1^*}$ to $N_2^* = \frac{L}{l_2^*}$.

The economy does not move to the new steady state instantaneously, as it takes time for the population and consumption to adjust. Figure 6.12 shows how the adjustment takes place in terms of the paths of consumption per worker and population. The economy is in a steady state before time T, at which time there is an increase in total factor productivity. Initially, the effect of this is to increase output, consumption, and consumption per worker, as there is no effect on the current population at time T. However, because consumption per worker has increased, there is an increase in population growth. As the population grows after period T, in panel (b) of the figure, consumption per worker falls (given the fixed quantity of land), until consumption per worker converges to c^*, its initial level, and the population converges to its new higher level N_2^*.

This then gives the pessimistic Malthusian result that improvements in the technology for producing food do not improve the standard of living in the long run. A better technology generates better nutrition and more population growth, and the extra population ultimately consumes all of the extra food produced, so that each person is no better off than before the technological improvement.

Population Control   How can society be better off in a Malthusian world? The prescription Malthus proposed was state-mandated population control. If the government were to institute something like the "one child only" policy introduced in China, this would have the effect of reducing the rate of population growth for each level of consumption per worker. In panel (b) of Figure 6.13, the function $g_1(c)$ shifts down to $g_2(c)$ as the result of the population control policy. In the steady state, consumption per worker increases from c_1^* to c_2^* in panel (b) of the figure, and this implies that the quantity of land per worker rises in the steady state in panel (a) from l_1^* to l_2^*. Because the quantity of land is fixed, the population falls in the steady state from $N_1^* = \frac{L}{l_1^*}$ to $N_2^* = \frac{L}{l_2^*}$. Here, a

FIGURE 6.11   The Effect of an Increase in z in the Malthusian Model

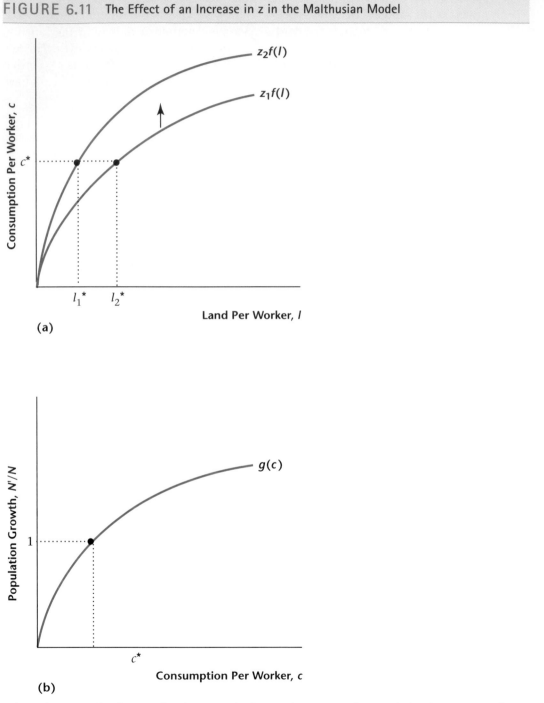

When z increases, land per worker decreases in the steady state (so the population increases) and consumption per worker remains the same.

FIGURE 6.12 Adjustment to the Steady State in the Malthusian Model When z Increases

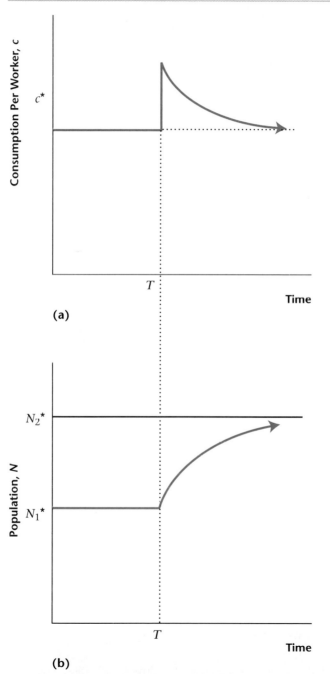

(a)

(b)

In the figure, z increases at time T, which causes consumption per worker to increase and then decline to its steady state value over time, with the population increasing over time to its steady state value.

FIGURE 6.13   Population Control in the Malthusian Model

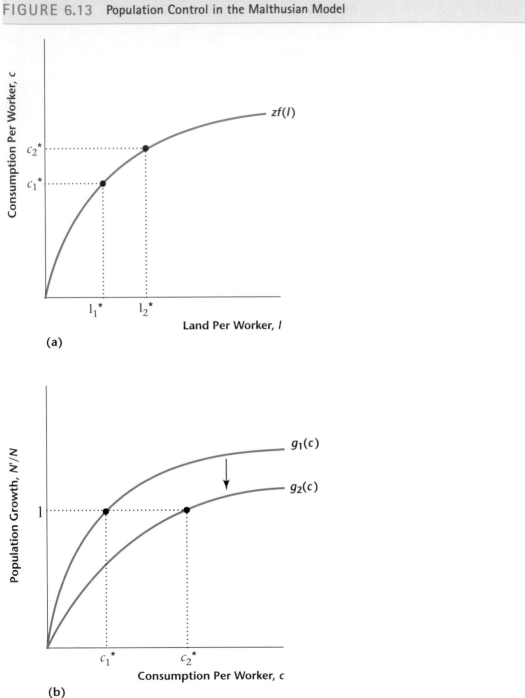

(a)

(b)

In the figure, population control policy shifts the function $g_1(c)$ to $g_2(c)$. In the steady state, consumption per worker increases and land per worker decreases (the population falls).

reduction in the size of the population increases output per worker and consumption per worker, and everyone is better off in the long run.

How Useful is the Malthusian Model of Economic Growth?

Given what was known in 1798, when Malthus wrote his essay, the Malthusian model could be judged to be quite successful. Our first economic growth fact, discussed at the beginning of this chapter, was that before the Industrial Revolution in about 1800, standards of living differed little over time and across countries. The Malthusian model predicts this, if population growth depends in the same way on consumption per worker across countries. Before the Industrial Revolution, production in the world was mainly agricultural; the population grew over time, as did aggregate production, but there appeared to have been no significant improvements in the average standard of living. This is all consistent with the Malthusian model.

As is well-known from the perspective of the early 21st century however, Malthus was far too pessimistic. There was sustained growth in standards of living in the richest countries of the world after 1800 without any significant government population control in place in the countries with the strongest performance. As well, the richest countries of the world have experienced a large drop in birth rates. Currently, in spite of advances in health care that have increased life expectancy dramatically in the richer countries, population in most of these richer countries would be declining without immigration. Thus, Malthus was ultimately wrong, both concerning the ability of economies to produce long-run improvements in the standard of living and the effect of the standard of living on population growth.

Why was Malthus wrong? First, he did not allow for the effect of increases in the capital stock on production. In contrast to land, which is limited in supply, there is no limit to the size of the capital stock, and having more capital implies that there is more productive capacity to produce additional capital. That is, capital can reproduce itself. The Solow growth model, which we develop later in this chapter, allows us to explore the role of capital accumulation in growth.

Second, Malthus did not account for all of the effects of economic forces on population growth. While it is clear that a higher standard of living reduces death rates through better nutrition and health care, there has also proved to be a reduction in birth rates. As the economy develops, there are better opportunities for working outside the home. In terms of family decisions, the opportunity cost of raising a large family becomes large in the face of high market wages, and more time is spent working in the market rather than raising children at home.

THE SOLOW MODEL: EXOGENOUS GROWTH

The Solow growth model is very simple, yet it makes sharp predictions concerning the sources of economic growth, what causes living standards to increase over time, what happens to the level and growth rate of aggregate income when the savings rate or the population growth rate rises, and what we should observe happening to relative living standards across countries over time. This model is much more optimistic about the prospects for long-run improvements in the standard of living than is the Malthusian model. Sustained increases in the standard of living can occur in the model, but sustained technological advances are necessary for this. As well, the Solow model does a good job of explaining the economic growth facts discussed early in this chapter.

In constructing this model, we begin with a description of the consumers who live in this environment and of the production technology. As with the Malthusian model we treat dynamics seriously here. We study how this economy evolves over time in a competitive equilibrium, and a good part of our analysis concerns the steady state of the model which we know, from our analysis of the Malthusian model, is the long-run equilibrium or rest point.

Consumers

As in the Malthusian model, there are many periods, but we will analyze the economy in terms of the "current" and the "future" period. In contrast to the Malthusian model we suppose that the population grows exogenously. That is, there is a growing population of consumers, with N denoting the population in the current period. As in the Malthusian model, N also is the labor force, or the quantity of employment. The population grows over time, with

$$N' = (1+n)N, \tag{6.9}$$

where N' is the population in the future period and $n > -1$. Here, n is the rate of growth in the population, which is assumed to be constant over time. We are allowing for the possibility that $n < 0$, in which case the population would be shrinking over time.

In each period, a given consumer has one unit of time available, and we assume that consumers do not value leisure, so that they supply their one unit of time as labor in each period. In this model, the population is identical to the labor force, because we have assumed that all members of the population work. We then refer to N as the number of workers or the labor force and to n as the growth rate in the labor force.

Consumers collectively receive all current real output Y as income (through wage income and dividend income from firms), because there is no government sector and no taxes. In contrast to all of the models we have considered to this point, consumers here face a decision concerning how much of their current income to consume and how much to save. For simplicity, we assume that consumers consume a constant fraction of income in each period; that is,

$$C = (1-s)Y, \tag{6.10}$$

where C is current consumption. For consumers, $C + S = Y$, where S is aggregate savings, so from Equation (6.10) we have $S = sY$ and s is then the aggregate savings rate. In Chapter 8 we discuss in more depth how consumers make their consumption–savings decisions.

The Representative Firm

Output is produced by a representative firm, according to the production function

$$Y = zF(K, N), \tag{6.11}$$

where Y is current output, z is current total factor productivity, K is the current capital stock, and N is the current labor input. The production function F has all of the properties that we studied in Chapter 4. As in the Malthusian model, constant returns to scale implies that, dividing both sides of equation (6.11) by N and rearranging, we get

$$\frac{Y}{N} = zF\left(\frac{K}{N}, 1\right) \tag{6.12}$$

In Equation (6.12), $\frac{Y}{N}$ is output per worker, and $\frac{K}{N}$ is capital per worker, and so (6.12) tells us that if the production function has constant returns to scale, then output per worker [on the left-hand side of (6.12)] depends only on the quantity of capital per worker [on the right-hand side of (6.12)]. For simplicity, as in the Malthusian model we can rewrite Equation (6.12) as

$$y = zf(k)$$

where y is output per worker, k is capital per worker, and $f(k)$ is the per-worker production function, which is defined by $f(k) \equiv F(k, 1)$. We use lowercase letters in what follows to refer to per-worker quantities. The per-worker production function is graphed in Figure 6.14. A key property of the per-worker production function is that

---

FIGURE 6.14 **The Per–Worker Production Function**

This function is the relationship between aggregate output per worker and capital per worker determined by the constant-returns-to-scale production function. The slope of the per-worker production function is the marginal product of capital, MP_K.

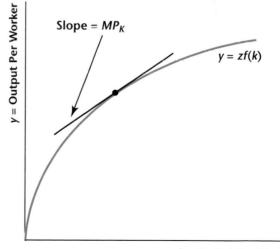

its slope is the marginal product of capital, MP_K. This is because adding one unit to k, the quantity of capital per worker, increases y, output per worker, by the marginal product of capital, because $f(k) = F(k, 1)$. As the slope of the per-worker production function is MP_K, and because MP_K is diminishing with K, the per-worker production function in the figure is concave—that is, its slope decreases as k increases.

We suppose that some of the capital stock wears out through use each period. That is, there is depreciation, and we assume that the depreciation rate is a constant d, where $0 < d < 1$. Then, the capital stock changes over time according to

$$K' = (1 - d)K + I, \tag{6.13}$$

where K' is the future capital stock, K is the current capital stock, and I is investment.

Competitive Equilibrium

Now that we have described the behavior of consumers and firms in the Solow growth model, we can put this behavior together and determine how consistency is achieved in a competitive equilibrium. In this economy, there are two markets in the current period. In the first market, current consumption goods are traded for current labor; in the second market, current consumption goods are traded for capital. That is, capital is the asset in this model, and consumers save by accumulating it. The labor market and the capital market must clear in each period. In the labor market, the quantity of labor is always determined by the inelastic supply of labor, which is N. That is, because the supply of labor is N no matter what the real wage, the real wage adjusts in the current period so that the representative firm wishes to hire N workers. Letting S denote the aggregate quantity of saving in the current period, the capital market is in equilibrium in the current period if $S = I$, that is, if what consumers wish to save equals the quantity of investment. However, because $S = Y - C$ in this economy—that is, national savings is aggregate income minus consumption as there is no government—we can write the equilibrium condition as

$$Y = C + I, \tag{6.14}$$

or current output is equal to aggregate consumption plus aggregate investment. From Equation (6.13) we have that $I = K' - (1 - d)K$, and so using this and Equation (6.10) to substitute for C and I in Equation (6.14), we get

$$Y = (1 - s)Y + K' - (1 - d)K,$$

or, rearranging terms and simplifying,

$$K' = sY + (1 - d)K; \tag{6.15}$$

that is, the capital stock in the future period is the quantity of aggregate savings in the current period ($S = Y - C = sY$) plus the capital stock left over from the current period that has not depreciated. Then if we substitute for Y in Equation (6.15) using the production function from Equation (6.11), we get

$$K' = szF(K, N) + (1 - d)K. \tag{6.16}$$

Equation (6.16) states that the stock of capital in the future period is equal to the quantity of savings in the current period (identical to the quantity of investment) plus the quantity of current capital that remains in the future after depreciation.

Now, it is convenient to express Equation (6.16) in per-worker terms, by dividing each term on the right-hand and left-hand sides of (6.16) by N, the number of workers, to get

$$\frac{K'}{N} = sz\frac{F(K, N)}{N} + (1 - d)\frac{K}{N},$$

and then multiplying the left-hand side by $1 = \frac{N'}{N'}$, which gives

$$\frac{K'}{N}\frac{N'}{N'} = sz\frac{F(K, N)}{N} + (1 - d)\frac{K}{N}.$$

Then we can rewrite this as

$$k'(1 + n) = szf(k) + (1 - d)k. \tag{6.17}$$

In Equation (6.17), $k' = \frac{K'}{N'}$ is the future quantity of capital per worker, $\frac{N'}{N} = 1 + n$ from Equation (6.9), and the first term on the right-hand side of (6.17) comes from the fact that $\frac{F(K,N)}{N} = F(\frac{K}{N}, 1)$ because the production function has constant returns to scale, and $F(\frac{K}{N}, 1) = f(k)$ by definition. We can then divide the right-hand and left-hand sides of Equation (6.17) by $1 + n$ to obtain

$$k' = \frac{szf(k)}{1 + n} + \frac{(1 - d)k}{1 + n}. \tag{6.18}$$

Equation (6.18) is a key equation that summarizes most of what we need to know about competitive equilibrium in the Solow growth model, and we use this equation to derive the important implications of the model. This equation determines the future stock of capital per worker, k' on the left-hand side of the equation, as a function of the current stock of capital per worker, k, on the right-hand side.

In Figure 6.15 we graph the relationship given by Equation (6.18). In the figure, the curve has a decreasing slope because of the decreasing slope of the per-worker production function $f(k)$ in Figure 6.14. In the figure, the 45° line is the line along which $k' = k$, and the point at which the 45° line intersects the curve given by Equation (6.18) is the steady state. Once the economy reaches the steady state, where current capital per worker $k = k^*$, then future capital per worker $k' = k^*$, and the economy has k^* units of capital per worker forever after. If the current stock of capital per worker, k, is less than the steady state value, so $k < k^*$, then from the figure $k' > k$, and the capital stock per worker increases from the current period to the future period. In this situation, current investment is sufficiently large, relative to depreciation and growth in the labor force, that the per-worker quantity of capital increases. However, if $k > k^*$, then we have $k' < k$, and the capital stock per worker decreases from the current period to the future period. In this situation, investment is sufficiently small that it cannot keep up with depreciation and labor force growth, and the per-worker quantity of capital declines from the current period to the future period. Therefore, if the quantity of capital per worker is smaller than its steady state value, it increases until it reaches the steady state, and if the quantity of capital per worker is larger than its steady state value, it decreases until it reaches the steady state.

FIGURE 6.15   Determination of the Steady State Quantity of Capital per Worker

The colored curve is the relationship between current capital per worker, k, and future capital per worker, k', determined in a competitive equilibrium in the Solow growth model. The steady state quantity of capital per worker is k^*, given by the intersection of the 45° line (the black line) with the colored curve.

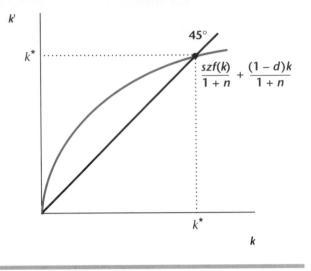

Because the Solow growth model predicts that the quantity of capital per worker converges to a constant, k^*, in the long run, it also predicts that the quantity of output per worker converges to a constant, which is $y^* = zf(k^*)$ from the per-worker production function. The Solow model then tells us that, if the savings rate s, the labor force growth rate n, and total factor productivity z are constant, then real income per worker cannot grow in the long run. Thus, if we take real GDP per worker as a measure of the standard of living, then there can be no long-run betterment in living standards under these circumstances. Why does this happen? The reason is that the marginal product of capital is diminishing. Output per worker can grow only as long as capital per worker continues to grow. However, the marginal return to investment, which is determined by the marginal product of capital, declines as the per-worker capital stock grows. That is, as the capital stock per worker grows, it takes more and more investment per worker in the current period to produce one unit of additional capital per worker for the future period. Therefore, as the economy grows, new investment ultimately only just keeps up with depreciation and the growth of the labor force, and growth in per-worker output ceases.

In the long run, when the economy converges to the steady state quantity of capital per worker, k^*, all real aggregate quantities grow at the rate n, which is the growth rate in the labor force. That is, the aggregate quantity of capital in the steady state is $K = k^*N$, and because k^* is a constant and N grows at the rate n, K must also grow at the rate n. Similarly, aggregate real output is $Y = y^*N = zf(k^*)N$, and so Y also grows at the rate n. Further, the quantity of investment is equal to savings, so that investment in the steady state is $I = sY = szf(k^*)N$, and because $szf(k^*)$ is a constant, I also grows at the rate n in the steady state. As well, aggregate consumption is $C = (1-s)zf(k^*)N$, so that consumption also grows at the rate n in the steady state. In the long run, therefore, if the savings rate, the labor force growth rate, and total factor productivity are constant, then growth rates in aggregate quantities are determined by the growth rate in the labor force. This is one sense in which the Solow growth model is an exogenous growth model. In the long run, the Solow model tells us that growth in key macroeconomic aggregates is determined by exogenous labor force growth when the savings rate, the labor force growth rate, and total factor productivity are constant.

Analysis of the Steady State

In this section, we put the Solow growth model to work. We perform some experiments with the model, analyzing how the steady state or long-run equilibrium is affected by changes in the savings rate, the population growth rate, and total factor productivity. We then show how the response of the model to these experiments is consistent with what we see in the data.

To analyze the steady state, we start with Equation (6.18), which determines the future capital stock per worker, k' given the current capital stock per worker, k. In the steady state, we have $k = k' = k^*$, and so substituting k^* in Equation (6.18) for k and k' we get

$$k^* = \frac{szf(k^*)}{1+n} + \frac{(1-d)k^*}{1+n},$$

multiplying both sides of this equation by $1 + n$ and rearranging, we get

$$szf(k^*) = (n+d)k^*. \tag{6.19}$$

Equation (6.19) solves for the steady state capital stock per worker, k^*. It is this equation we wish to analyze to determine the effects of changes in the savings rate s, in the population growth rate n, and in total factor productivity z on the steady state quantity of capital per worker, k^*.

We graph the left-hand and right-hand sides of Equation (6.19) in Figure 6.16, where the intersection of the two curves determines the steady state quantity of capital per worker, which we denote by k_1^* in the figure. The curve $szf(k^*)$ is the per-worker production function multiplied by the savings rate s, and so this function inherits the properties of the per-worker production function in Figure 6.14. The curve $(n+d)k^*$ in Figure 6.16 is a straight line with slope $n + d$.

The Steady State Effects of an Increase in the Savings Rate   A key experiment to consider in the Solow growth model is a change in the savings rate s. We can interpret a change in s as occurring due to a change in the preferences of consumers. For example, if consumers care more about the future, they save more, and s increases. A change in s could also be brought about through government policy, for example, if the government were to subsidize savings (though in Chapter 8, we show that this has opposing income and substitution effects on savings). With regard to government policy, we need to be careful about interpreting our results, because to be completely rigorous we should build a description of government behavior into the model.

In Figure 6.17 we show the effect of an increase in the savings rate, from s_1 to s_2, on the steady state quantity of capital per worker. The increase in s shifts the curve $szf(k^*)$

FIGURE 6.16   Determination of the Steady State Quantity of Capital per Worker

The steady state quantity of capital, k_1^*, is determined by the intersection of the curve $szf(k^*)$ with the line $(n+d)k^*$.

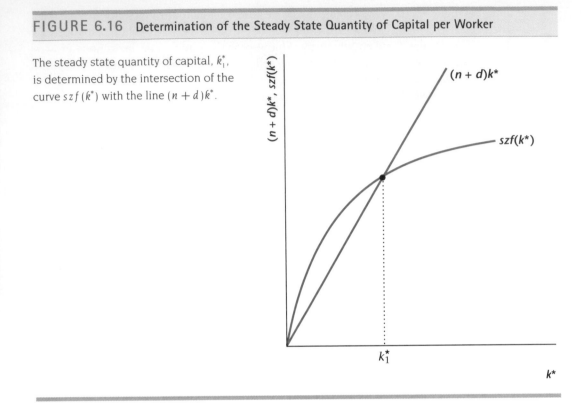

up, and k^* increases from k_1^* to k_2^*. Therefore, in the new steady state, the quantity of capital per worker is higher, which implies that output per worker is also higher, given the per-worker production function $y = zf(k^*)$. Though the levels of capital per worker and output per worker are higher in the new steady state, the increase in the savings rate has no effect on the growth rates of aggregate variables. Before and after the increase in the savings rate, the aggregate capital stock K, aggregate output Y, aggregate investment I, and aggregate consumption C grow at the rate of growth in the labor force, n. This is perhaps surprising, as we might think that a country that invests and saves more, thus accumulating capital at a higher rate, would grow faster.

Though the growth rates of aggregate variables are unaffected by the increase in the savings rate in the steady state, it may take some time for the adjustment from one steady state to another to take place. In Figure 6.18 we show the path that the natural logarithm of output follows when there is an increase in the savings rate, with time measured along the horizontal axis. Before time T, aggregate output is growing at the constant rate n (recall that if the growth rate is constant, then the time path of the natural logarithm is a straight line), and then the savings rate increases at time T. Aggregate output then adjusts to its higher growth path after period T, but in the transition to the new growth path, the rate of growth in Y is higher than n. The temporarily high growth rate in transition results from a higher rate of capital accumulation when the savings

---

FIGURE 6.17 **Effect of an Increase in the Savings Rate on the Steady State Quantity of Capital per Worker**

An increase in the savings rate shifts the curve $szf(k^*)$ up, resulting in an increase in the quantity of capital per worker from k_1^* to k_2^*.

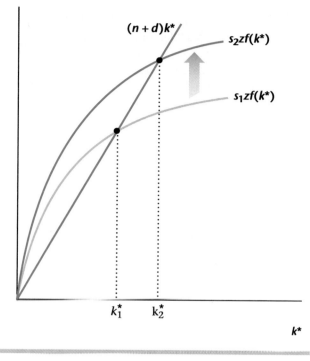

FIGURE 6.18 **Effect of an Increase in the Savings Rate at Time T**

The figure shows the natural logarithm of aggregate output. Before time T, the economy is in a steady state. At time T, the savings rate increases, and output then converges in the long run to a new higher steady state growth path.

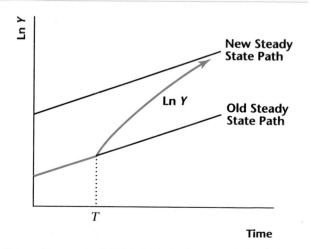

rate increases, which translates into a higher growth rate in aggregate output. As capital is accumulated at a higher rate, however, the marginal product of capital diminishes, and growth slows down, ultimately converging to the steady state growth rate n.

Consumption per Worker and Golden Rule Capital Accumulation   We know from Chapter 2 that GDP, or GDP per person, is often used as a measure of aggregate welfare. However, what consumers ultimately care about is their lifetime consumption. In this model, given our focus on steady states, an aggregate welfare measure we might want to consider is the steady state level of consumption per worker. In this subsection, we show how to determine steady state consumption per worker from a diagram similar to Figure 6.17. Then, we show that there is a given quantity of capital per worker that maximizes consumption per worker in the steady state. This implies that an increase in the savings rate could cause a decrease in steady state consumption per worker, even though an increase in the savings rate always increases output per worker.

   Consumption per worker in the steady state is $c = (1 - s)zf(k^*)$, which is the difference between steady state income per worker, $y^* = zf(k^*)$, and steady state savings per worker, which is $szf(k^*)$. If we add the per-worker production function to Figure 6.17, as we have done in Figure 6.19, then the steady state quantity of capital per worker in the figure is k_1^*, and steady state consumption per worker is the distance AB, which

---

FIGURE 6.19   Steady State Consumption per Worker

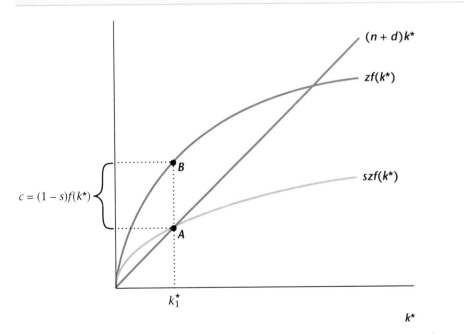

Consumption per worker in the steady state is shown as the distance AB, given the steady state quantity of capital per worker, k_1^*.

is the difference between output per worker and savings per worker. Consumption per worker in the steady state is also the difference between output per worker, $y^* = zf(k^*)$, and $(n+d)k^*$.

Next, because consumption per worker in the steady state is

$$c^* = zf(k^*) - (n+d)k^*$$

in Figure 6.20(a), we have in Figure 6.20(b) plotted c^* against the steady state quantity of capital per worker, k^*. There is a quantity of capital per worker for which consumption per worker is maximized, which we denote by k_{gr}^* in the figure. If the steady state quantity of capital is k_{gr}^*, then maximum consumption per worker is c^{**}. Here, k_{gr}^* is called the **golden rule quantity of capital per worker.** The golden rule has the property, from Figure 6.20(a), that the slope of the per-worker production function where $k^* = k_{gr}^*$ is equal to the slope of the function $(n+d)k^*$. That is, because the slope of the per-worker production function is the marginal product of capital, MP_K, at the golden rule steady state we have

$$MP_K = n + d.$$

Therefore, when capital is accumulated at a rate that maximizes consumption per worker in the steady state, the marginal product of capital equals the population growth rate plus the depreciation rate.

How can the golden rule be achieved in the steady state? In Figure 6.20(a), we show that if the savings rate is s_{gr}, then the curve $s_{gr}zf(k^*)$ intersects the line $(n+d)k^*$ where $k^* = k_{gr}^*$. Thus, s_{gr} is the **golden rule savings rate.** If savings takes place at the golden rule savings rate, then in the steady state the current population consumes and saves the appropriate amount so that, in each succeeding period, the population can continue to consume this maximum amount per person. The golden rule is a biblical reference, which comes from the dictum that we should treat others as we would like ourselves to be treated.

From Figure 6.20(b), if the steady state capital stock per worker is less than k_{gr}^*, then an increase in the savings rate s increases the steady state capital stock per worker and increases consumption per worker. However, if $k^* > k_{gr}^*$, then an increase in the savings rate increases k^* and causes a decrease in consumption per worker.

Suppose that we calculated the golden rule savings rate for the United States and found that the actual U.S. savings rate was different from the golden rule rate. For example, suppose we found that the actual savings rate was lower than the golden rule savings rate. Would this necessarily imply that the government should implement a change in policy that would increase the savings rate? The answer is no, for two reasons. First, any increase in the savings rate would come at a cost in current consumption. It would take time to build up a higher stock of capital to support higher consumption per worker in the new steady state, and the current generation may be unwilling to bear this short-term cost. Second, in practice, savings behavior is the result of optimizing decisions by individual consumers. In general, we should presume that private market outcomes achieve the correct trade-off between current consumption and savings, unless we have good reasons to believe that there exists some market failure that the government can efficiently correct.

FIGURE 6.20   **The Golden Rule Quantity of Capital per Worker**

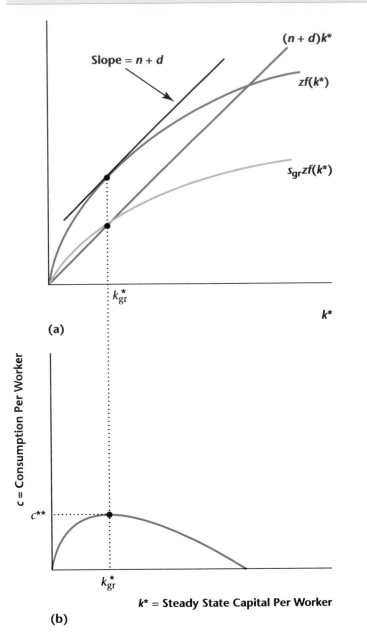

This quantity, which maximizes consumption per worker in the steady state, is k_{gr}^*, and the maximized quantity of consumption per worker is c^{**}. The golden rule savings rate s_{gr} achieves the golden rule quantity of capital per worker in a competitive equilibrium steady state.

FIGURE 6.21   Steady State Effects of an Increase in the Labor Force Growth Rate

An increase in the labor force growth rate from n_1 to n_2 causes a decrease in the steady state quantity of capital per worker.

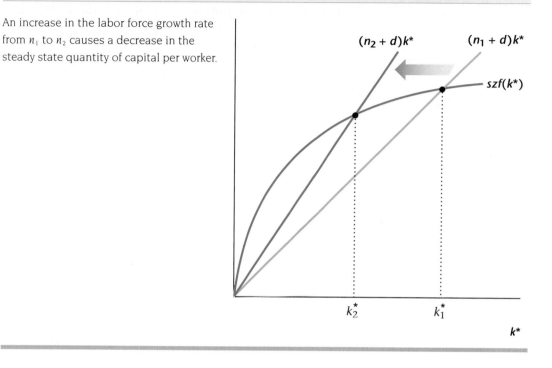

The Steady State Effects of an Increase in Labor Force Growth   The next experiment we carry out with the Solow model is to ask what happens in the long run if the labor force growth rate increases. As labor is a factor of production, it is clear that higher labor force growth ultimately causes aggregate output to grow at a higher rate. But what is the effect on output per worker in the steady state? With aggregate output growing at a higher rate, there is a larger and larger "income pie" to split up, but with more and more workers to share this pie. As we show, the Solow growth model predicts that capital per worker and output per worker will decrease in the steady state when the labor force growth rate increases, but aggregate output will grow at a higher rate, which is the new rate of labor force growth.

In Figure 6.21 we show the steady state effects of an increase in the labor force growth rate, from n_1 to n_2. Initially, the quantity of capital per worker is k_1^*, determined by the intersection of the curves $szf(k^*)$ and $(n_1 + d)k^*$. When the population growth rate increases, this results in a decrease in the quantity of capital per worker to k_2^* in the figure. Because capital per worker falls, output per worker also falls, from the per-worker production function. That is, output per worker falls from $zf(k_1^*)$ to $zf(k_2^*)$. The reason for this result is that, when the labor force grows at a higher rate, the current labor force faces a tougher task in building capital for next period's consumers, who are a proportionately larger group. Thus, output per worker and capital per worker are ultimately lower in the steady state.

We have already determined that aggregate output, aggregate consumption, and aggregate investment grow at the labor force growth rate n in the steady state. Therefore, when the labor force growth rate increases, growth in all of these variables must also increase. This is an example that shows that higher growth in aggregate income need not be associated, in the long run, with higher income per worker.

• •

THE SOLOW GROWTH MODEL, INVESTMENT RATES, AND POPULATION GROWTH

THEORY confronts the DATA

Now that we know something about the predictions that the Solow growth model makes, we can evaluate the model by matching its predictions with the data. It has only been relatively recently that economists have had access to comprehensive national income accounts data for essentially all countries in the world. The Penn World Tables, which are the work of Alan Heston, Robert Summers, and Bettina Aten at the University of Pennsylvania,[1] allow for comparisons of GDP, among other macroeconomic variables, across countries. Making these comparisons is a complicated measurement exercise, as GDP in different countries at a given point in time is measured in different currencies, and simply making adjustments using foreign exchange rates does not give the right answers. A limitation of the Penn World Tables is that they only extend back to 1950. A few decades of data may not tell us all we need to know, in terms of matching the long-run predictions of the Solow growth model. Can the steady state be achieved within a few decades? As we will see, however, two of the predictions of the Solow model appear to match the data in the Penn World Tables quite well.

Two key predictions of the Solow growth model are that, in the long run, an increase in the savings rate causes an increase in the quantity of income per worker, and an increase in the labor force growth rate causes a decrease in the quantity of income per worker. We examine in turn the fit of each of these predictions with the data.

The savings rate in the Solow growth model is the ratio of investment expenditures to GDP. The Solow model thus predicts that, if we look at data from a set of countries in the world, we should see a positive correlation between GDP per worker and the ratio of investment to GDP. This is the correlation that we discussed in the Economic Growth Facts section earlier in this chapter. In Figure 6.2 we observe that a positively sloped line would provide the best fit for the points in the figure, so that the investment rate and income per worker are positively correlated across the countries of the world. Clearly, as the Solow model predicts, countries with high (low) ratios of investment to GDP also have high (low) quantities of income per worker.

Next, the Solow model predicts that, in data for a set of countries, we should observe the labor force growth rate to be negatively correlated with output per worker. Using

---

[1] The income-per-worker statistics come from A. Heston, R. Summers, and B. Aten, *Penn World Table Version 6.1,* Center for International Comparisons at the University of Pennsylvania (CICUP), October 18, 2002, available at pwt.econ.upenn.edu.

population growth as a proxy for labor force growth, this is the fourth economic growth fact we discussed early in this chapter. In Figure 6.3, we observe a negative correlation between the population growth rate and income per worker across countries, as the Solow model predicts.

The Steady State Effects of an Increase in Total Factor Productivity   If we take real income per worker to be a measure of the standard of living in a country, what we have shown thus far is that, in the Solow model, an increase in the savings rate or a decrease in the labor force growth rate can increase the standard of living in the long run. However, increases in the savings rate and reductions in the labor force growth rate cannot bring about an ever-increasing standard of living in a country. This is because the savings rate must always be below 1 (no country would have a savings rate equal to 1, as this would imply zero consumption), and the labor force growth rate cannot fall indefinitely. The Solow model predicts that a country's standard of living can continue to increase in the long run only if there are continuing increases in total factor productivity, as we show here.

In Figure 6.22 we show the effect of increases in total factor productivity. First, an increase in total factor productivity from z_1 to z_2 results in an increase in capital per worker from k_1^* to k_2^* and an increase in output per worker as a result. A further increase in total factor productivity to z_3 causes an additional increase in capital per worker to k_3^* and an additional increase in output per worker. These increases in capital

---

FIGURE 6.22   **Increases in Total Factor Productivity in the Solow Growth Model**

Increases in total factor productivity from z_1 to z_2 and from z_2 to z_3 cause increases in the quantity of capital per worker from k_1^* to k_2^* and from k_2^* to k_3^*. Thus, increases in total factor productivity lead to increases in output per worker.

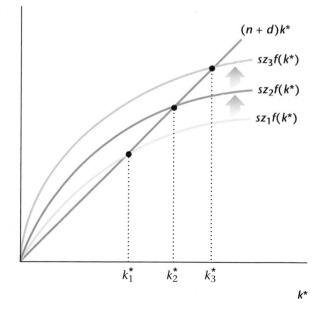

per worker and output per worker can continue indefinitely, as long as the increases in total factor productivity continue.

This is a key insight that comes from the Solow growth model. An increase in a country's propensity to save or a decrease in the labor force growth rate imply one-time increases in a country's standard of living, but there can be unbounded growth in the standard of living only if total factor productivity continues to grow. The source of continual long-run betterment in a country's standard of living, therefore, can only be the process of devising better methods for putting factor inputs together to produce output, thus generating increases in total factor productivity.

In contrast to the Malthusian model, where the gains from technological advance are dissipated by a higher population, the Solow model gives a more optimistic outlook for increases in the standard of living over time. If we accept the Solow model, it tells us that the steady increase in per-capita income that occurred since 1869 in the United States (see Figure 6.1) was caused by sustained increases in total factor productivity over a period of 134 years. If technological advances can be sustained for such a long period, there appears to be no reason why these advances cannot occur indefinitely into the future.

GROWTH ACCOUNTING

If aggregate real output is to grow over time, it is necessary for a factor or factors of production to be increasing over time, or for there to be increases in total factor productivity. Typically, growing economies are experiencing growth in factors of production and in total factor productivity. A useful exercise is to measure how much of the growth in aggregate output over a given period of time is accounted for by growth in each of the inputs to production and by increases in total factor productivity. This exercise is called **growth accounting,** and it can be helpful in developing theories of economic growth and for discriminating among different theories. Growth accounting was introduced in the 1950s by Robert Solow, one of the pioneering researchers in modern economic growth.[9]

Growth accounting starts by considering the aggregate production function from the Solow growth model,

$$Y = zF(K, N),$$

where Y is aggregate output, z is total factor productivity, F is the production function, K is the capital input, and N is the labor input. To use the aggregate production function in conjunction with data on output and factor inputs, we need a specific form for the function F. The widely used Cobb–Douglas production function, as discussed in Chapter 4, provides a good fit to U.S. aggregate data, and it is also a good analytical tool for growth accounting. For the production function to be Cobb–Douglas, the function

---

[9] See R. Solow, 1957, "Technical Change and the Aggregate Production Function," *Review of Economic Statistics* 39, 312–320.

F takes the form

$$F(K, N) = K^a N^{1-a}, \tag{6.20}$$

where a is a number between 0 and 1. Recall from Chapter 4 that, in a competitive equilibrium, a is the fraction of national income that goes to the capital input, and $1 - a$ is the fraction that goes to the labor input. In postwar U.S. data, the labor share in national income has been roughly constant at 64%,[10] so we can set $a = 0.36$, and our production function is then

$$Y = zK^{0.36} N^{0.64}. \tag{6.21}$$

If we have measures of aggregate output, the capital input, and the labor input, denoted $\hat{Y}$, $\hat{K}$, and $\hat{N}$, respectively, then total factor productivity z can be measured as a residual, as discussed in Chapter 4. The Solow residual, denoted $\hat{z}$, is measured from the production function, Equation (6.21), as

$$\hat{z} = \frac{\hat{Y}}{\hat{K}^{0.36} \hat{N}^{0.64}}. \tag{6.22}$$

The Solow residual is of course named after Robert Solow. This measure of total factor productivity is a residual, because it is the output that remains to be accounted for after we measure the direct contribution of the capital and labor inputs to output, as discussed in Chapter 4. Total factor productivity has many interpretations, as we studied in Chapters 4 and 5, and, hence, so does the Solow residual. Increases in measured total factor productivity could be the result of new inventions, good weather, new management techniques, favorable changes in government regulations, decreases in the relative price of energy, or any other factor that causes more aggregate output to be produced given the same quantities of aggregate factor inputs.

Solow Residuals and the Productivity Slowdown

A first exercise we work through is to calculate and graph Solow residuals from post–World War II U.S. data and then explain what is interesting in the resulting figure. Using GDP for $\hat{Y}$, measured aggregate output, total employment for $\hat{N}$, and a measure of the capital stock for $\hat{K}$, we calculated the Solow residual $\hat{z}$ using Equation (6.22) and plotted its natural logarithm in Figure 6.23, for the period 1948–2001. We can see that growth in total factor productivity was very high throughout most of the 1950s and 1960s, as evidenced by the steep slope in the graph during those periods. However, there was a dramatic decrease in total factor productivity growth beginning in the late 1960s and continuing into the 1980s, which is referred to as the **productivity slowdown**. The productivity slowdown is also seen in Table 6.1, where we show the average percentage growth in the Solow residual from 1950–1960, 1960–1970,

---

[10]See E. Prescott, 1986, "Theory Ahead of Business Cycle Measurement," *Federal Reserve Bank of Minneapolis Quarterly Review,* Fall, 9–22.

Table 6.1	**Average Annual Growth Rates in the Solow Residual**	
Years	Average Annual Growth Rate
1950–1960	1.45
1960–1970	1.60
1970–1980	0.50
1980–1990	1.02
1990–2000	1.33

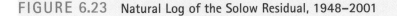

FIGURE 6.23   Natural Log of the Solow Residual, 1948–2001

The Solow residual is a measure of total factor productivity. Growth in total factor productivity slows from the early 1970s to the early 1980s.

Source: Bureau of Economic Analysis, Department of Commerce, and Bureau of Labor Statistics.

1970–1980, 1980–1990, and 1990–2000. Note in the table that total factor productivity growth, as measured by growth in the Solow residual, was high in the 1950s and very high in the 1960s. The growth rate fell considerably in the 1970s, picked up in the 1980s, and then was quite high again in the 1990s.

There are at least three reasons given by economists for the productivity slowdown:

1. The measured productivity slowdown might have been a measurement problem. Over this period, there was a shift in the United States from the production of manufactured goods to the production of services. Earlier, in Chapter 2, we discussed the problems associated with measuring real growth in GDP due to changes in the quality of goods and services over time. This measurement problem is especially severe in the service sector. Thus, if production is shifting from goods to services, then there tends to be an increase in the downward bias in measuring growth in GDP. GDP growth and total factor productivity growth can appear to be low, when they actually are not.

2. The productivity slowdown could have resulted from increases in the relative price of energy. There were two large increases in the price of oil imported to the United States in the 1970s: one in 1973–74, and one in 1979–80. An effect of the increase in oil prices was that old capital equipment that was not energy efficient—for example, buildings in cold climates with poor insulation—became obsolete. It was possible that obsolete plant and equipment were scrapped or fell out of use, and that this scenario was not adequately captured in the capital stock measure. That is, some of the measured capital stock was not actually productive. Essentially then, this is another type of measurement problem, but it is a problem in measuring inputs, whereas the measurement issue discussed in the first point is a problem in measuring output.

3. The productivity slowdown could have been caused by the costs of adopting new technology. Some economists—for example, Jeremy Greenwood and Mehmet Yorukoglu[11]—mark the early 1970s as the beginning of the information revolution, when computer and other information technology began to be widely adopted in the United States. With any dramatically new technology, time is required for workers to learn how to use the new technology, which is embodied in new capital equipment like computers. During this learning period, productivity growth can be low, because workers are spending some of their time investing in learning on the job, and they are, therefore, contributing less to measured output. The fact that productivity growth increased in the 1990s is consistent with this explanation for the productivity slowdown. The argument would be that, by the 1990s, older workers had become accustomed to working in the information age, and younger workers had been educated in how to use computers and other high-tech equipment.

The Cyclical Properties of Solow Residuals   From Figure 6.23, it is clear that there are cyclical fluctuations in Solow residuals about trend growth. In Figure 6.24 we plot percentage deviations from trend in Solow residuals for the years 1948–2001, along with percentage deviations from trend in GDP. Note that the fluctuations in Solow residuals about trend are highly positively correlated with the fluctuations in GDP about trend (recall our discussion of correlations and comovements from Chapter 3).

---

[11] See J. Greenwood and M. Yorukoglu, "1974," University of Rochester working paper.

FIGURE 6.24 **Percentage Deviations from Trend in Real GDP (black line) and the Solow Residual (colored line), 1948–2001**

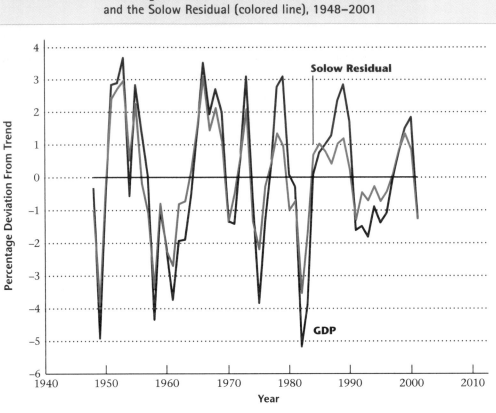

The Solow residual tracks GDP quite closely.

In fact, the Solow residual moves very closely with GDP, so that fluctuations in total factor productivity could be an important explanation for why GDP fluctuates. This is the key idea in real business cycle theory, which we will study in Chapter 11.

A Growth Accounting Exercise

Now that we know how the Solow residual is constructed and what some of its empirical properties are, we can do a full growth accounting exercise. By way of example, we show here how we can use the Cobb–Douglas production function (6.21) and observations on GDP, the capital stock, and employment to obtain measures of the contributions to growth in real output of growth in the capital stock, in employment, and in total factor productivity.

To do growth accounting, we use Equation (6.22) to calculate the Solow residual $\hat{z}$. In Table 6.2 we show data on real GDP, the capital stock, and employment at ten-year intervals from 1950 to 2000. This is the data we use to carry out our growth accounting exercise. The Solow residual $\hat{z}$ in the table was calculated using Equation (6.22).

Table 6.2 **Measured GDP, Capital Stock, Employment, and Solow Residual**[*]

Year	$\hat{Y}$ (billions of 1996 dollars)	$\hat{K}$ (billions of 1996 dollars)	$\hat{N}$ (millions)	$\hat{z}$
1950	1686.6	5553.1	58.89	5.574
1960	2376.7	7920.9	65.78	6.439
1970	3578.0	11547.1	78.67	7.548
1980	4900.9	15922.3	99.30	7.934
1990	6707.9	20871.1	118.80	8.784
2000	9191.4	26993.8	136.90	10.027

[*]*Source*: Bureau of Economic Analysis, Department of Commerce and Bureau of Labor Statistics.

Now, taking the data from Table 6.2, we calculate the average annual growth rates for measured output, capital, employment, and the Solow residual for the periods 1950–1960, 1960–1970, 1970–1980, 1980–1990, and 1990–2000. If X_n is the value of a variable in year n, and X_m is the value of that variable in year m, where $n > m$, then the average annual growth rate in X between year m and year n, denoted by g_{mn}, is given by

$$g_{mn} = \left(\frac{X_n}{X_m}\right)^{\frac{1}{n-m}} - 1.$$

For example, in Table 6.2, GDP in 1950 is 1,753.9 billion 1996 dollars, or $Y_{1950} = 1,686.6$. Further, $Y_{1960} = 2,376.7$ from Table 6.2. Then, we have $n - m - 10$, and the average annual growth rate in GDP from 1950 to 1960 in Table 6.3 is $\left(\frac{2,376.7}{1,686.6}\right)^{\frac{1}{10}} - 1 = 0.0349$, or 3.49%.

Table 6.3 shows that average annual growth in real GDP was very high during the 1960s, and somewhat lower in the 1950s, 1970s, 1980s, and 1990s. The very high growth in the 1960s came from all sources, as growth in capital was very high, growth in employment was somewhat high, and growth in total factor productivity (as measured by growth in $\hat{z}$) was high. Note that, in spite of the productivity slowdown in the 1970s, output still grew at a reasonably high rate, due to high growth in factors of production. During the 1970s, capital was accumulated at a high rate. Further, employment growth was unusually high, in part because of rapid increases in the female labor force participation rate. While growth in capital and employment declined in the 1980s and 1990s, there was a pickup in total factor productivity growth. This increase in total factor productivity growth was the driving force behind the high growth rate in aggregate output in the 1990s.

Table 6.3 **Average Annual Growth Rates**

Years	$\hat{Y}$	$\hat{K}$	$\hat{N}$	$\hat{z}$
1950–1960	3.49	3.62	1.11	1.45
1960–1970	4.18	3.84	1.81	1.60
1970–1980	3.20	3.27	2.36	0.50
1980–1990	3.19	2.74	1.81	1.02
1990–2000	3.20	2.61	1.43	1.33

MACROECONOMICS IN ACTION

East Asian Miracles and Total Factor Productivity Growth

If we examine the recent history of world growth, some countries stand out as growth miracles and others are growth disasters. A careful study of the causes of growth miracles and growth disasters is instructive, because we would like to know how a growth miracle could be replicated or how a disaster could be avoided. Four countries that stand out as growth miracles are the so-called "East Asian Tigers," Hong Kong, Singapore, South Korea, and Taiwan. From the data in Table 6.4, between 1966 and 1991, real GDP grew at an average annual rate of 7.3% in Hong Kong, and between 1966 and 1990 the average annual growth rates of real GDP in Singapore, South Korea, and Taiwan were 8.7%, 10.3%, and 9.4%, respectively. In the table annual average growth in real GDP in the United States over the period 1966 to 1990 was 3.0%. Thus, it seems extraordinary that such high growth rates could be sustained for about a quarter of a century in East Asia.

A prediction of the Solow growth model is that a country's standard of living can continue to increase over the long run only if there are sustained increases in total factor productivity. Thus, most economists (who are trained to view the world through the lens of the Solow growth model) would tend to think that the very high sustained rates of GDP growth experienced in East Asia had been driven primarily by very high total factor productivity growth.

Alwyn Young, in an article in the *Quarterly Journal of Economics*,[1] did a growth accounting exercise for each of Hong Kong, Singapore, South Korea, and Taiwan to evaluate whether or not it was high growth in total factor productivity that explained the high growth in real GDP in these countries. Surprisingly, Young found that total factor productivity growth in Hong Kong, Singapore, South Korea, and Taiwan was anything but miraculous. The high rates of GDP growth in these countries were mainly due to high growth rates in factor inputs.

From Table 6.4, the average growth rates in capital were extremely high in these East Asian countries, ranging from 7.7% per

[1]A. Young, 1995, "The Tyranny of Numbers: Confronting the Statistical Realities of the East Asian Growth Experience," *Quarterly Journal of Economics* 110, 641–680.

Table 6.4 **East Asian Growth Miracles (Average Annual Growth Rates)**

	Output	Capital	Labor	Total Factor Productivity
Hong Kong (1966–1991)	7.3%	7.7%	2.6%	2.3%
Singapore (1966–1990)	8.7%	10.8%	4.5%	0.2%
South Korea (1966–1990)*	10.3%	12.9%	5.4%	1.7%
Taiwan (1966–1990)*	9.4%	11.8%	4.6%	2.6%
United States (1966–1990)	3.0%	3.2%	2.0%	0.6%

*Excludes agriculture.

(*continued*)

year in Hong Kong to 12.9% per year in South Korea. These growth rates compare with an average growth rate in capital in the United States of 3.2% over the period 1966–1990. High rates of growth in the capital stocks of the East Asian countries were caused by high rates of investment. Also, average rates of growth in the labor force range from 2.6% per year in Hong Kong to 5.4% per year in South Korea, as compared with 2.0% in the United States over the period 1966–1990. The large increases in the labor force in East Asia were driven partly by population growth and partly by increases in labor force participation, particularly among women. For example, in Singapore the labor force participation rate for all workers increased from 27% to 51% from 1966 to 1990, and population grew at an average rate of 1.9% per year.

Ultimately, Young concluded that total factor productivity growth during this period in Hong Kong, Singapore, South Korea, and Taiwan was far short of miraculous, ranging from an average growth rate of 0.2% in Singapore to 2.6% in Taiwan. In the United States over the period 1966–1990, total factor productivity grew at an average annual rate of 0.6%. While total factor productivity growth exceeded that in the United States for three of these four countries, the difference is not as impressive as the difference in GDP growth rates. Therefore, while GDP growth in these four East Asian countries was extremely impressive, this high growth was mainly the result of unusually high growth rates in capital and labor.

There are two important implications of Young's analysis. The first is that the high growth in East Asia over the period from the mid-1960s to the early 1990s is probably not sustainable over a longer period. There is a limit to how much labor force participation rates can grow and thus contribute to growth in the labor force; namely, once the labor force participation rate reaches 100%, it cannot increase further. Also, consumers in these countries may not want to continue to forgo large quantities of current consumption to support the high rates of investment required to make the capital stock grow quickly. Second, Young's analysis makes it clear that the East Asian experience would be extremely difficult to replicate in the United States. The labor force participation rate is close to 70% in the United States, which is much higher than in East Asia, and so there is little scope in the United States for rapid growth in the labor force due to increased labor force participation. To mimic the East Asian experience would require that a very large fraction of U.S. GDP be devoted to investment, and this is not consistent with recent U.S. history. Note that growth in the U.S. capital stock averaged 3.2% per year over 1966–1990 and has slowed since then, while average growth in capital stocks ranged from 7.7% in Hong Kong to 12.9% in South Korea during the period of East Asian miracle growth.

In the next chapter, we study the persistence in disparities in standards of living across countries of the world and how the Solow growth model addresses these facts. As well, we introduce an endogenous growth model, which is used to discuss convergence in incomes across countries and the role of education in growth, among other issues.

CHAPTER SUMMARY

- We discussed eight economic growth facts. These were:
  1. Before the Industrial Revolution in about 1800, standards of living differed little over time and across countries.
  2. Since the Industrial Revolution, per capita income growth has been sustained in the richest countries. In the United States, average annual growth in per capita income has been about 2% since 1869.
  3. There is a positive correlation between the rate of investment and output per worker across countries.
  4. There is a negative correlation between the population growth rate and output per worker across countries.
  5. Differences in per capita incomes increased dramatically among countries of the world between 1800 and 1950, with the gap widening between the countries of Western Europe, the United States, Canada, Australia, and New Zealand, as a group, and the rest of the world.
  6. There is essentially no correlation across countries between the level of output per worker in 1960 and the average rate of growth in output per worker for the years 1960–1995.
  7. Among the richest countries, there is a negative correlation between the level of output per worker in 1960 and the average rate of growth in output per worker for the years 1960–1995.
  8. Among the poorest countries, there is essentially no correlation between the level of output per worker in 1960 and the average rate of growth in output per worker for the years 1960–1995.

- The first model was the Malthusian growth model, in which population growth depends positively on consumption per worker, and output is produced from the labor input and a fixed quantity of land.

- The Malthusian model predicts that an increase in total factor productivity has no effect on consumption per worker in the long run, but the population increases. The standard of living can only increase in the long run if population growth is reduced, perhaps by governmental population control.

- The Solow growth model is a model of exogenous growth in that, in the long-run steady state of this model, growth in aggregate output, aggregate consumption, and aggregate investment is explained by exogenous growth in the labor force.

- In the Solow growth model, output per worker converges in the long run to a steady state level, in the absence of a change in total factor productivity. The model predicts that output per worker increases in the long run when the savings rate increases or when the population growth rate decreases. Both of these predictions are consistent with the data.

- An increase in the savings rate could cause consumption per worker to increase or decrease in the Solow growth model. The golden rule savings rate maximizes consumption per worker in the steady state. The Solow growth model also predicts that a country's standard of living, as measured by income per worker, cannot increase in the long run unless there is ever-increasing total factor productivity.

- Growth accounting is an approach to measuring the contributions to growth in aggregate output from growth in the capital stock, in employment, and in total factor productivity. The latter is measured by the Solow residual.

- Measured Solow residuals for the United States using a Cobb–Douglas production function show a productivity slowdown occurring in the late 1960s and continuing into the 1980s. Suggested reasons for the productivity slowdown are (1) errors in measuring aggregate output, (2) errors in measuring the inputs to production, particularly capital, and (3) learning costs due to the adoption of new information technology.

- Cyclically, deviations from trend in the Solow residual track closely the deviations from trend in aggregate output. This empirical observation is important for real business cycle theory, discussed in Chapter 11.

KEY TERMS

Exogenous growth model: A model in which growth is not caused by forces determined by the model.

Endogenous growth model: A model in which growth is caused by forces determined by the model.

Steady state: a long run equilibrium or rest point. The Malthusian model and Solow model both have the property that the economy converges to a single steady state.

Per-worker production function: In the Malthusian model, $y = zf(l)$, where y is output per worker, z is total factor productivity, l is the quantity of land per worker, and f is a function. This describes the relationship between output per worker and land per worker, given constant returns to scale. In the Solow growth model, the per-worker production function is $y = zf(k)$, where y is output per worker, z is total factor productivity, k is the quantity of capital per worker, and f is a function. The per-worker production function in this case describes the relationship between output per worker and capital per worker, given constant returns to scale.

Golden rule quantity of capital per worker: The quantity of capital per worker that maximizes consumption per worker in the steady state.

Golden rule savings rate: The savings rate that implies consumption per worker is maximized in the steady state of a competitive equilibrium.

Growth accounting: uses the production function and data on aggregate output, the capital input, and the labor input, to measure the contributions of growth in capital, the labor force, and total factor productivity to growth in aggregate output.

Productivity slowdown: A decrease in the rate of measured total factor productivity growth beginning in the late 1960s and continuing into the 1980s.

QUESTIONS FOR REVIEW

1. What is the difference between exogenous growth and endogenous growth?

2. What are the eight economic growth facts?

3. What is the effect of an increase in total factor productivity on steady state population and consumption per worker in the Malthusian model?

4. What can increase the standard of living in the Malthusian model?

5. Was Malthus right? Why or why not?

6. What are the characteristics of a steady state in the Solow growth model?

7. In the Solow growth model, what are the steady state effects of an increase in the savings rate, of an increase in the population growth rate, and of an increase in total factor productivity?

8. Explain what determines the golden rule quantity of capital per worker and the golden rule savings rate.

9. In what sense does the Solow growth model give optimistic conclusions about the prospects for improvement in the standard of living, relative to the Malthusian model?

10. Why is a Cobb–Douglas production function useful for analyzing economic growth?

11. What is the parameter a in the production function in Equation (6.20)?

12. What does the Solow residual measure, and what are its empirical properties?

13. What are three possible causes for the productivity slowdown?

14. What are the three factors that account for growth in GDP?

15. What was miraculous about growth in East Asian countries over the period 1966–1991? What was not miraculous about growth in these countries at this time?

PROBLEMS

1. In the Malthusian model, suppose that the quantity of land increases. Using diagrams, determine what effects this has in the long-run steady state and explain your results.

2. In the Malthusian model, suppose that there is a technological advance that reduces death rates. Using diagrams, determine the effects of this in the long-run steady state and explain your results.

3. In the Solow growth model, suppose that the marginal product of capital increases for each quantity of the capital input, given the labor input.
   (a) Show the effects of this on the aggregate production function.
   (b) Using a diagram, determine the effects on the quantity of capital per worker and on output per worker in the steady state.
   (c) Explain your results.

4. Suppose that the depreciation rate increases. In the Solow growth model, determine the effects of this on the quantity of capital per worker and on output per worker in the steady state. Explain the economic intuition behind your results.

5. Suppose that the economy is initially in a steady state and that some of the nation's capital stock is destroyed because of a natural disaster or a war.
   (a) Determine the long-run effects of this on the quantity of capital per worker and on output per worker.
   (b) In the short run, does aggregate output grow at a rate higher or lower than the growth rate of the labor force?
   (c) After World War II, growth in real GDP in Germany and Japan was very high. How do your results in parts (a) and (b) shed light on this historical experience?

6. If total factor productivity decreases, determine using diagrams how this affects the golden rule quantity of capital per worker and the golden rule savings rate. Explain your results.

7. Modify the Solow growth model by including government spending, as follows. The government purchases G units of consumption goods in the current period, where $G = g N$ and g is a positive constant. The government finances its purchases through lump-sum taxes on consumers, where T denotes total taxes, and the government budget is balanced each

period, so that $G = T$. Consumers consume a constant fraction of disposable income—that is, $C = (1 - s)(Y - T)$, where s is the savings rate, with $0 < s < 1$.

(a) Derive equations similar to (6.17), (6.18), and (6.19), and show in a diagram how the quantity of capital per worker, k^*, is determined.

(b) Show that there can be two steady states, one with high k^* and one with low k^*.

(c) Ignore the steady state with low k^* (it can be shown that this steady state is "unstable"). Determine the effects of an increase in g on capital per worker and on output per worker in the steady state. What are the effects on the growth rates of aggregate output, aggregate consumption, and aggregate investment? Explain your results.

8. Determine the effects of a decrease in the population growth rate on the golden rule quantity of capital per worker and on the golden rule savings rate. Explain your results.

9. Alter the Solow growth model so that the production technology is given by $Y = zK$, where Y is output, K is capital, and z is total factor productivity. Thus, output is produced only with capital.

(a) Show that it is possible for income per person to grow indefinitely.

(b) Also show that an increase in the savings rate increases the growth rate in per capita income.

(c) From parts (a) and (b), what are the differences between this model and the basic Solow growth model? Account for these differences and discuss.

10. Consider the following data

Year	$\hat{Y}$ (billions of 1996 dollars)	$\hat{K}$ (billions of 1996 dollars)	$\hat{N}$ (millions)
1990	6709.9	20871.1	118.8
1991	6676.4	21207.6	117.7
1992	6880.0	21577.4	118.5
1993	7062.6	22027.7	120.3
1994	7347.7	22530.2	123.1
1995	7543.8	23072.9	124.9
1996	7813.2	23701.0	126.7
1997	8159.5	24383.6	129.6
1998	8508.9	25175.2	131.5
1999	8859.0	26033.2	133.5
2000	9191.4	26933.8	136.9
2001	9214.5	27711.2	136.9

(a) Calculate the Solow residual for each year from 1990 to 2001.

(b) Calculate percentage rates of growth in output, capital, employment, and total factor productivity for the years 1991 to 2001. In each year, what contributes the most to growth in aggregate output? What contributes the least? Are there any surprises here? If so, explain.

WORKING WITH THE DATA

1. The total capital stock consists of private equipment capital, private structures capital, private residential capital, and government capital. Determine the growth rates of each of these components of the capital stock for each decade from 1930 until 2000. Which component of capital was the most important, and which was the least important, as a contributor to growth in the total capital stock in each decade? Comment on your results.

2. For the periods 1950–1960, 1960–1970, 1970–1980, 1980–1990, and 1990–2000, determine the growth rates in the total population, in the labor force, and in employment. What explains the differences among these three growth rates for each period?

3. Determine the quantity of capital per worker for the years 1950, 1960, 1970, 1980, 1990, and 2000, and calculate the growth rates of capital per worker for the periods 1950–1960, 1960–1970, 1970–1980, 1980–1990, and 1990–2000. Relate these growth rates to the data on total factor productivity growth in Table 6.3.

CHAPTER 7

Income Disparity Among Countries and Endogenous Growth

This chapter extends the material in Chapter 6 to some additional issues related to the predictions of the Solow growth model and to the study of endogenous growth theory. Here, we are particularly interested in learning more about the reasons for the large income disparities that continue to exist among the countries of the world.

The Solow growth model makes strong predictions concerning the ability of poor countries to catch up with rich countries. That is, in this model income per worker converges among countries that are initially rich and poor but otherwise identical. The model tells us that countries that are initially poor in terms of income per worker grow at a faster rate than countries that are initially rich. This prediction is consistent with what we observe happening among the richest countries in the world. Since 1960, income per worker appears to have been converging among these countries. Among the poorest countries of the world, however, income per worker does not appear to be converging, and the poorest countries of the world seem to be falling behind the richest ones, rather than catching up. Therefore, if we suppose that all countries are identical, particularly with regard to the technology that they have access to, then the Solow model is not entirely consistent with the way in which the distribution of income is evolving in the world.

However, what if different countries do not have access to the same technology? This can arise if groups who might lose from technological change in particular countries have the power to prevent new technologies from being adopted. For example, if the legal structure in a country gives power to labor unions, then these unions might prevent firms from introducing technologies that make the skills of union members obsolete. As well, political barriers to international trade (tariffs, import quotas, and subsidies) shield firms from international competition and block the incentives to develop new technologies. Then, if different countries have different barriers to technology adoption, this can explain the differences in standards of living across countries, in a manner consistent with the Solow growth model.

An alternative set of models that can explain persistent differences in standards of living across countries is the set of endogenous growth models. In this chapter, we consider a simple model of endogenous growth, and we show how some of the predictions of this model differ from those of the Solow growth model. The endogenous growth model we study shows how the accumulation of skills and education is important to economic growth. We use the model to evaluate how economic policy might affect the quantity of resources allocated to skills and education and how this affects growth.

In contrast to the Solow growth model, the endogenous growth model we study does not predict convergence in levels of per capita income across countries when countries are identical except for being initially rich and initially poor. In fact, the endogenous growth model predicts that differences in per capita income persist forever. The model indicates some of the factors that can be important in explaining the continuing disparities in living standards between the richest and poorest countries of the world.

CONVERGENCE

There are remarkable differences in the levels of income per worker in the countries of the world. In 1995, income per worker in Mexico was 37.4% of what it was in the United States, in Egypt it was 22.0% of that in the United States, and in Burundi it was about 2.4% of the U.S. figure. The differences in the growth rates of income per worker are no less remarkable. Between 1960 and 1995, while income per worker was growing at an average rate of 1.77% in the United States, the comparable figure for Angola was −1.90%, for the Congo it was −3.37%, for Hong Kong it was 6.44%, and for Taiwan it was 6.41%. While these statistics tell us something about the wide variation in standards of living and in growth experience in the world, we would also like to know whether these disparities are increasing or decreasing over time and why. Is there a tendency for poor countries to catch up with rich countries with respect to standards of living? If the poor countries are not catching up, why is this so, and what could the poor countries do about it?

The Solow growth model makes strong predictions about the ability of poor countries to catch up with rich ones. For example, suppose two countries are identical with respect to total factor productivities (they share the same technology), labor force growth rates, and savings rates. However, the rich country initially has a higher level of capital per worker than does the poor country. Given the per-worker production function, the rich country also has a higher quantity of output per worker than the poor country. The Solow growth model predicts that both countries will converge to the same level of capital per worker and output per worker. Ultimately, the poor country will catch up to the rich country with regard to living standards.

In Figure 7.1, we show the relationship between current capital per worker, k, and future capital per worker, k' from the Solow growth model. The poor country initially has quantity k_p of capital per worker, while the rich country initially has quantity k_r of capital per worker. Capital per worker and output per worker grows in both countries, but in the long run, both countries have k^* units of capital per worker and the same quantity of output per worker. In Figure 7.2 we show the paths followed over time by real income per worker in the rich country and poor country. The initial gap between the rich and poor countries narrows over time and disappears in the long run.

The rich country and poor country in the example above also have identical growth rates of aggregate output (equal to their identical labor force growth rates) in the long run. Recall that the Solow growth model predicts aggregate output will grow at the rate of labor force growth in the long run, and so if the rich and poor countries have

FIGURE 7.1   Rich and Poor Countries and the Steady State

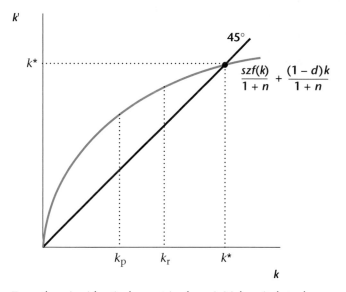

Two otherwise identical countries have initial capital stocks per worker of k_p (the poor country) and k_r (the rich country). Both countries converge in the long-run steady state to the quantity k^* of capital per worker.

the same labor force growth rate, their long-run growth rates in aggregate output will be identical. Supposing that the rich and poor countries also have the same initial labor force levels, the growth paths of aggregate output, as predicted by the Solow growth model, will be the same in the long run. In Figure 7.3 the black line denotes the long-run growth path of the natural logarithm of aggregate output in the rich and poor countries. As predicted by the Solow growth model, if aggregate output is initially lower in the poor country, its growth rate in aggregate output will be larger than that for the rich country, and this will cause the level of aggregate output in the poor country to catch up to the level in the rich country. In the long run, growth in aggregate output in the rich and poor countries converges to the same rate.

Therefore, given no differences among countries in terms of access to technology, the Solow model is quite optimistic about the prospects for countries of the world that are currently poor. Under these conditions the model predicts that, left alone, the countries of the world will converge to similar standards of living, with some differences across countries explained by differences in savings rates and population growth rates.

However, suppose that countries do not have access to the same technology. There are good reasons why significant barriers to the adoption of new technology exist,

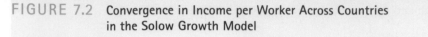

FIGURE 7.2   **Convergence in Income per Worker Across Countries in the Solow Growth Model**

Two otherwise identical countries, one with lower income per worker (the poor country) than the other (the rich country), both converge in the long-run steady state to the same level of income per worker, y_1^*.

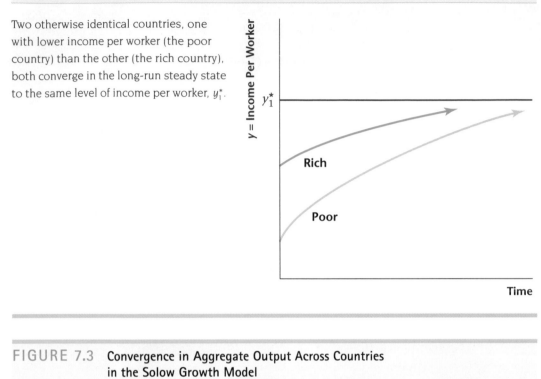

FIGURE 7.3   **Convergence in Aggregate Output Across Countries in the Solow Growth Model**

The initially rich country and the initially poor country converge in the long run to the same long-run growth path, where aggregate output grows at a constant rate.

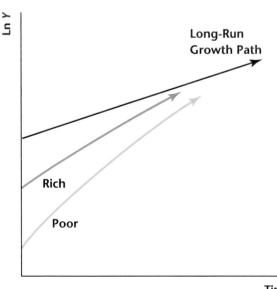

and these barriers can differ across countries.[1] Barriers to technology adoption arise for at least two reasons. First, if the government introduces laws that make it easy for labor unions to organize and gives them greater power in bargaining with firms, then unions will find it easier to block the introduction of new technologies. Powerful unions are able to negotiate high wages and benefits for their members, and they also try to prevent their members from being displaced from their jobs by new technologies that make union members' skills obsolete. For example, automobile industry unions would typically resist the use of robots that would displace labor in auto assembly plants.

Second, governments can introduce trade restrictions that shield domestic industries from foreign competition. This can have the effect of taking away the incentives for firms in those industries to develop more efficient technologies. For example, the United States currently imposes tariffs on imports of lumber from foreign countries, and grants large subsidies to American farmers. These government interventions act to reduce technological innovation by American lumber companies and American farmers, and this has a negative effect on total factor productivity in the United States.

To the extent that barriers to the adoption of new technology differ across countries, this causes total factor productivity to differ, and convergence in standards of living does not occur. To see how this works, consider Figure 7.4. Suppose that there are three different countries, which we call poor, middle income, and rich, and that these countries have levels of total factor productivity z_p, z_m, and z_r, respectively, where $z_p < z_m < z_r$. We also suppose that these countries have identical population growth rates and identical savings rates. Then in Figure 7.4, in the steady state the poor, middle income, and rich countries have levels of capital per worker of k_p^*, k_m^*, and k_r^*, respectively, so that output per worker in the steady state is ranked according to poor, middle income, and rich, in ascending order. In the steady state, standards of living are permanently different in the three countries, but aggregate output grows at the same rate in these countries. Thus, the Solow model can explain disparities across countries in income per worker, if there are differences in barriers to technology adoption across countries.

If the large disparity in incomes per worker across countries of the world is in part due to barriers to the adoption of technology, what can poor countries do to catch up to the rich countries?[2] First, governments can promote greater competition among firms. If monopoly power is not protected by governments, then firms have to develop and implement new technologies to remain competitive, so that productivity will be higher. Second, governments can promote free trade. Just as with greater domestic competition, greater competition between countries promotes innovation and the adoption of the best technologies. Third, governments should privatize production where there is no good economic case for government ownership. Government ownership where it is unnecessary often leads to protection of employment at the expense of efficiency, and this tends to lower total factor productivity.

---

[1] See S. Parente and E. Prescott, 2000. *Barriers to Riches*, MIT Press, Cambridge, MA.

[2] For an elaboration on these arguments, see S. Parente and E. Prescott, 2000. *Barriers to Riches*, MIT Press, Cambridge, MA.

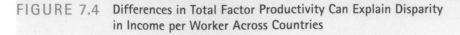

FIGURE 7.4 Differences in Total Factor Productivity Can Explain Disparity in Income per Worker Across Countries

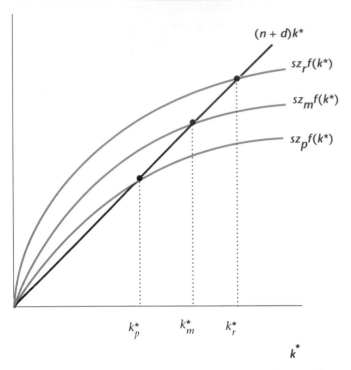

If countries have different levels of total factor productivity due to differing barriers to technology adoption, then capital per worker and income per worker differ across countries in the steady state.

IS INCOME PER WORKER CONVERGING IN THE WORLD?

If income per worker is converging among countries of the world, we would observe over time that the dispersion in income per worker was falling. As well, if we observed the countries of the world at a given point in time, we would see that income per worker was growing at a higher rate in poor countries than in rich countries. That is, we should see a negative correlation between the rate of growth in income per worker and the level of income per worker across countries.

In this section we look at the evidence for convergence in the world economy. From fact (6) in the Economic Growth Facts section in Chapter 6, recall that, when we look at all countries in the world, there is essentially no correlation between the level of output per worker in 1960 and the average growth rate of output per worker between 1960 and 1995. Fact (7) is that, when we look at the same data but include only the countries in the world that were the richest in 1960, there is a negative correlation. Finally, fact (8) is that including only the countries that were poorest in 1960 gives no correlation. Therefore, between 1960 and 1995 there appeared to be no convergence among all the countries in the world and among the poorest countries of the world. There is evidence, however, for convergence among the richest countries of the world for the same period.

The following story makes these observations on convergence from the data consistent with the predictions of the Solow growth model. First, we can think of the richest countries of the world in 1960 (the Western European countries, the United States, Canada, Australia, and New Zealand) as having access to roughly the same technology. The Solow growth model then tells us that we should expect convergence in standards of living among these countries, with some minor differences accounted for by differences in population growth and savings rates. Second, the tendency for differences in standards of living to persist among the poor countries of the world can be explained in the Solow model by different levels of total factor productivity in those countries brought about by differing barriers to technology adoption.

To support the idea that persistent disparity in incomes per worker across countries could be caused by barriers to technology adoption, we need additional evidence for the existence of such barriers and evidence that the barriers differ significantly among countries. In their book, *Barriers to Riches,* Stephen Parente and Edward Prescott provide considerable evidence of both types in examining experience in particular industries and countries.[1] They argue that evidence of resistance to the adoption of new technology can be found in the textiles industry and in the mining industry in the United States. Further, if we look at particular industries and measure productivities in those industries across countries, the evidence supports the idea that barriers to technology adoption are important for explaining the productivity differences.

A key feature of the data that supports the idea that there are barriers preventing poor countries from adopting the technologies used by the richest countries of the world, is that growth miracles have not occurred for the very rich. In the United States, as we observed in Chapter 6, the growth rate of income per capita has not strayed far from 2% per annum since 1869. The important growth miracles after World War II occurred in Japan, South Korea, Taiwan, Singapore, and Hong Kong. At the time when growth took off in these countries, they were all well behind the standard of living in the United States. The growth miracles in these countries are consistent with barriers to technology adoption being removed, which then allowed incomes per worker to quickly approach that of the United States. However, perhaps we need to be somewhat skeptical of this explanation, as our study of the East Asian growth miracles in Chapter 6 indicated that these growth miracles were due primarily to high growth in factors of production, not to high growth in total factor productivity.

---

[1]See S. Parente and E. Prescott, 2000. *Barriers to Riches,* MIT Press, Cambridge, MA.

ENDOGENOUS GROWTH: A MODEL OF HUMAN CAPITAL ACCUMULATION

Perhaps the primary deficiency of the Solow growth model is that it does not explain a key observation, which is growth itself. The Solow model relies on increases in total factor productivity coming from outside the model to generate long-run increases in per capita output, and this seems unsatisfactory, as we would like to understand the economic forces behind increases in total factor productivity. Total factor productivity growth involves research and development by firms, education, and training on the job, and all of these activities are responsive to the economic environment. We might like an economic growth model to answer the following questions: How does total factor productivity growth respond to the quantity of public funds spent on public education? How is total factor productivity growth affected by subsidies to research and development? Does it make sense to have the government intervene to promote economic growth? While the Solow growth model cannot answer these questions, a model of endogenous growth, where growth rates are explained by the model, potentially can.

The endogenous growth model that we work with here is a simplification of a model developed by Robert Lucas.[3] Another important earlier contributor to research on endogenous growth was Paul Romer.[4] In the model, the representative consumer allocates his or her time between supplying labor to produce output and accumulating **human capital,** where human capital is the accumulated stock of skills and education that a worker has at a point in time. The higher the human capital that workers have, the more they can produce, and the more new human capital they can produce. Thus, a higher level of human capital means that the economy can grow at a faster rate.

If we think in terms of real-world economies, at any given time some of the working age population is employed and producing goods and services, some are in school, and some are unemployed or not in the labor force. There is an opportunity cost associated with people of working age who are in school, as these people could otherwise be producing goods and services. By acquiring schooling, however, people accumulate skills (human capital), and a more highly skilled labor force in the future permits more future output to be produced. Also, a more highly skilled population can better pass on skills to others, and so human capital accumulation is more efficient if the level of human capital is higher.

Human capital accumulation, therefore, is an investment, just like investment in plant and equipment, as there are associated current costs and future benefits. However, there are good reasons to think that physical investment is fundamentally different from human capital investment, in addition to the obvious difference that physical investment is embodied in machines and buildings, and human capital investment is embodied in people. Recall that in the Solow growth model there are diminishing marginal returns to the accumulation of physical capital, because adding more capital to a fixed labor force should eventually yield lower increases in output at the margin. Human capital

---

[3]R. Lucas, 1988, "On the Mechanics of Economic Development," *Journal of Monetary Economics* 22, July, 3–42.

[4]See P. Romer, 1986, "Increasing Returns and Long-Run Growth," *Journal of Political Economy* 94, 500–521.

accumulation differs in that there appears to be no limit to human knowledge or to how productive individuals can become given increases in knowledge and skills. Paul Romer has argued that a key feature of knowledge is **nonrivalry.**[5] That is, a given person's acquisition of knowledge does not reduce the ability of someone else to acquire the same knowledge. Most goods are rivalrous; for example, my consumption of hotel services limits the ability of others to benefit from hotel services, as only a fixed number of hotel rooms is available in a given city at a given time. Physical capital accumulation also involves rivalry, as the acquisition of plant and equipment by a firm uses up resources that could be used by other firms to acquire plant and equipment. Thus, diminishing marginal returns to human capital investment seem unnatural. The lack of diminishing returns to human capital investment leads to unbounded growth in the model we study here, even though there are no exogenous forces propelling economic growth.

The Representative Consumer

Our endogenous growth model has a representative consumer, who starts the current period with H^s units of human capital. In each period, the consumer has one unit of time (as in the Malthusian model and the Solow model, the fact that there is one unit of time is simply a normalization), which can be allocated between work and accumulating human capital. For simplicity, we assume the consumer does not use time for leisure. Let u denote the fraction of time devoted to working in each period, so that the number of **efficiency units of labor** devoted to work is uH^s. That is, the number of units of labor that the consumer effectively supplies is the number of units of time spent working multiplied by the consumer's quantity of human capital. The consumer's quantity of human capital is the measure of the productivity of the consumer's time when he or she is working. For each efficiency unit of labor supplied, the consumer receives the current real wage w. For simplicity, we assume the consumer cannot save, and so the consumer's budget constraint in the current period is

$$C = wuH^s, \tag{7.1}$$

or consumption is equal to total labor earnings.

Though the consumer cannot save, he or she can trade off current consumption for future consumption by accumulating human capital. Because u units of time are used for work, the remainder, $1 - u$, is used for human capital accumulation. The technology for accumulating human capital is given by

$$H^{s'} = b(1 - u)H^s; \tag{7.2}$$

that is, the stock of human capital in the future period, denoted by $H^{s'}$, varies in proportion to the number of current efficiency units of labor devoted to human capital accumulation, which is $(1 - u)H^s$. Here, b is a parameter that captures the efficiency of the human capital accumulation technology, with $b > 0$. Thus, Equation (7.2) represents the idea that accumulating skills and education is easier, the more skills and education an individual (or society) has.

---

[5]See P. Romer, 1990, "Endogenous Technological Change," *Journal of Political Economy* 98, S71–S102.

The Representative Firm

The representative firm produces output using only efficiency units of labor, because for simplicity there is no physical capital in this model. The production function is given by

$$Y = zuH^d, \qquad (7.3)$$

where Y is current output, $z > 0$ is the marginal product of efficiency units of labor, and uH^d is the current input of efficiency units of labor into production. That is, uH^d is the demand for efficiency units of labor by the representative firm. The production function in Equation (7.3) has constant returns to scale, because there is only one input into production, efficiency units of labor, and increasing the quantity of efficiency units of labor increases output in the same proportion. For example, increasing efficiency units of labor uH^d by 1% increases current output by 1%.

The representative firm hires the quantity of efficiency units of labor, uH^d, that maximizes current profits, where profits are

$$\pi = Y - wuH^d,$$

which is the quantity of output produced minus the wages paid to workers. Substituting for Y from Equation (7.3), we get

$$\pi = zuH^d - wuH^d = (z - w)uH^d. \qquad (7.4)$$

Now, if $z - w < 0$, then in Equation (7.4) profits are negative if the firm hires a positive quantity of efficiency units of labor, so that the firm maximizes profits by setting $uH^d = 0$. If $z - w > 0$, then profits are $z - w$ for each efficiency unit hired, so that the firm wants to hire an infinite quantity of workers to maximize profits. If $z = w$, then the firm's profits are zero for any quantity of workers hired, so that the firm is indifferent about the quantity of efficiency units of labor hired. We conclude that the firm's demand curve for efficiency units of labor is infinitely elastic at $w = z$. In Figure 7.5 we show the firm's demand curve for efficiency units of labor, which is just a special case of the demand curve being identical to the marginal product schedule for efficiency units of labor. Here, the marginal product of efficiency units of labor is a constant, z. What this implies is that no matter what the supply curve for efficiency units of labor, the intersection between demand and supply always occurs, as in Figure 7.5, at a real wage of $w = z$. That is, the equilibrium real wage per efficiency unit of labor is always $w = z$. This then implies that the real wage per hour of work is $wH^d = zH^d$, and so the real wage as we would measure it empirically changes in proportion to the quantity of human capital of the representative consumer.

Competitive Equilibrium

Working out the competitive equilibrium here is quite straightforward. There is only one market each period, on which consumption goods are traded for efficiency units of labor, and we know already that this market always clears at a real wage of $w = z$.

FIGURE 7.5 **Determination of the Equilibrium Real Wage in the Endogenous Growth Model**

The figure shows the demand and supply of efficiency units of labor in the endogenous growth model. The equilibrium wage is z, the constant marginal product of efficiency units of labor.

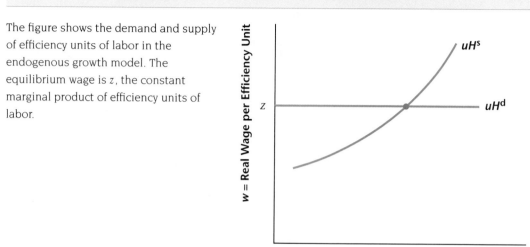

Market clearing gives $uH^s = uH^d$ (the supply of efficiency units of labor is equal to the demand), and so $H^s = H^d = H$. Therefore, substituting in Equations (7.1) and (7.2) for w and H^s, we get

$$C = zuH, \tag{7.5}$$

and

$$H' = b(1-u)H. \tag{7.6}$$

Therefore, Equation (7.6) determines future human capital H' given current human capital H, and we show this relationship in Figure 7.6. The slope of the colored line in the figure is $b(1-u)$, and if $b(1-u) > 1$, then we have $H' > H$, so that future human capital is always greater than current human capital, and, therefore, human capital grows over time without bound. From Equation (7.6), the growth rate of human capital is

$$\frac{H'}{H} - 1 = b(1-u) - 1, \tag{7.7}$$

which is a constant. What is important here is that the growth rate of human capital increases if b increases or if u decreases. Recall that b determines the efficiency of the human capital accumulation technology, which could be interpreted as the efficiency of the educational sector. Thus, the model predicts that countries with more efficient education systems should experience higher rates of growth in human capital. If u

FIGURE 7.6   Human Capital Accumulation in the Endogenous Growth Model

The colored line shows the quantity of future human capital H′ as a function of current human capital H. As drawn H′ > H for any H, so human capital continues to increase forever.

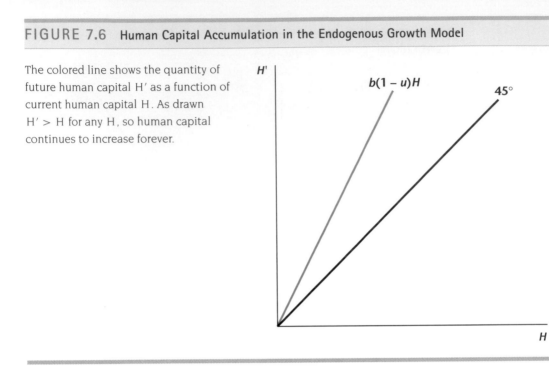

decreases, then more time is devoted to human capital accumulation and less to producing output in each period. As seems natural, this causes the growth rate in human capital to increase.

Now, Equation (7.5) will also hold in the future period, so that $C' = zuH'$ where C' is future consumption, and, therefore, from Equation (7.5) we can determine the growth rate of consumption, which is

$$\frac{C'}{C} - 1 = \frac{zuH'}{zuH} - 1 = \frac{H'}{H} - 1 = b(1-u) - 1,$$

that is, the growth rate of consumption is identical to the growth rate of human capital. Further, from Equations (7.3) and (7.5), $C = Y$, which we also know must hold in equilibrium, given the income–expenditure identity from Chapter 2 (our model has no investment, no government, and no net exports). Therefore, human capital, consumption, and output all grow at the same rate, $b(1-u) - 1$, in equilibrium.

This model economy does not grow because of any exogenous forces. There is no population growth (there is a single representative consumer), and the production technology does not change over time (b and z remain fixed). Growth occurs, therefore, because of endogenous forces, with the growth rate determined by b and u. The key element in the model that leads to unbounded growth is the fact that the production function, given by Equation (7.3), does not exhibit decreasing returns to scale in human capital. That is, the production function has constant returns to scale in human capital, because output increases in proportion to human capital, given u.

For example, if human capital increases by 10%, then, holding u constant, output increases by 10%. In the Solow growth model, growth is limited because of the decreasing marginal product of physical capital, but here the marginal product of human capital does not decrease as the quantity of human capital used in production increases. The marginal product of human capital does not fall as human capital increases, because knowledge and skills are nonrivalrous; additional education and skills do not reduce the extra output that can be achieved through the acquisition of more education and skills.

Economic Policy and Growth

Our endogenous growth model suggests that government policies can affect the growth rates of aggregate output and consumption. Because the common growth rate of human capital, consumption, and output depends on b and u, it is useful to think about how government policy might affect b and u. As b is the efficiency of the human capital accumulation technology, b could be affected by government policies that make the educational system more efficient. For example, this might be accomplished through the implementation of better incentives for performance in the school system, or possibly by changing the mix of public and private education. Exactly what policies the government would have to pursue to increase b we cannot say here without being much more specific in modeling the education system. However, it certainly seems feasible for governments to affect the efficiency of education, and politicians seem to believe this, too.

Government policy could also change the rate of economic growth by changing u. For example, this could be done through taxes or subsidies to education. If the government subsidizes education, then such a policy would make human capital accumulation more desirable relative to current production, and so u would decrease and the growth rate of output and consumption would increase.

Now, suppose that the government had the power to decrease u or to increase b, thus increasing the growth rate of consumption and output. Would this be a good idea or not? To answer this question, we would have to ask how the representative consumer's welfare would change as a result. Now, clearly a decrease in u increases the growth rate of consumption, which is $b(1-u)-1$, but there is also a second effect, in that the level of consumption goes down. That is, current consumption is $C = zuH$, and so in the very first period if u decreases, then C must also fall, because initial human capital H is given. Recall from Chapter 1 that if we graph the natural logarithm of a variable against time, then the slope of the graph is approximately the growth rate. Because consumption grows at the constant rate $b(1-u)-1$ in equilibrium, if we graph the natural log of consumption against time, this is a straight line. The slope of the graph of consumption increases as u decreases and the growth rate of consumption increases, and the vertical intercept of the graph decreases as u decreases, as this reduces consumption in the very first period. There is, therefore, a trade-off for the representative consumer when u decreases: consumption is sacrificed early on, but consumption grows at a higher rate, so that consumption ultimately is higher than it was with a higher level of u. Thus, the path for consumption shifts as in Figure 7.7. In the figure, consumption is lower after the change in u until period T, when after-change consumption is higher.

FIGURE 7.7 Effect of a Decrease in *u* on the Consumption Path in the Endogenous Growth Model

The figure shows the effect of a decrease in *u*, which increases the fraction of time spent accumulating human capital each period. The growth path for consumption (consumption is equal to income) pivots; thus, there is a short-run decrease in consumption, but consumption is higher in the long run.

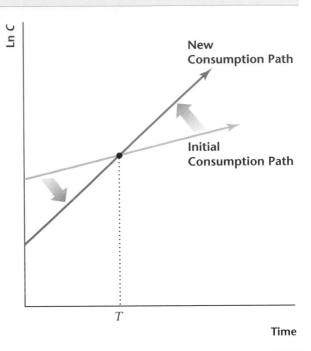

It is not clear that the consumer would prefer the new consumption path with the higher growth rate of consumption, even though consumption is higher in the long run. There is a cost to higher growth, which is that consumption in the near future must be forgone. Which consumption path the consumer prefers depends on how patient he or she is. Preferences could be such that the consumer is very impatient, in which case he or she would tend to prefer the initial consumption path with a low growth rate of consumption. Alternatively, the consumer might be very patient, tending to prefer the new consumption path with a high growth rate of consumption. The conclusion is that, even if the government could engineer a higher rate of growth by causing *u* to fall—say through education subsidies—this may not be desirable because of the near-term costs involved.

We could do a similar analysis for the case in which the government causes the growth rate of consumption to increase because of an increase in *b*, the parameter governing the efficiency of human capital accumulation. In this case, the model is not explicit about the near-term costs of increasing the growth rate of consumption by increasing *b*. That is, current consumption is given by $C = zuH$, and so consumption in the very first period does not depend on *b*. However, if the government were to increase *b* through education policy, for example, this would entail some real resource costs. Suppose that the government chose to make public education more efficient by increasing monitoring of teacher and student performance. Clearly, there would be a cost to this monitoring in terms of labor time. We might represent this cost in our model as a reduction in the level of consumption, as labor is diverted from goods production to government monitoring activities. Therefore, b would increase, which would increase the growth rate of consumption, but as in the case in which we examined the effects of a decrease in u, there would be a decrease in consumption in the very first period. Thus, the relationship between the new consumption path after the increase in b and the initial consumption path would be just as in Figure 7.7. As in the case where u falls, it is not clear whether the representative consumer is better off when the growth rate of consumption is higher, because there are short-term costs in terms of lost consumption.

Convergence in the Endogenous Growth Model

In the Solow growth model, with exogenous growth, countries that are in all respects identical, except for their initial quantities of capital per worker, have in the long run the same level and growth rate of income per worker. We showed in the previous section that this prediction of the Solow growth model is consistent with data on the evolution of incomes per worker in the richest countries of the world but not with data for poorer countries. To explain disparities among the poor countries with the Solow model, we must appeal to significant differences among countries in something exogenous in the Solow growth model, which could be total factor productivity.

In the endogenous growth model we have constructed here, convergence does not occur even if countries are identical in all respects except that there are differences in the initial level of human capital. To see this, note first that in the endogenous growth model, consumption is equal to income, and there is only one consumer, so that per capita income is identical to aggregate income. Accordingly, current consumption is given by $C = zuH$, and consumption grows at a constant rate $b(1 - u) - 1$, so that the natural log of consumption graphed against time is a straight line, as we showed in Figure 7.7. Now, suppose that we consider two countries that have the same technology and allocate labor in the same way between goods production and human capital accumulation. That is, b, z, and u are the same in the two countries. However, suppose that these countries differ according to their initial human capital levels. The rich country has a high level of initial human capital, denoted H_r, and the poor country has a low level of human capital, denoted H_p, which implies that consumption in the rich country is initially $C = zuH_r$, which is greater than initial consumption in the poor country, $C = zuH_p$. Now, because b and u are identical in the two countries, $b(1 - u) - 1$, the growth rate of consumption, is also identical for the rich and poor countries. Therefore, the growth paths of consumption for the rich country and the poor country are as in Figure 7.8. That is, initial differences in income and consumption across rich and poor countries persist forever, and there is no convergence.

How do we reconcile the predictions of the endogenous growth model concerning convergence with the facts? The model appears consistent with the fact that there are

FIGURE 7.8   No Convergence in the Endogenous Growth Model

In the endogenous growth model, two identical countries that differ only according to their initial incomes never converge.

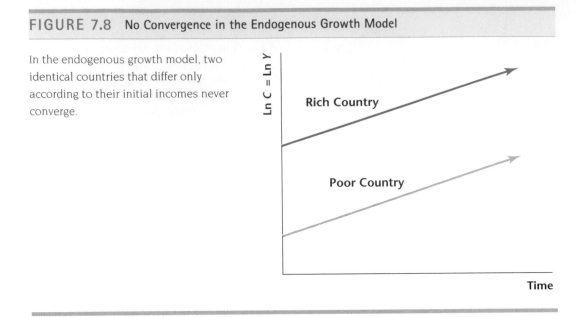

persistent differences in income per worker among poorer countries and persistent differences in income per worker between the poorer countries of the world and the richer countries. However, the model appears inconsistent with the fact that incomes per worker seem to be converging among the richer nations of the world. Perhaps an explanation for this is that, in regions of the world where labor and capital are mobile, and where skills are more easily transferred, there are important **human capital externalities,** as discussed by Robert Lucas.[6] A human capital externality exists when contact with others with high levels of human capital increases our human capital or makes us more productive. Human capital externalities can explain the existence of cities and the specialized activities that take place there. Why, for example, would people specializing in financial activities want to bear the congestion and pollution of New York City unless there were significant positive externalities involved in working there? In highly developed regions of the world where there are greater opportunities, through business contacts and education in other countries and regions, for taking advantage of human capital externalities, large differences in the levels of human capital across regions cannot persist, and there is convergence in income per worker. However, less developed countries interact to a low degree with highly developed countries, and people with high levels of human capital tend to move to the highly developed countries from the less developed countries (the "brain drain"). Thus, differences in human capital can persist across very rich and very poor countries.

[6]R. Lucas, 1988, "On the Mechanics of Economic Development," *Journal of Monetary Economics* 22, July, 3–42.

MACROECONOMICS IN ACTION

Education and Growth

Our endogenous growth model has some interesting implications for the relationship between the growth rate of real GDP and education. In the model, $1 - u$ represents the fraction of time that is devoted to the acquisition of education and skills by the average worker. The higher $1 - u$ is, the greater the growth rate in real GDP, and the greater is income per worker in the long run. In Figure 7.9 we display a

---

FIGURE 7.9   Growth and Education

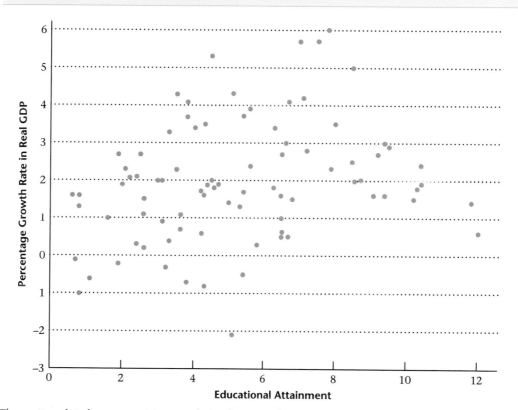

The scatter plot shows a positive correlation between the percentage growth rate in real GDP and average educational attainment among the countries of the world. This is consistent with the predictions of the endogenous growth model.

Source: Jones, C. 1998. *Introduction to Economic Growth*, W.W. Norton and Co., New York, Table B.2.

(continued)

scatter plot of data from Charles Jones's *Introduction to Economic Growth*, with the growth rate in output per worker on the vertical axis and the average number of years of schooling on the horizontal axis. Clearly, this data matches the predictions of the model, in that there is a positive correlation between the growth rate in income per worker and the average quantity of time spent in school by the average person. Similarly, Figure 7.10 shows a positive correlation between real income per worker (as a percentage of U.S. real income per worker) and educational attainment. The endogenous growth model shows how human capital investment is important for growth, and the data tell us that education (which represents the acquisition of human capital) is strongly positively related to growth in real income per worker and to the standard of living across countries.

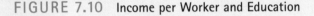

FIGURE 7.10   Income per Worker and Education

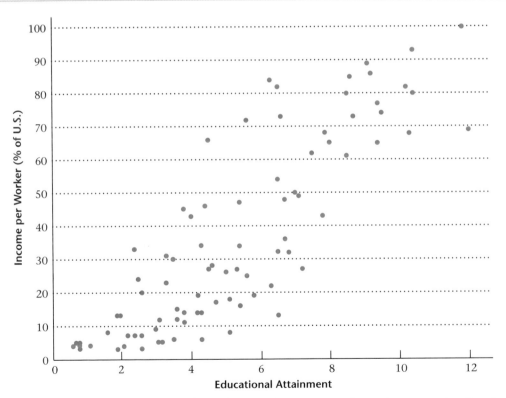

The scatter plot shows a positive correlation between income per worker and average educational attainment among the countries of the world. This is consistent with the predictions of the endogenous growth model.

Source: Jones, C. 1998. *Introduction to Economic Growth*, W.W. Norton and Co., New York, Table B.2.

(continued)

While education is important for growth, as the theory and the data tell us, there are many ways in which education can be delivered. There are key differences among countries, and among regions of the United States, in the public versus private provision of education, and in how public education is financed. The government plays a key role in making decisions determining the public versus private mix of education, and in financing decisions. These government decisions, therefore, potentially play an important role in determining economic growth and long-run living standards.

If we value an equitable distribution of income, public education has an advantage, in that equal access typically applies for elementary and secondary education. Further, public education can be more efficient. From society's point of view, it is preferable if scarce higher education is allocated by ability, as is typical of public education, rather than by the ability to pay, as can happen with private education. Investment in education is more productive if the highest-ability people are the ones who receive it. However, a disadvantage of public education is that taxpayers need to be convinced to support it. The benefits of education are indirect for most, and older people do not see any of the benefits, as the acquisition of an education takes decades. Thus, there is a tendency for public education to be underprovided.

Gerhard Glomm and B. Ravikumar[1] construct an endogenous growth model that is similar to ours in its basic structure but more sophisticated in that it allows for the consideration of public and private education and the financing of public education. They show that public education produces less income inequality in a country than does private education. However, with private education there is a tendency for per capita incomes to be higher in the long run.

---

[1] See G. Glomm and B. Ravikumar, 1992, "Public vs. Private Investment in Human Capital: Endogenous Growth and Income Inequality," *Journal of Political Economy* 100, 818–834.

We have now completed our study of economic growth in this part. In Part IV, we move on to a detailed examination of savings behavior and government deficits, and we begin building a model that is the basis for our study of business cycles.

CHAPTER SUMMARY

- If all countries are identical, except for initial differences in capital per worker, the Solow growth model predicts that there will be convergence among countries. That is, in the long run, all countries will have the same level of income per worker, and aggregate income will be growing at the same rate in all countries.

- In the data, there is evidence for conditional convergence among the richest countries of the world, but convergence does not appear to be occurring among all countries or among the poorest countries.

- The Solow growth model is consistent with the data if there are significant barriers to technology adoption, and these barriers differ among countries. This implies long-run differences in the level of total factor productivity and standards of living across countries.

- We constructed an endogenous growth model with human capital accumulation. This model has the property that, even with no increases in total factor productivity and no population growth, there can be unlimited growth in aggregate output and aggregate consumption, fueled by growth in the stock of human capital (i.e., skills and education).

- In the endogenous growth model, the rate of growth of output and consumption is determined by the efficiency of human capital accumulation and the allocation of labor time between goods production and human capital accumulation.

- If the government could introduce policies that altered the efficiency of human capital accumulation or the allocation of labor time, it could alter the rate of economic growth in the endogenous growth model.

- Increasing the rate of economic growth may or may not improve economic welfare, because an increase in the growth rate of aggregate consumption is always associated with lower consumption in the short run.

- In the endogenous growth model, per capita incomes do not converge across rich and poor countries, even if countries are identical except for initial levels of human capital.

KEY TERMS

Human capital: The accumulated stock of skills and education that a worker has at a point in time.

Nonrivalry: A feature of knowledge, in that acquisition of knowledge does not reduce the ability of others to acquire it.

Efficiency units of labor: The effective number of units of labor input after adjusting for the quantity of human capital possessed by workers.

Human capital externalities: Effects that exist if the human capital of others affects one's productivity.

QUESTIONS FOR REVIEW

1. If countries are initially identical, except with respect to levels of capital per worker, what does the Solow model predict will happen to these countries in the long run? Is this consistent with the data?

2. How is the Solow model consistent with evidence on convergence across countries?

3. What can cause barriers to the adoption of technology?

4. How can a country overcome barriers to technology adoption?

5. What causes economic growth in the endogenous growth model?

6. Why is knowledge nonrivalrous?

7. What two factors affect the growth rate of income and consumption in the endogenous growth model?

8. If the government could increase the rate of growth of consumption, should it? Why or why not?

9. Is there convergence in the levels and rates of growth of per capita income in the endogenous growth model? Why or why not?

10. What is the empirical relationship between education and growth and between education and national living standards?

PROBLEMS

1. Could differences across countries in population growth account for the persistence in income disparity across countries? Use the Solow growth model to address this question and discuss.

2. Suppose that z, the marginal product of efficiency units of labor, increases in the endogenous growth model. What effects does this have on the rates of growth and the levels of human capital, consumption, and output? Explain your results.

3. Introduce government activity in the endogenous growth model as follows. In addition to working u units of time in producing goods, the representative consumer works v units of time for the government and produces gvH goods for government use in the current period, where $g > 0$. The consumer now spends $1 - u - v$ units of time each period accumulating human capital.
   (a) Suppose that v increases with u decreasing by an equal amount. Determine the effects on the level and the rate of growth of consumption. Draw a diagram showing the initial path followed by the natural logarithm of consumption and the corresponding path after v increases.
   (b) Suppose that v increases with u held constant. Determine the effects on the level and the rate of growth of consumption. Draw a diagram showing the initial path followed by the natural logarithm of consumption and the corresponding path after v increases.
   (c) Explain your results and any differences between parts (a) and (b).

4. Suppose that the government makes a one-time investment in new public school buildings, which results in a one-time reduction in consumption. The new public school buildings increase the efficiency with which human capital is accumulated. Determine the effects of this on the paths of aggregate consumption and aggregate output over time. Is it clear that this investment in new schools is a good idea? Explain.

WORKING WITH THE DATA

1. Calculate the standard deviation of income per worker for the countries of the world for 1960 and 1995. Does this indicate that convergence is occurring or not? For the same years, calculate the standard deviation of income per worker for the poor countries (less than 20% of income per worker in the United States in 1960) and for the rich countries (greater than 50% of income per worker in the United States in 1960). What does this tell you about convergence among the rich and the poor?

2. Suppose that we divide the countries of the world into three groups: low income per worker in 1960 (less than 20% of income per worker in the United States), middle income per worker in 1960 (between 20% and 50% of income per worker in the United States), and high income (greater than 50% of income per worker in the United States).
   (a) Calculate average income per worker for the low income, middle income, and high income countries, respectively, for 1960 and 1995, and calculate the rates of growth of average income for the low, middle, and high income countries between 1960 and 1995.
   (b) Do the statistics you calculated in part (a) indicate any tendency for convergence among these three groups of countries?

PART IV

Savings, Government Deficits, and Investment

In this part, we explore further the macroeconomics of intertemporal decisions and dynamic issues. We start in Chapter 8 by considering the consumption-savings decisions of consumers, building on our knowledge of consumer behavior from Chapter 4. We then study the Ricardian equivalence theorem, which states that, under certain conditions, a change in the timing of taxes by the government has no effects on real macroeconomic variables or on the welfare of consumers. A key implication of the Ricardian equivalence theorem is that a cut in taxes by the government is not a free lunch. We also examine two important cases where Ricardian equivalence does not hold. In the first case, government tax policy affects the intergenerational distribution of wealth, and social security systems can increase economic efficiency. In the second case, there are credit market imperfections, and changes in the timing of taxes will affect the consumption–savings decisions of credit-constrained consumers.

In Chapter 9, we use what was learned about the microeconomics of consumption–savings behavior in Chapter 8, along with an analysis of the intertemporal labor supply behavior of consumers and the investment decisions of firms, to construct a complete intertemporal macroeconomic model. This model is the basis for most of what we do in the rest of this book. The model is used in Chapter 9 to show the effects of changes in government spending and in total factor productivity on output, employment, consumption, investment, the real wage, and the real interest rate. As well, we focus on the effects of expectations about the future on current events.

CHAPTER 8

A Two-Period Model: The Consumption–Savings Decision and Ricardian Equivalence

This chapter focuses on **intertemporal decisions** and the implications of intertemporal decision making for how government deficits affect macroeconomic activity. Intertemporal decisions involve economic trade-offs across periods of time. In Chapters 6 and 7, we studied the Solow growth model, where consumers made arbitrary intertemporal decisions about consumption and savings, consuming a constant fraction of income. In this chapter, we analyze these decisions at a deeper level, studying the microeconomic behavior of a consumer who must make a dynamic **consumption–savings decision.** In doing so, we apply what we learned in Chapter 4 concerning how a consumer optimizes subject to his or her budget constraint. We then study a model with many consumers and with a government that need not balance its budget and can issue debt to finance a government budget deficit. An important implication of this model is that the **Ricardian equivalence theorem** holds. This theorem states that there are conditions under which the size of the government's deficit is irrelevant, in that it does not affect any macroeconomic variables of importance or the economic welfare of any individual.

The consumption–savings decision involves intertemporal choice, as this is fundamentally a decision involving a trade-off between current and future consumption. Similarly, the government's decision concerning the financing of government expenditures is an intertemporal choice, involving a trade off between current and future taxes. If the government decreases taxes in the present, it must borrow from the private sector to do so, which implies that future taxes must increase to pay off the higher government debt. Essentially, the government's financing decision is a decision about the quantity of government saving or the size of the government deficit, making it closely related to the consumption–savings decisions of private consumers.

To study the consumption–savings decisions of consumers and the government's intertemporal choices, we work in this chapter with a **two-period model,** which is the simplest framework for understanding intertemporal choice and dynamic issues. We treat the first period in the model as the current period and the second period as the future period. In intertemporal choice, a key variable of interest is **the real interest rate,** which in the model is the interest rate at which consumers and the government can borrow and lend. The real interest rate determines the relative price of consumption in the future in terms of consumption in the present. With respect to consumer choice, we are interested in how savings and consumption in the present and in the future are affected by changes in the real interest rate and in present and future incomes. With respect to the effects of real interest rate changes, income and substitution effects are important, and we can apply here what was learned in Chapters 4 and 5 about how to isolate income and substitution effects in a consumer's choice problem.

An important principle in the response of consumption to changes in income is **consumption smoothing.** That is, there are natural forces that cause consumers to wish to have a smooth consumption path over time, as opposed to a choppy one. Consumption-smoothing behavior is implied by particular properties of indifference curves that we have already studied in Chapter 4. Consumption-smoothing behavior also has important implications for how consumers respond in the aggregate to changes in government policies or other features of their external environment that affect their income streams.

While it remains true here, as in the one-period model studied in Chapter 5, that an increase in government spending has real effects on macroeconomic activity, the Ricardian equivalence theorem establishes conditions under which the timing of taxation does not matter for aggregate economic activity. David Ricardo, for whom the Ricardian equivalence theorem is named, is best known for his work in the early nineteenth century on the theory of comparative advantage and international trade. Ricardian equivalence runs counter to much of public debate, which attaches importance to the size of the government deficit. We explain why Ricardian equivalence is important in economic analysis and why the Ricardian equivalence theorem is a useful starting point for thinking about how the burden of the government debt is shared. A key implication of the Ricardian equivalence theorem is that a tax cut is not a free lunch. A tax cut may not matter at all, or it may involve a redistribution of wealth within the current population or across generations.

We will study two cases where Ricardian equivalence does not hold. In the first case, consumers are finite-lived, and so changes in the timing of taxes matter for consumers' consumption and welfare. Here, social security programs have the potential to improve welfare for all consumers—social security can bring about a Pareto improvement. We study some alternative social security programs and explain the significance of our analysis for current social security policy in the United States. In the second case, we show how credit market imperfections imply that the timing of taxes matters, with a current tax cut matched by a future increase in taxes having the same effects as a government credit program for credit-constrained consumers.

To maintain simplicity and to retain focus on the important ideas in this chapter, our two-period model leaves out production and investment. In Chapter 9, we reintroduce production and add investment decisions by firms so that we can understand more completely the aggregate determination of output, employment, consumption, investment, the real wage rate, and the interest rate.

A TWO-PERIOD MODEL OF THE ECONOMY

A consumer's consumption–savings decision is fundamentally a decision involving a trade-off between current and future consumption. By saving, a consumer gives up consumption in exchange for assets in the present to consume more in the future.

Alternatively, a consumer can dissave by borrowing in the present to gain more current consumption, thus sacrificing future consumption when the loan is repaid. Borrowing (or dissaving) is thus negative savings.

A consumer's consumption–savings decision is a dynamic decision, in that it has implications over more than one period of time, as opposed to the consumer's static work-leisure decision considered in Chapters 4 and 5. We model the consumer's dynamic problem here in the simplest possible way, namely, in a two-period model. In this model, we denote the first period as the current period and the second period as the future period. For some economic problems, assuming that decision making by consumers takes place over two periods is obviously unrealistic. For example, if a period is a quarter, and because the working life of a typical individual is about 200 quarters, then a 200-period model might seem more appropriate. However, the results we consider in this chapter all generalize to more elaborate models with many periods or an infinite number of periods. The reason for studying models with two periods is that they are simple to analyze, while capturing the essentials of dynamic decision making by consumers and firms.

Consumers

There are no difficulties, in terms of what we want to accomplish with this model, in supposing that there are many different consumers rather than a single representative consumer. Therefore, we assume that there are N consumers, and we can think of N being a large number. We assume that each consumer lives for two periods, the current period and the future period. We further suppose that consumers do not make a work–leisure decision in either period but simply receive exogenous income. Assuming that incomes are exogenous allows us to focus attention on what we are interested in here, which is the consumer's consumption–savings decision. Let y be a consumer's real income in the current period, and y' be real income in the future period. Throughout, we use lowercase letters to refer to variables at the individual level and uppercase letters for aggregate variables. Primes denote variables in the future period (for example, y' denotes the consumer's future income). Each consumer pays lump-sum taxes t in the current period and t' in the future period. Suppose that incomes can be different for different consumers, but that all consumers pay the same taxes. If we let a consumer's savings in the current period be s, then the consumer's budget constraint in the current period is

$$c + s = y - t, \tag{8.1}$$

where c is current period consumption. Here, (8.1) states that consumption plus savings in the current period must equal disposable income in the current period. We assume that the consumer starts the current period with no assets. This does not matter in any important way for our analysis.

In (8.1), if $s > 0$, then the consumer is a lender on the credit market, and if $s < 0$, the consumer is a borrower. We suppose that the financial asset that is traded in the credit market is a bond. In the model, bonds can be issued by consumers as well as by the government. If a consumer lends, he or she buys bonds; if he or she borrows, there is a sale of bonds. There are two important assumptions here. The first is that all bonds are indistinguishable, because consumers never default on their debts, so that there is no risk associated with holding a bond. In practice, different credit instruments are associated with different levels of risk. Interest-bearing securities issued by the U.S. government are essentially riskless, while corporate bonds may be risky if investors feel that the corporate issuer might default, and a loan made by a bank to a consumer may also be quite risky. The second important assumption is that bonds are traded directly in the credit market. In practice, much of the economy's credit activity is channeled through financial intermediaries, an example of which is a commercial bank. For example, when a consumer borrows to purchase a car, the loan is usually taken out at a commercial bank or other depository institution; a consumer typically does not borrow directly from the ultimate lender (in the case of a commercial bank, the ultimate lenders include the depositors at the bank). For the problems we address with this model, we simplify matters considerably, without any key loss in the insights we get, to assume away credit risk and financial institutions like commercial banks. Credit risk and financial intermediation are discussed in detail in Chapter 15.

In our model, one bond issued in the current period is a promise to pay $1 + r$ units of the consumption good in the future period, so that the real interest rate on each bond is r. Because this implies that one unit of current consumption can be exchanged in the credit market for $1 + r$ units of the future consumption good, the relative price of future consumption in terms of current consumption is $\frac{1}{1+r}$. Recall from Chapter 1 that in practice the real interest rate is approximately the nominal interest rate (the interest rate in money terms) minus the inflation rate. We study the relationship between real and nominal interest rates in Chapter 10.

A key assumption here is that the real rate of interest at which a consumer can lend is the same as the real rate of interest at which a consumer can borrow. In practice, consumers typically borrow at higher rates of interest than they can lend at. For example, the interest rates on consumer loans are usually several percentage points higher than the interest rates on bank deposits, reflecting the costs for the bank of taking deposits and making loans. The assumption that borrowing and lending rates of interest are the same matters for some of what we do here, and we ultimately show what difference this makes to our analysis.

In the future period, the consumer has disposable income $y' - t'$ and receives the interest and principal on his or her savings, which totals $(1 + r)s$. Because the future period is the final period, the consumer chooses to finish this period with no assets, consuming all disposable income and the interest and principal on savings (we assume there are no bequests to descendants). We then have

$$c' = y' - t' + (1 + r)s, \tag{8.2}$$

where c' is consumption in the future period. In Equation (8.2), if $s < 0$, the consumer pays the interest and principal on his or her loan (retires the bonds he or she issued in the current period) and then consumes what remains of his or her future period disposable income.

The consumer chooses current consumption and future consumption, c and c', respectively, and savings s to make himself or herself as well off as possible while satisfying the budget constraints (8.1) and (8.2).

The Consumer's Lifetime Budget Constraint   We can work with diagrams similar to those used in Chapter 4 to analyze the consumer's work-leisure decision, if we take the two budget constraints expressed in Equations (8.1) and (8.2) and write them as a single lifetime budget constraint. To do this, we first use (8.2) to solve for s to get

$$s = \frac{c' - y' + t'}{1 + r}. \tag{8.3}$$

Then, substitute for s from (8.3) in (8.1) to get

$$c + \frac{c' - y' + t'}{1 + r} = y - t,$$

or rearranging,

$$c + \frac{c'}{1 + r} = y + \frac{y'}{1 + r} - t - \frac{t'}{1 + r}. \tag{8.4}$$

Equation (8.4) is the consumer's **lifetime budget constraint,** and it states that the **present value** of lifetime consumption $c + \frac{c'}{1+r}$ equals the present value of lifetime income $y + \frac{y'}{1+r}$ minus the present value of lifetime taxes $t + \frac{t'}{1+r}$. The present value here is the value in terms of period 1 consumption goods. That is, $\frac{1}{1+r}$ is the relative price of future consumption goods in terms of current consumption goods, because a consumer can give up 1 unit of current consumption goods and obtain $1 + r$ units of future consumption goods by saving for one period. The problem of the consumer is now simplified, in that he or she chooses c and c' to make himself or herself as well off as possible, while satisfying the budget constraint (8.4) and given r, y, y', t, and t'. Once we have determined what the consumer's optimal consumption is in the current and future periods, we can determine savings, s, from the current period budget constraint (8.1).

For a numerical example to illustrate present values, suppose that current income is $y = 110$ while future income is $y' = 120$. Taxes in the current period are $t = 20$, and taxes in the future period are $t' = 10$. Also suppose that the real interest rate is 10%, so that $r = 0.1$. In this example, the relative price of future consumption goods in terms of current consumption goods is $\frac{1}{1+r} = 0.909$. Here, when we discount future income and future taxes to obtain these quantities in units of current consumption goods, we multiply by the discount factor 0.909. The fact that the discount factor is less than 1 indicates that having a given amount of income in the future is worth less to the consumer than having the same amount of income in the current period. The present discounted value of lifetime income is

$$y + \frac{y'}{1 + r} = 110 + (120 \times 0.909) = 219.1,$$

and the present value of lifetime taxes is

$$t + \frac{t'}{1 + r} = 20 + (10 \times 0.909) = 29.1.$$

Then, in this example, we can write the consumer's lifetime budget constraint from Equation (8.4) as

$$c + 0.909c' = 190.$$

We label the present value of lifetime disposable income, the quantity on the right-hand side of Equation (8.4), as **lifetime wealth,** *we*, because this is the quantity of resources that the consumer has available to spend on consumption, in present-value terms, over his or her lifetime. We then have

$$we = y + \frac{y'}{1+r} - t - \frac{t'}{1+r},$$ (8.5)

and we can rewrite (8.4) as

$$c + \frac{c'}{1+r} = we.$$ (8.6)

In Figure 8.1 we graph the consumer's lifetime budget constraint as expressed in Equation (8.6). Writing this equation in slope-intercept form, we have

$$c' = -(1+r)c + we(1+r).$$ (8.7)

Therefore, in Equation (8.7) and in Figure 8.1, the vertical intercept, $we(1+r)$, is what could be consumed in the future period if the consumer saved all of his or her current-period disposable income and consumed lifetime wealth (after earning the real interest rate r on savings) in the future period. The horizontal intercept in Equation (8.7) and

---

FIGURE 8.1   **Consumer's Lifetime Budget Constraint**

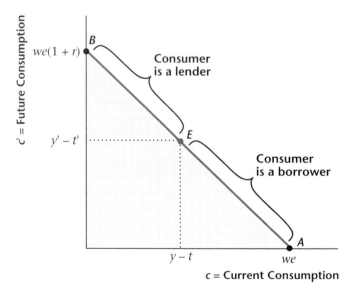

The lifetime budget constraint defines the quantities of current and future consumption the consumer can acquire, given current and future income and taxes, through borrowing and lending on the credit market. To the northwest of the endowment point E, the consumer is a lender with positive savings; to the southeast of E, he or she is a borrower with negative savings.

Figure 8.1, *we*, is what could be consumed if the consumer borrowed the maximum amount possible against future period disposable income and consumed all of lifetime wealth in the current period. The slope of the lifetime budget constraint is $-(1 + r)$, which is determined by the real interest rate. Point E in Figure 8.1 is the **endowment point**, which is the consumption bundle the consumer gets if he or she simply consumes disposable income in the current period and in the future period—that is, $c = y - t$ and $c' = y' - t'$—with zero savings in the current period. You can verify by substituting $c = y - t$ and $c' = y' - t'$ in Equation (8.4) that the endowment point satisfies the lifetime budget constraint. Now, any point along BE in Figure 8.1 implies that $s \geq 0$, so that the consumer is a lender, because $c \leq y - t$. Also, a consumption bundle along AE in Figure 8.1 implies that the consumer is a borrower with $s \leq 0$.

Any point on or inside AB in the shaded area in Figure 8.1 represents a feasible consumption bundle, that is, a combination of current-period and future-period consumptions that satisfies the consumer's lifetime budget constraint. As may be clear by now, the way we approach the consumer's problem here is very similar to our analysis of the consumer's work–leisure decision in Chapter 4. Once we describe the consumer's preferences and add indifference curves to the budget constraint as depicted in Figure 8.1, we can determine the consumer's optimal consumption bundle.

The Consumer's Preferences   As with the consumer's work–leisure decision in Chapter 4, the consumption bundle that is chosen by the consumer, which here is a combination of current-period and future-period consumptions, is determined jointly by the consumer's budget constraint and his or her preferences. Just as in Chapter 4, we assume that preferences have three properties, which are the following:

1. More is always preferred to less. Here, this means that more current consumption or more future consumption always makes the consumer better off.

2. The consumer likes diversity in his or her consumption bundle. Here, a preference for diversity has a specific meaning in terms of the consumer's desire to smooth consumption over time. Namely, the consumer has a dislike for consumption that is far from equal between the current period and the future period. Note that this does not mean that the consumer would always choose to have equal consumption in the current and future periods.

3. Current consumption and future consumption are normal goods. This implies that if there is a parallel shift to the right in the consumer's budget constraint, then current consumption and future consumption both increase. This is related to the consumer's desire to smooth consumption over time. If there is a parallel shift to the right in the consumer's budget constraint, this is because lifetime wealth *we* has increased. Given the consumer's desire to smooth consumption over time, any increase in lifetime wealth implies that the consumer chooses more consumption in the present and in the future.

As in Chapter 4, we represent preferences with an indifference map, which is a family of indifference curves. A typical indifference map is shown in Figure 8.2, where

FIGURE 8.2   A Consumer's Indifference Curves

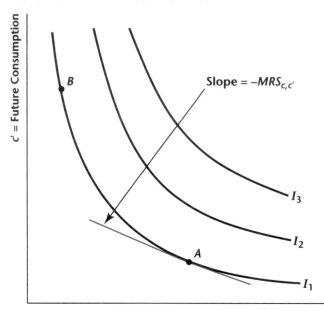

The figure shows the indifference map of a consumer. Indifference curves are convex and downward-sloping. Minus the slope of an indifference curve is the marginal rate of substitution of current consumption for future consumption.

the marginal rate of substitution of consumption in the current period for consumption in the future period, or $MRS_{c,c'}$, is minus the slope of an indifference curve. For example, $MRS_{c,c'}$ at point A in Figure 8.2 is minus the slope of a tangent to the indifference curve at point A. Recall that a preference for diversity, or diminishing marginal rate of substitution, is captured by the convexity in an indifference curve, which here also represents a consumer's desire to smooth consumption over time. On indifference curve I_1, at point A the consumer has a large quantity of current consumption and a small quantity of future consumption, and he or she needs to be given a large quantity of current consumption to willingly give up a small quantity of future consumption (minus the slope of the indifference curve at A is small). Conversely, at point B the consumer has a small quantity of current consumption and a large quantity of future consumption, and he or she needs to be given a large quantity of future consumption to give up a small quantity of current consumption (minus the slope of the indifference curve is large). Thus, the consumer does not like large differences in consumption between the two periods.

As an example to show why consumption smoothing is a natural property for preferences to have, suppose that Sara is a consumer living on a desert island, and that

Table 8.1   **Sara's Desire For Consumption Smoothing**

	Week 1 Coconuts	Week 2 Coconuts	Total Consumption
Bundle 1	5	15	20
Bundle 2	17	3	20
Preferred Bundle	11	9	20

she eats only coconuts. Suppose that coconuts can be stored for two weeks without spoiling, and that Sara has 20 coconuts to last for this week (the current period) and next week (the future period). One option that Sara has is to eat 5 coconuts this week and 15 coconuts next week. Suppose that Sara is just indifferent between this first consumption bundle and a second bundle that involves eating 17 coconuts this week and 3 coconuts next week. However, eating only 5 coconuts in the first week or only 3 coconuts in the second week leaves Sara rather hungry. She would, in fact, prefer to eat 11 coconuts in the first week and 9 coconuts in the second week, rather than either of the other two consumption bundles. This third consumption bundle combines half of the first consumption bundle with half of the second consumption bundle. That is, $\frac{5+17}{2} = 11$ and $\frac{15+3}{2} = 9$. Sara's preferences reflect a desire for consumption smoothing or a preference for diversity in her consumption bundle, that seems natural. In Table 8.1 we show the consumption bundles amongst which Sara chooses.

Consumer Optimization   As with the work–leisure decision we considered in Chapter 4, the consumer's optimal consumption bundle here is determined by where an indifference curve is tangent to the budget constraint. In Figure 8.3 we show the optimal consumption choice for a consumer who decides to be a lender. The endowment point is at E, while the consumer chooses the consumption bundle at point A, where $(c, c') = (c^*, c'^*)$. At point A, it is then the case that

$$MRS_{c,c'} = 1 + r; \tag{8.8}$$

that is, the marginal rate of substitution of current consumption for future consumption (minus the slope of the indifference curve) is equal to the relative price of current consumption in terms of future consumption ($1 + r$, which is minus the slope of the consumer's lifetime budget constraint). Recall from Chapter 4 that Equation (8.8) is a particular case of a standard marginal condition that is implied by consumer optimization (at the optimum, the marginal rate of substitution of good 1 for good 2 is equal to the relative price of good 1 in terms of good 2). Here, the consumer optimizes by choosing the consumption bundle on his or her lifetime budget constraint where the rate at which he or she is willing to trade off current consumption for future consumption is the same as the rate at which he or she can trade current consumption for future consumption in the market (by saving). At point A in Figure 8.3, the quantity of savings is $s = y - t - c^*$, or the distance BD. Similarly, Figure 8.4 shows the case of a consumer who chooses to be a borrower. That is, the endowment point is E and the

FIGURE 8.3   A Consumer Who Is a Lender

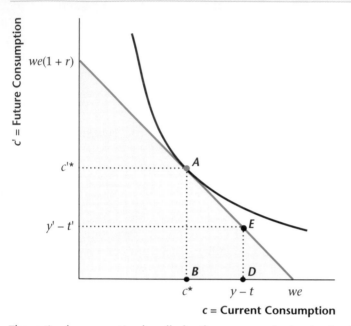

The optimal consumption bundle for the consumer is at point A, where the marginal rate of substitution (minus the slope of an indifference curve) is equal to $1 + r$ (minus the slope of the lifetime budget constraint). The consumer is a lender, as the consumption bundle chosen implies positive savings, with E being the endowment point.

consumer chooses point A, where $(c, c') = (c^*, c'^*)$. Here, the quantity the consumer borrows in the first period is $-s = c^* - y + t$, or the distance DB.

In the next stage in our analysis, we consider some experiments that tell us how the consumer responds to changes in current income, future income, and interest rates.

An Increase in Current-Period Income   From Chapter 4, we know that an increase in a consumer's dividend income or a reduction in taxes amounts to a pure income effect, which increases consumption and reduces labor supply. Here, we want to focus on how an increase in the consumer's current income affects intertemporal decisions. In particular, we want to know the effects of an increase in current income on current consumption, future consumption, and savings. As we show, these effects reflect the consumer's desire for consumption smoothing.

Suppose that, holding the interest rate, taxes in the current and future periods, and future income constant, a consumer receives an increase in period 1 income. Asking the consumer's response to this change in income is much like asking how an individual

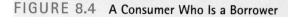

FIGURE 8.4   **A Consumer Who Is a Borrower**

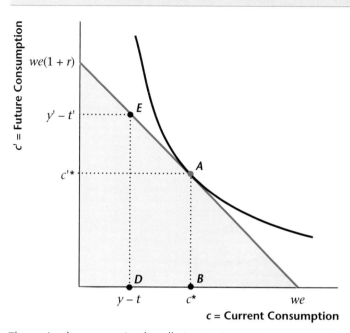

The optimal consumption bundle is at point A. Because current consumption exceeds current disposable income, saving is negative, and so the consumer is a borrower.

would react to winning a lottery. In Figure 8.5 the initial endowment point is at E_1, and the consumer initially chooses the consumption bundle represented by point A. In this figure we have shown the case of a consumer who is initially a lender, but it does not make a difference for what we want to show if the consumer is a borrower. We suppose that current-period income increases from y_1 to y_2. The result is that lifetime wealth increases from

$$we_1 = y_1 + \frac{y'}{1+r} - t - \frac{t'}{1+r}$$

to

$$we_2 = y_2 + \frac{y'}{1+r} - t - \frac{t'}{1+r},$$

and the change in lifetime wealth is

$$\Delta we = we_2 - we_1 = y_2 - y_1.$$

The effect is that the budget constraint shifts to the right by the amount $y_2 - y_1$, which is the distance $E_1 E_2$, where E_2 is the new endowment point. The slope of the budget constraint remains unchanged, as the real interest rate is the same.

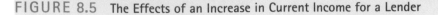

FIGURE 8.5   The Effects of an Increase in Current Income for a Lender

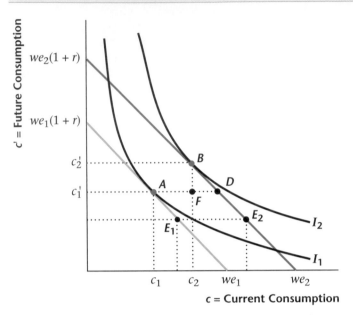

When current income increases, lifetime wealth increases from we_1 to we_2. The lifetime budget constraint shifts out, and the slope of the constraint remains unchanged, because the real interest rate does not change. Initially, the consumer chooses A, and he or she chooses B after current income increases. Current and future consumption both increase (both goods are normal), and current consumption increases by less than the increase in current income.

Because current-period consumption and future consumption are normal goods, the consumer now chooses a consumption bundle represented by a point like B, where consumption in both periods has risen from the previous values. Current consumption increases from c_1 to c_2, and future consumption increases from c_1' to c_2'. Thus, if current income increases, the consumer wishes to spread this additional income over both periods and not consume it all in the current period. In Figure 8.5 the increase in current income is the distance AD, while the increase in current consumption is the distance AF, which is less than the distance AD. The change in the consumer's savings is given by

$$\Delta s = \Delta y - \Delta t - \Delta c, \qquad (8.9)$$

and because $\Delta t = 0$, and $\Delta y > \Delta c > 0$, we have $\Delta s > 0$. Thus, an increase in current income causes an increase in consumption in both periods and an increase in savings.

Our analysis tells us that any one consumer who receives an increase in his or her current income consumes more during the current period but also saves some of the increase in income so as to consume more in the future. This behavior arises because of the consumer's desire to smooth consumption over time. This behavior certainly is intuitively reasonable. For example, consider a consumer, Paul, who is currently 25 years of age and wins $1 million in a lottery. Paul could certainly spend all of his lottery winnings on consumption goods within the current year and save nothing, but it would seem more sensible if he consumed a small part of his winnings in the current year and saved a substantial fraction to consume more for the rest of his life.

If all consumers act to smooth their consumption relative to their income, then aggregate consumption should likewise be smooth relative to aggregate income. Indeed, this prediction of our theory is consistent with what we see in the data. Recall from Chapter 3 that real aggregate consumption is less variable than is real GDP. The difference in variability between aggregate consumption and GDP is even larger if we take account of the fact that some of what is included in aggregate consumption is not consumption in the economic sense. For example, purchases of new automobiles are included in the NIPA as consumption of durables, but the purchase of a car might more appropriately be included in investment, because the car yields a flow of consumption services over its entire lifetime. In the data, expenditures on consumer durables are much more variable than actual consumption, measured as the flow of consumption services that consumers receive from goods. In Figure 8.6 we show the percentage deviations from trend in the consumption of durables, the consumption of nondurables and services, and in GDP for the period 1947–2003. Clearly, the consumption of durables is much more variable than aggregate income, while the consumption of nondurables and services is much less variable than income. Because the consumption of nondurables and services comes fairly close to measuring a flow of consumption services, the variability in this component of consumption reflects more accurately the tendency of consumers to smooth consumption.

Though aggregate data on consumption and income is clearly qualitatively consistent with consumption-smoothing behavior on the part of consumers, macroeconomists have been interested in the quantitative match between consumption theory and the data. The question is whether or not measured consumption is smooth enough relative to measured income to be consistent with theory. Generally, the conclusion from empirical work is that, while the theory points in the right direction, there is some **excess variability** of aggregate consumption relative to aggregate income. That is, while consumption is smoother than income, as the theory predicts, consumption is not quite smooth enough to tightly match the theory.[1] Thus, the theory needs some more work if it is to fit the facts. Two possible explanations for the excess variability in consumption are the following:

1. There are imperfections in the credit market. Our theory assumes that a consumer can smooth consumption by borrowing or lending at the market real interest rate r. In reality, consumers cannot borrow all they would like at the market interest rate, and market loan interest rates are typically higher than the interest rates at which consumers lend. As a result, in reality consumers may have less ability to

---

[1] See, for example, R. Hall, 1989. "Consumption," in R. Barro ed., *Modern Business Cycle Theory,* Harvard University Press, Cambridge, MA.

FIGURE 8.6   **Percentage Deviations from Trend in GDP and Consumption, 1947–2003**

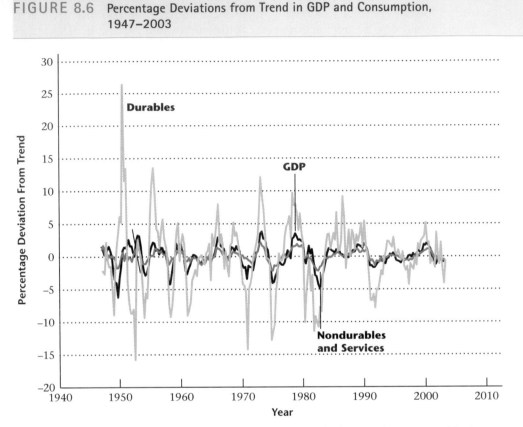

Consumption of durables is much more variable than GDP, which is much more variable than consumption of nondurables and services. The consumption-smoothing behavior of consumers is clearly reflected in the behavior of nondurables and services.

Source: Bureau of Economic Analysis, Department of Commerce.

---

smooth consumption than they do in the theory. We could complicate the model by introducing credit market imperfections, and this might help to explain the data better. However, this would make the model considerably more complicated. We further discuss credit market imperfections later in this chapter.

2. When all consumers are trying to smooth consumption in the same way simultaneously, this changes market prices. The consumption-smoothing theory we have studied thus far does not take into account the interaction of consumers with each other and with other sectors of the economy. All consumers may wish to smooth consumption over time, but aggregate consumption must fall during a recession because aggregate income is lower then, and similarly, aggregate consumption must rise in a boom. The way that consumers are reconciled to having high consumption

when output is high, and low consumption when output is low, is through movements in market prices, including the market interest rate. Shortly, we study how individual consumers react to changes in the real interest rate.

An Increase in Future Income   While a consumer's response to a change in his or her current income is informative about consumption-smoothing behavior, we are also interested in the effects on consumer behavior of a change in income that is expected to occur in the future. Suppose, for example, that Jennifer is about to finish her college degree in four months, and she lines up a job that starts as soon as she graduates. On landing the job, Jennifer's future income has increased considerably. How would she react to this future increase in income? Clearly, this would imply that she would plan to increase her future consumption, but Jennifer also likes to smooth consumption, so that she should want to have higher current consumption as well. She can consume more currently by borrowing against her future income and repaying the loan when she starts working.

In Figure 8.7 we show the effects of an increase for the consumer in future income, from y_1' to y_2'. This has an effect similar to the increase in current income on lifetime

FIGURE 8.7   An Increase in Future Income

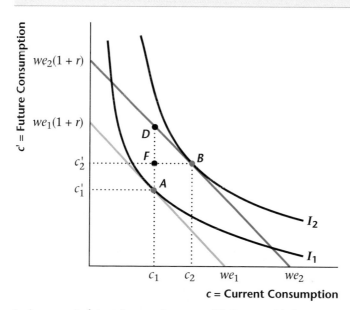

An increase in future income increases lifetime wealth from we_1 to we_2, shifting the lifetime budget constraint to the right and leaving its slope unchanged. The consumer initially chooses point A, and he or she chooses B after the budget constraint shifts. Future consumption increases by less than the increase in future income, saving decreases, and current consumption increases.

wealth, with lifetime wealth increasing from we_1 to we_2, and shifting the budget constraint up by the amount $y_2' - y_1'$. Initially, the consumer chooses consumption bundle A, and he or she chooses B after the increase in future income. Both current and future consumption increase; current consumption increases from c_1 to c_2, and future consumption increases from c_1' to c_2'. The increase in future consumption, which is the distance AF in Figure 8.7, is less than the increase in future income, which is the distance AD. This is because, as with the increase in current income, the consumer wants to smooth consumption over time. Rather than spend all the increase in income in the future, the consumer saves less in the current period so that current consumption can increase. The change in saving is given by Equation (8.9), where $\Delta t = \Delta y = 0$, and because $\Delta c > 0$, we must have $\Delta s < 0$—that is, savings decreases.

In the case of an expected increase in future income, the consumer acts to smooth consumption over time, just as when he or she receives an increase in current income. The difference is that an increase in future income leads to smoothing backward, with the consumer saving less in the current period so that current consumption can increase, whereas an increase in current income leads to smoothing forward, with the consumer saving more in the current period so that future consumption can increase.

Temporary and Permanent Changes in Income   When a consumer receives a change in his or her current income, it matters a great deal for his or her current consumption-savings choice whether this change in income is temporary or permanent. For example, Allen would respond quite differently to receiving a windfall increase in his income of $1,000, say by winning a lottery, as opposed to receiving a $1,000 yearly salary increase that he expects to continue indefinitely. In the case of the lottery winnings, we might expect that Allen would increase current consumption by only a small amount, saving most of the lottery winnings to increase consumption in the future. If Allen received a permanent increase in his income, as in the second case, we would expect his increase in current consumption to be much larger.

The difference between the effects of temporary and permanent changes in income on consumption was articulated by Milton Friedman in his **permanent income hypothesis.**[2] Friedman argued that a primary determinant of a consumer's current consumption is his or her permanent income, which is closely related to the concept of lifetime wealth in our model. Changes in income that are temporary yield small changes in permanent income (lifetime wealth), which have small effects on current consumption, whereas changes in income that are permanent have large effects on permanent income (lifetime wealth) and current consumption.

In our model, we can show the effects of temporary versus permanent changes in income by examining an increase in income that occurs only in the current period versus an increase in income occurring in the current period and the future period. In Figure 8.8 the budget constraint of the consumer is initially AB, and he or she chooses the consumption bundle represented by point H, on indifference curve I_1. Then, the consumer experiences a temporary increase in income, with current income increasing

---

[2] See M. Friedman, 1957, *A Theory of the Consumption Function*, Princeton University Press, Princeton, NJ.

FIGURE 8.8   **Temporary Versus Permanent Increases in Income**

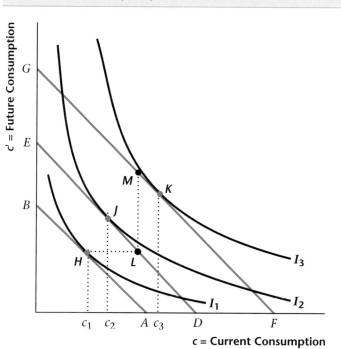

A temporary increase in income is an increase in current income, with the budget constraint shifting from AB to DE and the optimal consumption bundle changing from H to J . When there is a permanent increase in income, current and future income both increase, and the budget constraint shifts from AB to FG, with the optimal consumption bundle changing from H to K .

from y_1 to y_2, so that the budget constraint shifts out to DE. The real interest rate does not change, so that the slope of the budget constraint remains constant. The distance HL is equal to the change in current income, $y_2 - y_1$. Now, the consumer chooses point J on indifference curve I_2, and we know from our previous discussion that the increase in current consumption, $c_2 - c_1$, is less than the increase in current income, $y_2 - y_1$, as saving increases due to consumption-smoothing behavior.

Now, suppose that the increase in income is permanent. We interpret this as an equal increase of $y_2 - y_1$ in both current and future income. That is, initially future income is y_1' and it increases to y_2' with $y_2' - y_1' = y_2 - y_1$. Now, the budget constraint is given by FG in Figure 8.8, where the upward shift in the budget constraint from DE is the distance LM, which is $y_2' - y_1' = y_2 - y_1$. The consumer now chooses point K on indifference curve I_3. At point K, current consumption is c_3. Given that current and future consumption are normal goods, current consumption increases from point H to point J and from point J to point K. Therefore, if income increases permanently, this has a larger effect on current consumption than if income increases only temporarily.

If income increases only temporarily, there is an increase in saving, so that consumption does not increase as much as does income. However, if there is a permanent increase in income, then there need not be an increase in saving, and current consumption could increase as much as or more than does income.

Why is it important that consumers respond differently to temporary and permanent changes in their income? Suppose that the government is considering cutting taxes, and this tax cut could be temporary or permanent. For now, ignore how the government will go about financing this tax cut (we consider this later in the chapter). If consumers receive a tax cut that increases lifetime wealth, then this increases aggregate consumption. However, if consumers expect the tax cut to be temporary, the increase in consumption is much smaller than if they expect the tax cut to be permanent.

⦁ ⦁

CONSUMPTION SMOOTHING AND THE STOCK MARKET

THEORY confronts the DATA

Thus far, our theory tells us that, in response to increases in their lifetime wealth, consumers increase consumption, but in such a way that their consumption path is smoothed over time. One way in which consumers' wealth changes is through variation in the prices of stocks traded on organized stock exchanges, such as the New York Stock Exchange or NASDAQ.

How should we expect aggregate consumption to respond to a change in stock prices? On the one hand, publicly traded stock is not a large fraction of national wealth. That is, a large fraction of national wealth includes the housing stock and the capital of privately held companies, which are not traded on the stock market. Therefore, even if there is a large change in stock prices, this need not represent a large change in national wealth. On the other hand, financial theory tells us that, when the price of a stock changes, we should expect this price change to be permanent.

Financial theory tells us (with some qualifications) that stock prices are **martingales.** A martingale has the property that the best prediction of its value tomorrow is its value today. In the case of a stock price, the best prediction of tomorrow's stock price is today's stock price. The reason that stock prices follow martingales is that, if they did not, then there would be opportunities for investors to make profits. That is, suppose that a stock price does not follow a martingale, and suppose first that the best forecast is that tomorrow's stock price will be higher than today's stock price. Then, investors would want to buy the stock today so as to make a profit by selling it tomorrow. Ultimately, this would force up the market price of the stock today, to the point where the price today is what it is expected to be tomorrow. Similarly, if the price of the stock today were greater than what the stock's price was expected to be tomorrow, investors would want to sell the stock today so they could buy it at a cheaper price tomorrow. In this case, investors' actions would force the current stock price down to the point where it was equal to its expected price tomorrow. Because the current price of a stock is the best forecast of its future price, any change in prices is a surprise, and this change in prices is expected to be permanent.

A change in the overall value of the stock market does not represent a change in a large fraction of national wealth, and this would tend to dampen the effect of price movements in the stock market on aggregate consumption. However, the fact that any change in stock prices is expected to be permanent tends to amplify the effects of changes in stock prices, as we know that permanent changes in wealth have larger effects on consumption than do temporary changes in wealth. What do the data tell us? In Figure 8.9 we show a time series plot of the percentage deviations from trend in the Standard and Poor's composite stock price index for the United States, and percentage deviations from trend in real consumption of nondurables and services. The data plotted are quarterly data for the period 1985–2003. Here, note in particular that the stock price index is highly volatile relative to consumption. Deviations from

FIGURE 8.9   Stock Prices and Consumption of Nondurables and Services, 1985–2003

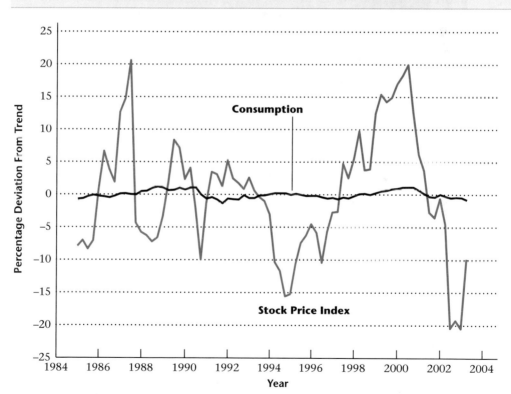

The graph shows that deviations from trend in stock prices (black line) and in nondurables consumption (colored line) are positively correlated. When there is a positive (negative) deviation from trend in stock prices, there tends to be a positive (negative) deviation from trend in consumption.

Source: Standard and Poor's; Bureau of Economic Analysis, Department of Commerce.

FIGURE 8.10   Scatter Plot of Percentage Deviations from Trend in Consumption of Nondurables and Services Versus Percentage Deviations from Trend in a Stock Price Index

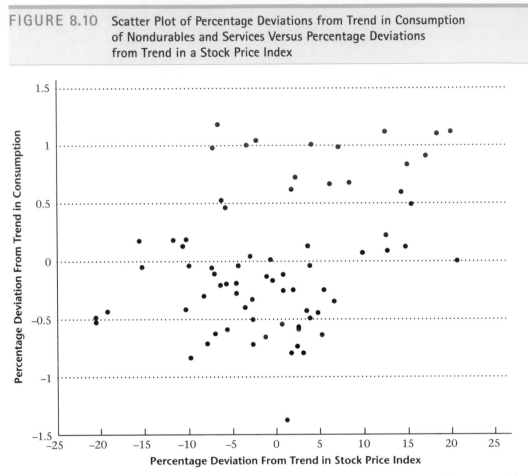

A positively sloped line would provide the best fit to the scatter plot, indicating that the two variables are positively correlated.

Source: Standard and Poor's; Bureau of Economic Analysis, Department of Commerce.

trend in the stock price index of 15 to 20% occur, while the deviations from trend in consumption are at most 1.5%. A close examination of Figure 8.9 indicates that deviations from trend in the stock price index are positively correlated with deviations from trend in consumption. Figure 8.10 shows this more clearly, where we graph the same data as in Figure 8.9, except in a scatter plot. A positively sloped line in Figure 8.10 would provide the best fit to the data in the scatter plot, indicating that the stock price and consumption are positively correlated.

The data indicate that the stock market is potentially an important channel for the effects of changes in wealth on aggregate consumption behavior. The fact that consumption and stock prices move together is consistent with the notion that shocks to the financial system that are reflected in the prices of publicly traded stocks can cause significant movements in aggregate consumption. Though the value of publicly traded stock is not a large part of national wealth, the fact that stock price changes are expected to be permanent potentially contributes to the influence of the stock market on consumption behavior.

An Increase in the Real Interest Rate   To this point, we have examined how changes in a consumer's current income and future income affect his or her choices of consumption in the current and future periods. These are changes that shift the consumer's budget constraint but do not change its slope. In this subsection, we study how the consumer responds to a change in the real interest rate, which changes the slope of the budget constraint. Changes in the market real interest rate are ultimately an important part of the mechanism by which shocks to the economy, fiscal policy, and monetary policy affect real activity, as we show in Chapters 9–12. A key channel for interest rate effects on real activity is through aggregate consumption.

Because $\frac{1}{1+r}$ is the relative price of future consumption goods in terms of current consumption goods, a change in the real interest rate effectively changes this intertemporal relative price. In Chapter 4, in the consumer's work–leisure choice problem, a change in the real wage was effectively a change in the relative price of leisure and consumption, and a change in the real wage had income and substitution effects. Here, in our two-period framework, a change in the real interest rate also has income and substitution effects in its influence on consumption in the present and the future.

Suppose that the consumer faces an increase in the real interest rate, with taxes and income held constant in both periods. First this makes the budget constraint steeper, because the slope of the budget constraint is $-(1+r)$. Further, under the assumption that the consumer never has to pay a tax larger than his or her income, so that $y' - t' > 0$, an increase in r decreases lifetime wealth we, as shown in Equation (8.5). Also from Equation (8.5), we have

$$we(1+r) = (y-t)(1+r) + y' - t',$$

and because $y > t$, there is an increase in $we(1+r)$ when r increases. Therefore, we know that an increase in r causes the budget constraint to pivot, as in Figure 8.11, where r increases from r_1 to r_2, resulting in a decrease in we from we_1 to we_2. We also know that the budget constraint must pivot around the endowment point E, because it must always be possible for the consumer to consume his or her disposable income in each period, no matter what the real interest rate is.

A change in r results in a change in the relative price of consumption in the current and future periods; that is, an increase in r causes future consumption to become cheaper relative to current consumption. A higher interest rate implies that the return on savings is higher, so that more future consumption goods can be obtained for a given sacrifice of current consumption goods. As well, for a given loan in the first period, the consumer has to forgo more future consumption goods when the loan is repaid. We can use what we learned about income and substitution effects in Chapter 4 to understand how an increase in the real interest rate affects the consumer's behavior. However, it turns out that the income effects of an increase in the real interest rate

FIGURE 8.11   An Increase in the Real Interest Rate

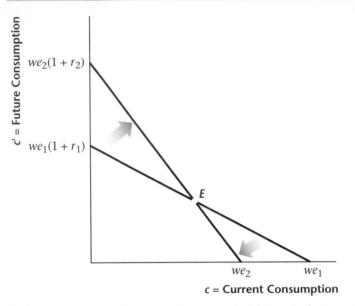

An increase in the real interest rate causes the lifetime budget constraint of the consumer to become steeper and to pivot around the endowment point E.

work in different directions for lenders and borrowers, which is what we want to show next.

First, consider the case of a lender. In Figure 8.12 consider a consumer who is initially a lender and faces an increase in the market real interest rate from r_1 to r_2. Initially, lifetime wealth is we_1, and this changes to we_2. The budget constraint pivots around the endowment point E. Initially, the consumer chose the consumption bundle A, and we suppose that the consumer chooses B after the increase in the real interest rate. To find the substitution effect of the real interest rate increase, we draw an artificial budget constraint FG, which has the same slope as the new budget constraint, and is just tangent to the initial indifference curve I_1. Thus, we are taking wealth away from the consumer until he or she is as well off as before the increase in r. Then, the movement from A to D is a pure substitution effect, and in moving from A to D future consumption increases and current consumption decreases, as future consumption has become cheaper relative to current consumption. The remaining effect, the movement from D to B, is a pure income effect, which causes both current-period and future-period consumption to increase (recall that we assumed that current and future consumption are normal goods). Therefore, future consumption must increase, as both the income and substitution effects work in the same direction. However, current-period consumption may increase or decrease, as the substitution effect causes current consumption to decrease, and the income effect causes it to increase. If the income effect is larger than the

FIGURE 8.12 An Increase in the Real Interest Rate for a Lender

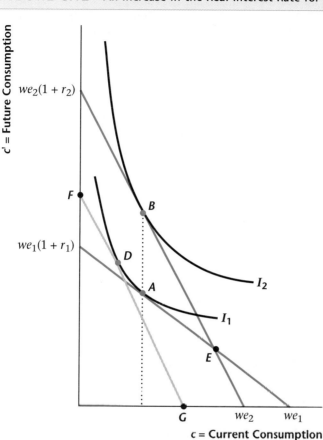

When the real interest rate increases for a lender, the substitution effect is the movement from A to D, and the income effect is the movement from D to B. Current consumption and saving may rise or fall, while future consumption increases.

substitution effect, then current consumption increases. The effect on savings depends on the change in current consumption, as we are holding constant current disposable income. Thus, saving may increase or decrease. Saving increases if the substitution effect is larger than the income effect, and saving decreases otherwise. An increase in the real interest rate makes saving more attractive, because the relative price of future consumption is lower (the substitution effect), but it makes saving less attractive as there is a positive income effect on period 1 consumption, which tends to reduce saving.

Consider the following example, which shows the intuition behind the income and substitution effects of a change in the real interest rate. Suppose Christine is currently a lender, whose disposable income in the current year is $40,000. She currently saves 30% of her current income, and she faces a real interest rate of 5%.

Her income next year will also be $40,000 (in current year dollars), and so initially she consumes $0.7 \times \$40,000 = \$28,000$ this year, and she consumes $\$40,000 + (1+0.05) \times \$12,000 = \$52,600$ next year. Now, suppose that the real interest rate rises to 10%. How should Christine respond? If she continues to consume $28,000 in the current year and saves $12,000, then she has future consumption of $53,200, an increase over initial future consumption, reflecting the substitution effect. However, if she consumes the same amount next year, she can now save less in the current year to achieve the same result. That is, she could save $11,454 in the current year, which would imply that she could consume $52,600 next year. Then, she consumes $\$40,000 - \$11,454 = \$28,546$, which is more than before, reflecting the income effect. What Christine does depends on her own preferences and how strong the relative income and substitution effects are for her as an individual.

Now, consider the effects of an increase in r for a borrower. In Figure 8.13, r increases from r_1 to r_2, and lifetime wealth changes from we_1 to we_2. The endowment point is at E, and the consumer initially chooses consumption bundle A; then, he or she chooses B after r increases. Again, we can separate the movement from A to B into substitution and income effects, by drawing an artificial budget constraint FG, which is parallel to the new budget constraint and tangent to the initial indifference curve I_1. Therefore, we are essentially compensating the consumer with extra wealth to make him or her as well off as initially when facing the higher interest rate. Then, the substitution effect is the movement from A to D, and the income effect is the movement from D to B. Here, the substitution effect is for future consumption to rise and current consumption to fall, just as was the case for a lender. However, the income effect in this case is negative for both current consumption and future consumption. As a result, current consumption falls for the borrower, but future consumption may rise or fall, depending on how strong the opposing substitution and income effects are. Savings must rise, as current consumption falls and current disposable income is held constant.

As an example, suppose that Christopher is initially a borrower, whose income in the current year and next year is $40,000 (in current year dollars). Initially, Christopher takes out a loan of $20,000 in the current year, so that he can consume $60,000 in the current year. The real interest rate is 5%, so that the principal and interest on his loan is $21,000, and he consumes $19,000 next year. Now, suppose alternatively that the real interest rate is 10%. If Christopher holds constant his consumption in the future, this must imply that his current consumption goes down, reflecting the negative income effect. That is, if he continues to consume $19,000 next year, given a real interest rate of 10%, he can borrow only $19,091 this year, which implies that his current year consumption is $59,091.

For both lenders and borrowers, there is an **intertemporal substitution effect** of an increase in the real interest rate. That is, a higher real interest rate lowers the relative price of future consumption in terms of current consumption, and this leads to a substitution of future consumption for current consumption and, therefore, to an increase in savings. In much of macroeconomics, we are interested in aggregate effects, but the above analysis tells us that there are potentially confounding income effects in

FIGURE 8.13 An Increase in the Real Interest Rate for a Borrower

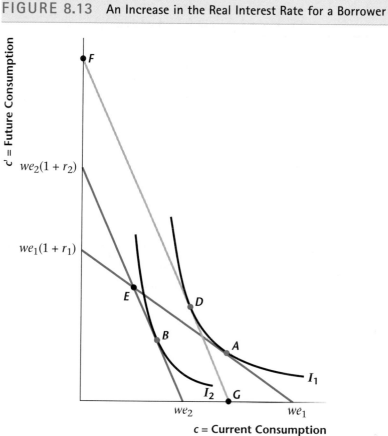

When the real interest rate increases for a borrower, the substitution effect is the movement from A to D, and the income effect is the movement from D to B. Current consumption decreases while saving increases, and future consumption may rise or fall.

determining the effect of an increase in the real interest rate on aggregate consumption. The population consists of many consumers, some of whom are lenders, and some of whom are borrowers. Though consumption decreases for each borrower when the real interest rate goes up, what happens to the consumption of lenders depends on the strength of opposing income and substitution effects. Though there is a tendency for the negative income effects on the consumption of borrowers to offset the positive income effects on the consumption of lenders, leaving us with only the substitution effects, there is no theoretical guarantee that aggregate consumption will fall when the real interest rate rises.

Tables 8.2 and 8.3 summarize our discussion of the effects of an increase in the real interest rate.

Table 8.2   **Effects of an Increase in the Real Interest Rate for a Lender**

Current Consumption	?
Future Consumption	Increases
Current Savings	?

Table 8.3   **Effects of an Increase in the Real Interest Rate for a Borrower**

Current Consumption	Decreases
Future Consumption	?
Current Savings	Increases

An Example: Perfect Complements   A convenient example to work with is the case in which a consumer has preferences with the perfect complements property. Recall from Chapter 4 that if two goods are perfect complements, they are always consumed in fixed proportions. In the case of current consumption and future consumption, the perfect complements property implies that the consumer always chooses c and c' such that

$$c' = ac, \tag{8.10}$$

where a is a positive constant. In Figure 8.14, the consumer's indifference curves, for example I_1 and I_2, are L-shaped with the right angles on the line $c' = ac$. Perfect complementarity is an extreme case of a desire for consumption smoothing, in that the consumer never wants to deviate from having current and future consumption in fixed proportions. The consumer's budget constraint is AB in the figure, which is described by the equation

$$c + \frac{c'}{1+r} = we, \tag{8.11}$$

where

$$we = y - t + \frac{y' - t'}{1+r}. \tag{8.12}$$

In Figure 8.14 the optimal consumption bundle is at a point such as D, which is on the consumer's budget constraint and on the line $c' = ac$. Therefore, we can solve algebraically for current and future consumption c and c', respectively, by solving the Equations (8.10) and (8.11) for the two variables c and c', given r and we. Using substitution, we get

$$c = \frac{we(1+r)}{1+r+a}, \tag{8.13}$$

$$c' = \frac{awe(1+r)}{1+r+a} \tag{8.14}$$

FIGURE 8.14   **Example with Perfect Complements Preferences**

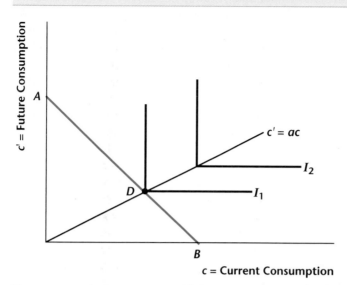

c = **Current Consumption**

The consumer desires current and future consumption in fixed proportions, with $c' = ac$. With indifference curves representing perfect complementarity between current and future consumption, the optimal consumption bundle is at point D on the lifetime budget constraint AB.

or substituting for *we* in (8.13) and (8.14) using (8.12), we obtain

$$c = \frac{(y - t)(1 + r) + y' - t'}{1 + r + a},\tag{8.15}$$

$$c' = a\left[\frac{(y - t)(1 + r) + y' - t'}{1 + r + a}\right].\tag{8.16}$$

From Equations (8.15) and (8.16) current and future consumption increase with current income *y* and with future income *y'*. The effects of a change in the interest rate *r* are more complicated, but essentially the effect of an increase in *r* on *c* and *c'* depends only on whether the consumer is a lender or a borrower. This is because there are no substitution effects when preferences have the perfect complements property. We explore this further in the problems at the end of this chapter.

The Demand for Current Consumption Goods   In later chapters, particularly Chapters 9–12, we work with models that are specified at the level of supply and demand curves. This is because it may sometimes be too complicated to be entirely explicit about consumers' preferences, particularly when we need to study the interaction among several markets in the economy. Thus, a less explicit but simpler approach is necessary.

One element of demand that is useful in later chapters is consumers' demand for current consumption goods. From the above analysis, we know that an individual's demand for current consumption goods increases with either current or future income. Further, if we assume that the intertemporal substitution effect of an increase in the real interest rate dominates the income effect when a consumer is a lender, then an increase in the real interest rate always causes the consumer's demand for current consumption goods to fall. Therefore, we can graph the demand for current consumption goods of an individual consumer, c^d, as a function of current income, as in Figure 8.15. Here, current income y is on the horizontal axis and current consumption c is on the vertical axis. The curve c^d in the figure is upward sloping. Further, because an increase in current income always produces a less than one-for-one increase in current consumption (given the consumption-smoothing motive, some of an increase in income is always saved), the slope of the c^d curve is less than 1, because this slope represents the increase in the consumer's current consumption that arises when current income increases by 1 unit. The slope of the c^d curve is defined to be the **marginal propensity to consume** or the *MPC*. We thus have $MPC < 1$. While we can say that the marginal propensity to consume must be less than 1, the *MPC* may vary with the level of income, depending on the consumer's preferences.

FIGURE 8.15   A Consumer's Demand for Current Consumption Goods,
c^d, as a Function of Current Income

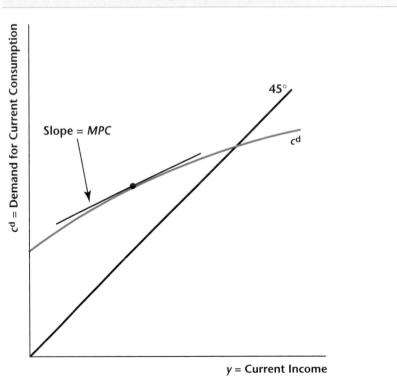

The slope of the c^d curve is the marginal propensity to consume, MPC, which is less than 1 for all y.

FIGURE 8.16 A Shift in a Consumer's Demand for Current Consumption

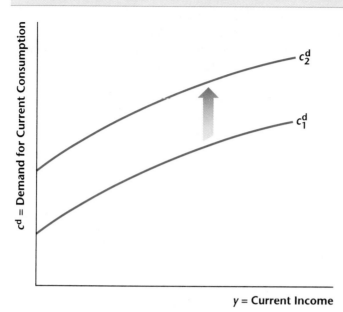

The c^d curve shifts up with a decrease in the real interest rate or an increase in future income.

The consumer's demand for consumption c^d shifts with either a change in the real interest rate or a change in the consumer's future income. Under the assumption that the intertemporal substitution effect of a change in the real interest rate always dominates the income effect, the c^d curve shifts up, as in Figure 8.16, if the real interest rate falls or if future income for the consumer increases.

Though we do not use the approach of Figures 8.15 and 8.16 in this chapter, it is applied in Chapters 9 and beyond.

Government

Now that we have studied how consumers behave, to complete our description of the model we need only describe what the government does. We can then explore the equilibrium effects of tax policy.

We suppose that the government wishes to purchase G consumption goods in the current period and G' units in the future period, with these quantities of government purchases given exogenously. The aggregate quantity of taxes collected by the government in the current period is T. Recall that there are N consumers who each pay a current tax of t, so that $T = Nt$. Similarly, in the future period total taxes are equal to T', and we have $T' = Nt'$. The government can borrow by issuing bonds. Recall that government bonds and private bonds are indistinguishable, with these bonds all bearing the same real interest rate r. Letting B denote the quantity of government bonds issued in the current period, the government's current-period budget constraint is

$$G = T + B; \tag{8.17}$$

that is, government spending is financed through taxes and the issue of bonds. Put another way, the current period government deficit, $G - T$, is financed by issuing bonds. In the future period, the government's budget constraint is

$$G' + (1 + r)B = T'. \tag{8.18}$$

The left-hand side of Equation (8.18) is total government outlays in the future, consisting of future government purchases and the principal and interest on the government bonds issued in the current period. These government outlays are financed through future taxes, the quantity on the right-hand side of Equation (8.18). The government's budget constraints allow for the possibility that $B < 0$. If $B < 0$ this would imply that the government was a lender to the private sector, rather than a borrower from it. In practice, the government engages in direct lending to the private sector, and it issues debt to private economic agents, so that it is a lender and a borrower.

Recall that, when we analyzed a consumer's budget constraint, we took the budget constraints for the current and future periods and collapsed them into a single lifetime budget constraint. Here, we can accomplish something similar, in taking the government's budget constraints expressed in Equations (8.17) and (8.18) and collapsing them into a single **government present-value budget constraint.** We obtain this constraint by first solving Equation (8.18) for B to get

$$B = \frac{T' - G'}{1 + r},$$

and then substituting in Equation (8.17) for B to get

$$G + \frac{G'}{1 + r} = T + \frac{T'}{1 + r}. \tag{8.19}$$

Equation (8.19) is the government present-value budget constraint, and it states that the present value of government purchases must equal the present value of taxes. This is similar to the consumer's lifetime budget constraint, which states that the present value of consumption is equal to the present value of lifetime disposable income. An interpretation of the government present-value budget constraint is that the government must eventually pay off all of its debt by taxing its citizens.

Competitive Equilibrium

Now that we have described the behavior of the consumers and the government in our model, we can proceed with the final step in putting the model into working order, which is to specify how a competitive equilibrium is achieved.

The market in which the N consumers in this economy and the government interact is the credit market, in which consumers and the government can borrow and lend. In trading in the credit market, consumers and the government are effectively trading future consumption goods for current consumption goods. Recall that the relative price at which future consumption goods trade for current consumption goods is $\frac{1}{1+r}$, which is determined by the real interest rate r.

In a competitive equilibrium for this two-period economy, three conditions must hold:

1. Each consumer chooses first- and second-period consumption and savings optimally given the real interest rate r.
2. The government present-value budget constraint, Equation (8.19), holds.
3. The credit market clears.

The credit market clears when the net quantity that consumers want to lend in the current period is equal to the quantity that the government wishes to borrow. Letting S^p denote the aggregate quantity of private savings—that is, the savings of consumers—the credit market equilibrium condition is

$$S^p = B, \tag{8.20}$$

or the aggregate quantity of private savings is equal to the quantity of debt issued by the government in the current period. Equation (8.20) also states that national saving, which is equal to aggregate private saving minus B, is equal to zero in equilibrium. Recall from Chapter 2 that a national income accounts identity states that $S^p + S^g = I + CA$, where S^g is government savings, I is investment, and CA is the current account surplus. Here, $S^g = -B$, $I = 0$ because there is no capital accumulation in this model, and $CA = 0$ because this is a closed economy model. Also recall that $S = S^p + S^g$, where S is national saving.

The equilibrium condition Equation (8.20) implies that

$$Y = C + G, \tag{8.21}$$

where Y is aggregate income in the current period (the sum of incomes across all N consumers) and C is aggregate consumption in the current period (the sum of consumptions across all N consumers). Recall from Chapter 2 that Equation (8.21) is the income–expenditure identity for this economy, because there is no investment, and no interaction with the rest of the world (net exports equal zero). To see why Equation (8.21) follows from Equation (8.20), note that

$$S^p = Y - C - T; \tag{8.22}$$

that is, aggregate private saving is equal to current period income minus aggregate current consumption minus aggregate current taxes. Also, from the government's current-period budget constraint, Equation (8.17), we have

$$B = G - T \tag{8.23}$$

Then, substituting in Equation (8.20) for S^p from Equation (8.22) and for B from Equation (8.23), we get

$$Y - C - T = G - T,$$

or, rearranging,

$$Y = C + G.$$

This result proves to be useful in the next section, as the economy can be shown to be in a competitive equilibrium if either Equation (8.20) or Equation (8.21) holds.

THE RICARDIAN EQUIVALENCE THEOREM

From Chapter 5, recall that an increase in government spending comes at a cost, in that it crowds out private consumption expenditures. However, in Chapter 5, we could not disentangle the effects of taxation from the effects of government spending, because the government was unable to borrow in the model considered there. That is certainly not true here, where we can independently evaluate the effects of changes in government spending and in taxes.

What we want to show here is a key result in macroeconomics, called the Ricardian equivalence theorem. This theorem states that a change in the timing of taxes by the government is neutral. By neutral, we mean that in equilibrium a change in current taxes, exactly offset in present-value terms by an equal and opposite change in future taxes, has no effect on the real interest rate or on the consumption of individual consumers. This is a very strong result, as it says that there is a sense in which government deficits do not matter, which seems to run counter to standard intuition. As we will see, however, this is an important starting point for thinking about why government deficits *do* matter, and a key message that comes from the logic of the Ricardian equivalence theorem is that *a tax cut is not a free lunch.*

DEFINITION

The Ricardian Equivalence Theorem: *If current and future government spending are held constant, then a change in current taxes with an equal and opposite change in the present value of future taxes leaves the equilibrium real interest rate and the consumptions of individuals unchanged.*

To show why the Ricardian equivalence theorem holds in this model, we need only make some straightforward observations about the lifetime budget constraints of consumers and the government's present-value budget constraint. First, because each of the N consumers shares an equal amount of the total tax burden in the current and future periods, with $T = Nt$ and $T' = Nt'$, substituting in the government's present-value budget constraint, Equation (8.19) gives

$$G + \frac{G'}{1+r} = Nt + \frac{Nt'}{1+r}, \tag{8.24}$$

and then rearranging we get

$$t + \frac{t'}{1+r} = \frac{1}{N}\left(G + \frac{G'}{1+r}\right), \tag{8.25}$$

which states that the present value of taxes for a single consumer is the consumer's share of the present value of government spending. Next, substitute for the present value of taxes from Equation (8.25) in a consumer's lifetime budget constraint, Equation (8.4) to get

$$c + \frac{c'}{1+r} = y + \frac{y'}{1+r} - \frac{1}{N}\left(G + \frac{G'}{1+r}\right). \tag{8.26}$$

Now, suppose that the economy is in equilibrium for a given real interest rate r. Each consumer chooses current consumption and future consumption c and c', respectively, to make himself or herself as well off as possible subject to the lifetime budget constraint, Equation (8.26), the present-value government budget constraint, Equation (8.19), holds, and the credit market clears, so current aggregate income is equal to current aggregate consumption plus current government spending, $Y = C + G$.

Next, consider an experiment in which the timing of taxes changes in such a way that the government budget constraint continues to hold at the interest rate r. That is, current taxes change by Δt for each consumer, with future taxes changing by $-\frac{\Delta t}{1+r}$ so that the government budget constraint continues to hold, from Equation (8.24). Then, from Equation (8.26) there is no change in the consumer's lifetime wealth, the right-hand side of Equation (8.26), given r, because y, y', N, G, and G' remain unaffected. Because the consumer's lifetime wealth is unaffected, then given r the consumer makes the same decisions, choosing the same quantities of current and future consumption. This is true for every consumer, so given r aggregate consumption C is the same. Thus, it is still the case that $Y = C + G$, so the credit market clears. Therefore, with the new timing of taxes and the same real interest rate, each consumer is optimizing, the government's present-value budget constraint holds, and the credit market clears, so r is still the equilibrium real interest rate.

Therefore, we have shown that a change in the timing of taxes has no effect on equilibrium consumption or the real interest rate. Because each consumer faces the same budget constraint before and after the change in the timing of taxes, all consumers are no better or worse off with the change in taxes. We have, thus, demonstrated that the Ricardian equivalence theorem holds in this model.

Though the timing of taxes has no effect on consumption, welfare, or the market real interest rate, there are effects on private saving and government saving. That is, because aggregate private saving is $S^P = Y - T - C$ and government saving is $S^g = T - G$, any change in the timing of taxes that increases current taxes T reduces current private saving and increases government saving by equal amounts. To give a more concrete example, suppose that there is a cut in current taxes, so that $\Delta t < 0$. Then, the government must issue more debt today to finance the tax cut, and it will have to increase taxes in the future to pay off this higher debt. Consumers anticipate this, and they increase their savings by the amount of the tax cut, because this is how much extra they have to save to pay the higher taxes they will face in the future. In the credit market, there is an increase in savings by consumers, which just matches the increase in borrowing by the government, so there is no effect on borrowing and lending among consumers, and therefore, no effect on the market real interest rate.

Ricardian Equivalence: A Numerical Example

To give a numerical example, assume an economy with 500 consumers who are all identical. Initially, the equilibrium real interest rate is 5%, and each consumer receives income of 10 units in the current period, and income of 12 units in the future period. In the current and future periods, each consumer initially pays taxes of 3 and 4 units, respectively. Lifetime wealth for each consumer is then

$$we = 10 - 3 + \frac{12 - 4}{1.05} = 14.61.$$

Suppose that each consumer initially finds it optimal to consume 6 units in the current period and 9.04 units in the future period. We can verify that this consumption bundle satisfies the consumer's lifetime budget constraint. That is,

$$6 + \frac{9.04}{1.05} = 14.61.$$

Then, each consumer saves $10 - 6 - 3 = 1$ in the current period, so that aggregate private saving is initially 500 units.

The government purchases 2,000 units in the current period and 1,475 units in the future period. Because aggregate taxes are 1,500 in the current period and 2,000 in the future period, the government borrows $B = 500$ in the current period. Thus, national saving is private saving plus government saving, or $500 - 500 = 0$. The government's present-value budget constraint is

$$2,000 + \frac{1,475}{1.05} = 1,500 + \frac{2,000}{1.05}.$$

Further, aggregate current income is 5,000, while aggregate current consumption is 3,000. This implies that $Y = C + G$, and so the credit market is in equilibrium.

Now, suppose that the government reduces taxes for each consumer in the current period to 2 units, and increases taxes for each consumer in the future period to 5.05 units. Suppose for now that the equilibrium real interest rate is unchanged at 5%. Then, the government's present-value budget constraint still holds, as

$$2,000 + \frac{1,475}{1.05} = 1,000 + \frac{2,525}{1.05}.$$

Further, lifetime wealth for each consumer is now

$$we = 10 - 2 + \frac{12 - 5.05}{1.05} = 14.61,$$

which is identical to lifetime wealth before the current tax cut, and so each consumer still wants to consume 6 units in the current period and 9.04 units in the future period. As a result, it must still be the case that $Y = C + G$, that is, the credit market clears. Therefore, 5% is still the equilibrium real interest rate, and each consumer's consumption decisions are unchanged.

Aggregate private saving has now increased by the amount of the tax cut, to 1,000, and government saving has decreased by the amount of the tax cut, to $-1,000$, with equilibrium national saving unchanged at 0.

Ricardian Equivalence: A Graph

We can show how the Ricardian equivalence theorem works by considering the effects of a current tax cut on an individual consumer. Here, the consumer also faces an increase in taxes in the future, as the government must pay off the current debt issued to finance the tax cut. Suppose that a consumer initially faces taxes t^* and t'^* in the current period

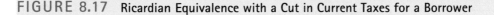

FIGURE 8.17   Ricardian Equivalence with a Cut in Current Taxes for a Borrower

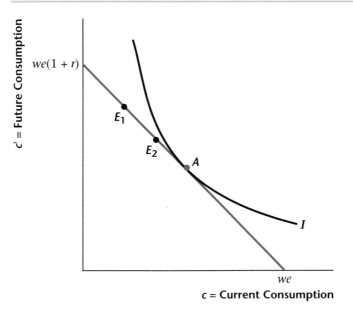

A current tax cut with a future increase in taxes leaves the consumer's lifetime budget constraint unchanged, and so the consumer's optimal consumption bundle remains at A. The endowment point shifts from E_1 to E_2, so that there is an increase in saving by the amount of the current tax cut.

and future period, respectively. In Figure 8.17 he or she has an endowment point E_1, and chooses consumption bundle A. Now, suppose there is a tax cut in the current period, so that $\Delta t < 0$. Therefore, the government must borrow $N\Delta t$ more in period 1 to finance the larger current government deficit, and taxes must rise for each consumer by $-\Delta t(1+r)$ in the future period to pay off the increased government debt. The effect of this on the consumer is that lifetime wealth we remains unchanged, as the present value of taxes has not changed. The budget constraint is unaffected, and the consumer still chooses point A in Figure 8.17. What changes is that the endowment point moves to E_2; that is, the consumer has more disposable income in the current period and less disposable income in the future period due to the tax cut in the current period. Because the consumer buys the same consumption bundle, what he or she does is to save all of the tax cut in the current period to pay the higher taxes that he or she faces in the future period.

Previously, when we looked at the effects of an increase in a consumer's current disposable income on current consumption, we determined that, because of the consumer's consumption-smoothing motive, some of the increase in disposable income would be saved. Thus, a temporary increase in disposable income would lead to a less than one-for-one increase in current consumption. In the real world, where individual consumption decisions are made over long horizons, any temporary increase in a consumer's disposable income should lead to a relatively small increase in his or her current income, in line with Friedman's permanent income hypothesis. Thus, Friedman's permanent income hypothesis would appear to imply that a temporary change in taxes leads to a very small change in current consumption. The Ricardian equivalence theorem carries this logic one step further by taking into account the implications of a current change in taxes for future taxes. For example, because any current tax cut must be paid for with government borrowing, this government borrowing implies higher future taxes to pay off the government debt. In making their lifetime wealth calculations, consumers recognize that the current tax cut is exactly offset by higher taxes in the future, and they save all of the current tax cut to pay the higher future taxes.

A key message from the Ricardian equivalence theorem is that a tax cut is not a free lunch. While a current tax cut can give all consumers higher current disposable incomes, and this seems like a good thing, consumers must pay for the current tax cut by bearing higher taxes in the future. Under the conditions studied in our model, the costs of a tax cut exactly offset the benefits, and consumers are no better off with the tax cut than without it.

Ricardian Equivalence and the Burden of the Government Debt

At the individual level, debt represents a liability that reduces an individual's lifetime wealth. The Ricardian equivalence theorem implies that the same logic holds for the government debt, which the theorem tells us represents our future tax liabilities as a nation. The government debt is a burden in that it is something we owe to ourselves; the government must pay off its debt by taxing us in the future. In the model in which we explained the Ricardian equivalence theorem above, the burden of the debt is shared equally among consumers. In practice, however, many issues in fiscal policy revolve around how the burden of the government debt is shared, among the current population and between generations. To discuss these issues, we need to address the role played by four key assumptions in our analysis of the Ricardian equivalence theorem.

1. The first key assumption is that when taxes change, in the experiment we considered above, they change by the same amount for all consumers, both in the present and in the future. For example, when a particular consumer received a tax cut in the current period, this was offset by an equal and opposite (in present-value terms) increase in taxes in the future, so that the present-value tax burden for each individual was unchanged. Now, if some consumers received higher tax cuts than others, then lifetime wealth could change for some consumers, and this would necessarily change their consumption choices and could change the equilibrium real interest rate. In the future, when the higher debt is paid off through higher future taxes, consumers might share unequally in this taxation, so that the burden of the debt might not be distributed equally. The government can redistribute wealth in society through tax policy, and the public debate concerning changes in taxes often focuses on how these tax changes affect consumers at different income levels.

2. A second key assumption in the model is that any debt issued by the government is paid off during the lifetimes of the people alive when the debt was issued. In practice, the government can postpone the taxes required to pay off the debt until long in the future, when the consumers who received the current benefits

of a higher government debt are either retired or dead. That is, if the government cuts taxes, then the current old receive higher disposable incomes, but it is the current young who will have to pay off the government debt in the future through higher taxes. In this sense, the government debt can be a burden on the young, and it can involve an intergenerational redistribution of wealth. In some instances, intergenerational wealth redistribution can improve matters for everyone, as with some social security programs. We explore this issue in the next subsection.

3. A third assumption made above was that taxes are lump sum. In practice, as mentioned in Chapter 4, all taxes cause distortions, in that they change the effective relative prices of goods faced by consumers in the market. These distortions represent welfare losses from taxation. That is, if the government collects $1 million in taxes, the welfare cost to the economy is something greater than $1 million, because of the distortions caused by taxation. The study of optimal taxation in public finance involves examining how large these welfare costs are for different kinds of taxes. For example, it could be that the welfare cost of income taxation at the margin is higher than the welfare cost of sales taxes at the margin. If the government taxes optimally, it minimizes the welfare cost of taxation, given the quantity of tax revenue it needs to generate. One of the trade-offs made by the government in setting taxes optimally is the trade-off between current taxation and future taxation. The government debt represents a burden, in that the future taxes required to pay off the debt will cause distortions. Some work on optimal taxation by Robert Barro,[3] among others, shows that the government should act to smooth tax rates over time, so as to achieve the optimal trade-off between current and future taxation.

4. A fourth key assumption made above is that there are **perfect credit markets,** in the sense that consumers can borrow and lend as much as they please, subject to their lifetime budget constraints, and they can borrow and lend at the same interest rate. In practice, consumers face constraints on how much they can borrow; for example, credit cards have borrowing limits, and sometimes consumers cannot borrow without collateral (as with mortgages and auto loans).[4] Consumers also typically borrow at higher interest rates than they can lend at. For example, the gap between the interest rate on a typical bank loan and the interest rate on a typical bank deposit can be 6 percentage points per annum or more. Further, the government borrows at lower interest rates than does the typical consumer. While all consumers need not be affected by **credit market imperfections,** to the extent that some consumers are credit-constrained, these credit-constrained consumers could be affected beneficially by a tax cut, even if there is an offsetting tax liability for these consumers in the future. In this sense, the government debt may not be a burden for some segments of the population; it may in fact increase welfare for these groups. We explore this idea further in the next subsection.

---

[3] See R. Barro, 1979, "On the Determination of the Public Debt," *Journal of Political Economy* 87, 940–971.

[4] Collateral is the security that a borrower puts up when the loan is made. If the borrower defaults on the loan, then the collateral is seized by the lender. With a mortgage loan, the collateral is the house purchased with the mortgage loan, and with an auto loan, the collateral is the car that was purchased.

The Ricardian equivalence theorem captures a key reality: current changes in taxes have consequences for future taxes. However, there are many complications associated with real-world tax policy that essentially involve shifts in the distribution of taxation across the population and in the distribution of the burden of the government debt. These complications are left out of our analysis of the Ricardian equivalence theorem. For some macroeconomic issues, the distributional effects of tax policy are irrelevant, but for other issues they matter a great deal. For example, if you were a macroeconomist working for a political party, how a particular tax policy affected the wealth of different consumers in different ways might be the key to your party's success, and you would want to pay close attention to this.

What Happens When Ricardian Equivalence Does Not Hold? Social Security and Credit Market Imperfections

We have just discussed how the Ricardian equivalence theorem would not hold if the tax burden were not shared equally among consumers, if there were intergenerational redistribution that resulted from a change in taxes, if there are tax distortions, or if there are credit market imperfections. The purpose of this section is to explore in more depth examples of the second and fourth cases. First, social security programs, if funded in particular ways, affect the distribution of the tax burden across generations, and we show how this occurs. Second, credit market imperfections imply that changes in the timing of taxes matter and can improve welfare for some consumers.

Social Security Programs   Social security programs are government-provided means for saving for retirement. There are essentially two types of programs: **pay-as-you-go** and **fully funded** social security, though in practice social security could be some mix of the two. With pay-as-you-go social security, the program simply involves transfers between the young and the old, while fully funded social security is a government-sponsored savings program where the savings of the young are used to purchase assets, and the old receive the payoffs on the assets that were acquired when they were young. We discuss the two types of social security program in turn.

Pay–As–You–Go Social Security   In the United States, social security operates as a pay-as-you-go system, in that taxes on the young are used to finance social security transfers to the old. While public discussion may make it appear that the system is in fact fully funded, as the difference between social security tax revenue and social security benefits is used to purchase interest-bearing federal government securities, this is merely an accounting convention and is unimportant for the economic consequences of U.S. social security.

To see the implications of pay-as-you-go social security for the distribution of wealth over time and across consumers, we assume for simplicity that social security has no effect on the market real interest rate r, which we suppose is constant for all time. Each consumer lives for two periods, youth and old age, and so in any period there is a young generation and an old generation alive. Let N denote the number of old consumers currently alive, and N' the number of young consumers currently alive.

Assume that

$$N' = (1+n)N, \tag{8.27}$$

so that the population is growing at the rate n, just as in the Solow growth model used in Chapters 6 and 7, though here people are finite-lived. A given consumer receives income y when young and income y' when old, and we allow (as we have throughout this chapter) for the fact that incomes can differ across consumers. For simplicity, assume that government spending is zero in all periods.

Now, suppose that no social security program exists before some date T, and that before date T the taxes on the young and old are zero in each period. Then, pay-as-you-go social security is established at date T and continues forever after. Here, for simplicity we suppose that the social security program guarantees each old-age consumer in periods T and later a benefit of b units of goods. Then, the tax for each old consumer in periods T and after is $t' = -b$. The benefits for old consumers must be financed by taxes on the young, and we assume that each young consumer is taxed an equal amount, t. Then, because total social security benefits equal total taxes on the young, we have

$$Nb = N't, \tag{8.28}$$

and so, using Equation (8.27) to substitute for N' in Equation (8.28), we can solve for t, obtaining

$$t = \frac{b}{1+n} \tag{8.29}$$

How do consumers benefit from social security? Clearly, the consumers who are old when the program is introduced in period T gain, as these consumers receive the social security benefit but do not have to suffer any increase in taxes when they are young. In Figure 8.18, the lifetime budget constraint of a consumer who is old in period T is AB if there is no social security program, where the slope of AB is $-(1+r)$ and the endowment point with no social security is E_1, determined by disposable income of y when young and y' when old. With the social security program, this consumer receives disposable income y when young and $y'+b$ when old and has an endowment point given by E_2 on the budget constraint DF (with slope $-(1+r)$) in the figure. The optimal consumption bundle shifts from H to J, and the consumer is clearly better off because his or her budget constraint has shifted out and he or she is able to choose a consumption bundle on a higher indifference curve.

What happens to consumers born in periods T and later? For these consumers, in Figure 8.19, the budget constraint would be AB without social security, with an endowment point at E_1 and the budget constraint having slope $-(1+r)$. With social security, disposable income when young is $y - t = y - \frac{b}{1+n}$ from Equation (8.29) and disposable income when old is $y'+b$, and the endowment point shifts to E_2 in the figure on the budget constraint DF. Because the market real interest rate has not changed, the slope of DF is $-(1+r)$. The slope of $E_1 E_2$ is $-(1+n)$, so in the figure we have shown the case where $n > r$. In this case, the budget constraint shifts out for this consumer, with the optimal consumption bundle shifting from H to J, and the consumer is better off. However, the budget constraint would shift in, and the consumer would be worse off if $n < r$.

FIGURE 8.18   Pay-As-You-Go Social Security for Consumers Who Are Old in Period T

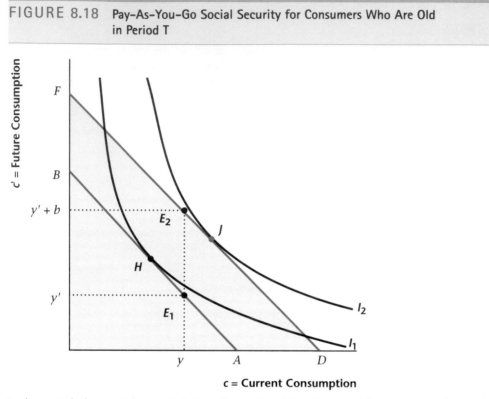

In the period when social security is introduced, the old receive a social security benefit. The budget constraint of an old consumer shifts from AB to DF, and he or she is clearly better off.

Therefore, social security makes everyone better off here only if the population growth rate is greater than the real interest rate. Otherwise, the old in the initial period are made better off at the expense of the current young and each future generation. The reason why social security can potentially improve welfare is that there is a kind of private market failure here that the government can exploit. That is, there is no way for people to trade with those who are not born yet, and the young and old alive in a given period cannot trade, as the young would like to exchange current consumption goods for future consumption goods, and the old would like to exchange current consumption goods for past consumption goods. The government is able to use its power to tax to bring about intergenerational transfers that may yield a Pareto improvement, whereby welfare increases for all consumers in the present and the future.

For pay-as-you-go social security to improve welfare for the consumers currently alive and those in future generations requires that the "rate of return" of the social security system be sufficiently high. This rate of return increases with the population growth rate n as the population growth rate determines how large a tax burden there is for the young generation in paying social security benefits to the old. The smaller

FIGURE 8.19   **Pay-As-You-Go Social Security for Consumers Born in Period T and Later**

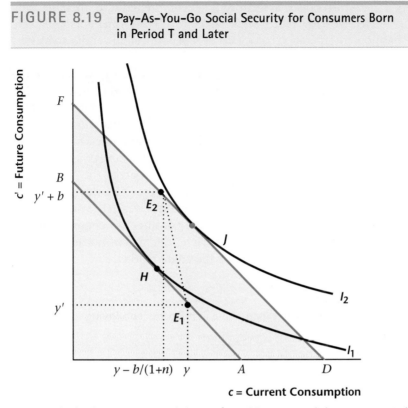

If $n > r$, the budget constraint shifts out from AB to DF, and the consumer is better off.

is this tax burden for each young person, the higher is the ratio of the social security benefit in old age to the tax paid to support social security when young, and this ratio is effectively the rate of return of the social security system. If n is larger than r, than the rate of return of the social security system is higher than the rate of return in the private credit market, and this is why social security increases welfare for everyone in this circumstance.

The issue of whether social security can bring about a Pareto improvement for consumers in all generations relates directly to contemporary issues facing the U.S. social security system. Currently, the social security taxes paid by the working population are more than sufficient to finance payments of social security benefits to the old. This will change, however, as the baby boom generation retires, roughly between 2010 and 2030. When this large cohort retires, if social security benefits are to remain at their current levels then this will require either a larger social security tax for the young or more immigration to increase the size of the working population that can pay the tax. Otherwise, benefits will have to be reduced. If we suppose that immigration will not change, then some group will have to lose. That is, if benefits remain at current levels, then the working population that pays the higher social security tax between 2010 and

2030 will receive a low return on social security. If benefits are reduced, then the baby boom generation will receive a low return on social security. The former is a more likely outcome, as the baby boom generation has a great deal of political power due to its size.

Fully Funded Social Security   To analyze fully funded social security, we can use the same apparatus as for the pay-as-you-go case. Again, suppose that government spending is zero forever, and in this case we assume for simplicity that taxes are zero as well.

In the absence of social security a consumer's lifetime budget constraint is given by AB in Figure 8.20, where the slope of AB is $-(1+r)$. The consumer's endowment is given by point E, and we suppose that this consumer optimizes by choosing point D, where saving is positive. Fully funded social security is a program whereby the government invests the proceeds from social security taxes in the private credit market, with social security benefits determined by the payoff the government receives in the private credit market. Alternatively, the government could allow the consumer to choose in which assets to invest his or her social security savings. Here, this makes no difference, as there is a single real rate of return, r, available on the credit market.

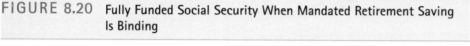

FIGURE 8.20   **Fully Funded Social Security When Mandated Retirement Saving Is Binding**

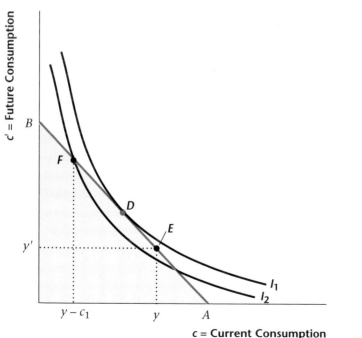

With binding mandated retirement saving, the consumer must choose point F rather than D and is, therefore, worse off.

In any event, fully funded social security is effectively a forced savings program, and it matters only if the amount of social security saving is a binding constraint on consumers. That is, fully funded social security makes a difference only if the social security system mandates a higher level of saving than the consumer would choose in the absence of the program. Such a case is illustrated in Figure 8.20, where the amount of social security saving required by the government is $y - c_1$, so that the consumer receives the consumption bundle F. Clearly, the consumer is worse off than he or she was at point D in the absence of the program. At best, fully funded social security is ineffective, if the amount of social security saving is not binding, or if consumers can undo forced savings by borrowing against their future social security benefits when young. If fully funded social security is a binding constraint on at least some people in the population, then it can only make things worse for optimizing consumers. Current proposals to "privatize" social security in the United States by allowing consumers to invest their social security savings in private assets are essentially proposals to move towards a fully funded rather than pay-as-you-go social security. Such proposals may in fact be welfare-improving for all generations, but this depends critically on how the transition to a fully funded social security system is financed by the federal government (see Macroeconomics in Action: Transitions From Pay-As-You-Go to Fully Funded Social Security).

MACROECONOMICS IN ACTION

Transitions From Pay-As-You-Go to Fully Funded Social Security

While the United States will not have to address the viability of its pay-as-you-go social security system until the baby boom generation begins to retire, European countries are already being forced to deal with the consequences for social security of an aging population. In some European countries, Germany and Italy for example, a transition from pay-as-you-go social security to some form of fully funded or partially funded social security is being considered. Research by Assaf Razin and Efraim Sadka analyzes some of the issues associated with such a transition.[1]

In our analysis of pay-as-you-go social security, we showed that the current young, the current old, and all future generations can benefit from such a social security program if the population growth rate exceeds the market real interest rate. However, in circumstances where there exists a very high ratio of current old to young, the current young would benefit from an immediate switch from pay-as-you-go to fully funded social security. The switch implies that the current young do not have to bear a high current tax in exchange for a standard-sized future retirement benefit. However, the transition from pay-as-you-go to fully funded would not be a Pareto improvement if the current old lost their retirement benefits (which they were expecting under the pay-as-you-go system that was in place when they were young).

(continued)

An alternative approach to a transition from pay-as-you-go to fully funded social security that could yield a Pareto improvement is to have the government issue debt to finance the payment of social security benefits to the current old. If the government issues debt in the present, this of course implies higher future taxes to pay off this debt. However, these higher future taxes will be paid by those who will benefit from the transition to a fully funded system. If the net benefits of the transition are positive, then the current young and future generations can be made better off as a result, and the current old are no worse off. Any Pareto-improving economic policy is something that the population as a whole will clearly vote for, so political economy arguments tell us that governments with a very old population should choose to abandon pay-as-you-go social security and run temporary deficits to finance benefits for the current old.

A problem with this scenario in Europe is that member countries of the European Monetary Union (EMU) have made commitments to keep their budget deficits within certain bounds. Under the Stability and Growth Pact, which came into effect in 1999 for all EMU countries, the government deficit of an EMU member cannot exceed 3% of GDP without penalties being imposed. Thus, in the case of a transition from pay-as-you-go to fully funded social security, the Stability and Growth Pact could block an economic policy that is Pareto improving. The framers of the Stability and Growth Pact clearly thought that the commitment outlined in the Pact was a good idea, as this would prevent some of the negative effects of large budget deficits. However, the Pact clearly did not account for the role of budget deficits in financing social security. As Razin and Sadka show, there are circumstances when a budget deficit can be a useful device in producing an intergenerational redistribution of wealth that makes an economic policy change (in this case a transition from pay-as-you-go to fully funded social security) produce positive benefits for everyone.

[1]A. Razin and E. Sadka, 2002. "The Stability and Growth Pact as an Impediment to Privatizing Social Security"

Credit Market Imperfections and Consumption   Here, we show how a consumer who is credit-constrained can be affected by a change in taxes that would not have any effect on the consumer's choices if there were perfect credit markets. Consider a consumer who lends at a real interest rate r_1 and borrows at a real interest rate r_2, where $r_2 > r_1$. This difference in borrowing and lending rates of interest arises in practice, for example, when borrowing and lending is carried out through banks, and it is costly for banks to sort credit risks. If the bank borrows from lenders (depositors in the bank) at the real interest rate r_1, and it makes loans at the real interest rate r_2, the difference $r_2 - r_1 > 0$ could arise in equilibrium to compensate the bank for the costs of making loans. The difference between borrowing and lending rates of interest leads to a more complicated lifetime budget constraint. As before, the current-period budget constraint of the consumer is given by Equation (8.1); but, the future-period budget constraint is

$$c' = y' - t' + s(1 + r_1),$$

if $s \geq 0$ (the consumer is a lender), and

$$c' = y' - t' + s(1 + r_2),$$

if $s \leq 0$ (the consumer is a borrower). Going through the same mechanics as before to derive the consumer's lifetime budget constraint, we obtain

$$c + \frac{c'}{1 + r_1} = y + \frac{y'}{1 + r_1} - t - \frac{t'}{1 + r_1} = we_1, \tag{8.30}$$

if $c \leq y - t$ (the consumer is a lender), and

$$c + \frac{c'}{1 + r_2} = y + \frac{y'}{1 + r_2} - t - \frac{t'}{1 + r_2} = we_2, \tag{8.31}$$

if $c \geq y - t$ (the consumer is a borrower).

We graph the consumer's budget constraint in Figure 8.21, where AB is given by Equation (8.30) and has slope $-(1 + r_1)$, and DF is given by Equation (8.31) and has slope $-(1 + r_2)$. The budget constraint is AEF, where E is the endowment point. Thus, the budget constraint has a kink at the endowment point, because the consumer lends at a lower interest rate than he or she can borrow at.

In a world where there are many different consumers, all having different indifference curves and different incomes, and where each consumer has a kinked budget

FIGURE 8.21   A Consumer Facing Different Lending and Borrowing Rates

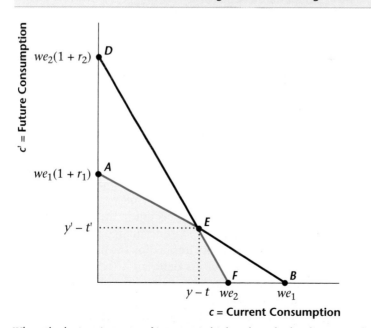

When the borrowing rate of interest is higher than the lending rate, there is a kinked budget constraint, AEF, with the kink at the endowment point E.

FIGURE 8.22   **Effects of a Tax Cut for a Consumer with Different Borrowing and Lending Rates**

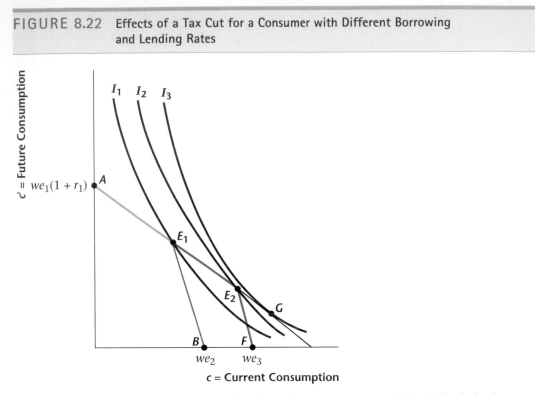

The consumer receives a current tax cut, with a future increase in taxes, and this shifts the budget constraint from AE_1B to AE_2F. The consumer's optimal consumption bundle shifts from E_1 to E_2, and the consumer consumes the entire tax cut.

constraint as in Figure 8.21, there is a significant number of consumers in the population whose optimal consumption bundle is the endowment point. For example, in Figure 8.22 the consumer faces budget constraint AE_1B, and the highest indifference curve on the budget constraint is reached at E_1, the endowment point. For this consumer, at the endowment point, the lending rate is too low to make lending worthwhile, and the borrowing rate is too high to make borrowing worthwhile.

Suppose in Figure 8.19 that the consumer receives a tax cut in the current period—that is, period 1 taxes change by $\Delta t < 0$, with a corresponding change of $-\Delta t(1+r_1)$ in future taxes. This is the consumer's future tax liability implied by the tax cut, assuming that the interest rate that the government pays on its debt is r_1, the lending rate of interest. Assume that interest rates do not change. The effect of the change in current and future taxes is to shift the endowment point to E_2, and given the way we have drawn the consumer's indifference curves, the consumer now chooses E_2 as his or her optimal consumption bundle on indifference curve I_2. Because he or she chooses the endowment point before and after the tax cut, period 1 consumption increases by the amount of the tax cut, $-\Delta t$. Contrast this with the Ricardian equivalence result where the consumer would save the entire tax cut and consumption would be unaffected.

The reason that the consumer's current consumption increases is that the government is effectively making a low interest loan available to him or her through the tax cut scheme. In Figure 8.22, the consumer would like to consume at point G if he or she could borrow at the interest rate r_1. Giving the consumer a tax cut of $-\Delta t$ with a corresponding future tax liability of $-\Delta t(1 + r_1)$ is just like having the government loan the consumer $-\Delta t$ at the interest rate r_1. Because the consumer would take such a loan willingly if it was offered, this tax cut makes the consumer better off.

Therefore, to the extent that credit market imperfections are important in practice, there can be beneficial effects of positive government debt. The government effectively acts like a bank that makes loans at below-market rates. If credit market imperfections matter significantly, then the people that are helped by current tax cuts are those who are affected most by credit market imperfections, and this might suggest to us that tax policy could be used in this way to increase general economic welfare. However, tax policy is quite a blunt instrument for relieving perceived problems due to credit market imperfections. A preferable policy might be to target particular groups of people—for example, small businesses, farmers, or homeowners—with direct government credit programs. In fact, there are many such programs in place in the United States, which are administered through government agencies such as the Small Business Administration. In considering government credit policies, though, careful evaluation needs to be done to determine whether direct lending by the government is a good idea in each particular circumstance. There may be good reasons for a particular private market credit imperfection. For example, real loan interest rates may be high in a particular segment of the credit market because the costs of screening and evaluating loans are very high, and the government would face the same high costs. This would then imply that the government has no special advantage in offering credit to these borrowers, and it would be inefficient for the government to get into the business of lending to them.

GEORGE H. W. BUSH AND THE WITHHOLDING REDUCTION

THEORY confronts the DATA

In his State of the Union Address on January 28, 1992, President George H. W. Bush made the following statement:

And I have, this evening, directed the Secretary of the Treasury to change the Federal tax withholding tables. With this change, millions of Americans from whom the Government withholds more than necessary can now choose to have the Government withhold less from their paychecks. Something tells me a number of taxpayers may take us up on this one. This initiative could return about $25 billion back into our economy over the next 12 months, money people can use to help pay for clothing, college, or to get a new car.[1]

[1]For the full text of President Bush's 1992 State of the Union Address, see http://www.thisnation.com/library/sotu/1992gb.html

The withholding change that President Bush referred to in his State of the Union Address was implemented immediately, as he stated, and continued for 10 months until the end of 1992. Each married person would have a reduction in tax withholding of $28.80 per month, while a single person would have a reduction of $14.40. Those in the highest tax bracket did not receive the benefit. The $25 billion effect appears to represent an estimate of the total withholding reduction for the U.S. population, based on a best guess as to the number of people affected for the 10 months of this program.

The withholding reduction comes as close as one might hope to a real-world Ricardian equivalence experiment. This is because the withholding reduction would not affect anyone's federal income taxes payable for 1992; the taxes were simply deferred until they were due in April 1993. Overlooking the relatively small amount of

FIGURE 8.23   **Real Consumption of Durables, 1991–1993**

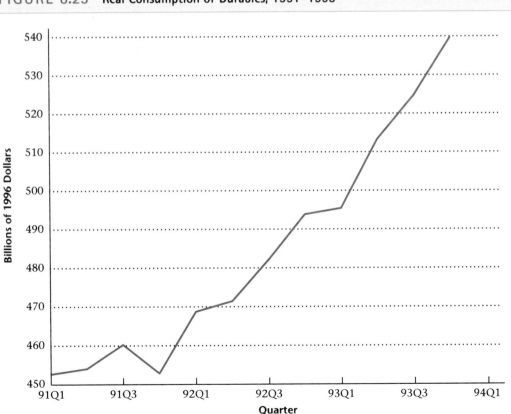

There appears to be no significant upward blip in durables consumption associated with the Bush withholding reduction.

Source: Bureau of Economic Analysis, Department of Commerce.

interest that consumers would earn on the withholding reduction until their taxes came due, lifetime wealth would be essentially unchanged for U.S. consumers. However, President Bush clearly did not put much stock in the Ricardian equivalence theorem, as he appeared convinced that the withholding reduction would increase private consumption expenditures. The Ricardian equivalence theorem predicts that U.S. taxpayers would essentially save the entire withholding reduction to pay their taxes in Spring 1993.

What is the evidence on the effects of the 1992 withholding reduction? In Figures 8.23 to 8.25, we show quarterly real consumption (billions of 1996 dollars, seasonally adjusted at annual rates) of durables, nondurables, and services, respectively, for the period 1991 to 1993. Suppose that we accept that disposable income increased by $25

FIGURE 8.24   Real Consumption of Nondurables, 1991–1993

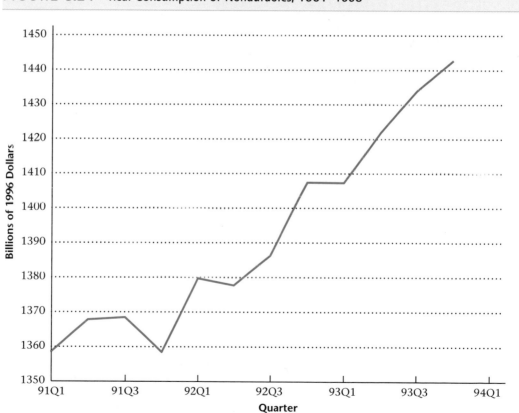

There appears to be no significant upward blip in nondurables consumption associated with the Bush withholding reduction.

Source: Bureau of Economic Analysis, Department of Commerce.

FIGURE 8.25 Real Consumption of Services, 1991–1993

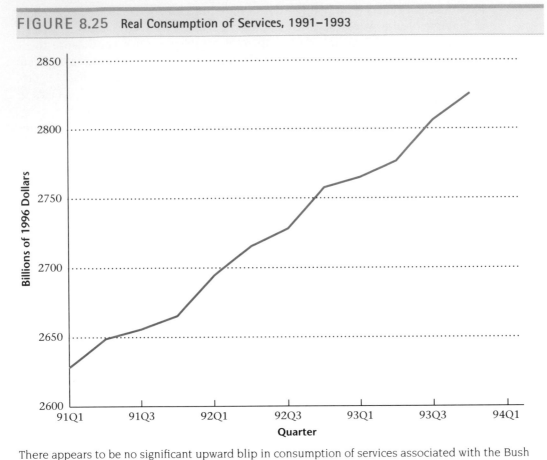

There appears to be no significant upward blip in consumption of services associated with the Bush withholding reduction.

Source: Bureau of Economic Analysis, Department of Commerce.

---

billion from first quarter 1992 to first quarter 1993, with a decrease of $25 billion in second quarter 1993 (when taxes are paid) as a result of the tax withholding experiment (this is the estimate by President Bush above). If all of the increase in income were spent on consumption goods in the period from 1992 first quarter to 1993 first quarter, with a corresponding reduction in consumption spending in 1993 second quarter, this would make a significant difference for consumption spending that we would see in Figures 8.23 to 8.25 as a sharp increase in some component(s) of consumer expenditure in the first quarter of 1992, with a sharp decrease or decreases in second quarter 1993. However, there appears to be no evidence of this in Figures 8.23 to 8.25. Instead, what we see is a more-or-less smooth recovery in the components of consumer spending from the 1991–92 recession. Thus, there was no apparent effect on aggregate consumption of the withholding reduction, in contrast to what President Bush expected. This evidence is consistent with the Ricardian equivalence theorem.

CHAPTER SUMMARY

- A two-period macroeconomic model was constructed to understand the intertemporal consumption-savings decisions of consumers and the effects of fiscal policy choices concerning the timing of taxes and the quantity of government debt.

- In the model, there are many consumers, and each makes decisions over a two-period horizon where a consumer's incomes in the two periods are given, and the consumer pays lump-sum taxes in each period to the government.

- The lifetime budget constraint of the consumer states that the present value of consumption over the consumer's two-period time horizon is equal to the present value of disposable income.

- A consumer's lifetime wealth is his or her present value of disposable income.

- A consumer's preferences have the property that more is preferred to less with regard to current and future consumption, there is a preference for diversity in current and future consumption, and current and future consumption are normal goods. A preference for diversity implies that consumers wish to smooth consumption relative to income over the present and the future.

- Consumption smoothing yields the result that, if income increases in the current period for a consumer, then current consumption increases, future consumption increases, and current saving increases. If future income increases, then consumption increases in both periods and current saving decreases. A permanent increase in income (when current and future income increase) has a larger impact on current consumption than does a temporary increase in income (only current income increases).

- If there is an increase in the real interest rate that a consumer faces, then there are income and substitution effects on consumption. Because an increase in the real interest rate causes a reduction in the price of future consumption in terms of current consumption, the substitution effect is for current consumption to fall, future consumption to rise, and current saving to rise when the real interest rate rises. For a lender (borrower), the income effect of an increase in the real interest rate is positive (negative) for both current and future consumption.

- The Ricardian equivalence theorem states that changes in current taxes by the government that leave the present value of taxes constant have no effect on consumers' consumption choices or on the equilibrium real interest rate. This is because consumers change savings by an amount equal and opposite to the change in current taxes to compensate for the change in future taxes.

- Ricardian equivalence depends critically on the notion that the burden of the government debt is shared equally among the people alive when the debt is issued. The burden of the debt is not shared equally when: (1) there are current distributional effects of changes in taxes; (2) there are intergenerational distribution effects; (3) taxes cause distortions; or (4) there are credit market imperfections.

- We explored the role of social security programs when Ricardian equivalence does not hold, and the effects of changes in taxes when there are credit market imperfections.

KEY TERMS

Intertemporal decisions: Decisions involving economic trade-offs across periods of time.

Consumption-savings decision: The decision by a consumer about how to split current income between current consumption and savings.

Ricardian equivalence theorem: Named for David Ricardo, this theorem states that changes in the stream of taxes faced by consumers that leave the present value of taxes unchanged have no effect on consumption, interest rates, or welfare.

Two-period model: An economic model where all decision makers (consumers and firms) have two-period planning horizons, with the two periods typically representing the present and the future.

Real interest rate: The rate of return on savings in units of consumption goods.

Consumption smoothing: The tendency of consumers to seek a consumption path over time that is smoother than income.

Lifetime budget constraint: Condition that the present value of a consumer's lifetime disposable income equals the present value of his or her lifetime consumption.

Present value: The value, in terms of money today or current goods, of a future stream of money or goods.

Lifetime wealth: The present value of lifetime disposable income for a consumer.

Endowment point: The point on a consumer's budget constraint where consumption is equal to disposable income in each period.

Excess variability: The observed fact that measured consumption is more variable than theory appears to predict.

Permanent income hypothesis: A theory developed by Milton Friedman that implies a consumer's current consumption depends on his or her permanent income. Permanent income is closely related to lifetime wealth in our model.

Martingale: An economic variable with the property that the best forecast of its value tomorrow is its value today. Finance theory implies that stock prices are martingales.

Intertemporal substitution effect: Substitution by a consumer of a good in one time period for a good in another time period, in response to a change in the relative price of the two goods. The intertemporal substitution effect of an increase in the real interest rate is for current consumption to fall and future consumption to rise.

Marginal propensity to consume (MPC): The increase in current consumption resulting from an increase of one unit in current income.

Government present-value budget constraint: Condition that the present value of government purchases is equal to the present value of tax revenues.

Perfect credit market: An idealized credit market in which consumers can borrow and lend all they want at the market interest rate, and the interest rate at which consumers lend is equal to the interest rate at which they borrow.

Credit market imperfections: Constraints on borrowing, or differences between borrowing and lending rates of interest.

Pay-as-you-go social security: A social security system where benefits to the old are financed by taxes on the working population.

Fully funded social security: A social security system where the social security payments of the working population are invested in assets, and the payoffs on these assets finance the social security benefits of those people in old age.

QUESTIONS FOR REVIEW

All questions refer to the macroeconomic model developed in this chapter.

1. Why do consumers save?
2. How do consumers save in the two-period model?

3. What factors are important to a consumer in making his or her consumption–savings decision?

4. What is the price of future consumption in terms of current consumption?

5. Show how to derive the consumer's lifetime budget constraint from the consumer's current-period and future-period budget constraints.

6. What is the slope of a consumer's lifetime budget constraint?

7. What are the horizontal and vertical intercepts of a consumer's lifetime budget constraint?

8. If a consumer chooses the endowment point, how much does he or she consume in each period, and how much does he or she save?

9. What are the three properties of a consumer's preferences?

10. How is the consumer's motive to smooth consumption captured by the shape of an indifference curve?

11. What are the effects of an increase in current income on consumption in each period, and on savings?

12. Give two reasons why consumption is more variable in the data than theory seems to predict.

13. What are the effects of an increase in future income on consumption in each period, and on savings?

14. What produces a larger increase in a consumer's current consumption, a permanent increase in the consumer's income or a temporary increase?

15. What does theory tell us about how the value of stocks held by consumers should be related to consumption behavior? Does the data support this?

16. What are the effects of an increase in the real interest rate on consumption in each period, and on savings? How does this depend on income and substitution effects and whether the consumer is a borrower or lender?

17. How does the government finance its purchases in the two-period model?

18. State the Ricardian equivalence theorem.

19. Give four reasons that the burden of the government debt is not shared equally in practice.

20. Under what conditions will a pay-as-you-go social security system improve welfare for those currently alive and for all future generations?

21. What are the effects of a fully funded social security system?

22. Does the existence of credit market imperfections imply that there is a useful role for government tax policy?

23. What does the Ricardian equivalence theorem tell us about the effects of the withholding reduction in 1992? What actually happened to aggregate consumption at that time?

PROBLEMS

1. A consumer's income in the current period is $y = 100$, and income in the future period is $y' = 120$. He or she pays lump-sum taxes $t = 20$ in the current period and $t' = 10$ in the future period. The real interest rate is 0.1, or 10%, per period.
   (a) Determine the consumer's lifetime wealth.
   (b) Suppose that current and future consumption are perfect complements for the consumer and that he or she always wants to have equal consumption in the current and future periods. Draw the consumer's indifference curves.

(c) Determine what the consumer's optimal current-period and future-period consumption are, and what optimal saving is, and show this in a diagram with the consumer's budget constraint and indifference curves. Is the consumer a lender or a borrower?

(d) Now suppose that instead of $y = 100$, the consumer has $y = 140$. Again, determine optimal consumption in the current and future periods and optimal saving, and show this in a diagram. Is the consumer a lender or a borrower?

(e) Explain the differences in your results between parts (c) and (d).

2. Suppose that a consumer's future income increases, and the real interest rate increases as well. In a diagram, determine how the consumer's optimal choice of current consumption and future consumption changes and how saving changes. Show how your results depend on income and substitution effects, and consider the case where the consumer is initially a lender and where he or she is initially a borrower.

3. An employer offers his or her employee the option of shifting x units of income from next year to this year. That is, the option is to reduce income next year by x units and increase income this year by x units.

(a) Would the employee take this option (use a diagram)?

(b) Determine, using a diagram, how this shift in income will affect consumption this year and next year and saving this year. Explain your results.

4. Consider the following effects of an increase in taxes for a consumer.

(a) The consumer's taxes increase by Δt in the current period. How does this affect current consumption, future consumption, and current saving?

(b) The consumer's taxes increase permanently, increasing by Δt in the current period and future period. Using a diagram, determine how this affects current consumption, future consumption, and current saving. Explain the differences between your results here and in part (a).

5. Suppose that the government introduces a tax on interest earnings. That is, borrowers face a real interest rate of r before and after the tax is introduced, but lenders receive an interest rate of $(1 - x)r$ on their savings, where x is the tax rate. Therefore, we are looking at the effects of having x increase from zero to some value greater than zero, with r assumed to remain constant.

(a) Show the effects of the increase in the tax rate on a consumer's lifetime budget constraint.

(b) How does the increase in the tax rate affect the optimal choice of consumption (in the current and future periods) and saving for the consumer? Show how income and substitution effects matter for your answer, and show how it matters whether the consumer is initially a borrower or a lender.

6. A consumer receives income y in the current period, income y' in the future period, and pays taxes of t and t' in the current and future periods, respectively. The consumer can borrow and lend at the real interest rate r. This consumer faces a constraint on how much he or she can borrow, much like the credit limit typically placed on a credit card account. That is, the consumer cannot borrow more than x, where $x < we - y + t$, with we denoting lifetime wealth. Use diagrams to determine the effects on the consumer's current consumption, future consumption, and savings of a change in x, and explain your results.

7. A consumer receives income y in the current period, income y' in the future period, and pays taxes of t and t' in the current and future periods, respectively. The consumer can lend at the real interest rate r_1. The consumer is given two options. First, he or she can borrow at the interest rate r_1 but can only borrow an amount x or less, where $x < we - y + t$. Second, he or she can borrow an unlimited amount at the interest rate r_2, where $r_2 > r_1$.

Use a diagram to determine which option the consumer chooses, and explain your results.

8. Assume a consumer who has current-period income $y = 200$, future-period income $y' = 150$, current and future taxes $t = 40$ and $t' = 50$, respectively, and faces a market real interest rate of $r = 0.05$, or 5% per period. The consumer would like to consume equal amounts in both periods; that is, he or she would like to set $c_1 = c_2$, if possible. However, this consumer is faced with a credit market imperfection, in that he or she cannot borrow at all, that is, $s = 0$.
   (a) Show the consumer's lifetime budget constraint and indifference curves in a diagram.
   (b) Calculate his or her optimal current-period and future-period consumption and optimal saving, and show this in your diagram.
   (c) Suppose that everything remains unchanged, except that now $t = 20$ and $t' = 71$. Calculate the effects on current and future consumption and optimal saving, and show this in your diagram.
   (d) Now, suppose alternatively that $y = 100$. Repeat parts (a) to (c), and explain any differences.

9. Assume an economy with 1,000 consumers. Each consumer has income in the current period of 50 units and future income of 60 units and pays a lump-sum tax of 10 in the current period and 20 in the future period. The market real interest rate is 8%. Of the 1,000 consumers, 500 consume 60 units in the future, while 500 consume 20 units in the future.
   (a) Determine each consumer's current consumption and current saving.
   (b) Determine aggregate private saving, aggregate consumption in each period, government spending in the current and future periods, the current-period government deficit, and the quantity of debt issued by the government in the current period.
   (c) Suppose that current taxes increase to 15 for each consumer. Repeat parts (a) and (b) and explain your results.

10. Use the social security model developed in this chapter to answer this question. Suppose that the government establishes a social security program in period T, which provides a social security benefit of b (in terms of consumption goods) for each old person forever. In period T, the government finances the benefits to the current old by issuing debt. This debt is then paid off in period $T + 1$ through lump-sum taxes on the young. In periods $T + 1$ and later, lump-sum taxes on the young finance social security payments to the old.
   (a) Show using diagrams that the young and old alive at time T all benefit from the social security program under any circumstances.
   (b) What is the effect of the social security program on consumers born in periods $T + 1$ and later? How does this depend on the real interest rate and the population growth rate?

11. Suppose in our two-period model of the economy that the government, instead of borrowing in the current period, runs a government loan program. That is, loans are made to consumers at the market real interest rate r, with the aggregate quantity of loans made in the current period denoted by L. Government loans are financed by lump-sum taxes on consumers in the current period, and we assume that government spending is zero in the current and future periods. In the future period, when the government loans are repaid by consumers, the government rebates this amount as lump-sum transfers (negative taxes) to consumers.
   (a) Write down the government's current-period budget constraint and its future-period budget constraint.
   (b) Determine the present-value budget constraint of the government.
   (c) Write down the lifetime budget constraint of a consumer.

(d) Show that the size of the government loan program (i.e., the quantity L) has no effect on current consumption or future consumption for each individual consumer and that there is no effect on the equilibrium real interest rate. Explain this result.

WORKING WITH THE DATA

1. Calculate and plot the ratio of aggregate consumption to GDP, and plot this data as a time series. Comment on the features of your time series plot. What principle of consumption behavior helps to explain what you see?

2. Calculate the value of real total government receipts by dividing current dollar total receipts by the implicit GDP price deflator. Then, calculate the quarterly percentage change in total government receipts and the quarterly percentage change in real GDP, starting in 1947, until 2003.
   (a) In a scatter plot, show the percentage change in real total government receipts against the quarterly percentage change in real GDP.
   (b) What do you see in the scatter plot in part (a)? Is there a positive or negative correlation between the two time series?
   (c) Is this data consistent with the Ricardian equivalence theorem? Why or why not?

3. Calculate the relative price of housing as the new housing price index divided by the implicit GDP deflator. Then, calculate quarterly percentage increases in the relative price of housing, and plot this against the quarterly percentage increase in real spending on consumer nondurables and services.
   (a) Do you notice a positive or negative correlation in the scatter plot?
   (b) How is your observation in part (a) consistent or not consistent with the theory of consumption behavior in this chapter? Explain.

CHAPTER 9

A Real Intertemporal Model with Investment

This chapter brings together the microeconomic behavior we have studied in previous chapters, to build a model that can serve as a basis for analyzing how macroeconomic shocks affect the economy, and that can be used for evaluating the role of macroeconomic policy. With regard to consumer behavior, we have examined work-leisure choices in Chapter 4 and intertemporal consumption–savings choices in Chapter 8. From the production side, in Chapter 4 we studied a firm's production technology and its labor demand decision, and then in Chapter 5 we showed how changes in total factor productivity affect consumption, employment, and output in the economy as a whole. In Chapter 8, we looked at the effects of choices by the government concerning the financing of government expenditure and the timing of taxes. While the Solow growth model studied in Chapters 6 and 7 included savings and investment, in this chapter we examine in detail how investment decisions are made at the the level of the firm.

In this chapter we complete a model of the real side of the economy. That is, the real intertemporal model we construct here shows how real aggregate output, real consumption, real investment, employment, the real wage, and the real interest rate are determined in the macroeconomy. To predict nominal variables, we need to add money to the real intertemporal model, which is done in Chapter 10. The intertemporal aspect of the model refers to the fact that both consumers and firms make intertemporal decisions, reflecting trade-offs between the present and the future.

Recall from Chapter 2 that the defining characteristic of investment—expenditure on plants, equipment, and housing—is that it consists of the goods that are produced currently for future use in the production of goods and services. For the economy as a whole, investment represents a trade-off between present and future consumption. Productive capacity that is used for producing investment goods could otherwise be used for producing current consumption goods, but today's investment increases future productive capacity, which means that more consumption goods can be produced in the future. To understand the determinants of investment, we must study the microeconomic investment behavior of a firm, which makes an intertemporal decision regarding investment in the current period. When a firm invests, it forgoes current profits so as to have a higher capital stock in the future, which allows it to earn higher future profits. As we show, a firm invests more the lower its current capital stock, the higher its expected future total factor productivity, and the lower the real interest rate.

A key determinant of investment is the real interest rate, which represents the opportunity cost of investment. A higher real interest rate implies that the opportunity cost of investment is larger, at the margin, and so investment falls. Movements in the real interest rate are an important channel by which shocks to the economy affect investment, as we show in this chapter. Further, monetary policy may affect investment through its influence on the real interest rate, as we show in Chapters 10 to 12.

A good part of this chapter involves model building, and there are several important steps we must take before we can use this model to address some important economic issues. This requires some patience and work, but the payoff arrives in the last part of this chapter and continues through the remainder of this book, where this model is the basis for our study of monetary factors in Chapter 10, business cycles in Chapters 11 and 12, and for other issues in later chapters.

This chapter focuses on the macroeconomic effects on aggregate output, investment, consumption, the real interest rate, and labor market variables of aggregate shocks to government spending, total factor productivity, and the nation's capital stock. While we have studied elements of these effects in Chapters 5 and 8, there are new insights in this chapter involving the effects on the interest rate and investment of these shocks, and the effects of permanent versus temporary shocks. For example, we see that the effects of permanent changes in government spending can be quite different from those of temporary changes, and that shocks to the economy that are expected in the future can have important implications for how the economy performs in the present.

As in Chapters 4 and 5, we work with a model that has a representative consumer, a representative firm, and a government, and, for simplicity, ultimately we specify this model at the level of supply and demand curves. We are able to capture the essential behavior in this model economy by examining the participation of the representative consumer, the representative firm, and the government in two markets: the market for labor in the current period, and the market for goods in the current period. The representative consumer supplies labor in the current labor market and purchases consumption goods in the current goods market, while the representative firm demands labor in the current labor market, supplies goods in the current goods market, and demands investment goods in the current goods market. The government demands goods in the current goods market in terms of government purchases.

THE REPRESENTATIVE CONSUMER

The behavior of the representative consumer in this model brings together the work–leisure choice from Chapter 4 with the intertemporal consumption behavior from Chapter 6. That is, the consumer makes a work–leisure decision in each of the current and future periods, and he or she makes a consumption–savings decision in the current period.

The representative consumer works and consumes in the current period and the future period. He or she has h units of time in each period and divides this time between work and leisure in each period. Let w denote the real wage in the current period, w' the real wage in the future period, and r the real interest rate. The consumer pays lump-sum taxes to the government of T in the current period and T' in the future period. His or her goal is to choose current consumption C, future consumption C', leisure time in the current and future periods, l and l', respectively, and savings in the current period, S^p, to make himself of herself as well off as possible, given his or her budget constraints in the current and future periods. The representative consumer is a price-taker who takes w, w', and r as given. Taxes are also given from the consumer's point of view.

In the current period, the representative consumer earns real wage income $w(h-l)$, receives dividend income π from the representative firm, and pays taxes T, so that his or her current-period disposable income is $w(h-l) + \pi - T$, just as in Chapter 4. As in Chapter 8, disposable income in the current period is then split between consumption and savings, and savings takes the form of bonds that earn the one-period real interest rate r. Just as in Chapter 8, savings can be negative, in which case the consumer borrows by issuing bonds. The consumer's current budget constraint is then

$$C + S^p = w(h-l) + \pi - T. \tag{9.1}$$

In the future period, the representative consumer receives real wage income $w'(h-l')$, receives real dividend income π' from the representative firm, pays taxes T' to the government, and receives the principal and interest on savings from the current period, $(1+r)S^p$. Because the future period is the last period and because the consumer is assumed to make no bequests, all wealth available to the consumer in the future is consumed, so that the consumer's future budget constraint is

$$C' = w'(h-l') + \pi' - T' + (1+r)S^p. \tag{9.2}$$

Just as in Chapter 8, we can substitute for savings S^p in Equation (9.1) using Equation (9.2) to obtain a lifetime budget constraint for the representative consumer:

$$C + \frac{C'}{1+r} = w(h-l) + \pi - T + \frac{w'(h-l') + \pi' - T'}{1+r}. \tag{9.3}$$

This constraint states that the present value of consumption (on the left-hand side of the equation) equals the present value of lifetime disposable income (on the right-hand side of the equation). A difference from the consumer's lifetime budget constraint in Chapter 8 is that the consumer in this model has some choice, through his or her current and future choices of leisure, l and l', over his or her lifetime wealth.

The representative consumer's problem is to choose C, C', l, and l' to make himself or herself as well off as possible while respecting his or her lifetime budget constraint, as given by Equation (9.3). We cannot depict this choice for the consumer conveniently in a graph, as the problem is four-dimensional (choosing current and future consumption and current and future leisure), while a graph is two-dimensional. It is straightforward, however, to describe the consumer's optimizing decision in terms of three marginal conditions we have looked at in Chapters 4 and 8. These are as follows:

1. The consumer makes a work-leisure decision in the current period, so that when he or she optimizes, we have

$$MRS_{l,C} = w; \tag{9.4}$$

that is, the consumer optimizes by choosing current leisure and consumption so that the marginal rate of substitution of leisure for consumption is equal to the real wage in the current period. This is the same marginal condition as in the work-leisure problem for a consumer that we considered in Chapter 4. Recall that, in general, a consumer optimizes by setting the marginal rate of substitution of one good for another equal to the relative price of the two goods. In Equation (9.4), the current real wage w is the relative price of leisure in terms of consumption goods.

2. Similarly, in the future the consumer makes another work-leisure decision, and he or she optimizes by setting

$$MRS_{l',C'} = w';\qquad(9.5)$$

that is, at the optimum, the marginal rate of substitution of future leisure for future consumption must be equal to the future real wage.

3. With respect to his or her consumption–savings decision in the current period, as in Chapter 8, the consumer optimizes by setting

$$MRS_{C,C'} = 1 + r;\qquad(9.6)$$

that is, the marginal rate of substitution of current consumption for future consumption equals the relative price of current consumption in terms of future consumption.

Current Labor Supply

Our ultimate focus is on interaction between the representative consumer and the representative firm in the markets for current labor and current consumption goods, and so we are interested in the determinants of the representative consumer's supply of labor and his or her demand for current consumption goods.

First, we consider the representative consumer's current supply of labor, which is determined by three factors—the current real wage, the real interest rate, and lifetime wealth. These three factors affect current labor supply as listed below.

1. *Current labor supply increases when the current real wage increases.* The consumer's marginal condition (9.4) captures the idea that substitution between current leisure and current consumption is governed by the current real wage rate w. Recall from Chapter 4 that a change in the real wage has opposing income and substitution effects on the quantity of leisure, so that an increase in the real wage could lead to an increase or a decrease in the quantity of leisure, depending on the size of the income effect. Here, we assume that the substitution effect of a change in the real wage is always larger than the income effect, implying that leisure decreases and hours worked increases in response to an increase in the real wage. This might seem inconsistent with the fact, pointed out in Chapter 4, that over the long run, income and substitution effects on labor supply appear to cancel. However, the model we are building here is intended mainly for analyzing short-run phenomena. As we argued in Chapter 4, the canceling of income and substitution effects in the long run can be consistent with the substitution effect dominating in the short run, as we assume here.

2. *Current labor supply increases when the real interest rate increases.* The consumer can substitute intertemporally not only by substituting current consumption for future consumption, as we studied in Chapter 8, but by substituting current leisure for future leisure. In substituting leisure between the two periods, the representative

consumer responds to the current price of leisure relative to the future price of leisure, which is $\frac{w(1+r)}{w'}$. Here, w is the price of current leisure (labor) in terms of current consumption, w' is the price of future leisure in terms of future consumption, and $1+r$ is the price of current consumption in terms of future consumption. Therefore, an increase in the real interest rate r, given w and w', results in an increase in the price of current leisure relative to future leisure. Assuming again that the substitution effect is larger than the income effect, the consumer wants to consume less current leisure and more future leisure. An example of how this **intertemporal substitution of leisure** effect works is as follows. Suppose that Paul is self-employed and that the market interest rate rises. Then, Paul faces a higher return on his savings, so that if he works more in the current period and saves the proceeds, in the future he can both consume more and work less. It may be helpful to consider that leisure, like consumption, is a good. When the real interest rate increases, and substitution effects dominate income effects for lenders, current consumption falls (from Chapter 6), just as current leisure decreases when the real interest rate increases and substitution effects dominate.

3. *Current labor supply decreases when lifetime wealth increases.* From Chapter 4, we know that an increase in current nonwage disposable income results in an increase in the quantity of leisure and a decrease in labor supply for the consumer, as leisure is a normal good. Further, in Chapter 8, we showed how income effects generalize to the intertemporal case where the consumer chooses current and future consumption. That is, an increase in lifetime wealth increases the quantities of current and future consumption chosen by the consumer. Here, when there is an increase in lifetime wealth, there is an increase in current leisure and, thus, a decrease in current labor supply, because current leisure is assumed to be normal. The key wealth effect for our analysis in this chapter is the effect of a change in the present value of taxes for the consumer. Any increase in the present value of taxes implies a decrease in lifetime wealth and an increase in current labor supply.

Given these three factors, we can construct an upward-sloping current labor supply curve as in Figure 9.1. Here, the current real wage w is measured along the vertical axis, and current labor supply N is on the horizontal axis. The current labor supply curve is labeled $N^s(r)$ to indicate that labor supply depends on the current real interest rate. If the real interest rate rises, say from r_1 to r_2, then the labor supply curve shifts to the right, as in Figure 9.2, because labor supply increases for any current real wage w. In Figure 9.3, an increase in lifetime wealth shifts the labor supply curve to the left from $N_1^s(r)$ to $N_2^s(r)$. Such an increase in lifetime wealth could be caused by a decrease in the present value of taxes for the consumer. In Figure 9.3 the real interest rate is held constant as we shift the current labor supply curve to the left.

The Current Demand for Consumption Goods

Now that we have dealt with the determinants of the representative consumer's current labor supply, we can turn to his or her demand for current consumption goods. The determinants of the demand for current consumption goods were studied in Chapter 8, where we showed that the primary factors affecting current consumption are lifetime

FIGURE 9.1 The Representative Consumer's Current Labor Supply Curve

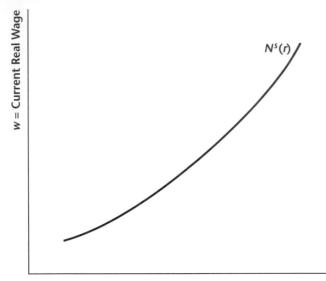

w = Current Real Wage

$N^s(r)$

N = Current Labor Supply

The current labor supply curve slopes upward, under the assumption that the substitution effect of an increase in the real wage outweighs the income effect.

wealth and the real interest rate. Further, lifetime wealth is affected by current income, by future income, and by the present value of taxes.

As in Chapter 8, we can construct a demand curve for current consumption by the representative consumer, as a function of current aggregate income Y, as shown in Figure 9.4. In the figure, the demand for consumption goods is on the vertical axis and aggregate income is on the horizontal axis. We let $C^d(r)$ denote the demand curve for current consumption goods, indicating the dependence of the demand for consumption on the real interest rate. Recall from Chapter 8 that the slope of the curve $C^d(r)$ in the figure is the *MPC* or marginal propensity to consume, which is the amount that current consumption increases when there is a unit increase in aggregate real income Y.

When there is an increase in the real interest rate, assuming again that the substitution effect of this increase dominates the income effect, there is a decrease in the demand for current consumption goods due to the intertemporal substitution of consumption. In Figure 9.5, if the real interest rate increases from r_1 to r_2, then the demand curve for current consumption shifts down from $C^d(r_1)$ to $C^d(r_2)$. Also, holding constant r and Y, if there is an increase in lifetime wealth then, as in Figure 9.6, the demand curve for current consumption shifts up from $C_1^d(r)$ to $C_2^d(r)$. Such an increase in lifetime wealth could be caused by a decrease in the present value of taxes for the consumer or by an increase in future income.

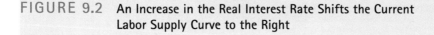

FIGURE 9.2 **An Increase in the Real Interest Rate Shifts the Current Labor Supply Curve to the Right**

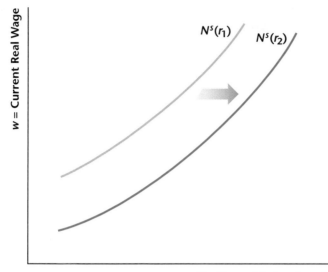

This is because the representative consumer consumes less leisure in the current period and more leisure in the future when r increases.

THE REPRESENTATIVE FIRM

Now that we have covered the important features of the consumer's current labor supply and current consumption demand decisions, we can turn to the key decisions of the representative firm for the current labor market and the current goods market.

The representative firm, as in Chapter 4, produces goods using inputs of labor and capital. The key differences here are that output is produced in both the current and future periods, and that the firm can invest in the current period by accumulating capital so as to expand future production capacity and, thus, produce more future output. In the current period, the representative firm produces output according to the production function

$$Y = zF(K, N), \tag{9.7}$$

where Y is current output, z is total factor productivity, F is the production function, K is current capital, and N is current labor input. Here, K is the capital with which the firm starts the current period, and this quantity is given. The production function F is identical in all respects to the production function we studied in Chapter 4.

Similarly, in the future period, output is produced according to

$$Y' = z'F(K', N'), \tag{9.8}$$

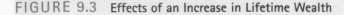

FIGURE 9.3   Effects of an Increase in Lifetime Wealth

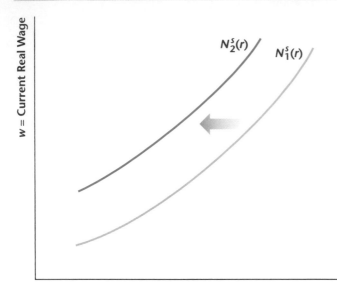

N = Current Labor Supply

More leisure is consumed in the present, due to an income effect, and the current labor supply curve shifts to the left.

where Y' is future output, z' is future total factor productivity, K' is the future capital stock, and N' is the future labor input.

Recall from Chapter 2 that investment, as measured in the NIPA, is expenditure on plant, equipment, housing, and inventory accumulation. Here, we model investment goods as being produced from output. That is, for simplicity we assume that it requires one unit of consumption goods in the current period to produce one unit of capital. The representative firm invests by acquiring capital in the current period, and the essence of investment is that something must be forgone in the current period to gain something in the future. What is forgone by the firm when it invests is current profits; that is, the firm uses some of the current output it produces to invest in capital, which becomes productive in the future. As in the Solow growth model introduced in Chapter 6, capital depreciates at the rate d when used. Letting I denote the quantity of current investment, the future capital stock is given by

$$K' = (1 - d)K + I. \tag{9.9}$$

That is, the future capital stock is the current capital stock net of depreciation plus the quantity of current investment that has been added in the current period. Further, the quantity of capital left at the end of the future period is $(1 - d)K'$. Because the future period is the last period, it would not be useful for the representative firm to retain this quantity of capital, and so the firm liquidates it. We suppose that the firm can take

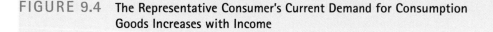

FIGURE 9.4   **The Representative Consumer's Current Demand for Consumption Goods Increases with Income**

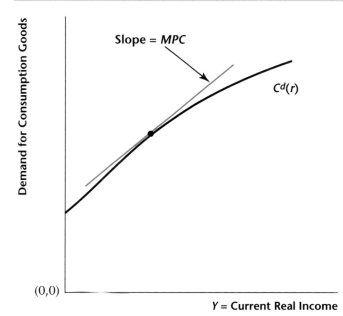

The slope of the demand curve for current consumption is the marginal propensity to consume, MPC. We have MPC < 1, because part of an increase in current income is saved.

the quantity $(1 - d)K'$, the capital left at the end of the future period, and convert it one-for-one back into consumption goods, which it can then sell. This is a simple way to model a firm's ability to sell off capital for what it can fetch on the secondhand market. For example, a restaurant that goes out of business can sell its used tables, chairs, and kitchen equipment secondhand in a liquidation sale.

Profits and Current Labor Demand

Now that we know how the firm produces output in the present and the future and how investment can take place, we are ready to determine present and future profits for the firm. The goal of the firm is to maximize the present value of profits over the current and future periods, and this allows us to determine the firm's demand for current labor, as well as the firm's quantity of investment, which we discuss in the next subsection. For the representative firm, current profits in units of the current consumption good are

$$\pi = Y - wN - I, \tag{9.10}$$

which is current output (or revenue) Y minus wages paid to workers in the current period minus current investment. The firm can produce one unit of capital using one unit of output, so that each unit of investment decreases current profits by one unit.

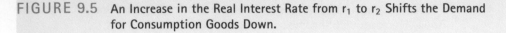

FIGURE 9.5   **An Increase in the Real Interest Rate from r_1 to r_2 Shifts the Demand for Consumption Goods Down.**

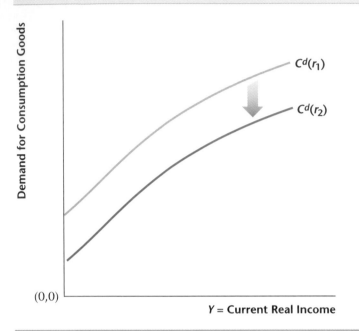

Future profits for the firm are

$$\pi' = Y' - w'N' + (1-d)K',$$
(9.11)

which is future output minus wages paid to workers in the future plus the value of the capital stock net of depreciation at the end of the future period.

Profits earned by the firm in the current and future periods are paid out to the shareholders of the firm as dividend income in each period. There is one shareholder in this economy, the representative consumer, and the firm acts in the interests of this shareholder. That implies that the firm maximizes the present value of the consumer's dividend income, which serves to maximize the lifetime wealth of the consumer. Letting V denote the present value of profits for the firm, the firm then maximizes

$$V = \pi + \frac{\pi'}{1+r}$$
(9.12)

by choosing current labor demand N, future labor demand N', and current investment I.

The firm's choice of current labor demand N affects only current profits π in Equation (9.10). As in Chapter 4, the firm hires current labor until the current marginal product of labor equals the current real wage, that is, $MP_N = w$. Also as in Chapter 4, the demand curve for labor in the current period is identical to the marginal product of labor schedule, as the MP_N schedule tells us how much labor the firm needs to hire

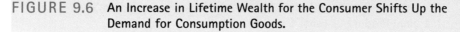

FIGURE 9.6 **An Increase in Lifetime Wealth for the Consumer Shifts Up the Demand for Consumption Goods.**

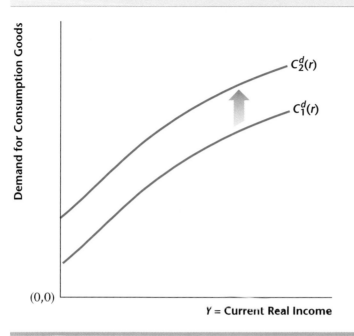

so that $MP_N = w$. In Figure 9.7 we show the representative firm's demand curve for labor, N^d, with the current real wage w on the vertical axis and the current quantity of labor N on the horizontal axis. Recall from Chapter 4 that the labor demand curve is downward-sloping because the marginal product of labor declines with the quantity of labor employed.

As in Chapter 4, the labor demand curve shifts with changes in total factor productivity z or with changes in the initial capital stock K. A higher current level of total factor productivity z or a higher level of K shifts the labor demand curve to the right, for example, from N_1^d to N_2^d in Figure 9.8.

The firm chooses labor demand in the future period in a similar way to its choice of current-period labor demand. We ignore, however, this future choice in our analysis, as this simplifies our model in a way that makes the model's predictions clearer while doing no harm.

The Representative Firm's Investment Decision

Having dealt with the representative firm's labor demand decision, and given its goal of maximizing the present value of its profits, we can proceed to a central aspect of this chapter, which is analyzing the investment choice of the firm.

The choice of investment by the representative firm involves equating the marginal cost of investment with the marginal benefit of investment. We let $MC(I)$ denote the

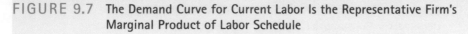

FIGURE 9.7   **The Demand Curve for Current Labor Is the Representative Firm's Marginal Product of Labor Schedule**

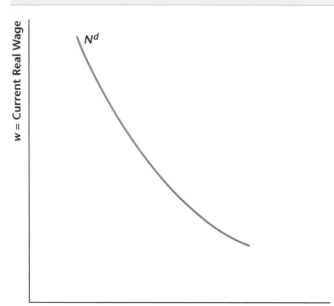

The curve slopes downward because the marginal product of labor declines as the labor input increases.

marginal cost of investment for the firm, where

$$MC(I) = 1. \tag{9.13}$$

That is, the marginal cost of investment for the firm is what it gives up, in terms of the present value of profits, V, by investing in one unit of capital in the current period. This marginal cost is 1, as from Equations (9.12) and (9.10), an additional unit of current investment I reduces current profits π by one unit, which reduces the present value of profits V by one unit.

The **marginal benefit from investment,** denoted by $MB(I)$, is what one extra unit of investment in the current period adds to the present value of profits, V. In Equation (9.11), all the benefits from investment come in terms of future profits π', and there are two components to the marginal benefit. First, an additional unit of current investment adds one unit to the future capital stock K'. This implies that the firm will produce more output in the future, and the additional output produced is equal to the firm's future marginal product of capital, MP'_K. Second, each unit of current investment implies that there will be an additional $1 - d$ units of capital remaining at the end of the future period (after depreciation in the future period), which can be liquidated. Thus, one unit of additional investment in the current period implies an additional $MP'_K + 1 - d$ units of future profits π'. In calculating the marginal benefit of investment we have to

FIGURE 9.8   **The Current Demand Curve for Labor Shifts Due to Changes in Current Total Factor Productivity z and in the Current Capital Stock K**

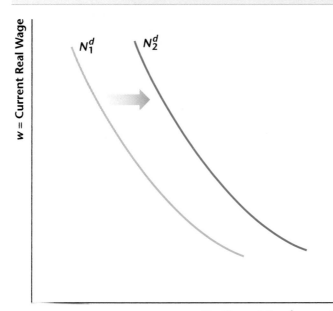

N = **Current Employment**

Here, an increase in *z* or in K shifts the curve to the right reflecting the resulting increase in the marginal product of labor.

discount these future profits, and so we then have

$$MB(I) = \frac{MP'_K + 1 - d}{1 + r}. \tag{9.14}$$

The firm invests until the marginal benefit from investment is equal to the marginal cost—that is, $MB(I) = MC(I)$—or from Equations (9.13) and (9.14),

$$\frac{MP'_K + 1 - d}{1 + r} = 1. \tag{9.15}$$

We can rewrite (9.15) as

$$MP'_K - d = r. \tag{9.16}$$

Equation (9.16) states that the firm invests until the **net marginal product of capital,** $MP'_K - d$, is equal to the real interest rate. The net marginal product of capital, $MP'_K - d$, is the marginal product of capital after taking account of the depreciation of the capital stock. The intuition behind the **optimal investment rule,** Equation (9.16), is that the opportunity cost of investing in more capital is the real rate of interest, which is the rate of return on the alternative asset in this economy. That is, in the model there are two assets: bonds traded on the credit market and capital held by the representative firm.

Effectively, the representative consumer holds the capital of the firm indirectly, because the consumer owns the firm and receives its profits as dividend income. From the consumer's point of view, the rate of return that he or she receives between the current and future periods when the firm engages in investment is the net marginal product of capital. As the firm acts in the interests of the consumer, it would not be optimal for the firm to invest beyond the point where the net marginal product of capital is equal to the real interest rate, as in Equation (9.16), because this would imply that the consumer was receiving a lower rate of return on his or her savings than could be obtained by lending in the credit market at the real interest rate r. Thus, the real interest rate represents the opportunity cost of investing for the representative firm.

In Figure 9.9 we graph the firm's **optimal investment schedule,** with the interest rate on the vertical axis and the demand for investment goods, I^d, on the horizontal axis. Given Equation (9.16), the optimal investment schedule is the firm's net marginal product of capital. In the figure, if the real interest rate is r_1 then the firm wishes to

FIGURE 9.9   Optimal Investment Schedule for the Representative Firm

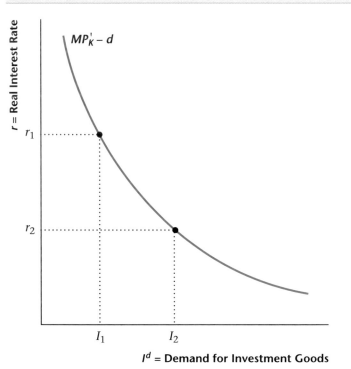

The optimal investment rule states that the firm invests until $MP'_K - d = r$. The future net marginal product schedule $MP'_K - d$ is the representative firm's optimal investment schedule, because this describes how much investment is required for the net marginal product of future capital to equal the real interest rate.

invest I_1, and if the real interest rate falls to r_2 then investment increases to I_2. Note the similarity here to the firm's current labor demand decision, as represented, for example, in Figure 9.7. When making its current labor demand decision, the relevant price to consider is the current real wage, and the firm hires labor until the marginal product of labor is equal to the real wage. In making its investment decision, the relevant price is the real interest rate, and the firm acquires capital (invests) until the net marginal product of capital is equal to the real interest rate.

Optimal investment I^d is determined in part by the market real interest rate r, as reflected in the negative slope of the optimal investment schedule in Figure 9.9. Also, the optimal investment schedule shifts due to any factor that changes the future marginal product of capital. Primarily, we are interested in the following two types of shifts in the optimal investment schedule:

1. The optimal investment schedule shifts to the right if future total factor productivity z' increases. From Chapter 4, recall that an increase in total factor productivity increases the marginal product of capital, for each level of the capital stock. Therefore, if total factor productivity is expected to be higher in the future, so that z' increases, this increases the future marginal product of capital, and the firm is more willing to invest during the current period. Higher investment in the current period leads to higher future productive capacity, so that the firm can take advantage of high future total factor productivity.

2. The optimal investment schedule shifts to the left if the current capital stock K is higher. A higher capital stock at the beginning of the current period implies, from Equation (9.9), that for a given level of current investment I, the future capital stock K' will be larger. That is, if K is larger, then there is more of this initial capital left after depreciation in the current period to use in future production. Therefore, higher K implies that the future marginal product of capital, MP'_K, will decrease for each level of investment, and the optimal investment schedule will then shift to the left.

In Figure 9.10 we show a shift to the right in the optimal investment schedule, which could be caused either by an increase in future total factor productivity z', or by a lower current quantity of capital K. Note that the optimal investment schedule also shifts if the depreciation rate d changes, but we ask the reader to determine the resulting shift in the curve as a problem at the end of this chapter.

This theory of investment can potentially explain why aggregate investment expenditures tend to be more variable over the business cycle than aggregate output or aggregate consumption. A key implication of consumer behavior is smoothing; consumers wish to smooth consumption over time relative to their income, and this explains why consumption tends to be less variable than income. However, investment behavior is not about smoothing but about the response of the firm's investment behavior to perceived marginal rates of return to investment. Provided that the real interest rate and anticipated future total factor productivity vary sufficiently over the business cycle, our theory of the business cycle can explain the variability in observed investment expenditures. That is, investment is variable if the real interest rate is variable, causing movements along the optimal investment schedule in Figure 7.9, or if there is

FIGURE 9.10   **The Optimal Investment Schedule Shifts to the Right if Current Capital Decreases or Future Total Factor Productivity Is Expected to Increase**

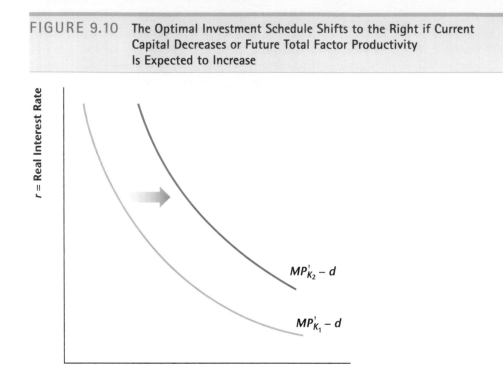

I^d = **Demand for Investment Goods**

This is because either of these changes causes the future marginal product of capital to increase. The figure shows the effect of a decrease in current capital from K_1 to K_2.

variability in anticipated future total factor productivity, causing the optimal investment schedule to shift over time.

Optimal Investment: A Numerical Example   To make the firm's optimal investment decision more concrete, consider the following numerical example. Paula, a small-scale farmer, has an apple orchard, which has 10 trees in the current period that is, $K = 10$. For simplicity, suppose that the quantity of labor required to operate the orchard does not depend on the number of trees Paula has, at least for the number of trees that Paula can plant on her land. In the current period, the 10 trees produce 100 bushels of apples, that is, $Y = 100$. Paula can invest in more trees by taking some of the apples, extracting the seeds (which we assume makes the apples useless), and planting them. Very few of the seeds grow, and it takes 1 bushel of apples to yield 1 tree that will be productive in the future period. The first extra tree that Paula grows is on her best land, and, therefore, it will have a high marginal product, bearing a relatively large amount of fruit. The second tree is planted on slightly worse land, and so will have a smaller marginal product, and so on. Each period, some trees die. In fact, at the end of each

Table 9.1 **Data For Paula's Orchard**

K' = trees in future	I	Y'	V	$MP_K' - d$
8	0	95	196.6	—
9	1	98	199.2	2.8
10	2	100	200.9	1.8
11	3	101	201.6	0.8
12	4	101.5	201.8	0.3
13	5	101.65	201.7	−0.05
14	6	101.75	201.6	−0.1
15	7	101.77	201.4	−0.18

period, Paula loses 20% of her trees, and so the depreciation rate is $d = 0.2$. At the end of the future period, Paula can liquidate her trees. Because each bushel of apples can produce a tree, it is possible to exchange 1 tree for 1 bushel of apples on the open market, so that the liquidation value of a tree remaining in the future period, after depreciation, is 1 bushel of apples. The real interest rate is 5%, or $r = 0.05$ in units of apples. Table 9.1 shows the quantity of future output that will be produced when the number of trees Paula has in the future is 8, 9, 10, ..., 15, as well as the associated level of investment, present discounted value of profits (in units of apples), and the net marginal product of capital (trees) in the future.

From Table 9.1, the present value of profits is maximized when the number of trees in the future is 12 and the quantity of investment is 4 bushels of apples. For each unit of investment from 1 to 4, the net marginal product of capital in the future is greater than the real interest rate, which is 0.05, and the net marginal product of capital is less than 0.05 for each unit of investment above 4. Therefore, it is optimal to invest as long as the net marginal product of future capital is greater than the real interest rate.

GOVERNMENT

We have now shown how the representative consumer and the representative firm behave in the markets for current goods and current labor. We need only to consider government behavior before we show how all these economic agents interact in a competitive equilibrium. Government behavior is identical to what it was in Chapter 8. The government sets government purchases of consumption goods exogenously in each period. The quantity of government purchases in the current period is G, and in the future government purchases are G'. The government finances government purchases in the current period through taxation and by issuing government bonds. Then in the future, the government pays off the interest and principal on its bonds and finances future government spending through future lump-sum taxation. As in Chapter 8, the government must satisfy its present-value budget constraint,

$$G + \frac{G'}{1+r} = T + \frac{T'}{1+r}. \qquad (9.17)$$

COMPETITIVE EQUILIBRIUM

Our analysis thus far has focused on the behavior of the representative consumer, the representative firm, and the government in two markets, the current-period labor market and the current-period market for goods. In this real intertemporal model, the representative consumer supplies labor in the current-period labor market, and demands consumption goods in the current-period goods market. The representative firm demands labor in the current period, supplies goods in the current period, and demands investment goods in the current period. Finally, the government demands goods in the current period, in terms of government purchases.

Perceptive readers might wonder why we have neglected the future markets for labor and goods and the market for credit. First, markets in the future are neglected to make our model simple to work with, and this simplification is essentially harmless at this level of analysis. Second, later in this chapter, we show that we have not actually neglected the credit market, as equilibrium in the current-period goods market implies that the credit market clears.

This section shows how a competitive equilibrium for our model, where supply equals demand in the current-period labor and goods markets, can be expressed in terms of diagrams. We put together the labor supply and labor demand curves to capture how the labor market functions; then, we derive an output supply curve that describes how the supply of goods is related to the real interest rate. Finally, we derive an output demand curve, which describes how the sum of the demand for goods from the representative consumer (consumption goods), the representative firm (investment goods), and the government (government purchases) is related to the real interest rate. Putting the output demand and supply curves together in a diagram with the labor market gives us a working model, which is used to address some key issues in macroeconomics in the following sections and in later chapters.

The Current Labor Market and the Output Supply Curve

First, we consider how the market for labor in the current period works. In Figure 9.11(a), we show the labor demand curve for the representative firm and the labor supply curve for the representative consumer, as derived in the previous sections, with the current real wage w on the vertical axis and the current quantity of labor, N, on the horizontal axis. Recall from earlier sections in this chapter that the labor supply curve slopes upward, as we are assuming that the substitution effect of an increase in the real wage dominates the income effect, and recall that the position of the labor supply curve depends on the real interest rate r. Also, we determined that an increase (decrease) in the real interest rate causes an increase (decrease) in labor supply for each real wage w, and the labor supply curve shifts to the right (left). Given the real interest rate r, the equilibrium real wage in Figure 9.11(a), is w^*, the equilibrium quantity of employment is N^*, and from the production function in Figure 9.11(b), we determine the quantity of aggregate output supplied (given the real interest rate), which is Y^*. Recall from Chapter 4 that the position of the production function is determined by current total factor productivity z and by the current capital stock K. An increase in z or K would shift the production function up.

FIGURE 9.11   Determination of Equilibrium in the Labor Market Given the Real
                Interest Rate r

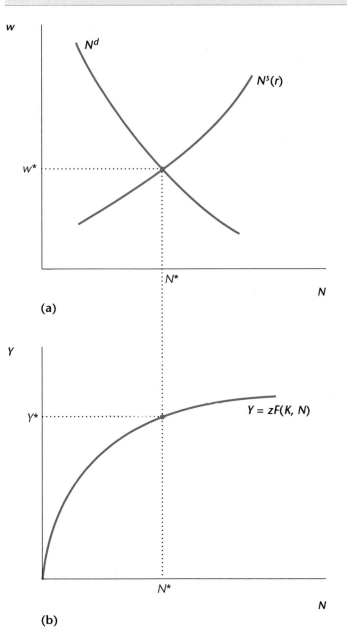

(a)

(b)

In (a), the intersection of the current labor supply and demand curves determines the current real wage
and current employment, and the production function in (b) then determines aggregate output.

Our next step is to use the diagrams in Figure 9.11 to derive an output supply curve, which describes how much output is supplied by firms for each possible level for the real interest rate. In Figure 9.12(a), the labor supply curves for two different interest rates, r_1 and r_2, are shown, where $r_1 < r_2$. Thus, with the increase in the real interest rate, the current labor supply curve shifts to the right, the current equilibrium real wage falls from w_1 to w_2, and current employment increases from N_1 to N_2. Further, current output increases from Y_1 to Y_2, in Figure 9.12(b), from the production function. We can then construct a curve, called the **output supply curve**, which is an upward-sloping curve consisting of all combinations of current output and real interest rates, (Y, r), for which the current labor market is in equilibrium. This curve is denoted Y^s in Figure 9.12(c). Two points on the Y^s curve are (Y_1, r_1) and (Y_2, r_2), because at real interest rate r_1 the labor market is in equilibrium when the representative firm produces current output Y_1 and at real interest rate r_2 the labor market is in equilibrium when the representative firm produces current output Y_2.

Shifts in the Output Supply Curve

When we work with our real intertemporal model, we must know how changes in particular exogenous variables shift supply and demand curves. In this subsection, we show how three factors—lifetime wealth, current total factor productivity, and the current capital stock—can shift the output supply curve. The latter two factors have much the same effect, so we deal with these together.

The output supply curve shifts either because of a shift in the current labor supply curve (not arising because of a change in the real interest rate; the output supply curve already takes this into account), because of a shift in the current labor demand curve, or because of a shift in the production function. From our analysis of consumer behavior, we know that a change in lifetime wealth shifts the labor supply curve, whereas a change in either current total factor productivity or the current capital stock shifts the labor demand curve and the production function. We deal with each of these shifts in turn.

Recall from our discussion of the representative consumer's behavior, earlier in this chapter, that a decrease in lifetime wealth reduces the consumer's demand for current leisure, due to an income effect, and so the consumer supplies more labor for any current real wage. Therefore, the labor supply curve shifts to the right. What would cause a reduction in lifetime wealth for the representative consumer? The key such factor of interest is an increase in government spending, either in the present or the future. From the present-value government budget constraint, Equation (9.17), any increase in government spending, either in the present or the future (that is an increase in G or G') must be reflected in an increase in the present value of taxes for the consumer, $T + \frac{T'}{1+r}$. Therefore an increase in G, in G', or in both, results in an increase in the lifetime tax burden for the representative consumer. In Figure 9.13(a), this causes a shift to the right in the labor supply curve from $N_1^s(r_1)$ to $N_2^s(r_1)$, as there is a negative income effect on current leisure.

The shift to the right in the labor supply curve in Figure 9.13(a) implies that, for a given real interest rate, the equilibrium quantity of employment in the labor market is higher; that is, employment rises from N_1 to N_2 in Figure 9.13(a), given a particular real interest rate r_1. From the production function in Figure 9.13(b), output rises from Y_1 to Y_2 given the real interest rate r_1. This then implies that the output supply curve

FIGURE 9.12   **Construction of the Output Supply Curve**

The output supply curve Y^s is an upward-sloping curve in panel (c) of the figure, consisting of real current output and real interest rate pairs for which the labor market is in equilibrium.

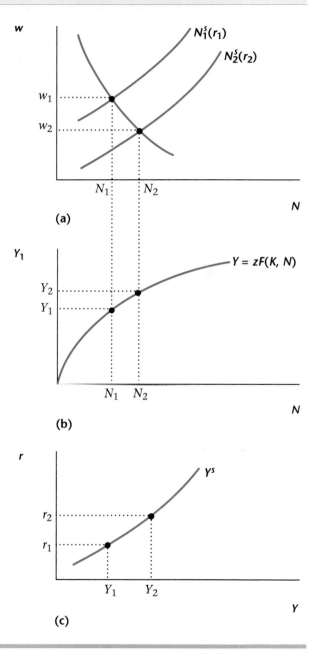

FIGURE 9.13   An Increase in Current or Future Government Spending Shifts the Y^s Curve

This is because the increase in government spending increases the present value of taxes for the representative consumer, and current leisure falls, shifting the labor supply curve to the right in (a) and shifting the output supply curve to the right in (c).

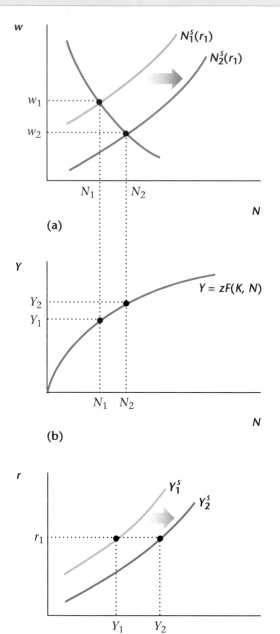

shifts to the right, from Y_1^s to Y_2^s, in 9.13(c). That is, output is higher for each possible value for the real interest rate. The conclusion is that *an increase in G or G' shifts the labor supply curve to the right and shifts the output supply curve to the right, because of the income effect on labor supply.*

From Chapter 4, recall that an increase in total factor productivity or in the capital stock shifts the production function up, because more output can be produced for any level of the labor input, and the labor demand curve shifts to the right, because the marginal product of labor increases. In our model, an increase in current total factor productivity z, or in the current capital stock K, causes the production function to shift up. In Figure 9.14(b) we show the results of an increase in z from z_1 to z_2, but the effect of an increase in K would be identical. The labor demand curve shifts to the right in Figure 9.14(a), from N_1^d to N_2^d. As a result, given the real interest rate r_1, the equilibrium quantity of employment rises from N_1 to N_2. Therefore, from the production function in Figure 9.14(b), as employment is higher and z is higher, output increases from Y_1 to Y_2. The same effects (an increase in employment and output) would happen for any level of the real interest rate, which implies that the output supply curve in Figure 9.14(c) must shift to the right. The results would be identical if there had been an increase in the current capital stock. The conclusion is that *an increase in z or K causes the production function to shift up, the labor demand curve to shift to the right, and the output supply curve to shift to the right.*

The Current Goods Market and the Output Demand Curve

Now that we understand how the current labor market works and how the output supply curve is constructed, we can turn to the functioning of the current-period goods market and the construction of the output demand curve. This then completes our model.

Total current aggregate income Y is the sum of the demand for current consumption goods by the representative consumer, $C^d(r)$, the demand for investment goods by the representative firm, $I^d(r)$, and government purchases of current goods, G:

$$Y = C^d(r) + I^d(r) + G. \tag{9.18}$$

Here, we use the notation $C^d(r)$ and $I^d(r)$ to reflect that the demand for current consumption goods and the demand for investment goods depend on the real interest rate r; this dependence is negative. Recall from our treatment of consumer behavior earlier in this chapter that the demand for current consumption goods also depends on the lifetime wealth of the representative consumer, one component of which is current income. In Figure 9.15 we show the total demand for goods, the right-hand side of Equation (9.18), as a function of current aggregate income Y. Because the demands for investment goods and government purchases do not depend on aggregate income, the slope of the curve $C^d(r) + I^d(r) + G$ in the figure is the marginal propensity to consume, *MPC*. What is the equilibrium demand for current goods in the market, given the real interest rate r? This is determined by the point at which the curve $C^d(r) + I^d(r) + G$ intersects the 45° line. Therefore, in Figure 9.15 the demand for current goods is Y_1, which is the quantity of aggregate income that generates a total demand for goods just equal to that quantity of aggregate income.

FIGURE 9.14   An Increase in Current Total Factor Productivity Shifts the Y^s Curve

This is because an increase in z increases the marginal product of current labor, shifting the labor demand curve to the right in (a), and also shifting the production function up in (b). As a result, the output supply curve shifts to the right in (c).

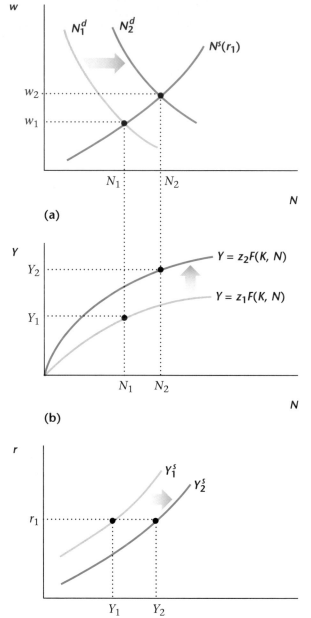

FIGURE 9.15 **The Demand for Current Goods**

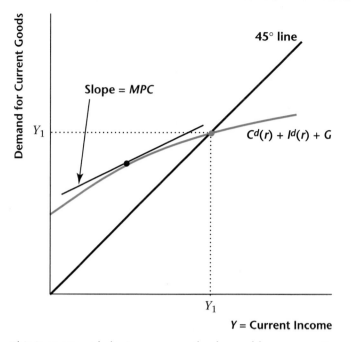

This is an upward-sloping curve, as the demand for consumption goods increases with current income. The slope of the demand curve for current goods is the marginal propensity to consume (MPC).

The next step is to construct the **output demand curve,** which is a negative relationship between current aggregate output and the real interest rate. In Figure 9.16(a), if the real interest rate is r_1, then the current demand for goods is $C^d(r_1) + I^d(r_1) + G$. If the real interest rate were r_2 with $r_2 > r_1$, then the current demand for goods falls for each level of aggregate current income Y, as the demand for current consumption goods and for current investment goods is lower. Thus, the demand for goods shifts down to $C^d(r_2) + I^d(r_2) + G$. As a result, the equilibrium quantity of goods demanded falls from Y_1 to Y_2. Now, in Figure 9.16(b), we can construct a downward-sloping curve in a diagram with the real interest rate r on the vertical axis, and current aggregate income Y on the horizontal axis. This curve, Y^d, is the output demand curve, and a point on the curve, (Y, r), represents the level of demand for goods (output), Y, given the real interest rate r. Two points on the output demand curve are (Y_1, r_1) and (Y_2, r_2), corresponding to Figure 9.16(a).

Shifts in the Output Demand Curve   Before we put all the elements of our real intertemporal model together—the output demand curve, the output supply curve, the production function, and the current labor supply and demand curves—we need to understand the important factors that shift the output demand curve. The output demand

FIGURE 9.16   Construction of the Output Demand Curve

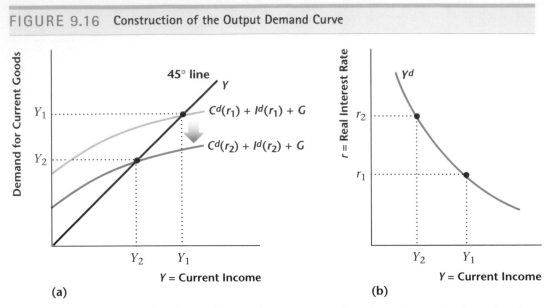

The output demand curve Y^d in (b) is a downward-sloping curve describing the combinations of real output and the real interest rate for which the current goods market is in equilibrium.

curve shifts as the result of a shift in the demand for current consumption goods, $C^d(r)$, a shift in the demand for investment goods, $I^d(r)$, or because of a change in the current quantity of government purchases G. In Figure 9.17 we show the effects of an increase in G. In Figure 9.17(a), the demand for current goods shifts up when current government purchases increase from G_1 to G_2. Then, given the real interest rate r_1, the quantity of current goods demanded increases from Y_1 to Y_2. As a result, in Figure 9.17(b), the output demand curve shifts to the right from Y_1^d to Y_2^d. That is, the quantity of current goods demanded is higher for any real interest rate, including r_1. Other important factors that shift the Y^d curve to the right, in a manner identical to the results for an increase in G in Figure 9.17, are the following:

- *A decrease in the present value of taxes shifts the Y^d curve to the right.* A decrease in the present value of taxes is caused by a reduction in current taxes, future taxes, or both. When this happens, the lifetime wealth of the representative consumer rises; therefore, the demand for consumption goods, $C^d(r)$, increases, which causes a shift to the right in the output demand curve.
- *An increase in future income Y' shifts the Y^d curve to the right.* If the representative consumer anticipates that his or her future income will be higher, then this is an increase in lifetime wealth, which causes $C^d(r)$ to increase and brings about a shift to the right in the output demand curve.
- *An increase in future total factor productivity z' causes the Y^d curve to shift to the right.* If the representative firm expects total factor productivity to be higher in the future,

FIGURE 9.17 **The Output Demand Curve Shifts to the Right if Current Government Spending Increases**

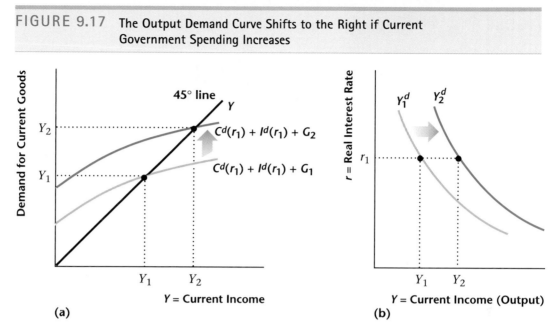

The curve shifts in a similar manner if the present value of taxes decreases, its future income increases, if future total factor productivity increases, or if the current capital stock declines.

this increases the firm's demand for goods, so that $I^d(r)$ increases. The output demand curve then shifts to the right.

- *A decrease in the current capital stock K causes the Y^d curve to shift to the right.* When there is a lower current capital stock, perhaps because of destruction, then the demand for investment goods, $I^d(r)$, increases for each r. As a result, the output demand curve shifts to the right.

The Complete Real Intertemporal Model

We now have all the building blocks for our real intertemporal model, and so we can put these building blocks together and use the model to address some interesting economic issues. Our model is presented in Figure 9.18, where a competitive equilibrium consists of a state of affairs where supply equals demand in the current labor market in panel (a) and in the current goods market in panel (b). In Figure 9.18(a), N^d is the current labor demand curve, while $N^s(r)$ is the current labor supply curve, which shifts with the real interest rate r. The equilibrium real wage is given by w^*, and the equilibrium quantity of employment is N^*, where w^* and N^* are determined by the intersection of the demand and supply curves for current labor. Equilibrium output and the equilibrium real interest rate are Y^* and r^*, respectively, in Figure 9.18(b), and they are determined by the intersection of the output demand curve Y^d with the output supply curve Y^s.

FIGURE 9.18 The Complete Real Intertemporal Model

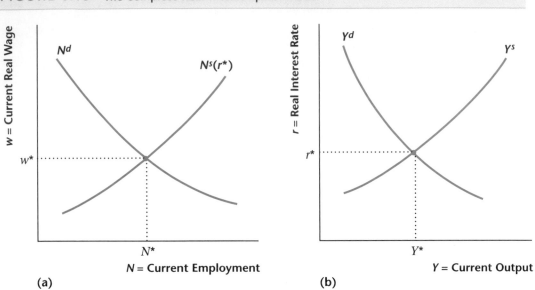

(a) The current real wage and current employment are determined by the intersection of the current labor supply and demand curves, given the real interest rate. (b) Current aggregate output and the real interest rate are determined by the intersection of the output supply and demand curves.

To use the model to help us understand how the macroeconomy works, we perform some experiments. These experiments each involve changing the value of some exogenous variable or variables, and then asking how the solution of the model is different as a result. We then show how we interpret the results of these experiments in terms of real-world macroeconomic events. Our experiments answer the following questions:

1. How does an increase in current government purchases, anticipated to be temporary, affect current macroeconomic variables?

2. How does an increase in government purchases that is expected to be permanent affect the macroeconomy?

3. What are the effects on current macroeconomic variables of a decrease in the current capital stock, brought about by a natural disaster or a war?

4. How does a temporary increase in total factor productivity affect macroeconomic variables, and how does this fit the key business cycle facts?

5. If total factor productivity is expected to increase in the future, how does this affect current macroeconomic variables?

6. What are the effects of a **sectoral shock** to the economy, which is a shock that causes some industries to expand and others to contract?

GOVERNMENT PURCHASES INCREASE TEMPORARILY: THE EQUILIBRIUM EFFECTS OF AN INCREASE IN G

Two key messages in this chapter are (1) the macroeconomic effects of a particular shock to the economy depend on whether that shock is temporary or permanent, and (2) the effects of a shock to the economy expected in the future will have important macroeconomic effects in the current period. Both of these messages will come through when we look at the effects of temporary and permanent changes in government purchases in this section and the next.

We will model a temporary increase in government spending as an increase in G, the quantity of government purchases in the current period, leaving future government purchases G' unchanged. When would the government choose to increase its expenditures on goods and services temporarily? An important example is a war. Typically, wars are known to be temporary (though the length of a war is typically uncertain), and the government commits spending to the war effort that does not remain in place when the war is over. Sometimes, however, a change in government spending can be essentially permanent. For example, when the U.S. government established the Environmental Protection Agency (EPA), this involved a commitment of resources that was as permanent as government commitments can be—no one expects the EPA to be abolished in the future.

Before the increase in current government purchases G, in Figure 9.19, the economy is in equilibrium with a current real wage w_1, current employment N_1, current output Y_1, and real interest rate r_1. When G increases this has two effects, one on output supply and one on output demand. First, because an increase in G increases the present value of government spending, the present value of taxes must rise, from the present-value government budget constraint, Equation (9.17), and the representative consumer's lifetime wealth falls. As a result, leisure decreases (leisure is a normal good) for the representative consumer, given the current real wage, and so the labor supply curve in Figure 9.19(a) shifts to the right from $N_1^s(r_1)$ to $N_2^s(r_1)$, and the output supply curve in Figure 9.19(b) shifts to the right from Y_1^s to Y_2^s. Second, the demand for consumption goods, $C_1(r)$, falls because of the drop in the consumer's lifetime wealth, and the demand for goods arising from government purchases increases, because G goes up. What happens on net to the demand for goods? We know that $MPC < 1$, that is, that the marginal propensity to consume is smaller than one. Thus, because for any real interest rate the present value of taxes increases by the increase in current government spending, the demand for current consumption goods must fall by less than government purchases rise. Therefore, the total demand for goods must rise for any real interest rate, and the output demand curve shifts to the right from Y_1^d to Y_2^d.

To determine all the equilibrium effects using the model, we start first with Figure 9.19(b). It is clear that current aggregate output must increase, as both the output demand and output supply curves shift to the right, and so Y increases from Y_1 to Y_2. It may appear that the real interest rate may rise or fall; however, there is strong theoretical support for an increase in the real interest rate. This is because the temporary increase in government spending should lead to only a small decrease in lifetime wealth for the consumer, which produces small effects on labor supply and on the demand for consumption goods. Therefore, there should be only a small shift to the right in the Y^s

FIGURE 9.19   **A Temporary Increase in Government Purchases**

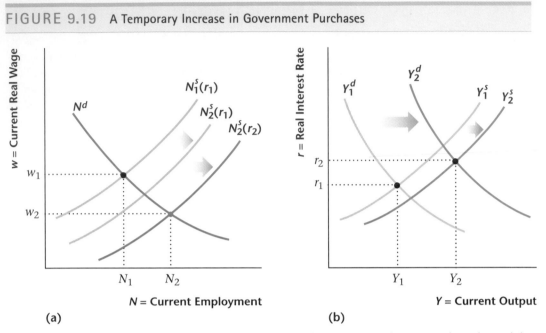

(a)   **(b)**

The increase in G shifts the labor supply curve to the right, the output supply curve to the right, and the output demand curve to the right. The real interest rate rises, and aggregate output increases in equilibrium. There is an additional shift to the right in the labor supply curve because of the increase in r, so employment rises and the real wage falls in equilibrium.

curve, and the small decrease in demand for consumption goods does not greatly offset the increase in demand for goods coming from the increase in G, so that the shift to the right in Y^d is relatively large. As a result, the real interest rate rises, as in Figure 9.19(b).

Current consumption expenditure could in principle rise or fall. This is because the decrease in the present value of taxes and the increase in the real interest rate reduce consumption, while the increase in current income causes consumption to go up. However, because the net effect on lifetime wealth of the increase in taxes and the increase in current income is small (as the increase in G is temporary) the real interest rate effect dominates, so that C falls. As well, investment expenditures must decrease, because of the increase in the real interest rate. Thus, both components of private expenditure (current consumption and investment) are crowded out by current government expenditure. Recall from Chapter 5, that when we analyzed the effects of an increase in government spending in a one-period model, without taking intertemporal substitution and investment into account, government spending crowded out only consumption expenditure. Because government spending is shown here to crowd out private investment expenditure, a further cost of government is that it reduces the economy's future productive capacity, as the future capital stock will be lower when government spending increases temporarily.

The next step is to work through the effects of the increase in the real interest rate for the labor market. In Figure 9.19(a) given the initial interest rate r_1, the labor supply curve shifts from $N_1^s(r_1)$ to $N_2^s(r_1)$. With an increase in the equilibrium real interest rate to r_2, the labor supply curve shifts further to the right, to $N_2^s(r_2)$. Therefore, the equilibrium real wage falls, from w_1 to w_2, and employment rises from N_1 to N_2.

What this analysis tells us is that increased temporary government spending, while it leads to higher aggregate output and employment, comes at a cost. With higher current government spending, the representative consumer consumes less and takes less leisure, and he or she also faces a lower real wage rate. Further, current investment spending is lower, which implies that the capital stock will be lower in the future, and the future capacity of the economy for producing goods will be lower.

GOVERNMENT PURCHASES INCREASE PERMANENTLY: THE EQUILIBRIUM EFFECTS OF AN INCREASE IN BOTH G AND G′

It turns out that the macroeconomic effects of a permanent increase in government spending are quite different from those of a temporary increase in spending. Again, a good example of a permanent increase in government purchases is the establishment of a new government agency, such as the EPA.

To set up the problem, suppose that government spending increases permanently by the amount ΔG. That is, current government spending G increases from G_1 to $G_1 + \Delta G$, and future government spending G' increases from G_1' to $G_1' + \Delta G$. Just as with a temporary increase in government purchases, there are two primary effects in the current period, which are the decrease in lifetime wealth for the representative consumer because of the increase in the present value of taxes, and the direct effect of an increase in current government purchases on the current demand for goods. In terms of the effect on output supply, from the present-value government budget constraint, Equation (9.17), the present value of taxes must rise for the consumer, given the real interest rate, because G and G' have increased. As a result, the lifetime wealth of the representative consumer goes down, which implies that he or she consumes less leisure and works harder in the current period. Therefore, in Figure 9.20(a) the supply curve for current labor shifts to the right from $N_1^s(r_1)$ to $N_2^s(r_1)$, where r_1 is the initial real interest rate. Because of this shift in the labor supply curve, the output supply curve in Figure 9.20(b) shifts to the right from Y_1^s to Y_2^s.

The decrease in lifetime wealth for the consumer, in addition to affecting labor supply, also causes a reduction in the consumer's current demand for consumption goods. At the same time, there is an increase in the demand for goods as a result of the increase in current government purchases. What, then, is the net impact on the current demand for goods? Milton Friedman's permanent income hypothesis, discussed in Chapter 8, implies that there would be no change in the demand for goods in the current period. That is, because government spending has increased permanently by ΔG, one way to finance this increase in spending would be for the government to increase taxes by ΔG in the present and the future. One way for the representative consumer to absorb the

FIGURE 9.20   **A Permanent Increase in Government Purchases**

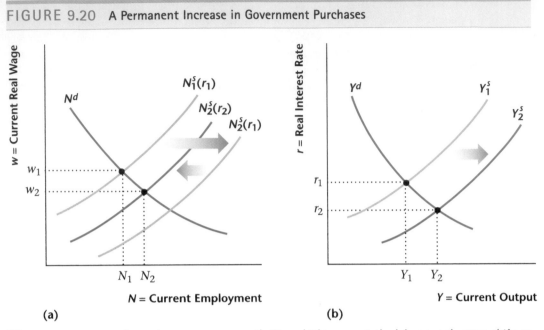

(a)   **(b)**

When government purchases increase permanently (G and G′ increase), the labor supply curve shifts to the right, and the output supply curve shifts right. There is no shift in output demand, and the real interest rate falls, with aggregate output rising. There is a further shift to the left in the labor supply curve, and employment rises with the real wage falling in equilibrium.

permanent increase in taxes would be to reduce his or her demand for consumption goods by ΔG in each of the current and future periods. In Friedman's language, the consumer's "permanent income" would decline by ΔG, and Friedman argued that the marginal propensity to consume out of permanent income is 1. This implies that the increase in the current demand for goods because of the increase in G, and the decrease in the demand for goods because of the negative income effect on current consumption, would exactly offset each other. This is what we have shown in Figure 9.20(b), where the output demand curve Y^d remains unaffected by the change in government purchases.

What is the impact of the permanent increase in government purchases on current variables in a competitive equilibrium? First, in Figure 9.20(b), the real interest rate must fall, from r_1 to r_2, and the quantity of aggregate output must rise, from Y_1 to Y_2. The decrease in the real interest rate results in an increase in investment expenditures. What happens to current consumption expenditures? There are three effects here. First, the lifetime wealth of the consumer is affected negatively by the increase in the present value of taxes, which reduces consumption; second, the decrease in the real interest rate increases consumption; third, the increase in current income increases consumption. Therefore, consumption may increase or decrease. An important key difference between the effects of a permanent and a temporary increase in government purchases on current macroeconomic activity is that the permanent increase does not have the same crowding-out effects as the temporary increase. With a permanent increase in government spending, investment expenditure rises rather than falls, and there is a positive effect on consumption from the decrease in the real interest rate. Note, however, that the crowding-out effect on consumption as the result of a reduction in the consumer's lifetime wealth is stronger when the increase in government purchases is permanent. As well, the wealth effect on labor supply implies that the representative consumer is working harder in equilibrium; this wealth effect is stronger with a permanent increase in government purchases than with a temporary increase.

To determine the ultimate effects of the changes in government spending on the labor market, we need to consider the impact of the decrease in the equilibrium real interest rate. When the real interest rate decreases in equilibrium from r_1 to r_2, this shifts the current labor supply curve in Figure 9.20(a) to the left from $N_2^s(r_1)$ to $N_2^s(r_2)$, because of the intertemporal substitution effect on labor supply. How do we know that the shift to the left in the labor supply curve is smaller than the initial rightward shift in this curve? In equilibrium, we know from Figure 9.20(b) that aggregate output in the current period must increase. For this to happen, from the production function, Equation (9.7), employment N must increase in equilibrium, as total factor productivity z and the current capital stock K have not changed. Thus, the shifts in the labor supply curve are as shown in the figure, and so employment increases from N_1 to N_2 and the real wage falls from w_1 to w_2.

Does current aggregate output increase more because of a temporary increase in government spending or a permanent increase? As sometimes occurs when we use economic theory to analyze a particular issue, the answer is that it depends. With the cases of permanent and temporary increases in government spending, there are two positive effects on aggregate output, an output demand effect and an output supply effect. The output demand effect is larger with a temporary increase in government purchases, whereas the output supply effect is larger with a permanent increase. Therefore, whether output increases more or less when government purchases increase temporarily is determined by the relative strengths of the output demand effect and the output supply effect.

How does macroeconomic theory help us understand the effects of changes in government purchases on aggregate output, if the answer here is ambiguous? Theory does help, as we have isolated what the relevant effects depend on, and so we have clear direction from the theory concerning what to look for in terms of measurement and empirical work. To get a clear answer to our question, we would want to know the empirical effects of a change in lifetime wealth on the demand for consumption goods and on labor supply, among other things, and this helps tell us about the size of the shifts in the output demand and output supply curves. The theory tells us what is important for answering the question, and as economists we can then proceed to find the information we need to obtain this answer. A more technical analysis of the problem by S. Rao Aiyagari, Lawrence Christiano, and Martin Eichenbaum[1] shows that

[1]S. R. Aiyagari, L. Christiano, and M. Eichenbaum, 1992, "The Output, Employment, and Interest Rate Effects of Government Purchases," *Journal of Monetary Economics* 30, 73–86.

output increases more when government spending increases permanently than when it increases temporarily.

. . . .

INVESTMENT SPENDING DURING WORLD WAR II

THEORY confronts the DATA

Recall that an example of a temporary increase in government purchases is what occurs during wartime. Here, we consider the macroeconomic effects of the increase in government spending during World War II in the United States. In Chapter 5, we studied data for the United States showing that, during World War II when there was an extremely large increase in real government spending, aggregate real output increased and aggregate consumption declined. This is certainly consistent with the results from our model above, where we showed that a temporary increase in government purchases causes an increase in output because of an increase in labor supply and causes a decrease in consumption. In addition, our model predicts that investment spending will decrease during a war, and so it would be interesting to check this prediction against the data.

Figure 9.21 shows the natural logarithm of real investment expenditures in the United States from 1929–2002. Note the extremely large drop in investment spending that occurred during World War II. Indeed, other than the decrease in investment spending during the Great Depression, there are no deviations from trend in investment of comparable magnitude. Recall from Chapter 5 that the crowding-out effect of government spending on consumption that appeared in the data during World War II was quite small, in that consumption expenditures dipped only slightly during this period. The drop in investment spending in the figure is extremely large, however, indicating that the empirical crowding-out effect of a temporary increase in government purchases may be much larger for investment than for consumption.

Although the decrease in investment in World War II is consistent with our theory, it appears that this drop in investment did not occur through an increase in the real interest rate, as in our model. In fact, real interest rates in the United States were quite low historically during World War II. For example, the nominal interest rate on U.S. Treasury bills (essentially the short-term interest rate on government debt) was less than 1% per annum during World War II, while the rate of inflation then was between 5% and 10%. Empirically, the real interest rate is approximately the nominal interest rate minus the inflation rate, so by this calculation the real interest rate during World War II was negative, which is historically low, as real interest rates are typically positive. Our model, therefore, cannot completely explain the behavior of the macroeconomy during World War II. One possible explanation for the problem in fitting our model to the data is that, in contrast to our assumption of market-clearing prices in the model, during World War II there was much government control over prices and the distribution of goods and raw materials (for example, through rationing). The large decrease in investment spending may have occurred in part because private producers of investment goods could not obtain material inputs (for example, gasoline and cement) at any price.

FIGURE 9.21   Natural Log of Real Investment, 1929–2002

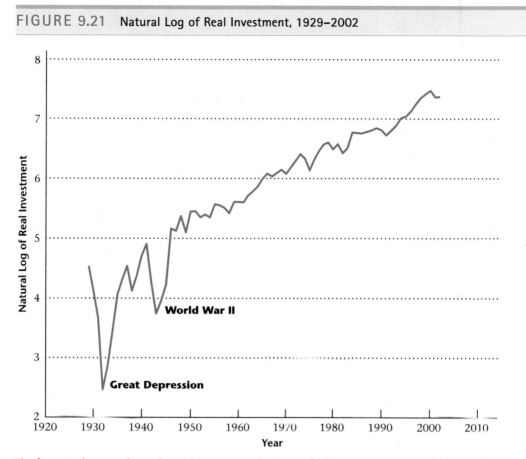

The figure indicates a large drop in investment during World War II, consistent with the predictions of the real intertemporal model.

Source: Bureau of Economic Analysis, Department of Commerce.

THE EQUILIBRIUM EFFECTS OF A DECREASE IN THE CURRENT CAPITAL STOCK, K

Over time, through investment, a nation adds to its capital stock, and this generally occurs slowly, as investment expenditure is typically quite small relative to the total capital stock. Thus, increases in capital do not contribute much to short-run fluctuations in aggregate output and employment. However, sometimes major reductions in the aggregate capital stock occur over a short period of time. For example, a war can leave a country with a much lower capital stock, as happened due to bombing in Germany, Great Britain, and Japan during World War II, in Vietnam during the Vietnam War, and in Iraq during the recent conflict. The capital stock can also be reduced because of natural disasters such as floods (see Macroeconomics in Action: The Macroeconomic Effects of the 1993 Upper Mississippi Basin Flood) or hurricanes.

In this subsection, we examine the effects of an experiment in our model in which the current capital stock K is reduced. That is, suppose that the representative firm begins the current period with a lower capital stock K. This affects both the supply and the demand for output. First, a decrease in K from K_1 to K_2 decreases the current marginal product of labor, which shifts the current demand for labor curve to the left from N_1^d to N_2^d in Figure 9.22(a). The output supply curve then shifts to the left, from Y_1^s to Y_2^s in Figure 9.22(b). Second, a decrease in K increases investment by the firm, because the future marginal product of capital will be higher. This shifts the output demand curve to the right in Figure 9.22(b), from Y_1^d to Y_2^d. The result is that, in equilibrium, in Figure 9.22(b), the real interest rate must rise from r_1 to r_2, but the effect on current aggregate output is ambiguous, depending on whether the output supply effect is larger or smaller than the output demand effect. In the figure, we have drawn the case where the output supply effect dominates, so that current real output falls. Empirically, there may be circumstances, such as with natural disasters (see Macroeconomics in Action: The Macroeconomic Effects of the 1993 Upper Mississippi Basin Flood), where aggregate output may not fall.

FIGURE 9.22 **The Equilibrium Effects of a Decrease in the Current Capital Stock**

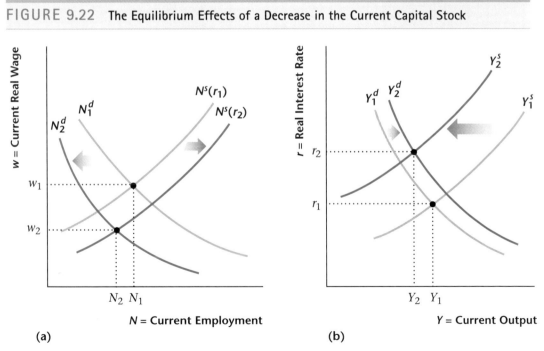

N = Current Employment

Y = Current Output

(a)

(b)

If the current capital stock falls—for example, because of a natural disaster—then the output demand curve shifts to the right and the output supply curve shifts to the left. The real interest rate rises, but current output may rise or fall.

In Figure 9.22 current consumption must fall, because the real interest rate has increased. The effects on investment appear to be ambiguous, because the decrease in K causes investment to increase, while the increase in the equilibrium real interest rate causes investment to fall. However, investment must rise, because less capital would otherwise cause ever-decreasing investment, which would be inconsistent with the fact that the marginal product of capital rises as the quantity of capital falls. That is, as the quantity of capital falls, the marginal product of capital rises, making the return on investment very high, so that ultimately investment must increase if the capital stock decreases.

Because of the increase in the real interest rate, there is intertemporal substitution of leisure, with the representative consumer working harder in the current period for each current real wage w. Therefore, the labor supply curve shifts to the right in Figure 9.22(a) from $N^s(r_1)$ to $N^s(r_2)$. This reinforces the effect of the increase in labor demand on the real wage, and so the real wage must fall, from w_1 to w_2. The equilibrium effect on the quantity of labor is ambiguous, because the effect on labor demand and on labor supply work in opposite directions on the quantity of employment. In Figure 9.22(a), we show employment falling from N_1 to N_2.

Now, suppose that we interpret these results in terms of the macroeconomic effects of a natural disaster or a war that destroys part of the nation's capital stock. The model shows that there are two effects on the quantity of output. The lower quantity of capital implies that less output can be produced for a given quantity of labor input, which tends to reduce output. However, the lower quantity of capital acts to increase investment to replace the destroyed capital, which tends to increase output. Theoretically, it is not clear whether output increases or decreases, and there appear to be empirical cases (see Macroeconomics in Action: The Macroeconomic Effects of the 1993 Upper Mississippi Basin Flood) in which the output supply and output demand effects roughly cancel.

MACROECONOMICS IN ACTION

The Macroeconomic Effects of the 1993 Upper Mississippi Basin Flood

In 1993, heavy rains centered in the midwestern United States caused the flooding of the Mississippi River and some of its tributaries, as well as the Missouri River. Measured in terms of quantity of rainfall, and the duration and extent of flooding, this flood was more severe than any other recorded in U.S. history. This flood represented an important macroeconomic shock, with the damage to the aggregate capital stock being quite significant. Many river towns were flooded, destroying part of the housing stock and the stock of plant and equipment. Further, there was damage to infrastructure, including roads, bridges, and water systems. In Des Moines, Iowa, the water system was out of commission for weeks, having been corrupted by flood waters. While publicly provided infrastructure—for example, *(continued)* roads, bridges, and water systems—is not a part of the private capital stock, it is nevertheless appropriately counted as part of the aggregate capital stock that contributes to aggregate production. According to the U.S. Geological Survey,[1] river flooding on average causes about $3 billion in damage annually, most of which we would include as damaged capital stock.

In spite of the widespread damage caused by the 1993 flood, there appears to have been no perceived effects on aggregate economic activity. Aggregate output and employment seem not to have been affected. Our real intertemporal model is entirely consistent with this. While the flood disrupted macroeconomic activity, in that activity in manufacturing, services, and agriculture was partially shut down, there was also much activity to repair flood damage. In the language of our model, the capital stock was reduced, thus reducing productive capacity, the demand for labor, and employment, which would ultimately reduce output supply. However, there was an opposing effect, an increase in the demand for investment goods (repairs to the capital stock), which increased output demand, and in the 1993 flood this appears to have roughly offset the negative effect on output of the reduced capital stock.

_____

[1]U.S. Geological Survey Yearbook 1994.

THE EQUILIBRIUM EFFECTS OF AN INCREASE IN CURRENT TOTAL FACTOR PRODUCTIVITY, z

Temporary changes in total factor productivity are an important cause of business cycles. Recall from Chapter 4 that an increase in total factor productivity could be caused by good weather, a favorable change in government regulations, a new invention, a decrease in the relative price of energy, or any other factor that results in more aggregate output being produced with the same factor inputs.

The experiment we examine here in our real intertemporal model is to increase current total factor productivity z, and then determine the effects of this change on current aggregate output, the real interest rate, current employment, the current real wage, current consumption, and investment. If current total factor productivity increases, the marginal product of labor goes up for each quantity of labor input, and so in Figure 9.23(a) the demand for labor curve shifts to the right, from N_1^d to N_2^d. Therefore, in Figure 9.23(b), the output supply curve shifts to the right, from Y_1^s to Y_2^s, and in equilibrium the quantity of output rises and the real interest rate must fall, from r_1 to r_2. The decrease in the real interest rate leads to increases in both consumption and investment.

In the labor market, the decrease in the real interest rate causes intertemporal substitution of leisure between the current and future periods, with current leisure increasing, and so the labor supply curve shifts to the left in Figure 9.23(a), from $N^s(r_1)$ to $N^s(r_2)$. In equilibrium, the real wage must increase from w_1 to w_2, but the net effect on the equilibrium quantity of employment is ambiguous. Empirically, however, the effect of the real interest rate on labor supply is small and, as in Figure 7.23(a), employment rises from N_1 to N_2.

FIGURE 9.23   **The Equilibrium Effects of an Increase in Current Total Factor Productivity**

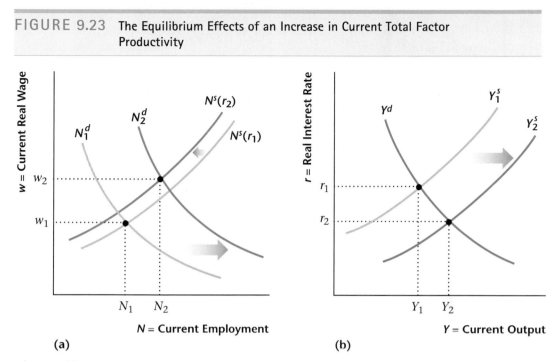

When total factor productivity increases temporarily, the output supply curve shifts to the right in (b), with the real interest rate falling and aggregate output rising. Investment and consumption rise, and employment and the real wage increase in (a).

When total factor productivity increases, this increases the current demand for labor, which raises the market real wage. With the real wage increase, workers are willing to supply more labor, employment increases, and output increases. In the goods market, the increased supply of goods decreases the market real interest rate, which results in an increased demand for investment goods and consumption goods, so that the demand for goods rises to meet the increased supply of goods on the market. As well, the increase in current income increases consumption.

From Chapter 3, recall that some key business cycle facts are that consumption, investment, employment, the real wage, and average labor productivity are procyclical. Our real intertemporal model predicts these comovements in the data if the economy receives temporary shocks to total factor productivity. That is, because Figure 9.23 predicts that a temporary increase in total factor productivity increases aggregate output, consumption, investment, employment, and the real wage, the model predicts that consumption, investment, employment, and the real wage are procyclical, just as in the data. As well, the average product of labor must be higher when z increases, because an increase in z makes the marginal product of labor higher for each quantity of labor, and the marginal product of labor is higher in equilibrium for the last worker hired. Thus, temporary shocks to total factor productivity are a candidate as a cause of business cycles. Indeed, the proponents of real business cycle theory, which we study in detail in Chapter 11, argue that total factor productivity shocks are the most important cause of business cycles.

THE EQUILIBRIUM EFFECTS OF AN INCREASE IN FUTURE TOTAL FACTOR PRODUCTIVITY, z'

The anticipation of future events can have important macroeconomic consequences currently, as when an increase in total factor productivity is expected to happen in the future. For example, firms might learn of a new invention, such as the design for a new production process, which is not available currently but will come on line in the future. We see that this shock increases current investment, current output, and current employment, and reduces the real wage.

Suppose that z' increases. This implies that the future marginal product of capital increases for the representative firm, and so the firm wishes to invest more in the current period, which increases the demand for current goods, shifting the output demand curve to the right in Figure 9.24(b). In equilibrium, this implies that aggregate

FIGURE 9.24   **The Equilibrium Effects of an Increase in Future Total Factor Productivity**

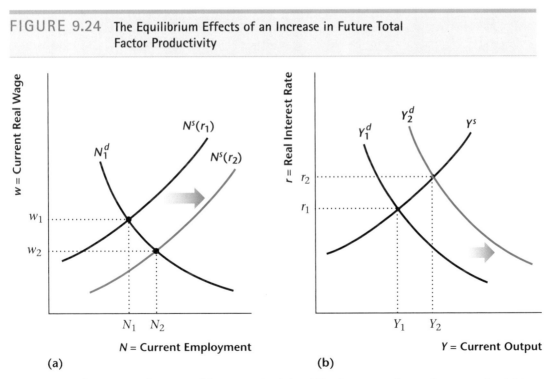

(a)   (b)

An anticipated increase in future total factor productivity shifts the output demand curve to the right, with current output and the real interest rate increasing in equilibrium. The real wage falls, and employment rises.

output increases from Y_1 to Y_2, and the real interest rate increases from r_1 to r_2. The increase in the real interest rate then causes current consumption to fall, but there is an opposing effect as consumption also tends to rise because of the increase in current income. In equilibrium, there are two effects on investment; the increase in z' causes investment to rise, and the increase in r causes it to fall. Consumption may rise or fall, but investment must rise, as the initial shock to the economy works through a positive effect on investment.

What are the effects in the labor market? The increase in the real interest rate leads to a rightward shift of the labor supply curve, from $N^s(r_1)$ to $N^s(r_2)$ in Figure 9.24(a). Therefore, in equilibrium, the quantity of employment increases from N_1 to N_2, and the real wage falls from w_1 to w_2.

In anticipation of a future increase in total factor productivity, firms increase investment expenditure, as the marginal payoff to having a higher future capital stock has increased. The increase in the demand for investment goods raises the market real interest rate, which increases labor supply and employment and generates an increase in aggregate output. The increase in labor supply causes the real wage to fall.

• •

THE "NEW ECONOMY" BECOMES OLD AGAIN

THEORY
confronts the
DATA

After the relatively mild 1991–92 recession, the 1990s was a time of great optimism. The stock market and investment expenditures boomed, and there was talk of a "new economy" of firms and consumers connected by advanced communications and information technologies in which business cycles would be a thing of the past. Widespread optimism was reflected in popular business strategy books such as Kevin Kelly's *New Rules for the New Economy: 10 Radical Strategies for a Connected World,* published in 1998.[1]

Figures 9.25–9.27 show, respectively, the percentage deviations from trend in real GDP and real investment, the ratio of investment to GDP, and the Standard and Poor's 500 stock price index. In Figure 9.25, we see that investment spending lead the economy out of the 1991–92 recession, with the trough in investment preceding the trough in GDP. In the figure, from 1991 until the beginning of 2000, investment increased from about 10% below trend to about 10% above trend. Another way of looking at the 1990s investment boom is to consider the ratio of investment to GDP, as shown in Figure 9.26, showing that the ratio of investment to GDP increased from close to 12% in 1991 to more than 19% at the beginning of 2000. Finally, in Figure 9.27, we see that stock prices increased by a factor of about 4 during the investment-boom period from 1991 to 2000.

The fact that a boom in investment is coupled in the 1990s with a boom in the stock market is strong evidence that investment was high because of high expectations

---

[1] K. Kelly, 1998. *New Rules for the New Economy: 10 Radical Strategies for a Connected World,* Viking Penguin, New York.

FIGURE 9.25 Percentage Deviations From Trend in GDP and Investment, 1990–2003

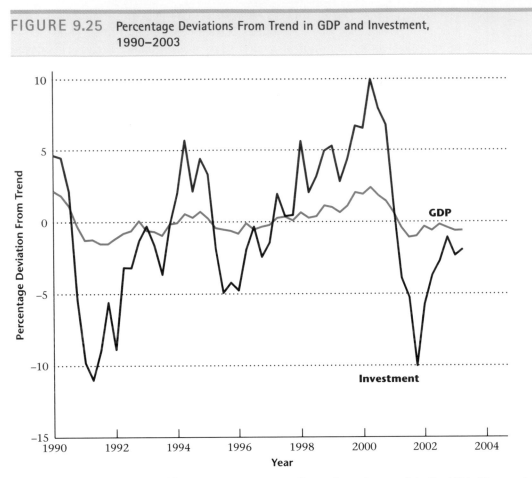

The figure shows the large buildup in investment expenditures from the trough in the 1991–92 recession to the peak in early 2000, followed by an investment crash to the trough of the 2001 recesssion.

Source: Bureau of Economic Analysis, Department of Commerce.

about future total factor productivity. In the real intertemporal model, an anticipated increase in z' leads to an increase in investment expenditures and GDP. The stock market is a convenient summary of sentiment among firms concerning the future. Increasing pessimism about future productivity is typically reflected in decreases in stock prices, while increasing optimism is reflected in increases in prices. Thus, what we see in Figures 9.25–9.27 is consistent with the story that investment was high in the 1990s because of optimism about future total factor productivity.

At the beginning of 2000, the optimism collapsed, with a dramatic contraction occurring in the high-technology sector of the economy. In Figures 9.25 and 9.26, investment expenditures fell from about 10% above trend to about 10% below trend

FIGURE 9.26   Investment as a Percentage of GDP, 1990–2003

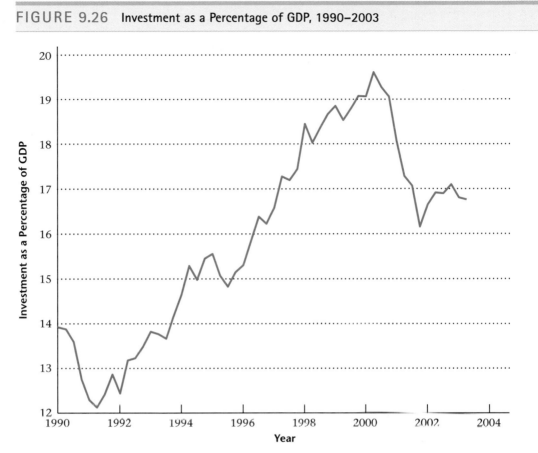

The fraction of GDP accounted for by investment increased dramatically from 1991 to 2000, and then decreased dramatically from 2000 to 2002.

Source: Bureau of Economic Analysis, Department of Commerce.

and from more than 19% of GDP to about 16% of GDP. Figure 9.27 shows that stock prices fell by more than 40% from the beginning of 2000 to the beginning of 2003, with the peak in stock prices in Figure 9.27 coinciding almost exactly with the peak in investment in Figure 9.25. Therefore, the dramatic decline in investment spending, which contributed in an important way to the recession of 2001, appears consistent with a decline in anticipated future total factor productivity.

As further evidence that the new economy may not yet be with us, hardcover copies of Kevin Kelly's book could be purchased on the internet for 20 cents in October 2003. It seems safe to say that fluctuations in GDP brought on by volatility in investment spending, in turn caused by waves of optimism and pessimism among investors, will be with us for a long time in the future.

FIGURE 9.27   Standard and Poor's 500 Stock Price Index, 1990–2003

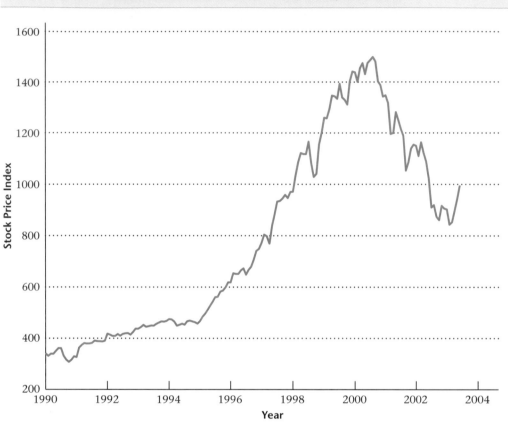

Stock prices increased dramatically from 1991 to 2000 and then fell, mirroring the behavior of investment in Figures 9.25 and 9.26.

Source: Standard and Poor's.

SECTORAL SHOCKS

A **sectoral shock** is any shock to the economy that results in a reallocation of factors of production from one or more industries in the economy to one or more other industries. Examples of sectoral shocks were the decline in the manufacturing sector in the United States relative to the service sector, beginning in the 1970s, and the increase in oil and natural gas production relative to production in other industries, induced by the energy price increases of 1974–75, 1979–80, 1991, 2001, and 2003. As we discuss in the next box item, one approach to analyzing the macroeconomic effects of the terrorist attacks of September 11, 2001, is to consider this as a type of sectoral shock.

On the one hand, a sectoral shock can occur because there is a shift in demand from one set of products to another, as was the case with the growth in services relative

FIGURE 9.28   The Effects of a Sectoral Shock

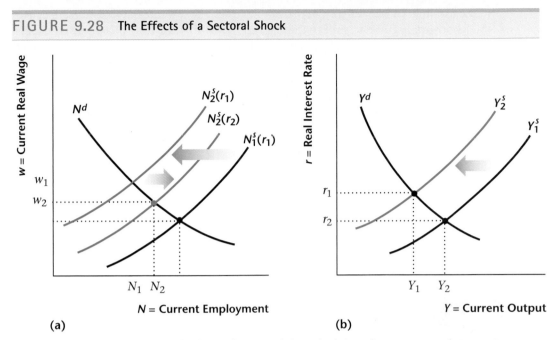

(a)   **(b)**

The labor supply curve shifts to the left, inducing a shift to the left in the output supply curve. In equilibrium, output falls, the real interest rate rises, consumption falls, investment falls, the real wage rises, and employment falls.

to manufacturing. On the other hand, a sectoral shock could occur because of a change in the relative productivities of sectors of the economy, as when manufacturing grew dramatically relative to agriculture during the Industrial Revolution. With either a shift in demand or a change in relative productivities, the shock results in workers being dislocated from jobs in the declining sector of the economy. It then takes time for these workers to find work in the expanding sector of the economy, and/or to receive training in the different skills that the expanding sector requires.

In Figure 9.28, we show the effects of a sectoral shock in the real intertemporal model. Because workers are temporarily dislocated from the declining sector and take time to find jobs in the expanding sector, there is effectively a temporary decrease in the supply of labor. Therefore, the labor supply curve shifts to the left from $N_1^s(r_1)$ to $N_2^s(r_1)$ in 9.28(b), and this shifts the output supply curve to the left from Y_1^s to Y_2^s in Figure 9.28(a). Whether the sectoral shock was the result of a shift in demand or a change in the relative productivities of different industries, on net there is no effect on the aggregate demand for consumption or investment goods or on the aggregate production technology. This is what makes this a sectoral shock—there are aggregate effects, but some aspects of the shock net out across sectors of the economy.

In equilibrium in Figure 9.28(a) there is an increase in the real interest rate from r_1 to r_2, and a decline in output from Y_1 to Y_2. Consumption decreases as the real interest rate has increased and income has fallen, and investment falls because of the increase in the real interest rate. Finally, in the labor market, the real interest rate increase causes the labor supply curve to shift to the right to $N_2^s(r_2)$, but the final position of the labor supply curve must be to the right of its initial position, as aggregate output has decreased (so employment must have decreased also). Therefore, employment falls from N_1 to N_2 and the real wage increases from w_1 to w_2.

Because of the frictions in the labor market that result in a period of adjustment as workers are reallocated from one industry to another, the economy contracts as a result of the sectoral shock. The shock, however, is temporary. After a period of time factors of production are reallocated as a result of the sectoral shock, and the economy returns to its initial equilibrium.

● ●

9/11 AS A SECTORAL SHOCK

THEORY confronts the DATA

The terrorist attacks that destroyed the World Trade Center in New York on September 11, 2001, had macroeconomic effects that can be understood in terms of three types of shocks to the economy. Aside from the tragic loss of life, which was the primary focus of national and international attention, the terrorist attacks represented a shock to total factor productivity, a shock to the capital stock, and a sectoral shock.

First, total factor productivity was reduced temporarily because of the immediate local effects of the terrorist attacks in New York City. Much financial activity was shut down or reduced dramatically for several days, and this had national and international implications as, for example, there was severe disruption to the U.S. payments system through which electronic payments are made among banks and other financial institutions. The fact that there was no air travel in the continental United States for several days also reduced total factor productivity temporarily, as this prevented firms from carrying on business and meant that checks could not be cleared effectively through the check-clearing system.

Second, and perhaps most obviously, the World Trade Center represented part of the nation's capital stock. The loss of capital stock in the terrorist attacks was similar in its effects to a natural disaster, and we analyzed this type of shock earlier in this chapter.

Third, the 9/11 terrorist attacks resulted in a sectoral shock to the economy. The attacks greatly reduced consumer demand for airline travel, and there was an associated decrease in the demand for tourism services (hotel services and restaurants, for example). However, this did not represent a reduction in the demand for all goods and services, but a shift from consumption of air travel and tourism to other goods and services. This sectoral shock caused the dislocation of workers from the airline and tourism sectors. These workers took time to retrain and find work in other sectors of the economy, with a resulting temporary loss in aggregate employment and output.

The sectoral shock aspect of the terrorist attacks is arguably the most important. This is because the reductions in total factor productivity and capital stock resulting from the attacks were apparently relatively small. The disruption to the financial system was temporary, the permanent inconvenience caused by increased security measures

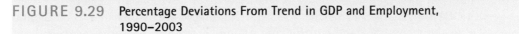

FIGURE 9.29   Percentage Deviations From Trend in GDP and Employment,
1990–2003

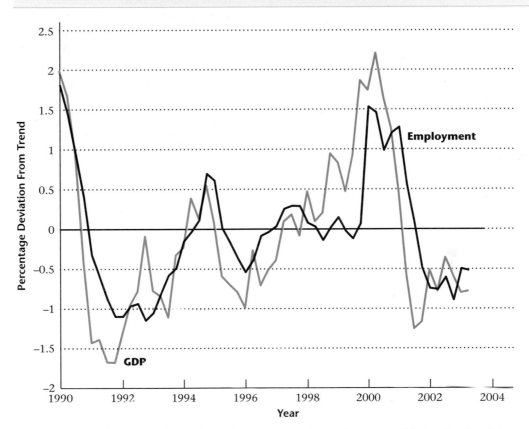

The sectoral shock associated with the 9/11 terrorist attacks may be responsible for the sluggish recovery from the recession of 2001.

Source: Bureau of Economic Analysis, Department of Commerce; Bureau of Labor Statistics.

seems negligible, and the World Trade Center accounted for a very small fraction of the nation's capital stock.

Figure 9.29 shows data on the percentage deviations from trend in quarterly GDP and employment for the period 1990Q1 to 2003Q2. Before the terrorist attacks occurred, which was late in the third quarter of 2001, GDP and employment were already well below trend, though the 2001 recession was less severe than the 1991–92 recession in terms of the deviation from trend in GDP at the trough of the recession (about −1.2% in 2001 vs. about −1.7% in 1990–91). In 2001, the trough in the deviation from trend in GDP occured in the third quarter. Even though the terrorist attacks happened only 19 days before the end of the quarter, they still could have caused GDP to be somewhat lower than it would have been otherwise during the third quarter of 1991. In the figure, after the third quarter of 2001 the economy began to recover, with GDP moving back somewhat toward trend. Employment appeared to be lagging GDP in the recovery phase, but this was not much different from the recovery from the 1990–91 recession (see Figure 9.29). Employment tends to be a lagging variable, as was discussed in Chapter 3. Though there is not quite enough data to go on, the recovery from the 2001 recession appears in the figure to be somewhat sluggish, with no apparent tendency for GDP and employment to be moving towards trend during 2002 and early 2003. This is certainly consistent with a lingering sectoral shock effect of the terrorist attacks, though there could be other causes of this as well.

Now that we have gained an understanding of the workings of our real intertemporal model, we can go on to use this model further, adding money and nominal variables in Chapter 10, and then using the model as a basis for studying business cycles in Chapters 11 and 12.

CHAPTER SUMMARY

- We developed a real intertemporal macroeconomic model that is useful for evaluating the macroeconomic effects of shocks to the economy, and which we can build on in later chapters. This model allows us to study the determinants of investment, consumption, aggregate output, the real interest rate, and employment, in an intertemporal setting.

- The model has two periods, the present and the future, and the representative consumer makes a work–leisure decision in each period and a consumption–savings decision in the current period. As the real interest rate increases, the consumer's demand for current consumption goods decreases, and his or her current labor supply increases. These effects are due to the intertemporal substitution of consumption and leisure between the present and the future in response to changes in the real interest rate.

- The representative firm produces output using labor and capital in each period. The firm's current demand for labor is determined by the usual marginal productivity condition (the marginal product of labor equals the real wage in the current period when the firm optimizes), and the firm invests in new capital in the current period until the net marginal product of capital in the future is equal to the real interest rate. An increase in the real interest rate leads to a decrease in the firm's optimal quantity of investment, and investment increases if the firm's initial quantity of capital decreases, or there is an anticipated increase in future total factor productivity.

- In equilibrium, the current goods market and the current labor market clear, and this implies that the credit market clears as well. For simplicity, we ignore markets in the future period.

- In the graphical representation of the model, there are two key elements: (1) output demand and supply, determining current aggregate output and the real interest rate; (2) current labor supply and current labor demand, determining current employment and the current real wage given the real interest rate.

- We conducted six experiments using the model:
  1. If current government purchases increase (a temporary increase in government spending), this increases the present value of taxes for the consumer, reducing lifetime wealth. As a result, the demand for current consumption goods falls, with the demand for current goods rising on net, and labor supply rises given the real interest rate. In equilibrium,

current output rises, current employment rises, the current real wage falls, and the real interest rate increases given that a temporary increase in government purchases implies that the output supply effect is small. Consumption and investment are crowded out. This is consistent with observations on U.S. investment during World War II, though the mechanism that caused investment to decrease then was somewhat different from what is depicted in the model.

2. If government spending increases permanently (both current and future government purchases increase), then the negative effect on current consumption demand roughly offsets the increase in the current demand for goods resulting from an increase in current government spending. There is then only an output supply effect, and aggregate output increases, the real interest rate falls, employment rises, the real wage falls, investment increases, and current consumption may rise or fall.

3. If the current capital stock decreases—for example, because of a natural disaster—then the optimal quantity of investment increases for the firm, given the real interest rate, so that output demand increases. Current output supply decreases, because the representative firm can produce less current output with a given input of labor. The real interest rate increases in equilibrium, but current aggregate output may rise or fall. If the output demand effect is small, then output falls.

4. If current total factor productivity increases (a temporary increase in total factor productivity), then output supply increases, the real interest rate falls, and consumption and investment increase in the current period. Current employment may rise or fall, but it rises provided the interest rate effect on labor supply is small. The current real wage rises. These predictions of the model replicate some of the key business cycle facts from Chapter 3.

5. An anticipated increase in future total factor productivity implies that the representative firm demands more investment goods, because the future marginal product of capital is expected to be higher. The demand for goods increases, causing the real interest rate and current aggregate output to rise. In the labor market, the real wage falls and employment rises, as the representative consumer substitutes leisure intertemporally in response to the real interest rate increase.

6. A sectoral shock is a shift in production from one sector of the economy to another, caused by a shift in demand or a change in relative productivities between sectors. This can be represented as a shift to the left in the labor supply curve. In equilibrium, employment falls, the real wage rises, output falls, the real interest rate rises, consumption decreases, and investment decreases.

KEY TERMS

Intertemporal substitution of leisure: The substitution of leisure between the current and future periods in response to the market real interest rate.

Marginal cost of investment: The profit forgone by the firm in the current period from investing in an additional unit of capital.

Marginal benefit of investment: The future marginal product of capital plus $1 - d$, where d is the depreciation rate.

Net marginal product of capital: The marginal product of capital minus the depreciation rate.

Optimal investment rule: Rule stating that the firm invests until the future net marginal product of capital is equal to the real interest rate.

Optimal investment schedule: A negative relationship between the firm's optimal quantity of investment and the market real interest rate.

Output supply curve: A positive relationship between the quantity of output supplied by firms and the real interest rate.

Output demand curve: A negative relationship between the quantity of output demanded (in the form of consumption expenditures, investment expenditures, and government expenditures) and the real interest rate.

Sectoral shock: any shock to the economy that results in a reallocation of factors of production from one or more industries in the economy to one or more other industries.

QUESTIONS FOR REVIEW

All questions refer to the macroeconomic model developed in this chapter.

1. Explain how intertemporal substitution is important for current labor supply and for the current demand for consumption goods.

2. What are three factors that determine current labor supply?

3. What determines the current demand for labor?

4. What is the goal of the representative firm in the real intertemporal model?

5. What rule does the representative firm follow in determining its optimal level of investment?

6. How is optimal investment for the firm affected by an increase in the current capital stock?

7. How is optimal investment affected by an increase in future total factor productivity?

8. What is the government's budget constraint in the real intertemporal model? Can the government run a deficit or run a surplus in the current period?

9. What are the factors that shift the output supply curve?

10. What are the factors that shift the output demand curve?

11. How are aggregate output and the real interest rate determined in competitive equilibrium?

12. What are the effects of a temporary increase in government purchases on the real interest rate, aggregate output, employment, the real wage, consumption, and investment?

13. What are the effects of a permanent increase in government purchases on the real interest rate, aggregate output, employment, the real wage, consumption, and investment? Explain why these results are different from the case in which government purchases increase temporarily.

14. What are the effects of a decrease in the current capital stock on the real interest rate, aggregate output, employment, the real wage, consumption, and investment?

15. What are the effects of an increase in total factor productivity on the real interest rate, aggregate output, employment, the real wage, consumption, and investment? Explain how these results relate to key business cycle facts and the causes of business cycles.

16. Determine the equilibrium effects of an anticipated increase in future total factor productivity in the real intertemporal model. Explain why these effects are different from the effects of an increase in current total factor productivity.

17. Explain what a sectoral shock is. What are the macroeconomic effects of a sectoral shock, and what are empirical examples of sectoral shocks?

PROBLEMS

1. What is the effect of an increase in d, the depreciation rate, on the representative firm's investment decision, and on its optimal investment schedule? Explain your results carefully.

2. Tom lives on an island and has 20 coconut trees in the current period, which currently produce 180 coconuts. Tom detests coconuts, but he can trade them with people on other neighboring islands for things that he wants. Further, Tom can borrow and lend coconuts with neighboring islands. In the coconut credit market, a loan of 1 coconut in the current period is repaid with 2 coconuts in the future period. Each period, Tom's trees produce, and then 10% of them die. If Tom plants a coconut in the ground in the current period, it will grow into a productive coconut tree in the future period. At the end of the future period, Tom can sell any remaining coconut trees for 1 coconut each. When Tom plants coconuts in the current period, he plants them in successively less fertile ground, and the less fertile the ground, the less productive is the coconut tree. For convenience, we assume here that fractions of coconuts can be produced by trees. Output in the future period, for given numbers of trees in production in the future period, is given in the following table:

Trees in Production in the Future	Future Output of Coconuts
15	155
16	162
17	168
18	173
19	177
20	180
21	182
22	183.8
23	184.8
24	185.2
25	185.4

   (a) Plot the level of output against the quantity of capital for the future period.
   (b) Plot the marginal product of capital against the quantity of capital for the future period.
   (c) Calculate Tom's present value of profits given each quantity of future trees.
   (d) Calculate the net marginal product of capital for each quantity of future trees.
   (e) Determine Tom's optimal quantity of investment, and explain your results.

3. The government wishes to bring about an increase in investment expenditures, and is considering two tax policies that policymakers think could bring this about. Under the first tax policy, firms would receive a subsidy in the current period of t per unit of current output produced. Policymakers reason that firms will use this subsidy for investment. The second policy under consideration is an investment tax credit, by which firms would receive a subsidy of s per unit of investment in the current period. Determine which tax policy would be more effective in accomplishing the government's goal of increasing current investment expenditures , and carefully explain your results.

4. Determine how the following affects the slope of the output demand curve, and explain your results:
   (a) The marginal propensity to consume increases.
   (b) The intertemporal substitution effect of the real interest rate on current consumption increases.
   (c) The demand for investment goods becomes less responsive to the real interest rate.

5. Determine how the following affects the slope of the output supply curve, and explain your results:
   (a) The marginal product of labor decreases at a faster rate as the quantity of labor used in production increases.
   (b) The intertemporal substitution effect of the real interest rate on current leisure decreases.

6. The government announces that an increase in government expenditure will occur next year. Use diagrams to determine the effects this will have on current aggregate output, current employment, the current real wage, the real interest rate, consumption, and investment. Explain your results.

7. Suppose that there is a shift in the representative consumer's preferences. Namely, the consumer prefers, given the market real interest rate, to consume less current leisure and more current consumption goods.
   (a) Determine the effects of this on current aggregate output, current employment, the current real wage, current consumption, and current investment.
   (b) Explain your results. What might cause such a change in the preferences of consumers?

8. Suppose that there is a permanent increase in total factor productivity. Determine the implications of this for current macroeconomic variables, and show how the impact differs from the case where total factor productivity is expected to increase only temporarily. Explain your results.

9. Suppose that z' increases and that K increases at the same time. Show that it is possible for the real interest rate to remain constant as a result. What does this say about the model's ability to explain the differences between poor and rich countries and to explain what happens as a country's economy grows?

10. There is a temporary increase in the relative price of energy. Determine how the response of current aggregate output to this shock depends on the marginal propensity to consume, and explain carefully why you get this result.

11. The nation experiences a major hurricane that destroys significant capital stock. Policymakers in the federal government reason that the destruction caused by the hurricane will reduce national income and that this should be counteracted through an increase in government expenditures.
    (a) Is the action suggested by these policymakers necessary, given what their goals appear to be?
    (b) What would be the net effects on the economy if government expenditures were temporarily increased after the hurricane?
    (c) Are there any circumstances when this course of action would make sense? Explain.

12. A war breaks out that is widely expected to last only one year. Show how the effect of this shock on aggregate output depends on the size of the intertemporal substitution effect of the real interest rate on current leisure, and carefully explain your results.

13. Explain, with the aid of diagrams, how you would distinguish empirically between a decrease in aggregate output caused by a reduction in total factor productivity and one caused by a sectoral shock.

WORKING WITH THE DATA

1. Calculate the ratio of real investment expenditures to GDP, quarterly, for the period 1947–2003, and calculate the real interest rate as the 3-month treasury bill rate minus the inflation rate (be careful that you calculate the inflation rate as an annualized rate), then plot the first variable against the second in a scatter plot. The theory of investment in this chapter predicts an optimal investment schedule that is a negative relationship between investment and the real interest rate. Is this what you observe in the data? Explain.

2. Calculate the ratio of total real government purchases to real GDP, quarterly, from first quarter 1947 to second quarter 2003. Also, calculate the real interest rate on a quarterly basis, as the 91-day Treasury bill rate in the last month of the quarter minus the inflation rate (measured as the percentage increase in the consumer price index from the last month of the previous quarter to the last month of the current quarter, multiplied by four to make this an annual rate).

   (a) Construct a scatter plot of the ratio of government purchases to GDP against the real interest rate.

   (b) Our real intertemporal model predicts that a temporary increase in government purchases causes an increase in the real interest rate. Is this implication of the model consistent with what you see in the scatter plot from part (a)? Explain why or why not.

3. Large increases in the relative price of energy occurred in 1974–75, 1979–80, in 1991 during the Persian Gulf War, in 2000, and in 2003. Is the behavior of detrended quarterly invesment expenditures consistent with the interpretation that increases in the relative price of energy are negative shocks to total factor productivity? Explain.

PART V

Money and Business Cycles

In this part, our first task is to integrate monetary factors into the real intertemporal model that was developed in Chapter 9. The resulting model, a monetary intertemporal model, is used in Chapter 10 to study the effects of changes in the quantity of money, the interaction between real and nominal phenomena, and monetary policy. In Chapters 11 and 12, we then use the monetary intertemporal model to study the causes of business cycles and the role of fiscal and monetary policy over the business cycle. In Chapter 11, we examine three equilibrium models of the business cycle, the first two of which imply that the government can at best make matters worse by smoothing business cycles, whereas the third is a modern Keynesian model in which government intervention to smooth business cycles can improve welfare. Chapter 12 is devoted to the examination of a traditional Keynesian sticky wage model, which justifies a role for government intervention to smooth business cycles. The alternative business cycle models we study highlight the many possible causes of business cycles, and in Chapters 11 and 12 we pay careful attention to the match between the predictions of business cycle models and the business cycle facts studied in Chapter 3.

CHAPTER 10

A Monetary Intertemporal Model: The Neutrality of Money

Money is important to the economy, for two reasons. First, the economy functions better with money than without it, because carrying out transactions by trading one kind of good for another is difficult, and because using credit in some transactions is costly or impossible. Second, changes in the quantity of money in existence matter for nominal quantities—for example, the price level—and can also affect real economic activity. The quantity of money in circulation is governed in most countries by a central bank, and the primary monetary policy decisions of the central bank concern the control of the money supply.

In this chapter, we construct a monetary intertemporal model, which builds on the real intertemporal model in Chapter 9. In the monetary intertemporal model, money is held so that consumers can carry out transactions. This model serves as the basis for our study of business cycles in Chapters 11 and 12.

The first result we show using the monetary intertemporal model is the **neutrality of money,** under which a one-time change in the money supply has no real consequences for the economy. Consumption, investment, output, employment, the real interest rate, and economic welfare remain unaffected. The neutrality of money is a good starting point for examining the role of money in the economy, but most macroeconomists agree that money is neutral only in the long run and that for various reasons changes in the money supply have real effects on the economy in the short run. We study these short-run nonneutralities of money in Chapters 11 and 12.

Our model determines a **money demand function,** which is a relationship between the quantity of money that economic agents wish to hold and other macroeconomic variables. We discuss some of the general empirical determinants of money demand and factors that cause the demand for money to shift over time. Shifts in the demand for money are a problem for monetary policy, particularly if monetary policy is formulated using monetarist doctrine. We show why monetarist-type monetary policy failed during the 1980s in the United States and other countries.

WHAT IS MONEY?

A traditional view of money is that it has three important functions. Namely, money is a **medium of exchange,** it is a **store of value,** and it is a **unit of account.** Money is a medium of exchange in that it is accepted in exchange for goods for the sole reason that it can in turn be traded for other goods, not because it is wanted for consumption purposes. Money is a store of value, like other assets such as stocks, bonds, housing, and so on, as it allows consumers to trade current goods for future goods. Finally, money is a unit of account because essentially all contracts are denominated in terms of money. For example, in the United States a typical labor contract is a promise to pay a specified number of U.S. dollars in exchange for a specified quantity of labor, and a typical loan contract is a promise to pay a specified number of U.S. dollars in the future in exchange for a specified quantity of U.S. dollars in the present. As well, U.S. firms keep their books in terms of U.S. dollars.

The distinguishing economic feature of money is its medium-of-exchange role. As mentioned above, there are other assets such as stocks, bonds, and housing that serve the store-of-value role that is served by money. However, there are difficulties in using these other assets in exchange. First, there is often imperfect information concerning the quality of assets. For example, it may be difficult to get the clerk in a convenience store to accept a stock certificate in exchange for a newspaper, as the clerk probably does not know the market value of the stock certificate, and it would be costly for him or her to sell the stock certificate. Second, some assets come in large denominations and are, therefore, difficult to use for small purchases. Even if the clerk in the convenience store knows the market value of a U.S. Treasury bill (a short-term debt instrument issued by the U.S. government), Treasury bills do not come in denominations less than $10,000, and so the clerk likely cannot make change for the purchase of a newspaper. Third, some assets take time to sell at their market value. For example, if I attempted to sell my house to the convenience store clerk, he or she would likely offer me much less for the house than I would receive if I searched the market for a buyer whose preferences best matched my house.

Measuring the Money Supply

As we discuss in more detail in Chapter 15, money has taken many forms historically. Money has circulated as commodity money (primarily silver and gold), circulating private bank notes (as was the case prior to the Civil War in the United States), commodity-backed paper currency (for example, under the gold standard), fiat money (for example, Federal Reserve notes in the United States), and transactions deposits at private banks. In the United States today, money consists mainly of objects that take the latter two forms, fiat money and transactions deposits at banks.

In modern developed economies, there are potentially many ways to measure the supply of money, depending on where we want to draw the line defining which assets satisfy the medium-of-exchange property and which do not. What is defined as money is somewhat arbitrary, and it is possible that we may want to use different definitions of money for different purposes. Table 10.1 shows measures of the standard **monetary aggregates** for September 2003, taken from the *Federal Reserve Bulletin*. A given monetary aggregate is simply the sum of a number of different assets for the U.S. economy.

The most narrowly defined monetary aggregate is M0, which is sometimes referred to as the **monetary base, outside money,** or **high-powered money.** The monetary

Table 10.1	**Monetary Aggregates, September 2003 (in $billions)**
M0	720.7
M1	1275.6
M2	6083.9
M3	8854.5

Source: Federal Reserve Bulletin.

base consists entirely of liabilities of the **Federal Reserve System** (the **Fed**), which is the central bank of the United States. The chief role of a central bank is to issue outside money. The liabilities making up M0 are U.S. currency outside the Fed and the deposits of depository institutions with the Fed. The quantity of M0 is called outside money, as it is the quantity of money outside of the banking system. The quantity of M1 is obtained by adding currency (outside the U.S. Treasury, the Fed, and the vaults of depository institutions), travelers' checks, demand deposits, and other checkable accounts at depository institutions. Thus, M1 is intended as a measure of the assets that are most widely used by the private sector in making transactions. The quantity of M2 is M1 plus savings deposits, small-denomination time deposits, and retail money market mutual funds. These additional assets are not directly used in transactions, but they are easily converted into currency and checkable deposits, which can be used in transactions. The quantity of M3 is M2 plus large-denomination time deposits, institutional money market mutual funds, repurchase agreements, and Eurodollars. The components added to M2 to obtain M3 are assets that can be converted into transactions assets fairly easily but with greater effort than for the components of M2.

The monetary aggregates are important, as they can be useful indirect measures of aggregate economic activity that are available on a more timely basis than GDP. Further, there are key regularities in the relationship between monetary aggregates and other aggregate variables, which make monetary aggregates useful in economic forecasting and in policy analysis. Finally, the paths followed by monetary aggregates over time can be useful in evaluating the performance of the Fed.

A MONETARY INTERTEMPORAL MODEL

Why do we use money in exchange? A useful analogy is that money is to economic exchange as oil is to an engine; money overcomes "frictions." Two important economic frictions that make money useful are the following. First, in modern economies, barter exchange—the exchange of goods for goods—is difficult. As Adam Smith recognized in his *Wealth of Nations,* specialization is key to the efficiency gains that come from economic development. Once economic agents become specialized in what they produce and what they consume, it becomes very time-consuming to trade what one has for what one wants through barter exchange. For example, if Sara specializes in giving economics lectures and wants to buy car repairs, to make a barter exchange she must not only find someone willing to repair her car—a **single coincidence of** wants,—but the car repair person must also want to receive a lecture in economics—a **double coincidence of wants.** Clearly, Sara may have to spend a great deal of time and energy searching for a trading partner! The double coincidence problem was first studied by William Stanley Jevons in the nineteenth century.[1] Money solves the double-coincidence problem because, if everyone accepts money in exchange, then would-be buyers need only satisfy a single-coincidence problem to buy a good, which is much easier. Sara can sell economics lectures for money and then exchange this money for car repairs.

A second reason that money is useful in exchange is that there are circumstances where credit transactions may be difficult or impossible to make. For example, it would be unlikely that a street vendor in New York City would accept my personal IOU in exchange for a hot dog. Because the street vendor does not know me or my credit history, he or she cannot evaluate whether my IOU is good or not, and it would be costly for him or her to take legal action should I not be willing to pay off my IOU. While modern credit card systems solve some of the information problems connected with the use of personal credit in transactions, these systems are costly to operate, and there are sellers of goods who do not accept credit under any circumstances. Because money is easily recognizable, there are essentially no information problems associated with the use of money in exchange, other than the problems that arise from counterfeiting.

There is much heated debate concerning how monetary exchange should be represented in macroeconomic models. According to one view,[2] if we are to understand the role of money in the economy and how monetary policy works, we need to model money at a deep level. That is, we need to model the fundamental reasons money is held—the frictions that make money useful—to make progress. In Chapter 15, we study a model that takes explicit account of the double-coincidence-of-wants problem in barter exchange discussed above and show how this problem gives rise to a role for money. A drawback of deep models of money is that they are sometimes difficult to work with, and such models are not typically useful for matching features of economic data. An alternative view is that, in many circumstances, it is sufficient in modeling money in a macroeconomic context to simply assume that money is used in all or some transactions and then proceed from there. This approach is relatively simple, and it yields a modeling framework that is more amenable to the problem of matching theory with data. It is this second, more practical, approach that we take in this chapter, but the deep approach to modeling money has much merit, particularly in advanced monetary economics.

In the model we construct here, we assume at the outset that all consumption goods must be purchased with cash on hand. In the macroeconomics literature, this type of model is called a **cash-in-advance model,** and it has been used extensively.

---

[1] See S. Jevons, 1910. *Money and the Mechanism of Exchange,* 23rd edition, Kegan Paul, London.

[2] See J. Kareken and N. Wallace, 1980. "Introduction," in J. Kareken and N. Wallace, eds., *Models of Monetary Economies,* Federal Reserve Bank of Minneapolis, Minneapolis, MN, pp. 1–12; and N. Wallace, 1998. "A Dictum for Monetary Theory," *Federal Reserve Bank of Minneapolis Quarterly Review,* Winter, 20–26.

The idea behind the cash-in-advance model originated with Robert Clower,[3] and Robert Lucas made important contributions to its development and applications.[4]

We use the details of the monetary intertemporal model in this chapter to examine the neutrality of money, the effects of shocks to the economy on nominal variables, and monetary policy issues.

Real and Nominal Interest Rates and the Fisher Relation

In the monetary intertemporal model that we construct, there are many periods but, just as in the economic growth models studied in Chapters 6 and 7, our analysis is mainly in terms of an arbitrary *current period* and the following period, which we refer to as the *future period*. There are two assets, money and nominal bonds. For simplicity, there are not any banks in the model (we consider banking in Chapter 15), and so the entire money stock is assumed to consist of currency. We use money as the numeraire here (recall that the numeraire is the object in which all prices are denominated in an economic model) with P denoting the current price level, or the current price of goods in terms of money. Similarly, P' denotes the price level in the future period. A **nominal bond** is an asset that sells for one unit of money (e.g., one dollar in the United States) in the current period and pays off $1 + R$ units of money in the future period. Therefore, R is the rate of return on a bond in units of money, or the **nominal interest rate.** Nominal bonds can be issued by the government, or by consumers, and all bonds bear the same nominal interest rate, as we are assuming that no one defaults on their debts.

As in Chapters 8 and 9, the real rate of interest, r, is the rate of interest in terms of goods. The real interest rate is the real rate of return that someone receives when holding a nominal bond from the current period to the future period. The real interest rate can be determined from the nominal interest rate, and the **inflation rate** i, which is defined by

$$i = \frac{P' - P}{P}.\tag{10.1}$$

That is, the inflation rate is the rate of increase in the price level from the current period to the future period. Then, the real interest rate is determined by the **Fisher relation,** named after Irving Fisher, which is

$$1 + r = \frac{1 + R}{1 + i}.\tag{10.2}$$

To derive the Fisher relation, recall that $1 + R$ is the return in terms of money in the future period from giving up one unit of money in the current period to buy a nominal bond. In real terms, someone acquiring a nominal bond gives up $\frac{1}{P}$ goods in the current period and receives a payoff of $\frac{1+R}{P'}$ goods in the future period. Therefore, from Equation (10.1),

---

[3]See R. Clower, 1967. "A Reconsideration of the Microfoundations of Monetary Theory," *Western Economic Journal* 6, 1–8.

[4]See R. Lucas, 1980. "Equilibrium in a Pure Currency Economy," in J. Kareken and N. Wallace, eds., *Models of Monetary Economies,* pp. 131–146, Federal Reserve Bank of Minneapolis, Minneapolis, MN; and R. Lucas and N. Stokey, 1987. "Money and Interest in a Cash-in-Advance Economy," *Econometrica* 55, 491–514.

the gross rate of return on the nominal bond, in real terms, is

$$1 + r = \frac{\frac{1+R}{P'}}{\frac{1}{P}} = \frac{1+R}{\frac{P'}{P}} = \frac{1+R}{1+i},$$

which gives us the Fisher relation (10.2).

Given a positive nominal interest rate on nominal bonds—that is, $R > 0$—the rate of return on nominal bonds exceeds the rate of return on money. The nominal interest rate on money is zero, and the real interest rate on money can be determined just as we determined the real interest rate associated with the nominal bond above. That is, if r^m is the real rate of interest on money, then as in Equation (10.2), we have

$$1 + r^m = \frac{1+0}{1+i} = \frac{1}{1+i},$$

and so if $R > 0$ then $r^m < r$, or the real interest rate on money is less than the real interest rate on the nominal bond. In our monetary intertemporal model, we need to explain why people are willing to hold money if they can receive a higher rate of return on the alternative asset, nominal bonds, when the nominal interest rate is positive.

Now, the Fisher relation can be rewritten by multiplying each side of Equation (10.2) by $1 + i$ and rearranging to get

$$r = R - i - ir.$$

Then, if the nominal interest rate and the inflation rate are small, ir is negligible; for example, if the inflation rate is 10% and the real interest rate is 8%, then $i = 0.1$, $r = 0.08$, and $ir = 0.008$. We can say that, for small inflation rates and interest rates,

$$r \approx R - i; \tag{10.3}$$

that is, the real interest rate is approximately equal to the nominal interest rate minus the inflation rate. For example, if the nominal interest rate is 5%, or 0.05, and the inflation rate is 3%, or 0.03, then the real interest rate is approximately 2%, or 0.02.

Empirically, there is a problem in measuring the real interest rate. Nominal interest rates on many different assets can be observed, but economic agents do not know the inflation rate that will be realized over the time they hold a particular asset. The correct inflation rate to use might be the one that an economic agent expects, but expectations cannot be observed. However, one approach to measuring the real rate of interest is to calculate it based on Equation (10.3), using the realized inflation rate for i. In Figure 10.1 we show data on the nominal interest rate, measured as the interest rate on 91-day U.S. Treasury bills over the period 1934–2003 and the corresponding real rate, calculated as the nominal interest rate minus the inflation rate. The measured real interest rate has varied considerably over time, and it has sometimes been quite low, dipping below 0% several times over this sample period, particularly during the early and late 1940s, early 1950s, and 1970s.

Representative Consumer

In constructing the monetary intertemporal model, we need to modify the real intertemporal model of Chapter 9 to account for the fact that transactions require money. For the analysis that we do in this chapter and in Chapters 11 and 12, we do not have

FIGURE 10.1   Real and Nominal Interest Rates, 1948–2003

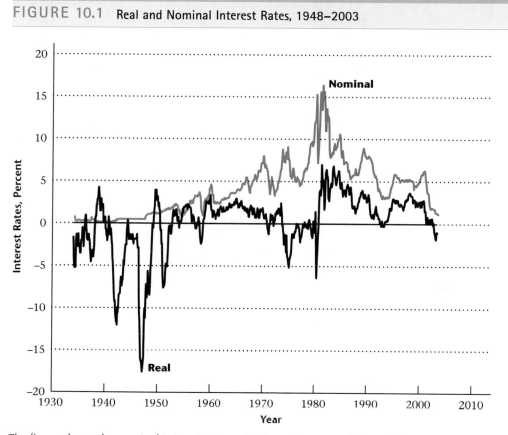

The figure shows the nominal interest rate on 91-day U.S. Treasury bills and the corresponding real interest rate, calculated as the nominal interest rate minus the rate of change in the consumer price index.

Source: Federal Reserve Bulletin and Bureau of Labor Statistics.

to alter how we model demand and supply in the labor market and goods market. However, we need to introduce a new market, the market for money. Here the demand for money is determined by the behavior of the representative consumer, and the supply of money is determined by the central bank. To understand the determinants of the demand for money, we need to be specific about how the representative consumer makes choices about how much money he or she should hold in conjunction with his or her consumption, savings, and labor supply decisions.

We assume in our model that the representative consumer carries out transactions during the period in a particular sequence. The order in which transactions occur may not always appear realistic, but it allows us to tell a simple story about the role that money plays in actual economies. The representative consumer begins the current period with supplies of the two available assets which were carried over from the previous period, nominal money M^- and nominal bonds B^-, each measured in units of money.

It is most convenient here to think of the money balances held by the consumer as being currency only. The consumer must then pay a lump-sum tax to the government in money, which is T in real terms or PT in nominal terms. Following this, the consumer goes to the credit market to rearrange his or her **asset portfolio** (an asset portfolio is just a collection of assets). We can think of these credit market exchanges as involving a trip to the bank or the ATM, though, as mentioned previously, there are no explicit banking institutions in the model. At the asset market, the consumer receives the payoff on the nominal bonds acquired last period. Each bond pays off $1 + R^-$ dollars at the beginning of the period (R^- is last period's nominal interest rate), so the total payoff to the consumer from bonds acquired last period is $B^-(1 + R^-)$. Then, the consumer chooses the quantity of nominal bonds B^d to purchase in the credit market in the current period, with each of these bonds being a promise to pay $1 + R$ units of money in the future period. As in the real intertemporal model, the consumer can lend or borrow on the credit market, so we could have $B^d \geq 0$ or $B^d \leq 0$, respectively. All transactions on the credit market are carried out using money. That is, the payoffs on bonds acquired in the previous period are received in money, new bonds are purchased using money, and the consumer borrows money if $B^d < 0$.

The consumer in our model cannot be in more than one place at once. After leaving the credit market, he or she goes to work for the firm, supplying $h - l$ units of labor (recall that h is the quantity of time the consumer has available, and l is the quantity of leisure consumed). The market real wage is w, so that the market nominal wage is Pw. The consumer does not receive his or her wages for this period until after the firm has sold its goods.

After finishing work, the consumer goes to the goods market to purchase consumption goods, and we assume that all consumption goods must be purchased with money. The assumption that all goods purchased are made using currency is clearly unrealistic, as much of the volume of transactions carried out in the U.S. economy makes use of credit cards, debit cards, checks, or some other alternative to currency. For our purposes, however, the conclusions would not be different if we introduced credit in our model, and we would lose simplicity. The consumer cannot spend more money on consumption goods than he or she has on hand when leaving the credit market. That is,

$$PC \leq M^- + B^-(1 + R^-) - PT - B^d, \qquad (10.4)$$

or the nominal value of consumption goods purchased (the quantity on the left-hand side of inequality (10.4)) cannot exceed (on the right-hand side of inequality (10.4)) the money balances the consumer has at the beginning of the period, plus the payoff on the nominal bonds held over from the previous period, minus nominal taxes, minus purchases of nominal bonds that pay off in the future period. The inequality (10.4) is a **cash-in-advance constraint** that states that nominal consumption cannot exceed the quantity of money on hand.

Finally, at the end of the period, after consumer goods are purchased, the consumer receives wages $Pw(h - l)$ and dividend income $P\pi$ from the firm, all paid in money, and decides how much nominal money balances M^d to carry over into the future period. Thus, the consumer's budget constraint can be written as

$$PC + B^d + M^d = M^- + B^-(1 + R^-) + Pw(h - l) + P\pi - PT, \qquad (10.5)$$

which states that nominal consumption purchases plus purchases of nominal bonds, plus money holdings at the end of the period, are equal to the consumer's money balances at the beginning of the period, plus total payoffs on bonds acquired last period, plus nominal wage income, plus nominal dividend income, minus nominal taxes.

During the period, the consumer chooses current consumption C, current leisure l, holdings of nominal bonds B^d, and money holdings M^d to make himself or herself as well off as possible, while satisfying the cash-in-advance constraint, inequality (10.4), and the budget constraint, Equation (10.5). A key feature of the consumer's problem is that wage and dividend income cannot be spent on consumption goods during the current period; current dividends and wages must be held as money until the future period when they can be spent.

Figure 10.2 illustrates the sequence of transactions and the flows of goods and assets during the period. At the beginning of the period, the consumer is holding all of the money in the economy. In the first stage, (a), the government collects taxes in the form of money from the consumer. Then, in stage (b), in the credit market, the government pays the interest and principal to consumers on bonds that the government issued in the previous period in money. As well, the government issues new nominal bonds, which are purchased by the consumer with money. After stage (b), the consumer and the government hold the total stock of money between them. In stage (c), the government spends all of its money making purchases from the firm, and the consumer buys consumption goods from the firm with money. Following this, in stage (d) the firm pays out all the money it acquired in stage (c) to the consumer as wage and dividend payments. Thus, at the end of the period after stage (d) the consumer is holding the total stock of money.

If the nominal interest rate is positive—that is $R > 0$—then the rate of return on bonds is greater than that on money, and this is the case we deal with here. Given a positive nominal interest rate, the consumer goes to the goods market with no more money than is necessary to purchase goods. This implies that the cash-in-advance constraint, inequality (10.4) is satisfied with equality. If the cash-in-advance constraint were not an equality, this would imply that the consumer was planning to carry money over from the credit market into the future period. But this would not be optimal, as bonds pay a higher return than money does; with a positive nominal interest rate, the consumer wishes to hold money only as a medium of exchange, not as a store of wealth.

Now, because money is acquired in the current period so that the consumer can purchase consumption goods in the future period, the consumer's demand for money, in real terms, is positively related to the consumer's lifetime wealth, as the higher is lifetime wealth the more goods the consumer wants to purchase. As well, because holding money implies that the consumer forgoes the nominal interest earned on bonds, with the nominal interest rate then representing the opportunity cost of holding money, real money demand depends negatively on the nominal interest rate. For convenience, we use real aggregate income as a proxy for the representative consumer's lifetime wealth, which implies that we can specify the demand for money in real terms as

$$\frac{M^d}{P} = L(Y, R), \tag{10.6}$$

FIGURE 10.2   The Sequence of Transactions During a Period in the Monetary Intertemporal Model

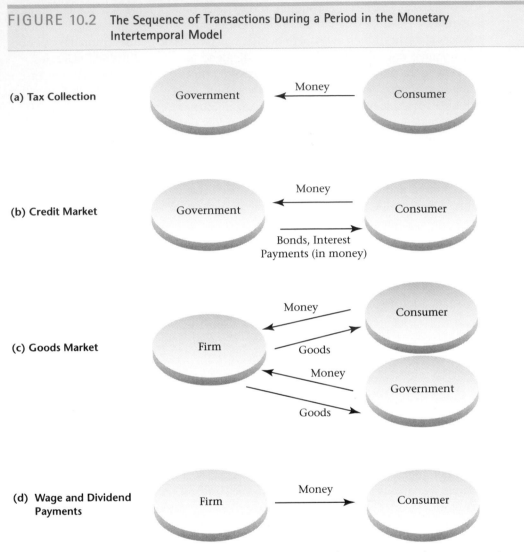

The figure shows how goods and assets are transferred among the government, the representative consumer, and the representative firm during the period.

where $\frac{M^d}{P}$ is money demand in terms of goods and L is a function that is increasing in real income Y and decreasing in the nominal interest rate R. We can rewrite Equation (9.9) by multiplying both sides by P, which gives

$$M^d = PL(Y, R). \tag{10.7}$$

In Equation (10.7), M^d is nominal money demand.

FIGURE 10.3   The Nominal Money Demand Curve in the Monetary
Intertemporal Model

Nominal money demand is a straight line
and it shifts with changes in real income
Y and the real interest rate r.

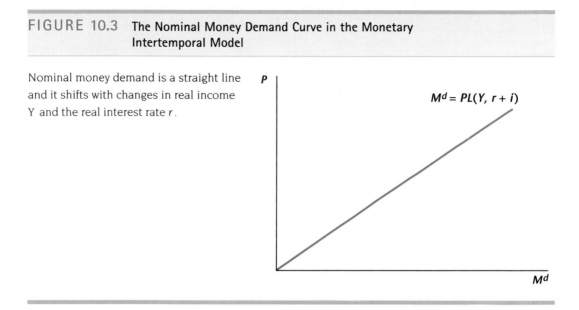

Now, taking the approximate Fisher relation (10.3) as an equality (that is, assuming the real interest rate and the inflation rate are small) implies that we can substitute $r + i$ for R in Equation (10.7) to get

$$M^d = PL(Y, r + i).\qquad(10.8)$$

For the analysis we do in this chapter and in Chapters 11 and 12, we look at economic experiments that do not deal with the effects of changes in long-run inflation. That is, all of the experiments we consider in these chapters leave i unaffected. When i is constant in Equation (10.8), it is harmless to set it to zero for convenience, which implies that Equation (10.8) becomes

$$M^d = PL(Y, r).\qquad(10.9)$$

With Y and r given, the function on the right-hand side of Equation (10.9) is linear in P with slope $L(Y, r)$, and we depict this function in Figure 10.3. If real income increases, for example from Y_1 to Y_2, then in Figure 10.4 the money demand curve shifts to the right from $PL(Y_1, r)$ to $PL(Y_2, r)$. We would obtain the same type of rightward shift in the money demand curve if the real interest rate r were to decrease.

Government

We have to expand on our treatment of government from Chapter 9 to take into account the ability of the government to issue money. For our purposes, it is convenient to assume that there is a single institution in our model called the government, which is responsible for both fiscal and monetary policy. Therefore, the government entity in this model is essentially what we would get if we merged the U.S. Treasury with the Federal Reserve System and placed them both under the control of the Congress. In the

FIGURE 10.4   The Effect of an Increase in Current Real Income on the Nominal Money Demand Curve

The current nominal money demand curve shifts to the right with an increase in current real income Y. The curve shifts in the same way if there is a decrease in the real interest rate r.

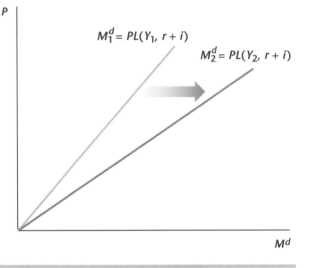

$M_1^d = PL(Y_1, r + i)$

$M_2^d = PL(Y_2, r + i)$

United States, the Federal Reserve System, which is the monetary authority, is essentially independent of the Treasury, which is the federal fiscal authority controlled by the U.S. government. The arrangement between the central bank and the federal government varies considerably across countries. In some countries, such as the United States, the central bank has considerable independence, while in other countries it does not.

In the current period, the government purchases G consumption goods and pays the nominal interest and principal on the government debt outstanding from the last period, $(1 + R^-)B^-$, where B^- is the quantity of one-period nominal bonds issued by the government in the previous period, which come due in the current period, with each of these bonds bearing a nominal interest rate of R^-. Current government purchases and the interest and principal on government debt, which sum to total current government outlays, are financed through taxation, the issue of new bonds, and by printing money. The government budget constraint in the current period is, therefore, given by

$$PG + (1 + R^-)B^- = PT + B + M - M^-. \tag{10.10}$$

The government budget constraint, Equation (10.10) is expressed in nominal terms, with the left-hand side denoting total government outlays during the period, and the right-hand side denoting total government receipts. On the right-hand side, PT denotes nominal taxes, B denotes government bonds issued in the current period, which come due in the future period, and the final term, $M - M^-$, is the change in the nominal money supply, where M is the total quantity of money outstanding in the current period, and M^- is the previous period's money supply.

Adding money creation, $M - M^-$, to the government budget constraint is an important step here over the kinds of models we considered in Chapters 5, 8, and 9, where we did not take account of the monetary transactions that take place in the economy. We are now able to consider the effects of monetary policy and how monetary and fiscal policy interact.

Competitive Equilibrium—The Complete Intertemporal Monetary Model

In the monetary intertemporal model there are three markets to consider—the market for current goods, the market for current labor, and the money market. As in the real intertemporal model studied in Chapter 9, equilibrium in the credit market is implied by equilibrium in these three other markets. The markets for current goods and current labor operate exactly as in the real intertemporal model, so the only important difference here from the model of Chapter 9 is the addition of the money market.

The nominal demand for money M^d is given by Equation (10.9), while the nominal money supply M^s is determined exogenously by the government, with $M^s = M$. When the money market is in equilibrium, the quantity of money supplied equals the quantity demanded, or $M^s = M^d$, so that from Equation (10.9),

$$M = PL(Y, r). \tag{10.11}$$

In Figure 10.5 we illustrate the workings of the money market, with the nominal money demand curve M^d being upward sloping and linear in P, as we saw previously. Here, we have added the money supply curve, which is a vertical line at the quantity M, because the money supply is exogenous. The intersection of the nominal money demand and nominal money supply curves determines the price level P. In the figure, the equilibrium price level is P^*.

Next, integrating the money market into the real intertemporal model of Chapter 9, we show in Figure 10.6 how the endogenous variables in the monetary intertemporal

---

FIGURE 10.5   The Current Money Market in the Monetary Intertemporal Model

The figure shows the current nominal demand for money curve M^d and the money supply curve M^s. The intersection of these two curves determines the equilibrium price level, which is P^* in the figure.

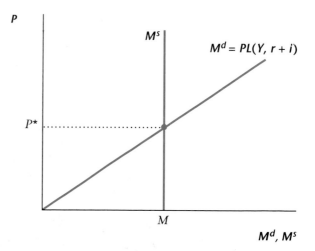

FIGURE 10.6   The Complete Monetary Intertemporal Model

In the model, the equilibrium real interest rate r and equilibrium current aggregate output Y are determined in panel (b). Then, the real interest rate determines the position of the labor supply curve in panel (a), where the equilibrium real wage w and equilibrium employment N are determined. Finally, the equilibrium price level P is determined in the money market in panel (c), given the equilibrium real interest rate r and equilibrium output Y.

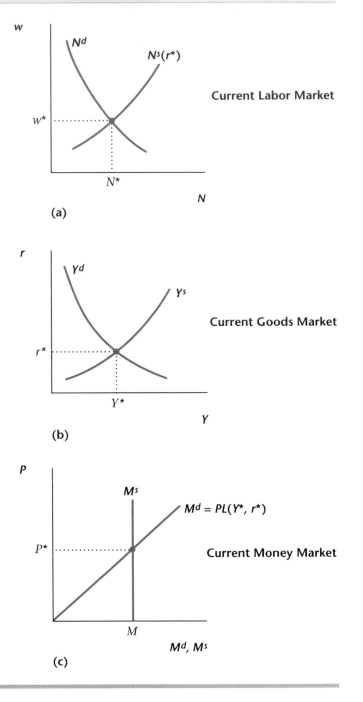

model are determined. In Figure 10.6(b), we depict equilibrium in the current goods market, where the output demand curve Y^d and the output supply curve Y^s jointly determine the equilibrium real interest rate r^* and the equilibrium quantity of aggregate output, Y^*. Then, in Figure 10.6(a), given the equilibrium real interest rate r^*, which determines the position of the labor supply curve $N^s(r^*)$, the labor demand curve N^d and the labor supply curve $N^s(r^*)$ jointly determine the equilibrium real wage w^* and the equilibrium quantity of employment, N^*. Then, in Figure 10.6(c), the equilibrium quantity of output, Y^*, and the equilibrium real interest rate r^* determine the position of the money demand curve M^d. Then, the money demand curve and the money supply curve in Figure 10.6(c) determine the equilibrium price level P^*.

A LEVEL INCREASE IN THE MONEY SUPPLY AND MONETARY NEUTRALITY

A government, through its central bank, has the power to increase the money supply by several different means. Historically, the power of a government to print money has been important, as the issue of new money can finance transfers to the private sector, can involve changing the quantity of interest-bearing assets held by the private sector, and can finance government expenditures. In this section, we would like to determine the effects on current macroeconomic variables of a one-time increase in the money supply. As we will see, a change in the level of the money supply of this sort is neutral, in that no real variables change, but all nominal quantities change in proportion to the change in the money supply. The neutrality of money is an important concept in monetary economics, and we want to understand the theory behind it and what it means in practice

In the experiment we perform in the model, we suppose that the money supply is fixed at the quantity $M = M_1$ until the current period, as in Figure 10.7. Until the current period, everyone anticipates that the money supply remains fixed at the quantity M_1 forever. During the current period, however, the money supply increases from M_1 to M_2 and then remains at that level forever. What could cause such an increase in the money supply? From the government budget constraint, Equation (10.10), the change in the money supply in the current period, $M - M^- = M_2 - M_1$, is positive, and so this positive change in the money supply in the current period needs to be offset by some other term in Equation (10.10). Because the nominal interest rate from the previous period, R^-, and the quantity of bonds issued by the government in the previous period, B^-, were determined last period based on the expectation that the quantity of money in circulation would be M_1 forever, only the other terms in Equation (10.10) could be affected. There are three possibilities:

1. The government could reduce current taxes T. The money supply increase, therefore, is reflected in a decrease in taxes on the household, which is the same as an increase in transfers. Milton Friedman referred to this method of increasing the money stock as a **"helicopter drop,"** because it is much like having a government helicopter fly over the countryside spewing money.

FIGURE 10.7   **A Level Increase in the Money Supply in the Current Period**

The figure shows a one-time increase in the money supply from M_1 to M_2.

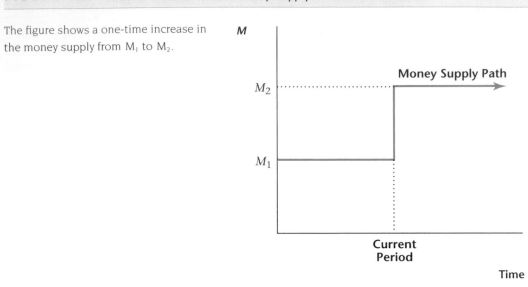

2. The government could reduce the quantity of bonds, B, that it issues during the current period. This is an **open market operation,** which in practice is carried out when the fiscal authority issues interest-bearing government debt, and then the monetary authority—the central bank—purchases some of this debt by issuing new money. An **open market purchase** is an exchange of money for interest-bearing debt by the monetary authority, and an **open market sale** is the sale of interest-bearing debt initially held by the monetary authority in exchange for money. In the case we examine here, where the money supply increases, there is an open market purchase. The day-to-day control of the money supply is accomplished in the United States mainly through open market operations by the Fed.

3. The government could temporarily increase the quantity of government spending, G, in the current period. Thus, the government would be printing money in order to finance government spending. When the government does this, it collects **seigniorage.** Seigniorage originally referred to the profit made by a seigneur, or ruler, from issuing coinage, but it has come to take on a broader meaning as the revenue earned by the government from issuing money. Seigniorage is also referred to as the revenue from the **inflation tax,** because the extra money that the government prints in general increases prices. Historically, seigniorage has been an important revenue-generating device. In the United States, seigniorage was a key source of revenue for the federal government during the Civil War and during World War I.

For our purposes here, it is most convenient for now to suppose that the money supply increase occurs through the first aforementioned method—a lump-sum transfer of money to the representative consumer. What happens in equilibrium when the money supply increases in the current period from M_1 to M_2? Here, because the level of the money supply does not matter for labor supply, labor demand, and the demand and supply of goods, the equilibrium determination of N, Y, r, and w in Figure 10.8 is unaffected by the current money supply M. That is, there a **classical dichotomy:** The model solves for all the real variables (output, employment, the real interest rate, and the real wage) in the labor market and the goods market in Figure 10.8, and the price level is then determined, given real output, in the money market. Real activity is completely separated from nominal variables (the money supply, the price level). In Figure 10.8(b), the real interest rate and current real output are given by r_1 and Y_1, respectively, and in Figure 10.8(a), the equilibrium real wage and level of employment are w_1 and N_1, respectively.

In the model, we want to investigate the effects of having a money supply of M_2 from the current period on, rather than a money supply of M_1. In Figure 10.8 there is no effect on real activity, because the labor market and goods market are unaffected by the level of the money supply. However, there is an effect on the price level. In Figure 10.8(c), the money supply curve shifts to the right because of the increase in the money supply from M_1 to M_2. The money demand curve is unaffected, because Y does not change and r does not change. As a result, the price level increases in equilibrium from P_1 to P_2. Further, we can say something about how much the price level increases. Because $M = PL(Y, r)$ in equilibrium (money supply equals money demand) and because Y, and r are unaffected by the increase in M, P must increase in proportion to M, so that $\frac{M}{P} = L(Y, r)$ remains unchanged. That is, if M increases by 10%, then P increases by 10%, so that the real money supply $\frac{M}{P}$ is unaffected. Note that the level increase in the money supply causes a level increase in the price level. There is only a one-time increase in the inflation rate (the rate of change in the price level), from the previous period to the current period, and no long-run increase in the inflation rate.

In this model, then, money is neutral. Money neutrality is said to hold if a change in the level of the money supply results only in a proportionate increase in prices, with no effects on any real variables. Thus, a change in the level of the money supply does not matter here. This does not mean, however, that money does not matter. In this model, if there were no money, then no goods could be consumed, because money is necessary to acquire these goods. In the real world, even if money were neutral, we know that if we eliminated money, then people would have to use more cumbersome means, such as barter, for making transactions. This would be much less efficient, and, in general, people would be worse off.

Is monetary neutrality a feature of the real world? In one sense, it almost obviously is. Suppose that the government could magically add a zero to all Federal Reserve notes. That is, suppose that overnight all \$1 bills become \$10 bills, all \$5 bills become \$50 bills, and so on. Suppose further that this change was announced several months in advance. It seems clear that, on the morning when everyone wakes up with their

FIGURE 10.8   The Effects of a Level Increase in M—The Neutrality of Money

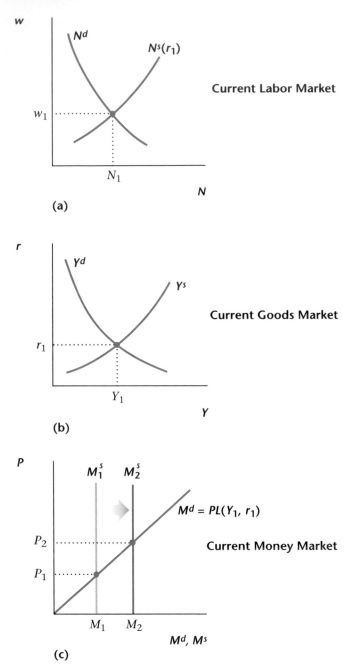

(a) Current Labor Market

(b) Current Goods Market

(c) Current Money Market

A level increase in the money supply in the monetary intertemporal model from M_1 to M_2 has no effects on any real variables, but the price level increases in proportion to the increase in the money supply. Money is neutral.

currency holdings increased by 10 times, all sellers of goods would have anticipated this change and would have increased their prices by 10 times as well, and that there would be no real change in aggregate economic activity. Though this thought experiment helps us understand the logic behind monetary neutrality, real-world increases in the money supply do not occur in this way, and there is in fact much debate about the extent of money neutrality in the short run.

Later, in Chapters 11 and 12, we explore the role of money in causing short-run fluctuations in real macroeconomic activity. Whether or not money is neutral in the short run can depend on how changes in the money supply are brought about, for example, through transfer payments, open market operations, or money-financed increases in government purchases. Also, it can matter whether a change in the money supply is widely anticipated or not. Key macroeconomic debates hinge on whether money is an important contributor to short-run fluctuations in aggregate economic activity, and just what mechanism causes money to be nonneutral in the short run. However, macroeconomists generally agree that money is neutral in the long run.

SHORT-RUN ANALYSIS IN THE MONETARY INTERTEMPORAL MODEL: A TEMPORARY DECREASE IN TOTAL FACTOR PRODUCTIVITY

The monetary intertemporal model developed here is a base for the analysis of business cycles in Chapters 11 and 12. We must understand, therefore, how the model is used to analyze short-run issues. As an example, we examine here the effects in the current period of a temporary decrease in total factor productivity. From Chapter 9, we already know the real effects of such a shock to the economy, which are a decrease in aggregate output, consumption, investment, the real wage, and employment and an increase in the real interest rate. We show here that a temporary decrease in total factor productivity also causes an increase in the price level.

As mentioned earlier, it is convenient to consider the case in which the current inflation rate is zero, or $i = 0$, so that nominal and real interest rates are equal. Our analysis would not change if the inflation rate i were positive or negative; setting $i = 0$ is simply a convenience.

In Chapters 5 and 9, we examined the effects on the real side of the economy of a change in total factor productivity. Recall that a decrease in total factor productivity z could arise because of an increase in the relative price of energy or because of new government regulations, among other causes. In Figure 10.9 we show the equilibrium effects in the monetary intertemporal model of a temporary decrease in current total factor productivity z. In Figure 10.9(a) and (b), the effects are exactly the same as in the real intertemporal model in Chapter 9. That is, a decrease in z decreases the current marginal product of labor, which shifts the labor demand curve to the left from N_1^d to N_2^d in Figure 10.9(a), and the output supply curve shifts to the left from Y_1^s to Y_2^s in Figure 10.9(b). In equilibrium, the real interest rate rises from r_1 to r_2, and current aggregate output falls from Y_1 to Y_2. Because of the increase in the real interest rate,

FIGURE 10.9   **Short-Run Analysis of a Temporary Decrease in Total Factor Productivity**

This is an example of how to use the monetary intertemporal model to examine the effects of short-run shocks. A decrease in current total factor productivity z reduces real output and raises the real interest rate. The money demand curve shifts to the left, and the equilibrium price level rises.

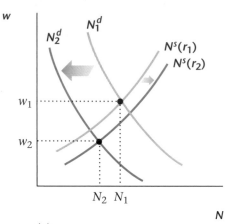

(a)

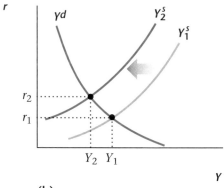

(b)

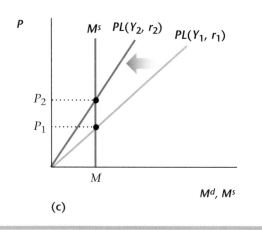

(c)

current consumption and current investment decrease. Also, the higher real interest rate results in intertemporal substitution of leisure, and the labor supply curve in Figure 10.9(a) shifts to the right, from $N^s(r_1)$ to $N^s(r_2)$. In equilibrium, the shift in the labor supply curve is sufficiently small that employment falls from N_1 to N_2 and the real wage falls from w_1 to w_2.

The effects that are new in the monetary intertemporal model occur in the money market in Figure 10.9(c). The equilibrium decrease in current real income Y reduces money demand, and the increase in the real interest rate r also reduces money demand. Therefore, the money demand curve shifts to the left, from $PL(Y_1, r_1)$ to $PL(Y_2, r_2)$. The money supply is fixed at M, and so in equilibrium the price level must rise from P_1 to P_2. The price level rises because, given the reduced real demand for money and the constant nominal money supply, the price level must rise to reduce the real supply of money so that it is equal to real money demand. Effectively, the same quantity of money is chasing a smaller quantity of goods, and so the price of goods, P, must rise.

Recall from Chapter 9 that the real intertemporal model responded to a change in total factor productivity in a manner consistent with the key business cycle facts that we studied in Chapter 3. That is, in the data, consumption, investment, employment, and the real wage are procyclical, just as the model predicts. The monetary intertemporal model not only matches these real business cycle facts, but it also is consistent with observed price level behavior. That is, the price level is observed to be countercyclical in post–World War II data, from Chapter 3, and the monetary intertemporal model predicts this countercyclical price level behavior. When total factor productivity decreases, real output falls and the price level increases. Therefore, aggregate output and the price level move in opposite directions in response to total factor productivity shocks.

• •

CHANGES IN THE RELATIVE PRICE OF ENERGY AND THE PRICE LEVEL

THEORY confronts the DATA

The monetary intertemporal model predicts that increases in the price level are associated with decreases in total factor productivity, and in Chapter 3 we discussed how an increase in the relative price of energy can be interpreted as a decrease in total factor productivity. In Figure 10.10 we show the relative price of energy in the United States, as in Chapters 3 and 9, and in Figure 10.11 we show data for a longer period for the detrended price level, that is, the deviations from trend in the GDP price deflator. There were large positive deviations from trend in the price level following the large increases in the relative price of energy that occurred in 1973–74, 1979–80, 1991, and 2002. However, the positive deviations from trend in the price level tend to lag the increases in the relative price of energy, which is something that our theory does not explain. Some macroeconomists would attribute this lag in the response of the price level to "stickiness" in nominal prices, caused by long-term contracting for goods in the economy. However, there is some disagreement concerning whether price stickiness is empirically important and what causes it. These are issues that we discuss more in Chapter 12.

FIGURE 10.10   Relative Price of Energy

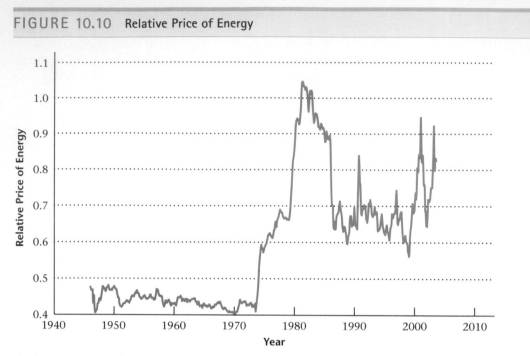

The key increases in the relative price of energy are in 1973–74, 1979–80, 1991, 2000, and 2002.

FIGURE 10.11   Percentage Deviations from Trend in the Price Level

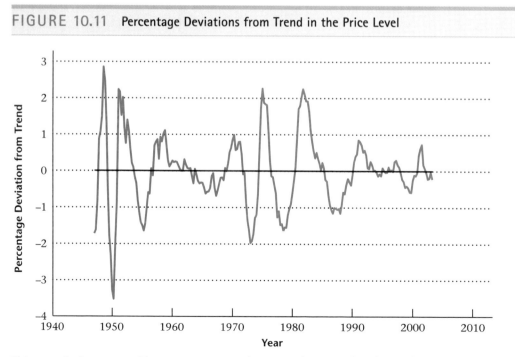

This quantity is measured here as percentage deviations from trend in the implicit GDP price deflator.

The theory predicts that a negative shock to the relative price of energy should cause a decrease in the price level. The data in Figures 10.10 and 10.11 seem consistent with this, particularly in that the negative deviations from trend in the price level in the late 1980s correspond to a decrease in the relative price of energy at that time.

SHIFTS IN MONEY DEMAND

In the monetary intertemporal model we are working with, the money demand relationship, which is determined by the real money demand function $L(Y, R)$, was taken as fixed. In practice, there has been a very unstable relationship between money demand and aggregate economic variables, and this instability has been quite important for central banks in determining monetary policy. There are many factors that cause money demand to shift, which we have not included in our monetary intertemporal model. In this section, we consider the empirical factors that cause shifts in money demand, and we look at the effects of shifts in money demand and some of their implications for monetary policy.

Shifts in the real demand for money—that is, changes in the function $L(Y, R)$—are associated with money's role as a medium of exchange and store of value. Thus, anything that changes what can be used as a medium of exchange or changes the costs of making transactions alters the demand for money. As well, in terms of the store-of-value role for money, because money is part of any consumer's portfolio of assets, changes in factors that affect the desirability of holding money relative to these other assets also change the demand for money. The most important factors that can lead to shifts in the demand for money are the following.

1. *A change in the costs of using alternatives to currency as means of payment.* If it becomes cheaper to use alternative means of payment (for example, if the cost of using debit cards falls), then the demand for currency falls, and the money demand curve shifts to the left.

2. *A change in the costs of converting other assets into currency.* If it becomes cheaper to convert other assets into currency, effectively other assets become more liquid relative to money, and consumers hold less money. The demand curve for money shifts to the left. An example is the cost of converting a checking or savings deposit into currency. This cost is essentially the time, and possibly the transaction fee, associated with a trip to the ATM machine. If the costs of visiting the ATM machine are smaller, say because there are more ATMs and a trip to the ATM takes less time, consumers will make more frequent trips to the ATM machine and hold less currency on average.

3. *A change in government regulations.* An example is the Depository Deregulation and Monetary Control Act of 1980, which permitted depository institutions (banks, savings and loan institutions, and credit unions) to pay interest on transactions accounts. If our definition of money is M1, which includes transactions accounts at banks, then such a change in government regulations would increase the demand

for money, because it reduces the opportunity cost of holding money. This amounts to a shift to the right in the money demand curve.

4. *A change in inflation risk.* Money is a risky asset, in that the real rate of return on money is affected by the inflation rate, and if inflation is uncertain (which it is in practice), then the real rate of return on money is uncertain. Everything else held constant, greater inflation risk implies that the money demand curve shifts to the left. Variability in the inflation rate is typically so small that, given the short holding period of money, it is essentially irrelevant. However, inflation variability tends to rise with the inflation rate, so that, particularly during periods of very high inflation, inflation variability matters.

5. A change in the riskiness of alternative assets. An increase in the riskiness of alternative assets causes an increase in the demand for money and a shift to the right in the money demand curve. During the Great Depression, widespread bank failures made households more uncertain about the value of their bank deposits, and there was a dramatic increase in the demand for currency. Greater volatility in the stock market can also lead to an increase in the demand for money.

As an example of the equilibrium effects of a shift in the demand for money, suppose that households perceive that banks are riskier, so that the demand for currency increases. For this experiment we again set the inflation rate $i = 0$, and the nominal interest rate is equal to the real interest rate, or $R = r$. If the demand for currency increases, the money demand curve shifts to the right in Figure 10.12, from $PL_1(Y, r)$ to $PL_2(Y, r)$. Here, Y and r are determined in the goods market and labor market,

---

FIGURE 10.12   **A Shift in the Demand for Money**

The money demand curve shifts to the right, causing a decrease in the equilibrium price level P, from P_1 to P_2.

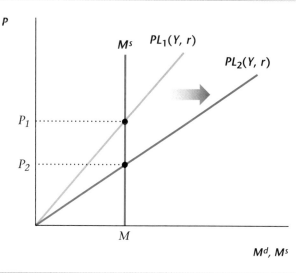

and they are unaffected by what happens to the supply and demand for money. Thus, the price level falls from P_1 to P_2. That is, because the real demand for money has risen, the real money supply $\frac{M}{P}$ must rise to meet the increased demand, and this can only happen if P falls. This is a potential explanation for the fall in the price level that occurred during the Great Depression. At the time, there were massive bank failures, and banks that remained in business were perceived by consumers as risky. As a result, consumers shifted their wealth from bank deposits to currency.

THE VELOCITY OF MONEY

THEORY
confronts the
DATA

The velocity of an asset is a measure of how fast that asset circulates. Typically, the most liquid assets (those assets that can be sold most quickly and at lowest cost for their market value) in the economy circulate faster (i.e., change hands more frequently) than the least liquid assets, and so money should have the highest velocity among assets, because it is the most liquid. The most common measure of the velocity of money is **income velocity,** which is defined as the ratio of nominal income to the nominal quantity of money:

$$V \equiv \frac{PY}{M}. \tag{10.12}$$

Because nominal income PY is a measure of the flow of nominal transactions over a given period of time, V is a measure of the number of times the money stock M turns over during the current period.

In studying the behavior of the velocity of money, we focus only on the behavior of M1 and the velocity of M1. The velocity of money can behave differently depending on the measure of money we use, but focusing on one monetary aggregate here allows us to make our essential points. In Figure 10.13 we plot M1, and in Figure 10.14 we plot the velocity of M1 for the period 1959–2003. In Figure 10.14, the velocity of M1 has changed considerably over time. Velocity approximately doubled from 1959 to the early 1980s, and it has fluctuated considerably since then.

Given our money demand function and market clearing from Equation (9.17), the velocity of money is

$$V = \frac{PY}{M} = \frac{Y}{L(Y, R)}, \tag{10.13}$$

so that the velocity of money depends on real income Y and the nominal interest rate R. Because money demand decreases with an increase in R, V increases when R increases. Whether V increases or decreases when Y increases depends on the form of the money demand function $L(Y, R)$. In the special case where $L(Y, R) = aYH(R)$, where $a > 0$

FIGURE 10.13   M1

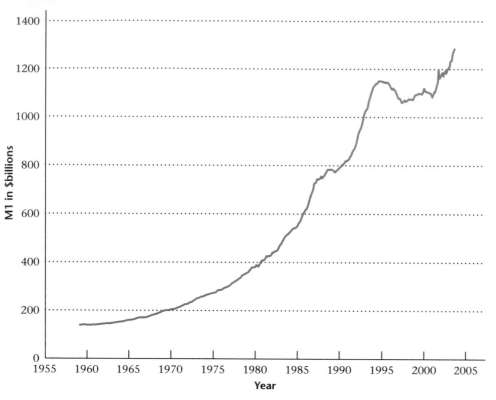

The figure shows the quantity, in billions, of M1 in the United States from 1959–2003.

is a constant and H is a decreasing function, we have

$$V = \frac{Y}{L(Y, R)} = \frac{1}{aH(R)},$$

so that the velocity of money does not change when aggregate income changes, as money demand simply increases in proportion to aggregate income. However, there is a positive relationship between the velocity of money and the nominal interest rate. Therefore, assuming the money demand function takes the form $L(Y, R) = aYH(R)$, if we plot the velocity of money against the nominal interest rate R, we should observe a positive correlation in the data. In Figure 10.15 we plot the velocity of M1 against the nominal interest rate, given quarterly observations for the period 1959–2003. In the figure, we can indeed observe the predicted positive relationship between the velocity of M1 and the nominal interest rate. However, this relationship is a noisy one, in that many of the observations fall far from a straight line fit to the data. Part of this noise arises because of the instability in the demand for money.

FIGURE 10.14   Velocity of M1

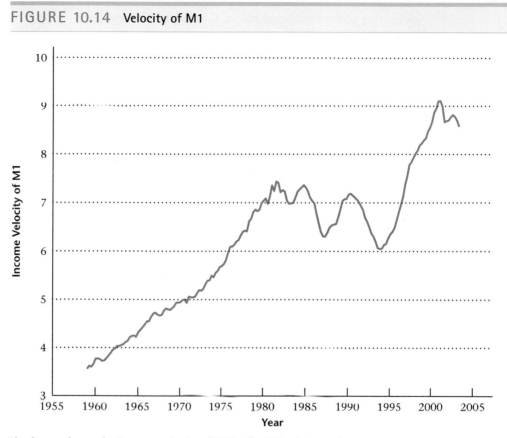

The figure shows the income velocity of M1 in the United States from 1959–2003.

THE QUANTITY THEORY OF MONEY AND MONETARISM

The quantity theory of money takes many forms, but in modern macroeconomics, it is most closely associated with the ideas of Milton Friedman. In its simplest form, the quantity theory starts with the definition of monetary velocity, rewritten as

$$M = \frac{1}{V}PY. \tag{10.14}$$

Then, if $V = \bar{V}$, a constant, it must be the case that any change in M is reflected in a proportional change in nominal aggregate income PY. Of course, the problem with this simple version of the quantity theory is that we know, from the previous section, that the velocity of money is not constant over time; velocity varies considerably. Thus, more advanced versions of the quantity theory, usually referred to as **monetarism**, argue that the money demand function $L(Y, R)$ is stable, that is, the function does not shift much

FIGURE 10.15   Scatter Plot of the Velocity of M1 vs. the Nominal Interest Rate,
1959–2003

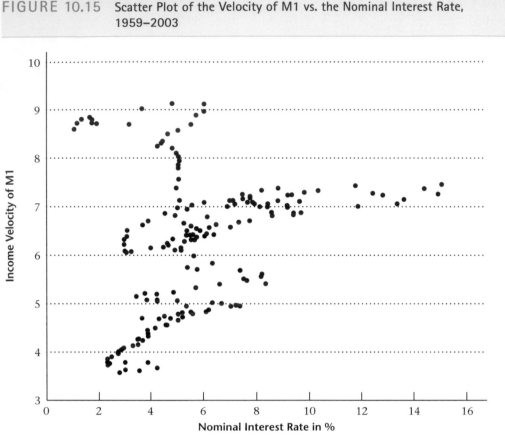

As the monetary intertemporal model predicts, the two variables are positively correlated.

over time. This then implies that V, from Equation (10.13), is a stable function of Y and R. As a result, in Equation (10.14) there is a predictable relationship between the money supply M and nominal income PY. Based on the assumption that the money demand function is stable, the two key elements of monetarism are as follows:

1. The money supply is the key measure of the level of aggregate economic activity, in that there is a systematic relationship between the money supply and aggregate nominal income.

2. The money supply is the key indicator of monetary policy.

Monetarist ideas became very influential in the 1970s, when many countries, including the United States, experienced high rates of inflation. Central bankers became convinced that the way to control inflation was to control growth in the money supply. Some central banks, including the U.S. Federal Reserve System, began to implement monetary policy in terms of explicit targets for the growth of specific monetary

FIGURE 10.16 **Central Bank Response Stabilizes Price Level**

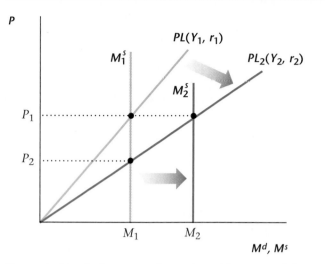

The central bank observes a change in real income and the real interest rate, and it correctly predicts the shift in the money demand curve to the right. Even though the central bank cannot observe the price level, it increases the money supply appropriately to hold the price level constant.

aggregates. A problem that many central banks encountered, however, particularly in the 1980s and 1990s, was unpredictable shifts in money demand functions. (See Macroeconomics in Action: The Usefulness of Monetary Aggregates in Monetary Policy Decisions.)

To see how unpredictable money demand shifts can be a problem for monetary policy when the monetary authority adopts a simple rule of controlling the money supply, consider the following example. Suppose that the monetary authority wishes to stabilize the price level-that is, hold the price level constant-in a short-run world where the inflation rate is zero, so that $R = r$. The monetary authority attempts to do this by setting the money supply appropriately. Suppose first that there is a stable money demand function $L(Y, r)$, and in Figure 10.16 the level of aggregate output is initially Y_1 and the real interest rate (equal to the nominal interest rate, as there is no inflation here) is r_1. Given the initial money supply M_1, the initial price level is P_1. Now suppose that there is a change in aggregate output and the real interest rate, and that the monetary authority observes these changes, as it has timely information on output and interest rates. However, it takes time for the monetary authority to observe the change in the price level. In the figure, the monetary authority assumes that the money demand function is stable so, given the changes in output and the interest rate to Y_2 and r_2 respectively, there is a shift to the right in the money demand curve. Because the monetary authority wants to hold the price level constant at P_1, it increases the money supply from M_1 to M_2. If the money supply had not increased, the price level would

FIGURE 10.17 Central Bank Does Not Observe the Price Level Response to a Shift in Demand for Money

In this case, the central bank cannot observe the decrease in the price level or the shift in the money demand curve to the left. The money supply should decrease from M_1 to M_2, but it does not.

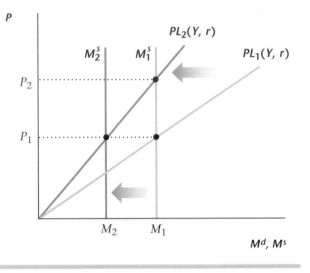

have fallen to P_2 in equilibrium. It turns out that in this case the monetary authority was correct in its assumption that the money demand function had not shifted because of factors other than income and the real interest rate, and it was successful in controlling the price level as desired.

However, suppose alternatively that the money demand function shifts to the left, as in Figure 10.17, from $PL_1(Y, r)$ to $PL_2(Y, r)$. If the monetary authority wants to control the price level, it should reduce the money supply from M_1 to M_2. However, the monetary authority does not immediately see the increase in the equilibrium price level that results, from P_1 to P_2, and so it does not change the money supply. Thus, in this case stabilizing the money supply without somehow accounting for the potential shift of the money demand function does not give the desired result of a stable price level.

We go on in Chapters 11 and 12 to use the monetary intertemporal model to study and assess alternative business cycle models.

MACROECONOMICS IN ACTION

The Usefulness of Monetary Aggregates in Monetary Policy Decisions

While the behavior of the Federal Reserve System in the 1970s and 1980s appears to have depended, at least somewhat, on what was happening to monetary aggregates over time, it seems that monetary aggregates *(continued)* no longer play on important role in Fed decisions, as evidenced by the published minutes of Federal Open Market Committee (FOMC) meetings (the FOMC is the policy-making body of the Fed). A recent article by Michael Dotsey, Carl Lantz, and Lawrence Santucci[1] studies how money should be used in making monetary policy decisions.

Dotsey, Lantz, and Santucci (DLS) point out that, even if monetary aggregates are not being explicitly targeted by a central bank, these aggregates can still be an important input into policymaking. First, current observations on the money supply might provide useful current information on economic variables that the central bank cares about but cannot observe in a timely fashion, such as real GDP, the price level, the inflation rate, employment, and the unemployment rate. Second, the money supply might help the central bank to forecast future variables that matter for economic welfare.

The relationship between the money supply and current variables that are unobserved, or are observed imperfectly, can be summarized by the money demand function. Therefore, if the money demand function is unstable (shifts over time), this makes monetary aggregates a noisy source of information. The more unstable is the money demand function, the less useful is the money supply in providing information about current economic variables. DLS find

that the demand functions for both M1 and M2 have been unstable over time, to the extent that neither M1 nor M2 should be used as an explicit target for monetary policy. This instability also varies over time. A key source of instability in money demand has been changes in financial regulation, such as changes in reserve requirements on banks, the relaxation of interest rate ceilings on some types of transactions deposits, changes in capital requirements on banks, and the allowance of "sweep accounts."

DLS find that both M1 and M2 have been useful in forecasting future economic variables. However, the usefulness of M1 in this respect has declined over time, with M2 appearing to be a more reliable forecasting tool.

Current Fed policy focuses on short-term nominal interest rates as a target for monetary policy, and this focus makes sense given the unstable relationship between monetary aggregates and other economic variables. Monetary aggregates, however, like other financial variables such as stock prices, long-term interest rates, and the quantity of loans, are likely to continue to play a useful role in monetary policymaking.

---

[1]M. Dotsey, C. Lantz, and L. Santucci, 2000. "Is Money Useful in the Conduct of Monetary Policy?" *Federal Reserve Bank of Richmond Economic Quarterly* 86, 23–48.

CHAPTER SUMMARY

- Money has three functions in the economy—it is a medium of exchange, a store of value, and a unit of account.

- The key measures of money are the monetary aggregates, which are the sums of quantities of assets having the functions of money. The monetary base, or M0, is the narrowest monetary aggregate, and it consists only of liabilities of the Federal Reserve System, in particular currency and the reserves of depository institutions. Other broader monetary aggregates, which include bank deposits and other assets, are M1 (broader than M0), M2 (broader than M1), and M3 (broader than M2).

- The monetary intertemporal model builds on the real intertemporal model of Chapter 9 by including supply and demand in the market for money. An important element of the monetary intertemporal model is the cash-in-advance constraint, which states that consumption goods must be purchased using the cash that the consumer has on hand when he or she goes to the goods market.

- In the monetary intertemporal model, money is neutral, in the sense that an increase in the level of the money supply leaves real variables—employment, output, consumption, the real interest rate, the real money supply, and the real wage—unaffected, and causes only a proportionate increase in all money prices.

- In the monetary intertemporal model, a short-run decrease in total factor productivity leads to an increase in the price level, which is consistent with evidence from U.S. historical episodes when the relative price of energy increased.

- Shifts in money demand can occur because of changes in financial technology, in government regulations, in the properties of money as an asset, and in the properties of alternative assets to money.

- Money demand shifts can be a particular problem for monetary policy, particularly if monetary policy is guided by monetarist principles.

KEY TERMS

Neutrality of money: Money is neutral if a change in its level has no real effects and causes only a proportionate increase in the price level.

Money demand function: The relationship between the quantity of money that economic agents wish to hold and other macroeconomic variables.

Medium of exchange: A property of money; a medium of exchange is accepted in transactions for the sole reason that it can in turn be exchanged for other goods and services.

Store of value: A property of money that is shared with other assets that permit current goods and services to be traded for future goods and services.

Unit of account: The object in an economy in which prices and contracts are denominated.

Monetary aggregates: These are measures of the money supply; each is the sum of a number of different types of assets in the economy.

Monetary base: The quantity of M0, consisting of U.S. currency outside the Federal Reserve System and the deposits of depository institutions with the Fed.

Outside money: This is identical to the monetary base.

High-powered money: This is identical to the monetary base.

Federal Reserve System (the Fed): The central bank of the United States.

Single coincidence of wants: Situation in which two people meet and one person has what the other wants.

Double coincidence of wants: Situation in which two people meet and the first person has what the second person wants and the second has what the first wants.

Cash-in-advance model: A macroeconomic model in which it is assumed that some goods must be purchased with cash on hand at the beginning of the period.

Nominal bond: A bond for which the payoff is defined in terms of money.

Nominal interest rate: If R is the nominal interest rate on an asset, then if 1 unit of money is exchanged for a given quantity of the asset in the current period, then this quantity of the asset pays off $1 + R$ units of money next period.

Inflation rate: The rate of change in the price level.

Fisher relation: Condition stating that $1 + r = \frac{1+R}{1+i}$, where r is the real interest rate from the current period to the future period, R is the nominal interest rate from the current period to the future period, and i is the rate of inflation between the current period and the future period.

Asset portfolio: A collection of assets.

Cash-in-advance constraint: A condition stating that a consumer's cash on hand must be at least as large as the nominal quantity of purchases of cash goods he or she wants to make.

Neutral: Describes a government policy that has no real effects.

Helicopter drop: Milton Friedman's thought experiment, which corresponds to an increase in the money supply brought about by transfers.

Open market operation: A purchase or sale of interest-bearing government debt by the central bank.

Open market purchase: An open market operation in which interest-bearing government debt is purchased by the central bank, increasing the money supply.

Open market sale: An open market operation in which interest-bearing government debt is sold by the central bank, decreasing the money supply.

Seigniorage: Revenue generated by the government through printing money.

Inflation tax: Inflation arising when the government prints money to extract seigniorage; this effectively taxes the private sector.

Classical dichotomy: Situation in an economic model where real variables are determined by real factors, and the money supply determines only the price level.

Income velocity: $V = \frac{PY}{M}$, where V is the income velocity of money, P is the price level, Y is real income, and M is the supply of money.

Monetarism: The tenets of monetarists, including Milton Friedman, who argue that the money demand function is stable, that money is the key measure of the level of aggregate economic activity, and that money is the key indicator for monetary policy.

QUESTIONS FOR REVIEW

1. What are the three functions of money?

2. List four monetary aggregates and the assets that these monetary aggregates include.

3. Why is money used in exchange when people could carry out transactions by trading goods or using credit?

4. How are the real interest rate, the nominal interest rate, and the inflation rate related to one another?

5. What is the real rate of interest on money?

6. How does the cash-in-advance constraint give rise to a demand for money in the monetary intertemporal model?

7. What are the effects of an increase in the money supply in the monetary intertemporal model?

8. What are three ways in which the government could bring about a change in the money supply?

9. What are the effects of a short-run decrease in total factor productivity in the monetary intertemporal model?

10. List five factors that lead to an increase in money demand.

11. How is the velocity of money related to the nominal interest rate?

12. How does the velocity of money behave empirically over short periods of time? Over long periods of time?

13. What are the key principles of monetarism?

14. Why are unpredictable shifts in the money demand function a problem for monetary policy?

PROBLEMS

1. In the monetary intertemporal model, suppose that the money supply is fixed for all time.
   (a) Determine the effects of a temporary increase in the quantity of government purchases on current equilibrium output, employment, the real wage, the real interest rate, the nominal interest rate, and the price level. Explain your results.
   (b) Now, suppose that the increase in government spending is permanent. How does this change your answers from part (a)? Explain.

2. In the monetary intertemporal model, suppose that the money supply is fixed for all time, and determine the effects of a decrease in the capital stock, brought about by a war or natural disaster, on current equilibrium output, employment, the real wage, the real interest rate, the nominal interest rate, and the price level. Explain your results.

3. A new technological innovation is announced that will come on line in the future period. What are the current effects on aggregate output, consumption, investment, employment, the real wage, the real interest rate, the nominal interest rate, and the price level? Explain your results.

4. Suppose, in the monetary intertemporal model, that the preferences of the representative household change in such a way that the worker in the household becomes more willing to work, in that he or she requires less compensation in terms of consumption goods to supply an extra unit of labor, given any consumption–leisure bundle.
   (a) If the money supply is fixed for all time, determine the effects of this change in preferences on current employment, current output, the real interest rate, the nominal interest rate, and the current price level. (Hint: The effect on the real interest rate is indeterminate; assume that r increases.)
   (b) Now, suppose that the monetary authority wishes to stabilize the price level (hold the price level constant). How would the money supply change in response to the change in preferences to accomplish this?
   (c) Suppose that there is a temporary increase in total factor productivity, and the monetary authority wishes to stabilize the price level. What would be the effects of the increase in total factor productivity on output, employment, the real interest rate, the nominal interest rate, the price level, and the money supply?
   (d) Now, suppose that there is an increase in total factor productivity, and that the monetary authority cannot observe output, the price level, and employment in the short run but can only observe the nominal interest rate. The monetary authority also cannot observe total factor productivity or household preferences. The monetary authority, in error, guesses that the nominal interest rate moved because there was a change in household preferences toward leisure and consumption. If it attempts to stabilize the price level

based on this belief, what will happen to the price level? Discuss the effects of the error that the monetary authority makes here.

5. Suppose that there is an increase in the number of ATM machines in service. What are the effects of this innovation on the demand for money and on the price level?

6. The issuers of credit cards demand payment every two weeks instead of every month. Determine the effects on money demand and on the price level, and explain your results.

7. The federal government increases expenditures permanently. Supposing that the goal of the central bank is to stabilize the price level, how should the central bank change the money supply in response to this permanent change in government spending? Explain with the aid of diagrams, and discuss what this shows about the importance of coordination between the central bank and the fiscal authority.

WORKING WITH THE DATA

1. Calculate the income velocities of M0 and M2 over the period 1959–2003, and plot these time series. Compare what you get with Figure 9.18, where we show the income velocity of M1, and comment on the differences you see. How does the behavior of these different velocity measures reflect shifts in demand among the monetary aggregates?

2. Construct a scatter plot of M1 against real GDP for the period 1959–2003.
   (a) Is there a positive or negative correlation in the scatter plot?
   (b) Is the correlation you observed in part (a) evidence that money is not neutral? Why or why not?

3. Plot the income velocity of M2 against the three-month Treasury bill rate for 1959–2003, and compare what you get to Figure 10.15. How would you explain the differences you see, if any?

CHAPTER 11

Market-Clearing Models of the Business Cycle

The publication of John Maynard Keynes's *A General Theory of Employment, Interest, and Money*[1] was a key departure from previous views of the causes of business cycles and the role of government policy. By the 1960s, Keynesian thought had come to dominate macroeconomics. At that time, most macroeconomists accepted Keynesian business cycle models as capturing the behavior of the economy in the short run. There appeared to be broad agreement that money was not neutral in the short run, and most macroeconomists viewed this nonneutrality as arising from the short-run inflexibility of wages and prices. Price and wage inflexibility, and the resulting possibility that all markets may not clear at each point in time, were the key to the mechanism by which shocks to the economy could cause aggregate output to fluctuate in Keynesian models. In the Keynesian view, the fact that prices and wages are slow to move to clear markets implies that there is a role for monetary and fiscal policy in stabilizing the economy in response to aggregate shocks.

By the 1960s, the main disagreements in macroeconomics were between monetarists and Keynesians. Monetarists tended to believe that monetary policy was a more effective stabilization tool than fiscal policy, but they were skeptical about the ability of government policy to fine-tune the economy; some monetarists argued that the short run over which policy could be effective was very short indeed. Keynesians believed that monetary policy was unimportant relative to fiscal policy, and that government policy should take an active role in guiding the economy along a smooth growth path. It may have seemed at the time that all the theoretical issues in macroeconomics had been resolved, in that most everyone agreed that the Keynesian model was a satisfactory model of the macroeconomy, and all that remained was for empirical work to sort out the disagreements between monetarists and Keynesians.

This view changed dramatically, however, with the advent of the rational expectations revolution in the early 1970s. Some important early contributors to the rational expectations revolution were Robert Lucas, Thomas Sargent, Neil Wallace, and Robert Barro. Two key principles coming out of the rational expectations revolution were: (1) macroeconomic models should be based on microeconomic principles—that is, they should be grounded in descriptions of the preferences, endowments, and technology and the optimizing behavior of consumers and firms; and (2) equilibrium models (as opposed to models with price and wage inflexibility where all markets need not clear) are the most productive vehicles for studying macroeconomic phenomena. There was

---

[1] See J. M. Keynes, 1936. *The General Theory of Employment, Interest, and Money,* Macmillan, London.

some resistance to following these two principles, but there was wide acceptance, at least of the first principle, by the 1980s. It became clear as well, with respect to the second principle, that equilibrium modeling does not automatically rule out an active role for government policy. Indeed, as we see in this chapter, some Keynesian ideas can be exposited using equilibrium models.

In this chapter, we study three models of the business cycle, which were each developed as explicit equilibrium models with optimizing consumers and firms. These models are the Friedman-Lucas money surprise model, the real business cycle model, and the Keynesian coordination failure model. Each model differs from the others in terms of what is important in causing business cycles and the role implied for government policy. However, we will show that we can describe each of these models by building on the monetary intertemporal model of Chapter 10 in straightforward ways. We study each model in turn, examine how well each matches the business cycle facts discussed in Chapter 3, and discuss each model's shortcomings.

We study equilibrium models of the business cycle first in this chapter, as this follows naturally from the theory we have developed in Chapters 4, 5, 8, 9, and 10. We study a traditional Keynesian model with inflexible (or "sticky") wages in Chapter 12.

Why is it necessary to study several different business cycle models? As we discussed in Chapter 3, business cycles are remarkably similar, in terms of the comovements among macroeconomic time series. However, business cycles can have many causes, and fiscal and monetary policymakers are constantly grappling to understand what macroeconomic shocks are driving the economy and what this implies for future aggregate activity. Each business cycle model we study allows us to understand one or a few features of the economy and some aspects of the economy's response to macroeconomic shocks. Putting all of these features into one model would produce an unwieldy mess that would not help us understand the fundamentals of business cycle behavior and government policy.

Different business cycle models, however, sometimes give contradictory advice concerning the role of government policy. Does this mean that business cycle theory has nothing to say? The contradictory advice that different business cycle models give concerning the role of government policy reflects the reality of macroeconomic policymaking. Policymakers in federal and state governments and in central banks often disagree about the direction in which policy should move. To make persuasive arguments, however, policymakers have to ground their arguments in well-articulated macroeconomic models. This chapter shows, in part, how we can evaluate and compare macroeconomic models and come to conclusions about their relative usefulness.

THE FRIEDMAN–LUCAS MONEY SURPRISE MODEL

The theory behind the money surprise model was sketched out by Milton Friedman[2] in 1968, and it was formalized by Robert Lucas in 1972.[3] Lucas's work marked the start of the rational expectations revolution, and Lucas was awarded the Nobel Prize in economics in 1995 for this research.

---

[2]See M. Friedman, 1968. "The Role of Monetary Policy," *American Economic Review* 58, 1–17.

[3]See R. Lucas, 1972. "Expectations and the Neutrality of Money," *Journal of Economic Theory* 4, 103–124.

In the 1960s, macroeconomists had regarded any short-run nonneutralities of money as being the result of out-of-equilibrium behavior of the economy arising from sticky wages or prices. The Friedman-Lucas model was the first attempt to construct a theory where changes in the level of the money supply could have real effects, with all markets clearing all the time.

The key element of the theory is that workers have imperfect information, in the short run, about aggregate variables that are important to their decision making. In the theory, a worker, who we will call Bob, has complete information about things that directly concern him, for example, the current nominal wage. However, because Bob is not buying all goods all the time, he has imperfect information about the price level. Further, Bob cannot immediately observe aggregate shocks, like changes in total factor productivity and changes in the money supply, that hit the economy. Under these circumstances, Bob might misperceive an increase in his nominal wage as an increase in his real wage, when it is really not, and Bob is fooled into working harder. Money "surprises" can then cause output to fluctuate, and this is a bad thing. The role for the central bank in this model is to make the money supply predictable.

The Friedman-Lucas money surprise model is a modification of the monetary intertemporal model from Chapter 10, with changes to account for the imperfect information problem. During the current period, Bob observes his current nominal wage W, where $W = wP$, with w the current real wage and P the price level. In terms of making his current labor supply decision, Bob cares about his real wage, not the nominal wage, but there would be no problem determining the real wage if Bob knew the current price level. Then, he could calculate the real wage as $w = \frac{W}{P}$. The problem is that Bob buys many goods, and he does not purchase all of these goods in any one period. For example, consumers in practice typically buy groceries and restaurant food every week, clothing perhaps monthly or seasonally, and a new car every two years or more. Suppose, for simplicity, that Bob simply does not know the current price level P during the current period. This implies that he also does not observe his current real wage w.

We suppose that there are two shocks that may hit the macroeconomy. The first is a temporary change in z, total factor productivity, and the second is a permanent increase in M, the money supply. We assume that Bob cannot observe either z or M during the current period. However, he does know that either temporary z-shocks or permanent M-shocks can hit the economy. Though Bob cannot observe the price level or the real wage directly, he can make inferences about the chances of a particular shock having hit the economy, based on how his nominal wage moves in the current period.

Given the environment that Bob lives in, how does he make decisions? Suppose that in the current period Bob sees an increase in his nominal wage W. Given what he knows about how the world works, Bob knows that W may have increased because the money supply went up permanently or because there was a temporary increase in total factor productivity. If Bob knows how frequently total factor productivity shocks and money supply shocks hit the economy, he then knows the chances that W increased in the current period as the result of either shock. Recall from Chapter 10 that if there is perfect information (Bob can observe all variables in the economy), then a permanent increase in the level of the money supply would cause a proportionate increase in the price level and there would be no real effects, so that the current real wage w would remain unchanged. Bob, therefore, would not change labor supply. Also, from

Chapter 10, if there were a temporary increase in z under perfect information, then the real wage w would increase and the current price level P would fall. We assume that the nominal wage, wP, increases. Thus, in this case, Bob would want to increase labor supply in response to the increase in the real wage, and an increase in the nominal wage effectively signals an increase in the real wage.

The problem is that Bob does not know whether the current nominal wage increased because the money supply increased permanently or because total factor productivity increased temporarily. This implies that if the money supply actually went up, causing the nominal wage to increase, then Bob infers that there is some chance that the nominal wage increased because of a temporary productivity shock and, therefore, he increases labor supply. Higher labor supply then causes output to go up.

To show how this works in the monetary intertemporal model, consider Figure 11.1. Initially, the economy is in equilibrium with current real output Y_1, real interest rate r_1, current price level P_1, current employment N_1, and current real wage w_1. Now, suppose that the money supply increases from M_1 to M_2 in Figure 11.1(c). However, Bob infers that z may have increased temporarily when he sees the increase in his nominal wage W. In terms of the actual real wage, which is the variable on the vertical axis in Figure 11.1(a), Bob then perceives the real wage to be higher than it actually is, and this implies that the labor supply curve shifts rightward from $N_1^s(r_1)$ to $N_2^s(r_1)$. That is, a money supply increase does not increase the real wage, a total factor productivity increase causes the real wage to increase, and the consumer thinks there is some chance that either event happened, so that the consumer's estimate is that the real wage increased. Thus, when it was really the money supply that increased, Bob's estimate of the real wage is higher than the actual real wage. We know that when the labor supply curve shifts to the right, the output supply curve also shifts to the right, so there is a shift in Y^s from Y_1^s to Y_2^s in Figure 11.1(b). In equilibrium, the level of output increases to Y_2, and the real interest rate falls to r_2. Consumption increases as real income has increased and the real interest rate has fallen, and investment increases because of the decrease in the real interest rate. In Figure 11.1(c), the nominal money demand curve shifts rightward from $PL(Y_1, r_1)$ to $PL(Y_2, r_2)$, because real income has increased and the real interest rate has gone down. The money supply curve has also shifted to the right, with the increase in the money supply from M_1 to M_2, but on net the price level increases, from P_1 to P_2.

In Figure 11.1(a), the labor demand curve shifts leftward from $N_2^s(r_1)$ to $N_2^s(r_2)$ when the real interest rate falls, but the shift to the left in the labor supply curve cannot be greater than the initial rightward shift, because we know that output must increase, and output could not increase unless employment increased. Therefore, employment goes up to N_2 and the actual real wage falls to w_2, though the perceived real wage of the consumer has risen. The perceived real wage of the consumer must have increased, as this is why the consumer is supplying more labor in equilibrium. As employment increases and there is no change in total factor productivity, average labor productivity must fall.

The key feature of the money surprise model is that money is not neutral. An increase in the nominal money supply in the short run causes the real interest rate and the real wage to fall, and real output and employment to rise. Because $\frac{M}{P} = L(Y, r)$ in equilibrium, and because real output has increased and the real interest rate has

FIGURE 11.1 The Effects of an Unanticipated Increase in the Money Supply in the Money Surprise Model

An unanticipated increase in the money supply shifts the labor supply curve to the right, as the actual real wage is lower than the real wage that the worker perceives. The output supply curve shifts to the right, output rises, and the real interest rate falls, increasing the demand for money, and causing the price level to rise. Money is not neutral.

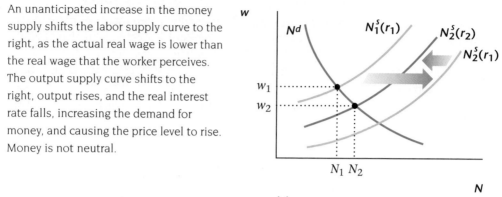

(a)

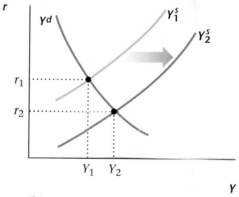

(b)

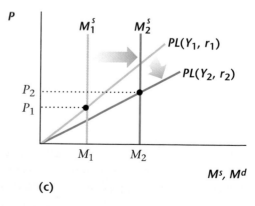

(c)

decreased, causing real money demand $L(Y, r)$ to rise, $\frac{M}{P}$ (the real money supply) rises. That is, the price level rises less than proportionally to the increase in the money supply.

Implications of the Money Surprise Model for Monetary Policy

In the Friedman-Lucas money surprise model, an unanticipated increase in the money supply causes employment and output to increase, and it might seem that this is a good thing. In Keynesian models, like the Keynesian sticky wage model that we study in Chapter 12, it is economically efficient in some circumstances for the central bank to increase the money supply so as to increase output and employment. In the money surprise model, however, an engineered money surprise by the central bank is always a bad thing.

Output increases as the result of a money supply increase in the money surprise model only because people are fooled. An optimal state of affairs in this model is when consumers and firms are perfectly informed about what is happening to the economy. Under perfect information, all markets clear, the optimal quantity of labor is bought and sold in the labor market, and the optimal quantity of goods is bought and sold in the goods market. That is, if there were perfect information in the money surprise model, then the equilibrium allocation of resources would be Pareto optimal (recall our discussion from Chapter 5).

Market prices carry important signals about shocks that are hitting the economy. If those signals are transmitted clearly to market participants, then this aids in the appropriate allocation of resources in the economy. For example, an increase in the relative price of peaches signals a scarcity in the quantity of peaches. People who buy peaches respond by buying fewer peaches and substituting other goods, and people who sell peaches respond by trying to bring more peaches to market. Any variability in the money supply adds noise to price signals, and this can mean that market participants receive the wrong messages. For example, in the money surprise model, an increase in the nominal wage that is a purely nominal increase can be misinterpreted as an increase in the real wage.

The appropriate policy for the monetary authority to adopt in an environment like this, as emphasized by Friedman and Lucas, is to make the money supply as predictable as possible. Friedman's recommendation[4] was that the monetary authority should follow a **constant money growth rule**, according to which some monetary aggregate (and Friedman argued that it did not matter which one) should grow at a constant rate over time. Here, using monetary policy to increase output and employment is not appropriate. We see in Chapter 12 that the Keynesian sticky wage model has quite different policy implications.

Critique of the Friedman–Lucas Money Surprise Model

The Friedman–Lucas money surprise model tells a coherent story about the non-neutrality of money based on the actions of optimizing consumers and firms. In this sense, the model is appealing; however, there are some shortcomings in the ability of

---

[4]See M. Friedman, 1968. "The Role of Monetary Policy," *American Economic Review* 58, 1–17.

Table 11.1 **Data Versus Predictions of the Money Surprise Model with Monetary Shocks**

Variable	Data	Model
Consumption	Procyclical	Procyclical
Investment	Procyclical	Procyclical
Price Level	Countercyclical	Procyclical
Money Supply	Procyclical	Procyclical
Employment	Procyclical	Procyclical
Real Wage	Procyclical	Countercyclical
Average Labor Productivity	Procyclical	Countercyclical

the money surprise model to mimic the key business cycle regularities over the period 1947–2003 (see Chapter 3). Table 11.1 shows the features of the data from Chapter 3 relative to what the money surprise model predicts. The money surprise model predicts that if money variability is the primary explanation for business cycles, as argued by Lucas,[5] then consumption and investment are procyclical, money is procyclical, and employment is procyclical, as in the data. But the real wage is countercyclical, average labor productivity is countercyclical, and the price level is procyclical, and these three predictions are inconsistent with the data.

One can argue that the mechanism by which money affects output in the money surprise model is not plausible. That is, information on aggregate price indices and the money supply is widely available on a timely basis, and so it seems hard for people to be fooled as happens in the model. Further, the Federal Reserve System has become increasingly open about how it conducts monetary policy. All of these factors make it hard to believe that imperfect information about the money supply and/or the price level could contribute much to fluctuations in aggregate GDP.

In spite of its shortcomings, there is a key insight of the Friedman-Lucas money surprise model that has been quite influential among macroeconomic policymakers. This is the idea that the economy functions less efficiently when the behavior of policymakers is not well understood or when policy decisions are difficult to predict. Since the 1970s, central banks in particular have taken greater pains to provide information about their policy decisions and to help the public understand the reasons for their decisions. The Federal Reserve Board now announces its decisions following the key Federal Open Market Committee meetings, and it provides more details concerning likely future policy moves.

THE REAL BUSINESS CYCLE MODEL

Now that we know the basic features of the Friedman-Lucas money surprise model, we can move on to study the real business cycle model, which was developed later. Real business cycle theory was introduced by Finn Kydland and Edward Prescott[6]

---

[5]See R. Lucas, 1980. "Methods and Problems in Business Cycle Theory," *Journal of Money, Credit, and Banking* 12.

[6]See F. Kydland and E. Prescott, 1982. "Time to Build and Aggregate Fluctuations," *Econometrica* 50, 1345–1370.

FIGURE 11.2   Solow Residuals and GDP

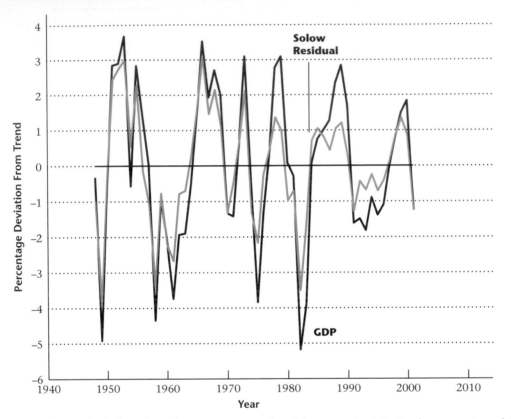

The Solow residual (the colored line), a measure of total factor productivity, tracks aggregate real GDP (the black line) quite closely.

in the early 1980s. Kydland and Prescott asked whether or not a standard model of economic growth subjected to random productivity shocks (that is, "real" shocks, as opposed to monetary shocks) could replicate, qualitatively and quantitatively, observed business cycles. Kydland and Prescott were perhaps motivated to pursue this question by the observation we made in Chapter 6, and replicate in Figure 11.2, that the detrended Solow residual (a measure of total factor productivity z) closely tracks detrended real GDP. Thus, productivity shocks appear to be a potential explanation for business cycles.

Recall that many factors can lead to changes in total factor productivity. Essentially, any change implying that an economy can produce more aggregate output with the same factor inputs is an increase in total factor productivity, that is, an increase in z. Factors that increase z include good weather, technological innovations, the easing of government regulations, and decreases in the relative price of energy.

The version of the real business cycle model we study here is the monetary intertemporal model from Chapter 10. Though Kydland and Prescott studied a model where there was no role for money, Thomas Cooley and Gary Hansen showed, in a cash-in-advance real business cycle model, that adding money made little difference to the results.[7]

The Solow residual, as observed in Figure 11.2, is a persistent variable. When it is above (below) trend, it tends to stay there. This tells us that total factor productivity shocks are persistent, so that when there is a current increase in z, we would expect future total factor productivity z' to be higher as well. This implies that, in analyzing how the real business cycle model reacts to a total factor productivity shock, we need to combine the results of two different shocks from Chapter 9, a shock to z and a shock to z'.

Now, suppose that there is a persistent increase in total factor productivity in the monetary intertemporal model, so that there are increases in z and z', current and future total factor productivity respectively. In Figure 11.3 we show the equilibrium effects. The increase in current total factor productivity z increases the marginal product of labor for each quantity of labor input, so that the labor demand curve shifts rightward from N_1^d to N_2^d in Figure 11.3(a), and this shifts the output supply curve rightward from Y_1^s to Y_2^s in Figure 11.3(b). There are additional effects because of the anticipated increase in future total factor productivity z'. First, the demand for investment goods increases, as the representative firm anticipates an increase in the future marginal productivity of capital. Second, the representative consumer anticipates that higher future total factor productivity implies higher future income, so that lifetime wealth increases and the demand for consumption goods goes up. Both of these factors cause the output demand curve Y^d to shift rightward from Y_1^d to Y_2^d.

In equilibrium, in Figure 11.3(b), aggregate output must rise, but it is not clear whether the real interest rate rises or falls. However, the output demand curve probably shifts less than the output supply curve, because the direct effect of the increase in total factor productivity on the supply of goods is likely to be larger than the effects of the anticipated increase in future total factor productivity on the demand for goods. Thus, the real interest rate falls, as in Figure 11.3(b), from r_1 to r_2. Current consumption expenditures then increase because of the decrease in the real interest rate, the increase in current real income, and the increase in future real income stemming from the increase in future total factor productivity. Current investment rises because of the decrease in the real interest rate and the increase in future total factor productivity. In the money market, in Figure 11.3(c), because equilibrium real output rises and the real interest rate falls, money demand increases, and the nominal money demand curve shifts rightward from $PL(Y_1, r_1)$ to $PL(Y_2, r_2)$. Therefore, in equilibrium, the price level falls from P_1 to P_2. In the labor market, in Figure 11.3(a), the labor supply curve shifts leftward from $N^s(r_1)$ to $N^s(r_2)$ because of the fall in the real interest rate. However, as in Chapter 7, the labor supply curve shifts less than the labor demand curve, since the

---

[7]See T. Cooley and G. Hansen, 1989. "The Inflation Tax in a Real Business Cycle Model," *American Economic Review* 79, 733–748.

FIGURE 11.3　**Effects of a Persistent Increase in Total Factor Productivity in the Real Business Cycle Model**

With a persistent increase in total factor productivity, the output supply curve shifts to the right because of the increase in current total factor productivity, and the output demand curve shifts to the right because of the anticipated increase in future total factor productivity. The model replicates the key business cycle facts.

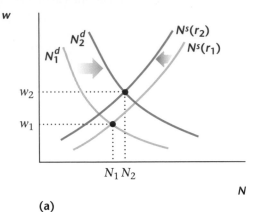

(a)

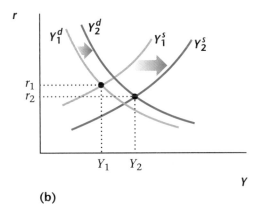

(b)

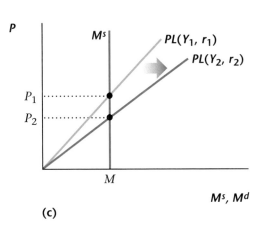

(c)

FIGURE 11.4   **Average Labor Productivity with Total Factor Productivity Shocks**

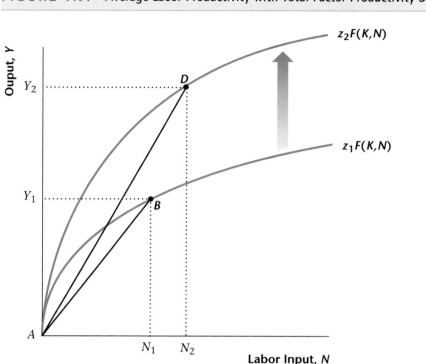

When output and employment are high, average labor productivity is also high, as in the data.

intertemporal substitution effect on labor supply from the change in the real interest rate is relatively small. Hence, current equilibrium employment rises from N_1 to N_2, and the current real wage rises from w_1 to w_2. In Figure 11.4, we show the response of average labor productivity. Initially employment is N_1 and output is Y_1, and average labor productivity is the slope of AB. After the increase in current and future total factor productivity, employment increases to N_2 and output to Y_2, with average labor productivity being the slope of AD in the figure. Thus, average labor productivity increases. We could have drawn the figure so that employment increased sufficiently that the slope of AD was smaller than the slope of AB. However, Figure 11.4 is consistent with the results from Kydland and Prescott's model, where N would increase in this circumstance but not enough that Y/N would decrease.

Therefore, as shown in Table 11.2, the real business cycle model qualitatively explains essentially all of the key business cycle regularities. Consumption, investment, employment, the real wage, and average labor productivity are procyclical, and the price level is countercyclical. Perhaps more importantly, the real business cycle model can also quantitatively replicate some important observations about business cycles, as can be shown if a more sophisticated version of this model is put on a computer and simulated.

Table 11.2 **Data Versus Predictions of the Real Business Cycle Model with Productivity Shocks**

Variable	Data	Model
Consumption	Procyclical	Procyclical
Investment	Procyclical	Procyclical
Price Level	Countercyclical	Countercyclical
Money Supply	Procyclical	—
Employment	Procyclical	Procyclical
Real Wage	Procyclical	Procyclical
Average Labor Productivity	Procyclical	Procyclical

The model can explain the fact that consumption is less variable than output and that investment is more variable than output. Further, it can approximately replicate the observed relative variabilities in consumption, investment, output, and employment, which were discussed in Chapter 3.[8] As we see in Table 11.2, one feature of the data that the model in this form cannot replicate is the procyclicality of the money supply. We discuss this further in the next subsection.

Real Business Cycles and the Behavior of the Money Supply

In the real business cycle model, money is neutral; level changes in M have no effect on real variables and cause a proportionate increase in the price level. It might seem, then, that the real business cycle model cannot explain two key business cycle regularities from Chapter 3, which are the following:

1. The nominal money supply is procyclical.
2. The nominal money supply tends to lead real GDP.

As we show, however, the real business cycle model can be made consistent with these two facts through some straightforward extensions.

First, in the real business cycle model, the procyclicality of the nominal money supply can be explained by way of **endogenous money.** That is, in practice, the money supply is not determined exogenously by the monetary authority but responds to conditions in the economy. Endogenous money can explain the procyclicality of money in two ways, supposing that business cycles are caused by fluctuations in z. First, if our money supply measure is M1, M2, or some broader monetary aggregate, then part of the money supply consists of bank deposits. When aggregate output increases, all sectors in the economy, including the banking sector, tend to experience an increase in activity at the same time. An increase in banking sector activity is reflected in an increase in the quantity of bank deposits and, therefore, in an increase in M1, M2, and the broader monetary aggregates, and we observe the money supply increasing

---

[8]See E. Prescott, 1986. "Theory Ahead of Business Cycle Measurement," *Federal Reserve Bank of Minneapolis Quarterly Review,* Fall, 9–22.

FIGURE 11.5 **Procyclical Money Supply in the Real Business Cycle Model with Endogenous Money**

A persistent increase in total factor productivity increases aggregate real income and reduces the real interest rate, causing money demand to increase. If the central bank attempts to stabilize the price level, this increases the money supply in response to the total factor productivity shock.

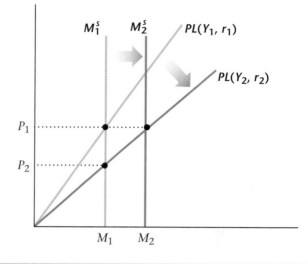

when total factor productivity increases. Second, the money supply could increase in response to an increase in z because of the response of monetary policy. Suppose that the central bank wishes to stabilize the price level. When there is a persistent increase in total factor productivity, this causes an equilibrium increase in Y, and the real interest rate falls, as we showed above. In Figure 11.5 output increases from Y_1 to Y_2 and the real interest rate falls from r_1 to r_2, so that the nominal money demand curve shifts rightward from $PL(Y_1, r_1)$ to $PL(Y_2, r_2)$. If the central bank did nothing, the price level would fall from P_1 to P_2. However, because the central bank wishes to stabilize the price level, it increases the money supply from M_1 to M_2, shifting the money supply curve from M_1^s to M_2^s. As a result, the money supply is procyclical, as it increases when output increases, in response to the persistent total factor productivity increase.

Fact (2) above, that the nominal money supply tends to lead real GDP, appears to be a particular problem, because this might be viewed as strong evidence that money supply fluctuations cause the fluctuations in real GDP. Indeed, this was the interpretation given to fact (2) by Milton Friedman and Anna Schwartz.[9] However, the weak link in Friedman and Schwartz's interpretation of the data is that **statistical causality** need not tell us anything about true causality. A variable a statistically causes a variable b if current a helps predict future b. For example, every year we observe birds flying south before the onset of winter, and so the flight patterns of birds statistically predict

_____

[9]See M. Friedman and A. Schwartz, 1963. *A Monetary History of the United States, 1867–1960,* National Bureau of Economic Research, Cambridge, MA.

the winter. However, birds flying south do not cause winter; it is winter that is causing the birds to fly south.

There is an explanation for the tendency of money to lead output that is analogous to the example of birds flying south for the winter. There are two reasons that productivity shocks could cause money to lead output, again through the process of endogenous money. First, the banking sector tends to lead other sectors of the economy, as banks provide loans for real activity that will occur at a later date. When bank loans increase, so do bank deposits, as a bank borrows by way of bank deposits to finance its lending. Thus, bank deposits tend to be procyclical and to lead real GDP, and, therefore, M1, M2, and broader monetary aggregates tend to lead real GDP. Second, if the monetary authority is trying to stabilize prices, and it uses all available information efficiently, it can predict an increase in output due to an increase in z before the output increase is observed. Because an increase in the money supply may take time to affect prices, the monetary authority may want to act on this information before the increase in output and the decrease in the price level actually occur. Thus, money can lead real GDP because of preemptive monetary policy actions.

Implications of Real Business Cycle Theory for Government Policy

Now that we know how the real business cycle model works and have discussed how it fits the data, we can explore what the model implies for government policy. In the basic real business cycle model, there is no role for government stabilization policy. First, level changes in the money supply are neutral, and so attempts to smooth out business cycles through monetary policy actions have no effect. Second, because all markets clear, and there are no inefficiencies (for example, distorting taxes or externalities) in the basic model which government policy should correct, there is also no reason that the government should vary its spending in response to fluctuations in total factor productivity. Government spending can have an effect on output, but the level of such spending should be set according to the appropriate long-run role of the government in providing public goods (goods and services, such as national defense, that cannot or should not be provided by the private sector), not to smooth short-run fluctuations in aggregate GDP. In the basic real business cycle model, business cycles are essentially optimal responses of the economy to fluctuations in total factor productivity, and nothing should be done about them. Given the first fundamental theorem of welfare economics, from Chapter 5, if the allocation of resources in the economy is Pareto optimal, there is no need for the government to intervene, unless we think the government should redistribute income and wealth.

Though there is no role for government in the basic real business cycle model, other more elaborate versions of this model explain a role for government arising from the need to correct market failures and distortions.[10] For example, in practice all taxes are distorting. Income taxes distort labor supply decisions because firms and workers

---

[10]See T. Cooley, 1995. *Frontiers of Business Cycle Research,* Princeton University Press, Princeton, NJ.

face different effective wage rates, and sales taxes distort consumer purchasing patterns because firms and consumers do not face the same effective prices for all goods. Over time, it is efficient for the government to smooth out these distortions, or welfare losses, that arise from taxation. This can tell us that tax rates should be smooth over time, which then implies that the government should let total tax revenues rise in booms and fall in recessions, as tax revenue increases with income if the income tax rate is constant. This is a kind of countercyclical government policy, which may look like it is intended to stabilize output but is actually aimed at smoothing tax distortions.

Critique of Real Business Cycle Theory

The real business cycle model certainly fits the data better than does the Friedman–Lucas money surprise model. As well, the theory is internally consistent, and it helps focus our attention on how government policy should act to correct market failures and distortions, rather than on attempting to correct for the fact that prices and wages may not clear markets over short periods of time, as in older Keynesian models of the type we study in Chapter 12.

Real business cycle theory certainly has shortcomings, however, in its ability to explain business cycles. One problem is that the assessment of whether or not real business cycle theory fits the data is based on using the Solow residual to measure total factor productivity. There is good reason to believe that there is a large cyclical error in how the Solow residual measures total factor productivity z, and that the close tracking of detrended GDP by the Solow residual in Figure 11.2 might at least partly be accounted for by measurement error. During a boom, the aggregate capital stock is close to being fully utilized. Most machinery is running full time, and many manufacturing plants are in operation 24 hours per day. Further, the workers who are operating the plant and equipment are very busy. These workers are under pressure to produce output, because demand is high. There are few opportunities to take breaks, and overtime work is common. Thus, workers are being fully utilized as well. Alternatively, in a temporary recession, the aggregate capital stock is not fully utilized, in that some machinery is sitting idle and plants are not running 24 hours per day. Further, during a temporary recession, a firm may not wish to lay workers off (even though there is not much for them to do), because this may mean that these workers would get other jobs and the firm would lose workers having valuable skills that are specific to the firm. Thus, workers employed at the firm during a recession might not be working very hard—they might take long breaks and produce little. In other words, the workforce tends to be underutilized during a recession, just as the aggregate capital stock is. This phenomenon of underutilization of labor during a recession is sometimes called **labor hoarding.**

The underutilization of capital and labor during a recession is a problem for the measurement of total factor productivity, because during recessions the capital stock and the labor input would be measured as being higher than they actually are. Thus, in terms of measurement, we could see a drop in output during a recession and infer that total factor productivity dropped because the Solow residual decreased. But output may have dropped simply because the quantity of inputs in production dropped, with no change in total factor productivity.

To see how this works, consider the following example. Suppose that the production function is Cobb-Douglas with a capital share in output of 36%, as we assumed in calculating Solow residuals in Chapter 6. Namely, the production function takes the form

$$Y = zK^{0.36}N^{0.64}, \tag{11.1}$$

where Y is aggregate output, z is total factor productivity, K is the capital stock, and N is employment. Now, suppose initially that $z = 1$, $K = 100$, and $N = 50$, so that, from Equation (11.1), we have $Y = 64.2$, and capital and labor are full utilized. Then, suppose that a recession occurs that is not the result of a drop in total factor productivity, so that $z = 1$ as before. Firms still have capital on hand equal to 100 units, and employment is still 50 units, and so measured capital is $K = 100$ and measured employment is $N = 50$. However, suppose only 95% of the capital in existence is actually being used in production (the rest is shut down), so that actual capital is $K = 95$. Further, suppose the employed workforce is being used only 90% as intensively as before, with workers actually only putting in 90% of the time working that they were formerly. Thus, actual employment is $N = 45$. Plugging $z = 1$, $K = 95$, and $N = 45$ into Equation (11.1), we get $Y = 58.9$. Now, if we mistakenly used the measured capital stock, measured employment, and measured output to calculate the Solow residual, we would obtain

$$\hat{z} = \frac{58.9}{(100)^{0.36}(50)^{0.64}} = 0.918,$$

where $\hat{z}$ is the Solow residual or measured total factor productivity. Therefore, we would measure total factor productivity as having decreased by 8.2%, when it really had not changed at all. This shows how decreases in the utitilization of factors of production during recessions can lead to biases in the measurement of total factor productivity and to biases in the evaluation of the importance of total factor productivity shocks for business cycles.

. . . .

MONETARY SHOCKS, REAL SHOCKS, AND POST-1970 RECESSIONS

THEORY confronts the DATA

If the Solow residual were a highly accurate measure of total factor productivity, we would take Figure 11.2 as strong evidence that the primary cause of business cycles in the United States after World War II was fluctuations in total factor productivity. We would then have little reason to go beyond the real business cycle model to explain why we have booms and recessions. However, as was explained in the previous section, there is good reason to believe that there is significant bias in the Solow residual as a measure of total factor productivity. Therefore, in determining the causes of particular recessions, for example, it is useful to look at other sources of evidence than just the behavior of the Solow residual. This is also important because movements in the Solow residual, even if they accurately reflect movements in total factor productivity, may be caused by one or several out of a set of many factors.

FIGURE 11.6 **Percentage Deviations From Trend in Money Supply and GDP**

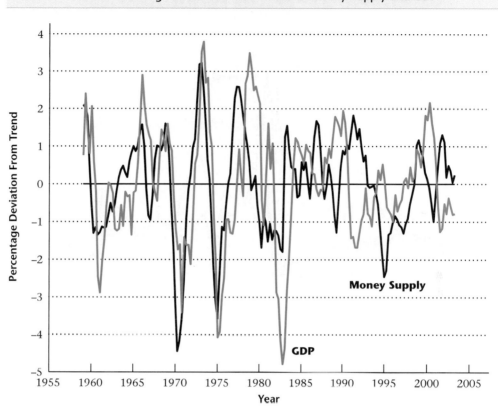

In the 1974–75 recession, money leads output and tracks it closely. Money decreases below trend prior to the 1981–82 recession. In the recessions of 1990–91 and 2001, money is above trend.

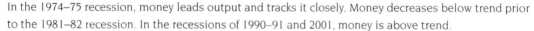

As an example of how we can use available evidence to sort out the causes of particular business cycle events, suppose that we focus on recessions that have occurred since 1970. These are the recessions of 1974–75, 1981–82, 1990–91, and 2001. Further, in terms of evidence on what the underlying shocks were that caused these recessions, we focus on movements in the money supply and interest rates as indicators of monetary shocks and on movements in the relative price of energy as a source of total factor productivity shocks. This evidence is displayed in Figures 11.6, 11.7, and 11.8.

First, consider the 1974–75 recession. Conventional wisdom is that this recession was caused by a negative shock to total factor productivity arising from a sharp increase in the relative price of energy. This is certainly consistent with Figures 11.6–11.8. In Figure 11.8, there was a large increase in the relative price of energy in 1973, which resulted from a cutback in crude oil output by OPEC countries. While Figure 11.6 shows a reduction in the money supply below trend in 1974–75 that lead the decrease in real GDP below trend, this is consistent with an endogenous money story. As well,

FIGURE 11.7 Real and Nominal Interest Rates

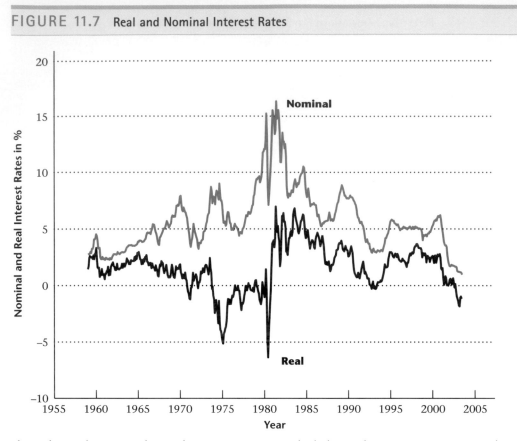

The real rate of interest is low in the 1974–75 recession, high during the 1981–82 recession, and decreasing during the 1991–92 and 2001 recessions.

there is a decline in the real interest rate in 1974–75 in Figure 11.7. In the real business cycle model, a reduction in total factor productivity would cause an increase in the real interest rate, while in the money surprise model if the central bank increases the money supply the real interest rate falls. Thus, the money supply could have decreased because of a contraction in bank deposits during the recession, but the Fed caused the money supply to fall less than it otherwise would have, with the result that the real interest rate fell.

What about the recession of 1981–82? This is often referred to as the "Volcker recession," as it is commonly believed that the Federal Reserve Chairman, Paul Volcker, instigated a tightening in monetary policy to reduce inflation which then caused the recession. There is certainly evidence for this, as Figure 11.6 shows the money supply dropping below trend before the onset of the 1981–82 recession, and in Figure 11.7 there is a sharp jump in the real interest rate in 1981 to unprecedented high levels. However, we cannot entirely discount real factors as a contributing cause to the 1981–82

FIGURE 11.8 Relative Price of Energy

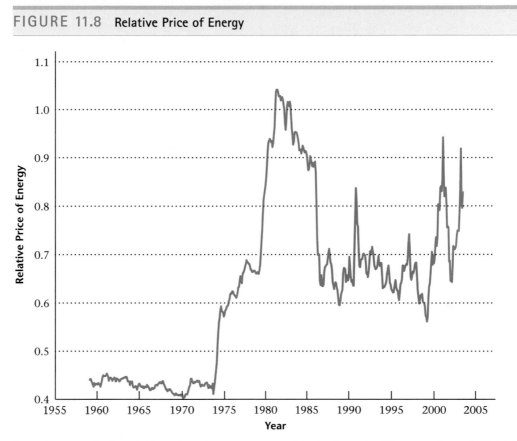

Large increases in the relative price of energy are associated with each of the recessions of 1974–75, 1981–82, 1991–92, and 2001. However, the increase in the relative price of energy preceded the 1981–82 recession by at least a year, and the increase in the relative price of energy prior to the 1991–92 recession was very short-lived.

recession, as there was a very large increase in the relative price of energy, shown in Figure 11.8, in 1979–80.

For the 1990–91 recession, it is somewhat more difficult to pinpoint causes. There was a spike in the relative price of energy in late 1990/early 1991 caused by the Persian Gulf War, as shown in Figure 11.8, but it seems unlikely that this temporary price increase would have had much effect on total factor productivity. With regard to monetary policy, the money supply was above trend in 1990–91 in Figure 11.6, and in Figure 11.7 the real interest rate was falling. Thus, the recession does not appear to have been caused by tight monetary policy, though we could say that monetary policy likely prevented the recession from being more severe.

We have already discussed the 2001 recession to some extent in Chapter 9. The most likely primary cause in this case was a collapse in investment spending because of pessimism about future total factor productivity. This does not show up in Figures 11.6–11.8. However, an important contributing cause would appear to be the increase in the relative price of energy in 2000, observed in Figure 11.8. As with the 1990–91 recession, monetary policy appears to have made the recession less severe, as the money supply was above trend in 2001 and the real interest rate was falling, as we see in Figures 11.6 and 11.7.

MACROECONOMICS IN ACTION

Business Cycle Models and the Great Depression

The Great Depression was a unique event in U.S. macroeconomic history. The Great Depression began in 1929, and real GDP declined for about four years, decreasing by 31% from 1929 to 1933. It then took another seven years for real GDP to recover to its 1929 level. Relative to the average post–World War II recession, the length and size of the decline in output during the Great Depression were very large, and the recovery took a particularly long time. In the average post–World War II recession, GDP declined by 2.9% after about one year and then recovered in one-and-a-half years. Was the Great Depression essentially a larger-scale version of a recession that otherwise looks much like a typical post–World War II recession, or do standard macroeconomic theories of the business cycle fail to explain the behavior of the U.S. economy during the Great Depression? In an article in the *Federal Reserve Bank of Minneapolis Quarterly Review*,[1] Harold Cole and Lee Ohanian set out to answer this question.

Cole and Ohanian look at versions of the three business cycle theories that we have examined or will examine—a Keynesian sticky wage model, a money surprise model, and a real business cycle

model (among other explanations)—to see how well these models fit the data for the Great Depression. The Keynesian sticky wage model does not fare very well. During the Great Depression, there was a large decline in the money supply. In the Keynesian sticky wage model that we study in Chapter 12, this would reduce the price level, and then, given a sticky nominal wage, the real wage would rise, and this would cause firms to hire less labor, with output decreasing. In the manufacturing sector, real wages increased while output was declining from 1929 to 1933, but outside of manufacturing the real wage fell precipitously over this period, and nonmanufacturing real wages were still much below trend in 1939. These data do not appear to be consistent with broad-based stickiness in nominal wages being a major influence during the Great Depression.

Cole and Ohanian find that shocks to total factor productivity can explain the decline in aggregate output from 1929 to 1933, but cannot explain the slow recovery. Similar results are obtained for the money surprise model. Estimated total factor productivity shocks and money surprises during the Great Depression predict that the

(continued)

recovery should have happened much earlier than it did.

Thus, the problem with standard theories of the business cycle, when confronted with the Great Depression, is primarily in explaining the long and weak recovery. What is Cole and Ohanian's alternative explanation for the length of the recovery during the Great Depression? They conjecture that regulation was the culprit. The National Industrial Recovery Act of 1933 suspended U.S. antitrust laws and permitted more collusion among firms, particularly in the manufacturing sector. More collusion among firms in an industry tends to reduce output, raise prices, and lower investment—all features consistent with the Great Depression.

_____

[1]See H. Cole and L. Ohanian, 1999. "The Great Depression in the United States from a Neoclassical Perspective," *Federal Reserve Bank of Minneapolis Quarterly Review,* Winter, 2–24.

A KEYNESIAN COORDINATION FAILURE MODEL

The two equilibrium theories of the business cycle that we have discussed thus far in this chapter—the Friedman-Lucas money surprise theory and real business cycle theory—are in the classical tradition, in that they imply that the government should at best stay out of the way and allow markets to work. However, this does not mean that all equilibrium theories of the business cycle imply no role for the government in smoothing business cycles. Many modern Keynesians adopt an approach to macroeconomics very similar to that of classical economists, in assuming that prices and wages are fully flexible and that all markets clear. Some of these modern Keynesians explore an idea that one can find in Keynes's *General Theory,* the notion of **coordination failure.** In macroeconomics, coordination failures were first studied rigorously by Peter Diamond in the early 1980s,[11] and later contributions were by Russell Cooper and Andrew John,[12] Jess Benhabib and Roger Farmer,[13] and Roger Farmer and Jang-Ting Guo.[14] The basic idea in coordination failure models is that it is difficult for private sector workers and producers to coordinate their actions, and there exist **strategic complementarities,** which imply that one person's willingness to engage in some activity increases with the number of other people engaged in that activity.

An example of an activity with a strategic complementarity is a party. If Paul knows that someone wishes to hold a party and that only a few other people will be going, he will probably not want to go. However, if many people are going, this will be much

_____

[11]See P. Diamond, 1982. "Aggregate Demand in Search Equilibrium," *Journal of Political Economy* 90, 881–894.

[12]R. Cooper and A. John, 1988. "Coordinating Coordination Failures in Keynesian Models," *Quarterly Journal of Economics* 103, 441–463.

[13]See J. Benhabib and R. Farmer, 1994. "Indeterminacy and Increasing Returns," *Journal of Economic Theory* 63, 19–41.

[14]See R. Farmer and J. Guo, 1994. "Real Business Cycles and the Animal Spirits Hypothesis," *Journal of Economic Theory* 63, 42–72.

more fun, and Paul will likely go. Paul's potential enjoyment of the party increases with the number of other people who are likely to go. We might imagine that there are two possible outcomes (equilibria) here. One outcome is that no one goes, and another is that everyone goes. These are equilibria because, if no one goes to the party, then no individual would want to go, and if everyone goes to the party, then no individual would want to stay at home. If Paul could coordinate with other people, then everyone would certainly agree that having everyone go to the party would be a good idea, and they could all agree to go. However, without coordination, it is possible that no one goes.

If we use the party as an analogy to aggregate economic activity, the willingness of one producer to produce may depend on what other producers are doing. For example, if Jennifer is a computer software producer, the quantity of software she can sell depends on the quantity and quality of computer hardware that is sold. If more hardware is sold, it is easier for Jennifer to sell software, and if Jennifer sells more software, it is easier to sell hardware. Computer hardware and computer software are complementary. Many such complementarities exist in the economy, and different producers find it difficult to coordinate their actions. Thus, it is possible that there may be **multiple equilibria** for the aggregate economy, whereby output and employment might be high, or output and employment might be low. Business cycles might simply be fluctuations between these high and low equilibria, driven by waves of optimism and pessimism.

To formalize this idea in an economic model, we start with the notion that there are aggregate increasing returns to scale, which implies that output more than doubles if all inputs double, as discussed in Chapter 4. Until now, we have assumed constant returns to scale, which implies that the marginal product of labor is diminishing when the quantity of capital is fixed. Increasing returns to scale at the aggregate level can be due to the strategic complementarities that we discussed above. We can then have increasing returns to scale at the aggregate level in a situation where, for each individual firm, there are constant returns to scale in production. With sufficient aggregate increasing returns to scale, the aggregate production function, fixing the quantity of capital, can be convex, as in Figure 11.9. Then, because the slope of the production function in the figure increases with the labor input, the marginal product of labor for the aggregate economy is increasing rather than decreasing. Because the aggregate demand for labor is just the aggregate marginal product of labor schedule, this implies that the aggregate labor demand curve N^d can be upward sloping as in Figure 11.10.

Now, for the coordination failure theory to work, the aggregate labor demand curve must have a greater slope than the labor supply curve, as in Figure 11.11. To repeat the exercise from Chapter 9 where we derived the output supply curve Y^s, suppose that the real interest rate is r_1, with the labor supply curve $N^s(r_1)$ in Figure 11.12(c). Then the equilibrium quantity of employment would be N_1 and output would be Y_1, from the production function in Figure 11.12(b). Therefore, an output-real interest rate pair implying equilibrium in the labor market is (Y_1, r_1) in Figure 11.12(a). Now, if the real interest rate is higher, say r_2, then the labor supply curve shifts rightward to $N^s(r_2)$ in Figure 11.12(c), because workers wish to substitute future leisure for current leisure. As a result, the equilibrium quantity of employment falls to N_2 and output falls to Y_2.

FIGURE 11.9 A Production Function with Increasing Returns to Scale

Strategic complementarities among firms imply that there can be increasing returns to scale at the aggregate level, which can give a convex production function as depicted, where the marginal product of labor increases as the quantity of labor input increases.

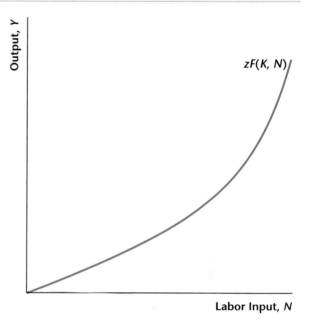

FIGURE 11.10 Aggregate Labor Demand with Sufficient Increasing Returns to Scale

With sufficient increasing returns to scale, the aggregate labor demand curve slopes upward, as the aggregate marginal product of labor increases with aggregate employment.

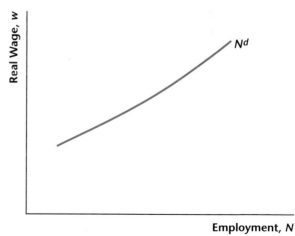

FIGURE 11.11 **The Labor Market in the Coordination Failure Model**

With sufficient increasing returns, the labor demand curve is steeper than the labor supply curve, which is required for the coordination failure model to work.

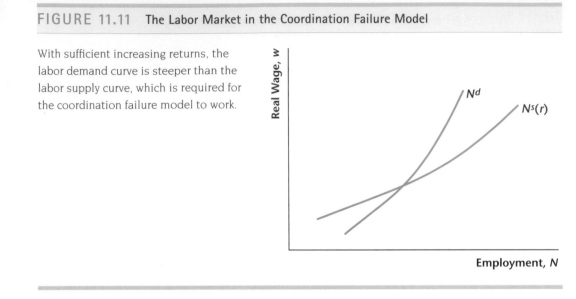

Thus, another point on the output supply curve in Figure 11.12(a) is (Y_2, r_2), and the Y^s curve is downward sloping.

The Coordination Failure Model: An Example

We now consider a simple example that shows some of the key insights that come from coordination failure models. Suppose that the downward-sloping Y^s curve and the downward-sloping Y^d curve intersect in just two places (though this need not be the case; there could be more than two intersections, or there could be only one), as in Figure 11.13(b). Here, the economy could be in one of two equilibria. In the first, the "bad equilibrium," output is Y_1, the real interest rate is r_1, the price level is P_1, the real wage is w_1, and employment is N_1. In the second, the "good equilibrium," output is Y_2, the real interest rate is r_2, the price level is P_2, the real wage is w_2, and employment is N_2. In a more explicit version of this model, which would have a description of consumers' preferences, consumers would be better off in the good equilibrium with high output and employment than in the bad equilibrium with low output and employment.

Will the economy be in the good equilibrium or the bad equilibrium? There is certainly nothing to prevent the bad equilibrium from arising. Even though everyone prefers the good equilibrium, the bad equilibrium could arise if everyone is pessimistic and expects bad things to happen. Similarly, the good equilibrium arises if everyone is optimistic. In this model, business cycles could result if consumers and firms are alternately optimistic and pessimistic, so that the economy alternates between the good equilibrium and the bad equilibrium. This seems much like what Keynes referred to as "animal spirits," the waves of optimism and pessimism that he viewed as being an important determinant of investment.

FIGURE 11.12   **The Output Supply Curve in the Coordination Failure Model**

The figure shows the construction of the output supply curve Y^s in the coordination failure model. An increase in the real interest rate shifts the labor supply curve to the right, reducing employment and output.

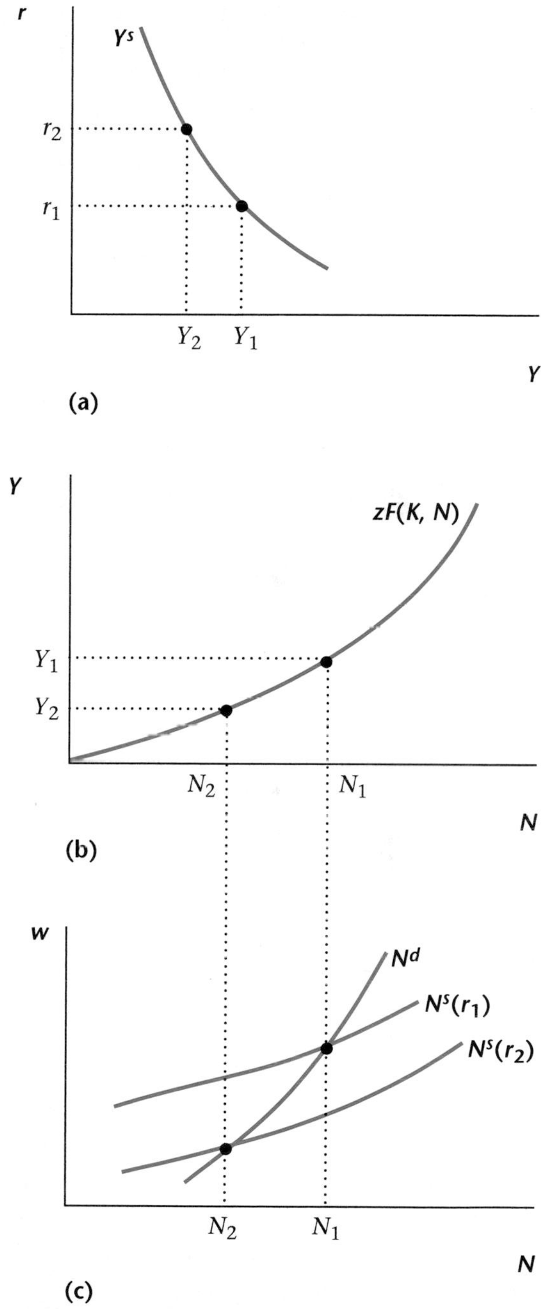

(a)

(b)

(c)

FIGURE 11.13 Multiple Equilibria in the Coordination Failure Model

Because the output supply curve is downward-sloping in the coordination failure model, there can be two equilibria, as in this example. In one equilibrium, aggregate output is low and the real interest rate is high; in the other, aggregate output is high and the real interest rate is low.

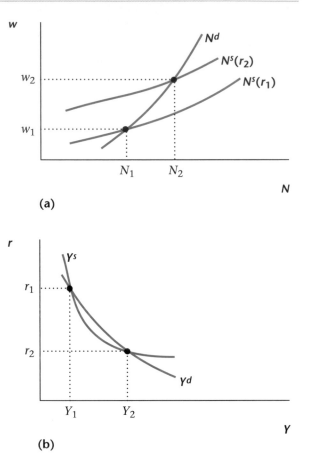

(a)

(b)

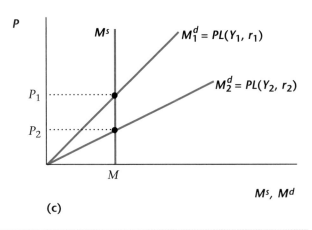

(c)

In the coordination failure model, it is possible that extraneous events that are completely unrelated to economic fundamentals (technology, preferences, and endowments) can "cause" business cycles. Macroeconomists sometimes call such extraneous events **sunspots,** in analogy to the irregular occurrence of dark spots observed on the sun, because a dark spot on the sun does not affect production possibilities, preferences, or available resources (i.e., anything fundamental) on Earth. However, sunspots are in principle observable to everyone. Therefore, if workers and firms all treat the observation of a sunspot as a sign of optimism, then the economy goes to the good equilibrium when a sunspot is observed, and it goes to the bad equilibrium when no sunspot is observed. It then appears that sunspots are causing business cycles. The behavior of the stock market is perhaps most indicative of the presence of "sunspot behavior," in that there is much more variability in stock prices than can be explained by fluctuations in fundamentals (the earnings potential of firms). Alan Greenspan, the current chairman of the Federal Reserve Board, once referred to the stock market as being under the influence of "irrational exuberance." Sunspot behavior in the economy need not literally be driven by sunspots, but by events with no connection to anything fundamentally important to preferences, endowments, and technology.

Predictions of the Coordination Failure Model

From Figure 11.13, the good equilibrium has a low real interest rate, a high level of output, a low price level, a high level of employment, and a high real wage. The bad equilibrium has a high real interest rate, a low level of output, a high price level, a low level of employment, and a low real wage. Thus, given the low (high) real interest rate, the good (bad) equilibrium has a high (low) level of consumption and investment. Therefore, if business cycles are fluctuations between the good and bad equilibrium, then, as in Table 11.3, consumption, investment, and employment are procyclical, the price level is countercyclical, and the real wage is procyclical, just as observed in the data. As well, in Figure 11.14 average labor productivity (the slope of a ray from the origin to the relevant point on the production function) must be procyclical, as it is higher in the good equilibrium than in the bad equilibrium. Further, Roger Farmer

Table 11.3 **Data Versus Predictions of the Coordination Failure Model**

Variable	Data	Model
Consumption	Procyclical	Procyclical
Investment	Procyclical	Procyclical
Price Level	Countercyclical	Countercyclical
Money Supply	Procyclical	—
Employment	Procyclical	Procyclical
Real Wage	Procyclical	Procyclical
Average Labor Productivity	Procyclical	Procyclical

FIGURE 11.14   Average Labor Productivity in the Keynesian Coordination Failure Model

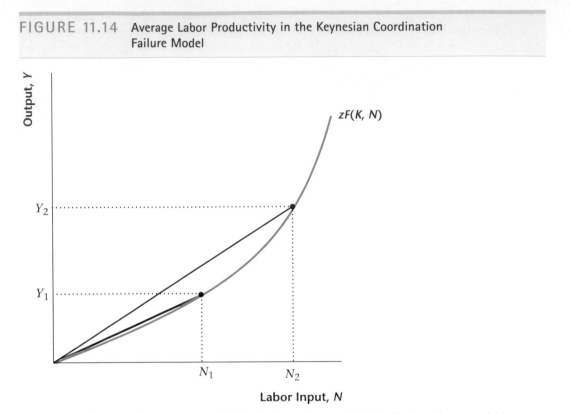

In the good (bad) equilibrium, output is high (low), employment is high (low), and average labor productivity is high (low).

and Jang-Ting Guo have shown that a version of the coordination failure model does essentially as well as the real business cycle model in quantitatively replicating U.S. business cycle behavior.[15]

Though money is neutral in the coordination failure model, as it is in the real business cycle model, the coordination failure model can explain why the nominal money supply is procyclical. Suppose that the money supply fluctuates between M_1 and M_2, where $M_2 > M_1$. Also, suppose that money acts as a sunspot variable. That is, when consumers and firms observe a high money supply, they are optimistic, and when they observe a low money supply, they are pessimistic. Therefore, when the money supply is high, the economy is in the good equilibrium, and when the money supply is low, the economy is in the bad equilibrium, and people's expectations are

---

[15] See R. Farmer and J. Guo, 1994. "Real Business Cycles and the Animal Spirits Hypothesis," *Journal of Economic Theory* 63, 42–72.

FIGURE 11.15 Procyclical Money Supply in the Coordination Failure Model

If the money supply is a sunspot variable in the coordination failure model, then money may appear to be nonneutral because people believe it to be. When the money supply is high (low), everyone is optimistic (pessimistic), and output is high (low).

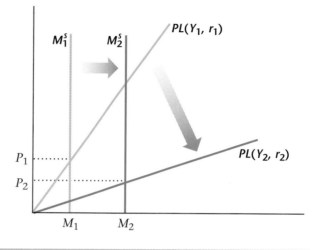

self-fulfilling. In Figure 11.15, we can still have the price level moving countercyclically, provided money supply does not fluctuate too much. In the good equilibrium, nominal money demand is $PL(Y_2, r_2)$, and in the bad equilibrium, nominal money demand is $PL(Y_1, r_1)$. Money supply increases in the good equilibrium from M_1 to M_2, and the price level falls from P_1 to P_2. Here, though money is actually neutral, it can appear to be causing business cycles.

Policy Implications of the Coordination Failure Model

In terms of how they match the data, the coordination failure and real business cycle models are essentially indistinguishable. However, the two models have very different policy implications. In the real business cycle model, decreases in output and employment are just optimal responses to a decline in total factor productivity, while in the coordination failure model, the good equilibrium is in principle an opportunity available in the aggregate economy when the bad equilibrium is realized. Thus, if we believe this model, then government policies that promote optimism would be beneficial. For example, encouraging statements by public officials, such as the treasury secretary or the chairman of the Federal Reserve Board, could in principle bump the economy from the bad equilibrium to the good equilibrium.

Policy could also be designed to smooth business cycles or to eliminate them altogether in the coordination failure model. As an example, consider Figure 11.16, where there are initially two equilibria, a bad equilibrium where the real interest rate is r_1 and the level of output is Y_1, and a good equilibrium where the real interest rate is r_2 and the level of output is Y_2. Then, suppose that the government reduces current government spending G. Recall from Chapter 9 that a decrease in current government

FIGURE 11.16 Stabilizing Fiscal Policy in the Coordination Failure Model

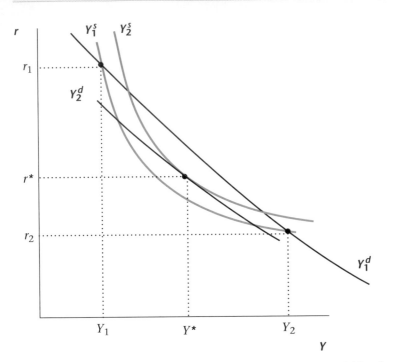

Fiscal policy can stabilize output in the coordination failure model by eliminating multiple equilibria. Here, with a decrease in government spending, the output demand curve shifts left and the output supply curve shifts right and this can produce a unique equilibrium where $Y = Y^*$ and $r = r^*$.

spending reduces the present value of taxes, causing a decrease in current labor supply. Here, this shifts the output supply curve to the right (not to the left as in Chapter 9) from Y_1^s to Y_2^s in the figure. Further, recall from Chapter 9 that we know that a decrease in G shifts the output demand curve leftward from Y_1^d to Y_2^d. If the government reduces G by just the right amount, then there is only one equilibrium, where $Y = Y^*$ and $r = r^*$, as in the figure. Effectively, the bad equilibrium gets better and the good equilibrium gets worse, because of the decrease in G, and there are no business cycles. It is not clear whether eliminating business cycles in this manner is advantageous. For example, if in the absence of the decrease in G the economy was in the good equilibrium most of the time, then average welfare could go down when business cycles are eliminated. It could be, however, that there are benefits from reduced uncertainty when business cycles are eliminated, so that even though average output might go down, the benefits from reduced uncertainty from smoothing business cycles could be beneficial.

MACROECONOMICS IN ACTION

Are Business Cycles Disappearing?

In the United States, the last severe recession, the 1981–82 recession, is now in the seemingly distant past, and the two most recent recessions, in 1990–91 and 2001, were comparatively mild and short. Further, there has been no post–World War II recession that remotely compares to the Great Depression in length and severity. It may seem that the U.S. economy has become less erratic in its behavior, and an explanation for this might be that monetary and fiscal policy have become much more effective over time. Perhaps, according to a Keynesian view of business cycles, monetary and fiscal policy are now conducted in a way that better stabilizes the economy. Alternatively, according to a classical view of business cycles, the monetary and fiscal authorities may have learned how to stay out of the way.

Christina Romer, in an article in the *Journal of Economic Perspectives*,[1] looks at some evidence that can be used to compare business cycles before World War I with those after World War II. She finds that the reduction in the volatility of real GDP is not that great from the earlier to the later period. In the United States from 1886–1916, the standard deviation of percentage changes in real GDP was 3.0%, while for 1948–1997, the comparable figure is 2.5%. The United States did not have a central bank before 1914 to engage in monetary policy, and the government sector accounted for a very small fraction of GDP before World War I, so that fiscal policy could have had only small effects if the government had chosen

to use it. Thus, if we are to measure the contribution of fiscal and monetary policy by the reduction in the volatility of real GDP from the 1886–1916 period to the 1948–1997 period, this contribution appears to be quite small.

More recent history does appear consistent with the view that business cycles are being successfully wrung out of the system by sound monetary and fiscal policy. Some recessions, in particular the 1981–82 recession, appear to have been policy induced. That is, according to one interpretation, the 1981–82 recession was caused by tight monetary policy, which was necessary to quell the high inflation brought on by the monetary policy errors of the 1970s. Since the mid-1980s, however, the inflation rate in the United States has been relatively low, in part because the Fed has been focused on keeping it low, and so surprise tightening in monetary policy to reduce inflation, with the side effect of a recession, has not been necessary.

A more pessimistic view is that we have just been lucky recently, in that there have been no important external shocks to the economy that would give rise to major recessions. The most recent recession in 2001 was short, but the recovery from the recession was not strong; growth in real output and employment remain weak into 2003.

---

[1] C. Romer, 1999. "Changes in Business Cycles: Evidence and Explanations," *Journal of Economic Perspectives* 13, 23–44.

Critique of the Coordination Failure Model

The key insight of the coordination failure model is that business cycles can result simply from self-fulfilling waves of optimism and pessimism. As mentioned previously, the existence of these self-fulfilling expectations appears to be most evident in the case of the stock market, where it seems difficult to explain the wild gyrations that occur daily as being the result of changes in fundamental economic factors.

There are some potential weaknesses, however, in coordination failure theories of the business cycle. First, a critical element of the coordination failure theory is that there exist sufficient increasing returns to scale in aggregate production that the aggregate labor demand curve slopes upward and is steeper than the aggregate labor supply curve. If aggregate production is subject to constant returns to scale or decreasing returns to scale, then this theory is a nonstarter. In practice, the measurement of returns to scale in aggregate production is very imprecise. Some researchers claim to find evidence of increasing returns in the data, but others do not. A good reference for this issue is the work of Harold Cole and Lee Ohanian.[16] At best, the evidence supporting the existence of increasing returns to scale at the aggregate level is weak.

Second, a problem with this model is that the underlying shocks that cause business cycles are expectations, and expectations are essentially unobservable. This makes it difficult to use the theory to understand historical recessions and booms.

This completes our study of equilibrium models of the business cycle. In Chapter 12 we analyze an early-generation Keynesian model in which the nominal wage is sticky and the labor market may not always clear.

CHAPTER SUMMARY

- In this chapter, we constructed three different equilibrium models of the business cycle, and we evaluated these models in terms of how they fit the data, their policy predictions, and their plausibility.

- In the first model, the Friedman–Lucas money surprise model, workers in the short run do not have perfect information on aggregate economic variables, in that they do not observe the money supply, the price level, or total factor productivity, but they know that the economy could be hit by permanent shocks to the money supply or temporary shocks to total factor productivity. If the money supply increases, then workers observe an increase in their nominal wage, but they do not know if this is because the money supply increased or there was a positive shock to total factor productivity. In the latter case, the increase in the nominal wage would also signal an increase in the real wage, and so workers increase labor supply, implying that output increases.

- Money is not neutral in the money surprise model, because workers can be fooled by unanticipated increases in the money supply. The money surprise model fits most features of the data, but it implies that the price level is procyclical and that the real wage and average labor productivity are countercyclical, and these predictions are not consistent with

---

[16]See H. Cole and L. Ohanian, 1999. "Aggregate Returns to Scale: Why Measurement Is Imprecise," *Federal Reserve Bank of Minneapolis Quarterly Review,* Summer, 19–28.

the key business cycle facts from Chapter 3. The policy conclusion implied by the money surprise model is that monetary policy should be carried out in a predictable fashion.

- The second model studied in this chapter is the real business cycle model, in which business cycles are explained by persistent fluctuations in total factor productivity. The real business cycle model is consistent with all the business cycle facts from Chapter 3, and endogenous money can explain the regularities in the behavior of the nominal money supply relative to real aggregate output.

- The basic real business cycle model has no role for government policy, since business cycles are simply optimal responses to fluctuations in total factor productivity.

- The real business cycle model is not always successful in explaining historical business cycle events, and there are measurement problems in using the Solow residual as a measure of total factor productivity.

- The third model studied here is the Keynesian coordination failure model, which is based on the existence of strategic complementarities giving rise to increasing returns to scale at the aggregate level. This implies that there can be multiple equilibria, and we considered an example in which the model had two equilibria: a good equilibrium with high output, consumption, investment, employment, and real wage, and a low real interest rate and price level; and a bad equilibrium with low output, consumption, investment employment, and real wage, and a high real interest rate and price level. The economy could then fluctuate between these two equilibria, with fluctuations driven by waves of optimism and pessimism.

- Money is neutral in the Keynesian coordination failure model, but it could be a sunspot variable that produces optimism and pessimism, thus making it appear that money is not neutral.

- The coordination failure model does as well as the real business cycle model in fitting the data. The role for government policy in the coordination failure model could be to produce optimism, and there may be a role for fiscal policy in smoothing out business cycles.

KEY TERMS

Constant money growth rule: A monetary policy rule advocated by Milton Friedman, which specifies that the money supply should grow at a constant rate.

Endogenous money: The concept that the money supply is not exogenous but depends on other aggregate economic variables because of the behavior of the banking system and the central bank.

Statistical causality: When an economic variable a helps predict the future values of an economic variable b, we say that a statistically causes b.

Labor hoarding: The process by which firms may not lay off workers during a recession, even though those workers are not as busy on the job as they might be.

Coordination failure: Situation in which economic agents cannot coordinate their actions, producing a bad equilibrium.

Strategic complementarities: Relationships in which actions taken by others encourage a particular firm or consumer to take the same action.

Multiple equilibria: The presence of more than one equilibrium in an economic model.

Sunspot: An economic variable that has no effect on aggregate production possibilities or on consumers' preferences.

QUESTIONS FOR REVIEW

1. What were the two main principles introduced in the rational expectations revolution?

2. Why is it useful to study different models of the business cycle?

3. Explain why money is nonneutral in the money surprise model.

4. Should the government act to stabilize output in the money surprise model? Why or why not?

5. Does the money surprise model fit the data?

6. What causes output to fluctuate in the real business cycle model?

7. Why is money neutral in the real business cycle model?

8. How can the real business cycle model explain the behavior of the money supply over the business cycle?

9. Should the government act to stabilize output in the real business cycle model?

10. Does the real business cycle model fit the data?

11. What are the important shortcomings of the real business cycle model?

12. Describe an example of a coordination failure problem.

13. What causes business cycles in the coordination failure model?

14. Why is money neutral in the coordination failure model?

15. Does the coordination failure model fit the data?

16. Which is the better macro model, the real business cycle model or the coordination failure model? Explain.

PROBLEMS

1. In the money surprise model, suppose that total factor productivity increases temporarily. What are the equilibrium effects of this, and how does this differ from what happens in the monetary intertemporal model of Chapter 9? Explain your results.

2. Suppose that the central bank wishes to reduce the price level and announces that it will reduce the money supply to accomplish this. Use the money surprise model to answer the following questions:
   (a) Suppose that the public does not believe that the central bank is serious about reducing the price level. What happens to real aggregate variables and the price level?
   (b) Suppose, alternatively, that the public believes the central bank announcement. What happens to real variables and the price level now?
   (c) Compare your results in parts (a) and (b). In which case does the price level change more for a given reduction in the money supply? What do you think a central bank can do to make its policy announcements more credible?

3. In the money surprise model, compare the performance of the economies in two countries, which in all respects but one are identical. In country a, the money supply is highly variable, while in country b, there is little variability in the money supply. For a given surprise increase in the money supply, determine with the aid of diagrams how the economy in country a responds relative to the economy in country b. Explain your results.

4. In the real business cycle model, suppose that government spending increases temporarily. Determine the equilibrium effects of this. Could business cycles be explained by fluctuations in G? That is, does the model replicate the key business cycle facts from Chapter 3 when subjected to temporary shocks to government spending? Explain carefully.

5. Suppose that temporary increases in government spending lead to permanent increases in total factor productivity, perhaps because some government spending improves infrastructure and makes private firms more productive. Show that temporary shocks to government spending of this type could lead to business cycles that are consistent with the key business cycle facts, and explain your results.

6. In the real business cycle model, suppose that firms become infected with optimism and they expect that total factor productivity will be much higher in the future.
   (a) Determine the equilibrium effects of this.
   (b) If waves of optimism and pessimism of this sort cause GDP to fluctuate, does the model explain the key business cycle facts?
   (c) Suppose that the monetary authority wants to stabilize the price level in the face of a wave of optimism. Determine what it should do, and explain.

7. Suppose that money plays the role of a sunspot variable in the coordination failure model, so that the economy is in the bad equilibrium when the money supply is low and in the good equilibrium when the money supply is high. Explain what the monetary authority could do to make consumers better off. Compare this prescription for monetary policy with the one coming from the money surprise model, and discuss.

8. In the coordination failure model, suppose that consumers' preferences shift so that they want to consume less leisure and more consumption goods. Determine the effects on aggregate variables in the good equilibrium and in the bad equilibrium, and explain your results.

9. In the coordination failure model, suppose that there is a permanent increase in government spending. Determine how this affects output, the real interest rate, employment, the real wage, and the price level in the good equilibrium and in the bad equilibrium. Will real output be more or less volatile over time if there are waves of optimism and pessimism? Explain your results.

10. Suppose that there is a natural disaster that destroys some of the nation's capital stock. The central bank's goal is to stabilize the price level. Given this goal, what should the central bank do in response to the natural disaster? Explain with the aid of diagrams.

WORKING WITH THE DATA

1. Construct scatter plots of: (i) detrended monetary base vs. detrended real GDP; (ii) detrended M1 vs. detrended real GDP; (iii) detrended M2 vs. detrended real GDP.
   (a) What differences do you notice among the scatter plots?
   (b) How would you explain the differences you observed in part (a), if any?

2. Construct a times series plot of detrended real government expenditures and detrended real GDP, and construct a scatter plot of these two variables.
   (a) What do you observe in the plots you constructed? Is government spending a counter-cyclical or procyclical variable? Does it appear to be a leading, lagging, or coincident variable?

(b) Do any of the business cycle models studied in this chapter explain the features of the data in your answer to part (a)? If not, suggest an explanation or explanations for these regularities in the data.

3. Construct a times series plot of the detrended S and P 500 stock price index and detrended real GDP, and construct a scatter plot of these two variables.
   (a) What do you observe in the plots you constructed?
   (b) With what business cycle theory or theories are the observations from part (a) consistent? Explain.

CHAPTER 12

Keynesian Business Cycle Theory: The Sticky Wage Model

In this chapter, we study a business cycle model in the spirit of Keynes's General Theory.[1] Keynesian business cycle models have been very influential with both academics and policymakers. The basic formal modeling framework underlying these models was developed by Hicks in the late 1930s,[2] and popularized in Paul Samuelson's textbook in the 1950s. In the 1960s, large-scale versions of these Keynesian business cycle models were fit to data, and they are still used by some economists for forecasting and policy analysis. Though Keynesian models certainly have some strong adherents,[3] they have many detractors as well.[4] Part of what we do in this chapter is to critically evaluate the Keynesian sticky wage model, just as we evaluated equilibrium business cycle models in Chapter 11. We see how well the Keynesian sticky wage model fits the key business cycle facts we discussed in Chapter 3, and we examine how useful it is for guiding the formulation of economic policy.

In constructing the Keynesian sticky wage model, we do not start from scratch but build on the monetary intertemporal model studied in Chapter 10. The primary feature that makes a Keynesian macroeconomic model different from the models that we have examined thus far is that all prices and wages are not completely flexible—that is, some prices or wages are sticky. If some prices and wages cannot move so as to clear markets, then this will have important implications for how the economy behaves and for economic policy. The Keynesian sticky wage model studied in this chapter is essentially identical to the monetary intertemporal model in Chapter 10, except that the nominal wage rate is not sufficiently flexible for the labor market to clear in the short run. Given the failure of the labor market to clear, the Keynesian sticky wage model has far different properties from the monetary intertemporal model, and we need to take a quite different graphical approach to analyzing how it works.

In contrast to the monetary intertemporal model in Chapter 10, the Keynesian sticky wage model has the property that money is not neutral. When the monetary authority increases the money supply, there is an increase in aggregate output and

---

[1] See J. M. Keynes, 1936. *The General Theory of Employment, Interest, and Money,* Macmillan, London.

[2] J. Hicks, 1937. "Mr. Keynes and the Classics: A Suggested Interpretation," *Econometrica* 5, 147–159.

[3] L. Ball and N. G. Mankiw, 1994. "A Sticky-Price Manifesto," *Carnegie-Rochester Conference Series on Public Policy* 41, 127–151.

[4] See R. Lucas, 1980. "Methods and Problems in Business Cycle Theory," *Journal of Money, Credit, and Banking* 12.

employment. In general, monetary policy can then be used to improve economic performance and welfare. Keynesians typically believe strongly that the government should play an active role in the economy, through both monetary and fiscal policy, and Keynesian business cycle models support this belief.

Because the nominal wage does not move in the short run to clear the labor market in the Keynesian sticky wage model, there may be unemployment in that, given the market real wage, some people who wish to work cannot find employment. This is the first instance in this book of a genuine theory of unemployment; all of the macroeconomic models we have studied thus far explain only the quantity of employment and not the amount of unemployment. In Chapter 16, we study other models of unemployment that take account of the search behavior of the unemployed and incentive problems in the workplace.

In this chapter, we first construct the Keynesian sticky wage model, starting first with the labor market (where the critical difference in behavior from the monetary intertemporal model is), and then proceed to the construction of the *IS* and *LM* curves, which capture behavior in the goods market and money market, respectively. Then, we show how the aggregate demand and aggregate supply curves are constructed, which jointly determine equilibrium aggregate output and the price level. A key feature of the model is that it does not exhibit the classical dichotomy—the price level and real variables are simultaneously determined. Once we have put the Keynesian sticky wage model together, we put it to work, first in showing that money is not neutral. Then, we study the match between the model and the key business cycle facts from Chapter 3. Finally, we show how active monetary and fiscal policy can smooth out business cycles in the model by reacting to extraneous shocks to the economy.

THE LABOR MARKET IN THE KEYNESIAN STICKY WAGE MODEL

What makes the Keynesian sticky wage model different is the functioning of the labor market, and so we start with a description of how this market works. Keynesians argue that, in the short run, the nominal market wage W is imperfectly flexible. The rationale for this is that there are institutional rigidities in how nominal wages are set. For example, it is costly to get workers and firms together frequently to negotiate wage agreements, so that wages are typically set at a given firm for a year or more. Further, it is also costly for workers and firms to write complicated contracts, that is, contracts that provide for every contingency that might arise during the course of a labor contract. For example, workers might want to have a provision in a labor contract for nominal wages to rise faster in the event that inflation is higher than anticipated, and the firm might want nominal wages to rise at a slower rate if inflation is lower than anticipated. A labor contract in which future wage increases are geared to inflation is an **indexed** contract. Indexation to the inflation rate is relatively simple, because there are observed measures of inflation, such as the consumer price index, that could be used for this purpose. In spite of this, most labor contracts in the United States do not provide for complete indexation to inflation, though indexation was more common when inflation rates were higher, such as in the 1970s.

Given that indexation of wages to observed inflation rates in labor contracts seems relatively low cost and yet is typically not done, we can understand why more complicated types of contingencies do not find their way into labor contracts. For example, consider a bakery that is negotiating a contract with its workers. It might be efficient for the workers to receive a higher wage over the course of the contractual period in the event that the firm sells an unexpectedly large quantity of bread or that an individual worker should receive a lower wage in the event that the worker's health is unexpectedly bad. However, it may be difficult for the workers to monitor the firm's output, or for the firm to monitor each worker's health, so that these particular features do not find their way into the labor contract. As well, the more factors that are included in a labor contract, the more difficult it is to negotiate the contract. Simple labor contracts arise in part because contract negotiation is costly.

If workers and firms negotiate wage contracts in nominal terms, we could represent this as a fixed nominal wage W for the economy as a whole. We must recognize that the nominal wage should be thought of as being fixed only in the short run. Though the nominal wage W does not respond to factors affecting the labor market in the short run, we think of the nominal wage as being flexible over the long run. Given that the nominal wage is fixed in the short run, we could have a situation as in Figure 12.1, where the market-clearing real wage rate is w_{mc}, but the market or actual real wage is w^*, which is greater than w_{mc}. This situation could arise because the nominal wage was negotiated in the past, with the expectation by workers and firms that it would be a

---

FIGURE 12.1 The Labor Market in the Keynesian Sticky Wage Model

In the Keynesian sticky wage model, the labor market need not clear. In the figure, the market real wage w^* is greater than the market-clearing real wage w_{mc}. The quantity of employment is N^*, determined by the quantity of labor that the representative firm wishes to hire, and $N^{**} - N^*$ is Keynesian unemployment.

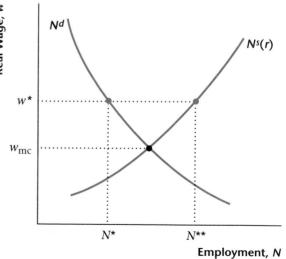

market-clearing wage, but then unforeseen circumstances caused unanticipated shifts in the labor supply or labor demand curves. At the real wage w^*, employment is determined by how much labor the representative firm wants to hire, which is N^*. However, the representative consumer wants to supply N^{**} units of labor at the real wage w^*, and we can then think of the difference $N^{**} - N^*$ as **Keynesian unemployment;** that is, workers cannot work as much as they would like at the going wage. In the sticky wage model, the quantity of labor is always determined by how much labor the representative firm wants to hire, that is, by the labor demand curve. The justification for this is that, in most employment relationships, the firm determines how many workers are employed with the firm, and what their hours of work are.

Though the sticky wage model can capture an element of the phenomenon of unemployment, because in the model there potentially are would-be workers who would like to be employed but cannot find jobs, the Keynesian depiction of unemployment is perhaps unsatisfactory. One problem is that unemployment, as measured in the U.S. unemployment survey, is job search activity. In the Keynesian sticky wage model, the representative consumer is not making choices about how hard to search for work or what job offers to accept. A second problem is that, in practice, some unemployment always exists, while in the labor market in the Keynesian sticky wage model, as we have set it up, there are circumstances in which there is no unemployment. If employment is determined as the quantity of labor desired by the representative firm at the market real wage—that is, by the quantity determined by the labor demand curve—then there is no unemployment if the market real wage is less than the market-clearing real wage. In this case, as in Figure 12.2, the market real wage is w^*, which is less than the

---

FIGURE 12.2   The Labor Market in the Keynesian Sticky Wage Model When There Is Excess Demand

In this circumstance, the market real wage w^* is less than the market-clearing real wage w_{mc}. The quantity of employment, determined by labor demand, is N^*, which is greater than N^{**}, the quantity of labor that the representative consumer wishes to supply.

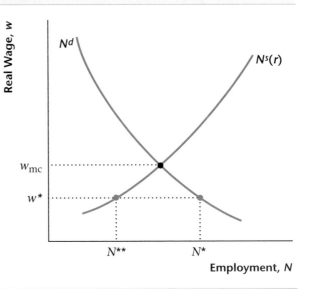

market-clearing real wage w_{mc}. At the market real wage, N^* is the quantity of employment, determined by the representative firm, but N^{**} is the quantity of labor that the representative consumer wants to supply. Thus, in this case the consumer is working more than he or she would like, which seems unpalatable.

To make the model more palatable, we might suppose instead that, in the situation depicted in Figure 12.2, the quantity of employment is determined by how much the representative consumer wants to work. In this case, employment would be N^{**}, and there would be an excess demand for labor of $N^* - N^{**}$, because the representative firm wants to hire a larger quantity of labor at the market wage than the representative consumer wants to supply. Though this fix is somewhat more appealing, there remains the undesirable feature that in this circumstance there is no unemployment, whereas in practice there are always some people who are not employed but are searching for work. In Chapter 16, we analyze a model of search and unemployment in which the unemployment rate is determined by the choices of the unemployed concerning what job offers they take. In that model, the unemployment rate will always be positive.

In the remainder of this chapter, we stick to circumstances in which the market real wage is no lower than the equilibrium real wage and employment is determined by the labor demand curve. This allows us to consider only cases where the model predicts positive unemployment.

THE STICKY WAGE AGGREGATE SUPPLY CURVE

Now that we have introduced the key element of the Keynesian sticky wage model, which is the labor market, we can fill in the other components of the model. An important difference in the Keynesian model from the monetary intertemporal model in Chapter 10 is that given the fixed nominal wage W, the real wage $\frac{W}{P}$ depends on the price level. Therefore, because employment is determined by labor demanded at the market real wage, employment and output depend on the price level. In this section, the component of the model we construct is the **aggregate supply curve**, which is a positive relationship between real output and the price level.

The aggregate supply curve is derived in Figure 12.3. Because the nominal wage W is fixed in the short run here, the real wage $w = \frac{W}{P}$ changes when the price level changes. In Figure 12.3(a), if the price level is P_1, then the quantity of employment is determined by the labor demand curve N^d, with employment $N = N_1$. Because the labor supply curve is irrelevant for determining employment in the sticky wage model, we leave it out of the diagram. This also implies that the supply of output does not depend on the real interest rate r, in contrast to the monetary intertemporal model. Given employment equal to N_1, from the production function in Figure 12.3(b) we determine real aggregate output, which is Y_1. Thus, the point (Y_1, P_1) in Figure 12.3(c) represents a level of output and a price level such that the representative firm is willing to supply the quantity of output Y_1 given the nominal wage W and the price level P_1. This point is then on the aggregate supply curve AS.

Suppose that the price level is higher, say $P_2 > P_1$. This implies, because the nominal wage is fixed, that the real wage is lower, that is, $\frac{W}{P_2} < \frac{W}{P_1}$. Seeing a lower real wage, the representative firm hires more labor, with the quantity of employment given by

FIGURE 12.3   Construction of the Aggregate Supply Curve

Given the fixed nominal wage W, an increase in the price level reduces the market real wage, which increases employment as the representative firm hires more labor. This results in more output being produced. Thus, a higher price level implies that more output is produced, which yields the upward-sloping aggregate supply curve AS in panel (c).

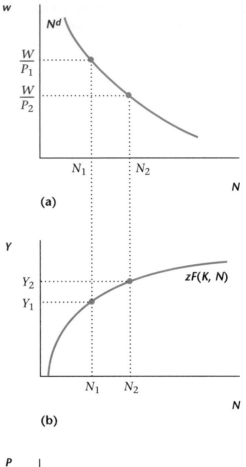

(a)

(b)

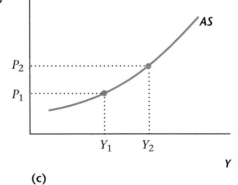

(c)

the labor demand curve N^d, or employment equal to N_2. Then, from the production function in Figure 12.3(b), output is $Y_2 > Y_1$, and in Figure 12.3(c) we have another point on the aggregate supply curve AS, namely (Y_2, P_2). Similarly, we could ask how much output would be supplied by the representative firm for any value of the price level and trace out an upward-sloping aggregate supply curve AS. The aggregate supply curve implies that, given a fixed nominal wage W, an increase in the price level reduces the real wage, which increases labor demand and employment, and this implies that more output gets produced. Thus, the AS curve is upward sloping.

Factors Shifting the Sticky Wage Aggregate Supply Curve

Now that we have constructed the aggregate supply curve, we must determine what factors shift the curve, so that we can correctly use the curve as part of our model. In general, two factors can shift the AS curve.

- An increase in the nominal wage W shifts the aggregate supply curve to the left. If the nominal wage increases, then for any price level P, the real wage, $w = \frac{W}{P}$, is higher. This then implies that labor demand, which equals employment in the sticky wage model, must fall, and, therefore, output falls. Thus, for any price level, the quantity of output is lower, and so an increase in the real wage causes a shift to the left in the aggregate supply curve. In Figure 12.4 the aggregate supply curve shifts from AS to AS'.

FIGURE 12.4   **The Effect of an Increase in W or a Decrease in z**

An increase in W or a decrease in z implies that the representative firm hires less labor given the price level P, and output supplied therefore decreases. Thus, the aggregate supply curve shifts to the left.

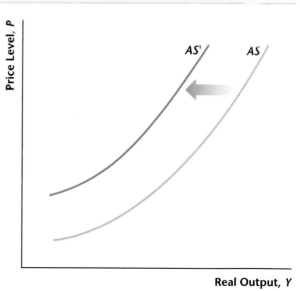

- A decrease in current total factor productivity z shifts the aggregate supply curve to the left. If there is a decrease in z, total factor productivity, this causes a downward shift in the production function and a shift to the left in the labor demand function. Given the nominal wage and the price level, which determine the real wage, less labor is demanded, and output supplied falls because employment is lower and because labor and capital are less productive. Again, the aggregate supply curve shifts to the left, as in Figure 12.4.

AGGREGATE DEMAND: THE IS AND LM CURVES

Early Keynesian models often neglected aggregate supply and concentrated on aggregate demand. These aggregate demand Keynesian models are often referred to as $IS - LM$ models, because Hicks, in his formalization of Keynes's General Theory, used the terms IS and LM to refer to the curves in his model.

The **IS curve** in the Keynesian sticky wage model is identical to the output demand curve Y^d in the monetary intertemporal model in Chapter 10. As in Chapters 9 and 10, the curve, as depicted in Figure 12.5, is downward sloping because an increase in the real interest rate r causes consumers to substitute future consumption for current consumption and causes firms to reduce investment, so that the demands for consumption and investment goods fall when r rises.

FIGURE 12.5   **The IS Curve**

The IS curve is identical to the output demand curve Y^d derived in Chapter 10 in the monetary intertemporal model. The curve represents the demand for current goods given the real interest rate r.

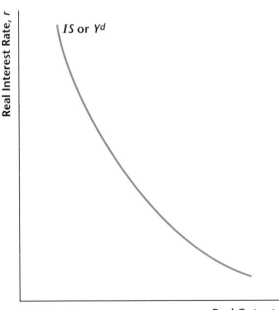

Now, to derive the **LM curve**, we need to consider again the approach from the monetary intertemporal model that determines the demand for money. As when we considered short-run analysis in the monetary intertemporal model in Chapter 10, it is convenient to suppose for now that there is no long-run inflation. This implies, given the Fisher relation from Chapter 10, that the nominal and real interest rates are equal, or $R = r$. Then, from Chapter 10, the demand for real money balances is given by $L(Y, r)$; that is, the real demand for money is increasing in aggregate real income Y and decreasing in the real interest rate r. (Recall from Chapter 10 that an increase in Y increases lifetime wealth, increasing the demand for goods purchased with money, and an increase in r increases the opportunity cost of holding money, so that the demand for real cash balances decreases.) Given that the nominal money supply M is determined exogenously by the government, equilibrium in the money market is determined by

$$M = PL(Y, r),$$

or nominal money supply equals nominal money demand. In Figure 12.6(a), with the real interest rate (rather than the price level; note the difference from Chapter 10) on

---

FIGURE 12.6   Money Demand, Money Supply, and the LM Curve

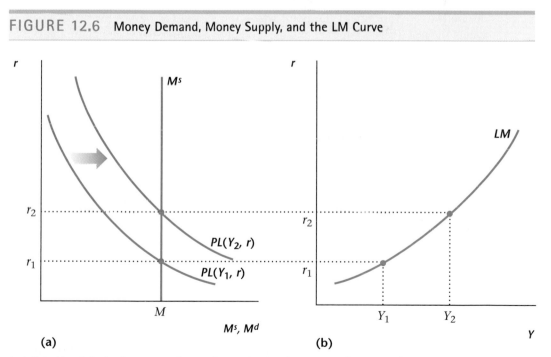

(a)   **(b)**

A shift to the right in the money demand curve in panel (a) occurs because of an increase in income, implying that the real interest rate must rise to restore equilibrium in the money market. This implies that the LM curve, representing (Y, r) combinations for which the money market is in equilibrium, is upward-sloping in panel (b).

the vertical axis, the money supply curve is given by the vertical line $M^s = M$, and the current nominal money demand curve $PL(Y_1, r)$ is downward sloping because the quantity of money demanded falls as the interest rate increases, given the level of real income Y_1 and the price level P. Thus, given real income Y_1 and the price level P, the money market is in equilibrium where money supplied equals money demanded, or where the real interest rate is r_1. We, therefore, have an output-interest rate pair (Y_1, r_1) for which the money market is in equilibrium (given P), in Figure 12.6(b).

Now, suppose that the level of real income is higher, say Y_2, while the price level remains the same at P. This implies that money demand increases for each real interest rate, or the current nominal money demand curve shifts rightward to $PL(Y_2, r)$ from $PL(Y_1, r)$. This then implies that the money market is in equilibrium at a higher real interest rate, $r_2 > r_1$. Now, we have another output-interest rate pair (Y_2, r_2) for which the money market is in equilibrium, given P, in Figure 12.6(b). Similarly, if we consider all possible levels of income and the associated levels of the real interest rate for which the money market is in equilibrium, we derive an upward-sloping curve, which is the *LM* curve in Figure 12.6(b). The curve is upward-sloping because, given the real money supply $\frac{M}{P}$, real money demand increases when income increases, and so for the money market to be in equilibrium the real interest rate must rise to reduce real money demand.

In Figure 12.7, given the price level P, the goods market and the money market are both in equilibrium at the point where the *IS* and *LM* curves intersect, which is where the real interest rate is r^* and the level of real income is Y^*. The figure then gives a complete picture of the demand side of the model, which determines, given the price level P, the level of aggregate output and the real interest rate.

FIGURE 12.7   Determination of r and Y Given P

Given the price level P, the IS and LM curves determine the level of real output and the real interest rate for which the goods market and money market clear.

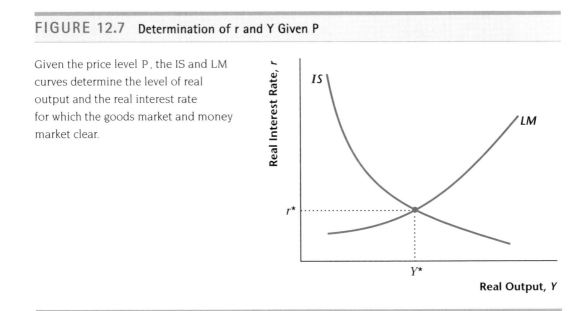

Shifts in the IS Curve

The factors we considered previously that lead to shifts in the output demand curve Y^d also shift the IS curve, because the IS curve is the same thing as the output demand curve. For our short-run analysis, as in Chapter 10, the IS curve shifts to the right as the result of any of the following changes:

- *An increase in current government purchases G*. Recall that this increases the demand for goods consumed by the government.
- *A decrease in the present value of taxes*. This increases the demand for current consumption goods by the representative consumer.
- *An anticipated increase in future income*. This increases lifetime wealth for the consumer, thus increasing the demand for consumption goods.
- *A decrease in the current capital stock K*. Recall that, if the capital stock decreases, then the future marginal product of capital will rise, which will increase the demand for investment goods.
- *An increase in future total factor productivity z'*. If total factor productivity is expected to increase in the future, the future marginal product of capital will rise, and there is an increase in the demand for investment goods.

Shifts in the LM Curve

In examining factors that shift the LM curve, the key things that we are interested in are changes in the nominal money supply M, changes in the price level P, and shifts in the money demand function $L(Y, r)$.

- *If the money supply M increases, the LM curve shifts to the right.* In Figure 12.8(a) suppose that the monetary authority increases the money supply from M_1 to M_2 with the price level held constant at P and aggregate income held constant at Y_1. Initially, the nominal demand for money is given by $PL(Y_1, r)$, and the money market is in equilibrium at the real interest rate r_1. When the money supply increases, the money demand curve does not shift, but the money supply curve shifts to the right from M_1^s to M_2^s. Now, the money market is in equilibrium for a real interest rate of r_2. Therefore, in Figure 12.8(b), the point (Y_1, r_1) is on the initial LM curve, LM_1, as this is a real income/real interest rate combination such that the money market is in equilibrium. After the money supply increases, the point (Y_1, r_2) is on the new LM curve, LM_2. That is, for any level of real income, the real interest rate must now be lower so that money demand rises to meet the higher money supply. Therefore, the LM curve shifts down, or to the right, when the money supply increases.
- *If P increases, the LM curve shifts to the left.* In Figure 12.9(a), with the money supply and aggregate income held constant at M and Y_1, respectively, the price level increases from P_1 to P_2. This causes the money demand curve to shift rightward from $P_1L(Y_1, r)$ to $P_2L(Y_1, r)$. Then, in equilibrium, the real interest rate must increase from r_1 to r_2. We then know that, in Figure 12.9(b), a point on the initial

FIGURE 12.8   The Effect of an Increase in the Money Supply on the LM Curve

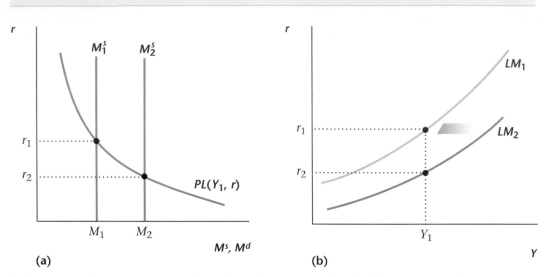

(a)   **(b)**

An increase in the money supply reduces the real interest rate for which the money market is in equilibrium given the level of real income, which shifts the LM curve to the right.

FIGURE 12.9   The Effect of an Increase in the Price Level on the LM Curve

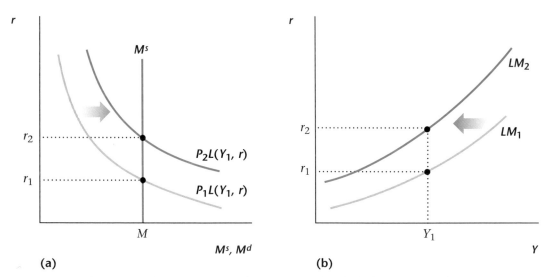

(a)   **(b)**

An increase in the price level increases the real interest rate for which the money market is in equilibrium given the level of the real interest rate, which shifts the LM curve to the left.

FIGURE 12.10 **A Positive Shift in Money Demand Shifts the LM Curve to the Left**

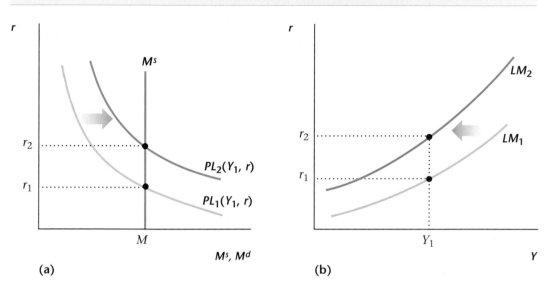

(a)

(b)

If there is a positive shift in money demand, this has a similar effect to a decrease in the money supply. The real interest rate for which the money market is in equilibrium increases, given the level of real income, shifting the LM curve to the left.

LM curve, LM_1, is (Y_1, r_1), while a point on the new LM curve, LM_2, is (Y_1, r_2). For any level of real income, an increase in the price level increases the demand for money, so that the real interest rate must rise to decrease the demand for money so that demand equals the constant supply of money. Therefore, the LM curve shifts up or to the right.

- *If there is a positive shift in the money demand function $L(Y, r)$, the LM curve shifts to the left.* In Figure 12.10(a) the money market is initially in equilibrium, given the price level P and the level of current real income Y_1, for the real interest rate r_1. The initial real demand for money is $L_1(Y_1, r)$. Then, suppose that the demand for money rises, which could occur if there were an increase in the risk associated with holding alternative assets to money. Then, the nominal demand for money shifts to the right in Figure 12.10(a), from $PL_1(Y_1, r)$ to $PL_2(Y_1, r)$. As a result, given the level of real income Y_1, the equilibrium real interest rate is now $r_2 > r_1$. Thus, in Figure 12.10(b), (Y_1, r_1) is a point on the initial LM curve, LM_1, while (Y_1, r_2) is a point on the new LM curve, LM_2. Because money demand is higher for any level of income, given the price level P, the real interest rate must be higher to reduce money demand to equal the fixed money supply. Thus, the LM curve shifts up or to the left with a positive shift in the money demand function.

The Aggregate Demand Curve

Now that we have constructed the aggregate supply curve, and the IS and LM curves, the final component of the Keynesian sticky wage model is the **aggregate demand curve,** which we derive from the $IS - LM$ diagram. Recall that the $IS - LM$ diagram is constructed for a given price level P. In Figure 12.11(a) the initial LM curve, LM_1, is drawn for price level P_1. Thus, (Y_1, P_1) denotes a real output and price level pair such that the money market and goods market are in equilibrium in Figure 12.11(b). Now, suppose that the price level is higher, say $P_2 > P_1$. Then, the increase in the price level causes the LM curve to shift leftward to LM_2. As a result, the money market and goods market are in equilibrium at a lower level of output, Y_2. Then, in Figure 12.11(b),

---

FIGURE 12.11   The Aggregate Demand Curve

An increase in the price level reduces the level of real income for which the money market and goods market are in equilibrium in panel (a). This implies that the AD curve, describing (Y, P) combinations for which the goods and money markets are in equilibrium is downward sloping as in panel (b).

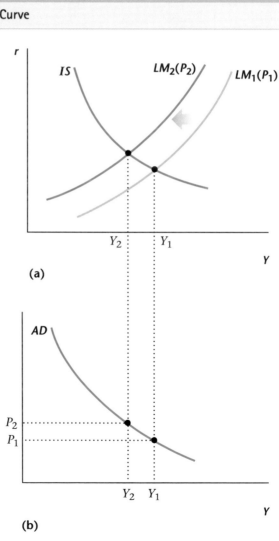

(Y_2, P_2) is another output and price level combination for which the money market and goods market are in equilibrium. If we considered all possible values for the price level and determined the associated levels of income for which the money market and goods market were in equilibrium, we would then trace out the aggregate demand curve AD, which is a downward-sloping curve in Figure 12.11(b). The curve is downward-sloping because an increase in the price level reduces the real money supply, causing a reduction in the level of output at which the money market and goods market are in equilibrium, given the price level.

Shifts in the Aggregate Demand Curve

To complete our knowledge of how the Keynesian sticky wage model works, we need to know how the aggregate demand curve shifts in response to changes in exogenous variables. Basically, anything that causes a shift in either the IS curve or the LM curve also shifts the AD curve.

- *If the IS curve shifts to the right, then the AD curve shifts to the right.* In Figure 12.12(a) the IS curve shifts to the right. Recall that the LM curve depends on the price level, and we suppose here that the price level is P_1. When the IS curve shifts, the level of income for which the goods market and money market are in equilibrium rises from Y_1 to Y_2. Therefore, a point on the initial aggregate demand curve in Figure 12.12(b) is (Y_1, P_1) and a point on the new aggregate demand curve is (Y_2, P_1). The aggregate demand curve must shift to the right from AD_1 to AD_2 as, for any price level, the level of real income at which the money market and goods market are in equilibrium has increased.

- *If the LM curve shifts to the right, then the aggregate demand curve shifts to the right.* In Figure 12.13(a), given the price level P_1, an increase in the money supply or a negative shift in the money demand function shifts the LM curve to the right, from LM_1 to LM_2. Therefore, the money market and goods market are now in equilibrium at the level of income Y_2 rather than at Y_1, as initially. Therefore, the point (Y_1, P_1) in Figure 12.13(b) is on the initial aggregate demand curve AD_1 and the point (Y_2, P_1) is on the new aggregate demand curve AD_2. As we could conduct the same experiment for all possible values for the price level, the new aggregate demand curve AD_2 is to the right of the initial curve AD_1.

Therefore, given what we know from the previous sections about the factors that shift the IS and LM curves, and the relationship between shifts in the IS and LM curves and the AD curve, we know that the AD curve shifts to the right when any of the following occur:

- Government spending G increases.
- The present value of taxes decreases.
- The current capital stock K decreases.
- Future total factor productivity z' will increase.
- The money supply increases.
- There is a negative shift in the money demand function.

A shift to the right in the IS curve implies that, given the price level P, the money and goods markets are in equilibrium for a higher level of real output, which shifts the aggregate demand curve to the right.

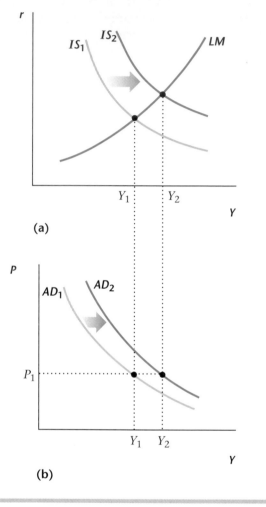

(a)

(b)

THE COMPLETE KEYNESIAN STICKY WAGE MODEL

Now that we have constructed the aggregate supply curve, the IS and LM curves, and the aggregate demand curve, we can put these elements of the Keynesian sticky wage model together into a useful working model. Again, recall that this is the same structure as we worked with in the monetary intertemporal model, except that the sticky nominal wage makes the model work in a quite different way. A key feature of the Keynesian sticky wage model is that the classical dichotomy does not hold, in contrast to the monetary intertemporal model. That is, the price level and real variables are jointly determined, and money is not neutral, as we will see.

FIGURE 12.13 **A Shift to the Right in the LM Curve Shifts the AD Curve to the Right**

A shift to the right in the LM curve implies that, given the price level P, the money and goods markets are in equilibrium for a higher level of real output, which shifts the aggregate demand curve to the right.

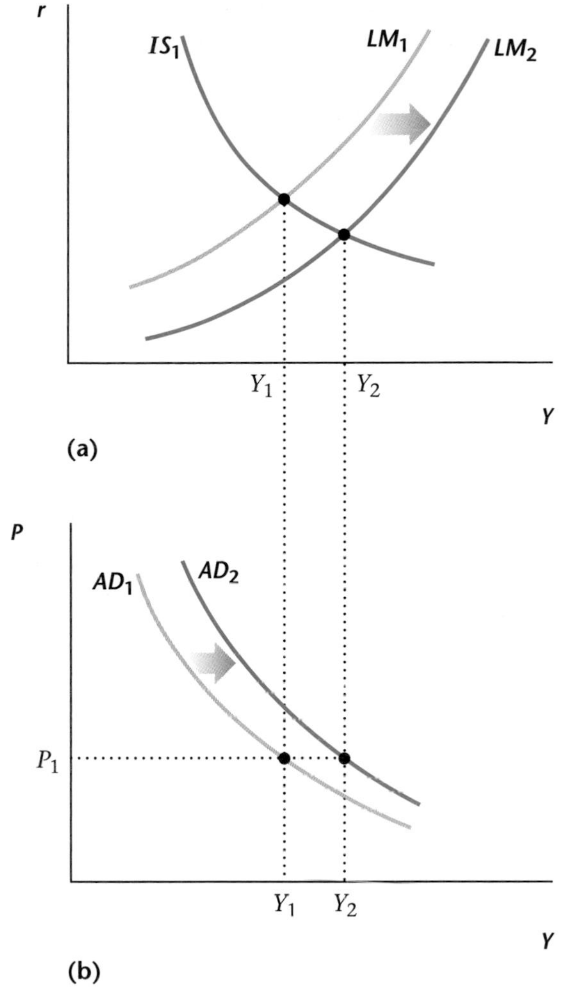

Figure 12.14 shows the complete Keynesian sticky wage model, where we determine the real interest rate, the level of output, the price level, the real wage, and employment, as r^*, Y^*, P^*, $\frac{W}{P^*}$, and N^*, respectively. Here, Y and P are determined by the intersection of the aggregate demand and aggregate supply curves in Figure 12.14(b). Because the nominal wage W is fixed, when we know the price level we know the real wage $w = \frac{W}{P}$, which determines employment in Figure 12.14(c). Given the price level, we know the position of the LM curve in Figure 12.14(a), which then determines the real interest rate r from the intersection of the IS and LM curves.

FIGURE 12.14   The Keynesian Sticky Wage Model

The figure shows the complete Keynesian sticky wage model. The AD and AS curves determine the price level P and level of output Y in panel (b). Then, given the nominal wage W, the real wage $\frac{W}{P}$ determines employment from the labor demand curve N^d in panel (c). Finally, given P, the real interest rate is determined by the intersection of the IS and LM curves in panel (a).

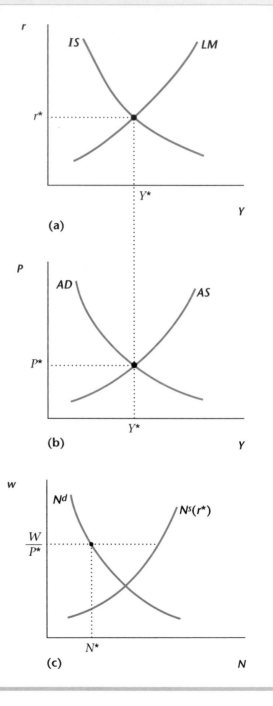

The Nonneutrality of Money When Wages Are Sticky

Given our complete description of the Keynesian sticky wage model, we can proceed with an experiment, which illustrates how money fails to be neutral in this model. In general, a change in the supply of money has real effects in the Keynesian sticky wage model, and the price level does not change in proportion to the change in the money supply.

In Figure 12.15 we show the effects of an increase in the money supply. Initially the money supply is M_1, and it increases to M_2. This increase shifts the aggregate demand curve to the right, from AD_1 to AD_2 in Figure 12.15(b). In equilibrium, the price level rises from P_1 to P_2, and real output rises from Y_1 to Y_2. In the $IS - LM$ diagram in Figure 12.15(a), the increase in the money supply from M_1 to M_2 shifts the LM curve rightward from LM_1 to LM_2. However, we know that in equilibrium the price level rises, and this shifts the LM curve back to the left to LM_3. We know that the leftward shift in LM does not completely offset the rightward shift in LM, as we know from the $AD - AS$ diagram in Figure 12.15(b) that output must increase in equilibrium. Therefore, in equilibrium the real interest rate must fall, from r_1 to r_2. Further, we know that the real money supply $\frac{M}{P}$ must rise in equilibrium, because it is $\frac{M}{P}$ that determines the position of the LM curve; if the LM curve shifted to the right from LM_1 to LM_3, then $\frac{M}{P}$ must have risen, so that the price level increased less than in proportion to the money supply.

In the labor market diagram in Figure 12.15(c), the real wage falls from $\frac{W}{P_1}$ to $\frac{W}{P_2}$, because the nominal wage W is fixed and the price level has increased. As employment is determined by the labor demand curve, employment increases from N_1 to N_2; that is, firms hire more labor because the real wage has fallen. Further, because the real interest rate falls in equilibrium, workers wish to supply less labor (they wish to supply less labor today and more in the future), and the labor supply curve shifts to the left from $N^s(r_1)$ to $N^s(r_2)$. The result is that, because employment rises from N_1 to N_2, and desired labor supply falls from N_1^s to N_2^s, Keynesian unemployment falls from $N_1^s - N_1$ to $N_2^s - N_2$.

Therefore, to summarize, money is not neutral, because the increase in the money supply has real effects; the real interest rate falls, real output increases, the real wage falls, employment increases, and Keynesian unemployment decreases. Keynesians think of money having these real effects through the **Keynesian transmission mechanism for monetary policy.** That is, an increase in the money supply has its first effects in financial markets; the real interest rate falls to equate money demand with the increased money supply. Because the interest rate is lower, this increases the demand for consumption goods (through intertemporal substitution), and for investment goods. The increase in the demand for goods raises the price level, which lowers the real wage (given the fixed nominal wage), and increases employment.

Most Keynesians regard money as being neutral in the long run. While Keynesians argue that money is not neutral in the short run because of sticky wages (or prices), they also believe that the nominal wage eventually adjusts so that supply equals demand in the labor market, in which case money is neutral as in the monetary intertemporal model we studied in Chapter 10.

FIGURE 12.15   **An Increase in the Money Supply in the Sticky Wage Model**

An increase in the money supply is not neutral. The real interest rate falls, the price level rises less than proportionally to the money supply increase, the real wage falls, and employment and output rise.

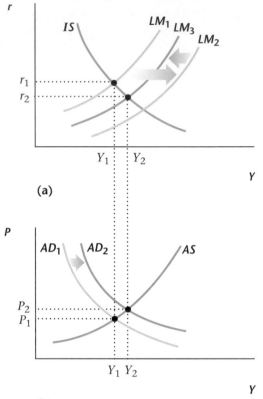

(a)

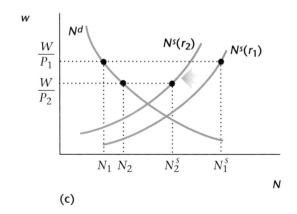

(b)

(c)

CAN STICKY WAGES AND MONEY SUPPLY FLUCTUATIONS EXPLAIN BUSINESS CYCLES?

THEORY confronts the DATA

Because changes in the money supply can cause output to change in the Keynesian sticky wage model, a key prediction of the model is that, if the money supply fluctuates, then so does aggregate output. The model then gives a monetary theory of business cycles. That is, the model predicts that fluctuations in the money supply could cause business cycles. As economists, we would then like to ask whether this is a good or bad theory of business cycles. To answer this question, we have to ask how the predictions of the model fit the key business cycle regularities that we outlined in Chapter 3.

In Table 12.1 we show how the predictions of the Keynesian sticky wage model with money supply fluctuations fit features of the post–World War II data we examined in Chapter 3. Some features of the model clearly fit the data. For example, when the money supply increases, output increases, which is consistent with the fact that money is procyclical in the data. As well, when the money supply increases, the fall in the real interest rate causes investment to rise, so that investment is procyclical, as in the data. Consumption is procyclical (as in the data) as the decrease in the real interest rate and the increase in real income both lead to increases in C. Further, an increase in the money supply causes an increase in employment, and so employment is procyclical, as is the case in the data.

However, other results do not fit. When the money supply increases, the price level goes up, so that if money supply fluctuations are a primary cause of business cycles, the price level is procyclical. However, the price level is countercyclical in the data. As well, the real wage falls when the money supply increases and so the model predicts that the real wage is countercyclical, but it is procyclical in the data. Further, because employment increases with an increase in the money supply and there is no change in the production function, there is a decline in the average productivity of labor. Therefore, in the model average labor productivity is countercyclical, but in the data it is procyclical.

We conclude that, at least for the post–World War II period in the United States, it does not appear that fluctuations in the stock of money could have been the most

Table 12.1   **Data vs. Predictions of the Keynesian Sticky Wage Model with Monetary Shocks**

Variable	Data	Model
Consumption	Procyclical	Procyclical
Investment	Procyclical	Procyclical
Price Level	Countercyclical	Procyclical
Money Supply	Procyclical	Procyclical
Employment	Procyclical	Procyclical
Real Wage	Procyclical	Countercyclical
Average Labor Productivity	Procyclical	Countercyclical

important cause of business cycles, if money affects the economy as captured in the Keynesian sticky wage model. It is possible, however, that fluctuations in the money supply, acting through the Keynesian transmission mechanism for monetary policy, made significant contributions (though not the primary ones) to fluctuations in GDP over the post–World War II period. As well, before World War II in the United States, the price level was procyclical, rather than countercyclical as in the post–World War II period, which is consistent with monetary shocks being important for business cycles during this earlier period.

We must regard conclusions from Table 12.1 with caution, as in practice the money supply in the United States is controlled by the Fed, which reacts to events in the economy. Federal Reserve policymakers living in the Keynesian sticky wage world would come to realize that fluctuations in the money supply could cause output and employment to fluctuate. In circumstances where no other shocks were impinging on the economy, the Fed would have no reason to change the money supply, and so we would not observe events in which a change in the money supply was the obvious cause of a change in output. As we study in more detail later in this chapter, the Fed might have good reasons to change the money supply in response to other shocks to the economy, but then it would be hard to disentangle the effects of monetary policy on real activity from the effects of other shocks.

MACROECONOMICS IN ACTION

Monetary Policy and the "Volcker Recession"

Though the evidence from the previous section appears to indicate that monetary policy was relatively unimportant in causing business cycles during the post–World War II period, the 1981–82 recession is widely attributed to the actions of the Federal Reserve System under Chairman Paul Volcker. Volcker was appointed as chairman of the Federal Reserve Board by President Carter in 1979, at a time when the inflation rate in the United States was at a historically high level. Under a Keynesian interpretation of subsequent events, Volcker decided that inflation had to be reduced through contractionary monetary policy, which had the side effect of producing a severe recession in 1981–82, dubbed the "Volcker recession." Then, according to the story, once U.S. residents had borne the short-run pain of a recession, they could enjoy the relatively low inflation rates of the later 1980s and 1990s.

An examination of the behavior of real GDP, the money supply, and interest rates certainly appears to support this view. In Figure 12.16 the money supply dips below trend beginning in 1979–80, and this is followed by a large drop in real GDP below trend in 1981–82, as it took some time for the tightening in monetary policy to have its real effects on the economy. In Figure 12.17

(continued)

there is an increase in real and nominal interest rates in 1979–80, which is consistent with the monetary tightening seen in the behavior of the money supply. The data in Figures 12.16 and 12.17, therefore, appear consistent with the Keynesian sticky wage model and with the view that monetary policy can have large effects on real output.

The evidence from Figures 12.16 and 12.17 is not, however, the end of the story. Typically, there are many different shocks hitting the economy simultaneously, and sophisticated statistical analysis is required to separate out the effects of these shocks from the effects of monetary policy. It turns out that the results from this type of sophisticated statistical analysis are not entirely conclusive. Work by Eric Leeper, Christopher Sims, and Tao Zha summarizes much of the research in this area. They generally find that contractionary monetary policy has significant negative effects on real

FIGURE 12.16 Money Supply and GDP

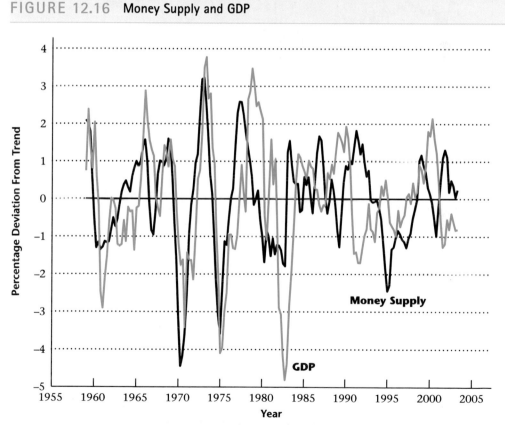

The figure shows detrended money supply and detrended real GDP for the post–World War II period in the United States. A drop in money below trend precedes the 1981–82 recession.

(continued)

FIGURE 12.17   Real and Nominal Interest Rates

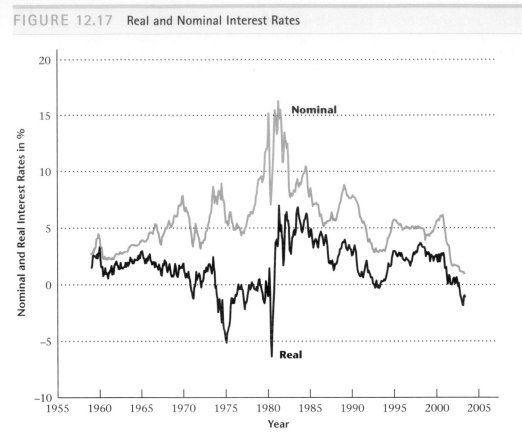

The figure shows the short-term nominal interest rate and the corresponding real interest rate, measured as the nominal rate minus the actual inflation rate, for the post–World War II period in the United States. Increases in the real and nominal interest rates precede the 1981–82 recession.

output.[1] Harald Uhlig argues, however, that much of this research is tainted, and he suggests that the evidence is consistent with money being neutral.[2]

During the 1981–82 recession in the United States, most casual observers attributed the severity of the recession to high interest rates, and they assigned responsibility for those high interest rates to the Federal Reserve System and Chairman Volcker. The statistical evidence, however, though tending to favor this view of the cause of the 1981–82 recession, is not entirely conclusive.

---

[1]See E. Leeper, C. Sims, and T. Zha, 1996. "What Does Monetary Policy Do?" *Brookings Papers on Economic Activity*, series 2, 1–63.

[2]See H. Uhlig, 2001. "What Are the Effects of Monetary Policy on Output? Results From an Agnostic Identification Procedure," working paper, Humboldt University.

KEYNESIAN AGGREGATE DEMAND SHOCKS AS CAUSES OF BUSINESS CYCLES

Though monetary shocks in the Keynesian sticky wage model may not be able to explain the key business cycle regularities discussed in Chapter 3, some other shock to the economy might successfully explain observed business cycles in this model. Keynes argued in his *General Theory of Employment, Interest, and Money* that a principal cause of business cycles is fluctuations in aggregate demand, and what he appears to have had in mind was shocks to investment, which would be captured here as shifts in the *IS* curve. That is, suppose that firms become more optimistic about future total factor productivity, so that they view the future marginal product of capital as having increased (Keynes referred to such waves of optimism as being due to the "animal spirits" of investors). This increases the demand for investment goods, shifts the *IS* curve to the right, and shifts the *AD* curve to the right.

An increase in the demand for investment goods leads to a rightward shift in the *IS* curve from IS_1 to IS_2 in Figure 12.18(a) and a rightward shift in the *AD* curve from AD_1 to AD_2 in Figure 12.18 (b). In equilibrium, in Figure 12.18(b), the price level increases from P_1 to P_2, and real output increases from Y_1 to Y_2. In Figure 12.18(a), when the price level increases, this causes the *LM* curve to shift leftward from LM_1 to LM_2. Ultimately, the real interest rate increases from r_1 to r_2. The increase in the real interest rate causes investment to fall. However, the initial shock to the economy increased the demand for investment goods, and so investment rises on net. For consumption, the real interest rate causes a decrease, and the rise in real income causes an increase. On net, it is not clear whether consumption rises or falls, but to give the model the benefit of the doubt we say that the real interest rate effect is small and consumption increases. In the labor market, in Figure 12.18(c), the real wage falls from $\frac{W}{P_1}$ to $\frac{W}{P_2}$, and employment increases from N_1 to N_2. We leave the labor supply curve out of Figure 12.18(c) as labor supply is important only for determining unemployment in this model, and this is not critical for our arguments. Because employment has increased and the production function is unchanged, average labor productivity must fall.

Table 12.2 summarizes the key business cycle facts from Chapter 3 and the predictions of the Keynesian sticky wage model under investment shocks. From Figure 12.18,

Table 12.2 **Data vs. Predictions of the Keynesian Sticky Wage Model with Investment Shocks**

Variable	Data	Model
Consumption	Procyclical	Procyclical
Investment	Procyclical	Procyclical
Price Level	Countercyclical	Procyclical
Money Supply	Procyclical	Procyclical
Employment	Procyclical	Procyclical
Real Wage	Procyclical	Countercyclical
Average Labor Productivity	Procyclical	Countercyclical

FIGURE 12.18   **An Increase in the Demand for Investment Goods in the Sticky Wage Model**

An anticipated increase in future total factor productivity increases the demand for investment goods, shifting the IS curve to the right. Output, employment, and the price level increase, and the real wage declines. Consumption may rise or fall, and investment increases in equilibrium.

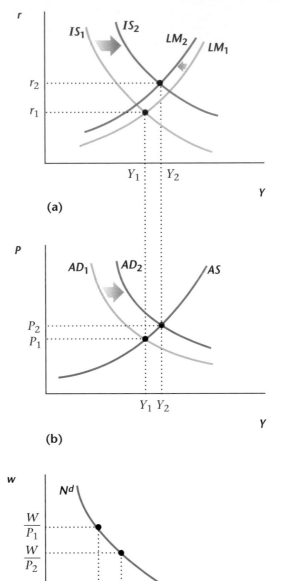

an increase in output coincides with an increase in investment, an increase in consumption, an increase in the price level, an increase in employment, a decrease in the real wage, and a decrease in average labor productivity. Therefore, in contrast to the data, the price level is procyclical, the real wage is countercyclical, and average labor productivity is countercyclical. As well, the model provides no explanation for why the money supply is procyclical. Our conclusion is that the fit to the data could be better, and so investment shocks in the Keynesian sticky wage model do not appear to completely explain business cycle facts.

The Role of Government Policy in the Sticky Wage Model

In macroeconomics, some important disagreements focus on the issue of whether or not the government should act to smooth out business cycles. This smoothing, or what is sometimes referred to as **stabilization policy,** involves carrying out government actions that increase aggregate real output when it is below trend and decrease it when above trend. Using government policy to smooth business cycles may appear to be a good idea. For example, we know that a consumer whose income fluctuates behaves optimally by smoothing consumption relative to income, so why shouldn't the government take actions that smooth aggregate real income over time? As we saw in Chapter 11, in the real business cycle model, this logic need not apply when considering the rationale for government policy intervention with respect to macroeconomic events.

Keynesians tend to believe that government intervention to smooth out business cycles is appropriate, and the Keynesian sticky wage model provides a justification for this belief. We start by considering a situation in which an unanticipated shock has hit the economy, causing the real wage to be higher than its equilibrium level in the labor market, as in Figure 12.19(c). For example, there may have been an unanticipated increase in the relative price of energy, which led to a decrease in total factor productivity. After the shock hits the economy, the nominal wage is W_1, the price level is P_1, and the real wage is $\frac{W_1}{P_1}$, which implies, in Figure, 12.19(c), that employment is N_1 and there is Keynesian unemployment, given the labor supply curve $N^s(r_1)$. In Figure 12.19(b) aggregate output is Y_1 and the price level is P_1, while in Figure 12.19(a) the real interest rate is r_1.

Now, after the shock has hit the economy, the allocation of resources is not economically efficient. Recall from Chapter 5 that the first fundamental theorem of welfare economics implies that a competitive equilibrium is Pareto optimal, but in Figure 12.19 the economy is not in a competitive equilibrium, as initially labor demand is not equal to labor supply. One response of the government to the economic inefficiency caused by the shock to the economy would be to do nothing, and let the problem cure itself. Because the real wage is initially above its equilibrium level, there is a tendency for the nominal wage to fall. This causes the aggregate supply curve to shift to the right, which puts downward pressure on the price level. This in turn causes the *LM* curve to shift to the right, reducing the real interest rate. In the long run, the nominal wage and the price level decrease to the point where the price level is P_2 in Figure 12.19(b), output is Y_2, and in Figure 12.19(c) the nominal wage has fallen to W_2, and the real wage $\frac{W_2}{P_2}$ is such that supply is equal to demand in the labor market. The labor supply curve comes

FIGURE 12.19   Long–Run Adjustment of the Nominal Wage

If the real wage is initially higher than its equilibrium value, the nominal wage tends to fall. In the long run, the nominal wage decreases, the price level decreases, output increases, and the real interest rate falls, until supply is equal to demand in the labor market.

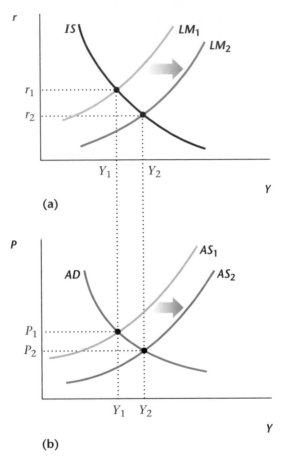

(a)

(b)

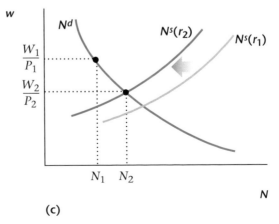

(c)

to rest at $N^s(r_2)$ given the decrease in the real interest rate. The fall in the price level leads to a shift in the LM curve to LM_2 in the long run, and the real interest rate falls to r_2. Ultimately, then, long-run reductions in the nominal wage and the price level result in increases in real output, employment, consumption, and investment (because the real interest rate falls).

Keynesian macroeconomists argue that the long run is too long to wait. In Figure 12.20 suppose an initial situation just as in Figure 12.19, where the economy has been hit by a shock that causes the initial real wage, $\frac{W}{P_1}$ in Figure 12.20(c), to be too high relative to its equilibrium level. One possible response to the economic inefficiency that exists would be an increase in the money supply M by the monetary authority. Initially, the LM curve shifts to LM_2 in Figure 12.20(a), given the initial price level P_1, determined by the intersection of the initial aggregate demand curve AD_1 and the aggregate supply curve AS in Figure 12.20(b). If M is increased just the right amount by the monetary authority, the aggregate demand curve shifts to AD_2 and the equilibrium price level rises to P_2 while output rises to Y_2 from Y_1. The increase in the price level causes a leftward shift in the LM curve from LM_2 to LM_3, with the ultimate result being that the real interest rate falls from r_1 to r_2. In the labor market, the labor supply curve shifts from $N^s(r_1)$ to $N^s(r_2)$ because of the fall in the interest rate, and the real wage falls to $\frac{W}{P_2}$ because of the increase in the price level. If the increase in the money supply is just right, then full employment is achieved with the quantity of employment being N_2.

After the increase in the money supply, the economy is in exactly the same situation, in real terms, as it would have been in the long run if the monetary authority did nothing and allowed the nominal wage and price level to fall (compare Figure 12.20 with Figure 12.19). The only difference is that the nominal wage and the price level are higher in the case where the monetary authority intervenes. The advantage of intervention is that an efficient outcome is achieved faster than if the monetary authority lets events take their course.

The return to full employment could also be achieved through an increase in government expenditures G, but with some different results. In Figure 12.21 we show a similar initial situation to Figures 12.19 and 12.20, where initial employment is N_1, which is less than the quantity of labor that the representative consumer wants to supply at the market real wage $\frac{W}{P_1}$. If the government increases government purchases G by just the right amount, then the IS curve shifts to the right in Figure 12.21(a) from IS_1 to IS_2, and the aggregate demand curve in Figure 12.21(b) shifts rightward from AD_1 to AD_2. In equilibrium, the price level increases from P_1 to P_2, and aggregate output increases from Y_1 to Y_2 in Figure 12.21(b). Then, in Figure 12.21(a), the increase in the price level causes the LM curve to shift leftward from LM_1 to LM_2, which is just enough that the intersection of IS_2 with LM_2 is at the level of income Y_2, as determined in the aggregate demand/aggregate supply diagram in Figure 12.21(b). In equilibrium, the real interest rate increases from r_1 to r_2. With the increase in the price level, the real wage falls from $\frac{W}{P_1}$ to $\frac{W}{P_2}$, and the increase in the real interest rate causes the labor supply curve to shift to the right, from $N^s(r_1)$ to $N^s(r_2)$ in Figure 12.21(c). Given that the government increases G by the right amount, in equilibrium the quantity of employment is N_2, and supply is equal to demand in the labor market.

FIGURE 12.20 Stabilization Policy in the Sticky Wage Model–Monetary Policy

A shock to the economy initially causes the real wage to be above its equilibrium value. The monetary authority increases the money supply, causing the real interest rate to fall, the price level to rise, the real wage to fall, and employment and output to rise. An appropriate increase in the money supply restores equilibrium in the labor market.

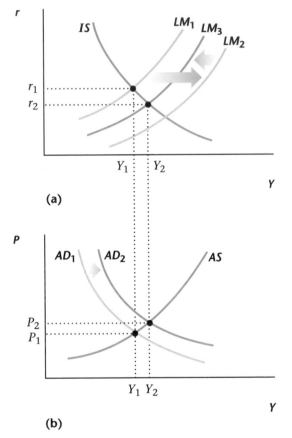

(a)

(b)

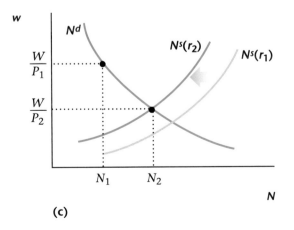

(c)

FIGURE 12.21 **Stabilization Policy in the Sticky Wage Model—Fiscal Policy**

The figure shows stabilization policy by way of a temporary increase in government spending. Equilibrium is restored in the labor market through an increase in G, which increases the real interest rate, reduces consumption and investment, increases the price level, reduces the real wage, and increases employment and output.

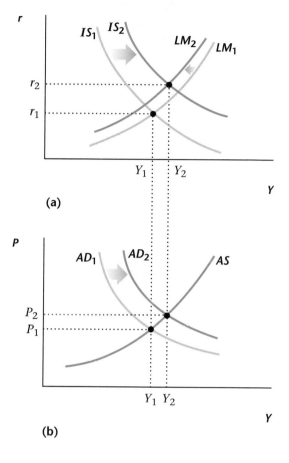

(a)

(b)

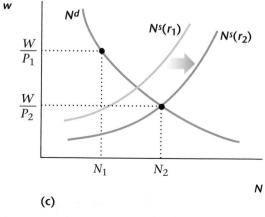

(c)

Now, note the differences in final outcomes between Figures 12.21 and 12.20. In Figure 12.21, with the increase in *G* the real interest rate has risen, while it falls in Figure 12.20 when the money supply is increased. The increase in the real interest rate in Figure 12.21 causes investment and consumption to fall; that is, there is crowding out of private expenditure by government expenditure. In contrast, the decrease in the real interest rate causes an increase in investment and consumption in Figure 12.20. The increase in the real interest rate leads to a rightward shift in the labor supply curve in Figure 12.21, while the labor supply curve shifts to the left in Figure 12.20. The conclusion is that, when government expenditures are used to increase employment rather than having the monetary authority increase the money supply, investment is lower, and employment is higher, so that output is also higher. Consumption may be higher or lower, as the higher real interest rate reduces consumption, but higher real income increases consumption. Thus, it matters whether fiscal or monetary policy is used for stabilization purposes, as this will affect the level of aggregate output and the public and private uses of that output.

Whether fiscal or monetary policy is used to smooth business cycles, the Keynesian sticky wage model provides a rationale for stabilization policy. If shocks kick the economy out of equilibrium, because there is a failure of private markets to clear in the short run, then if fiscal or monetary policymakers can move fast enough, they can restore the economy to equilibrium before self-adjusting markets achieve this on their own. Thus, the important elements of the Keynesian view of government's role in the macroeconomy are the following:

1. Private markets fail to operate smoothly on their own, in that not all wages and prices are perfectly flexible, implying that supply is not equal to demand in all markets, and economic efficiency is not always achieved in a world without government intervention.

2. Fiscal policy and/or monetary policy decisions can be made quickly enough, and information on the behavior of the economy is good enough, that the fiscal or monetary authorities can improve efficiency by countering shocks that cause a deviation from a full-employment equilibrium.

MACROECONOMICS IN ACTION

George W. Bush, Alan Greenspan, and the Timing of the Effects of Fiscal and Monetary Policy

In the 2000 federal election, George W. Bush ran for president on a platform that included a proposal for a large reduction in federal income taxes. Soon after the election, the U.S. economy showed signs of weakness. After taking office, in an address to a joint session of Congress on February 27, 2001, President Bush stated:

(continued)

The Chairman of the Federal Reserve Board has testified before Congress that tax cuts often come too late to stimulate economic recovery. So I want to work with you to give our economy an important jump-start by making tax relief retroactive.

Like his father, George W. Bush does not appear to put much stock in the Ricardian equivalence theorem, which was discussed in Chapter 8. Recall that the Ricardian equivalence theorem states that a change in taxes has no effect, as the present value of tax liabilities for consumers remains unaffected. George W. Bush's father, President George H. W. Bush, declared in his State of the Union address in January 1992 that proposed changes in tax withholding would cause a large increase in consumer spending, while Ricardian equivalence predicts no effect.

Suppose, however, that we accept that the fiscal policy action of cutting taxes does increase the demand for consumption goods (perhaps because a large fraction of consumers are credit-constrained), which shifts the IS and AD curves to the right in the Keynesian sticky wage model, thus increasing aggregate output. How then should we interpret George W. Bush's statement above?

President Bush, in the quote above, refers to a statement by Alan Greenspan, the chairman of the Federal Reserve Board, in testimony before Congress, concerning the timing of the effects of fiscal policy actions. While the effects of fiscal and monetary policy are instantaneous in the Keynesian sticky wage model, in practice it takes time to formulate policy, and it takes time for policy to affect the economy. First, policymakers do not have complete information. The national income accounts, employment data, and price data are time-consuming to compile, and policymakers in the federal government and at the Fed have good information only for what was happening in the economy months previously. Second, when information is available, it may take time for policymakers to agree among themselves concerning a course of action. Finally, once policy is implemented, there is a time lag before policy has its effects on aggregate economic activity.

While the first stage of policymaking (information collection) is essentially the same for fiscal and monetary policy, it is generally recognized that the second stage (decision making) takes much longer for fiscal policy than for monetary policy in the United States. The congressional process of passing a budget can take months, while the Federal Open Market Committee, the decision-making body of the Fed, meets every six weeks, and it can make decisions between these meetings if necessary.

Alan Greenspan clearly alluded to this longer decision lag for fiscal policy in the statement mentioned by President Bush. The problem with a long decision lag in making fiscal policy is that the need for corrective action may have gone away by the time such action is taken. President Bush recognizes that the decision lag is there, and he uses this as an argument for haste in quickly passing a budget with his tax cut and, better still, making the tax cuts retroactive. Presumably, this means that consumers would see immediate increases in their disposable incomes, rather than a delay of several months.

For the third stage in the timing of the effects of fiscal and monetary policy— that is, the lag between a policy decision and when its effects are realized in the economy—it is not clear whether fiscal or

(*continued*)

monetary policy takes longer. While Alan Greenspan appeared to have implied that monetary policy might have some advantage over fiscal policy in terms of the total length of time to make a decision and see its effects, he is not necessarily on firm ground here. Indeed, one of the points of Milton Friedman and Anna Schwartz's study of the role of money in the U.S. economy, *A Monetary History of the United States, 1867–1960,* is that the lag between a monetary policy action and its effects is "long and variable." That is, it can take a long time for monetary policy to have its effects, perhaps six months to a year, and this length of time is always uncertain.

The conclusion is that, even if we believe that stabilizing the economy through the use of fiscal and monetary policy is appropriate, as the Keynesian sticky wage model tells us, there is still much that can go wrong. Guiding the economy can be much like trying to steer a car with a faulty steering mechanism; one has to see the bumps and curves in the road well in advance to avoid driving into the ditch or otherwise having a very uncomfortable ride. This is in part why Milton Friedman, among others, has encouraged abstinence from stabilization policy altogether. Friedman argued that well-intentioned stabilization policy could do more harm than good, as the lags in policy could lead to stimulative action being taken when tightening the screws on the economy would be more appropriate, and vice versa.

Shifts in Money Demand and Monetary Control

In Chapter 10 we discussed some implications of shifts in money demand for monetary policy in a world where money is neutral and the central bank is interested in controlling the price level. The Keynesian sticky wage model implies an important stabilization policy problem for a central bank when the money demand function is unstable. As we show, a shift in the money demand function causes output and employment to change. This can be counteracted with an appropriate change in the money supply. Essentially, if money demand increases (decreases), then the money supply should increase (decrease) to accommodate this. With unstable money demand, we show that in the short run it is preferable for the central bank to target the interest rate rather than the money supply.

Suppose that the economy is initially in a long-run equilibrium with the price level equal to P_1 and output at the level Y_1 as in Figure 12.22(b), given initial aggregate demand and aggregate supply curves AD_1 and AS, respectively. In Figure 12.22(c), the real wage $\frac{W}{P_1}$ initially clears the labor market, given the labor demand curve N^d and the initial labor supply curve $N^s(r_1)$.

Then, suppose that there is a positive shift in money demand, for example, because of an increase in the riskiness of alternative assets to money. This causes the *LM* curve in Figure 12.22(a) to shift leftward to LM_2, given the initial price level P_1. As a result, the aggregate demand curve in Figure 12.22(b) shifts to the left from AD_1 to AD_2, and in equilibrium the price level falls to P_2 and aggregate output drops to Y_2. The decrease in the price level shifts the *LM* curve rightward from LM_2 to LM_3, implying an

FIGURE 12.22   **The Equilibrium Effects of a Positive Money Demand Shift**

A positive shift in money demand increases the real interest rate, reduces the price level, increases the real wage, and reduces employment and aggregate output.

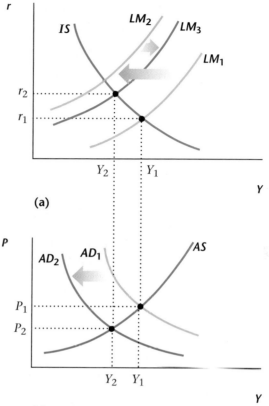

(a)

(b)

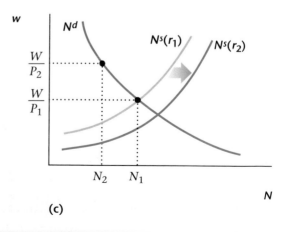

(c)

equilibrium level of income of Y_2 in Figure 12.22(a). In equilibrium, the real interest rate rises to r_2. In Figure 12.22(c), the real wage rises to $\frac{W}{P_2}$, and the labor supply curve shifts rightward to $N^s(r_2)$, implying that employment falls from N_1 to N_2 and there is now unemployment. Therefore, the positive shift in money demand leads to a bad short-run outcome where output and employment are inefficiently low.

The central bank can correct the short-run inefficiency resulting from the shift in money demand by changing the money supply appropriately. In this case, the central bank should accommodate the increase in money demand by increasing the money supply. This shifts the LM curve to the right. If the central bank increases the money supply by just the right amount, the LM curve shifts to LM_1 in Figure 12.22(a), the aggregate demand curve shifts to AD_1 in Figure 12.22(b), the real wage falls to $\frac{W}{P_1}$, in Figure 12.22(c) and the real interest rate falls to r_1 in Figure 12.22(a), shifting the labor supply curve in Figure 12.22(c) leftward to $N^s(r_1)$. The result is that efficiency is restored, with all real and nominal variables identical to what they were before the shift in money demand.

In the discussion above, it may appear straightforward for a central bank to manipulate the money supply to respond to unexpected shifts in money demand. However, central banks face a problem of imperfect information. The central bank can observe market interest rates on a minute-by-minute basis, it can observe the money supply on a somewhat less timely basis, and real variables such as aggregate output are observable even less frequently. For simplicity, suppose that the central bank wants to control aggregate output but cannot observe it in the short run. The central bank can, however, observe the money supply and the real interest rate. If there are unexpected shocks to money demand hitting the economy, which of the observable variables should the central bank choose to control as a short-run target, the money supply or the real interest rate? Our analysis above tells us that the central bank should control the interest rate. In Figure 12.22 control of the money supply (that is, holding it constant) in the short run would imply that the positive shock to money demand would cause output to fall from Y_1 to Y_2, which is undesirable. However, controlling the real interest rate by holding it constant at r_1 implies that the money supply has to increase, and output stays constant at Y_1.

Beginning in the 1970s, many central banks, including the U.S. Federal Reserve System, experimented with the short-run targeting of monetary aggregates. However, instability in money demand in the 1980s led most of the world's central banks to lessen considerably the attention paid to the behavior of monetary aggregates in setting monetary policy. In Chapter 10, we showed how the instability of money demand can lead to price level fluctuations when the money stock is targeted, and our analysis here suggests Keynesian arguments that money demand instability can lead to undesirable fluctuations in real variables.

KEYNESIAN STICKY PRICE MODELS

In Keynesian macroeconomics, the sticky wage model is not the only approach to studying how the economy functions and for understanding the role of policy. Alternatives to the sticky wage model are models where prices are sticky, so that goods markets do not always clear. These **sticky price models** have similar properties to those of the sticky wage model, in that money is not neutral in the short run and there is a role for government stabilization policy.

Why might goods prices be sticky in the short run? Some Keynesians argue that it is costly for firms to change prices, and even if these costs are small, this could lead firms to fix the prices for their products for long periods of time.[5] Consider a restaurant, which must print new menus whenever it changes its prices. Printing menus is costly, and this causes the restaurant to change prices infrequently. Given that prices change infrequently, there may be periods when the restaurant is full and people are being turned away. If menus were not costly to print, the restaurant might increase its prices under these circumstances. Alternatively, there may be periods when the restaurant is not full and prices would be lowered if it were not for the costs of changing prices. The restaurant example is a common one in the economic literature on sticky price models. Indeed, sticky price models are often referred to as **menu cost models.**

Criticisms of Keynesian Sticky Wage and Sticky Price Models

Critics of Keynesian sticky wage and sticky price models, who we refer to as **classical macroeconomists,** argue that these models fall short in several respects. First, as we have already pointed out, the sticky wage model does not fully replicate the key business cycle regularities. Perhaps most importantly, the model implies that the real wage and average labor productivity are countercyclical, which does not fit the facts. Second, classical economists argue that the theory underlying the sticky wage model is poor or nonexistent. In the sticky wage model, it is argued that the nominal wage is fixed because of long-term labor contracts, but the model does not take explicit account of the reasons that firms and workers write such contracts. To properly understand why wages might be sticky and exactly how this matters for macroeconomic activity, we need to be explicit in our theories about the features of the world that are important to labor contracting and to show how a model with such features explains reality.

Menu cost models are a response to the criticisms by classical economists of Keynesian models. In these models, firms face explicit costs of changing prices, firms maximize profits in the face of these costs, and the result is that prices are in fact sticky and the models have implications much like those of our sticky wage model. However, menu cost models have certainly not been immune from criticism. Classical economists point out that the costs of changing prices are minuscule compared with the short-run costs of changing the quantity of output. Consider the case of a restaurant. On the one hand, the cost of changing menu prices is the cost of making a few keystrokes on a computer keyboard, and then running off a few copies of the menu on the printer in the back room. Indeed, a restaurant will be printing new menus frequently anyway, because restaurant patrons tend to spill food on the menus. On the other hand, if the restaurant wants to increase output in response to higher demand, it will have to move in more tables and chairs and hire and train new staff. Why would the restaurant

---

[5]See L. Ball and N. G. Mankiw, 1994. "A Sticky Price Manifesto," *Carnegie-Rochester Conference Series on Public Policy* 41, 127–151.

want to change output in response to a temporary increase in demand rather than just increasing prices temporarily?

The questions we have raised above help in framing the debate as to whether Keynesian sticky wage and sticky price models on the one hand or equilibrium business cycle models on the other hand are more useful. As we saw in Chapter 11, equilibrium models in general have quite different implications for the role of fiscal and monetary policy than does the Keynesian sticky wage model, with some equilibrium models implying that government intervention is detrimental. However, in the Keynesian coordination failure model (an equilibrium business cycle model) active government stabilization policy could be justified. The reader may wonder at this point why we should study different business cycle models that appear to have contradictory implications. The reason is that business cycles can have many causes, and each of the business cycle models we have examined contains an element of truth that is useful in understanding why business cycles occur and what, if anything, can or should be done about them.

This chapter completes our study of the macroeconomics of business cycles in closed economies. We go on in Chapters 13 and 14 to study macroeconomics in an open economy context.

CHAPTER SUMMARY

- We constructed a Keynesian sticky wage model of the business cycle, where the nominal wage is fixed in the short run and does not move to equate supply and demand in the labor market. As a result there may be Keynesian unemployment, in that the representative consumer wishes to supply more labor than the representative firm wants to hire.

- Given the fixed nominal wage, there exists an aggregate supply relationship, whereby an increase in the price level reduces the real wage, firms hire more labor (in the model, we assume that the labor demand curve determines employment), and more output is produced. The aggregate supply curve is a positive relationship between the price level and level of output. This curve shifts to the right if the nominal wage falls or if total factor productivity increases.

- The aggregate demand side of the model is constructed from the $IS - LM$ diagram, where the IS curve is identical to the output demand curve in the monetary intertemporal model of Chapter 10. The IS curve describes real interest rate/real output combinations such that the goods market is in equilibrium. The LM curve describes real interest rate/real output combinations such that the money market is in equilibrium, given the price level. The aggregate demand curve is a negative relationship between the price level and the level of aggregate output, which describes price level/output combinations for which the goods market and money market are in equilibrium.

- The IS curve shifts to the right with an increase in government spending, a decrease in the present value of taxes, an increase in future income, a decrease in the current capital stock, or an increase in future total factor productivity. The LM curve shifts to the right if the money supply increases, if there is a negative shift in the money demand function, or if the price level decreases. If the IS curve or LM curve shifts to the right, the aggregate demand curve shifts to the right (excepting changes in the price level, which involve movements along the aggregate demand curve).

- In the complete Keynesian sticky wage model, the price level and output are determined in the aggregate demand/aggregate supply diagram. Then, given the price level, employment and the real wage are determined in the labor market, and the real interest rate is determined by the $IS - LM$ diagram.

- Money is not neutral in the Keynesian sticky wage model. An increase in the money supply, through the Keynesian transmission mechanism for monetary policy, causes the real interest rate to fall, which leads to an increase in the demand for investment goods and consumption goods, causing the price level to increase and the real wage to fall (given the fixed nominal wage). As a result, the firm hires more labor and output rises.

- Money supply shocks in the Keynesian sticky wage model are inconsistent with key business cycle facts in that the model predicts a procyclical price level, a countercyclical real wage, and countercyclical average labor productivity.

- With investment shocks, the model is inconsistent with some business cycle facts in that it predicts a procyclical price level, a countercyclical real wage, and countercyclical average labor productivity.

- Because the nominal wage does not adjust to clear the labor market in the model, there is a role for monetary policy and/or fiscal policy to smooth business cycles over time.

- Shifts in money demand in the Keynesian sticky wage model cause real effects, and these real effects can be offset by the appropriate monetary policy. When the central bank has difficulty observing real output on a timely basis, it is appropriate for the central bank to control the interest rate rather than the money supply in the short run, in the face of an unstable money demand function.

- Alternative Keynesian models have sticky prices, motivated by the existence of menu costs.

- The Keynesian sticky wage model's faults are that it is not entirely consistent with the data and that the model is silent as to why wages are sticky. Sticky price models are more explicit about the reasons for stickiness.

KEY TERMS

Indexed: Describes the situation in which the rate of increase of a price or wage is tied to the rate of increase in a measure of the price level, such as the consumer price index.

Keynesian unemployment: Given the market real wage, the difference between the quantity of labor that workers want to supply and actual employment (the quantity demanded).

Aggregate supply curve: In the Keynesian sticky wage model, a positive relationship between the price level and the level of real output.

IS curve: A curve that is identical to the output demand curve in the monetary intertemporal model of Chapter 10; in the Keynesian sticky wage model, this is a downward-sloping relationship between the real interest rate and the level of output, and it represents a set of (Y, r) combinations such that the goods market is in equilibrium.

LM curve: In the Keynesian sticky wage model, an upward-sloping relationship between the real interest rate and the level of output; a set of (Y, r) combinations such that the money market is in equilibrium, given the price level.

Aggregate demand curve: In the Keynesian sticky wage model, a downward-sloping relationship between the price level and the level of real output; a set of (Y, P) combinations such that the goods market and the money market are in equilibrium.

Keynesian transmission mechanism for monetary policy: The real effects of monetary policy in the Keynesian model. In the model, money is not neutral, because an increase in the money supply causes the real interest rate to fall, increasing the demand for consumption and investment, and causing the price level to increase. The real wage then falls, the firm hires more labor, and output increases.

Stabilization policy: Fiscal or monetary policy justified by Keynesian models, which acts to offset shocks to the economy.

Sticky price models: Keynesian models that are closely related to sticky wage models except that there are costs to changing prices, which cause prices to adjust slowly to clear goods markets.

Menu cost models: Identical to sticky price models.

Classical macroeconomists: The alternative to Keynesian macroeconomists; a classical macroeconomist believes that market-clearing models are useful and tends to believe that the government should not engage in stabilization policy.

QUESTIONS FOR REVIEW

1. Are Keynesian business cycle models still used? If so, what for?
2. Why is the nominal wage sticky in the sticky wage model?
3. Is there unemployment in the sticky wage model? If so, why?
4. Does the unemployment in the sticky wage model correspond to unemployment as we observe it? Why or why not?
5. What are two factors that shift the aggregate supply curve in the sticky wage model?
6. Give five factors that shift the *IS* curve.
7. Give three factors that shift the *LM* curve.
8. What are seven factors that shift the aggregate demand curve in the sticky wage model?
9. Explain why money is not neutral in the sticky wage model.
10. Do money supply shocks explain recent business cycles in the United States? Why or why not?
11. Do investment shocks explain recent business cycles in the United States? Why or why not?
12. Should the government act to stabilize output in the sticky wage model? If so, how should it do this?
13. Does it matter if output is stabilized using fiscal policy or monetary policy? Why or why not?
14. Why should the central bank target the interest rate if money demand is unstable?
15. Why are prices sticky in a sticky price model?
16. Explain what faults Keynesian sticky wage and sticky price models have.

PROBLEMS

1. Suppose that total factor productivity decreases in the sticky wage model. Determine the effects on output, the real interest rate, consumption, investment, employment, the price level, and the real wage. Compare these predictions with those of the monetary intertemporal model. Are there any important differences? Explain.

2. Suppose that nominal wages are negotiated between the representative firm and the representative consumer to be perfectly indexed to the price level. That is, if the price level rises by $x\%$, then the nominal wage will increase by $x\%$. This implies that the real wage is fixed over the course of the contract.

   (a) Determine the aggregate supply curve when the real wage is fixed.

   (b) Suppose initially that supply equals demand in the labor market. Then, assume that the money supply increases. Determine the effects on real output, employment, the real interest rate, the real wage, the nominal wage, and Keynesian unemployment, and explain your results.

   (c) Now, suppose again that supply initially equals demand in the labor market, and that total factor productivity falls. Determine the effects on real output, employment, the real interest rate, the real wage, the nominal wage, and Keynesian unemployment. Explain your results and any differences from part (b).

3. Suppose that government spending increases temporarily in the sticky wage model.

   (a) What are the effects on real output, consumption, investment, the price level, employment, and the real wage?

   (b) Are these effects consistent with the key business cycle facts from Chapter 3? What does this say about the ability of government spending shocks to explain business cycles?

4. In the Keynesian sticky wage model, suppose that supply is initially equal to demand in the labor market and that there is a negative shock to the demand for investment goods, because the firm anticipates lower total factor productivity in the future.

   (a) Determine the effects on real output, the real interest rate, the price level, employment, and the real wage, if the government did nothing in response to the shock.

   (b) Determine the effects if monetary policy is used to stabilize the economy, with the goal of the monetary authority being zero Keynesian unemployment.

   (c) Determine the effects if government spending is used to stabilize the economy, with the goal of the fiscal authority being zero Keynesian unemployment.

   (d) Explain and comment on the differences in your results among parts (a), (b), and (c).

5. If there is a reduction in government spending in the Keynesian sticky wage model, show what difference it makes if this reduction is temporary or permanent. What do you conclude about how fiscal policy should be used as a stabilization device? If government spending changes to offset a shock to the economy, should this spending change be announced to be temporary or permanent? Why?

6. The nominal interest rate cannot be less than zero, because if the nominal interest rate were negative, then no one would want to hold bonds. In terms of our model, this can be represented as the demand for money being perfectly elastic with respect to the nominal interest rate when the nominal interest rate is zero.

   (a) Suppose the nominal interest rate (equal to the real interest rate in the Keynesian sticky wage model) is currently equal to zero. What does this imply about the slope of the *LM* curve?

   (b) Suppose the nominal interest rate is currently zero and the monetary authority increases the money supply. What are the short-run equilibrium effects?

   (c) Recently, nominal interest rates have been at or close to zero in Japan. What implications does this have for Japanese monetary policy?

7. Suppose that the goal of the fiscal authority is to set government spending so as to achieve zero Keynesian unemployment, while the goal of the monetary authority is to achieve stability of the price level. Now, the economy is hit by a temporary decrease in total factor productivity.

Show that the goals of the fiscal authority and monetary authority are in conflict, suggest a remedy for this conflict, and discuss.

8. Suppose that the monetary authority's goal is to stabilize aggregate output, but that it cannot observe aggregate output in the short run. If there are shocks to the demand for investment goods, would it be preferable for the monetary authority to target the interest rate or the money supply in the short run? Explain your results.

9. Some macroeconomists have argued that it would be beneficial for the government to run a deficit when the economy is in a recession and a surplus during a boom. Does this make sense? Carefully explain why or why not, using the Keynesian sticky wage model.

10. Suppose that investment and consumption expenditures change very little with a change in the real interest rate. Show what this implies for the slopes of the *IS* curve and *AD* curve and for the relative effectiveness of monetary and fiscal policy in stabilizing real output. Explain your results.

WORKING WITH THE DATA

1. The Keynesian sticky wage model predicts that there is a negative relationship between the quantity of Keynesian unemployment and the deviation of real output from potential. Suppose that Keynesian unemployment is measured as the deviation from trend in the unemployment rate, and the deviation of output from potential is the percentage deviation of real GDP from trend.
    (a) Plot the deviation from trend in the unemployment rate and the percentage deviation from trend in real GDP in a scatter plot.
    (b) What do you observe in the scatter plot? Is this consistent with what the Keynesian sticky wage model predicts? Explain.

2. Construct a time series plot of the percentage deviations from trend in the monetary base and in real GDP, and construct a scatter plot of the two variables. Are these plots consistent or inconsistent with the nonneutrality of money that the Keynesian sticky wage model predicts? Explain.

3. Construct a time series plot of the percentage deviations from trend in total real government expenditures and in real GDP, and construct a scatter plot of the two variables. Does it appear from these plots that the government is engaging in stabilizing fiscal policy? Explain.

PART VI

International

Macroeconomics

Because of globalization—the continuing integration of world markets in goods, services, and assets—international factors are increasingly important for the performance of the domestic economy and for the conduct of fiscal and monetary policy. In this part, we study models of open economies in which there is trade between the domestic economy and the rest of the world. We use these models in Chapter 13 to study the benefits from international trade, the effects of changes in world prices and interest rates, the determinants of the current account surplus, and the implications of current account deficits. In Chapter 14, we examine the role of money in the world economy, the determination of exchange rates, the effects of fixed and flexible exchange rates, and the implications of shocks occurring abroad for domestic business cycles.

CHAPTER 13

International Trade in Goods and Assets

Our goal in this chapter is to extend the models developed in Chapters 5, 8, and 9, so that they can address issues in international macroeconomics. Until now, we have looked at closed-economy macroeconomic issues using closed-economy models, but for many interesting macroeconomic problems, we must do our analysis in an open-economy context. This chapter is confined to issues relating to real international macroeconomics. In Chapter 14, we address the monetary side of international interaction.

During the twentieth and twenty-first centuries, international trade has become increasingly important for two reasons. First, the costs of transporting goods and assets across international boundaries has fallen dramatically, permitting a freer flow of international trade. Second, government-imposed barriers to trade, such as import quotas, tariffs, and restrictions on international financial activity, have been relaxed. A relaxation of trade restrictions was carried out under the General Agreement on Tariffs and Trade (GATT) between 1947 and 1995, when the GATT framework was replaced by the World Trade Organization. Trade restrictions have also been reduced through regional agreements, for example, the North American Free Trade Agreement (NAFTA), signed in 1992, and the European Union (EU). Given the increasing importance of trade in the world economy, we must understand its implications for domestic macroeconomic activity.

In this chapter, we study the importance for domestic aggregate economic activity of trade with the rest of the world in goods and assets. We are interested particularly in how the current account surplus and domestic output, employment, consumption, and investment are affected by events in the rest of the world. To study this, we extend some of the models we have worked with in Chapters 5, 8, and 9.

Throughout this chapter, we confine attention to small open-economy models, which are models in which actions by consumers and firms in the domestic economy have no collective effect on world prices. Some countries are clearly small relative to the rest of the world, such as New Zealand, Singapore, and Luxembourg, and for these countries it is clear that the small open-economy assumption is quite realistic. However, for large countries such as the United States, which play a particularly important role in the world economy, the assumption of price-taking on world markets is perhaps less plausible. There are three reasons that we study small open-economy models here and use them to explain events in large open economies (the United States in particular). The first is that small open-economy models are relatively simple to work with; for example, it is easy to modify closed-economy models so as to construct small open-economy models. Second, many of the conclusions we derive from small open-economy models are identical to the ones we would obtain in more complicated large open-economy models. Third, as time passes, the small open-economy assumption becomes more realistic for a country such as the United States. Given development in the rest of the world, GDP in the United States relative to GDP in the rest of the world falls, and it becomes a closer approximation to the truth that the United States is a price-taker in world goods and asset markets.

In this chapter, we study three small open-economy models that build, respectively, on the one-period model in Chapter 5, the two-period model in Chapter 8, and the real intertemporal model in Chapter 9. The first model focuses on the determinants of domestic production and consumption of goods and the volume of trade between the domestic economy and the rest of the world. This model is used to study how the welfare of domestic consumers can be improved through free trade in goods with the rest of the world and to study the effects of changes in world prices on domestic consumption, production, and the volume of trade.

In the second model, there are two periods, so that we can examine the impact of borrowing and lending between the domestic economy and the rest of the world. Here, we are primarily interested in the determinants of the current account surplus, and the importance of the current account surplus in domestic policymaking. An important idea is that international borrowing and lending permits the smoothing of aggregate consumption over time for the domestic economy, just as a single consumer can smooth consumption by borrowing and lending.

In the third and final model, we include investment and production, so that we can study the relationships among domestic consumption, output, investment, government spending, and the current account balance. This model is used to examine the relationship between the current account deficit and the government budget deficit, and we can apply this analysis to understanding the so-called twin deficits problem of the 1980s. We also examine the role of investment in determining the current account deficit, and we address to what extent a current account deficit is good or bad for a nation's welfare.

A TWO-GOOD MODEL OF A SMALL OPEN ECONOMY

The first international model we consider is closely related to the one-period model we constructed in Chapter 5, and the analysis we developed there is also useful here. We use this international model to understand why countries trade, and the primary determinants of the volume of trade. This is a model of a **small open economy (SOE).** The economy is small, in the sense that economic activity in this country does not affect the world prices of goods. That is, the firms and consumers in this economy are individual price-takers—they treat market prices as being given—and collective price-takers—their collective actions have no effect on the world prices for goods. The economy is also open, in that we explore the consequences of trade between this economy and the rest of the world. Until now, we have considered macroeconomic models of closed economies where there is no trade with the rest of the world.

In the SOE, there are two goods that are produced and consumed, which we will call good a and good b. From the viewpoint of people in the SOE, the price of good a in terms of good b, denoted by TOT_{ab}, is given. This price is the **terms of trade** or the

real exchange rate, because TOT_{ab} is the rate at which the residents of the SOE can trade good b for good a on world markets. The model tells us under what conditions the SOE imports good a and exports good b, or exports good a and imports good b.

Allowing the two goods in the model, a and b, to stand in for all of the goods produced and consumed in the economy is an important simplification. Clearly, a given country imports and exports many different kinds of goods, and so assuming that there are only two goods may seem unrealistic. For many countries, however, the assumption of two broad categories of goods fits the facts of their trade patterns well. For example, New Zealand's exports are primarily agricultural products, and its main imports are manufactured goods. Similarly, Kuwait exports crude oil and imports manufactured goods. For the United States, the story is somewhat more complicated, as the U.S. imports and exports goods that may appear to be the same. For example, the U.S. exports wine produced in California and imports wine from Australia and France. Also, a good portion of trade between the United States and its largest trading partner, Canada, is trade in automobiles. The Ford Motor Company, for example, assembles cars in Oakville, Ontario, for export to the United States, and it also builds cars in Detroit, Michigan, for export to Canada. For our purposes, however, it is convenient to think of exports and imports as different goods. For wine, this is clearly the case. Wine consumers definitely draw a distinction between California wine and French wine. However, most of the trade between the United States and Canada in automobiles is explained by factors that are quite specific to the nature of production in the auto industry. These factors are unimportant for the issues we wish to address.

The SOE has a production possibilities frontier (PPF), which describes the combinations of good a and good b that the SOE can produce, and this PPF is depicted in Figure 13.1. The PPF is similar to the ones that we constructed in Chapter 5, where

---

FIGURE 13.1 **Production Possibilities Frontier for the SOE**

The figure depicts the production possibilities frontier (PPF) for the small open economy. The slope of the PPF is minus the marginal rate of transformation, and the PPF is concave.

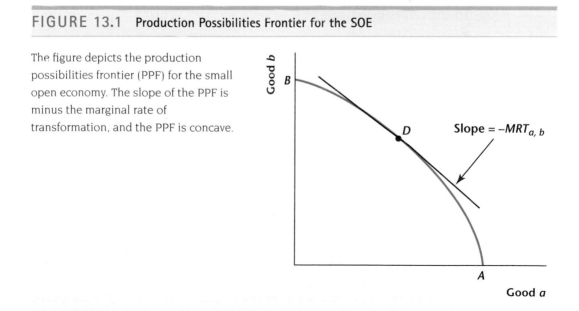

we considered the combinations of consumption and leisure that could be produced in a closed economy. We do not formally derive the *PPF* for the SOE in the figure as we did in Chapter 5, but we can give some intuition for why it has the shape that it does. In the SOE, goods *a* and *b* are produced using labor and capital. At point *A* on the *PPF* in the figure, only good *a* is produced; at point *B*, only good *b* is produced. Now, consider what happens if we begin at point *B*, and move along the *PPF* toward point *A*. As we do so, more of good *a* is produced and less of good *b* is produced, with labor and capital being reallocated from production of good *b* to production of good *a*. Because the *PPF* represents combinations of goods *b* and *a* that can be produced efficiently in the SOE, when labor and capital are reallocated from production of good *b* to production of good *a*, these factors of production are those that are most productive at the margin in producing good *a* relative to good *b*. Thus, the *PPF* is not very steep at point *B*, as only a small amount of good *b* is sacrificed at the margin to obtain another unit of good *a*. As we move down the *PPF* from point *B* to point *A*, however, the *PPF* becomes steeper, as the labor and capital reallocated from production of good *b* to production of good *a* become relatively more productive at the margin in industry *b* than in industry *a*, and we need to sacrifice more of good *b* at the margin to obtain another unit of good *a*. Recall that the slope of the *PPF* is minus the marginal rate of transformation, which is denoted by $MRT_{a,b}$. The marginal rate of transformation, $MRT_{a,b}$, is the quantity of good *b* that must be forgone in the economy if another unit of good *a* is produced. At point *D* in Figure 13.1, $MRT_{a,b}$ is minus the slope of a tangent to the *PPF*. Thus, as for the *PPF* in Chapter 5, the marginal rate of transformation increases as we move down the *PPF* from point *B* to point *A*. That is, the *PPF* is concave.

The residents of the SOE consume only goods *a* and *b*, and we assume that we can capture their preferences using the representative consumer device, as in Chapter 4. That is, there is a representative consumer in the SOE whose preferences are represented by indifference curves, as in Figure 13.2. As we assumed in Chapter 4, the representative consumer prefers more to less and has a preference for diversity, so that the indifference curves in Figure 13.2 slope downward and are convex. Further, goods *a* and *b* are both normal, in that an increase in income, holding prices constant, will imply that domestic consumption of both goods increases.

Competitive Equilibrium in the Small Open Economy Without Trade

Now that we know the basic characteristics of the SOE, given by the production possibilities frontier and the representative consumer's indifference curves, our first goal is to understand what determines the pattern of trade. That is, we want to know what factors determine whether the SOE imports *a* and exports *b*, or vice versa, and how this is important for the welfare of consumers in the SOE.

To show the effects of trade in the SOE, we want to first determine the characteristics of a competitive equilibrium if the SOE could not engage in trade. Just as in Chapter 5, a competitive equilibrium for this economy is Pareto optimal, and the competitive equilibrium quantities of goods *a* and *b* produced and consumed are determined by

FIGURE 13.2 Indifference Curves of the Representative Consumer in the SOE

The indifference curves of the representative consumer in the SOE are downward-sloping and convex.

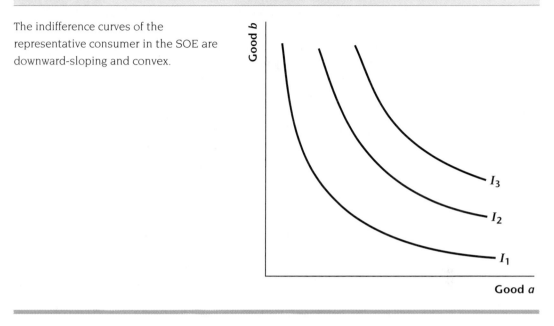

the point at which an indifference curve is tangent to the *PPF*. That is, the competitive equilibrium is point *A* in Figure 13.3. Recall that, at the competitive equilibrium point *A*, the marginal rate of substitution of good *a* for good *b* is equal to the marginal rate of transformation, or

$$MRS_{a,b} = MRT_{a,b},$$

because the marginal rate of substitution is minus the slope of the indifference curve at point *A*, and the marginal rate of transformation is minus the slope of the *PPF* at point *A*. Further, the equilibrium price of good *a* relative to good *b*, or p_{ab}, is minus the slope of a line tangent to the indifference curve and the *PPF* at point *A*. This is because, first, in equilibrium the representative consumer optimizes by setting

$$MRS_{a,b} = p_{ab}. \tag{13.1}$$

Recall from Chapter 4 that consumer optimization implies that a consumer sets the marginal rate of substitution of one good for another equal to the price of one good relative to the other, which implies that Equation (13.1) holds in this model in equilibrium. Second, optimization by firms will imply that

$$MRT_{a,b} = p_{ab}. \tag{13.2}$$

This second condition holds for the following reason. The marginal rate of transformation, $MRT_{a,b}$, tells us how many units of good *b* must be given up to produce one additional unit of good *a*, while p_{ab} is the price that can be received in the market for one unit of good *a* in units of good *b*. If $MRT_{a,b} < p_{ab}$, then a firm could profit

FIGURE 13.3 Equilibrium in the SOE with No Trade

If there is no trade in the SOE, equilibrium is determined by the tangency between the PPF and an indifference curve for the representative consumer. In equilibrium, the slope of the PPF is equal to minus the price of good a relative to good b.

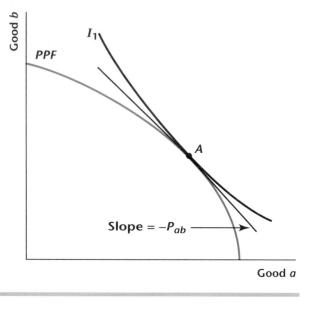

by taking capital and labor from the production of good b and producing good a, whereas if $MRT_{a,b} > p_{ab}$, then a firm could profit by taking capital and labor from the production of good a and producing good b. Therefore, profit maximization implies that Equation (13.2) holds in equilibrium.

The Effects of Trade in the Small Open Economy

We now know the characteristics of a competitive equilibrium in the SOE in the case where there is no trade with the rest of the world. Of course, our objective is to show the determinants of the pattern and volume of trade between the SOE and the rest of the world and to show how trade affects welfare. Thus, at this stage, we will suppose that the SOE can trade with the rest of the world at world prices given by TOT_{ab}; that is, the relative price of good a in terms of good b is now determined on world markets, rather than in domestic markets in the SOE. Recall that the SOE is a price-taker on world markets, so that economic activity in the SOE does not affect the terms of trade TOT_{ab}.

Trade opens up consumption opportunities that are not available to the representative consumer in the SOE in the absence of trade. That is, in equilibrium, the representative consumer need no longer consume the consumption bundle that is produced in the SOE, as was the case in Figure 13.3. When the SOE can trade with the rest of the world, the terms of trade determine what is produced. Namely, optimization by firms implies that

$$MRT_{a,b} = TOT_{ab},$$

FIGURE 13.4 **Production and Consumption in the SOE with Trade**

When the SOE trades with the rest of the world at market prices given by the terms of trade, consumption occurs at point E and production occurs at point D, with the slope of DE equal to minus the terms of trade.

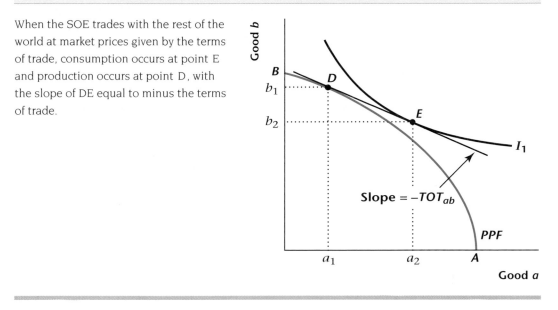

so that the quantities of goods a and b that are produced in the SOE are given by point D in Figure 13.4, where the slope of DE is equal to $-TOT_{ab}$. The quantity of good a produced is a_1, and the quantity of good b produced is b_1. To determine what is consumed in a competitive equilibrium with trade, we think of the consumption bundle that is produced in the SOE as being an endowment available to the consumer, which then determines the representative consumer's budget constraint. Essentially, the representative consumer receives what is produced as income, through wages and the dividends distributed by firms. Then, if the consumer is endowed with a_1 units of good a and b_1 units of good b and can exchange good b for good a on world markets at the rate TOT_{ab}, the terms of trade, then the representative consumer's budget constraint is

$$TOT_{ab}q_a + q_b = TOT_{ab}a_1 + b_1. \tag{13.3}$$

In the consumer's budget constraint, q_a and q_b are the quantities of good a and good b consumed, respectively, and the budget constraint is written in terms of good b. Thus, the quantity on the right-hand side of Equation (13.3) is the representative consumer's income in terms of good b, and the quantity on the left-hand side is the consumer's expenditure on goods a and b, again in units of good b. The budget constraint, Equation (13.3) then runs through points D and E in Figure 13.4.

Next, the representative consumer optimizes, just as in Chapter 4, by choosing the consumption bundle for which an indifference curve is tangent to his or her budget constraint. In Figure 13.4, the consumer chooses point E, where the quantity of good a consumed is $q_a = a_2$ and the quantity of good b consumed is $q_b = b_2$. In the figure, the SOE then is an importer of good a and an exporter of good b, because $a_2 > a_1$ and $b_2 < b_1$. The value of imports, in units of good b, is $TOT_{ab}(a_2 - a_1)$, and the value of exports is $b_1 - b_2$. Recalling the definition of the current account surplus from Chapter 2, which is net exports plus net factor payments from abroad, the current account surplus in the SOE in units of good b, is the value of exports minus the value of imports (because net factor payments are zero here), which is

$$CA = b_1 - b_2 - TOT_{ab}(a_2 - a_1).$$

But from the consumer's budget constraint, Equation (13.3), we then have $CA = 0$; that is, the current account surplus is zero. This is a one-period model where the SOE cannot borrow and lend abroad, which implies that the current account surplus must be zero in equilibrium. In this model, the value of goods exported always equals the value of goods imported in equilibrium.

The pattern of trade between the SOE and the rest of the world is determined in part by two factors. The first is the principle of **comparative advantage.** In Figure 13.4, the SOE imports good a and exports good b, so that the SOE tends to have a comparative advantage in producing good b. Comparative advantage is determined by the slope of the production possibilities frontier. The steeper the production possibilities frontier is, the greater is the SOE's comparative advantage in producing good b relative to good a, because more of good b needs to be sacrificed at the margin to produce another unit of good a. A steeper PPF also implies that more of good b is produced, and less of good a is produced, when the SOE can trade with the rest of the world, and so there is a tendency to export more of good b.

The second factor that determines the pattern of trade is consumer preferences. Even if the SOE has a strong comparative advantage in producing a good, if the representative consumer has a strong preference for that good, it could be imported rather than exported. The important characteristic of consumer preferences for determining the pattern of trade is the marginal rate of substitution, $MRS_{a,b}$. As $MRS_{a,b}$ increases, the indifference curves of the representative consumer become steeper, and the SOE has a greater tendency to import good a and export good b.

An important result is that the representative consumer is always better off with trade than without it. To show this, we consider two cases. In the first case, the domestic price of good a in terms of good b (when there is no trade) is greater than the terms of trade, as in Figure 13.5. Here, when there is no trade, the consumption bundle produced and consumed is given by point A, but when the SOE is opened up to world trade, production occurs at point B, and the representative consumer chooses point D. The terms of trade are given by minus the slope of the line EF. With trade, the consumer is on a higher indifference curve; that is, indifference curve I_2 represents a higher level of welfare than indifference curve I_1. In the second case, as in Figure 13.6, the domestic price of good a in terms of good b (when there is no trade) is smaller than the terms of trade. In this case, consumption and production when the economy is closed are at point A, but when the economy is open, production occurs at point B and consumption at point D. Again, the representative consumer's welfare improves with free trade. This result—trade increases opportunities and makes the nation better off—is a fundamental economic principle.

FIGURE 13.5   An Increase in Welfare When Good a Is Imported

When there is no trade, consumption and production occur at point A, but when the SOE trades with the rest of the world, production occurs at B and consumption at D. In this case, good *a* is imported, and welfare is higher with trade, as the representative consumer attains a higher indifference curve.

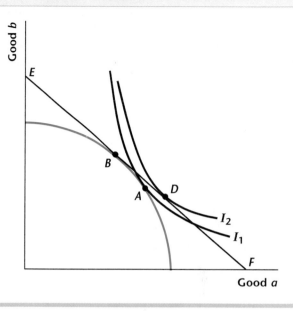

FIGURE 13.6   An Increase in Welfare When Good b Is Imported

Here, in contrast to Figure 13.5, good *b* is imported when the SOE can trade with the rest of the world. Trade improves welfare, as the consumer attains a higher indifference curve.

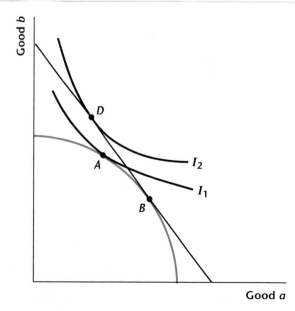

Our model captures the effects of trade on the average consumer, showing that trade always makes this average consumer (the representative consumer) better off. In practice, however, eliminating trade restrictions typically harms some people while benefiting others, though we argue the net effect on welfare is positive. For example, U.S. residents were not all in agreement that NAFTA, signed in 1992 by Canada, Mexico, and the United States, was a good idea. NAFTA tended to harm those industries in the United States for which Mexico and Canada had comparative advantages. In those industries, product prices and real wages tended to fall, and workers were displaced. However, in industries for which the United States has a comparative advantage relative to Mexico and Canada, prices and real wages tended to rise, and employment expanded. The fact that someone almost always stands to lose in circumstances where trade restrictions are relaxed makes it difficult to pass laws that free up international trade.

A Change in the Terms of Trade: Effects on Production, Consumption, and Welfare

A key macroeconomic shock for an open economy is a change in the price of imports relative to the price of exports, that is, a change in the terms of trade. The terms of trade could move against a country if imports became more expensive relative to exports, as, for example, in New Zealand if the prices of manufactured goods were to increase relative to the prices of agricultural goods. In this case, economic welfare would decrease in New Zealand. The terms of trade could also move in favor of a country if imports became cheaper relative to exports. This would happen in Kuwait if there were an increase in the relative price of crude oil, which would increase economic welfare for the residents of Kuwait. As we show in this section, a change in the terms of trade has similarities to a change in total factor productivity in a closed economy, as considered in Chapter 5. This is because there are in general income and substitution effects associated with a change in the terms of trade.

In an open economy, changes in the terms of trade affect domestic production, domestic consumption, exports, and imports. In the model, we must consider the two cases where the terms of trade move in favor of, and against the SOE. In the first case, the SOE imports good a before an increase in the terms of trade, and in the second, the SOE initially imports good b. This matters for the results because of the effects on economic welfare, and because there is a difference in income effects on consumption of both goods. In the first case, there is a negative income effect on consumption and in the second case a positive income effect. Substitution effects work in the same way in each case.

In Figure 13.7 we show the first case, where initially the consumption bundle produced is given by point A, and the initial terms of trade are given by the negative of the slope of a line tangent at point A. The initial consumption bundle is at point B, where this line is tangent to indifference curve I_1. With an increase in the terms of trade, production is at point D, where the terms of trade (minus the slope of a line tangent to the PPF at point D) is higher. Production of good a must increase, while production of good b decreases, as the relative price of good a has risen, encouraging more production of a and less production of b. The new consumption bundle is given

FIGURE 13.7 **An Increase in the Terms of Trade when Good a Is Initially Imported**

The terms of trade increase, with the price of good a increasing relative to good b. When good a is initially imported, welfare falls. The substitution effect on consumption is the movement from B to F, the income effect the movement from F to E. Consumption of good a falls, and consumption of good b may rise or fall. The production point moves from A to D.

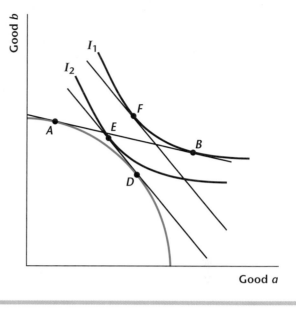

by point E, where in this case the representative consumer consumes less of good a and more of good b. In fact, the SOE now imports good b and exports a.

We can separate the effect of the change in the terms of trade on consumption into income and substitution effects. Namely, if we draw a tangent to the initial indifference curve I_1 in Figure 13.7, the slope of which is minus the new terms of trade, then this line is tangent to I_1 at point F, and the substitution effect of the change in the terms of trade is the movement from B to F. That is, the substitution effect is for consumption of good a to decrease and that of good b to increase. There is a negative income effect, which is the movement from F to E. Recall that we assumed that both goods are normal, so that the income effect is for consumption of goods a and b to decrease.

On net, then, the consumption of good a must decrease, and the consumption of good b may increase or decrease, depending on the size of the income effect relative to the substitution effect. Production of good a increases, and production of good b decreases. The quantity of a good imported is given by consumption minus production. Therefore, we can conclude that the quantity of good a imported must decrease, as consumption decreases and production increases. For good b, however, there is an ambiguous effect on the quantity imported, as production decreases, but consumption may increase or decrease. However, if substitution effects dominate income effects, then the quantity of good b imported rises.

In terms of the value of imports and exports, in units of good b, the results are ambiguous. The value of imports is

$$\text{Quantity of imports} \times TOT_{ab},$$

FIGURE 13.8 An Increase in the Terms of Trade when Good b Is Initially Imported

An increase in the terms of trade increases welfare when good b is initially imported. The substitution effect on consumption is the movement from B to F, the income effect the movement from F to E. Consumption of good a may rise or fall, and consumption of good b rises. Production moves from A to D.

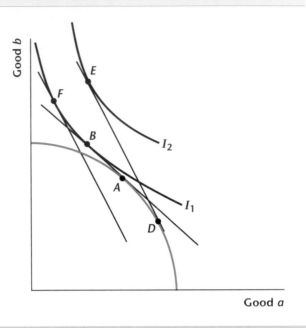

and though we know that the quantity of imports decreases, the terms of trade TOT_{ab} increases, and so the product of quantity and terms of trade could either increase or decrease. Because we have already determined that the quantity of good b exported could increase or decrease, we know that the value of good b exported, in units of good b (which is the same thing), could increase or decrease. Though the effects on the value of exports and imports are ambiguous here, we know that there is no effect on the current account surplus from a change in the terms of trade, because the current account surplus is always zero in this model.

Now consider the second case, in Figure 13.8, where there is an increase in the terms of trade when the SOE initially imports good b and exports good a. Initially, production of goods a and b is given by point A, with consumption at point B. The slope of the line AB is equal to minus the initial terms of trade. When the terms of trade increases, the production point shifts to D, with domestic output of good a rising and output of good b falling, just as in the first case. The representative consumer now chooses point E, with the slope of DE equal to minus the new terms of trade. Here, there is a positive income effect on consumption of goods a and b. Separating the effect of the change in the terms of trade into income and substitution effects, the substitution effect is the movement from B to F, while the income effect is the movement from F to E. As before, the substitution effect leads to an increase in consumption of good b and a decrease in consumption of good a. Here, however, the income effect leads to an increase in consumption of both goods a and b (again under the assumption that both goods are normal). Therefore, consumption of good *b* must rise, but consumption of good *a* may rise or fall.

In the second case, then, imports of good *b* may rise or fall, because less is produced and less is consumed as well. Exports of good *a* may also rise or fall, because more is produced, but consumption may increase or decrease. What happens to the value of imports and exports is also ambiguous, but again there is no effect on the current account surplus, which is always zero.

What happens to the representative consumer's welfare differs between the first case and the second. When good *a* is initially imported, and the terms of trade change so that the relative price of good *a* increases, the representative consumer is worse off. That is, in Figure 13.7, the representative consumer initially chooses a consumption bundle on indifference curve I_1, and chooses a consumption bundle on a lower indifference curve, I_2, when the terms of trade changes. This is the case in which the terms of trade turn against the SOE, in the sense that the goods that are being sold abroad (good *b*) become cheaper relative to the goods that are purchased abroad (good *a*). In Figure 13.8, however, the change in the terms of trade is favorable to the SOE, in that the representative consumer is on a higher indifference curve after the terms of trade change. In this case, imported goods (good *b*) become cheaper relative to exports, and this is good for economic welfare in the SOE.

MACROECONOMICS IN ACTION

How Important Are Shocks to the Terms of Trade for Business Cycles?

Because the terms of trade cause changes in the makeup of domestic consumption and production and they affect aggregate economic welfare, shocks to the terms of trade could be sources of business cycles. Indeed, one of the shocks to the economy that we have previously analyzed as a shock to total factor productivity—a change in the relative price of energy—can also be modeled as a change in the terms of trade. The large increases in the world price of crude oil that occurred in 1973, in the late 1970s, in 1991, in 2000, and in 2002, were adverse changes in the terms of trade for the United States. In all these cases, the terms of trade turned against the United States,

which is a net importer of crude oil. After the shifts in the terms of trade in these episodes, the results in the United States were just as our model predicts. Domestic production of crude oil and other alternative sources of energy increased, while domestic consumption of energy decreased. A reduction in economic welfare was reflected in a short-run decrease in GDP.

Though the United States can be vulnerable to terms of trade shocks, particularly those resulting from changes in the world price of crude oil, it is not as sensitive to changes in the terms of trade as some other countries. Though imports and
(continued)

exports are significant relative to GDP in the United States, foreign trade is much more important for some other countries, particularly Canada, Mexico, and the countries of Western Europe. As well, U.S. imports and exports are diversified across a wide array of goods and services. In some countries, there is a dependence on one commodity as a major export. For example, Kuwait is primarily an exporter of crude oil, so that fluctuations in the world price of this one commodity can have dramatic effects for the economy of Kuwait.

For all countries of the world, how important are terms of trade shocks for busi-

ness cycles? Using a real business cycle model and data from many countries, Enrique Mendoza finds that half of the variability in real GDP is explained by terms of trade shocks.[1] This is a highly significant finding, and it indicates that accounting for shocks from abroad is very important for analyzing business cycles. If attention is confined to a closed-economy analysis of the factors determining business cycles, we lose at least half of the picture.

[1] See E. Mendoza, 1993. "The Terms of Trade, the Real Exchange Rate, and Economic Fluctuations," *International Economic Review* 36, 101–138.

A TWO-PERIOD SMALL OPEN-ECONOMY MODEL: THE CURRENT ACCOUNT

The previous one-period model was useful for understanding the benefits from trade and the effects of changes in the terms of trade. However, some important issues in international macroeconomics are related to intertemporal choices. In particular, we would like to study the determinants of the current account surplus. We know from Chapter 2 that a current account surplus must always be reflected in an excess of domestic savings over domestic investment and by an increase in the net claims of domestic residents on foreign residents. Thus, to analyze the current account, we need a model where, at the minimum, consumers make borrowing and lending and consumption-savings decisions. A useful model of borrowing and lending and consumption-savings decisions is the two-period model we developed in Chapter 8. Here, we modify that model by having a single representative consumer, capturing the average behavior of all domestic consumers, and we allow borrowing and lending between domestic and foreign residents.

We suppose that there is a single representative consumer in the SOE, and that this consumer lives for two periods, the current and future periods. For the representative consumer, income is exogenous in both periods, with Y denoting current real income and Y' future real income. The consumer also pays lump-sum taxes to the SOE government of T in the current period and T' in the future period. Because this economy is small and open, the actions of the representative consumer do not affect the world real interest rate, and so we assume that the consumer in the SOE can borrow and lend as much as he or she wishes at the world real interest rate r. Just as in Chapter 8, the representative consumer chooses consumption in the current and future periods, C and C', respectively, to make himself or herself as well off as possible given his or her

FIGURE 13.9 **The Two-Period Small Open-Economy Model**

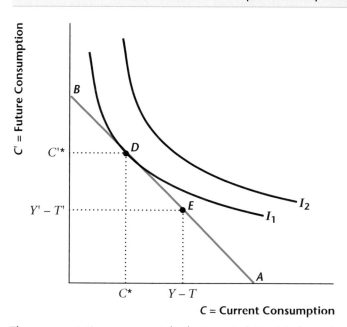

The representative consumer's budget constraint is AB, the endowment point is E, and the consumer chooses point D.

lifetime budget constraint

$$C + \frac{C'}{1+r} = Y - T + \frac{Y'-T'}{1+r}. \tag{13.4}$$

In Figure 13.9 we show the consumer's lifetime budget constraint as the line AB. Point E is the endowment point, and the representative consumer chooses point D on his or her lifetime budget constraint, which is the point where an indifference curve is tangent to the lifetime budget constraint. In the figure, consumption in the current and future periods is C^* and C'^*, respectively. Private saving in the current period is then given by $S^P = Y - T - C = Y - T - C^*$, and so in the figure the consumer saves a positive amount.

   Now, to complete the model, we need to describe the behavior of the government in the SOE. Government spending in the current and future periods is G and G', respectively, and these quantities are exogenous. The government then sets current and future taxes on the representative consumer, T and T', respectively, to satisfy the government's present-value budget constraint

$$G + \frac{G'}{1+r} = T + \frac{T'}{1+r}. \tag{13.5}$$

Then, the quantity of government saving is given by $S^g = T - G$, and in this economy where there is no investment, the current account surplus in the current period, from Chapter 2, is

$$CA = S - I = (S^p + S^g) - 0 = Y - C - G.$$

In this model, we are interested in understanding the key factors that affect the current account surplus CA, which are the following:

- *Current period income.* Recall from Chapter 8 that an increase in current income increases current consumption and future consumption, and current consumption increases by less than the increase in current income, because the consumer wishes to smooth consumption over his or her lifetime. An increase in Y, therefore, leads to an increase in the current account surplus. Because of the consumption-smoothing motive, a country that experiences an increase in current income saves more by lending abroad, and this is reflected in an increase in the current account surplus.

- *Current government spending.* An increase in government spending, given the government's present-value budget constraint, Equation (13.5), leads to a decrease by an equal amount in the present value of taxes for the consumer. Therefore, the consumer's lifetime wealth falls by the increase in government spending. We know then that the consumer's current consumption falls, but by less than the increase in government spending, because the consumer smooths consumption between the current and future periods. The current account surplus, therefore, decreases with an increase in government spending.

- *Taxes.* Given the Ricardian equivalence theorem from Chapter 8, changes in taxes have no effect on aggregate consumption, because consumers simply adjust savings to account for the change in their future tax liabilities. As consumption is unaffected, there is no effect on the current account surplus. Just as in the closed-economy model in Chapter 8, however, if there are significant credit market imperfections, then a change in current taxes in general affects current consumption, and this matters for the trade balance.

- *The real interest rate.* Recall from Chapter 8 that the effect of a change in the real interest rate on current consumption depends on whether the representative consumer is initially a net borrower or a net lender. If the consumer is a net lender, then current consumption may rise or fall when the real interest rate rises, because there is a positive income effect on consumption, and the substitution effect implies that current consumption falls and future consumption rises. If the consumer is a net borrower, the income and substitution effects work in the same direction, and an increase in the real interest rate causes a decrease in current consumption. In general, then, if income effects are not too large, an increase in the real interest rate causes a decrease in current consumption and an increase in the current account surplus.

IS A CURRENT ACCOUNT DEFICIT A BAD THING?

THEORY confronts the DATA

It may seem that a current account deficit is undesirable, because if a country runs a current account deficit, it is borrowing from the rest of the world and accumulating debt. However, just as is the case for individual consumers, lending and borrowing is the means by which a nation smooths consumption. If a given country runs current account deficits when aggregate income is low and runs current account surpluses when aggregate income is high, this allows the residents of that country to smooth their consumption over time. This state of affairs is preferable to one in which the country always has a current account surplus of zero and consumption is as variable as income.

Thus, there are good reasons for expecting that countries should run current account surpluses in good times and current account deficits in bad times. Government policy aimed at correcting this tendency could be counterproductive. But do countries actually smooth consumption over time as theory predicts? In Figure 13.10 we show the deviations from trend in real GDP and the current account surplus for the United States over the period 1960–2003. For real GDP, the deviations are percentage deviations from trend, and for the current account surplus these are the absolute deviations from trend, scaled to match reasonably closely the average percentage deviation from trend in real GDP. In the figure, there is a tendency for the current account surplus to be above (below) trend when real GDP is below (above) trend, so that deviations from trend in GDP and the current account surplus are negatively correlated. This is the opposite of consumption smoothing, in that the United States tended to export goods and lend more abroad when output was low, and to borrow more abroad when output was high.

Why would the data not exhibit obvious evidence of consumption smoothing when economic theory tells us that nations should smooth consumption by lending (borrowing) abroad when income is high (low)? A potential explanation may be that the timing and severity of business cycles in the rest of the world and in the United States are similar. For example, the data in Figure 13.10 are consistent with consumption smoothing if business cycles coincided in the United States and the rest of the world, but the upturns and downturns were more severe in the rest of the world. Then, the United States could in equilibrium be lending to other countries when its own output was low and borrowing from other countries when its own output was high.

THE TWIN DEFICITS OF THE 1980s

THEORY confronts the DATA

Our two-period small open-economy model predicts that an increase in government spending causes a decrease in the current account surplus and that, given Ricardian equivalence, a decrease in current taxes has no effect. With a decrease in current taxes, consumers understand that their future taxes have increased by an equal amount, in present-value

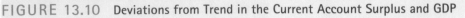

FIGURE 13.10 Deviations from Trend in the Current Account Surplus and GDP

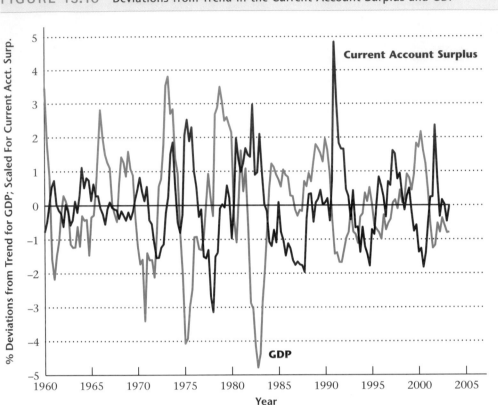

In U.S. data for 1960–2003, there does not appear to be evidence of national consumption smoothing, as deviations from trend in net exports and GDP are negatively correlated. This may be the result of synchronization in business cycles across countries.

Source: Bureau of Economic Analysis, Department of Commerce.

terms, and current consumption is unaffected, leaving the current account surplus unchanged.

During the 1980s, an interesting fiscal policy experiment was carried out by the Reagan administration, in that there was a sharp increase in government spending, accounted for mainly by an increase in defense spending, coupled with a sharp reduction in income taxes. Figure 13.11 shows total U.S. taxes (receipts) and government spending relative to GDP, where we see a dramatic increase in spending as a fraction of GDP in the early 1980s and a corresponding sharp decrease in receipts. Figure 13.12 then shows the total U.S. government surplus and the U.S. current account surplus, again relative to GDP, over the same period. Our theory predicts that net exports should fall in the face of an increase in government spending, and this is certainly consistent with what occurred

FIGURE 13.11   Government Spending and Taxes

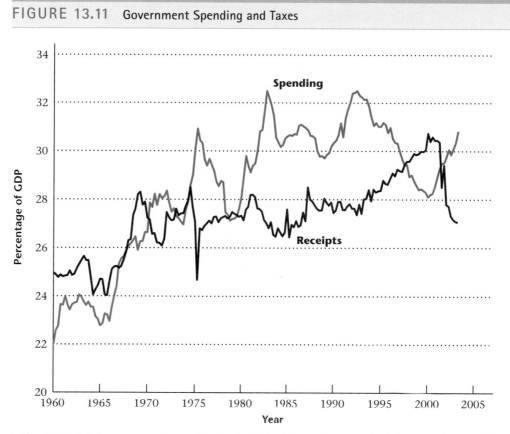

In the 1980s, total government spending in the United States increased, while taxes decreased, as percentages of GDP.

Source: Bureau of Economic Analysis, Department of Commerce.

in the 1980s in Figure 13.12, where a decrease in the government surplus in the 1980s corresponds to a decrease in the current account surplus. While many other factors could have influenced the current account surplus during the 1980s, this is a case where there appears to be a clear connection between the government budget surplus and the current account surplus. This is often referred to as the **twin deficits,** as both the government surplus and the current account surplus were negative in the 1980s. The data for the 1980s are consistent with the increase in government spending causing an increase in the government budget deficit and the current account deficit and the decrease in taxes having no effect on the current account deficit because of Ricardian equivalence.

The clear connection between the government budget deficit and the current account deficit in the 1980s certainly does not apply for all periods in Figure 13.12.

FIGURE 13.12   The Twin Deficits

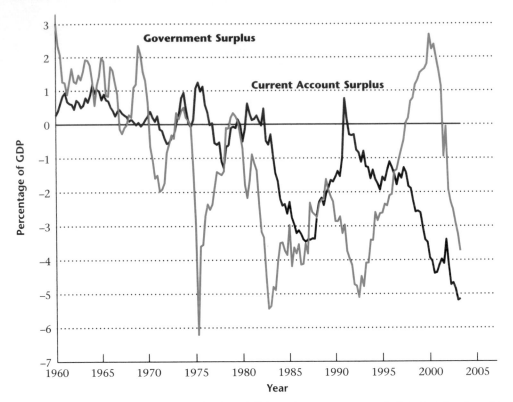

The twin deficits are the government budget deficit and current account deficit that developed in the 1980s. The government budget surplus and the current account surplus tended to move in opposite directions after 1990.

Source: Bureau of Economic Analysis, Department of Commerce.

Before the 1970s and after 1990, we do not see this relationship. Indeed, since 1990 the current account surplus and the government surplus have tended to move in opposite directions (see Figure 13.12). Recall from Chapter 2 that national income accounts identities imply that

$$CA = S - I;$$

that is, the current account surplus is equal to national saving minus investment expenditures. If private saving and investment are unchanged and there is a decrease in government saving (an increase in the government deficit), then, from this equation, the current account surplus must fall. This is roughly what appears to have happened during the 1980s. After 1990, it seems that private saving and investment did not remain constant when government saving increased and then decreased, and so we did not see an increase and then a rapid decrease in the current account surplus. It is particularly important to pay careful attention to the behavior of investment in explaining the behavior of the current account surplus since 1990. In the next section, we study a model of international trade that takes account of investment expenditures.

PRODUCTION, INVESTMENT, AND THE CURRENT ACCOUNT

While the previous model yields some useful insights concerning the role of the current account in national consumption smoothing, and some explanations for the behavior of the current account, we must understand more completely the relationship between the current account surplus and events in the domestic economy. In this section, we study a model based on the real intertemporal model in Chapter 9, which includes production and investment behavior.

In this model, just as in the previous one, the SOE faces a given world real interest rate. As in Chapter 9, output supply is given by the upward-sloping curve Y^s in Figure 13.13. Here, however, we assume that goods can be freely traded with foreign

FIGURE 13.13 A Small Open–Economy Model with Production and Investment

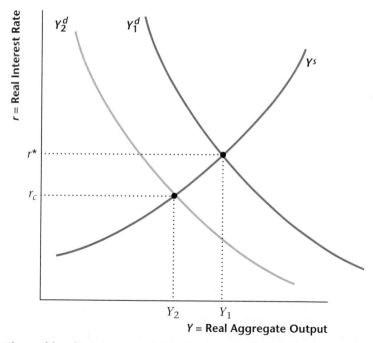

The world real interest rate, determined on world credit markets, is r^*. Net exports adjusts so that the Y^d curve intersects the Y^s curve at the world real interest rate. Here, NX > 0, and in the absence of trade, the domestic real interest rate would be r_c.

countries, and so from the income-expenditure identity $Y = C + I + G + NX$, the demand for goods also includes net exports, NX. In Figure 13.13, the world real interest rate is r^*, which then determines the domestic demand for consumption goods and investment goods. If total domestic demand, $C + I + G$, exceeds the domestic supply of goods at the world real interest rate, then goods are imported and net exports are negative; and if domestic demand is less than the domestic supply of goods at the world real interest rate, then goods are exported and net exports are positive. The equilibrium quantity of net exports is the quantity NX, which yields a downward-sloping output demand curve Y_1^d that intersects the Y^s curve in Figure 13.13 at the world real interest rate r^*. We have depicted a case in Figure 13.13 where $NX > 0$, that is, if there were no trade in goods with the rest of the world, then the output demand curve would be Y_2^d, to the left of Y_1^d, and the domestic real interest rate would be r_c. In general, it could be the case that that $r^* < r_c$ or $r^* > r_c$. Given the world real interest rate r^*, the quantity of aggregate output produced in the SOE is Y_1, but in this case the domestic demand for goods, $C + I + G$, is less than Y_1. The domestic demand for goods, $C + I + G$, is sometimes referred to as **absorption,** as this is the quantity of aggregate output that is absorbed by the domestic economy. The quantity NX is then the current account surplus, or net exports. Recall that the current account surplus is net exports plus net factor payments from abroad, but net factor payments from abroad equal zero in this model. In Figure 13.13, the SOE has a positive current account surplus; that is, $NX > 0$, which implies that the SOE is accumulating assets from the rest of the world.

The Effects of an Increase in the World Real Interest Rate

Because the model here is essentially identical to the real intertemporal model with a real interest rate that is fixed on world credit markets, it is straightforward to use the model to analyze the effects of particular shocks to the domestic economy. The output demand curve and output supply curve shift in the same ways in response to shocks as in the real intertemporal model of Chapter 9, with the only modification in the analysis being that NX adjusts so that the output demand curve intersects the output supply curve at the world real interest rate r^*. The first experiment we carry out is to look at the effects in the model of an increase in the world real interest rate. Such a change could have many causes; it could result from, for example, a negative total factor productivity shock in other countries (recall our analysis of domestic total factor productivity shocks from Chapter 9).

Suppose, in Figure 13.14, that the world real interest rate increases from r_1 to r_2. Then the current account surplus increases causing the output demand curve to shift to the right from Y_1^d to Y_2^d. Domestic investment must decrease, as the real interest rate increases, but domestic consumption may rise or fall as there is a negative effect from the increase in r and a positive effect from the increase in Y.

These results have the interesting implication that a negative total factor productivity shock abroad, which would *decrease* foreign output and cause the world real interest rate to rise, also causes an *increase* in domestic output. Therefore, a foreign shock of this sort, when transmitted to the domestic economy, does not cause output in the domestic economy and in the rest of the world to move together.

FIGURE 13.14 **An Increase in the World Real Interest Rate**

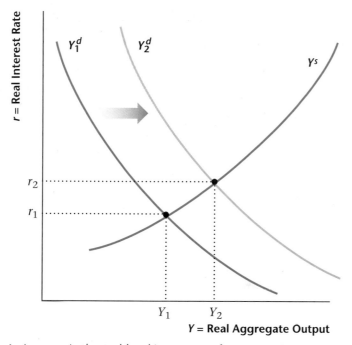

An increase in the world real interest rate from r_1 to r_2 increases output and the current account surplus.

Temporary and Permanent Increases in Government Expenditure and the Effects on the Current Account

For our second experiment, we consider the effects of increases in domestic government expenditure. As we will see, the results depend in important ways on whether the increase in government spending is temporary or permanent, particularly for the response of the current account surplus.

First, we consider the effects of a temporary increase in government spending, that is, an increase in G. Just as in Chapter 9, there is a negative income effect on leisure for the representative consumer, because of the increase in the present value of taxes, and so labour supply increases, shifting the output supply curve rightward from Y_1^s to Y_2^s in Figure 13.15. There is a shift to the right in the output demand curve resulting from the net increase in output demand caused by the increase in G. The current account surplus then adjusts so that the output demand curve ultimately shifts from Y_1^d to Y_2^d (see Figure 13.15). As in Chapter 9, the initial shift in the output supply curve is small relative to the shift in the output demand curve (because the increase in government spending is temporary, so that the effects on lifetime wealth are small). The current account surplus, therefore, must decrease.

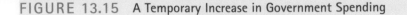

FIGURE 13.15   A Temporary Increase in Government Spending

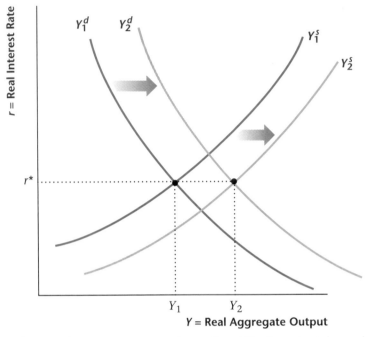

An increase in current government spending shifts the output demand curve and the output supply curve to the right (the output demand curve shifts to a greater extent). Output increases and the current account surplus decreases.

Next, suppose that the increase in government spending is permanent. That is, as in Chapter 9, assume that there are equal increases in current government purchases G, and in future government purchases G'. Then, in Figure 13.16, there is no shift in the output demand curve Y^d as a result of the change in government spending, as the demand for current consumption falls by as much as current government spending rises, given the reduction in lifetime wealth resulting from the tax increases necessary to finance government spending. The output supply curve shifts rightward from Y_1^s to Y_2^s, because of the negative effect of the decrease in lifetime wealth on current leisure. The current account surplus increases until the output demand curve has shifted form Y_1^d to Y_2^d.

The effect of an increase in government spending is quite different depending on whether the increase in government spending is temporary or permanent. A temporary increase in government spending results in a decrease in the current account surplus, consistent with what occurred in the twin deficits episode in the United States during the 1980s (see Figure 13.12). However, a permanent increase in government spending causes an increase in the current account surplus. Therefore, to be consistent with this

FIGURE 13.16   A Permanent Increase in Government Spending

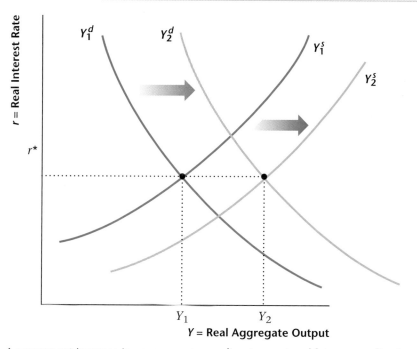

A permanent increase in government spending (current and future spending increase by the same amount) shifts the output supply curve to the right. Domestic output increases, and the current account surplus increases.

model, it would have had to be the case that consumers in the 1980s anticipated that the increase in government spending was temporary. Perhaps this is plausible, as the increase in defense spending during the Reagan administration could have been viewed as temporary spending to finish off the Cold War with the Soviet Union. Permanent decreases in government spending are then a candidate explanation for the decrease in the current account surplus observed during the 1990s in Figure 13.12, though in this case it seems hard to rationalize a public belief that these reductions in government spending were permanent.

The Effects of Increases in Current and Future Total Factor Productivity

In Chapters 5 and 9, we showed how total factor productivity matters for domestic real aggregate activity. An increase in current total factor productivity in a closed economy increases labor demand, and it leads to increases in the real wage, employment, and output, and a decrease in the real interest rate. An anticipated increase in future total factor productivity increases the current demand for investment goods and consumption

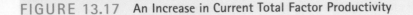

FIGURE 13.17   **An Increase in Current Total Factor Productivity**

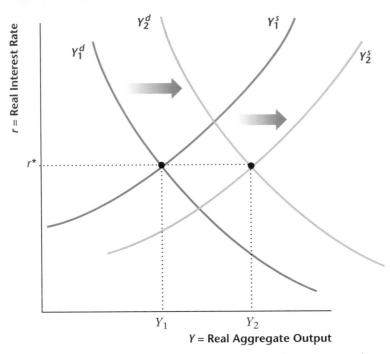

An increase in current total factor productivity shifts the output supply curve to the right. Aggregate output increases, and the current account surplus increases.

goods in a closed economy, and it increases current aggregate output and the real interest rate. In an SOE, some of these results are somewhat different, as the real interest rate is determined on the world credit market. We are also able to determine the effects of total factor productivity shocks on the current account.

Suppose first that current total factor productivity increases. Recall from Chapter 9 that this causes a shift to the right in the output supply curve. In Figure 13.17 the output supply curve shifts from Y_1^s to Y_2^s. Then, the current account surplus increases, shifting the output demand curve to the right from Y_1^d to Y_2^d. As a result, aggregate output increases from Y_1 to Y_2, and there is an increase in the current account surplus. Domestic consumption increases because of the increase in real income, but given that the real interest rate is unchanged there is no effect on investment. In a closed economy, the real interest rate falls when total factor productivity increases, causing increases in C and I. However, the real interest rate is determined on world markets here, and so an increase in total factor productivity in the domestic economy has no effect on the real interest rate. Typically, though, different countries simultaneously experience increases in total factor productivity at the same time, as changes in production technology tend to be transmitted across international borders. Therefore, an increase in total factor productivity domestically would also tend to be associated with a decrease in the world real interest rate and increases in domestic consumption and investment.

Next, suppose that an increase in future total factor productivity is anticipated. Recall from Chapter 9 that this implies the representative firm expects an increase in the future marginal product of capital, which causes an increase in the demand for investment goods. Further, the representative consumer anticipates higher future income as the result of the increase in future total factor productivity, and this causes an increase in the demand for current consumption goods. The increase in the demand for current consumption and investment goods shifts the output demand curve in Figure 13.18 rightward, but there is a corresponding decrease in the current account surplus so that demand equals supply for domestically produced goods. In equilibrium, aggregate output remains fixed at Y_1, but the current account surplus falls.

The above provides a potential explanation, perhaps more plausible than permanent negative government spending shocks, for the reduction in the current account surplus that occurred in the 1990s, observed in Figure 13.12. In particular, in Figure 13.19, there was a large increase in investment expenditures during the 1990s to more

FIGURE 13.18 **An Increase in Future Total Factor Productivity**

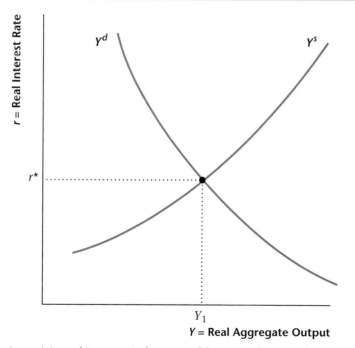

An anticipated increase in future total factor productivity shifts the output demand curve to the right. Aggregate output remains unchanged, and the current account surplus declines.

FIGURE 13.19 Investment as a Percentage of GDP

There was a large increase in investment expenditure as a fraction of GDP in the United States during the 1990s. This is a possible explanation for the increase in the U.S. current account deficit at that time.

Source: Bureau of Economic Analysis, Department of Commerce.

than 19% of GDP in 1999 (before a rapid decrease). This is consistent with anticipated increases in future total factor productivity causing increases in investment spending, which reduced the current account surplus, as in Figure 13.18.

Current Account Deficits, Consumption, and Investment

We have already discussed how a current account deficit need not be a bad thing, as current account deficits help domestic consumers smooth consumption over time. A current account deficit can also serve another purpose, which is to finance domestic investment, as was the case when we considered the effects of an anticipated shock to future total factor productivity in the previous subsection. When a country runs a current account deficit so as to finance an increase in domestic investment expenditures, this increases the capital stock and future productive capacity. In the

FIGURE 13.20 **An Increase in the Capital Stock**

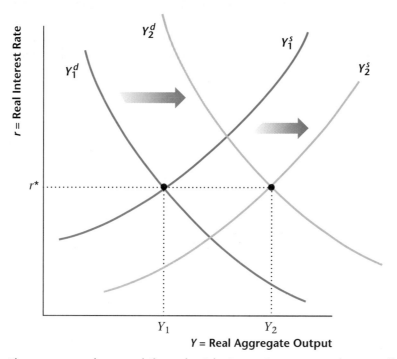

The output supply curve shifts to the right, increasing output and potentially eliminating the current account deficit. Thus, investment financed by a current account deficit can eliminate the current account deficit in the long run.

future, the current account deficit can be eliminated because of this higher productive capacity.

In Figure 13.20 the SOE is initially running a current account deficit. The output demand curve is Y_1^d, the output supply curve is Y_1^s, and current output is Y_1. Now, if the current account deficit is financing domestic investment, in the future the capital stock K will be higher. This will increase the demand for labor and shift the output supply curve to the right, to Y_2^s. Then, the current account surplus increases, shifting the output demand curve to the right to Y_2^d. Thus, if the current account deficit finances domestic investment, this increases future productive capacity, more goods can be sold abroad, and the current account deficit can be eliminated.

Historically, borrowing abroad has been quite useful in promoting development in some countries. For example, the takeoff in economic growth in the United States in the nineteenth century was spurred in part by the construction of railroads, which were partially financed by borrowing abroad. The sizable current account deficit that developed in the United States in the 1990s also appeared to be financing domestic investment in plants, equipment, and housing, and this will permit a higher standard of living in the future and possibly cause an elimination of the current account deficit.

This chapter explored the real macroeconomic implications of having trade in goods and assets among nations. In Chapter 14, we integrate money into the third model that we studied in this chapter so as to understand the determination of nominal exchange rates, the importance of flexible and fixed exchange rates, and why capital controls are important for macroeconomic activity.

CHAPTER SUMMARY

- In this chapter we studied the implications of international trade in goods and assets for domestic welfare, output, consumption, investment, and the current account surplus. We constructed three small open-economy models and showed how these models can be used to understand the importance of openness for the domestic economy. In a small open economy (SOE), domestic residents are price-takers with respect to the rest of the world.

- The first model is one where there are two goods, a and b, consumed and produced in an SOE. The relative price of good a in terms of good b is the terms of trade, or the real exchange rate, and this is the rate at which good b can be traded for good a on world markets.

- The representative consumer in the SOE is always better off by trading on world markets at the terms of trade than by not trading. In equilibrium, domestic production is determined by the condition that the marginal rate of transformation of good a for good b equals the terms of trade, and domestic consumption satisfies the property that the marginal rate of substitution of good a for good b equals the terms of trade.

- An increase in the terms of trade, which here means that good a becomes more expensive relative to good b, always implies that production in the SOE shifts away from production of good b and toward production of good a. However, whether the consumption of goods a or b increases or decreases depends on whether the SOE was an importer or exporter of good a before the change in the terms of trade and on income and substitution effects.

- The second model we considered was a two-period model of a SOE, where the representative consumer has exogenous income in the current and future periods, and the consumer pays taxes to the government in both periods. Government spending is exogenous in each period, and the government and the representative consumer can borrow and lend in the current period.

- In the model, the current account surplus increases whenever national saving increases. An increase in current income leads to an increase in the current account surplus in equilibrium, an increase in government spending leads to a decrease in the current account surplus, a change in taxes has no effect under Ricardian equivalence, and a change in the real interest rate has an indeterminate effect on the current account surplus.

- Current account deficits need not be a bad thing, as this implies borrowing abroad, which helps domestic consumers to smooth their consumption over time.

- In the third small open-economy model, we allowed for the determination of production and investment, with the domestic economy facing an interest rate determined on world markets. Here, the current account surplus is the difference between consumption and absorption, where absorption is the domestic demand for goods, or consumption plus investment plus government spending.

- An increase in the world real interest rate increases domestic output, reduces absorption, and increases the current account surplus.

- A temporary increase in government spending increases domestic absorption and decreases the current account surplus, whereas a permanent increase in government spending increases aggregate output and the current account surplus.

- An increase in current total factor productivity increases domestic output and increases the current account surplus, whereas an anticipated increase in future total factor productivity causes no change in current aggregate output and reduces the current account surplus.

- A current account deficit that finances investment increases the future capital stock and acts to increase future output and reduces the current account deficit in the future.

KEY TERMS

Small open economy (SOE): An economy that trades with the rest of the world, and for which the collective actions of domestic consumers and firms have negligible effects on prices on world markets.

Terms of trade: The relative price at which imports trade for exports on world markets.

Real exchange rate: The terms of trade.

Comparative advantage: How efficient a country is at producing one good relative to another, as compared with the rest of the world. Comparative advantage is determined by the slope of the production possibilities frontier.

Twin deficits: A current account deficit coupled with a government budget deficit.

Absorption: Consumption plus investment plus government expenditures; the quantity of domestically produced goods absorbed through domestic spending.

QUESTIONS FOR REVIEW

1. What is a small open economy?

2. Why is it appropriate to use a small open-economy model to explain events in the United States?

3. In the first model in this chapter, with two goods, what are the conditions that determine production and consumption in the SOE when there is no trade?

4. What are the conditions that determine production and consumption in the SOE when there is trade with the rest of the world?

5. Are the residents of the SOE better off or worse off when they can trade with the rest of the world? Why is this the case?

6. If the terms of trade increase and the SOE initially imports good a, what are the effects on consumption and production of goods a and b in the SOE?

7. If the terms of trade increase and the SOE initially imports good b, what are the effects on consumption and production of goods a and b in the SOE?

8. In the second model in this chapter, what are the four determinants of the current account surplus, and how does each of these determinants affect it?

9. Why could it be a good thing for a country to run a current account deficit?

10. What were the twin deficits of the 1980s, and what caused them?

11. What are the effects of an increase in the world real interest rate on output, absorption, and the current account surplus?

12. What are the effects of temporary and permanent increases in government expenditure on output, absorption, and the current account surplus?

13. What are the effects of an increase in current and future total factor productivity on output, absorption, and the current account balance?

14. If an increase in the current account deficit finances an increase in domestic investment, what implications does this have for the future performance of the economy?

PROBLEMS

1. Suppose that, in the model where two goods a and b are produced domestically and traded internationally, the representative consumer's preferences change so that the marginal rate of substitution of good a for good b increases for each consumption bundle. That is, the consumer is now less willing to give up good a in exchange for good b. Determine the effects of this change in preferences on the production of goods a and b in the SOE, on consumption of goods a and b, and on the quantities of goods a and b imported and exported. Explain your results.

2. Suppose that there is an improvement in the technology for producing good b in the SOE. This implies that the marginal rate of transformation, $MRT_{a,b}$, increases for each quantity of good a. Determine the effects of this technology change on the consumption of goods a and b, the production of goods a and b, and the quantities of goods a and b imported and exported. Explain your results in terms of income and substitution effects, and interpret.

3. The government imposes a quota on imports. Determine the effect of this on production and consumption of goods a and b in the first model in this chapter. Also determine the effect on the consumer's welfare. Explain your results.

4. Assume a two-period model where the representative consumer has income of 100 in the current period, income of 120 in the future period, and faces a world real interest rate of 10% per period. The consumer always wishes to set current consumption equal to future consumption, which implies perfect-complements preferences.
   (a) Suppose that current and future government expenditures are 15 and 20, respectively in the future. Determine consumption in the current and future periods, and the current account surplus. Draw a diagram to illustrate your results.
   (b) Now, suppose that current government expenditures increases to 25, with everything else unchanged. Again, determine consumption in the current and future periods and the current account surplus, and show these in your diagram.
   (c) Explain the difference in your results in parts (a) and (b).

5. Modify the second model in this chapter as follows: Suppose that real interest rates are determined on world markets. The government can borrow and lend on world markets at the interest rate r, but the representative consumer lends at the interest rate r and borrows at the interest rate r^*, which is also determined on world markets. Assume that $r^* > r$, perhaps because of the costs of operating international banks that make loans to consumers.
   (a) Suppose that r^* increases, with r unchanged. Determine the effects on consumption in the current and future periods, and on the current account balance, and explain your results in terms of income and substitution effects.
   (b) Now, suppose that the government cuts current taxes and increases future taxes, holding constant government spending in the current and future periods. Assume, before the tax cut is put into effect, that the current account surplus is zero. Determine the effects of the tax cut in period 1 on consumption in the current and future periods, the trade balance, and the welfare of the representative consumer. Explain your results.

6. Use the third model in this chapter to answer this question. The government in a small open economy is concerned that the current account deficit is too high. One group of economic advisers to the government argues that high government deficits cause the current account deficit to be high and that the way to reduce the current account deficit is to increase taxes. A second group of economic advisers argues that the high current account deficit is caused by high domestic investment and proposes that domestic investment should be taxed, with these investment taxes returned to consumers as lump-sum transfers.

   (a) Which advice should the government take if its goal is to reduce the current account deficit? Explain.

   (b) Is the government's goal of reducing the current account deficit sensible? Why or why not? What will happen if the government takes the advice that achieves its goal, as in part (a)?

7. In the second model in this chapter, determine the effects of an increase in future government spending on current consumption, future consumption, and the current account surplus, and explain your results.

8. In Chapter 11, we studied how persistent total factor productivity shocks in a closed economy can provide an explanation for business cycles. In the third model studied in this chapter, determine the effects of a persistent increase in total factor productivity on domestic output, consumption, investment, and the current account surplus. Are the predictions of the model consistent with what you observe in Figure 13.10? Explain why or why not.

9. An increase in government spending is anticipated in the future. What effects does this have on current output, consumption, investment, and the current account surplus? Explain your results.

WORKING WITH THE DATA

1. Answer the following:
   (a) Calculate the relative price of energy, as the ratio of the producer price index for fuels and related products and power to the producer price index, and plot this as a time series.

   (b) Calculate the real quantity of imports of petroleum and petroleum products, as the ratio of imports of petroleum and petroleum products (nominal) to the consumer price index, and plot this as a time series.

   (c) Calculate the annual percentage increase in the relative price of energy (December to December) and the annual percentage increase in the real quantity of imports of petroleum and petroleum products (fourth quarter to fourth quarter), and plot one variable against the other in a scatter plot.

   (d) Explain what you see in time series and scatter plots from parts (a) to (c), and interpret this in terms of the predictions of the first model in this chapter concerning the effects of changes in the terms of trade.

2. Answer the following:
   (a) Calculate consumption (C), investment (I), government spending (G), and net exports (NX), as percentages of GDP (Y) for the years 1947–2003.

   (b) Construct scatter plots of NX/Y vs. C/Y, NX/Y vs. I/Y, and NX/Y vs. G/Y for the years 1947–2003. What do you observe? What do these data tell us about the primary causes of fluctuations in the current account?

CHAPTER 14

Money in the Open Economy

Many issues in international macroeconomics can be well understood without the complication of monetary exchange in the picture, as we saw in Chapter 13. However, there are also many intriguing issues in international finance—particularly those involving the determination of nominal exchange rates, the effects of having flexible or fixed exchange rates, the transmission of nominal macroeconomic shocks among countries, the effects of capital controls, and the role of international financial institutions—that we need monetary models to understand. In this chapter, we build on the third small open-economy model we studied in Chapter 13 to integrate money into a monetary small open-economy model that can address some key issues in international monetary economics.

We will first consider the notion of purchasing power parity, or the law of one price, which is a cornerstone of the monetary small open-economy model in this chapter. Purchasing power parity would hold if the prices of all goods in the world economy were equal, corrected for nominal exchange rates, where a nominal exchange rate is the price of one currency in terms of another. While there are economic forces that result in a long-run tendency toward purchasing power parity, in reality there can be fairly large and persistent deviations from purchasing power parity, some examples of which we study in this chapter. However, although purchasing power parity may not be the best approximation to reality in the short run, it proves to be very useful in simplifying the model used in this chapter.

The monetary small open-economy model we construct and put to work in this chapter builds on the third small open-economy model from Chapter 13, in that the goods markets in the two models are identical. The model of this chapter also has much in common with the monetary intertemporal model in Chapter 10. In particular, the monetary small open-economy model features a classical dichotomy, in that nominal variables—in this case, the price level and the nominal exchange rate—are determined independently of real variables. Further, money is neutral. This is a useful starting point for international monetary economics, because adding some of the frictions that we considered in the business cycle models of Chapters 11 and 12—sticky wages, the money surprise mechanism, and coordination failures—involves straightforward extensions of this basic framework.

The first experiments we carry out with the model in this chapter emphasize the effects of shocks from abroad under flexible and fixed nominal exchange rates. A flexible exchange rate is free to move according to supply and demand in the market for foreign exchange, whereas under a fixed exchange rate the domestic government commits in some fashion to supporting the nominal exchange rate at a specified value. A flexible exchange rate has the property that monetary policy can be set independently in the domestic economy, and the domestic price level is not affected by changes in foreign prices. Under a fixed exchange rate, however, the domestic central bank cannot control its money supply independently, and price level changes originating abroad are essentially imported to the domestic economy. Flexible and fixed exchange rate regimes each have their own advantages and disadvantages, as we discuss.

Finally, we examine the effects of capital controls on the behavior of the domestic economy. Capital controls are restrictions on the international flow of assets, and these controls tend to dampen the fluctuations that result from some shocks to the economy. Capital controls are detrimental, however, in that they reduce economic efficiency.

THE NOMINAL EXCHANGE RATE, THE REAL EXCHANGE RATE, AND PURCHASING POWER PARITY

The model we work with in this chapter is a monetary small open-economy model, which builds on the third small open-economy model of Chapter 13 and the monetary intertemporal model in Chapter 10. Key variables in this model are the nominal exchange rate and the real exchange rate, which are defined in this section. Further, in this section we derive the purchasing power parity relationship, which determines the value of the real exchange rate.

In the model in this chapter, just as in the monetary intertemporal model, all domestically produced goods sell at a price P, in terms of domestic currency. Foreign-produced goods sell at the price P^*, in terms of foreign currency. In the model, there is a market for foreign exchange, on which domestic currency can be traded for foreign currency, and we let e denote the price of one unit of foreign currency in terms of domestic currency. That is, e is the **nominal exchange rate.** Therefore, if a domestic resident holding domestic currency wished to buy goods abroad, assuming that foreign producers of goods accept only foreign currency in exchange for their goods, one unit of foreign goods costs eP^* in units of domestic currency. This is because the domestic resident must first buy foreign currency with domestic currency, at a price of e, and then buy foreign goods with foreign currency at a price of P^*. To give an example, suppose that a book in England costs five British pounds, and that the exchange rate between U.S. dollars and British Pounds is two U.S. dollars per British Pound, that is, $e = 2$. Then, the cost of the book in U.S. dollars is $2 \times 5 = 10$.

Because the price of domestic goods in domestic currency is P, and the price of foreign goods in terms of domestic currency is eP^*, the real exchange rate (or the terms of trade), which is the price of foreign goods in terms of domestic goods, is

$$\text{Real exchange rate} = \frac{eP^*}{P}.$$

Now, suppose that it is costless to transport goods between foreign countries and the domestic country and that there are no trade barriers, such as government-set import quotas and tariffs (import taxes). Then, if $eP^* > P$, it would be cheaper to buy goods domestically than abroad, so that foreign consumers would want to buy domestic goods rather than foreign goods, and this would tend to increase P. Alternatively, if $eP^* < P$, then foreign goods would be cheaper than domestic goods, and so domestic consumers would prefer to purchase foreign goods rather than domestic goods, in which case P would tend to fall. Thus, with no transportation costs and no trade barriers, we should expect to observe that

$$P = eP^*, \tag{14.1}$$

and this relationship is called **purchasing power parity (PPP).** This relationship is also called the **law of one price,** as, if it holds, the price of goods is the same, in terms of domestic currency, at home and abroad. If PPP holds, then the real exchange rate is 1.

In the real world, we would not in general expect PPP to hold exactly if we measure P and P^* as the price levels in two different countries. Any measure of the price level, such as the consumer price index or the implicit GDP price deflator, includes the prices of a large set of goods produced and consumed in the economy. Some of these goods are traded on world markets, such as agricultural commodities and raw materials, while other goods are only traded domestically, such as local services like haircuts. While we would expect that there would be a tendency for the law of one price to hold for goods that are traded internationally, we would not expect it to hold for nontraded goods. For example, crude oil can be shipped at relatively low cost over large distances by pipeline and in large oil tankers, and there is a well-organized world market for crude oil, so that crude oil sells almost anywhere in the world at close to the same price (plus transport costs). However, there is not a world market in haircuts, as the cost of traveling to another country for a haircut is in most cases very large relative to the cost of the haircut. The law of one price should hold for crude oil but not for haircuts.

In general, there are strong economic forces that tend to make market prices and nominal exchange rates adjust so that PPP applies. For example, if PPP does not apply, then even if there are large costs of transporting goods across countries, consumers would want to move to where goods are relatively cheaper, and firms would want to move their production where goods are relatively more expensive, and ultimately we would expect PPP to hold over the long run. Unless it is very difficult to move goods, labor, and capital across international borders, purchasing power parity should hold, at least as a long-run relationship. Though PPP may be a poor description of short-run reality, as we show in the next section, and the adjustment to PPP may be quite slow, it simplifies our models considerably to make the PPP assumption, and this simplification helps us focus on the issues of this chapter.

• •

THE BIG MAC INDEX AND THE PPP RELATIONSHIP FOR THE UNITED STATES AND CANADA

THEORY confronts the DATA

If purchasing power parity (PPP) holds for each good, then a particular good should sell at the same price worldwide, corrected for foreign exchange rates. At the aggregate level, if PPP holds, then the real exchange rate, in terms of price indices, should remain fixed over time. In this section, we show that there are important deviations from purchasing power parity for Big Macs—a homogeneous good sold worldwide—and that the real exchange rate varies significantly for two countries with a close trading relationship—the United States and Canada.

Table 14.1   **Purchasing Power Parity and the Big Mac Index**

Country	P*	e	$\frac{eP^*}{P}$
Argentina	4.10	0.347	0.525
Australia	3.00	0.621	0.686
Brazil	4.55	0.326	0.547
Britain	1.99	0.633	0.465
Canada	3.20	0.690	0.814
Chile	1400	0.0014	0.722
China	9.90	0.121	0.441
Czech Republic	56.57	0.035	0.722
Denmark	27.75	0.147	1.510
Euro Area	2.71	0.909	0.909
Japan	262	0.0083	0.806
Mexico	23	0.095	0.806
New Zealand	3.95	0.562	0.819
Russia	41	0.032	0.486
Sweden	30	0.120	1.327
Thailand	59	0.023	0.510

Source: *The Economist*, April 26–May 2, 2003 pg. 68.

An interesting example of deviations from purchasing power parity for a single good is the **Big Mac index,** published by *The Economist*. The Big Mac is a homogeneous product; it is essentially identical wherever it is sold by McDonald's. Table 14.1 shows data from April 2003 for a set of 16 countries, which shows the price in local currency of a Big Mac (P^*), the exchange rate e between the U.S. dollars and the local currency, and the real exchange rate in terms of Big Macs, $\frac{eP^*}{P}$. The price of a Big Mac in the United States in April 2003 was $P = \$2.71$.

Table 14.1 shows that there are sometimes large deviations from purchasing power parity in terms of Big Macs. While PPP predicts a real exchange rate of 1, the real exchange rate for Big Macs is less than 1 for most countries. For example, the real exchange rate for China is 44.1% of what PPP predicts. Only Sweden and Denmark have Big Mac real exchange rates greater than 1. Thus, it would typically be cheaper to exchange U.S. dollars for foreign currency and purchase a Big Mac in a foreign country (except for Scandinavian countries), rather than purchasing a Big Mac in the United States. This of course ignores the cost of travelling to the foreign country. While Big Macs are essentially the same product no matter where they are sold, they are not traded between countries, so it should not be surprising that hamburgers might be relatively cheaper in other countries of the world than in the United States.

A case where we might expect relatively small deviations from PPP involves the relationship between the United States and Canada. Historically, there has been a high volume of trade between these two countries. The United States and Canada signed a free trade agreement in 1989, which was replaced in 1992 by the North American Free Trade Agreement (NAFTA), which included Mexico. An earlier trade agreement was the Canada-U.S. Auto Pact, signed in 1965, which permitted the shipment of autos and auto parts across the Canada-U.S. border by manufacturers. Given the close proximity of Canada and the United States, and natural north-south transportation links, transportation costs between the United States and Canada are quite low. Not only are goods easy to move between these two countries, but NAFTA now permits freer movement of labor across the Canada-U.S. border as well. Capital is also relatively free to move between these two countries. Therefore, there are especially strong forces in place in the U.S.-Canada case that would cause us to be surprised if PPP did not apply, at least approximately.

In Figure 14.1 we show the real exchange rate, $\frac{eP^*}{P}$, for Canada versus the United States for the years 1950–2003. Here, e is the price of Canadian dollars in terms of U.S. dollars, P^* is the Canadian consumer price index, and P is the CPI in the United States. The real exchange rate has been scaled for convenience, so that its value is 100 in

FIGURE 14.1 The Real Exchange Rate for Canada vs. the United States

Purchasing power parity predicts that the real exchange rate should be a constant, but there have been large and persistent deviations from PPP in this case.

Source: Statistics Canada and Bureau of Labor Statistics.

October 1950. Purchasing power parity predicts that the real exchange rate in the figure should be constant, but it is certainly not. In the figure, the real exchange rate has fluctuated significantly. The fluctuations are not small short-run fluctuations around a constant value but are more persistent in nature. Indeed, there appears to be no tendency for the real exchange rate to fluctuate more closely around some long-run value after the free trade agreement in 1989. Between 1989 and 2002, the real exchange rate decreased by more than 40%. If there are such large deviations from PPP for Canada and the United States, we should expect PPP relationships to be even more loose in the short run between the United States and other countries of the world.

FLEXIBLE AND FIXED EXCHANGE RATES

In addition to PPP, another important component of the monetary small open-economy model is the exchange rate regime. As we show, a key determinant of how the domestic economy responds to shocks, and an important factor for the conduct of domestic monetary and fiscal policy, is the set of rules for government intervention in foreign exchange markets. Roughly speaking, the polar extremes in foreign exchange market intervention are a **flexible exchange rate regime** and a **fixed exchange rate regime.** Currently, there are countries in the world that conform closely to an idealized flexible exchange rate regime, others that fix the exchange rate, and some countries that mix the two approaches.

Under a flexible or floating exchange rate, there is no intervention by the domestic fiscal or monetary authorities to specifically target the nominal exchange rate e. If the nominal exchange rate is truly flexible, it is free to move in response to market forces. Some countries with flexible exchange rates[1] are India, South Korea, Brazil, Australia, New Zealand, Canada, and the United States. For reasons we discuss ahead, essentially all countries care about short-run movements in their nominal exchange rate, and they therefore intervene from time to time, through monetary and fiscal policy to influence the value of the nominal exchange rate, even under a flexible exchange rate regime.

There are several different important fixed exchange rate systems, which can be roughly characterized as **hard pegs** and **soft pegs.** Under a hard peg, a country commits to a fixed nominal exchange rate relative to some other currency for the indefinite future. With a soft peg, there is no long-term commitment to a particular value for the exchange rate, but the exchange rate can be fixed relative to another currency for long periods of time, with periodic **devaluations** (increases in the nominal exchange rate e) and **revaluations** (decreases in e).

A hard peg can be implemented in basically three different ways. First, a country could abandon its national currency and **dollarize.** Dollarization essentially involves using the currency of another country as the national medium of exchange. For example, Ecuador currently uses the U.S. dollar as its national currency, though dollarization can refer to a situation in which a country uses a currency other than the U.S. dollar.

---

[1] See http://fx.sauder.ubc.ca/currency_table.html.

A disadvantage of dollarizing is that a country relinquishes its ability to collect seignorage (discussed in Chapter 10); that is, it cannot print money to finance government spending.

The second way to implement a hard peg is through the establishment of a **currency board.** With a currency board, there is a centralized institution, which could be the country's central bank, that holds interest-bearing assets denominated in the currency of the country against which the nominal exchange rate is being fixed. This institution then stands ready to exchange domestic currency for foreign currency at a specified fixed exchange rate, and it can buy and sell interest-bearing assets in order to carry out these exchanges. A country that currently uses a currency board is Hong Kong, which fixes its nominal exchange rate relative to the U.S. dollar. Under a currency board, a country maintains its ability to collect seignorage.

Finally, a third approach to implementing a hard peg is through mutual agreement among countries to a common currency, as in the **European Monetary Union (EMU)**, which was established in 1999. Most European countries are EMU members, with some notable exceptions such as the United Kingdom. The common currency of the EMU is the **Euro**, and the supply of Euros is managed by the **European Central Bank (ECB)**. The rules governing the operation of the ECB specify how the seignorage revenue from the printing of new Euros is to be split among the EMU members.

Soft pegs involve various degrees of commitment to a fixed exchange rate or to target bands for the exchange rate. For example, under the **European Monetary System (EMS)**, which was established in 1979 and preceded the EMU, member European countries committed over the short run to target their exchange rates within specified ranges. In this arrangement, coordination was required among the EMS members, and there were periodic crises and changes in target bands for exchange rates. Another soft peg was the **Bretton Woods arrangement**, the rules for which were specified in an agreement negotiated at Bretton Woods, New Hampshire, in 1944. The Bretton Woods arrangement governed post–World War II international monetary relations until 1971. Under Bretton Woods, the United States fixed the value of the U.S. dollar relative to gold, by agreeing to exchange U.S. dollars for gold at a specified price. All other countries then agreed to fix their exchange rates relative to the U.S. dollar. This was, thus, a modified gold standard arrangement. For reasons we discuss later in this chapter, soft peg arrangements have tended to be unstable; the arrangements typically collapse and are replaced by alternative systems, as was the case with the EMS and the Bretton Woods arrangement.

A key international monetary institution that plays an important role in exchange rate determination is the **International Monetary Fund (IMF)**, the framework for which was discussed at Bretton Woods in 1944, with the IMF established in 1946. The IMF currently has 184 member countries, and it performs a function that is in some ways similar to the one carried out by a central bank relative to the domestic banks under its supervision. Namely, the IMF plays the role of a **lender of last resort** for its member countries, just as a central bank is a lender of last resort for domestic financial institutions (as we discuss in Chapter 15). The IMF stands ready to lend to member countries in distress, though IMF lending comes with strings attached. Typically, IMF lending is conditional on a member country submitting to a program set up by the IMF, which typically specifies corrective policy actions.

A MONETARY SMALL OPEN–ECONOMY MODEL WITH A FLEXIBLE EXCHANGE RATE

Now that we have discussed some of the institutional arrangements governing the determination of exchange rates, we can proceed to work with a monetary small open-economy model in which there is international monetary interaction. This model is in part based on the monetary intertemporal model in Chapter 10. This is a small open-economy model that essentially involves adding a money market to the third real small open-economy model in Chapter 13. In this model, we assume for now that the exchange rate is flexible, and we study the properties of a fixed exchange rate system in the next section.

In Figure 14.2 we show the goods market for the monetary small open-economy model, which is identical to the goods market for the third real small open-economy model of Chapter 13. The curve Y^d is the output demand curve, which is downward-sloping because of the negative effect of the real interest rate on the demand for consumption and investment goods, and Y^s is the output supply curve, which is upward sloping because of the intertemporal substitution effect of the real interest rate on labor supply. The output supply and output demand curve shift as the result of factors discussed in detail in Chapter 13. Just as in Chapter 13, the small open-economy assumption implies that domestic firms and consumers are collectively price-takers on world markets. In equilibrium, the income-expenditure identity holds, so that $Y = C + I + G + NX$. Given that the domestic economy is, as a whole, a price-taker on world markets, any output not absorbed domestically as C, I, or G is exported (if net exports are positive) or any excess of domestic absorption over domestic output is purchased abroad (if net exports are negative).

We assume that PPP holds, so that

$$P = eP^*, \tag{14.2}$$

where P is the domestic price level, e is the price of foreign exchange in terms of domestic currency, and P^* is the foreign price level. Though we know from above that the PPP relationship typically does not hold in the short run, assuming PPP simplifies our model greatly and essentially implies that we are ignoring the effects of changes in the terms of trade (discussed in Chapter 13), which would cloud some of the issues we want to discuss here. Given the assumption of a small open economy, events in the domestic economy have no effect on the foreign price level P^*, and so we treat P^* as exogenous. However, the domestic price level P and the exchange rate e are endogenous variables. The exchange rate is flexible, in that it is determined by market forces, as we show below.

Next, we want to determine how the money market works in our equilibrium model. As in Chapter 10, money demand is given by

$$M^d = PL(Y, r^*), \tag{14.3}$$

FIGURE 14.2 The Goods Market in the Monetary Small Open–Economy Model

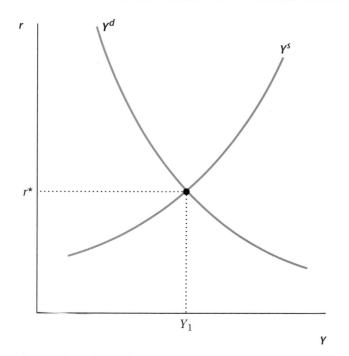

The goods market in this model is identical to the goods market in the real small open-economy model with investment in Chapter 13. The world real interest rate is r^*, and equilibrium real output is Y_1. The current account surplus adjusts so that the Y^d curve intersects the Y^s curve at the world real interest rate r^*.

where $L(Y, r^*)$ denotes the demand for real money balances, which depends positively on aggregate real income Y and negatively on the real interest rate. Here, recall that the domestic real interest rate is identical to the world real interest rate r^*, and we are assuming no long-run money growth, so that the domestic inflation rate is zero and the real interest rate is equal to the nominal interest rate given the Fisher relation (see Chapter 10). Now, given the PPP relation, Equation (14.2), we can substitute in Equation (14.3) for P to get

$$M^d = eP^*L(Y, r^*).$$

We take the nominal money supply to be exogenous, with $M^s = M$. In equilibrium, money supply equals money demand, so that $M^s = M^d$, or

$$M = eP^*L(Y, r^*). \tag{14.4}$$

In Figure 14.3, money demand and money supply are on the horizontal axis, while e, the exchange rate, is on the vertical axis. Then, given Y and r^*, money demand M^d is a

FIGURE 14.3   **The Money Market in the Monetary Small Open-Economy Model with a Flexible Exchange Rate**

With a flexible exchange rate, and given purchasing power parity, the equilibrium nominal exchange rate is e_1, determined by the intersection of the nominal money supply and nominal money demand curves.

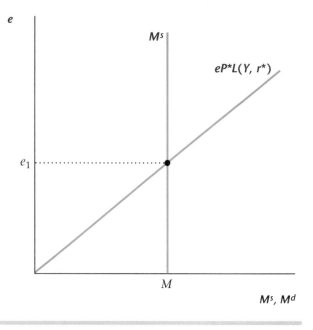

straight line through the origin in the figure, while money supply M^s is a vertical line at $M^s = M$. The intersection of the supply and demand curves for money then determines the nominal exchange rate e, so that the equilibrium exchange rate in the figure is e_1. Once we have determined e, we have also determined the domestic price level P from the PPP equation, (14.2).

Thus, in this model, the nominal exchange rate is determined by the nominal demand for money relative to the nominal supply of money. Because the nominal exchange rate is a nominal variable, this seems natural. Movements in the exchange rate are caused either by a shift in money demand or a shift in money supply.

The Neutrality of Money with a Flexible Exchange Rate

Now that we have set up the model, we can proceed to study its properties. Just as in the monetary intertemporal model we studied in Chapter 10, this model features a classical dichotomy, in that real variables (the level of output, the current account surplus, consumption, and investment) are determined independently of nominal variables (the domestic price level P and the nominal exchange rate e). In Figure 14.3, the nominal exchange rate is determined by the supply and demand for money, and the level of the nominal exchange rate has no bearing on real variables.

If the central bank increases the money supply, say from M_1 to M_2 in Figure 14.4, this has the effect of shifting the money supply curve rightward from M_1^s to M_2^s.

FIGURE 14.4   **An Increase in the Money Supply in the Monetary Small
Open-Economy Model with a Flexible Exchange Rate**

Money is neutral in the monetary small open-economy model with a flexible exchange rate. An increase in the money supply causes the nominal exchange rate and the price level to increase in proportion to the increase in the money supply, with no effect on real variables.

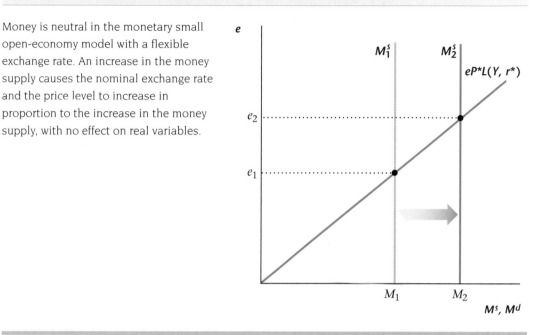

In equilibrium, the nominal exchange rate increases from e_1 to e_2, and there is no effect on the level of real output, the real interest rate (which is the real interest rate on world markets, r^*), consumption, investment, or the current account surplus. Because the price of foreign currency has risen in terms of domestic currency, we say that there is a **depreciation** of the domestic currency. Ultimately, because Equation (14.4) implies that

$$\frac{M}{e} = P^*L(Y, r^*),$$

and because P^*, Y, and r^* remain unaffected by the change in the money supply, $\frac{M}{e}$ remains unchanged. Thus, the nominal exchange rate increases in proportion to the money supply; for example, if the money supply increased by 5%, the nominal exchange rate would also increase by 5%. Further, because PPP holds, or $P = eP^*$, and because P^* is fixed, the price level P also increases in proportion to the increase in the money supply.

Thus, money is neutral in this model economy with a flexible exchange rate. There are no real effects of an increase in the nominal money supply, but all money prices, including the nominal exchange rate, increase in proportion to the increase in the money supply. While most macroeconomists adopt the view that money is neutral in the long run in an open economy, there are differences of opinion about the short-run neutrality of money and the explanations for any nonneutralities of money, just as in closed-economy macroeconomics. As mentioned earlier, it is possible to extend this model to include frictions such as the money surprise mechanism or sticky wages from Chapters 11 and 12, under which money is not neutral in the open economy in the short run. In this chapter we cannot do everything, and we stick to the basic monetary small open-economy model.

A Nominal Shock to the Domestic Economy from Abroad: P* Increases

We would like to use the monetary small open-economy model to investigate how the domestic economy is affected by events in the rest of the world. The first example we consider is the case of an increase in the price level in the rest of the world, which is essentially a nominal shock to the domestic economy. We see that a flexible exchange rate system has an insulating property with respect to increases in the foreign price level. That is, the nominal exchange rate adjusts to exactly offset the increase in the foreign price level, and there are no effects on the domestic price level or domestic real variables. In particular, the temporary foreign inflation resulting from the increase in the foreign price level is not imported to the domestic economy.

Suppose that P^* increases from P_1^* to P_2^*, perhaps because central banks in foreign countries increase the quantity of foreign money in circulation. Then, in Figure 14.5, the

---

FIGURE 14.5   **An Increase in the Foreign Price Level in the Monetary Small Open-Economy Model with a Flexible Exchange Rate**

If the foreign price level increases, this shifts the nominal money demand curve to the right, with the nominal exchange rate falling from e_1 to e_2 in equilibrium. The decrease in the nominal exchange rate exactly offsets the increase in the foreign price level, and there is no effect on the domestic price level.

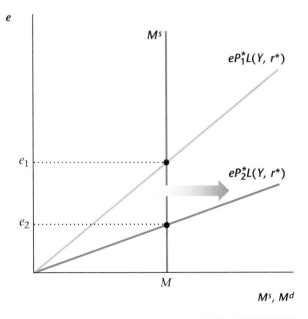

money demand curve shifts rightward from $eP_1^*L(Y, r^*)$ to $eP_2^*L(Y, r^*)$. In equilibrium, there is no effect on real variables, but the nominal exchange rate falls from e_1 to e_2, so that there is an **appreciation** of the domestic currency. Because $P = eP^*$, from Equation (14.4) we have

$$\frac{M}{P} = L(Y, r^*),$$

and because M, Y, and r^* remain unchanged, P is also unchanged. Therefore, no domestic variables were affected by the price level change in the rest of the world. In particular, the appreciation of the domestic currency was just sufficient to offset the effect of the increase in P^* on the domestic price level. That is, the flexible exchange rate insulated the domestic economy from the nominal shock from abroad. This is certainly a desirable property of a flexible exchange rate regime. Under flexible exchange rates, the domestic price level, and by implication the domestic inflation rate, is determined by the quantity of domestic money supplied by the domestic central bank, and it is not influenced by how monetary policy is conducted by foreign central banks.

A Real Shock to the Domestic Economy from Abroad

As an experiment to determine how real domestic variables, the nominal exchange rate, and the price level respond to a real disturbance transmitted from abroad, we examine the effects of an increase in the world real interest rate. Such a shock could result, for example, from a decrease in total factor productivity in the rest of the world (recall our analysis of the effects of total factor productivity shocks from Chapter 9). As we show, a flexible exchange rate cannot shield the domestic economy from the effects of a change in the world real interest rate; the nominal exchange rate appreciates (e falls), and the price level falls.

In Figure 14.6 the world real interest rate increases from r_1^* to r_2^*. The real effects of this are the same as we considered for the third real small open-economy model in Chapter 12. In Figure 14.6(a), the current account surplus increases, shifting the output demand curve to the right until it comes to rest at Y_2^d. Output increases from Y_1 to Y_2 because of the increase in labor supply that results from intertemporal substitution of leisure by the representative consumer. The increase in the real interest rate causes domestic consumption expenditures and investment expenditures to fall, though the increase in current income causes consumption to rise. On net, consumption may rise or fall. Total domestic absorption, $C + I + G$, may rise or fall, but any increase in absorption is smaller than the increase in domestic output, so that the current account surplus rises.

The nominal effects of the increase in the world real interest rate depend on how the demand for money changes. The increase in the real interest rate causes the demand for money to fall, while the increase in domestic output causes the demand for money to rise. It is not clear whether $L(Y_2, r_2^*) < L(Y_1, r_1^*)$ or $L(Y_2, r_2^*) > L(Y_1, r_1^*)$. However, if real money demand is much more responsive to real income than to the interest rate, then money demand will rise, and the money demand curve in Figure 14.6(b) shifts to

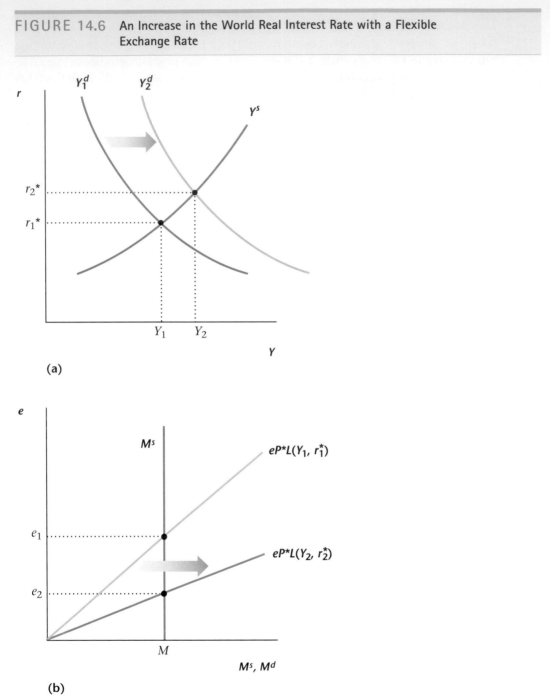

(a)

(b)

Under a flexible exchange rate, if the world real interest rate increases, this causes real output to rise, and the money demand curve shifts to the right, assuming money demand is much more responsive to real income than to the real interest rate. The nominal exchange rate decreases in equilibrium.

the right. In equilibrium, the exchange rate appreciates, with the nominal exchange rate decreasing from e_1 to e_2. As purchasing power parity holds—that is, $P = eP^*-$, with P^* constant, P falls in proportion to the decrease in e. Thus, the increase in the world real interest rate leads to an exchange rate appreciation and a decrease in the price level. Clearly, the flexible exchange rate cannot automatically insulate the domestic economy from real shocks that occur abroad. For example, if the central bank wished to stabilize the price level in the face of the increase in the world real interest rate, it would have to increase the money supply in response to the increase in money demand resulting from the shock.

MACROECONOMICS IN ACTION

The Asian Crisis

In 1997, there was a sharp depreciation in nominal exchange rates in East Asia, primarily in Indonesia, South Korea, Malaysia, and Thailand, and these exchange rate depreciations were the first symptoms of what became known as the Asian crisis. From 1996 until the fall of 1997, the nominal exchange rate (the price of a U.S. dollar in terms of domestic currency) increased by 98.5% in Indonesia, 110.7% in South Korea, 54.4% in Malaysia, and 86.5% in Thailand.[1] What could cause nominal exchange rates to depreciate so dramatically in East Asia over so short a time period? Some answers are provided in a National Bureau of Economic Research working paper, "What Caused the Asian Currency and Financial Crisis?" by Giancarlo Corsetti, Paolo Pesenti, and Nouriel Roubini, hereafter referred to as CPR.

At the time of the Asian crisis, Indonesia, South Korea, Malaysia, and Thailand were under flexible exchange rate regimes; thus, the model we worked with above should be useful in understanding the large exchange rate depreciation that oc-

curred. The model tells us that a large exchange rate depreciation (a large increase in e) would have to occur because the demand for money fell abruptly or because there was a large increase in the domestic money supply. In our model, money demand could fall because real GDP fell, and so let us first consider the possibility that money demand fell because of a reduction in real GDP in East Asia. This was certainly not the case. Economic growth had been quite strong in East Asia before and during the 1990s. Indeed, in Chapter 8, we discussed the miraculous growth performance of the "East Asian tigers," which included South Korea. From CPR, the growth rates in real GDP in 1996 for Indonesia, South Korea, Malaysia, and Thailand were 7.98%, 7.10%, 8.58%, and 5.52%, respectively. These rates of growth were very high relative to average growth rates in GDP in other countries, and growth continued to be high for most of these countries in 1997, though lower than in 1996. The exception is Thailand, which had negative real GDP growth in 1997.

(continued)

In general, though, for these countries money demand would have been increasing rather than decreasing because of growth in real GDP, and so this does not seem to explain the large nominal exchange rate depreciations.

To consider a second possibility, the exchange rate depreciations could have been caused during the Asian crisis by rapid growth in the money supply. However, rapid growth in the money supply typically results in a high domestic inflation rate (recall our analysis from Chapter 9), and inflation rates in Indonesia, South Korea, Malaysia, and Thailand, in 1997, from CPR, were 11.62%, 4.45%, 2.66%, and 5.61%, respectively, which are certainly moderate relative to the size of the exchange rate depreciations. Thus, money supply growth does not seem to be a potential explanation.

The only other potential explanation could be a dramatic shift in the demand for the currencies of Indonesia, South Korea, Malaysia, and Thailand, and this explanation appears to be in agreement with the analysis of CPR. They argue that these four countries were running large current account deficits prior to the Asian crisis, and that these current account deficits were financing investment that would ultimately have poor returns. That is, the domestic financial institutions in these countries were badly regulated, and they were borrowing abroad to make loans to finance domestic investment projects that would ultimately have poor returns. In terms of our analysis of current account deficits from Chapter 12, international lenders became concerned that the large current account deficits in East Asia were not sustainable. That is, to ultimately pay off the foreign debt resulting from large current account deficits, these countries would have to generate large current account surpluses in the future. International lenders to these countries did not appear to believe that the capital stocks in these countries would increase sufficiently to produce high enough future current account surpluses.

The result was a loss in confidence in East Asia on the part of international lenders, who discontinued lending to these countries. Effectively, this loss in confidence works much like a loss in confidence in the domestic banking system. In a domestic banking panic, deposits are withdrawn from banks and converted into domestic currency. In the case of the Asian crisis, the deposits of foreign lenders were withdrawn from East Asian banks and converted into assets denominated in non-East Asian currencies. This is effectively a fall in the demand for East Asian currencies, and it results in an exchange rate depreciation, as in our model.

Why was the Asian crisis a crisis? The main risk from the large exchange rate depreciations was the possibility of a widespread failure of East Asian financial institutions. These institutions were having difficulty borrowing abroad to finance long-term lending, and the exchange rate depreciation implied that the real value of the liabilities of these institutions had increased a great deal relative to the real value of their assets. East Asian financial institutions could then become insolvent and fail. The Asian crisis had temporary and fairly small effects for countries outside of East Asia, in part because of the intervention of the IMF and the world's central banks.

---

[1] See G. Corsetti, P. Pesenti, and N. Roubini, 1998. "What Caused the Asian Currency and Financial Crisis?" working paper, National Bureau of Economic Research.

A MONETARY SMALL OPEN-ECONOMY MODEL WITH A FIXED EXCHANGE RATE

Now that we have studied how the economy behaves under a flexible exchange rate regime, we explore how real and nominal variables are determined when the exchange rate is fixed. The type of fixed exchange rate regime we consider is a type of soft peg, where the government fixes the nominal exchange rate for extended periods of time, but might devalue or revalue the domestic currency at some times.

Under the fixed exchange rate regime we model, the government chooses a level at which it wants to fix the nominal exchange rate, which is e_1 in Figure 14.7. The government must then, either through its central bank or some other authority, stand ready to support this exchange rate. For simplicity, we suppose that the fixed exchange rate is supported through the government standing ready to exchange foreign currency for domestic currency at the fixed exchange rate e_1. To see how this happens, consider the simplified government balance sheet in Table 14.2. This is a consolidated balance sheet for the central bank and the fiscal authority. To support a fixed exchange rate, the government must act to buy or sell its foreign exchange reserves (think of this as foreign currency) for outside money (domestic currency) in foreign exchange markets, whenever there are market forces that would tend to push the exchange rate away from the fixed value the government wants it to have. For example, if there are forces tending to increase the exchange rate and, thus, cause a depreciation

FIGURE 14.7 **The Money Market in the Monetary Small Open-Economy Model with a Fixed Exchange Rate**

With a fixed exchange rate, the money supply is endogenous. Given the fixed exchange rate e_1, the money supply M is determined so that the money supply curve M^s intersects the money demand curve for an exchange rate equal to e_1.

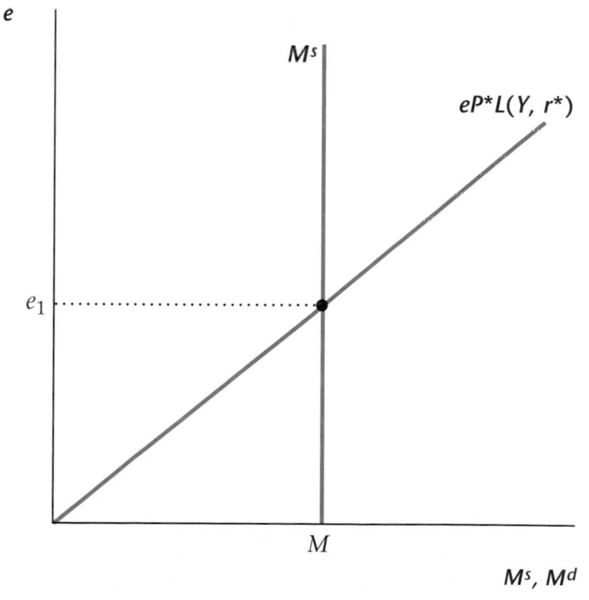

Table 14.2   **A Simplified Government Balance Sheet**

Assets	Liabilities
Foreign exchange reserves	Outside money
	Interest-bearing government debt

of the domestic currency, the government should sell foreign currency and buy domestic currency to offset those forces. If there are forces pushing down the exchange rate (appreciation), the government should buy foreign currency and sell domestic currency.

With a fixed exchange rate, the domestic central bank necessarily loses control over the domestic stock of money. To see this, consider Figure 14.7, where the nominal exchange rate is fixed at e_1. If the domestic central bank attempted to increase the money supply above M, its current value, the effect of this would be to put upward pressure on the exchange rate. Given the tendency for the price of foreign currency to rise in terms of domestic currency as a result, participants in foreign exchange markets would want to trade domestic currency for foreign currency, and the government would have to carry out these exchanges to support the fixed exchange rate. This would tend to reduce the stock of domestic money in circulation, and the attempt by the central bank to increase the money supply would be completely undone by actions in the foreign exchange market to support the fixed exchange rate. The money supply would remain at M, with the exchange rate and the domestic price level P unchanged. Similarly, if the domestic central bank attempted to engineer a reduction in the money supply below M, this would put downward pressure on the exchange rate, participants in the foreign exchange market would want to exchange foreign currency for domestic currency, and the government would be forced to exchange domestic currency for foreign currency, thus reducing the supply of money. The money supply could, therefore, not be reduced below M. The implication of this is that, under a fixed exchange rate regime, the supply of money cannot be determined independently by the central bank. Once the government fixes the exchange rate, this determines the domestic money supply.

A Nominal Foreign Shock Under a Fixed Exchange Rate

Suppose that the foreign price level increases when the domestic economy is under a fixed exchange rate. In Figure 14.8 P^* increases from P_1^* to P_2^*. As a result, the demand for money shifts rightward from $eP_1^*L(Y, r^*)$ to $eP_2^*L(Y, r^*)$. This increase in the demand for money results in downward pressure on the exchange rate, so that domestic currency becomes more attractive relative to foreign currency. On foreign exchange markets, the government must exchange domestic currency for foreign currency, and this leads to an increase in the domestic money supply from M_1 to M_2. Because $P = eP^*$, and the exchange rate is fixed, the domestic price level increases in proportion to the increase in the foreign price level. Thus, under a fixed exchange rate regime, in contrast to the flexible exchange rate regime, the domestic economy is not insulated from nominal

---

FIGURE 14.8 An Increase in the Foreign Price Level in the Monetary Small Open-Economy Model with a Fixed Exchange Rate

---

With a fixed exchange rate, an increase in the foreign price level shifts the money demand curve to the right, which causes the domestic money supply to increase. The domestic price level increases in proportion to the increase in the foreign price level.

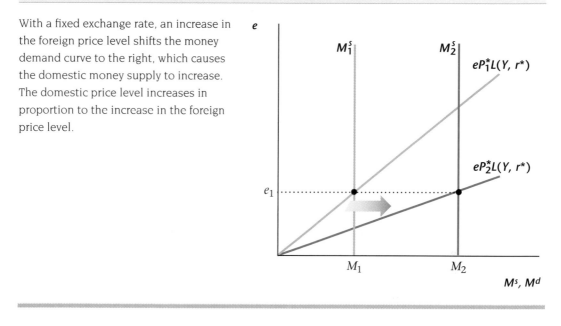

shocks that occur abroad. When the foreign price level changes, this price level change is imported, and the domestic price level increases in proportion. Because domestic monetary policy is not independent under a fixed exchange rate, the domestic central bank is forced to adopt the world's inflation rate domestically.

A Real Foreign Shock Under a Fixed Exchange Rate

Now, we consider the effects of an increase in the world real interest rate from r_1^* to r_2^*, just as we did for the case of a flexible exchange rate. In Figure 14.9(a), as under the flexible exchange rate regime, the real effects of the interest rate increase are an increase in domestic output from Y_1 to Y_2, a decrease in investment, consumption may increase or decrease, and the current account surplus increases. Assuming that the effect of the increase in real income on money demand is much larger than that of the increase in the real interest rate, the demand for money shifts rightward in Figure 14.9(b), from $eP^*L(Y_1, r_1^*)$ to $eP^*L(Y_2, r_2^*)$. Then, with the exchange rate fixed at e_1, the domestic money supply must rise from M_1 to M_2. Because $P = eP^*$ and e and P^* do not change, the domestic price level does not change. Thus, a fixed exchange rate can insulate the domestic price level from real shocks that occur abroad. The same result could be achieved under a flexible exchange rate, but this would require discretionary action by the domestic central bank, rather than the automatic response that occurs under a fixed exchange rate.

Under a fixed exchange rate, an increase
in the world real interest rate causes an
increase in real output and a shift to the
right in nominal money demand. The
money supply increases to accommodate
the increase in money demand, and the
domestic price level remains unchanged.

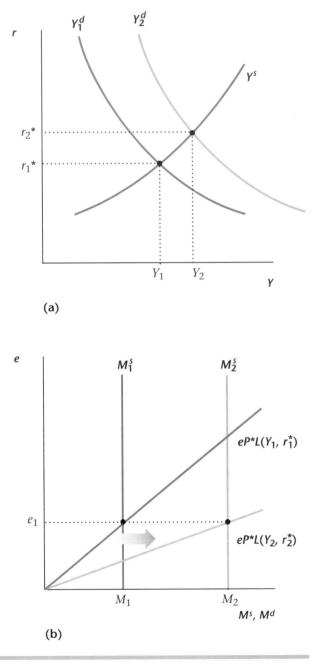

(a)

(b)

Exchange Rate Devaluation

Under a fixed exchange rate regime, a devaluation of the domestic currency (an increase in the fixed exchange rate e) might be a course the government chooses in response to a shock to the economy. In this section, we show how a temporary reduction in domestic total factor productivity would lead to a reduction in foreign exchange reserves that the government may not desire. In this case, the decrease in foreign exchange reserves can be prevented by a devaluation of the domestic currency. The total factor productivity shock also causes a decrease in the current account surplus, but the devaluation has no effect in offsetting this current account change.

Suppose in Figure 14.10 that the domestic economy is initially in equilibrium with the output demand curve Y_1^d and the output supply curve Y_1^s determining domestic output Y_1 in panel (a), given the world real interest rate r^*. In Figure 14.10(b), the exchange rate is fixed at e_1 at first, nominal money demand is initially $eP^*L(Y_1, r^*)$, and the money supply is M_1. Now, suppose that there is a temporary negative shock to domestic total factor productivity. This shifts the output supply curve leftward from Y_1^s to Y_2^s in Figure 14.10(a), as in Chapter 9. The current account surplus falls, shifting the output demand curve to the left, until it comes to rest at Y_2^d. In equilibrium, output falls to Y_2, domestic absorption falls because of the decrease in consumption (as income falls), and the current account surplus falls. In Figure 14.10(b), the money demand curve shifts leftward to $eP^*L(Y_2, r^*)$ with the fall in real income. If the government were to continue to support the fixed nominal exchange rate at e_1, this would imply, given the fall in the demand for the domestic currency, that the government would have to sell foreign currency on the foreign exchange market and buy domestic currency. This implies that the money supply would contract from M_1 to M_2.

Suppose, however, that the government does not wish to sell any of its foreign exchange reserves or that it does not have the foreign exchange reserves to sell, when the demand for domestic money falls. The government can avoid selling foreign exchange by fixing the exchange rate at e_2 in Figure 14.10(b). This implies that the money supply remains fixed at M_1, and there is a devaluation in the exchange rate, as the price of foreign currency has risen relative to domestic currency.

An important point is that the devaluation of the domestic currency has no effect here on the current account deficit. We might think that a devaluation would make domestic goods cheaper relative to foreign goods, thus increasing the real exchange rate, and that this would cause imports to fall, exports to rise, and the current account deficit to fall. While this might be true in the short run in some types of Keynesian analysis with sticky prices (but there are income and substitution effects to be concerned with, in terms of the effect on the current account deficit), with purchasing power parity there is no effect on the real exchange rate. Ultimately, if the government determined that the current account deficit that results here is a problem—for example, if the current account deficit is caused by excessive government spending—then this is a real problem that should be corrected through real means. That is, the real current account deficit could be reduced through a reduction in government spending, which we know from Chapter 13 can reduce the current account deficit in Figure 14.10(a). Trying to reduce the current account deficit through a devaluation in the domestic currency essentially

FIGURE 14.10   A Devaluation in Response to a Temporary Total Factor Productivity Shock

A temporary decrease in total factor productivity shifts the output supply curve to the left, reducing output and the current account surplus. The nominal money demand curve shifts to the left. If the government wants to avoid a loss in foreign exchange reserves, it can increase the fixed exchange rate from e_1 to e_2 and devalue the domestic currency.

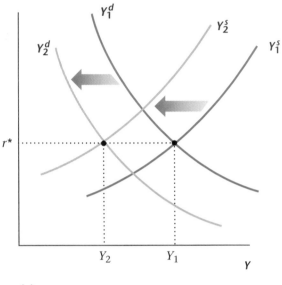

(a)

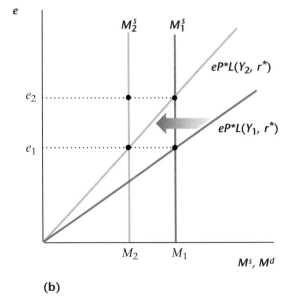

(b)

involves trying to make a real change through nominal means, which cannot work in the long run.

Flexible versus Fixed Exchange Rates

Governments face important choices concerning exchange rate policy, and a key choice is whether a flexible or fixed exchange rate regime should be adopted. What are the arguments for the adoption of flexible versus fixed exchange rates? In the previous subsections, we have seen that the exchange rate regime affects how the domestic economy is insulated from shocks from abroad. If a country's central bank seeks to stabilize the price level, then our analysis tells us that if nominal shocks from abroad are important, then a flexible exchange rate is preferable to a fixed exchange rate, because a flexible exchange rate absorbs a shock to the foreign price level and stabilizes the domestic price level. Alternatively, if real shocks from abroad are important, then a fixed exchange rate is preferable to a flexible exchange rate, as this acts to prevent the domestic price level from moving in response to real shocks from abroad, because the domestic money supply acts as a shock absorber. Thus, in this respect, whether a particular country should choose a fixed or flexible exchange rate depends on its circumstances. It is possible that a particular country might want to move from a fixed to a flexible exchange rate over time and then back again.

It is sometimes argued that a flexible exchange rate allows the domestic central bank to implement a monetary policy independent of what happens in the rest of the world. In our model, with a flexible exchange rate the domestic government can set the domestic money supply independently, but with a fixed exchange rate, the money supply is not under the control of the domestic government. However, giving the domestic central bank the power to implement an independent monetary policy is useful only if the central bank can be trusted with this power. Some central banks, such as those in the United States, Canada, and parts of Europe, have excellent track records in controlling the rate of inflation after World War II. In other countries, the track record is not so good. For example, Argentina suffered very high rates of inflation until its nominal exchange rate was fixed relative to the U.S. dollar. If the central bank is weak, in that it has difficulty in controlling the domestic money supply, then a fixed exchange rate can be a very important commitment device. If the exchange rate is fixed against the currency of a country with a strong central bank, then this implies, given PPP, that the weak-central-bank country essentially adopts the monetary policy of the strong-central-bank country. With a fixed exchange rate, the price level of the domestic economy is tied to the foreign price level, which is essentially determined by foreign monetary policy.

In conclusion, there is no clear case for flexible versus fixed exchange rates in all circumstances. For the United States, where the central bank is relatively independent of political pressures and appears to be well focused on controlling inflation, a flexible exchange rate seems appropriate. The Federal Reserve System appears to be sufficiently trustworthy relative to foreign central banks that allowing the Fed to pursue a monetary policy geared to U.S. interests seems advisable. However, for other countries, particularly some in Latin America and Africa, a fixed exchange rate regime makes good sense.

There are many long-standing instances of fixed exchange rates that we take for granted. For example, rates of exchange between different denominations of Federal Reserve notes have always been fixed in the United States. Why should it necessarily be the case that five one-dollar bills trade for one five-dollar bill in all circumstances in the United States? This is because the Federal Reserve always stands ready to trade one five-dollar bill for five ones; essentially, the Fed maintains fixed exchange rates among notes of different denominations. Further, all of the regional Federal Reserve Banks in the United States issue different notes that are clearly marked according to the Federal Reserve Bank of issue (check your wallet, and you will see that this is true; for example, I9 denotes the ninth Federal Reserve district—a note issued by the Minneapolis Federal Reserve Bank). Why should a one-dollar bill issued by the Kansas City Federal Reserve Bank trade one-for-one for a one-dollar bill issued by the Richmond Federal Reserve Bank? The answer is that all Federal Reserve Banks stand ready to exchange all Federal Reserve notes at their face value for other Federal Reserve notes. Again, the Fed maintains fixed exchange rates in this respect.

Essentially, all countries maintain fixed exchange rates within their borders. There is a national currency that is accepted as legal tender, and typically this currency circulates nationally as a medium of exchange, though in some countries foreign currencies, in particular U.S. dollars, circulate widely. What then determines the natural region, or **common currency area,** over which a single currency dominates as a medium of exchange? Clearly, a common currency area need not be the area over which there is a single political or fiscal authority. In the United States, each state has the power to tax state residents, but the states cede monetary authority to the Federal Reserve System, for which the central decision-making unit resides with the Board of Governors in Washington, D.C. In the EMU, member countries maintain their fiscal independence, but monetary policy is in the hands of the ECB. An advantage of having a large trading area with a common currency is that this simplifies exchange; it is much easier to write contracts and trade across international borders without the complications of converting one currency into another or bearing the risk associated with fluctuating exchange rates. However, in joining a **currency union** such as the EMU, a country must give up its monetary independence to the group. The formation of the EMU clearly has created tensions among EMU members, concerning matters that include the choice of the leaders of the European Central Bank, and the monetary policy stance this central bank should take. Great Britain, which has the world's oldest central bank, the Bank of England, chose not to join the EMU so as to maintain its monetary independence.

CAPITAL CONTROLS

A useful application of the monetary small open-economy model is to the problem of the role of capital controls in the international economy. Capital controls refer broadly to any government restrictions on the trade of assets across international borders. We show here that capital controls can reduce movements in the nominal exchange rate in response to some shocks under a flexible exchange rate regime, and they can reduce fluctuations in foreign exchange reserves under a fixed exchange rate regime. We argue, however, that capital controls are in general undesirable, because they introduce welfare-decreasing economic inefficiencies.

The Capital Account and the Balance of Payments

To understand capital controls, we have to first understand the accounting practices behind the **capital account.** The capital account is part of the **balance of payments,** which includes the current account and the capital account. The capital account includes all transactions in assets, in which entries in the capital account where a foreign resident purchases a domestic asset are recorded as a positive amount—a **capital inflow**—and entries where a domestic resident purchases a foreign asset are recorded as a negative amount—a **capital outflow.** For example, if a British bank lends to a U.S. firm, this is a capital inflow, as the loan to the U.S. firm is an asset for the British bank. If a U.S. automobile manufacturer builds a new plant in Britain, this is a capital outflow for the United States, and it is part of **foreign direct investment** in Britain. Foreign direct investment is distinct from **portfolio inflows and outflows,** which are capital account transactions involving financial assets, including stocks and debt instruments. A helpful rule of thumb in counting asset transactions in the capital account is that the transaction counts as a capital inflow if funds flow into the domestic country to purchase an asset, and as an outflow if funds flow out of the domestic country to purchase an asset.

The balance of payments is defined to be the current account surplus plus the capital account surplus. That is, letting *BP* denote the balance of payments, and *KA* the capital account surplus, we have

$$BP = KA + CA,$$

where *CA* is the current account surplus. A key element in balance of payments accounting is that the balance of payments is always zero (though it is not measured as such because of measurement error), so that

$$KA = -CA.$$

Therefore, the capital account surplus is always the negative of the current account surplus. If the current account is in deficit (surplus), then the capital account is in surplus (deficit). We have not discussed the capital account until now for this reason—the capital account surplus is just the flip side of the current account surplus, so that when we know the current account surplus, we know exactly what the capital account surplus is.

The balance of payments is always zero, because any transaction entering the balance of payments always has equal and opposite entries in the accounts. For example, suppose that a U.S. firm borrows the equivalent of $50 million in British pounds from a British bank so that it can purchase $50 million worth of auto parts in Britain to ship to the United States. The loan from the British bank enters as a capital inflow, because the British bank has accumulated a U.S. asset, and so there is an entry of +$50 million in the capital account for the United States. Next, when the auto parts are purchased and imported into the United States, this enters as −$50 million in the current account.

FIGURE 14.11   A Temporary Total Factor Productivity Shock, With and Without Capital Controls

With a temporary decrease in total factor productivity, under a flexible exchange rate there is a larger decrease in aggregate output and the current account surplus and a larger increase in the nominal exchange rate in the case without capital controls.

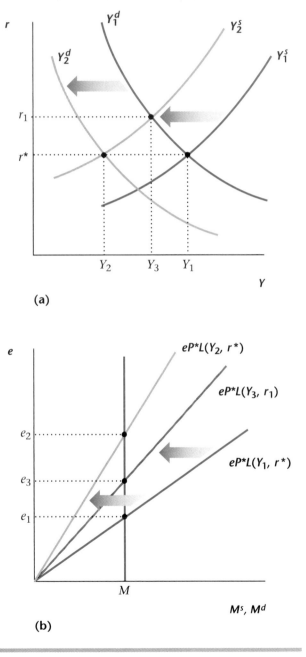

(a)

(b)

Thus, in this as in all cases, the net effect on the balance of payments is zero. The offsetting entries associated with a given transaction need not be in the current account and the capital account, but in some cases could be all in the current account or all in the capital account.

The Effects of Capital Controls

In practice, capital controls can be imposed in terms of capital inflows or capital outflows, and they sometimes apply to foreign direct investment and sometimes to portfolio inflows and outflows. For example, restrictions on capital outflows were introduced in Malaysia in 1998 after the Asian crisis, and Chile used controls on capital inflows extensively from 1978 to 1982 and from 1991 to 1998. In both cases, the capital controls were in terms of portfolio inflows and outflows. Countries sometimes also restrict foreign direct investment, which is a control on capital inflows. Controls on foreign direct investment are sometimes put in place because of concern (perhaps misplaced) over the foreign ownership of the domestic capital stock.

What are the macroeconomic effects of capital controls? Essentially, capital controls alter the way in which the domestic economy responds to a shock. For example, suppose that there is a temporary negative shock to domestic total factor productivity under a flexible exchange rate. In Figure 14.11(a), suppose that the output demand curve is Y_1^d and the initial output supply curve is Y_1^s, and assume that initially the current account surplus is zero, with output equal to Y_1 at the world real interest rate r^*. In Figure 14.11(b), the initial money demand curve is $eP^*L(Y_1, r^*)$, and the initial nominal exchange rate is e_1, given the nominal money supply M.

Now, suppose there is a temporary decrease in domestic total factor productivity, which shifts the output supply curve leftward to Y_2^s in Figure 14.11(a) With no capital controls in place, this implies that the current account surplus falls (with the current account then running a deficit), shifting the output demand curve to the left until it comes to rest at Y_2^d. Real output falls to Y_2 from Y_1, and consumption falls because of the decrease in income. In Figure 14.11(b), nominal money demand shifts leftward to $eP^*L(Y_2, r^*)$, and there is an exchange rate depreciation, with the nominal exchange rate increasing to e_2.

Now, assume an extreme form of capital controls where the government prohibits all capital inflows and outflows. This implies that the capital account surplus must be zero in equilibrium, and so the current account surplus must be zero as well. With a temporary decrease in domestic total factor productivity in Figure 14.11, the domestic real interest rate rises to r_1, which is above the world real interest rate r^*. In equilibrium, foreign investors would like to purchase domestic assets, as the return on domestic assets is greater than it is in the rest of the world, but they are prohibited from doing so. Thus, in this case, real output decreases to Y_3 in equilibrium. Assuming that money demand is much more responsive to real income than to the real interest rate, the money demand curve shifts to the left in Figure 14.11(b), though by less than it does in the case with no capital controls. The nominal exchange rate rises to e_3.

The results are that the nominal exchange rate increases by a smaller amount when capital controls are in place than when they are not, output falls by a smaller amount, and there is a smaller change in the current account deficit. Thus, capital controls tend to dampen aggregate fluctuations in output, the current account surplus, and the nominal exchange rate resulting from shocks of this type to the economy. If a country is concerned about the effects of fluctuations in the nominal exchange rate under a flexible exchange rate regime (for reasons that are not modeled here), capital controls tend to mitigate this problem, at least if the major source of shocks is temporary changes in total factor productivity. This solution is quite costly, however, as it produces an economic inefficiency. As in Chapter 5, the equilibrium allocation of resources is Pareto optimal in this model in the absence of capital controls. With no capital controls, in this example, the domestic economy would face a lower real interest rate after the total factor productivity shock, and this means that lenders would be worse off and borrowers better off. Though some would win and some would lose from getting rid of capital controls, there would in general be an average gain in welfare.

Under a fixed exchange rate, Figure 14.11(a) still applies, but the money market works as in Figure 14.12. The nominal exchange rate is assumed to be fixed at e_1. Initially, the money supply is M_1, and in the absence of capital controls, the money supply declines to M_2, but with capital controls there is a decline in the money supply only to M_3. Here, fluctuations in the money supply are smaller with capital controls, which implies that foreign exchange reserves drop by a smaller amount with capital

---

FIGURE 14.12   **A Total Factor Productivity Shock Under a Fixed Exchange Rate, With and Without Capital Controls**

Under a flexible exchange rate, capital controls dampen the reduction in the money supply that occurs when there is a temporary decline in total factor productivity.

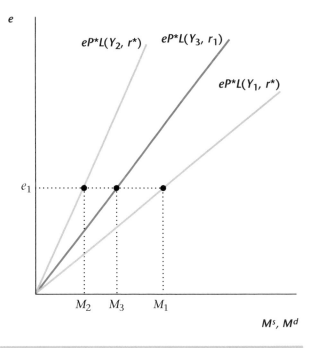

controls. Therefore, with capital controls in place a government can better support a fixed exchange rate, if exhausting the stock of foreign exchange reserves on hand is potentially a problem without controls. Again, though, capital controls come at a cost in lost economic efficiency.

While there are many more interesting issues to study in international macroeconomics, this chapter ends our discussion of this topic in this book. In Part VII, we move on to study topics in money and banking, unemployment, and inflation, which involve in-depth issues in closed-economy macroeconomics.

MACROECONOMICS IN ACTION

Do Capital Controls Work in Practice?

With regard to how capital controls work in practice, we are primarily interested in two questions: (1) Can capital controls be effectively enforced, so that they have the intended effects? (2) How large are the economic inefficiencies that capital controls cause? In an article in the *Journal of Economic Perspectives*, Sebastian Edwards sets out to answer these questions, using the example of Chile.[1]

Edwards argues that there is little support by economists for restrictions on capital outflows, but that some economists have pointed to Chile as an example of how restrictions on capital inflows appeared to have worked well in practice. One aim of his article is to dismiss these latter arguments by studying the details of what happened in Chile, where controls on capital inflows were in place from 1978 to 1982 and from 1991 to 1998. These restrictions mainly applied to portfolio inflows of short-maturity securities, and they took the form of reserve requirements on these inflows. That is, if a foreigner purchased short-term, interest-bearing Chilean assets (a capital inflow), then a fraction of the value of these assets would have to be held as a non-interest-

bearing deposit with the central bank of Chile. This had the same effect as would a tax on short-term capital inflows, as the noninterest-bearing deposits could otherwise be held in interest-bearing form.

What were the effects of the capital controls in Chile? Edwards finds that apparently many investors learned how to avoid the controls. While capital inflows appeared to have shifted somewhat toward longer-term inflows from shorter-term inflows, the shift was not that large, and investors seemed to have found many clever schemes for disguising short-term capital inflows as long-term ones. Edwards argues that the severe affects of the capital controls were on small and medium-sized Chilean firms, which faced much higher costs of borrowing.

Thus, the conclusion of Edwards's article is that the welfare costs of capital controls are small on average, mainly because the controls are ineffective, but the costs are large for some groups in the population. Edwards argues that capital controls should be phased out in countries where they still exist. However, he argues that in some cases

(continued)

this phaseout should be gradual. The inefficiencies caused by capital controls may in some cases be small relative to the potential inefficiencies arising from a poorly regulated banking system. If restrictions on capital inflows are relaxed quickly, then domestic banks can borrow more easily abroad so as to finance domestic lending. However, if domestic banks are improperly regulated (as we study in more depth in Chapter 15), then they take on too much risk, and this problem can be exacerbated in a wide-open international lending environment. The relaxation of capital controls sometimes needs to be coupled with improvements in the regulation of domestic financial institutions.

[1]S. Edwards, 1999. "How Effective Are Capital Controls?" *Journal of Economic Perspectives* 13, 65–84.

CHAPTER SUMMARY

- We first studied purchasing power parity, or the law of one price, which predicts that prices are equated across countries in terms of the same currency. While there can be large and persistent deviations from purchasing power parity in practice, there are strong economic forces that move prices and exchange rates toward purchasing power parity over the long run. The purchasing power parity assumption is very useful in the model studied in this chapter.

- In the monetary small open-economy model the real interest rate and the foreign price level are determined on world markets.

- Under a flexible exchange rate, money is neutral, and the domestic economy is insulated from nominal shocks from abroad, in that no real or nominal domestic variables are affected by a change in the foreign price level. The nominal exchange rate moves in equilibrium to absorb completely a shock to the foreign price level. However, the flexible exchange rate does not insulate the domestic price level against real shocks from abroad.

- A fixed exchange rate causes the domestic price level to increase in proportion to an increase in the foreign price level, but the fixed exchange rate regime insulates the domestic price level from foreign real shocks. Under a fixed exchange rate regime, a devaluation of the domestic currency might occur if the government's foreign exchange reserves are depleted. A devaluation raises the domestic price level.

- Whether a flexible exchange rate regime is preferred to a fixed exchange rate regime depends on a country's circumstances, but a flexible exchange rate regime implies that domestic monetary policy can be independent, whereas a fixed exchange rate regime implies that the domestic economy adopts the monetary policy of a foreign central bank.

- Capital controls involve restrictions on capital inflows and outflows, which are items in the capital account, where the asset transactions for a nation are added up. The balance of payments surplus is the sum of the capital account surplus and the current account surplus, and the balance of payments surplus is always zero.

- Capital controls can dampen fluctuations in output, the current account surplus, and the exchange rate (under a flexible exchange rate) or the money supply (under a fixed exchange rate), but these controls reduce economic efficiency. In practice, capital controls appear not to have been very effective, and in this sense they have not had large effects on efficiency.

KEY TERMS

Nominal exchange rate: The price of foreign currency in terms of domestic currency, denoted by e in the model of this chapter.

Purchasing power parity (PPP): The same thing as the law of one price, except that P is the domestic price level and P^* is the foreign price level.

Law of one price: $P = eP^*$ where P is the domestic price, P^* is the foreign price, and e is the exchange rate.

Big Mac index: The ratio of the prices of Big Macs in two different countries, published by *The Economist*.

Flexible exchange rate regime: A system under which a nation's nominal exchange rate is determined by market forces.

Fixed exchange rate regime: A system under which the domestic government supports the value of the exchange rate at a specified level in terms of a foreign currency or currencies.

Hard pegs: Exchange rate systems where there is a firm commitment to a fixed exchange rate, either through dollarization or a currency board.

Soft pegs: Exchange rate systems where the government commits to a fixed exchange rate for periods of time, but sometimes changes the value at which the exchange rate is fixed.

Devaluations: Increases in the price of foreign exchange in terms of domestic currency.

Revaluations: Decreases in the price of foreign exchange in terms of domestic currency.

Dollarize: For a nation to abandon its own currency and adopt the currency of another country as its medium of exchange.

Currency board: An institution that fixes the exchange rate by holding foreign-currency-denominated interest-bearing assets and committing to buying and selling foreign exchange at a fixed rate of exchange.

European Monetary Union (EMU): An organization of European countries, established in 1999, which shares a common currency, the Euro.

Euro: The currency shared by the members of the EMU.

European Central Bank (ECB): The central bank of the EMU countries.

European Monetary System (EMS): A cooperative exchange rate system in place among European countries from 1979 until 1999.

Bretton Woods arrangement: A worldwide cooperative exchange rate system, in place from 1946 to 1971, under which the price of gold was fixed in terms of U.S. dollars, and there were fixed exchange rates for all other currencies in terms of the U.S. dollar.

International Monetary Fund (IMF): An international monetary institution established in 1946, which was intended as a lender of last resort for its member countries, which now number 183.

Lender of last resort: A centralized institution that lends to economic agents in distress; examples are central banks, which lend to domestic banks, and the IMF, which lends to its member countries.

Depreciation (of the exchange rate): A rise in the price of foreign currency in terms of domestic currency.

Appreciation (of the exchange rate): A fall in the price of foreign currency in terms of domestic currency.

Common currency area: A region over which a single currency dominates as a medium of exchange.

Currency union: A group of countries that agrees to become a common currency area.

Capital account: The component of the balance of payments in which all international asset transactions between the domestic economy and foreign countries are added up.

Balance of payments: A system of accounts for a country for adding up all international transactions in goods and assets.

Capital inflow: The purchase of a domestic asset by a foreign resident, recorded as a positive entry in the capital account.

Capital outflow: The purchase of a foreign asset by a domestic resident, recorded as a negative entry in the capital account.

Foreign direct investment: A capital inflow that involves the acquisition of a new physical asset by a foreign resident.

Portfolio inflows and outflows: Capital account transactions involving international transactions in financial assets.

QUESTIONS FOR REVIEW

1. Does purchasing power parity hold in practice in the short run? Why or why not? Does it hold in the long run? Why or why not?

2. What countries in the world have flexible exchange rates? Which have fixed exchange rates?

3. What are the different systems for fixing the exchange rate? Describe how each works.

4. Describe the role of the International Monetary Fund.

5. In the model constructed in this chapter, what are the effects on the domestic economy of an increase in the foreign price level under a flexible exchange rate and under a fixed exchange rate?

6. In the model, what are the effects on the domestic economy of an increase in the world real interest rate under a flexible exchange rate and under a fixed exchange rate?

7. In the model, is money neutral under a flexible exchange rate? Explain why or why not. Can we say that money is neutral under a fixed exchange rate? Explain.

8. Explain why domestic monetary policy is not independent under a flexible exchange rate.

9. What are the effects of a devaluation of the domestic currency under a fixed exchange rate?

10. List the key pros and cons of fixed versus flexible exchange rate regimes.

11. Give two examples of fixed exchange rates within the United States.

12. What are the advantages and disadvantages of a common currency area or currency union?

13. If the capital account surplus is positive, what can we say about the current account surplus?

14. Give two examples of countries where capital controls were imposed.

15. What do capital controls imply for the response of the economy to shocks?

16. Are capital controls a good idea? Why or why not?

17. Are capital controls effective in practice? Explain.

PROBLEMS

1. In the equilibrium small open-economy model, suppose that total factor productivity increases temporarily.
   (a) If the exchange rate is flexible, determine the effects on aggregate output, absorption, the current account surplus, the nominal exchange rate, and the price level.
   (b) Repeat part (a) for the case of a fixed exchange rate. If the goal of the domestic government is to stabilize the price level, would it be preferable to have a fixed exchange rate or a flexible exchange rate regime when there is a change in total factor productivity?

(c) Now, suppose that under a flexible exchange rate regime, the domestic monetary authority controls the money supply so as to stabilize the price level when total factor productivity increases. Explain the differences between the outcome in this case and what happens in part (b) with a fixed exchange rate.

2. Suppose in the model that government expenditures increase temporarily. Determine the effects on aggregate output, absorption, the current account surplus, the nominal exchange rate, and the price level. What difference does it make if the exchange rate is flexible or fixed?

3. Suppose that better transaction technologies are developed that reduce the domestic demand for money. Use the monetary small open-economy model to answer the following:
   (a) Suppose that the exchange rate is flexible. What are the equilibrium effects on the price level and the exchange rate?
   (b) Suppose that the exchange rate is flexible, and the domestic monetary authority acts to stabilize the price level. Determine how the domestic money supply changes and the effect on the nominal exchange rate.
   (c) Suppose that the exchange rate is fixed. Determine the effects on the exchange rate and the price level, and determine the differences from your results in parts (a) and (b).

4. A country is under a fixed exchange rate regime, and the government decides to reduce government spending permanently.
   (a) Show that if the government has no foreign exchange reserves, it must devalue the domestic currency. Determine the equilibrium effects of this.
   (b) What effect does the change in government spending have on the current account surplus? Does the exchange rate devaluation affect the current account surplus? Explain your results.

5. Consider a country with a flexible exchange rate, and which initially has a current account surplus of zero. Then, suppose there is an anticipated increase in future total factor productivity.
   (a) Determine the equilibrium effects on the domestic economy in the case where there are no capital controls. In particular, show that there will be a current account deficit when firms and consumers anticipate the increase in future total factor productivity.
   (b) Now, suppose that the government dislikes current account deficits, and that it imposes capital controls in an attempt to reduce the current account deficit. With the anticipated increase in future total factor productivity, what will be the equilibrium effects on the economy? Do the capital controls have the desired effect on the current account deficit? Do capital controls dampen the effects of the shock to the economy on output and the exchange rate? Are capital controls sound macroeconomic policy in this context? Why or why not?

6. The domestic central bank increases the supply of money under a flexible exchange rate regime, leading to a depreciation of the nominal exchange rate. If the government had imposed capital controls before the increase in the money supply, would this have had any effect on the exchange rate depreciation? Explain your results, and comment on their significance.

WORKING WITH THE DATA

1. Using the data from Figure 14.1, where e is the value of a Canadian dollar in terms of U.S. dollars, P^* is the U.S. consumer price index, and P is the Canadian consumer price index, construct a time series plot of e, $\frac{P^*}{P}$, and $\frac{eP^*}{P}$. What explains most of the variability in $\frac{eP^*}{P}$?

Is it variability in e or in $\frac{P^*}{P}$? What does this tell us about the causes of changes in the real exchange rate in the short run?

2. Construct a time series plot of the German exchange rate relative to the U.S. dollar, the Japanese exchange rate relative to the dollar, and the Canadian exchange rate relative to the dollar. For comparability, scale these exchange rates so that they all are equal to 100 for the first data point. What do you observe in the time series plot? What does this tell us about how central banks in these countries control their exchange rates relative to the U.S. dollar?

3. Construct a scatter plot of the annual percentage changes (use December-to-December) in the U.S. trade-weighted exchange rate and the annual percentage changes in the monetary base. What do you observe? Is this consistent with the model constructed in this chapter?

PART VII

Money, Banking, Unemployment, and Inflation

In this part, we deal with some in-depth topics. In Chapter 15, we study at a more detailed level the role of money in the economy, the forms that money has taken historically, the effects of long-run inflation on aggregate activity and economic welfare, and the role of banks and other financial intermediaries in the economy. Then, in Chapter 16 we study two models of unemployment, the search model and the efficiency wage model. Both models help explain why there are always unemployed people, even in a well-functioning economy, and they also help us understand the main determinants of the unemployment rate. Finally, in Chapter 17 we explain why central banks may cause inflation, even though it is well known that inflation is harmful. We use recent inflation history in the United States as a backdrop in examining the role of central bank learning and commitment in inflation policy.

CHAPTER 15

Money, Inflation, and Banking

In the monetary analysis we have done so far in this book, particularly in Chapters 10–12 and 14, we began by assuming that money was needed to make transactions and proceeded from there. This allowed us to understand the effects of changes in the quantity of money, the role of money in the business cycle, and how money influences foreign exchange rates. In this chapter, we wish to gain a deeper understanding of the functions of money in the economy, to understand the long-run effects of inflation on aggregate economic activity and economic welfare, and to study the role of banks and other financial intermediaries in the economy.

In this chapter we first discuss how historical monetary systems worked, and we study the basic role of money in the economy in overcoming the difficulty of carrying out exchange using only commodities. Then, we return to the monetary intertemporal model developed in Chapter 10 and use this model to study the long-run effects of inflation. Empirically and in our model, long-run inflation is caused by growth in the money supply. We see that higher rates of money growth and inflation tend to reduce employment and output. This is because inflation erodes the purchasing power of money in the period between when labor income is earned and when it is spent. Thus, inflation tends to distort labor supply decisions. We show that an optimal long-run inflation policy for a central bank is to follow a **Friedman rule**, according to which the money supply grows at a rate that makes the rate of return on money identical to the rate of return on alternative assets and drives the nominal interest rate to zero. We discuss why real-world central banks do not appear to follow Friedman rules.

Finally, we examine the role of banks and other financial intermediaries in the economy. A **financial intermediary** is any financial institution that borrows from one large group of people and lends to another large group of people, transforms assets in some way, and processes information. Banks and other depository institutions are financial intermediaries that are of particular interest to macroeconomists for two reasons. First, some of the liabilities depository institutions issue are included in measures of the money supply and compete with currency as media of exchange. Second, depository institutions interact closely with the central bank and are typically on the receiving end of the first-round effects of monetary policy.

We study a simple model of a bank, which is the Diamond–Dybvig banking model. This model shows how banks supply a kind of insurance against the need to make transactions using liquid assets, why bank runs can occur (as happened in the Great Depression and before the existence of the Federal Reserve System), and why government-provided deposit insurance might prevent bank runs. We discuss the incentive problem that deposit insurance creates for banks.

ALTERNATIVE FORMS OF MONEY

In Chapter 10 we discussed how money functions as a medium of exchange, a store of value, and a unit of account, with the key distinguishing feature of money being its medium-of-exchange property. Though all money is a medium of exchange, historically there have been many different objects that have performed this role. The most important forms of money have been commodity money, circulating private bank notes, commodity-backed paper currency, fiat money, and transactions deposits at private banks. We discuss each of these in turn.

Commodity money: This was the earliest money, in common use in Greek and Roman civilizations and in earlier times, and it was typically a precious metal, for example, gold, silver, or copper. In practice, commodity money systems involved having the government operate a mint to produce coins from precious metals, which then circulated as money. Control over the mint by the government was important, because the ability to issue money provided an important source of seigniorage revenue for the government. Commodity money systems, however, had several problems. First, the quality of any commodity is difficult to verify. For example, gold can be adulterated with other cheaper metals, so that there is an opportunity for fraud in the production of commodity money. Also, in the exchange of commodity monies, bits could be clipped off coins and melted down, with the hope that this would go undetected. Second, commodity money is costly to produce. For example, gold has to be dug out of the ground, minted, and then reminted when the coins wear out. Third, the use of a commodity as money diverts it from other uses. Gold and silver, for example, can also be used as jewelry and in industrial applications. In spite of these three problems, at the time commodity monies were used there were no good alternatives, mainly because any laws against the counterfeiting of paper currency would have been difficult or impossible to enforce. What may seem paradoxical is that the high cost of producing a commodity money was a virtue. To avoid inflation, the quantity of money must be in limited supply, and one characteristic of gold and silver that made them function well as commodity monies is their scarcity.

Circulating private bank notes: In the **Free Banking Era** in the United States (1837–1863), and earlier, banks chartered by state governments issued pieces of paper that were exchanged hand-to-hand, much as currency is today. A system of note issue by private banks was also in place in Canada before 1935.[1] A problem during the Free Banking Era was that there were thousands of banks issuing notes, so that it was very difficult for a person offered a note in a particular location to evaluate its quality. For example, a storekeeper in Boston offered a note issued by a New Orleans bank may not have known whether this was an insolvent bank that might ultimately not redeem the note or if the New Orleans bank indeed even existed. Some characterize

---

[1] See S. Williamson, 1989. "Restrictions on Financial Intermediaries and Implications for Aggregate Fluctuations: Canada and the United States 1870–1913," in *NBER Macroeconomics Annual 1989,* pp. 303–340, edited by Olivier Blanchard and Stanley Fischer, MIT Press, Cambridge MA; and B. Champ, B. Smith, and S. Williamson, 1996. "Currency Elasticity and Banking Panics: Theory and Evidence," *Canadian Journal of Economics* 29, 828–864.

the Free Banking Era as chaotic, but the efficiency of free banking is an issue that is much debated by economic historians.[2]

Commodity-backed paper currency: In this type of monetary system, there is government-issued paper currency, but the currency is backed by some commodity, as for example under the **gold standard.** The United States operated under the gold standard before 1933. Under the rules of the gold standard, the U.S. government stood ready to exchange currency for gold at some specified price, so that government currency was always redeemable in gold. Effectively this was a commodity money system, but it saved on some of the costs of a commodity money, in that consumers did not have to carry large quantities of the commodity (in this case gold) around when they wanted to make large purchases.

Fiat money: This is at least part of the monetary system in place in most modern economies. In the United States, fiat currency is the stock of Federal Reserve notes issued by the Fed. Fiat money consists of pieces of paper that are essentially worthless in that, for example, most people do not value U.S. Federal Reserve notes for their color or for the pictures on them. However, U.S. Federal Reserve notes are valued in that they can be exchanged for consumable goods. Why is fiat money accepted in exchange for goods? We accept fiat money because we believe that others will accept this money in exchange for goods in the future. This notion of the value of money supported by belief is intriguing, and it is part of what excites those who study monetary economics.

Transactions deposits at private banks: In the United States, widespread deposit banking and the use of checks in transactions was mainly a post–Civil War phenomenon, and the U.S. financial system (and similarly the financial systems in most developed economies) has evolved to the point where much of the total volume of transactions is carried out through banks. With a bank deposit that is checkable or can be used in conjunction with a debit card, consumers can make purchases without the use of fiat money. A check or debit card transaction is a message that specifies that a given quantity of value is to be debited from the account of the person writing the check or using the debit card and credited to the account of the person on the other end of the transaction. If the accounts of the buyer and the seller are in different banks, then, for the correct accounts to be debited and credited, the transaction needs to be cleared. In the case of a transaction using a check, the check needs to pass through the **check-clearing system.** Check clearing is one mechanism by which banks carry out exchanges with each other.

Some readers may be concerned that we have not mentioned credit cards as a form of money. There is a good reason we have not done this—money and credit are fundamentally different. When a credit card purchase is made, the vendor of goods or services extends credit to the purchaser, and then this credit is transferred to the credit card issuer (Visa, Mastercard, or American Express, for example).

---

[2]See, for example, B. Smith and W. Weber, 1999. "Private Money Creation and the Suffolk Banking System," *Journal of Money, Credit and Banking* 31, 624–659; and A. Rolnick and W. Weber, 1983. "New Evidence on the Free Banking Era," *American Economic Review* 73, 1080–1091.

The credit extended is not money in the sense that currency or a bank deposit is money, because the issuer of credit cannot use what is effectively an IOU of the purchaser as a medium of exchange. Forms of credit, however, particularly credit cards, are a substitute for money in making transactions, and, therefore, they are important in terms of how we think about the monetary system.

MACROECONOMICS IN ACTION

Commodity Money and Commodity-Backed Paper Money: Yap Stones and Playing Cards

A commodity money system that appears unusual on the surface but has several features common to other commodity money systems, is the exchange of so-called Yap stones on the island of Yap in Micronesia, as studied by the anthropologist William Henry Furness III in 1903.[1] On the island of Yap, there were large stones that served as money and measured from 1 foot to 12 feet in diameter.[2] These stones were quarried from limestone deposits on another island about 400 miles from Yap and transported back by boat. What the Yap stones had in common with other commodity monies, such as gold and silver, was scarcity. It was quite costly in time and effort to create a new Yap stone, and the value of the stones increased with the difficulty in acquiring them, which might include weathering storms on the trip back to Yap. What seems different about the Yap stones as a commodity money is that they were extremely difficult to move around; an attractive feature of gold and silver as commodity monies was that the quantities required to make moderate-sized transactions were extremely portable. However, the Yap islanders did not typically move the Yap stones when transactions were made. Yap stones were most often used to make large land transactions and to make large gifts,

but the stones themselves usually stayed in a fixed location. It was well known to most of the small population of Yap who owned which stones, and a transaction involving a Yap stone was public knowledge, but there was no written record of ownership. Thus, it appears that exchange was actually carried out on the island of Yap using commodity-backed money. What "changed hands" in a transaction was the record of the ownership of the stone, which was stored in the collective memories of the islanders, and the stones were just the backing for the "currency," which was not physical objects at all, but an entry in public memory.

Yap stones had much in common with the earliest known paper money used in North America, in New France, in 1685. There had been difficulties in keeping coins minted in France in circulation in New France (now the province of Quebec in Canada), as the coins were often used in payment for imports from France and, thus, left the colony. Therefore, the coins constantly had to be replenished by shipments from France in the form of payments to the troops in New France. In 1685, the shipment of coins was late in arriving from France, and De Meulles, the Intendant (governor of the colony) of New France authorized the issue of playing card money.

De Meulles requisitioned the playing cards in the colony, and the cards were issued, signed by him in different denominations, as payment to the troops. These playing cards were essentially IOUs, which promised payment in coin when the shipment arrived from France. The playing cards then circulated as a medium of exchange in New France, and they were subsequently retired, as promised. These cards were then issued repeatedly in later years, but ultimately the government of France lost interest in its colony in New France, and the shipments of coins did not arrive from France in the quantities promised, so that the IOUs that the playing cards represented could not be honored in full. There were problems with inflation, because of the temptation to issue the playing card money in excess of the promises that the Intendant could actually keep.[3]

Like the ownership rights to the Yap stones that circulated on the island of Yap, playing card money in New France was a commodity-backed money. However, the New France playing card monetary system seems to have been less successful than the Yap system, because the commodity backing of the playing card money was uncertain (due to the inability of public officials to keep their promises), whereas the existence of the Yap stones was well known to essentially everyone on the island of Yap.

[1]W. Furness, 1910. *The Island of Stone Money: Uap and the Carolines*, J. P. Lippincott Co., Philadelphia and London.

[2]You can see a picture and description of a Yap stone housed in the Federal Reserve Bank of Richmond's money museum at http://www.rich.frb.org/research/econed/museum/2.html.

[3]See http://collections.ic.gc.ca/bank/english/emar76.htm for a description and photograph of card money in New France from the Bank of Canada currency museum.

MONEY AND THE ABSENCE OF DOUBLE COINCIDENCE OF WANTS: THE ROLE OF COMMODITY MONEY AND FIAT MONEY

Now that we know something about what objects have served as a medium of exchange, we consider in more detail what it means for some object to be a medium of exchange, which is the distinctive function of money. In this section, we consider a model that formalizes why money is useful as a medium of exchange. This model helps us understand the role of the two simplest types of money, commodity money and fiat money.

A fundamental question in monetary economics is why market exchange is typically an exchange of goods for money (monetary exchange) rather than of goods for goods (barter exchange). Jevons[3] argued that money helped to solve a problem of an **absence of double coincidence of wants** associated with barter exchange. To understand the double-coincidence-of-wants problem, imagine a world where there are many goods and people are specialized in what they wish to produce and consume. For example, suppose person *I* produces corn but wants to consume wheat. If person *I* meets another

[3]See S. Jevons, 1910. *Money and the Mechanism of Exchange*, 23rd edition: Kegan Paul.

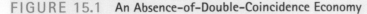

FIGURE 15.1   **An Absence–of–Double–Coincidence Economy**

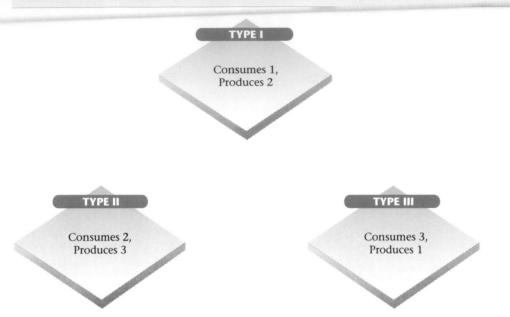

In the model there are three types of people. A type I person consumes good 1 and produces good 2, a type II person consumes good 2 and produces good 3, and a type III person consumes good 3 and produces good 1.

person *II* who has wheat, that would be a single coincidence of wants, because *II* has what *I* wants. However, *II* may not want corn in exchange for her wheat. If *II* wanted to consume corn, there would be a double coincidence of wants, because *I* wants what *II* has and *II* wants what *I* has. Barter exchange can only take place if there is a double coincidence. Now, searching for a trading partner is costly in time and resources (for example, hauling corn from place to place looking for a double coincidence of wants), particularly if there are many goods in the economy, so that there are many would-be sellers to search among. It would be much easier if, in selling corn, person *I* only needs to satisfy a single coincidence of wants, that is, find a person who wants corn. This would be the case if everyone accepted some object, called money. Then, in selling corn in exchange for wheat, all person *I* needs to do is to sell corn for money in a single-coincidence meeting, then sell money for wheat in another single-coincidence meeting.

To see how this might work, consider the following simple economy, depicted in Figure 15.1. This is an example from the work of Nobuhiro Kiyotaki and Randall Wright,[4] who formalized Jevons's notion of the role of money using modern dynamic methods. There are three types of people in this economy. Type *I* people consume good 1 and produce good 2, type *II* people consume good 2 and produce good 3,

---

[4]N. Kiyotaki and R. Wright, 1989. "On Money as a Medium of Exchange," *Journal of Political Economy* 97, 927–954.

and type *III* people consume good 3 and produce good 1. There are many people of each type in the economy, and everyone lives forever, with people meeting each other pairwise and at random each period. That is, each person meets one other person each period, and that other person is someone he or she bumps into at random. If the people in this economy each produce their good, and then wait until they meet another person with whom they can engage in a barter exchange, everyone will wait forever to trade, because this economy has an absence of double coincidence of wants. This is the simplest type of example in which there are no possible pairwise meetings where a double coincidence of wants occurs.

How might trade be accomplished here? One solution would be for people to use a commodity money. Suppose, for example, that good 1 can be stored at a relatively low cost. Then good 1 might be used as a commodity money, in that type *II* people accept good 1 in exchange for good 3 when meeting type *III* people. Why does type *II* accept good 1 even though it is not something he or she consumes? This is because type *II* knows that type *I* accepts good 1 in exchange for good 2 (this is a double-coincidence trade). Good 1 in this example is then a commodity money—a medium of exchange—as it is accepted in exchange by people who do not ultimately consume it. We show the equilibrium patterns of trade in Figure 15.2.

FIGURE 15.2   Good 1 as a Commodity Money in the Absence-of-Double-Coincidence Economy

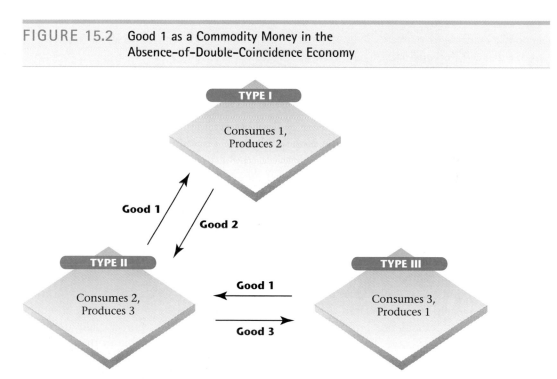

Given the absence-of-double-coincidence problem, one solution is to have good 1 serve as a commodity money. A type II person accepts good 1 even though he or she does not consume it. Good 1 is held by type II until he or she can exchange it for good 2 with a type I person.

FIGURE 15.3   Fiat Money in the Absence-of-Double-Coincidence Economy

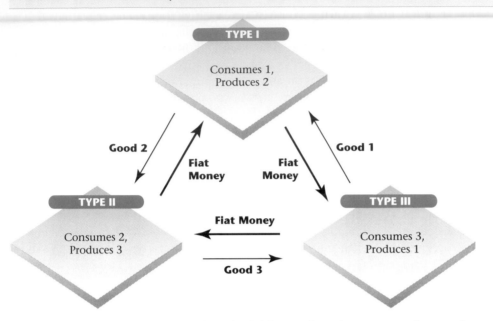

The double-coincidence problem can be solved if the people in this economy all accept fiat money. Money circulates clockwise in the figure, while goods are passed counterclockwise.

Another solution to the absence-of-double-coincidence problem would be the introduction of a fourth good, fiat money, which no one consumes but is acceptable to everyone in exchange for goods. A possible equilibrium pattern of exchange is shown in Figure 15.3. Here, when types *I* and *II* meet, *II* buys good 2 with money; when *I* and *III* meet, *I* buys good 1 with money; and when *III* and *II* meet, *III* buys good 3 with money. Thus, money circulates clockwise in Figure 15.3, and goods are passed counterclockwise.

For this model to say something interesting about the conditions under which commodity money would be useful, and when a fiat money system would be better than having commodity money, we would have to introduce costs of counterfeiting, the resource costs of producing commodity money, and so forth. This would be quite complicated to do. However, this simple model captures the essentials of the absence-of-double-coincidence problem and why this helps to make money socially useful in promoting exchange. Barter exchange is difficult, in fact impossible in this example, unless individuals accept in exchange objects that they do not consume. That is, a medium of exchange—money—is essential in allowing people to exchange what they do not want for what they want, and it, therefore, increases welfare. In fact, in this example the institution of money is a Pareto improvement (recall our discussion from Chapter 5), because it increases welfare for everyone over what it would be otherwise.

LONG-RUN INFLATION IN THE MONETARY INTERTEMPORAL MODEL

The institution of monetary exchange matters for the determination of real macro-economic quantities and contributes in important ways to economic welfare in modern economies. Once this institution is in place, however, the money supply can change in ways that have no consequences at all for real macroeconomic variables or for welfare. Though short-run monetary nonneutralities might arise because of money surprises (studied in Chapter 11) or sticky nominal wages (studied in Chapter 12), in the long run money is neutral (as we showed in Chapter 10), in that a one-time level increase in the stock of money only changes prices in proportion and has no long-run effects on real variables.

Though money is neutral in the long run, in that a change in the *level* of the money supply has no long-run real effects, changes in the *growth rate* of the money supply are not neutral. It should not be surprising, because an increase in the level of the money supply causes an increase in the price level, that an increase in the rate of growth in the money supply causes an increase in the rate of growth in the price level, that is, an increase in the inflation rate. Using the monetary intertemporal model we constructed in Chapter 10, we are able to show why money growth and inflation are costly in terms of lost aggregate output and misallocation of resources. Further, we determine an optimal prescription for monetary growth, often referred to as the Friedman rule for monetary policy, after Milton Friedman. The Friedman rule for optimal money growth is that money should grow at a rate that implies that the nominal interest rate is zero. It turns out that the optimal money growth rate and the implied optimal inflation rate are negative.

There are many factors that can cause changes in the price level, some of which we have explored in Chapters 9 to 12. For example, a change in total factor productivity changes equilibrium aggregate output Y and the equilibrium real interest rate r, and this shifts the money demand curve and causes a change in the price level. However, sustained inflations, where the price level continues to increase over a long period of time, are usually the result of sustained growth in the money supply. In Figure 15.4 we plot the rate of inflation in the United States (the quarterly percentage rate of increase in the CPI) for the period 1960–2003 against the quarterly percentage rate of growth in the monetary base, M0. There is a positive relationship between the two, in that the positively sloped straight line in the figure is the best fit to the set of points, but the relationship is quite noisy, which reflects that there are factors in addition to money growth affecting the rate of inflation in the short run. The causal link between money growth and inflation was emphasized by Milton Friedman and Anna Schwartz in *A Monetary History of the United States 1867–1960.*[5]

To understand the effects of long-run inflation, we allow the money supply to grow forever at a constant rate in the monetary intertemporal model. We suppose that the

---

[5]M. Friedman and A. Schwartz, 1960. *A Monetary History of the United States 1867–1960,* Princeton University Press, Princeton, NJ.

FIGURE 15.4   Scatter Plot of the Inflation Rate vs. the Growth Rate
in M0 for the United States, 1960–2003

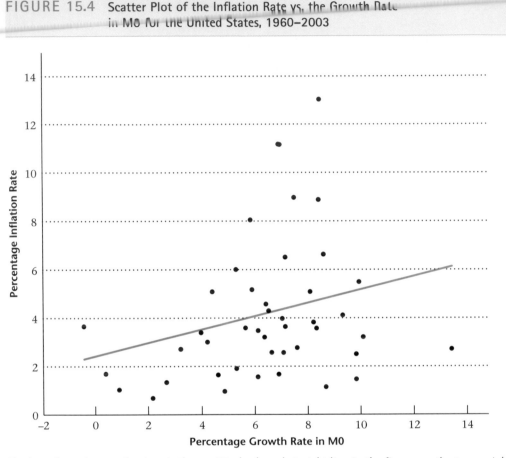

The best fit to the set of points is the positively sloped straight line in the figure, so the two variables are positively correlated, though not strongly so.

government permits the money supply to grow by making lump-sum transfers to the representative household each period, with the money supply growing according to

$$M' = (1 + x)M \tag{15.1}$$

where M' is the future money supply, M is the current money supply, and x is the growth rate of the money supply from the current period to the future period. For simplicity, we suppose that the economy looks exactly the same in every period, in that total factor productivity, real government spending, and consumer preferences are identical in every period. The only exogenous variable that changes over time is the money supply, which grows according to Equation (15.1). This implies that all of the endogenous variables in the model, except the price level, remain the same for all time. That is, the real wage, employment, aggregate output, the real interest rate, and the inflation rate are constant for all time. In the current period, money supply is equal to money demand in equilibrium, and so from Chapter 10, we have

$$M = PL(Y, r + i). \tag{15.2}$$

Recall from Chapter 10 that, on the left-hand side of Equation (15.2), M is the nominal money supply and, on the right-hand side of Equation (15.2), $PL(Y, r + i)$ is nominal money demand. From the Fisher relation, recall that $r + i$ (the real interest rate plus the inflation rate) is equal (approximately) to the nominal interest rate. It must also be the case in equilibrium that money supply is equal to money demand in the future period, so that

$$M' = P'L(Y', r' + i'), \tag{15.3}$$

where P' is the price level in the future period, Y' is future aggregate output, r' is the future real interest rate, and i' is the future inflation rate. Then, from Equations (15.2) and (15.3), we have

$$\frac{M'}{M} = \frac{P'L(Y', r' + i')}{PL(Y, r + i)} \tag{15.4}$$

But in equilibrium, aggregate output, the real interest rate, and the inflation rate remain constant over time, which implies that $Y' = Y$, $r' = r$, and $i' = i$. This then gives $L(Y', r' + i') = L(Y, r + i)$, so that the real demand for money is the same in the future and current periods. Then, from Equation (15.4), we get

$$\frac{M'}{M} = \frac{P'}{P},$$

so that the growth rates of the money supply and the price level are the same in equilibrium. This implies, from Equation (15.1), that the inflation rate is given by

$$i = \frac{P'}{P} - 1 = \frac{M'}{M} - 1 = x,$$

so that the inflation rate is equal to the money growth rate. The equality of the money growth rate and the inflation rate is special to this situation in which real variables remain constant over time. From Equation (15.4), if the real demand for money changes over time, so that $L(Y', r' + i') \neq L(Y, r + i)$, then the money growth rate is not equal to the inflation rate. However, it is still true that the inflation rate will increase as the money growth rate increases.

We wish to determine the effects of an increase in x on output, the real interest rate, employment, and the real wage in the monetary intertemporal model. To do this, we first need to understand how inflation affects labor supply and the demand for current consumption goods in this model. Recall from Chapter 10 that, in the monetary intertemporal model, consumption goods are purchased using currency acquired by the representative consumer before the goods market opens and that the consumer receives his or her wage income after goods are purchased, so that wage income must be held in the form of currency before it is spent in the future period. Just as in Chapter 8, when the representative consumer optimizes, he or she sets the marginal rate of substitution of current consumption goods for future consumption goods equal to $1 + r$, or

$$MRS_{C,C'} = 1 + r. \tag{15.5}$$

As well, because current wages cannot be spent on consumption goods until the future period, the effective real wage for the consumer is $\frac{Pw}{P'}$, which is the current nominal wage divided by the future price level. Therefore (recall Chapter 4), when the consumer optimizes, he or she sets the marginal rate of substitution of current leisure for future consumption equal to $\frac{Pw}{P'}$ or

$$MRS_{l,C'} = \frac{Pw}{P'} \tag{15.6}$$

Now, because Equations (15.5) and (15.6) tell us how the consumer substitutes at the optimum between current and future consumption and between current leisure and future consumption, we can derive from these two equations a marginal condition for substitution at the optimum between current leisure and current consumption. That is, at the optimum it must be the case that

$$MRS_{l,C} = \frac{MRS_{l,C'}}{MRS_{C,C'}} = \frac{Pw}{P'(1+r)},$$

from Equations (15.5) and (15.6). Therefore, from the Fisher relation in Chapter 10, we have

$$MRS_{l,C} = \frac{w}{1+R}, \tag{15.7}$$

where R is the nominal interest rate. To understand the marginal condition, Equation (15.4), it helps to run through how the consumer would substitute between current consumption and current leisure, which is roundabout because of the cash-in-advance constraint. If the consumer wishes to supply one extra unit of time during the current period as labor, he or she earns additional real wages of w, which then must be held over to the future period, when their value in terms of future consumption goods is $\frac{Pw}{P'}$. To consume more current goods, the consumer can borrow against this amount in the credit market before he or she arrives in the goods market. The real quantity that can be borrowed is $\frac{Pw}{P'(1+r)} = \frac{w}{1+R}$, which then must be the relative price of current leisure for current consumption.

Given Equation (15.7), a higher nominal interest rate R causes substitution away from consumption goods and towards leisure. Equation (15.4) then tells us that, from the approximate Fisher relation $R = r + i$, given the real interest rate r and the real wage w, and assuming that substitution effects dominate income effects, an increase in the inflation rate i causes substitution from consumption goods to leisure.

In Figure 15.5 we show the effects in the current period of an increase in the money growth rate from x_1 to x_2, which takes place for all periods, and is anticipated by everyone. In equilibrium the inflation rate in every period then increases from x_1 to x_2, given our analysis above where we showed that the money growth rate equals the inflation rate in equilibrium. The increase in the inflation rate causes substitution

FIGURE 15.5 **The Long-Run Effects of an Increase in the Money Growth Rate**

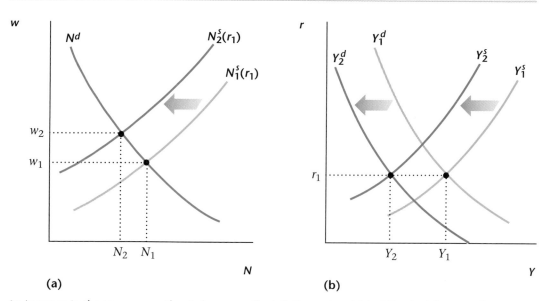

(a)   **(b)**

An increase in the money growth rate increases the inflation rate, which shifts the labor supply curve to the left, the output supply curve to the left, and the output demand curve to the left. The real wage rises, employment falls, and output falls. The real interest rate may rise or fall, but for simplicity we show the case where it stays constant.

by the representative consumer from consumption goods to leisure. This causes the labor supply curve to shift to the left in Figure 15.5(a), which in turn shifts the output supply curve to the left in Figure 15.5(b). As well, because the consumer substitutes away from consumption goods, the output demand curve shifts to the left in Figure 15.5(b). Now, in Figure 15.5(b), it is not clear whether the real interest rate rises or falls. For simplicity, we show the case where the output demand and output supply effects on the real interest rate just cancel, so that the real interest rate does not change. This also implies that investment and the capital stock are unaffected (assume that we are in a steady state where the capital stock is constant over time), which also greatly simplifies matters.

In Figure 15.5, in equilibrium output falls from Y_1 to Y_2, employment falls from N_1 to N_2, and the real wage rises from w_1 to w_2. In the figure the real interest rate remains constant, so that investment expenditures are unaffected, but consumption must fall as real income has decreased. From the approximate Fisher relation, $R = r + i$, where R is the nominal interest rate. Therefore, because r is constant, and i increases from x_1 to x_2, the nominal interest rate increases by the amount of the money growth rate increase (the **Fisher effect**; in the long run, an increase in the inflation rate is reflected one-for-one in an increase in the nominal interest rate). Also, given equilibrium in the money market,

$$\frac{M}{P} = L(Y, r + i),\tag{15.8}$$

real output Y has decreased, r is the same, and i has increased; therefore, real money demand on the right-hand side of Equation (15.8) has decreased, and so the current real money supply on the left-hand side of Equation (15.8) must also decrease. Higher money growth and inflation causes the consumer to hold a smaller quantity of real cash balances in equilibrium.

Though money is neutral in this economy, in that a change in the level of the money supply has no real effects, a change in the growth rate of the money supply is not neutral. If a change in the money growth rate had no real effects, we would say that money was **superneutral.** However, money is not superneutral here, as an increase in the money growth rate leads to decreases in consumption, output, and employment. These effects occur because higher money growth leads to higher inflation, which affects the consumer's decisions concerning how much to work in the current period and how much and what to consume. Higher inflation increases the nominal interest rate, which is the opportunity cost of holding money for transactions purposes. As a result, the household economizes on money balances. The resulting costs of inflation are lost output and consumption.

Optimal Monetary Policy: The Friedman Rule

At this point, we would like to demonstrate the key economic inefficiencies that result from inflation, and then show how these inefficiencies can be corrected by the appropriate long-run monetary policy. Recall from Chapter 5 that economic efficiency is achieved when the allocation of resources in an economy is Pareto optimal, that is, when there is no way to rearrange production or the allocation of goods so that someone is better off and no one worse off. A key condition for Pareto optimality that we derived in Chapter 5 was that the marginal rate of substitution of leisure for consumption must be equal to the marginal rate of transformation of leisure for consumption, that is

$$MRS_{l,C} = MRT_{l,C}.\tag{15.9}$$

This condition applies at the Pareto optimum because it is efficient for the rate at which the consumer is just willing to substitute leisure for consumption to be equal to the rate at which leisure can be converted into consumption goods using the production technology. Now in this model, as in the model of Chapter 5, the marginal rate of transformation of leisure for consumption is equal to the marginal product of labor, MP_N. In a competitive equilibrium, profit maximization by the representative firm implies that $MP_N = w$, so it is also true in a competitive equilibrium that

$$MRT_{l,C} = w.\tag{15.10}$$

Therefore, substituting for w in Equation (15.7) using Equation (15.10) gives

$$MRS_{l,C} = \frac{MRT_{l,C}}{1 + R}. \tag{15.11}$$

Therefore, because (15.11) holds in competitive equilibrium in this model, Equation (15.9) does not hold, and so the competitive equilibrium is not Pareto optimal, in general, as long as the nominal interest rate is positive, or $R > 0$. That is, a positive nominal interest rate drives a "wedge" between the marginal rate of substitution and the marginal rate of transformation, thus, creating an inefficiency. The fact that the nominal interest rate is positive implies that too much leisure is consumed, too little output is produced, consumption is too low, and real money balances are too low.

We know that an increase in the money growth rate x causes an increase in the nominal interest rate, so that higher money growth, which is associated with higher inflation, implies a larger wedge separating the marginal rate of substitution from the marginal rate of transformation. If the money growth rate and inflation were reduced, then it appears that this would promote economic efficiency, but what would be the best money growth rate for the government to set? Clearly, if the nominal interest rate were reduced to zero, then the marginal rate of substitution would be equal to the marginal rate of transformation in Equation (15.11). What is the money growth rate x that would drive the nominal interest rate to zero? Because in equilibrium the nominal interest rate is $R = r + x$, if $R = 0$, then it is optimal for the money growth rate to be $x = -r$. Because the real interest rate is positive ($r > 0$), then at the optimum $x < 0$ and the money supply decreases over time. Further, if the money supply is decreasing over time, there is **deflation**, because the inflation rate is $i = x = -r < 0$. Thus, it is optimal for the government to generate a deflation that continues forever, implying that the nominal interest rate is zero in every period.

The fact that the optimal monetary policy drives the nominal interest rate to zero is of prime importance in understanding why this policy works to maximize welfare. A positive nominal interest rate on bonds implies that the representative consumer economizes too much on money balances in favor of holding bonds. The consumer also consumes too small a quantity of goods and too much leisure. If the nominal interest rate is driven to zero through deflation, giving money a higher real return, then the household becomes indifferent between holding bonds and money, and this is optimal.

This type of optimal deflationary monetary policy is called a Friedman rule, after Milton Friedman.[6] In practice, the Friedman rule means that the nominal interest rate on riskless securities should always be zero. This does not mean that all nominal interest rates should be zero (this would be impossible), but that the nominal interest rate on short-term government debt (for example, U.S. Treasury bills) should be zero. The Friedman rule is probably the most robust policy conclusion that comes from monetary economics, but it is a policy that essentially no central bank currently follows

---

[6] See "The Optimum Quantity of Money," in M. Friedman, 1969. *The Optimum Quantity of Money and Other Essays*, pp. 1–50, Aldine Publishing, Hawthorne, NY.

or ever has followed. No central bank pursues long-run deflation as a goal, and no central bank advocates pushing the nominal interest rate to zero. Thus, central banks are doing something wrong, our model leaves out some important aspect(s) of the problem at hand, or inflation just does not matter much.

To pursue the last explanation, one possible reason central banks do not follow the Friedman rule is that, at low levels of inflation, say below 10% per annum, the gains from reducing inflation are very small. Indeed, Thomas Cooley and Gary Hansen[7] conclude that, in a monetary model similar to the one we have studied here, the welfare loss from an inflation rate of 10% per annum is about 0.5% of consumption for the average consumer, and the welfare loss from a monetary rule with 0% inflation versus the Friedman rule rate of deflation is about 0.14% of consumption for the average consumer.

Though most macroeconomic models tell us that the welfare losses from moderate inflations are quite small, the costs of extremely high rates of inflation—that is, **hyperinflations**—are clearly very large. Some prominent hyperinflations occurred in Austria, Hungary, Germany, and Poland in the early 1920s following World War I. For example, the inflation rate in Austria averaged 10,000% per annum between January 1921 and August 1922. Typically hyperinflations occur because the government is unwilling or unable to finance large government outlays through taxation or borrowing, and so it must resort to seigniorage. For example, the German hyperinflation following World War I occurred in part because the German government financed large war reparations to other European countries by printing money at a very high rate. The key to stopping a hyperinflation, as Thomas Sargent points out,[8] is gaining control over fiscal policy by reducing the government deficit.

Another reason that central bankers are wary of deflation and low nominal interest rates is that these have been characteristics of poorly performing economies. For example, there were deflation and low nominal interest rates in the United States during the Great Depression and more recently in Japan. The Japanese economy has performed poorly since the early 1990s, and short-term nominal interest rates there have been essentially zero. Keynes argued that, at a low nominal interest rate, there could be a **liquidity trap.** That is, if the nominal interest rate on government securities is zero, then money and government securities are essentially identical assets. If the central bank attempts to increase the money supply through an open market sale of government securities when the nominal interest rate is zero, this will have no effect, as the central bank is simply exchanging one type of asset for another identical asset. Perhaps central bankers fear a liquidity trap, but the logic of the Friedman rule tells us that a liquidity trap is a good place to be, and, in any event, an escape from the liquidity trap is possible if the government simply prints money and increases the money supply through transfers.

---

[7]See T. Cooley and G. Hansen, 1989. "The Inflation Tax in a Real Business Cycle Model," *American Economic Review* 79, 733–748.

[8]See "The Ends of Four Big Inflations," in T. Sargent, 1993. *Rational Expectations and Inflation,* 2nd edition, pp. 43–116, Harper Collins, New York.

MACROECONOMICS IN ACTION

Should the Fed Reduce the Inflation Rate to Zero or Less?

Our monetary intertemporal model tells us that the optimal rate of inflation is negative, which implies that the Fed should engineer a rate of growth in the money supply that would give permanent deflation. However, as we pointed out, no central bank appears to have attempted to bring about a deflation. At most, some policymakers are willing to recommend that the inflation rate be reduced to zero, so that the price level will remain constant over time. For example, in 1989 a bill was introduced in the House of Representatives that would have directed the Fed to reduce the inflation rate to zero over a five-year period. Does this imply that there is something that the monetary intertemporal model is missing in terms of the costs and benefits of inflation? Could the optimal inflation rate be higher than zero? S Rao Aiyagari, in "Deflating the Case for Zero Inflation,"[1] makes the case that the costs of reducing the inflation rate to zero would exceed the benefits. In making his argument, Aiyagari appeals to some of the costs of inflation that are contained in our monetary intertemporal model, but he considers other costs and benefits of inflation as well.

First, as in our model, Aiyagari argues that a cost of inflation arises because the nominal interest rate is positive, which causes people to economize too much on money balances. He points out that some of these costs could be eliminated if the government permitted the payment of interest on some components of the money stock. For example, the Fed currently does not pay interest on reserves that depository institutions (including banks) hold with the Fed. As well, it is currently prohibited for de-

pository institutions to pay interest on demand deposits, which are transactions deposits held by businesses. If interest were paid at the market interest rate on reserves and demand deposits, then only currency would be a noninterest-bearing asset. Currency is a fraction of the total money supply, and at that most U.S. currency is held by foreigners or held for illegal purposes. Inflation acts as a tax on currency holding, but if this tax falls mostly on foreigners and people engaged in illegal transactions, then inflation is not so costly for U.S. residents, and it might deter crime.

While the costs of inflation are very small, as Aiyagari argues, the short-run costs of reducing the inflation rate might potentially be large. Keynesian economists argue that price and wage stickiness can cause short-run decreases in aggregate output if the Fed were to reduce money supply growth to bring about a reduction in inflation, as we studied in Chapter 12. As well, if the private sector doubts the Fed's resolve to reduce inflation, this can cause a short-run drop in aggregate activity until the Fed proves that it is serious, an issue we address in Chapter 17. Given these potentially large short-run costs, Aiyagari concludes that a reduction in the inflation rate to zero would not be worthwhile, but that relaxing regulations on the banking sector—for example, by permitting the payment of interest on all transactions deposits and reserves—would certainly be beneficial.

---

[1] See S. R. Aiyagari, 1990. "Deflating the Case for Zero Inflation," *Federal Reserve Bank of Minneapolis Quarterly Review*, Summer, 2–11.

FINANCIAL INTERMEDIATION AND BANKING

The purpose of this section is to study the place of banking in the monetary system. Earlier, in this chapter we discussed the historical importance of currency issued by private banks and how in modern economies much of transactions activity takes place using bank deposits. The role that banks and other financial intermediaries play in the economy is intimately related to the properties that different assets have, and so in the following subsection we discuss the characteristics of assets and their economic importance.

Properties of Assets

The four most important properties of assets are rate of return, risk, maturity, and liquidity; we discuss each of these in turn.

Rate of return: The rate of return on an asset is the payoff on the asset over some specified period of time divided by the initial investment in the asset, minus one. For example, the one-period rate of return on an asset that is bought at price q_t in period t, sold at price q_{t+1} in period $t + 1$, with a payout (say a dividend on a stock) of d in period $t + 1$, would be

$$r_t^a = \frac{q_{t+1} + d}{q_t} - 1.$$

Everything else held constant, consumers prefer assets that bear higher rates of return.

Risk: In modern finance theory, the risk that matters for a consumer's behavior is the risk that an asset contributes to the consumer's entire portfolio, where a portfolio is the entire set of assets the consumer holds. For example, a set of stocks might be quite risky on an individual basis, in that their rates of return fluctuate a great deal over time. However, when all these stocks are held together in a well-diversified portfolio, the entire portfolio may not be very risky. For instance, holding all of one's wealth in shares of Joe's Restaurant might be quite risky, but holding shares in all the restaurants in town might not be very risky at all. Even though diversifying one's portfolio by holding many different assets reduces risk, because the rates of return on some assets can go up while other rates of return go down, there is a limit to the risk reduction that can be gained from diversification. Risk that cannot be diversified away is aggregate or macroeconomic risk, and it is the amount of this **nondiversifiable risk** present in a particular asset that matters for economic behavior. Here, we assume that consumers are **risk-averse,** so that, everything else held constant, a consumer prefers to hold assets with less nondiversifiable risk.

Maturity: Maturity refers to the time it takes for an asset to pay off. For some assets, maturity is a straightforward concept. For example, a 91-day U.S. Treasury bill is a security issued by the U.S. government that pays its face value 91 days from the date of issue, so maturity in this case is 91 days. For some other assets, however, this is not so clear, as in the case of a long-maturity bond. Many bonds provide for coupon payments, which are amounts the bearer receives at fixed intervals until the bond matures, when it pays its face value. Thus, a 30-year bond that provides for coupon payments at monthly intervals does not have a maturity of 30 years, but something less than that, because the payoffs on the asset take place during the 30-year period until all payoffs are received. All other things held constant, a consumer prefers a short-maturity asset to a long-maturity asset. Short-maturity assets imply more flexibility in meeting unanticipated needs for funds, and even if a consumer is certain that the funds will not be needed until far in the future (suppose the consumer is saving for a child's education, for example), it is possible to meet this need by holding a string of short-maturity assets rather than a long-maturity asset.

Liquidity: The final asset characteristic is liquidity, which is a measure of how long it takes to sell an asset for its market value, and of how high the costs are of selling the asset. Because money is widely acceptable in exchange and can, therefore, essentially be sold for its market value instantaneously, it is the most liquid asset. A good example of an illiquid asset is a house, which can often take weeks to sell, with a high transaction fee paid to an intermediary—the real estate agent—to find a buyer. Liquidity is important to an asset holder, because investors face uncertainty about when they want to purchase goods or assets. For example, consumers may face unforeseen expenses such as medical bills, or they may want to take advantage of an unanticipated investment opportunity. All else held constant, consumers prefer more liquidity to less liquidity.

Financial Intermediation

Now that we know something about the properties of assets, we can examine the role of financial intermediaries in the monetary system.

A financial intermediary is defined by the following characteristics:

1. It borrows from one group of economic agents and lends to another.
2. The group of economic agents it borrows from is large, and so is the group it lends to. That is, a financial intermediary is well diversified.
3. It transforms assets. That is, the properties of its liabilities are different from the properties of its assets.
4. It processes information.

Examples of financial intermediaries are insurance companies, mutual funds, and depository institutions. The economic role that these intermediaries play is intimately related to their four defining characteristics. Suppose that we consider depository institutions as an example. Depository institutions include commercial banks, thrift institutions (savings and loan associations and mutual savings banks), and credit unions. These institutions exist in part because of difficulties in getting ultimate borrowers and ultimate lenders together. To see why this is so, consider how the borrowing and lending done by a depository institution would take place in the absence of this institution. An individual wanting to borrow to purchase a house, for example, would have to first find a lender willing to loan him or her the funds to make the purchase. Even if the would-be borrower were well known to the would-be lender, the would-be lender may not have good information on the would-be borrower's ability to repay the loan, and some time and effort would have to be forgone to acquire this information. Further, given that the loan required is sizable, the would-be borrower might have to approach several would-be lenders to finance the house purchase, and each of these would-be lenders would have to incur information costs to ascertain the riskiness of lending to the would-be borrower. Now, supposing the loan is made, each of the lenders would bear some risk, given that there is always some chance that the borrower will not repay the loan. Further, unless the lenders had the means to enforce the loan contract, the borrower might try to abscond with the loan without repaying, even though he or she could repay. Finally, after the loan is made, it would be difficult for the lender to sell the loan to someone else should he or she require funds at short notice. That is, the loan is illiquid, in part because it has a long maturity. In fact, given the high value of the loan relative to the would-be borrower's income, the maturity of the loan may be so long that few would-be lenders would want to tie up funds for this length of time. To summarize, there are six potential problems with direct lending from ultimate lenders to ultimate borrowers, without the benefit of a financial intermediary:

1. Matching borrowers with lenders is costly in time and effort.
2. The ultimate lenders may not be skilled at evaluating credit risks.
3. Because several lenders would often be required to fund any one borrower, there would be replication of the costs required to evaluate credit risk.
4. Because lenders economize on information costs by lending to few borrowers, lending is risky.
5. Loans tend to be illiquid.
6. Loans tend to have longer maturities than lenders would like.

Without financial intermediaries, few loans would be made, and the only lending would be to the least risky borrowers. However, in our running example, consider what a depository institution can do to alleviate the aforementioned six difficulties. First, the depository institution is a well-defined place of business, and people know where to go if they wish to borrow or lend, and so this eliminates the search costs involved in getting borrowers and lenders together. Second, the depository institution is specialized in evaluating credit risks, and so can do this at a lower cost per loan than would be the case for an unspecialized individual. That is, there are economies of scale in acquiring information. Third, because the financial intermediary pools the funds of many lenders, it can avoid the replication of costs that occurs when there is direct lending. Fourth, because the financial intermediary is well diversified with respect to both its assets and liabilities, it can transform risky, illiquid, long-maturity assets into relatively safe, liquid, short-maturity liabilities.

Taking a depository institution specializing in mortgage lending as an example, each mortgage may be risky, illiquid, and of long maturity. However, because the depository institution holds many mortgages (it is well diversified on the asset side of its balance sheet), the payoff on the bank's entire asset portfolio is relatively predictable, because the fraction of mortgage loans that default should be predictable. Further, even though all the assets of the depository institution are illiquid and of long maturity, the institution's liabilities can be liquid and of short maturity because of the diversification of its liabilities. That is, suppose that the depository institution has many depositors, all holding transactions accounts. An individual depositor could decide to make with-drawals and deposits or to write checks at random times, but taken as a group, the behavior of depositors is predictable. Thus, though a transactions deposit is highly liquid and has as short a maturity as the depositor might wish for, the institution can make highly illiquid and long-maturity loans based on its ability to predict the aggregate behavior of a large number of depositors.

The Diamond–Dybvig Banking Model

This banking model was developed in the early 1980s by Douglas Diamond and Philip Dybvig.[9] It is a simple model that captures some of the important features of banks and helps to explain why bank runs might occur (as they did historically) and what role the government might have in preventing banking runs.

In the model, there are three periods: 0, 1, and 2. There are N consumers, where N is very large, and each consumer is endowed with one unit of a good in period 0, which can serve as an input to production. The production technology takes one unit of the input good in period 0 and converts this into $1 + r$ units of the consumption good in period 2. However, this production technology can also be interrupted in period 1. If interruption occurs in period 1, then one unit of consumption goods can be obtained for each unit of the good invested in period 0. If production is interrupted, then nothing is produced in period 2.

A given consumer might wish to consume early—in period 1—or to consume late—in period 2. However, in period 0, individual consumers do not know whether they are early or late consumers; they learn this in period 1. In period 0, each consumer knows that they have a probability t of being an early consumer and probability $1 - t$ of being a late consumer, and in period 1, tN consumers learn that they are early consumers and $(1 - t)N$ consumers learn that they are late consumers. We have $0 < t < 1$. For example, if $t = \frac{1}{2}$ then a consumer has equal probabilities of being an early or late consumer, as if consuming early or late were determined by the flip of a coin.

The production technology captures liquidity in a simple way. That is, using the production technology is much like investing in a long-maturity asset that could be sold with some loss before it matures. For a consumer, the possibility that he or she might consume early captures the idea that there exist random needs for liquid assets, that is unforeseen circumstances when transactions need to be made. In practice we make many transactions over the course of a day or a week, and not all of these transactions are anticipated. For example, one might see a book in a store window and wish to purchase it, or one might be caught in an unexpected rainstorm and need to buy an umbrella, etc.

Whether consumption takes place early or late, the utility (or pleasure) that the consumer receives is given by $U(c)$, where U is a utility function and c is consumption. The utility function is concave, as in Figure 15.6, because the marginal utility of consumption declines as consumption increases. The **marginal utility of consumption,**

[9]Diamond, D. and Dybvig, P. 1983. "Bank Runs, Liquidity, and Deposit Insurance," *Journal of Political Economy* 91, 401–419.

FIGURE 15.6 The Utility Function For a Consumer in the Diamond–Dybvig Model

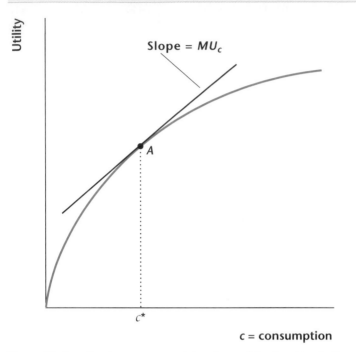

The utility function is concave, and the slope of the function is the marginal utility of consumption, MU_c.

MU_c, is given by the slope of the utility function. For example, in Figure 15.6 the MU_c when $c = c^*$ is given by the slope of a tangent to the utility function at point A.

Given the world that an individual consumer lives in here, he or she needs to make decisions under uncertainty in period 0. In economics, a productive approach to modelling consumer choice under uncertainty is to assume that a consumer maximizes expected utility, which here is

$$\text{Expected Utility} = tU(c_1) + (1 - t)U(c_2),$$

where c_1 is consumption if the consumer needs to consume early and c_2 is consumption if the consumer is a late consumer. That is, expected utility is a weighted average of utilities that occur if the particular events happen (early or late consumption), where the weights are the probabilities that the particular events occur, which in this case are t and $1 - t$.

We can represent a consumer's expected utility preferences in terms of indifference curves, with c_1 (early consumption) on the horizontal axis and c_2 (late consumption) on the vertical axis in Figure 15.7. As in Chapters 4 and 8, these indifference curves are

FIGURE 15.7   The Preferences of a Diamond–Dybvig Consumer

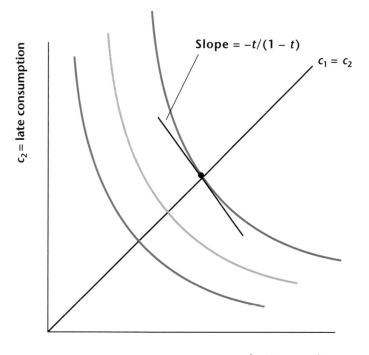

c_1 = early consumption

The figure shows the indifference curves for a Diamond–Dybvig consumer, who has preferences over early consumption and late consumption.

downward sloping and convex. The marginal rate of substitution of early consumption for late consumption for the consumer is given by

$$MRS_{c_1,c_2} = \frac{tMU_{c_1}}{(1-t)MU_{c_2}},$$ (15.12)

where MRS_{c_1,c_2} is minus the slope of an indifference curve in Figure 15.7. When $c_1 = c_2$, so that early consumption and late consumption are equal, we have $MU_{c_1} = MU_{c_2}$ (if consumption is the same, the marginal utility of consumption must also be the same). From Equation (15.12) we have

$$MRS_{c_1,c_2} = \frac{t}{(1-t)},$$

when $c_1 = c_2$. Therefore, in Figure 15.7, an important property of the indifference curves is that, along the line $c_1 = c_2$, the slopes of each of the indifference curves is $\frac{-t}{1-t}$.

Now, suppose that each consumer must invest independently. On his or her own, what would a consumer do? Clearly, he or she invests all of his or her one unit of endowment in the technology in period 0. Then, in period 1, if he or she is an early consumer, then he or she interrupts the technology and is able to consume $c_1 = 1$. If he or she is a late consumer, then the technology is not interrupted and the consumer gets $c_2 = 1 + r$ in period 2 when the investment matures. What we would like to show is that a bank can form that allows all consumers to do better than this.

A Diamond–Dybvig Bank   In this model, a bank is an institution that offers deposit contracts to consumers. These deposit contracts allow consumers to withdraw c_1 units of goods from the bank in period 1 if they wish or to leave their deposit in the bank until period 2 and receive c_2 units of goods then. In period 1, consumers are served in sequence by the bank; that is, if a consumer wishes to withdraw his or her deposit in period 1, he or she is randomly allocated a place in line. We assume that the bank cannot tell the difference between early consumers and late consumers. While an early consumer would not want to pose as a late consumer by not withdrawing early, as this could only make him or her worse off, it is possible that there might be circumstances in which a late consumer might want to withdraw early. We suppose that a late consumer who withdraws in period 1 can store goods until period 2 and then consume them.

What determines the deposit contract (c_1, c_2) that the bank offers? We suppose that there is one bank in which all consumers make their deposits and that this bank behaves competitively. There is free entry into banking, implying that the bank earns zero profits in equilibrium. The bank makes each depositor as well off as possible, while earning zero profits in periods 1 and 2, because if it did not behave in this way, then some other bank could enter the market offering an alternative deposit contract and attract all consumers away from the first bank. Because all consumers deposit in the bank in period 0, the bank has N units of goods to invest in the technology in period 0. In period 1, the bank must choose the fraction x of the investment to interrupt so that it can pay c_1 to each depositor who wishes to withdraw at that time. Supposing that only early consumers show up at the bank to withdraw in period 1, we must have

$$Ntc_1 = xN \tag{15.13}$$

or the total quantity of withdrawals equals the quantity of production interrupted. Then, in period 2, the quantity of uninterrupted production matures, and this quantity is used to make payments to those consumers who chose to wait, who we are supposing are only the late consumers. Then, we have

$$N(1 - t)c_2 = (1 - x)N(1 + r). \tag{15.14}$$

That is, the total payout to the late consumers (on the left-hand side of Equation (15.14)) is equal to the total return on uninterrupted production (on the right-hand side of Equation (15.14)). If we substitute in Equation (15.14) for x using Equation (15.13) and simplify, we get

$$tc_1 + \frac{(1 - t)c_2}{1 + r} = 1, \tag{15.15}$$

and Equation (15.15) is like a lifetime budget constraint for the bank that governs how the deposit contract (c_1, c_2) can be set. We can rewrite the bank's lifetime budget constraint in slope-intercept form as

$$c_2 = -\frac{t(1+r)}{1-t}c_1 + \frac{1+r}{1-t},\tag{15.16}$$

and the bank's lifetime budget constraint is depicted in Figure 15.8; in the figure, points A, B, and D lie on the constraint. The constraint has a vertical intercept of $\frac{1+r}{1-t}$, which is the maximum payout to late consumers if the bank does not interrupt any of its production, and the horizontal intercept is $\frac{1}{t}$, which is the maximum amount that could be withdrawn by early consumers in the case where all production is interrupted by the bank. The slope of the bank's lifetime budget constraint is $\frac{-t(1+r)}{1-t}$. The equilibrium deposit contract offered by the bank is at point A in Figure 15.8, where an

---

FIGURE 15.8 **The Equilibrium Deposit Contract Offered by the Diamond–Dybvig Bank**

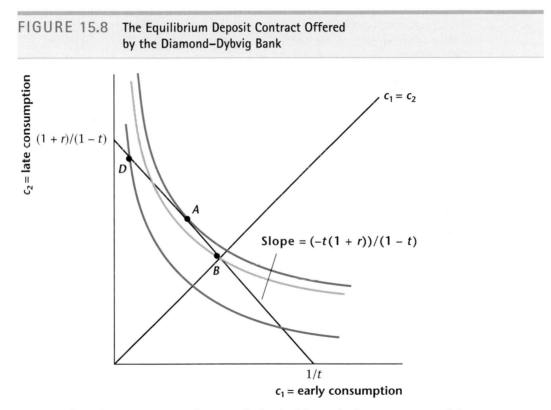

Point A, where there is a tangency between the bank's lifetime budget constraint and the consumer's indifference curve, is the equilibrium deposit contract. Point B would have equal consumption for early and late consumers, and point D is what the consumer could achieve in the absence of the bank.

indifference curve for the consumer is tangent to the bank's lifetime budget constraint. The equilibrium deposit contract has two important properties, which are:

1. The equilibrium deposit contract, at point A in Figure 15.8, lies to the northwest of point B, which is the point on the bank's lifetime budget constraint where the bank's payouts to early and late consumers are the same. We know from above that at point B the marginal rate of substitution of early consumption for late consumption is $\frac{-t}{1-t}$, and so an indifference curve running through point B is less steep than the lifetime budget constraint of the bank. Therefore, A must lie to the northwest of B in the figure. The importance of this observation is that late consumers consume more than early consumers, given the equilibrium deposit contract; that is $c_2 > c_1$. Thus, if all other late consumers do not withdraw, any individual late consumer prefers not to withdraw in period 1. A late consumer is not tempted to pose as an early consumer if other late consumers do not do this.

2. The equilibrium deposit contract, at point A in Figure 15.8, lies to the southeast of point D, which is what the consumer would choose in the absence of the bank. By substituting in the bank's lifetime budget constraint, Equation (15.15), the deposit contract $(1, 1+r)$ (point D in the figure) satisfies this constraint, so that the consumption profile chosen by the consumer in the absence of the bank is a choice open to the bank as well. To guarantee that point D lies to the northwest of point A in the figure requires an extra assumption, essentially that there is enough curvature in the utility function depicted in Figure 15.6. Without getting into the technical details concerning why this makes sense, we simply assume here that D lies to the northwest of A in the figure. The reason this is important is that it guarantees that $c_1 > 1$ and $c_2 < 1+r$, so that there is a sense in which the bank provides insurance against the event that the consumer needs liquidity in period 1 to make a transaction (to consume). By accepting the banking contract, the consumer is able to consume more in period 1 than he or she could otherwise, at the expense of lower consumption in period 2.

The Diamond–Dybvig bank has some of the properties of financial intermediaries that we mentioned above. While it does not lend but instead holds assets directly and does not process information, the bank in this model borrows from a large number of depositors (it is well diversified), and it carries out an asset transformation. The fact that the bank is well diversified is important for its role in transforming assets. That is, because the bank holds the deposits of a large number of depositors, the number of depositors who wish to withdraw is predictable, and so the bank need only interrupt that fraction of production required to satisfy the withdrawal needs of the early consumers. The bank holds illiquid assets and is able to convert these assets into liquid deposits, providing depositors with a type of insurance against the need for liquid assets.

Bank Runs in the Diamond–Dybvig Model   The fact that the Diamond–Dybvig bank supplies consumers with insurance against the need for liquidity also leaves the bank open to bank runs. Given the banking contract at point A in Figure 15.8, where $c_1 > 1$ and $c_2 < 1+r$, there is a *good equilibrium* where each early consumer lines up at the bank to withdraw their deposit in period 1, each late consumer waits to withdraw until period 2, and everyone is happy. Given these circumstances, no late consumer has the incentive to withdraw in period 1, as $c_1 < c_2$ at point A in Figure 15.8, so withdrawing early would only make a late consumer worse off. However, suppose that a late consumer believes that all other late consumers will go to the bank to withdraw in period 1. Because all early consumers withdraw in period 1, the individual late consumer then believes that everyone else will go to the bank in period 1. Because $c_1 > 1$ at point A in Figure 15.8, even if the bank liquidates all of its assets in period 1, which yields the quantity N in consumption goods, it cannot satisfy total withdrawal demand, which is $(N-1)c_1$ (recall that N is large, so that $(N-1)c_1 > N$ at point A in the figure). Thus, the individual late consumer is faced with two choices. He or she can run to the bank and hope to get a place close to the front of the line, in which case he or she gets c_1, while risking the chance of being too close to the rear of line, in which case he or she gets nothing. If he or she chooses to wait until period 2 to withdraw, there will definitely be nothing left. Therefore, the choice is clear; if a late consumer anticipates in period 1 that everyone else will run to the bank to withdraw their deposit, he or she will want to do it as well. Thus, there is a *bad equilibrium*, which is a **bank run.** Everyone runs to the bank in period 1; some consume c_1, but others consume nothing. This outcome is no better for some consumers (the early consumers who manage to get to the bank before it runs out of funds) and is worse for everyone else than the good equilibrium.

The Diamond–Dybvig model, thus, has multiple equilibria, much like the Keynesian coordination failure model we studied in Chapter 11. Multiple equilibria are used here to explain why bank runs have occurred historically. In the United States before the establishment of the Federal Reserve System in 1914, there were recurring **banking panics** during the **National Banking era** (1863–1913). During these panic episodes, which were typically triggered by the failure of a large financial institution or institutions, there were large deposit withdrawals from banks that sometimes appeared to be contagious. As well, widespread bank runs occurred during the Great Depression in the United States. The Diamond–Dybvig model provides an explanation for why an otherwise sound bank could experience a bank run and fail. According to the logic of the model, because a bank provides a liquidity transformation service to consumers, this leaves it open to bank runs. Because bank deposits are liquid, if all depositors show up at the bank in the anticipation that the bank will fail, then their expectations are self-fulfilling, and the bank will indeed fail.

Deposit Insurance   A potential solution to the problem of bank runs is government-provided deposit insurance. In the Diamond–Dybvig model, if the government steps in and guarantees each depositor that they will receive the quantity c_2 given by the banking contract at point A in Figure 15.11, then no late consumer would have a reason to run to the bank. This leaves aside the question of who the government will tax if it has to make good on its deposit insurance guarantees. However, in the model the bad equilibrium will never occur with deposit insurance in place, so the government will never have to make any payouts related to its insurance program. The model tells us that promises by the government can serve to prevent a bad outcome.

In the United States, deposits in depository institutions are insured up to $100,000 by the Federal Deposit Insurance Corporation (FDIC). This means that, if a depository institution fails, the depositors are guaranteed that they will receive the value of their deposits up to $100,000. The FDIC was established in 1934, mainly in response to the failure of about one-third of all depository institutions during the Great Depression.

The main cost of deposit insurance is that it creates a **moral hazard** problem, and this problem is something that is not taken into account in the Diamond–Dybvig banking model. Moral hazard arises in essentially all insurance situations, because the insured individual tends to take less care in preventing the event against which he or she is insured. For example, if the owner of a car is completely insured against damages to his or her car, he or she takes less care in driving in parking lots, and, therefore, is more likely to have an accident. It is difficult for the insurance company to correct for this problem, because the amount of care taken by the driver of the car is hard to observe. Moral hazard can explain the existence of deductibles in insurance contracts, which require the insured party to bear the cost of small losses.

For a depository institution, moral hazard arises because deposit insurance encourages the depository institution to take on more risk. This happens because the riskiness of a bank's assets is difficult to observe and because with deposit insurance the depositors have no interest in whether the depository institution is risky or not. Therefore, though deposit insurance can prevent the failures of sound depository institutions that might occur because of self-fulfilling panics, it could produce more failures because of the increased riskiness of banks. Thus, the existence of deposit insurance requires that the regulators of depository institutions impose restrictions on depository institution activities to assure that these institutions do not take on too much risk.

The Deregulation and Monetary Control Act of 1980 introduced many needed reforms into the regulation of depository institutions in the United States. Among these reforms were relaxations in restrictions on the kinds of assets that thrift institutions—savings and loans institutions and mutual savings banks—could hold. Unfortunately, there was inadequate supervision of these thrift institutions in the 1980s, and consequently they took on some very risky assets, with the result that many thrifts failed in the later 1980s. The resources of deposit insurers were insufficient to compensate depositors, and U.S. taxpayers incurred a cost of hundreds of billions of dollars to bail out thrift institutions. This is an example of what can happen because of the moral hazard problem induced by deposit insurance.

Another element of moral hazard in the U.S. monetary system results from the **too-big-to-fail doctrine.** This represents the belief that the regulators of the U.S. financial system would not tolerate losses by depositors at any large depository institution in the country, because of the fear that such losses would lead to widespread financial panic. Indeed, in 1984 when the Continental Illinois Bank failed (which at the time was one of the 10 largest banks in the United States), the FDIC compensated not only depositors with deposits less than $100,000 but also large depositors and bondholders as well. Given that large banks know that all or most of the holders of their liabilities are implicitly insured against loss, these large banks have an even greater incentive than small banks to take on too much risk.

This completes our study of money and banking in this book. In Chapter 16 we examine some issues in unemployment, and in Chapter 17 we return to the study of inflation to explain why central banks may resort to inflation in situations in which they know inflation is a bad thing.

MACROECONOMICS IN ACTION

Bank Failures and Banking Panics in the United States and Canada

Canada and the United States are in many ways economically similar, but they have very different banking systems.[1] The two countries have also had very different historical experiences with banking panics and bank failures, and this represents a challenge to the Diamond–Dybvig banking model.

While the United States has a unit banking system, with thousands of banks that typically serve small geographical areas (though this is changing), Canada has a branch banking system, with only a handful of commercial banks that branch nationally. On the one hand, the United States has had a network of regulations designed to keep banks small, and it is relatively easy to open a new bank. On the other hand, in Canada banks are typically not prevented from becoming large, and it requires federal legislation for a bank to obtain a charter and open for business.

United States banking history has many episodes of widespread bank failures and banking panics, as we have discussed. There were recurrent banking panics during the National Banking era in the United States, from 1863 to 1913. The Federal Reserve System, established in 1914, was supposed to correct the institutional problems that caused banking panics, but missteps in monetary policy in the Great Depression contributed to a situation in which about one-third of U.S. banks failed between 1929 and 1933.

Before the establishment of the Canadian central bank, the Bank of Canada, in 1935, there were no banking panics of note in Canada. Canada was a latecomer to

deposit insurance, introducing it in 1967, but in spite of this there were few bank failures before that time. No commercial banks failed in the Great Depression in Canada, and the most recent bank failure before 1985 was the failure of the Home Bank in 1923. The most recent commercial bank failures were those of the Northland Bank and the Canadian Commercial Bank in 1985.

Why have the experiences with bank failures and panics been so different in Canada and the United States? This seems hard to explain using the Diamond–Dybvig banking model, where bank runs arise simply because banks are performing a useful intermediation service; in this sense U.S. banks and Canadian banks are no different. The evidence points to two factors (not included in the Diamond–Dybvig banking model), that appear to be important in explaining these differences between the United States and Canada. First, in the period before 1935, much of the circulating currency in Canada was issued by commercial banks (see the discussion earlier in this chapter). This private currency was viewed by the public as being quite safe. At times of the year when the demand for currency was particularly high (typically during the fall harvest) relative to bank deposits, it was easy for the chartered banks to convert deposit liabilities into notes in circulation by printing more notes to issue when depositors chose to withdraw. In periods of high demand for currency in the United States between 1863 and 1913, a panic could result, but this was averted in Canada because

(continued)

of the note-issuing ability of Canadian commercial banks. Bank failures are also averted in Canada by the fact that Canadian banks are relatively large and well-diversified geographically. One of the reasons for the failures of the Northland Bank and Canadian Commercial Bank in 1985 was that these banks did most of their lending in one western province of Canada, which exposed them to the risks associated with local shocks. In this case the local shock was a sharp drop in the prices of oil and natural gas that caused a reduction in local asset prices, resulting in borrowers at these banks defaulting on their loans. U.S. banks, which are typically not well-diversified geographically, are exposed to the same kind of risk and, thus, are more likely to fail than a well-diversified Canadian branch bank.

[1]The material here relies heavily on Williamson, S. 1989. "Restrictions on Financial Intermediaries and Implications for Aggregate Fluctuations: Canada and the United States, 1870–1913," in O. Blanchard and S. Fischer, eds., *NBER Macroeconomics Annual 1989,* NBER, Cambridge, MA; and Champ, B., Smith, B., and Williamson, S. 1996. "Currency Elasticity and Banking Panics: Theory and Evidence," *Canadian Journal of Economics* 29, 828–864.

CHAPTER SUMMARY

- Money functions as a medium of exchange, a store of value, and a unit of account. Historically, the objects that have played the role of money are commodity money, circulating private bank notes, commodity-backed paper currency, fiat money, and transactions deposits at private banks.

- We considered a simple model capturing the absence-of-double-coincidence-of-wants problem that can exist in barter economies where people only have goods to trade. In the model, commodity money or fiat money can overcome the double-coincidence problem by providing a universally acceptable medium of exchange.

- The monetary intertemporal model from Chapter 10 was used to study the effects of long-run inflation. A higher money growth rate causes an increase in the rate of inflation, an increase in the nominal interest rate, and decreases in output, consumption, and employment.

- A positive nominal interest rate represents a distortion that drives a wedge between the marginal rate of substitution of leisure for consumption and the marginal rate of transformation of leisure for consumption.

- An optimal long-run monetary policy in the monetary intertemporal model is for the central bank to follow a Friedman rule, whereby the money growth rate and the inflation rate are equal to minus the real interest rate. This implies that the nominal interest rate is zero at the optimum.

- In the Diamond–Dybvig banking model, a bank provides its depositors with insurance against the event that they need liquid assets to make transactions. The bank converts illiquid assets into liquid deposits.

- In the Diamond–Dybvig model, there is a good equilibrium where all early consumers withdraw their deposits from the bank early and all late consumers withdraw late. There is also a bad equilibrium (a bank run) where all consumers choose to withdraw early, and the bank fails. The bank run equilibrium can be prevented through government-provided deposit insurance.

- There is a moral hazard problem associated with deposit insurance, in that an unregulated bank with insured deposits takes on too much risk. According to the too-big-to-fail doctrine, the implicit insurance of the deposits and other liabilities of large banks makes these banks especially prone to the moral hazard problem.

KEY TERMS

Friedman rule: An optimal rule for monetary policy, whereby the money supply grows at a rate that implies a zero nominal interest rate.

Financial intermediary: Any financial institution that borrows from one large group of people and lends to another large group of people, transforms assets in some way, and processes information.

Free banking era: The period running from 1837–1863 in the United States characterized by the issuance of currency by many private banks.

Gold standard: An arrangement whereby a country stands ready to exchange its money for gold at a fixed price.

Check-clearing system: The system that allows for debiting and crediting of the appropriate bank deposit accounts when a check deposited in a bank is written on an account in another bank.

Absence of double coincidence of wants: Situation in which there are two would-be trading partners, but it is not true that each has the good the other wants.

Fisher effect: The increase in the nominal interest rate resulting from an increase in the rate of inflation.

Superneutral: Describes money in the situation where a change in the money supply growth rate has no real effects.

Deflation: Decrease in the price level over time.

Hyperinflations: Situations where the inflation rate is extremely high.

Liquidity trap: A situation where, if the nominal interest rate is zero, then open market operations by the central bank have no effect.

Nondiversifiable risk: Risk that an individual cannot diversify away by holding a large portfolio of assets.

Risk-averse: Describes an individual who does not like risk.

Marginal utility of consumption: The slope of the utility function, or the marginal increase in utility (happiness) resulting from a one-unit increase in consumption.

Bank run: A situation where a bank's depositors panic and simultaneously attempt to withdraw their deposits.

Banking panics: Situations where bank runs are widespread.

National banking era: The period in the United States between 1863 and 1913.

Moral hazard: The tendency of insured individuals to take less care to prevent a loss against which they are insured.

Too-big-to-fail doctrine: The doctrine according to which U.S. regulatory agencies should intervene to prevent the failure of any large financial institution.

QUESTIONS FOR REVIEW

1. What are five forms that money has taken historically?

2. What do Yap stones and the playing card money of New France have in common? What is different about these two forms of money?

3. How does an absence of double coincidence of wants make money socially useful?

4. What are the effects of an increase in the money supply growth rate in the monetary intertemporal model?

5. What are the costs of inflation?

6. Should the monetary authority manipulate the money supply to hold the price level constant over time?

7. Why don't real-world central banks follow the Friedman rule?

8. List four properties of assets, and explain why these properties are important.

9. What are the four defining characteristics of a financial intermediary?

10. What are three types of financial intermediaries?

11. What is unusual about depository institutions relative to other financial intermediaries?

12. In the Diamond–Dybvig banking model, why does a consumer do better by depositing in a bank rather than investing on his or her own?

13. What features of real-world banks does a Diamond–Dybvig bank have?

14. Why are there two equilibria in the Diamond–Dybvig banking model? How do the two equilibria compare?

15. How can bank runs be prevented?

16. Explain what moral hazard is and why and how deposit insurance and the too-big-to-fail doctrine induce a moral hazard problem.

PROBLEMS

1. Consider the absence-of-double-coincidence economy depicted in Figure 15.1. Determine who would trade what with whom if good 2 were used as a commodity money. Explain your results.

2. As an alternative to the economy depicted in Figure 15.1, suppose that there are three types of people, but now the person who consumes good 1 produces good 3, the person who consumes good 2 produces good 1, and the person who consumes good 3 produces good 2.
   (a) Determine who trades what with whom if good 1 is used as a commodity money, and compare this with what happens when good 1 is used as a commodity money in the economy in Figure 15.1. Explain.
   (b) Determine who trades what with whom if fiat money is used in exchange, and commodity money is not used. Explain.

3. Suppose, in the monetary intertemporal model, that the quantity of government purchases increases permanently, and that this increase in government spending is financed by an increase in the growth rate x of the money supply. That is, the increase in government spending is financed through seigniorage. Determine the effects on current equilibrium inflation, employment, output, the real wage, the real interest rate, and the nominal interest rate. Explain your results.

4. Suppose, in the monetary intertemporal model, that the government can pay interest on money, financing this interest with lump-sum taxes on consumers. If the nominal interest

rate on money is the same as the nominal interest rate on bonds, determine the effects in the model, illustrating this in a diagram. Explain your results.

5. Consider the following assets: (i) a work of art; (ii) a United States Treasury bill; (iii) a share in Microsoft; (iv) a loan to a close relative; (v) a loan to General Motors. For each asset, answer the following questions:
   (a) Does the asset have a high rate of return or a low rate of return (on average)?
   (b) Is the asset high risk or low risk?
   (c) Is the asset a long-maturity asset or a short-maturity asset?
   (d) Is the asset highly liquid, less liquid, somewhat illiquid, or highly illiquid?
   (e) Explain why the asset has the above four properties.
   (f) Which of the properties of money (medium of exchange, store of value, unit of account) does the asset have? Would we consider it money and why or why not?

6. In the Diamond–Dybvig banking model, suppose that the banking contract includes a "suspension of convertibility" provision according to which the bank allows only the first tN depositors in line in period 1 to withdraw their deposits. Will there still be a bank run equilibrium? Carefully explain why or why not.

7. Alter the Diamond–Dybvig model in the following way. Suppose that there are two assets, an illiquid asset that returns $1 + r$ units of consumption goods in period 2 for each unit invested in period 0, and a liquid asset that returns one unit of consumption goods in period 1 for each unit invested in period 0. The illiquid asset production technology cannot be interrupted in period 1. The model is otherwise the same as outlined in this chapter.
   (a) Determine a consumer's lifetime budget constraint when there is no bank, show this in a diagram, and determine the consumer's optimal consumption when an early consumer and when a late consumer in the diagram.
   (b) Determine a bank's lifetime budget constraint, show this in your diagram, and determine the optimal deposit contract for the bank in the diagram. Are consumers who deposit in the bank better off than in part (a)? Explain why or why not.
   (c) Is there a bank run equilibrium? Explain why or why not.

8. Explain how moral hazard arises in each of the following situations:
   (a) A mother promises her daughter that she will help her with her homework during the coming school year but only if the daughter has difficulty with her homework.
   (b) An individual's house is insured against damage by fire for its full value.
   (c) An individual is appointed to manage an investment portfolio for a group of coworkers.
   (d) The same individual in part (c) is appointed to manage the investment portfolio, and the government guarantees that all investors in the group will receive a 5% return per year. That is, the government will make up the difference if the return on the portfolio falls below 5% in a given year.

WORKING WITH THE DATA

1. Answer the following questions:
   (a) Calculate the monthly percentage increases in the consumer price index and in M1, and display these in a scatter plot. What do you observe? Explain.
   (b) Now, calculate percentage increases in the consumer price index and in M1 over five-year periods, and display these in a scatter plot. How does this scatter plot compare to the one you constructed in part (a)? Explain.

2. Display the 3-month Treasury bill interest rate, the interest rate on a 10-year Treasury note, and the interest rate on a 3-month certificate of deposit in a time series plot. What do you observe? How do the properties of assets explain the regularities in this interest rate data?

3. Plot the 3-month treasury bill interest rate and the rate of inflation over the previous year in a time series plot. To what extent does the nominal interest rate reflect the actual inflation rate? Is this consistent with the predictions of the monetary intertemporal model in this chapter? Explain.

CHAPTER 16

Unemployment: Search and Efficiency Wages

To study the reasons for unemployment, we need to understand in more detail how people use their time. In the macroeconomic models we have used in previous chapters, consumers typically divide their time between leisure and market work, but in this chapter we would like to explore explanations for a third activity—unemployment—which, as measured by the Bureau of Labor Statistics in the United States, is neither leisure nor market work. There are two key features of unemployment that set it apart. One is that unemployment entails searching for work, which is costly. The reason the unemployed are willing to bear the costs of searching for work is that there is a chance that they will find a job and be better off. Thus, the fact that searching for work is painful implies the second key feature of unemployment, which is that the unemployed are worse off, in some sense, than the employed. Though unemployment is painful, and the unemployed would typically be better off working at some job, unemployment is a necessary evil in modern economies. Indeed, it would be impossible to eliminate all unemployment, and some government policies that could reduce unemployment would in fact be detrimental to overall economic welfare.

Our first goal in this chapter is to examine the behavior of the unemployment rate in the United States. As well, we study the behavior of another key labor market variable, the participation rate. We show how the unemployment rate and participation rate move over the business cycle, and discuss some of the determinants of these two variables.

Next, we study two models that permit us to organize our thinking about the determinants of the unemployment rate. The first model is a search model of unemployment, in which unemployed workers look for jobs and accept a job when the welfare they receive from working at the wage offered exceeds the welfare from turning down the job offer and continuing to search. The search model allows us to show how unemployment insurance benefits, taxation, and other government interventions affect the behavior of unemployed workers and the unemployment rate.

The second model we consider is the efficiency wage model, which builds on the idea that workers' effort on the job depends on the real wage they receive. This can imply that, in equilibrium, the real wage is higher than the market-clearing real wage, because the higher real wage allows the firm to elicit more effort from its workers. Thus, the real wage is "sticky," and there can be equilibrium unemployment. This model, thus, is related to the Keynesian sticky wage model in Chapter 12, though in that model it was the nominal wage rather than the real wage that was sticky. Once we have constructed the efficiency wage model and have showed how it works, we will examine how well the efficiency wage model fits the business cycle facts discussed in Chapter 3.

THE BEHAVIOR OF THE UNEMPLOYMENT RATE AND THE PARTICIPATION RATE IN THE UNITED STATES

Before studying models of unemployment, we explore the empirical behavior of the unemployment rate and the participation rate in the United States. Recall from Chapter 2 that, if E is the number of working age persons who are employed, U is the number of unemployed, and NL denotes those who are not in the labor force, then the unemployment rate and participation rate are defined by

$$\text{unemployment rate} = \frac{U}{E + U},$$

$$\text{participation rate} = \frac{E + U}{E + U + NL},$$

where the total labor force is equal to $E + U$.

Figure 16.1 shows a plot of the monthly unemployment rate for the United States for the years 1948 to 2003. The unemployment rate is a countercyclical variable, in that it is high during recessions and low during booms. In particular, note in the figure that the unemployment rate spiked up during the recessions of 1974–75, 1981–82, 1991–92, and 2001 and decreased during the economic booms of the late 1970s, the late 1980s, and the 1990s following the 1990–91 recession. In addition to the cyclical behavior of the unemployment rate, there also appear to be longer-run movements in the unemployment rate in the figure. For example, from about 1970 until the mid-1980s, there was a trend increase in the unemployment rate and a trend decrease from the mid-1980s through the 1990s. We would like to understand the reasons for both the cyclical behavior and long-run behavior of the unemployment rate.

The key determinants of the unemployment rate are the following:

Aggregate Economic Activity: When aggregate real GDP is high relative to trend, the unemployment rate tends to be low. As mentioned above, the unemployment rate is a countercyclical variable. In Figure 16.2, which shows the deviations from trend in the unemployment rate and in real GDP (percentages in this case), we see that the unemployment rate tends to be below (above) trend when real GDP is above (below) trend.

Demographics: Demography is the study of population. The age structure of the population matters a great deal for the unemployment rate, as workers of different ages behave quite differently in the labor market. The unemployment rate for the young tends to be higher than that for the old, as younger workers have a weaker attachment to the labor force and switch jobs more frequently early in their careers, thus suffering more frequent spells of unemployment. In Figure 16.1, part of the increase in the average unemployment rate in the 1970s was because this was the period when many members of the post–World War II baby boom generation entered the labor force. Then, the average unemployment rate fell during the 1980s and 1990s as baby boomers aged.

Government intervention: A key government program that affects the unemployment rate over the long run is government-provided unemployment insurance (UI). Workers who suffer a spell of unemployment typically experience a drop in their

FIGURE 16.1   The U.S. Unemployment Rate, 1948–2003

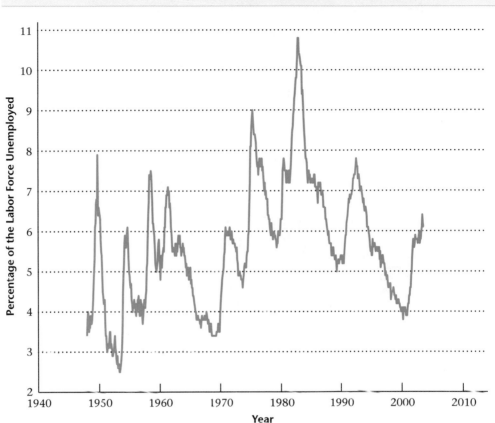

The unemployment rate shows considerable cyclical volatility. In the United States, there was also a trend increase in the unemployment rate from 1970 until the mid-1980s, and a trend decrease from the mid-1980s through the 1990s.

consumption. Why shouldn't this loss be insurable, just as is the loss from an automobile accident, a fire, or ill health? The problem is that UI is not supplied by private firms, and the government has taken on this insurance role in most developed countries. In the United States, UI programs are run by state governments, and the rules governing UI vary state by state. Typically, unemployed workers in the United States can draw UI benefits for about six months, and the **replacement ratio,** the ratio of UI benefits to the wage the unemployed worker was earning when employed, is about 0.5. Thus, the typical UI benefit in the United States is about one-half of the wage earned when employed. Just as happens with other types of insurance, there is moral hazard associated with UI. That is, the behavior of an insured person changes in a way that makes a loss more likely, as we discussed in connection with deposit

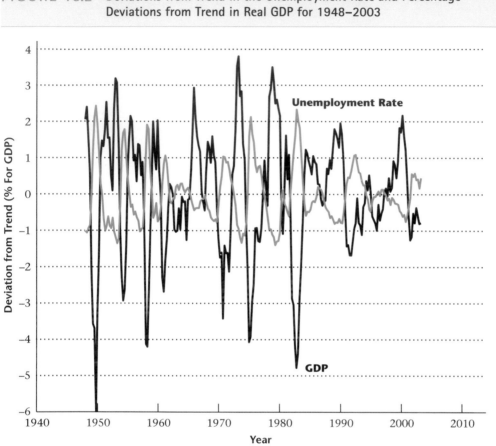

FIGURE 16.2   Deviations from Trend in the Unemployment Rate and Percentage Deviations from Trend in Real GDP for 1948–2003

The unemployment rate is countercyclical, as it tends to be above (below) trend when real GDP is below (above) trend.

insurance in Chapter 15. In the case of UI programs, more generous UI benefits tend to make unemployed workers more picky concerning the kinds of jobs they will take, and this tends to increase the duration of unemployment spells and increase the unemployment rate, as we show in a search model of unemployment later in this chapter. Also see "Macroeconomics in Action: Unemployment Insurance and Incentives."

Sectoral shifts: A sectoral shift is a change in the economy's aggregate structure of production, as discussed in Chapter 9. For example, in the United States recently, there has been a shift away from manufacturing (the production of tangible goods) and toward services (intangible goods). As a result, workers in manufacturing industries such as steel and textiles have been displaced. Displacement can imply a long period of unemployment, particularly for older workers, as displaced workers may have obsolete skills and may need to acquire new ones, and finding work in a different sector of the economy takes time. Given the level of aggregate economic activity, the greater the restructuring occurring among industries in the economy, the higher the unemployment rate will tend to be.

Now that we have gained some understanding of the determinants of the unemployment rate, which are reinforced by our study of models of unemployment later in this chapter, we can turn to the other key labor market variable, the participation rate, which is depicted in Figure 16.3 for the years 1948–2003. Here, the fraction of the

FIGURE 16.3 **The U.S. Participation Rate, 1948–2003**

The participation rate increased in the United States from about 59% in 1948 to about 67% in 1999 before a slight decrease began in 2000.

FIGURE 16.4   Labor Force Participation of Women and Men

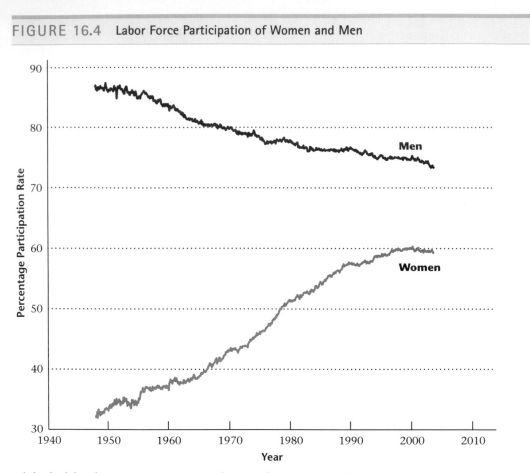

While the labor force participation rate of women has increased almost continuously since 1948 before levelling off recently, the participation rate of men has decreased.

working age population in the labor force increased substantially, from less than 60% in the early 1950s to about 67% in 1999, before decreasing slightly. In Figure 16.4 we show the participation rates of men and women, which show a decline for men and a huge increase for women. Therefore, the increase in the total participation rate in Figure 16.3 until 1999 is accounted for solely by an increase in the labor force participation rate for women. Some point to sociological explanations for the increase in the participation rate of women, but economists do not find it surprising that more women would choose market work in the face of large increases in market real wages in the post–World War II period. The declining participation rate of men is closely connected to the increasing participation rate of women, because family decisions concerning labor market participation are made jointly.

FIGURE 16.5   Deviations from Trend in the Participation Rate and GDP

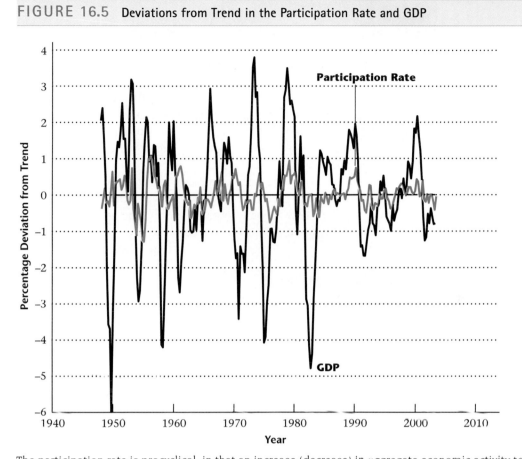

The participation rate is procyclical, in that an increase (decrease) in aggregate economic activity tends to cause an increase (decrease) in labor force participation.

In Figure 16.5 we show the percentage deviations from trend in the participation rate and real GDP in the United States. The participation rate is a procyclical variable, in that it tends to be above trend when real GDP is above trend. With increases in aggregate economic activity, more workers tend to enter the labor force. That is, when GDP increases, employment tends to go up, and naturally some of this increase in employment arises because of a flow of people from the unemployment pool to the employment pool. However, some of the increased employment also arises because people who were formerly not in the labor force choose to work when aggregate economic activity increases.

MACROECONOMICS IN ACTION

Unemployment in Europe

A common view of unemployment in Europe versus the United States is that unemployment is high in Europe and low in the United States because European labor markets are overregulated and, therefore, unnecessarily rigid. In an article in the *Journal of Economic Perspectives,* Stephen Nickell argues that this view is in part correct, but that the story is considerably more complicated.[1]

Table 16.1 shows average unemployment rates in the member countries of the Organization for Economic Co-operation and Development (OECD) for the period 1983–1996, from Table 1 of Nickell's

article. While it is true that, of the 15 European countries in the table, 9 had average unemployment rates greater than the U.S. rate, ranging as high as 19.7% for Spain, there were 6 countries that had lower average unemployment rates than the 6.5% rate in the United States. Further, as Nickell points out, these low-unemployment-rate countries have labor markets with considerably more rigidity than in the United States, which appears to be inconsistent with the story that greater labor market rigidities create greater unemployment. The greater labor market rigidities that are present in most European countries include laws that

Table 16.1 **Average Unemployment Rates in OECD Countries, 1983–1996**

Australia	8.7%
Austria	3.8%
Belgium	9.7%
Canada	9.8%
Denmark	9.9%
Finland	9.1%
France	10.4%
Germany(W)	6.2%
Ireland	15.1%
Italy	7.6%
Japan	2.6%
Netherlands	8.4%
New Zealand	6.8%
Norway	4.2%
Portugal	6.4%
Spain	19.7%
Sweden	4.3%
Switzerland	1.8%
United Kingdom	9.7%
United States	6.5%

encourage the formation of labor unions, tougher legal restrictions on the hiring and firing of employees, relatively generous unemployment compensation, high minimum wages, and high taxes. In general, we would expect all of these factors to make it more difficult for those searching for jobs to find them, but Nickell shows that this need not always be the case.

Nickell's empirical work shows that high unemployment tends to be associated with poorly designed unemployment insurance systems, a high degree of unionization, high taxes on labor, high minimum wages, and poor educational standards. One of Nickell's surprising findings is that

unemployment insurance compensation can be quite generous and still have little effect on the unemployment rate, provided that the benefits are limited in duration, and that sufficient incentives are given for finding employment when unemployed. Also, high unionization does not always mean higher unemployment, if there is a high degree of coordination among employers in wage negotiations; presumably, this prevents inefficiencies such as costly strikes.

---

[1] S. Nickell, 1997. "Unemployment and Labor Market Rigidities: Europe Versus North America," *Journal of Economic Perspectives* 11, 55–74.

A SEARCH MODEL OF UNEMPLOYMENT

Now that we know some of the features of labor market data, we can proceed to study models that explain the behavior of the unemployment rate. In explaining the unemployment rate, we need to construct a more complicated model of how people use their time. In the models we have worked with to this point, consumers typically use their time for only two different purposes, market work and leisure. Unemployment, however, is an economic activity distinct from either work or leisure, being an activity that involves search. The first search models were developed in the late 1960s,[1] and they have since been refined and put into wide use in labor economics and macroeconomics. This model allows us to think about the factors that motivate the search behavior of unemployed workers, and it permits us to analyze the determinants of the unemployment rate.

The Welfare of Employed and Unemployed Workers

For simplicity, the workers in our model are all in the labor force; that is, they are either employed or unemployed, with U denoting the fraction of workers who are unemployed and $1 - U$ the fraction who are employed. The jobs of the employed differ according to the wages that they pay, where w denotes the real wage associated with a particular job. Let $V_e(w)$ denote the value of being employed. This is the welfare of a worker who is employed and earning a real wage w, and it takes into account the taxes that a worker pays and all possible future events, including the chances of the worker being separated from his or her job and what will happen to the worker in such an event. We let s denote the **separation rate**; that is, s is the fraction of workers who

---

[1] See J. McCall, 1970. "Economics of Information and Job Search," *Quarterly Journal of Economics* 84, 113–126.

become randomly separated from their jobs every period. This is a simple way to capture job separations that occur in practice because of firings and quits arising from poor matches between workers and firms. We depict the function $V_e(w)$ in Figure 16.6. $V_e(w)$ increases with w, as the worker is better off with higher-paying jobs, and $V_e(w)$ is concave because the worker experiences diminishing marginal utility from higher-paying jobs. That is, the increase in welfare for the worker from an extra unit of real wage income becomes smaller as real wage income increases, reflected in the declining slope of $V_e(w)$. Shifts in the function $V_e(w)$ result as follows:

- The function $V_e(w)$ shifts down if the separation rate s increases. Given an increase in the separation rate, there is a greater chance of an employed worker losing his or her job and becoming unemployed. This makes employment less attractive, and the welfare from being employed at any wage must fall.

- The function $V_e(w)$ shifts down if taxes on wage income increase. Clearly, an increase in such taxes implies that effective wages are lower, which will decrease the welfare of an employed worker for each real wage.

Now, we want to consider the welfare of an unemployed worker, which we denote by V_u. The key determinant of V_u is the size of the UI benefit that an unemployed worker receives. For simplicity, we assume that the UI benefit is a constant real amount b that does not depend on the wage the unemployed worker earned when he or she was employed. Another important determinant of V_u is the frequency with which the unemployed worker receives job offers, and we denote this frequency by p. That is, each period a fraction p of all the unemployed workers receive job offers. Three important facts are the following:

- V_u increases when b increases. An increase in the unemployment benefit increases an unemployed worker's welfare.

FIGURE 16.6 **The Welfare of an Employed Worker**

The worker's welfare is increasing in the real wage w that he or she earns on the job, and the function is concave because the marginal benefit from a higher real wage declines as the real wage increases.

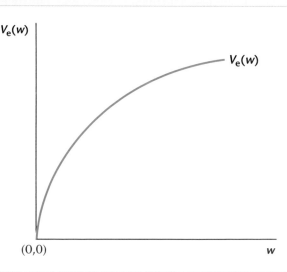

- V_u increases when p increases. With a higher p, the chances are better for the unemployed worker of receiving a job offer he or she will take, and this will increase welfare.

- V_u decreases if taxes on unemployment benefits increase. This decreases the effective unemployment benefit and reduces the welfare of the unemployed.

The Reservation Wage

Now that we know how a worker's welfare is determined when employed and unemployed, we can work out how the unemployed worker makes choices. When an unemployed worker receives a job offer, it is a job offer at a particular wage, w. The key decision for the unemployed worker on receiving a job offer is whether to take the offer or to continue searching for work. If a low-wage job is turned down, there is some possibility of receiving a higher-wage offer in the future, but the worker must bear a period of unemployment and uncertainty before this higher-wage offer is received. Therefore, if a bad job is turned down, there is a trade-off in this decision between the short-run losses from unemployment and the uncertain long-run benefits from a good job. Clearly, some wage offer is sufficiently high that the unemployed worker accepts it, and he or she would also accept any wage offer that was higher than this amount. We call this the **reservation wage** and denote it by w^*.

When a wage offer w is received, this implies a level of welfare for the job, $V_e(w)$. The unemployed worker accepts the job if the welfare from taking it is higher than the welfare of being unemployed and declines it otherwise. That is, the worker accepts the job if $V_e(w) \geq V_u$ and turns it down if $V_e(w) < V_u$. In Figure 16.7 we have $V_e(w) \geq V_u$ if $w \geq w^*$ and $V_e(w) < V_u$ if $w < w^*$, and so w^* is the reservation wage that determines acceptance or rejection of job offers.

FIGURE 16.7 **The Reservation Wage**

The reservation wage w^* is determined by the intersection of the $V_e(w)$ curve (the welfare from employment) and the V_u curve (the welfare from unemployment).

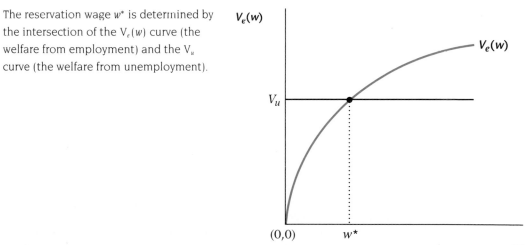

FIGURE 16.8   **An Increase in the Unemployment Insurance Benefit b**

The increase in benefits increases the welfare from unemployment from V_u^1 to V_u^2. The reservation wage then increases from w_1^* to w_2^*.

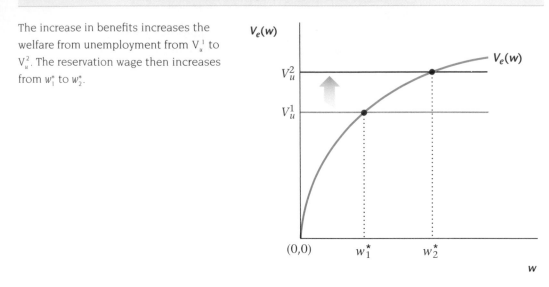

The reservation wage changes if there are shifts in either $V_e(w)$ or V_u. We consider two examples. First, suppose that the unemployment benefit increases. This causes an increase in V_u from V_u^1 to V_u^2 in Figure 16.8. As a result, the reservation wage increases from w_1^* to w_2^*. Therefore, with an increase in the unemployment benefit, there is a smaller cost to turning down a job to hold out for a higher wage offer, and an unemployed worker then becomes more picky concerning the jobs that he or she will take. Second, suppose that there is an increase in the tax on wage income, which in Figure 16.9 causes a shift down in the welfare of an employed worker from $V_e^1(w)$ to $V_e^2(w)$. As a result, the reservation wage increases from w_1^* to w_2^*. This occurs because, for a given wage offer w, there is now a smaller difference between welfare when employed and when unemployed, and so the net loss from turning down any job offer and waiting for a better one is now smaller. Unemployed workers are then more picky and, therefore, have a higher reservation wage.

The Determination of the Unemployment Rate

Having shown how an unemployed worker chooses his or her reservation wage, we can complete our search model of unemployment and show how it determines the long-run rate of unemployment. In the model, there are flows between the pool of employed workers and the pool of unemployed workers each period. Some employed workers are separated from their jobs and become unemployed, while some unemployed workers receive job offers that are sufficiently attractive to accept. If U is the unemployment rate—that is, the fraction of the labor force that is unemployed—then given that the

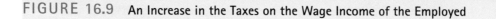

FIGURE 16.9 **An Increase in the Taxes on the Wage Income of the Employed**

The tax increase reduces the welfare from employment, and increases the reservation wage from w_1^* to w_2^*.

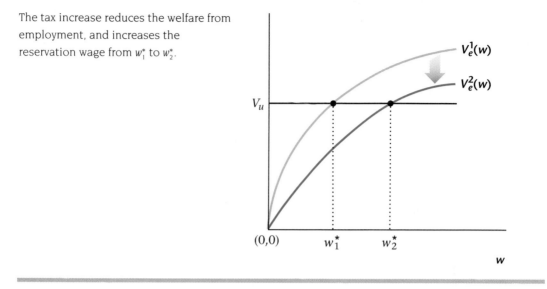

separation rate is s, the flow of workers from employment to unemployment is $s(1-U)$. Now, let $H(w)$ denote the fraction of unemployed workers receiving a wage offer whose offer is greater than w, where $H(w)$ is depicted in Figure 16.10. $H(w)$ is decreasing in w. Now, if unemployed workers choose a reservation wage w^*, then given that a fraction p of the unemployed receive a job offer and a fraction $H(w^*)$ of those receiving an offer are offered a wage greater than w^*, the portion of the unemployed who will be employed next period is the fraction who receive a wage offer that is at their reservation wage or above. Therefore, the flow of workers from unemployment to employment is $UpH(w^*)$.

In a long-run equilibrium, the flow of workers from employment to unemployment must be equal to the flow of workers from unemployment to employment, and so we must have

$$s(1-U) = UpH(w^*). \tag{16.1}$$

This is an equation that determines the unemployment rate U given s, p, and the reservation wage w^*. In Figure 16.11 we depict the left-hand and right-hand sides of Equation (16.1), with the intersection of these two curves determining the long-run equilibrium unemployment rate, denoted by U^*.

Now, Figure 16.12 shows how the reservation wage and the unemployment rate are determined in equilibrium. In Figure 16.12(a), the reservation wage w^* is determined by the intersection of the V_u and $V_e(w)$ curves, while Figure 16.12(b) determines the unemployment rate given the reservation wage w^*.

FIGURE 16.10   The Fraction of Unemployed Workers Receiving a Wage Offer Greater than w

As w increases, the fraction of unemployed workers, H(w), who receive a wage offer greater than w falls.

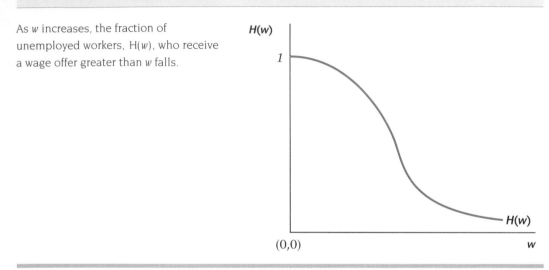

FIGURE 16.11   The Determination of the Unemployment Rate U* in the Search Model

In the figure, $s(1-U)$ is the flow of workers from employment to unemployment, and $UpH(w^*)$ is the flow of workers from unemployment to employment. The long-run unemployment rate U^* is determined by the intersection of the two lines.

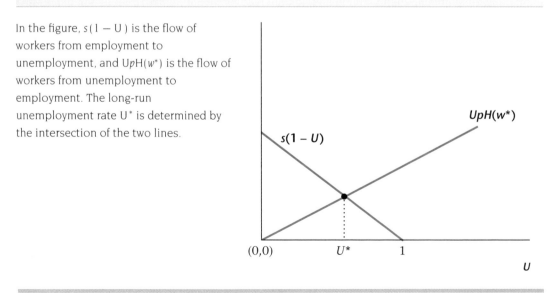

FIGURE 16.12 The Determination of the Reservation Wage and the Unemployment Rate in the Search Model

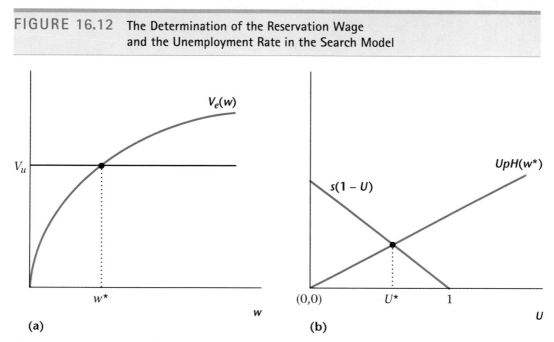

(a) **(b)**

The reservation wage w^* is determined in panel (a) by the intersection of the curves $V_e(w)$ and V_u. Then, given the reservation wage, the long-run unemployment rate is determined in panel (b).

Now that we have a complete model that determines the reservation wage and the long-run unemployment rate, we can use this model to analyze the effects on these two variables of changes in the economic environment.

An Increase in Unemployment Insurance Benefits The first experiment we carry out is to look at the effects of a change in unemployment insurance benefits. In Figure 16.13(a) an increase in UI benefits b increases the welfare of the unemployed, V_u, from V_u^1 to V_u^2. The effect of this is to increase the reservation wage from w_1^* to w_2^*. This then implies that the fraction of unemployed workers receiving an acceptable wage offer is smaller. That is, because $H(w)$ is decreasing in w, we have $H(w_2^*) < H(w_1^*)$. In Figure 16.13(b), this implies that the line $UpH(w_1^*)$ shifts down to $UpH(w_2^*)$. As a result, the unemployment rate increases from U_1 to U_2 in the long run.

The intuition behind this result is that more generous UI benefits imply that unemployed workers can afford to be more picky about the jobs they accept. On average, then, spells of unemployment tend to be longer, and the long-run unemployment rate must increase. Relatively higher unemployment insurance benefits in part explain higher average unemployment rates in Europe and Canada than in the United States.

FIGURE 16.13   **An Increase in the Unemployment Insurance Benefit b**

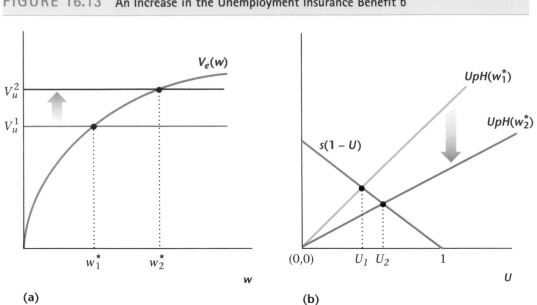

(a)   (b)

The rise in UI benefit increases the value of unemployment from V_u^1 to V_u^2 in panel (a), causing the reservation wage to increase. This decreases the flow of workers from unemployment to employment in panel (b), and the unemployment rate rises in the long run.

An Increase in the Job Offer Rate   A second experiment is to look at the effects of an increase in the job offer rate p on the reservation wage and the long-run unemployment rate. Suppose that the job offer rate p increases. Such a change would result from an increase in the efficiency with which firms and unemployed workers are matched. This could occur for two reasons. First, there might be technological change, such as better information technology, which could increase the likelihood of matches between unemployed workers and firms with vacancies. For example, the Internet greatly increases an unemployed worker's ability to find work at low cost. Second, p could increase because of government intervention. In many countries, the government plays an active role in finding work for unemployed workers, through government-run employment centers and the like.

In Figure 16.14 we show the long-run equilibrium effects of an increase in p. Here, when p increases, this raises the welfare of the unemployed from V_u^1 to V_u^2 in Figure 16.14(a). As a result, the reservation wage increases from w_1^* to w_2^*, because unemployed workers can now afford to be more picky, as they do not have to wait as long for another wage offer if the current offer is turned down. In Figure 16.14(b), there are two effects on the flow of workers from unemployment to employment. The direct effect is that an increase in p from p_1 to p_2 increases the flow of workers from

FIGURE 16.14 **An Increase in the Job Offer Rate p**

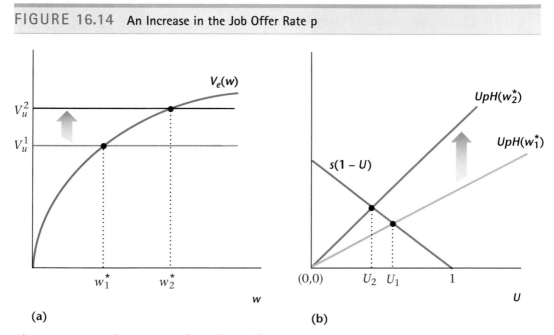

(a)

(b)

When p increases, this increases the welfare of the unemployed, who are now more likely to find work, and the reservation wage increases from w_1^* to w_2^* in panel (a). In panel (b), there are two effects on $UpH(w^*)$, in that p has increased, which increases the flow of workers from unemployment to employment, but w^* has increased, which reduces this flow. It is not clear how the unemployment rate is affected, but we show it decreasing in the figure.

unemployment to employment, because job offers are now received at a higher rate. This shifts up the line $UpH(w^*)$. The indirect effect is that the reservation wage rises, reducing $H(w^*)$, the fraction of workers receiving a job offer who accept the offer. On net, it is not clear whether $UpH(w^*)$ will rise or fall, but in Figure 16.14 we show it increasing from $Up_1 H(w_1^*)$ to $Up_2 H(w_2^*)$, which implies that the unemployment rate falls in long-run equilibrium from U_1 to U_2. However, if the indirect effect is greater than the direct effect, then the unemployment rate rises.

The implications of this for government policy are important. If the government uses resources to find work for unemployed workers, then this may be counterproductive if its goal is to decrease the unemployment rate. It may be the case that unemployed workers simply become picky enough concerning the jobs they will take that the unemployment rate rises. Also, workers may or may not be better off as a result. The welfare of the unemployed is affected positively, because unemployed workers have better choices, and the employed are in general working at higher-paying jobs, but there is a cost of the government's unemployment program, which ultimately is financed through taxation, and this reduces the welfare of those who are taxed. The net effect on economic welfare is, therefore, uncertain.

FIGURE 16.15 **An Increase in Taxes on Labor Income**

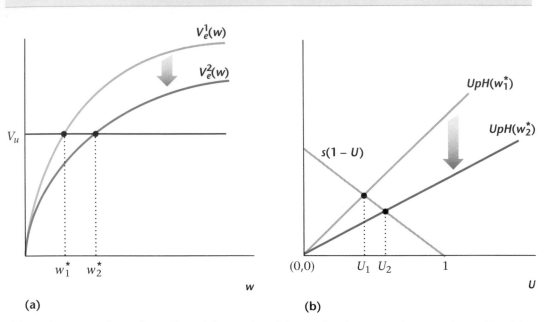

This tax increase reduces the welfare of the employed, increasing the reservation wage from w_1^* to w_2^* in panel (a). In panel (b), the flow of workers from unemployment to employment goes down, which causes the unemployment rate to rise in the long run.

Taxes on Labor Income and Unemployment Insurance Benefits Our next set of experiments involves looking at the effects of taxing the labor income of the employed and the UI benefits of the unemployed. First, in Figure 16.15 we show the effects of a tax on labor income. This reduces the welfare of the employed in Figure 16.15(a), with $V_e^1(w)$ shifting down to $V_e^2(w)$. Therefore, the reservation wage increases from w_1^* to w_2^*. Then, the fraction of workers receiving wage offers who accept these offers falls from $H(w_1^*)$ to $H(w_2^*)$, which implies that, in Figure 16.15(b), the line $UpH(w_1^*)$ shifts down to $UpH(w_2^*)$. In equilibrium, the unemployment rate increases from U_1 to U_2.

The effect of the labor income tax is to discourage employment, so that in the long run the unemployment rate increases. This effect is neutralized if the income tax is levied on both labor income and UI benefits. In this case, $V_e(w)$ and V_u both shift down by the same amount, in Figure 16.16(a), so that the reservation wage remains unchanged at w^*. Then, in Figure 16.16(b), the long-run unemployment rate also stays constant at U^*. In the United States, UI benefits are taxed at the same rates as other income, so that employment is not discouraged.

FIGURE 16.16   **Taxes on Labor Income and Unemployment Benefits**

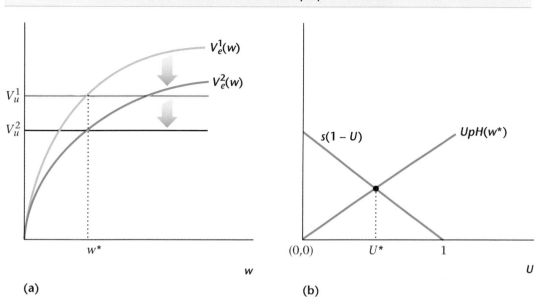

(a)

(b)

If taxes fall equally on labor income and unemployment benefits, there is no effect on the reservation wage and no effect on the unemployment rate.

MACROECONOMICS IN ACTION

Unemployment Insurance and Incentives

The search model of unemployment illustrates one effect of UI, which is that higher UI benefits tend to make the unemployed more selective concerning the job offers they will accept. This increases the average duration of an unemployment spell and increases the unemployment rate. There are also other effects of UI which we have not included in our simple search model. A second effect has to do with the influence of UI on on-the-job performance. For those employed, effort is required to retain a job. If

an employer feels that a worker does not meet some threshold level of effort, then the worker could be fired. Of course, it is difficult for the employer to observe a worker's effort level perfectly, so, in general, some errors might be made by the employer in that workers with good levels of effort might at times be fired and some workers with poor levels of effort might be retained. However, in general, if a worker increases his or her effort level on

(continued)

the job, the chance of being fired is reduced. With higher UI benefits, though, the cost of being fired from a job is lower, and workers, therefore, exert less effort on the job and stand a greater chance of losing their jobs. Higher UI benefits, therefore, act to increase the rate of transition from employment to unemployment through this effect, and this increases the unemployment rate.

A third effect of UI is its influence on the effort that the unemployed put into searching for work. Just as the unemployed become more choosy concerning the job offers they take with higher UI benefits, they also tend to search less intensively, because higher UI benefits decrease the cost of being unemployed.

A key feature of the three effects of UI on behavior—the effect on job acceptances, the effect on on-the-job effort, and the effect on search effort—is that all of these effects are imperfectly observable. That is, there are moral hazard problems associated with UI, just as there are moral hazard problems for other forms of insurance (including deposit insurance, as discussed in Chapter 15), as we mentioned earlier in this chapter. It is difficult for the provider of UI to observe whether the unemployed are turning down good job offers, whether workers are being fired because their effort is too low, or whether long spells of unemployment are the result of low search effort. Indeed, the fact that UI is provided by the government in the United States may indicate that the moral hazard problems associated with UI are so severe that UI would not be provided by a private insurer in the absence of government provision.

UI systems need to be designed with moral hazard problems in mind, and the UI system in the United States certainly has features that, at least partially, correct for moral hazard. For example, the level of benefits does not imply full insurance, in that (as pointed out earlier in this chapter) the replacement rate (the ratio of benefits when unemployed to wages when employed) is about 0.5, and benefits are limited in duration for individuals, typically extending for only about six months of unemployment. An optimal UI system achieves an optimal tradeoff between the benefits of insurance and the costs of moral hazard. If there is too much insurance (for example if the unemployed receive benefits equal to their wages on the job forever) then workers and the unemployed have poor incentives; but, if there is too little insurance, unemployment is too painful.

What would an optimal unemployment insurance system look like, and how close does the UI system in the United States come to such an optimal system? Several articles in the economics literature have attempted to address these questions. An approach that is useful in this context is a dynamic contracting model, which allows us to think about economic problems in a dynamic framework where information is not perfect, as is the case with unemployment insurance. An early article by S. Shavell and L. Weiss[1] shows that the optimal unemployment insurance benefit decreases over time. That is, in contrast to the UI system in the United States, where benefits are constant for six months of unemployment and then go to zero, optimally benefits should decrease over time continuously and extend indefinitely. The optimal benefit schedule looks like this because the longer a person has been unemployed, the more likely it is that they are not looking very hard for a job, and so a person should be penalized with lower benefits the longer they have been unemployed. However, a person may have been unemployed for a long time simply because he or she was unlucky, so it does not make sense to reduce benefits to zero for the long-term unemployed.

A more recent paper by Cheng Wang and Stephen Williamson[2] broadens the approach of Shavell and Weiss. Wang and Williamson show that an optimal unemployment insurance system should be more individual-specific, while having the Shavell-Weiss feature that UI benefits decline with the duration of unemployment. That is, the level of benefits for an unemployed person should depend not only on the length of time since the person became unemployed and the wage when employed but also on the whole history of employment and unemployment for that person. Such an optimal system would be implemented by having each U.S. citizen hold an account with the UI authority that would be credited during periods of employment and debited during periods of unemployment when the individual is drawing UI benefits. The level of the current UI benefit allowed would depend on the balance in the account at that time. While such a system looks far different from the UI system currently in place in the United States, the discouraging news is that the welfare gain from moving to an optimal system would be small. Wang and Williamson's estimate is that a welfare increase equivalent to about 1% of GDP, at most, would result from switching from the current UI system in the United States to an optimal system.

---

[1] S. Shavell and L. Weiss, 1979. "The Optimal Payment of Unemployment Insurance Benefits Over Time," *Journal of Political Economy* 87, 1347–1362.

[2] C. Wang and S. Williamson, 2002. "Moral Hazard, Optimal Unemployment Insurance, and Experience Rating," *Journal of Monetary Economics* 49, 1337–1337.

THE EFFICIENCY WAGE MODEL

An alternative to search theory in modeling unemployment is the efficiency wage model, which takes seriously the notion that workers' wages affect their on-the-job performance.[2] In the efficiency wage model, a firm may be willing to pay its workers a real wage that is higher than the wage that would be competitively determined, because this induces the firm's employees to work harder. In equilibrium, more workers than are employed would like to work, but it is not efficient for firms to hire them; thus, there is unemployment. Efficiency wage considerations make the labor market work quite differently from the standard competitive labor market we studied in previous chapters, as we will see.

In the efficiency wage model, a worker's effort increases with the wage he or she receives. To capture this, we let $e(w)$ denote the effort of each worker on the job, where w is the real wage, and the function $e(w)$, an increasing function, is depicted in Figure 16.17. Then, if N denotes hours worked by all workers, the effective labor input for the firm is $e(w)N$, or effort per worker multiplied by total hours worked, which gives total effort.

There are two reasons that worker effort would tend to increase with the real wage, both of which are associated with information problems in the labor market. First, there

---

[2] For a survey, see L. Katz, 1986. "Efficiency Wage Theories: A Partial Evaluation," *NBER Macroeconomics Annual* 1, 235–276.

FIGURE 16.17   Effort of the Worker as a Function of His or Her Wage

The curve $e(w)$ gives the effort of the worker as a function of the real wage w. Effort increases because of adverse selection and moral hazard problems.

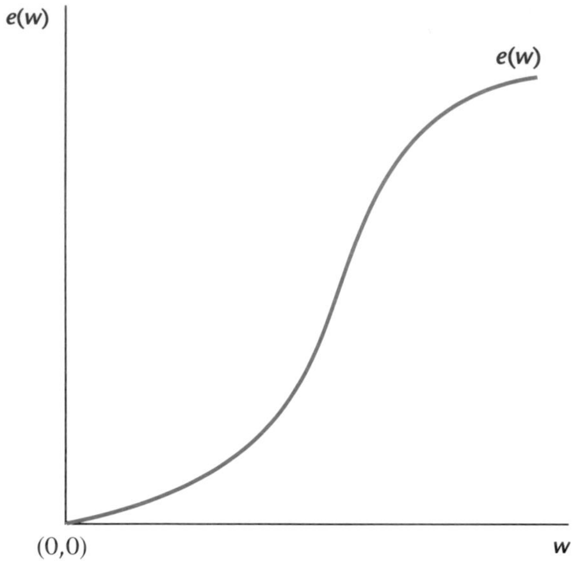

can be problems of **adverse selection** in the labor market. Adverse selection problems generally occur in markets where there are different types of market participants and it is difficult for other market participants to distinguish among these different types. In a labor market context, there can be workers of different abilities, but firms may have difficulty distinguishing high-ability workers from low-ability workers. Now, if high-ability workers tend to have higher reservation wages than low-ability workers, because in general they have better options in the labor market, then a higher wage offered by a particular firm implies that the quality of the firm's job applicants will increase. Therefore, a higher real wage implies that average effort by workers is higher. Second, there may be a moral hazard problem in the relationship between a firm and its workers (recall our earlier discussion of moral hazard in this chapter and in Chapter 15). A moral hazard problem can arise if a firm has difficulty in monitoring the on-the-job effort of its workers. However, if the firm can threaten to fire a worker if it detects shirking, then the loss to the worker from being fired is larger the greater the gap between market real wages and the real wage offered by the firm. Therefore, effort by the worker increases with the real wage paid by the firm.

Optimization by the Firm: The Choice of Employment and the Efficiency Wage

Now, given that the effective quantity of labor hired by the firm is $e(w)N$, the production function for the firm is given by

$$Y = zF(K, e(w)N),$$

where Y is output, z is total factor productivity, and K is the capital stock, assumed fixed in the short run. The firm's goal is to maximize profits. In a competitive environment where a firm is a price-taker, typically the firm does not want to offer a real wage to its workers above the market real wage, as this would not be profit maximizing. In the efficiency wage model, however, it may be profit maximizing for the firm to pay a real wage higher than the market wage. Therefore, one of the choices for the firm here concerns what real wage it should pay. The firm then chooses the wage rate w and employment N to maximize profits, where profits are given by

$$\pi = F(K, e(w)N) - wN.$$

The firm hires labor N until the marginal product of labor is equal to the real wage. In this case, the marginal product of labor is

$$MP_N = e(w)MP_{e(w)N}.$$

That is, the marginal product of labor is the effort of the worker at the real wage offered by the firm multiplied by the marginal product of effective units of labor. Then, the firm hires labor until $MP_N = w$, or

$$e(w)MP_{e(w)N} = w. \tag{16.2}$$

Equation (16.2) describes a relationship between w and N that we can interpret as the firm's demand curve for labor. Under certain conditions, this demand curve does not slope downward everywhere, but we assume that $e(w)$ and the production function have properties that guarantee that the implied demand curve for labor N^d is downward sloping, as in Figure 16.18. The demand curve tells us how much labor N the firm wants to hire given any real wage w.

Now, in choosing the real wage, the firm wants to minimize the cost of inducing each worker to supply effort. If the firm offers its workers a higher wage, this induces more effort on the part of workers, but this is of course more costly for the firm. What the firm wants to do is to maximize $\frac{e(w)}{w}$, which is the effort received from the worker per unit of real wages paid to the worker. In Figure 16.19, if a worker receives a real wage w', then effort is $e(w')$. Then, $\frac{e(w')}{w'}$ is the slope of a line from the origin to point A in Figure 16.19. Now, given that the goal of the firm is to maximize $\frac{e(w)}{w}$, the firm chooses a wage such that a line from the origin to a point on the curve $e(w)$ is just tangent to the curve, as in Figure 16.20. Here, w^* is the optimal wage for the firm to choose, and we call this wage the **efficiency wage.** If the firm sets the real wage at the efficiency wage, then workers will supply the optimal amount of effort on the job.

Labor Market Equilibrium in the Efficiency Wage Model

The efficiency wage model implies that there can be unemployment in equilibrium. In Figure 16.21(a) the efficiency wage is w^*, which is above the market-clearing wage w^{**} that would imply equality between the supply and demand for labor. The representative firm does not reduce the real wage to w^{**} because this would decrease its profits, as workers would supply an inefficient quantity of effort. In equilibrium, the

FIGURE 16.18 The Demand for Labor in the Efficiency Wage Model

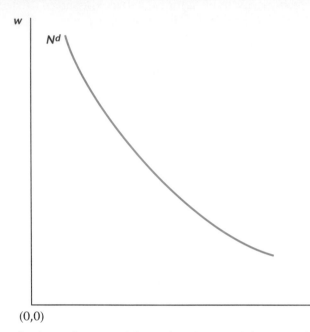

The demand curve for labor, N^d, is downward sloping in this model.

FIGURE 16.19 The Ratio of Effort to the Real Wage

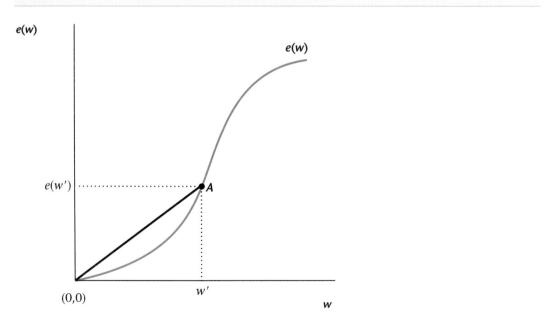

Given the real wage w', the ratio of effort to the real wage is the slope of a line from the origin to point A.

FIGURE 16.20   Determination of the Efficiency Wage

The efficiency wage w^* is chosen so as to maximize the ratio of effort to the real wage, $\frac{e(w)}{w}$. Point B is the point of tangency between the curve $e(w)$ and a line from the origin.

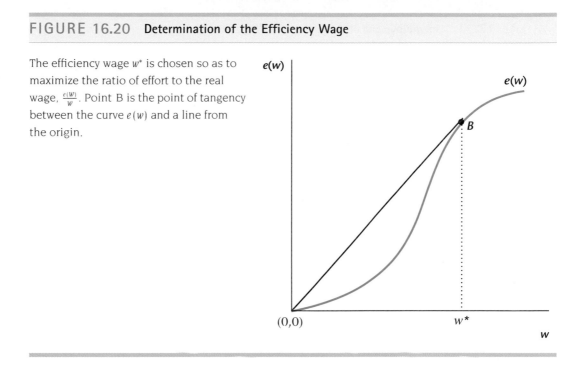

firm sets the real wage at the efficiency wage w^*, which implies that the equilibrium quantity of employment is N^*, and the quantity of unemployment is $N_1^s - N^*$, which is equal to the hours that workers want to supply at the efficiency wage minus the quantity of labor firms want to hire. This looks very similar to Keynesian unemployment, though in the efficiency wage model we can have permanent real wage rigidity, as opposed to the temporary nominal wage rigidity in the Keynesian sticky wage model of Chapter 12. In the Keynesian model, unemployment disappears in the long run as the nominal wage adjusts.

Alternatively, it is possible for the efficiency wage to be smaller than the market-clearing real wage, as in Figure 16.21(b). Here, the equilibrium quantity of employment is N^* and the equilibrium real wage is w^{**}. In this case, at the efficiency wage the firm cannot hire all the labor it would like, and, therefore, it is forced to bid up wages to the point at which the market real wage implies that the quantity of labor the firm wants to hire is equal to the quantity that workers want to supply.

The Efficiency Wage Model and Business Cycles

If there is unemployment in the efficiency wage model, then this implies that the quantity of employment is determined by the labor demand curve. Therefore, labor supply has no effect on employment and output. As a result, the output supply curve is vertical, as in Figure 16.22(c), because the real interest rate does not affect the labor demand curve. In the figure, the equilibrium real interest rate is r^*, aggregate output

FIGURE 16.21   Unemployment in the Efficiency Wage Model

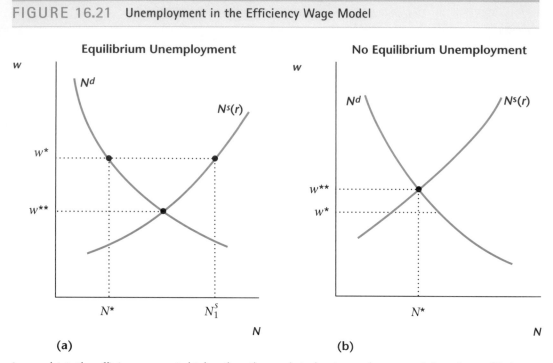

In panel (a), the efficiency wage is higher than the market-clearing real wage, and there is equilibrium unemployment, whereas in panel (b), the efficiency wage is lower than the market-clearing wage and there is no unemployment.

is Y^* [in panels (b) and (c)], employment is N^*, and the equilibrium real wage is the efficiency wage w^* [in panels (a) and (b)].

Given the vertical output supply curve, aggregate output changes only if there is a shift in the output supply curve. If there is a shock that increases some component of output demand—for example, if government spending G increases—then this shifts the output demand curve rightward in Figure 16.23(b) from Y_1^d to Y_2^d. The labor supply curve shifts rightward from $N_1^s(r_1)$ to $N_2^s(r_1)$ because of the negative wealth effect of an increase in government spending. In equilibrium, the real interest rate increases from r_1 to r_2, with output remaining unchanged at Y_1. In Figure 16.23(a), the labor supply curve shifts rightward from $N_2^s(r_1)$ to $N_2^s(r_2)$ given the increase in the real interest rate, as consumers substitute leisure in the future for leisure in the present. There is then an increase in unemployment with no change in employment.

The only shock to the economy that can cause aggregate output to fluctuate in the efficiency wage model is a shock that shifts the output supply curve. A candidate shock is a change in total factor productivity. Now, suppose that total factor productivity increases. In Figure 16.24(a) the labor demand curve then shifts rightward from

FIGURE 16.22 **The Output Supply Curve in the Efficiency Wage Model**

The output supply curve in panel (c) is vertical, because in panel (a) the quantity of employment is determined by the labor demand curve, which does not depend on the real interest rate.

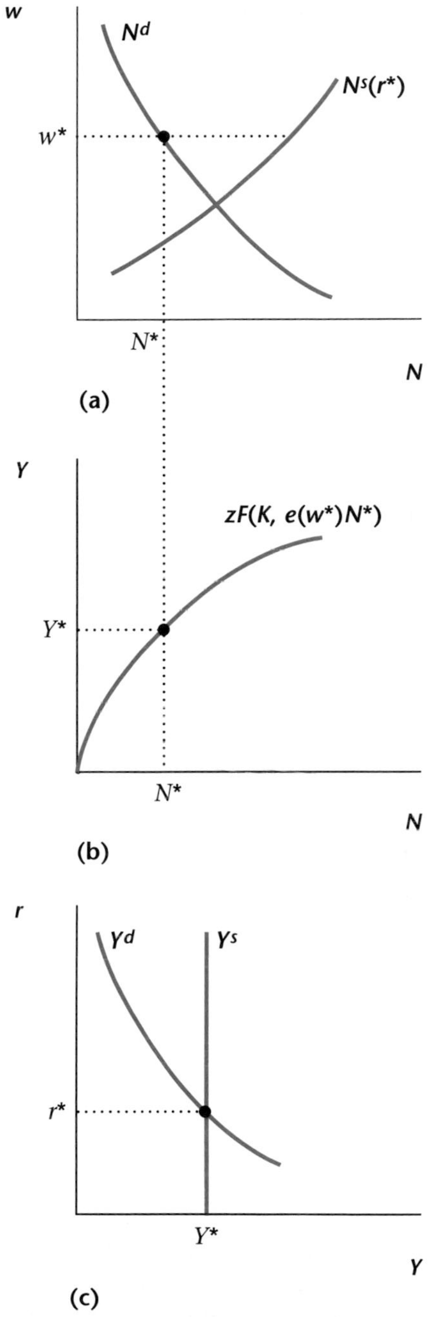

(a)

(b)

(c)

FIGURE 16.23   **An Increase in G in the Efficiency Wage Model**

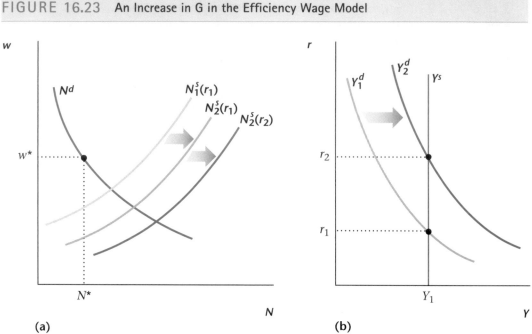

(a)   **(b)**

An increase in government spending shifts the output demand curve to the right in panel (b) of the figure. This increases the real interest rate but has no effect on aggregate output in equilibrium.

N_1^d to N_2^d. However, there is no change in the efficiency wage w^*, because the efficiency wage is determined by the schedule $e(w)$, as in Figure 16.20. The output supply curve shifts rightward from Y_1^s to Y_2^s in Figure 16.24(b), which implies that the real interest rate falls from r_1 to r_2, causing a leftward shift in the labor supply curve from $N^s(r_1)$ to $N^s(r_2)$. In equilibrium, the level of employment rises from N_1 to N_2 and unemployment falls. The model is, thus, consistent with most of the business cycle facts that are discussed in Chapter 3. That is, the model predicts that, under productivity shocks, consumption and investment are procyclical [because the decrease in r in Figure 16.24(b) causes C and I to increase], and employment is procyclical. However, the model does not predict the procyclicality of the real wage, because the efficiency wage does not respond to productivity shocks.

The only way that the efficiency wage model could be consistent with a procyclical real wage under total factor productivity shocks is if the change in total factor productivity somehow affects the efficiency wage. It would be useful to explore this possibility. If an increase in total factor productivity is the result of better management practices, this change might also imply that firms develop improved methods for monitoring workers in the firm and this could change $e(w)$. Effort then increases for each level of the real wage. In Figure 16.25 the effort function shifts up from $e_1(w)$ to $e_2(w)$, which

FIGURE 16.24 **An Increase in Total Factor Productivity in the Efficiency Wage Model**

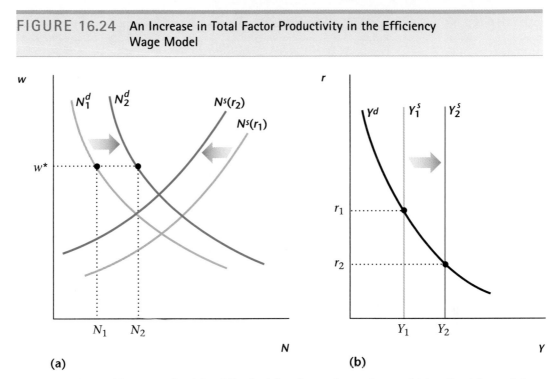

(a)   **(b)**

An increase in total factor productivity shifts the labor demand curve in panel (a) to the right, and the output supply curve in panel (b) to the right. The efficiency wage remains unchanged, and employment and output increase.

implies that the efficiency wage decreases from w_1^* to w_2^*. Therefore, this would result in a decrease in the real wage in conjunction with an increase in aggregate output. Then, the model would predict that the real wage is countercyclical, which is inconsistent with the data.

To conclude, the efficiency wage model is not consistent with all of the business cycle regularities, though in this respect it is no worse than the Keynesian sticky wage model studied in Chapter 12 or the Friedman–Lucas money surprise model in Chapter 11. A perhaps unexpected feature of the efficiency wage model is that it has a Keynesian-type sticky real wage, but the other properties of the model are actually quite different from those of the Keynesian sticky wage model. We typically think of Keynesian models as having the feature that shocks to the demand for output cause aggregate output to fluctuate. In the efficiency wage model, however, shocks that affect output demand have no effect on aggregate output, and changes in government spending are completely ineffective in changing the quantity of output produced.

This chapter ends our detailed study of the causes of unemployment. In Chapter 17, we examine why well-intentioned policymakers can generate inflation and the problems in obtaining commitment by a central bank to low inflation.

FIGURE 16.25 An Increase in the Effectiveness of Monitoring by the Firm

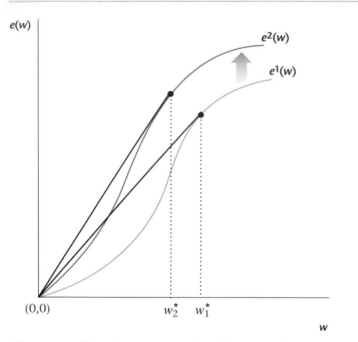

If firms more effectively monitor workers, this causes the effort function $e(w)$ to shift up and reduces the efficiency wage from w_1^* to w_2^*.

CHAPTER SUMMARY

- The key determinants of the unemployment rate are aggregate economic activity, demographics, government intervention, and sectoral shifts.

- The participation rate is affected by demographics and by the different labor market behavior of men and women.

- The unemployment rate is a countercyclical variable, whereas the participation rate is procyclical.

- In the search model of unemployment, the welfare of an employed worker increases with the real wage the worker earns, decreases with the chances of separation from his or her current job, and decreases as taxes on wage income increase. The welfare of an unemployed worker increases as unemployment insurance benefits increase, increases as the chances of receiving job offers increase, and decreases as taxes on unemployment benefits rise.

- The reservation wage is the wage at which an unemployed worker is indifferent between accepting a job offer and continuing to search for work. When an unemployed worker receives a wage offer, the wage offer is accepted if that wage offer is at or above the worker's reservation wage. The reservation wage increases as UI benefits increase and as taxes on wage income increase.

- In the search model, the long-run unemployment rate is determined by the condition that the flow of workers between unemployment and employment is equal to the flow in the opposite direction.

- An increase in UI benefits increases the unemployment rate, but an increase in the job offer rate has an indeterminate effect on the unemployment rate. Thus, government intervention designed to make it easier for unemployed workers to find jobs may not reduce the unemployment rate. Taxes on labor income increase the unemployment rate, but if labor income and unemployment benefits are taxed equally, then there is no effect on the unemployment rate.

- In the efficiency wage model, worker effort increases with the real wage as the result of adverse selection in the labor market and moral hazard on the job. The efficiency wage is the wage set by the firm that maximizes the ratio of worker effort to the real wage. In equilibrium, there may be unemployment, but the firm does not lower its wages, as this reduces worker effort and causes profits to fall.

- The efficiency wage model has the property that, if there is unemployment in equilibrium, then aggregate output is determined by the vertical output supply curve, and labor supply does not matter for employment.

- An increase in government spending has no effect on output and employment, and an increase in total factor productivity increases output and employment but has no effect on the efficiency wage or the equilibrium real wage. The efficiency wage model is not entirely consistent with the key business cycle facts.

KEY TERMS

Demography: The study of population.

Replacement ratio: For an unemployed worker receiving unemployment insurance, this is unemployment benefits divided by the person's wages when they were working.

Separation rate: The rate at which employed workers become separated from their jobs.

Reservation wage: The wage such that an unemployed worker will accept any job offering this wage or more.

Adverse selection: Phenomenon that occurs in a market where there are different types of market participants, and other market participants have difficulty distinguishing among them.

Efficiency wage: In the efficiency wage model, this is the wage the firm sets to maximize the effort of workers relative to the wage they are paid.

QUESTIONS FOR REVIEW

1. What are the four key determinants of the unemployment rate?
2. Is the unemployment rate procyclical or countercyclical?
3. How do demographic factors affect the participation rate?
4. Is the participation rate procyclical or countercyclical?
5. What causes shifts in the welfare of the employed in the search model?
6. What causes shifts in the welfare of the unemployed in the search model?
7. What determines the reservation wage in the search model?
8. How does an increase in the UI benefit affect the reservation wage in the search model and why?

9. How does an increase in the tax on wage income affect the reservation wage in the search model and why?

10. How does an increase in the UI benefit affect the long-run unemployment rate in the search model and why?

11. How does an increase in the job offer rate affect the reservation wage and the long-run unemployment rate in the search model? What implications does this have for government policy?

12. Explain why it matters whether or not UI benefits are taxed.

13. Give two reasons that the effort of workers on the job can depend on the real wage workers are paid.

14. Why can there be unemployment in the efficiency wage model?

15. What are the effects of an increase in government spending in the efficiency wage model?

16. What are the effects of an increase in total factor productivity in the efficiency wage model?

17. Which business cycle facts does the efficiency wage model fit, and which does it not?

PROBLEMS

1. Determine the effects of an increase in the separation rate s on the reservation wage and on the long-run unemployment rate in the search model of unemployment. Explain your results.

2. Suppose that there is an increase in total factor productivity, which implies that all firms offer higher wages. In the search model of unemployment, determine the effects of this on the reservation wage and on the long-run unemployment rate. Explain your results.

3. Suppose that the government introduces an unemployment insurance program in which UI benefits are financed by taxes on employed workers. Determine the effects on the reservation wage and on the long-run unemployment rate in the search model of unemployment, and explain your results.

4. Suppose that the government makes it more difficult to qualify for unemployment insurance, for example, by increasing the duration of employment required before collecting UI benefits during an unemployment spell. Determine the effects of this change in government policy on the reservation wage and the long-run unemployment rate in the search model of unemployment.

5. Suppose that, in the efficiency wage model, it becomes more difficult for the firm to distinguish high-ability workers from low-ability workers in the labor market. What effects does this have on $e(w)$ and the efficiency wage? Explain your results.

6. Suppose in the efficiency wage model that some of the firm's capital stock is destroyed. Determine the effects on aggregate output, employment, unemployment, the real wage, and the real interest rate, and explain your results.

7. Because the real wage is sticky in the efficiency wage model, does this mean that efficiency wages imply that money is not neutral, as was the case in the Keynesian sticky wage model? Explain with the use of diagrams.

8. Suppose that government spending increases permanently in the efficiency wage model. What are the effects on equilibrium output, employment, unemployment, the real wage, consumption, investment, and the real interest rate? Is there crowding out caused by government spending? Explain your results and discuss.

WORKING WITH THE DATA

1. Construct a time series plot of the median duration of unemployment. What do you notice? How does the median duration of unemployment move over the business cycle? Can you make sense of these observations by appealing to the search model of unemployment? Why or why not?

2. Construct time series plots of the unemployment rates of white males 20 years old and over and white males 16–19. How do these compare? How would you explain the differences?

3. Construct time series plots of the unemployment rates of white males 20 years old and over, black males 20 and over, white females 20 and over, and black females 20 and over. What patterns do you notice here and how have they changed over time? Can a search model or an efficiency wage model explain the key features of this data?

CHAPTER 17

Inflation, the Phillips Curve, and Central Bank Commitment

R ecently, the inflation rate has been quite low in the United States. Using the rate of growth in the implicit GDP price deflator as a measure of inflation, the quarterly inflation rate in the United States, at annual rates, has been below 4% since 1991, and an inflation rate in excess of 10% was last seen in the United States in 1980. Further, the United States has never had a hyperinflationary episode on the order of the 10,000% inflation rate achieved in Austria in 1921–22, or the 20,000% inflation rate in Argentina in 1989–90. Inflation is of little public concern currently in the United States, and Americans have been able to avoid some of the truly calamitous experiences with inflation of other countries.

From Chapter 15, we know some of the economic costs of inflation, which arise from the distortions inflation causes in intertemporal rates of return. Inflation causes the public to hold an inefficiently low aggregate stock of real money balances, and it reduces aggregate output and employment below their efficient levels. The costs of inflation are certainly obvious to anyone who has lived through a hyperinflation. Significant public concern can even arise about inflation during relatively moderate inflations, such as what occurred in the United States during the 1970s when the average inflation rate was below 10%.

If it is widely recognized that inflation is undesirable, why then do governments let it happen? In some circumstances, inflation clearly results from problems associated with fiscal policy. Indeed, essentially all hyperinflations can be traced to the existence of large government budget deficits. A government may have high expenditures, perhaps because it must fight a war. However, the public may be unwilling to pay for these expenditures through taxation, or the government may be unwilling to increase taxes. As a result, the government may resort to printing money to finance the government deficit. Moderate inflations, though, need not result from high government budget deficits and the necessity of resorting to the inflation tax. For example, the moderate inflation in the United States in the 1970s was not associated with large government budget deficits and would not have generated much seigniorage, so what motivated the Fed to increase the money supply at a high rate so as to cause what appeared to be excessive inflation? In this chapter, we use a version of the Friedman–Lucas money surprise model studied in Chapter 11 to evaluate two potential explanations for the behavior of the Fed in the post–World War II period. The post–World War II U.S. inflation experience serves as a convenient example here to illustrate some general principles concerning the causes of inflation.

The Friedman–Lucas money surprise model provides an explanation for the Phillips curve, which is the sometimes-observed positive relationship between the inflation rate and real aggregate economic activity (as discussed in Chapter 3). In U.S. data, the Phillips curve is readily discernible during some time periods, while during other periods it is not. The Friedman–Lucas money surprise model is a useful aid in understanding why we should sometimes observe a Phillips curve, and sometimes not, in that the model tells us that the Phillips curve is an unstable relationship that shifts with the inflation rate that the private sector expects.

Two competing explanations for the behavior of the Fed over the post–World War II period are the "central bank learning story," and the "central bank commitment story." In the central bank learning story, high inflation in the 1970s was caused by a lack of knowledge on the part of the Fed concerning how the economy works. Once the Fed understood, by the early 1980s, that higher inflation could not permanently increase aggregate output, it acted quickly to reduce inflation. In the central bank commitment story, high inflation in the 1970s was caused by an inability of the Fed to commit to not using surprise inflation to increase output in the short run.

Ultimately, we conclude that central bank commitment was probably not an important element in recent U.S. inflation history. However, this does not mean that commitment is unimportant for central banks in all countries and under all circumstances. Indeed, as we discuss, central bank commitment appears to have been critical in controlling inflation in Hong Kong since 1983.

THE PHILLIPS CURVE

In the 1950s, A. W. Phillips noticed, in data for the United Kingdom,[1] that there was a negative relationship between the rate of change in nominal wages and the unemployment rate. Other researchers found that such a relationship existed in data for other countries. Further, because the rate of change in nominal wages is highly positively correlated with the rate of change in other money prices and the unemployment rate is highly negatively correlated with the deviation of aggregate economic activity from trend, it should not be surprising that if there is a negative correlation between the rate of change in nominal wages and the unemployment rate, there is also a positive correlation between the inflation rate and the deviation of aggregate economic activity from trend. Indeed, the term *Phillips curve* has come to denote any positive correlation between aggregate economic activity and the inflation rate. For our purposes, we conveniently define the Phillips curve to be a positive relationship between the rate of inflation and the deviation of real aggregate output from trend. If we let Y^T denote trend real aggregate output and Y denote actual real aggregate output then a Phillips curve is described by the relationship

$$i = H(Y - Y^T),$$

where i is the inflation rate and H is an increasing function. We depict this relationship in Figure 17.1.

---

[1] See A.W. Phillips, 1958. "The Relationship Between Unemployment and the Rate of Change of Money Wages in the United Kingdom, 1861–1957," *Economica* 25, 283–299.

FIGURE 17.1 The Phillips Curve

This is an idealized Phillips curve, which is a positive relationship between the inflation rate and aggregate real output.

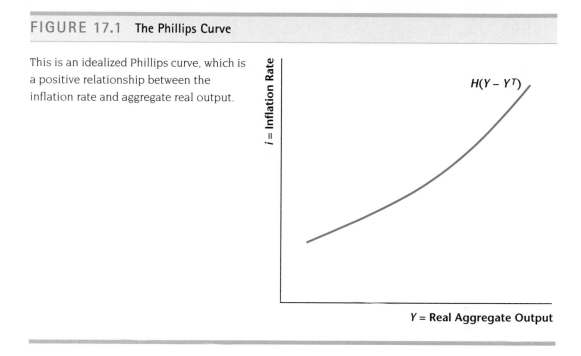

Is there a clear Phillips curve relationship in U.S. data? As we show, this depends on what time period we examine. The post-war data we have is for 1947–2003, and we divide this up into the sub-periods 1947–1959, 1960–1969, 1970–1979, 1980–1989, and 1990–2003. For each of these sub-periods, in Figures 17.2 through 17.6, we graph the inflation rate, measured as the quarterly percentage change in the implicit GDP price deflator, against the percentage deviation of real GDP from trend. In each figure, the solid colored line represents the best statistical fit to the scatter plot. In Figures 17.2 and 17.3, the Phillips curve relationship is clearly discernible in that a line with a positive slope most closely fits the data. The Phillips curve relationship, however, is quite noisy in these two figures; the observations graphed in Figures 17.2 and 17.3 do not fall close to the colored straight line in these figures. In Figure 17.4, it is apparent that the Phillips curve is beginning to disappear in the data. A positively sloped line still provides the best fit to the data, but the slope of this line is small, and the correlation between the inflation rate and the percentage deviation of GDP from trend is close to zero in the 1970s. In Figures 17.5 and 17.6, the Phillips curve is essentially gone. In these figures the line that best fits the data has a slope that is not statistically different from zero. Thus, it appears from the U.S. data that a clear Phillips curve relationship that existed in the period 1947 to 1969 began to disintegrate in the 1970s and was absent from the data after 1980.

Now, if we show the data in their time series form in Figures 17.7 and 17.8, we see in Figure 17.7 that there was a large increase in the inflation rate from low levels in the late 1940s and 1950s (except for the temporarily high inflations in the late 1940s and during the Korean War in the early 1950s) and 1960s to very high levels during the

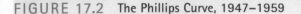

FIGURE 17.2   **The Phillips Curve, 1947–1959**

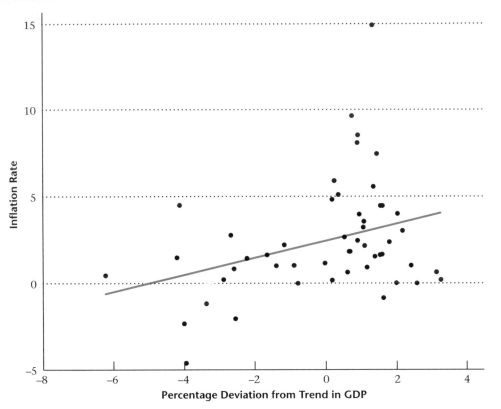

During this period there is a clear Phillips curve relationship represented by the positively sloped line, which is the best statistical fit to the scatter plot.

1970s. In the early 1980s the inflation rate began to fall, and it has continued to fall on trend since then. This average behavior of inflation appears unrelated to the behavior of the deviations of GDP from trend in Figure 17.8. That is, the fact that inflation is high or low for an extended period of time does not seem to matter for how output moves about trend. Therefore, we can make two observations about empirical Phillips curve relations:

1. Clear Phillips curve relations do not exist in all data sets. In U.S. data, we can observe a Phillips curve in the 1970s and before, but not after.

2. The Phillips curve relation, where it does exist, appears to shift over time. Over some extended periods the inflation rate is high, but it is low over other extended periods. However, this average behavior of the inflation rate seems unrelated to the behavior of deviations of real GDP from trend.

FIGURE 17.3 The Phillips Curve, 1960–1969

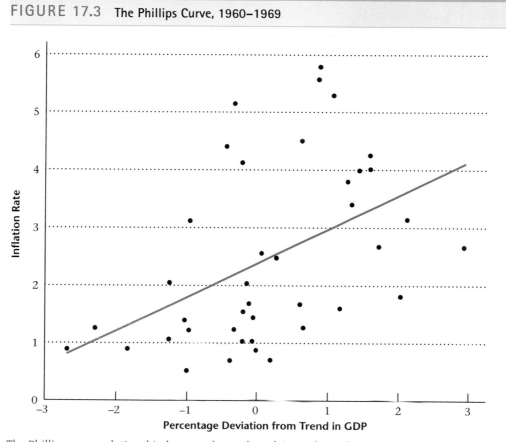

The Phillips curve relationship has not changed much from the earlier period in Figure 17.2.

The Friedman–Lucas Money Surprise Model and the Phillips Curve

Now that we have studied empirical Phillips curve relations for the United States, and uncovered the important characteristics of the relationship between cyclical aggregate economic activity and inflation, our goal is to construct a version of the Friedman–Lucas money surprise model that we ultimately use to understand this data. In Chapter 11, we showed that money is not neutral in the Friedman–Lucas money surprise model. If the central bank brings about a surprise increase in the money supply, then because workers have imperfect information on aggregate variables, the increase in money wages is mistaken for an increase in the real wage, and labor supply, employment, and output increase. The money surprises we studied in Chapter 12 were unanticipated changes in the level of the money supply, but in an environment where there is long-run growth in the money supply, it is straightforward to extend the Friedman–Lucas money surprise model to address the effects of surprise changes in the money supply growth rate. Then,

FIGURE 17.4 The Phillips Curve, 1970–1979

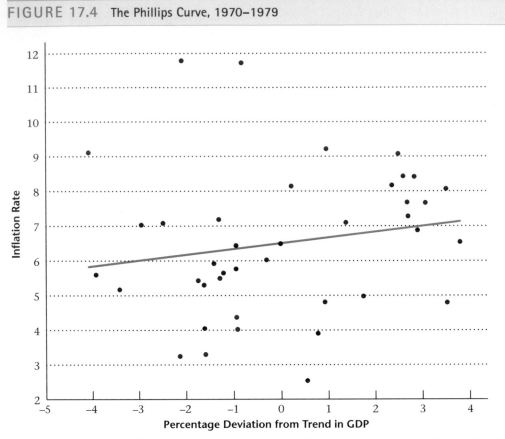

During the 1970s the Phillips curve began to disintegrate. The correlation between the inflation rate and the percentage deviation of GDP from trend is quite low, and the slope of the estimated Phillips curve (the straight line in the figure) is low as well.

if there is a surprise change in the money supply growth rate, this implies that there is a surprise increase in the inflation rate, and workers mistake the increase in the growth rate of money wages for an increase in the growth rate of real wages, so that labor supply, employment, and output increase above trend.

Then, in an environment where there is trend growth in the money supply and the price level, the Friedman–Lucas money surprise model can be summarized by the simplified relationship

$$i - i^e = a(Y - Y^T), \qquad (17.1)$$

where i is the actual inflation rate, i^e is the expected inflation rate, or the inflation rate perceived by the private sector, a is a positive constant, Y is aggregate output, and Y^T

FIGURE 17.5 **The Phillips Curve, 1980–1989**

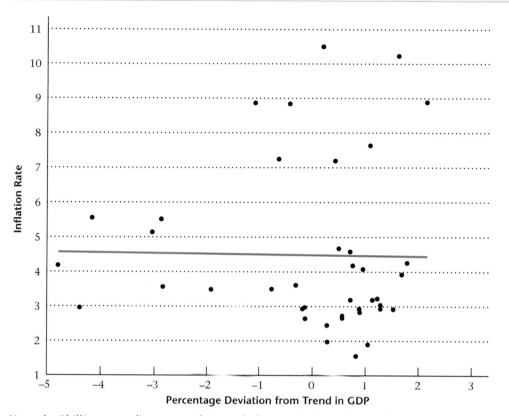

Here, the Phillips curve disappears. The straight line in the figure that best fits the scatter plot has a negative slope.

is trend aggregate output.[2] Equation (17.1) states that there is a positive relationship between the deviation of the inflation rate from what it is expected to be and the deviation of real output from trend. This relationship arises because real output only deviates from trend in the model if the central bank increases the growth rate of the money supply in a surprise way, causing a surprise increase in the inflation rate. We can rewrite Equation (17.1) as

$$i = i^e + a(Y - Y^T),$$ \(17.2\)

---

[2]There are some dangers to representing the Friedman–Lucas money surprise model by Equation (17.1). For example, the constant a, in general, depends, as Lucas pointed out, on particular features of central bank behavior. However, for what we wish to accomplish in this chapter, there is not much harm in using (17.1) as a reduced form for the Friedman–Lucas money surprise model.

FIGURE 17.6   The Phillips Curve, 1990–2003

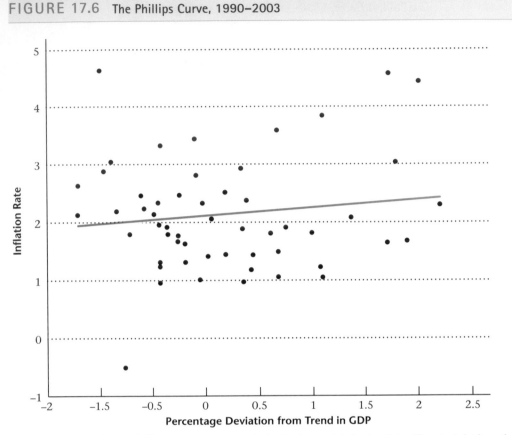

During this period, the Phillips curve is not statistically detectable in the data. The straight line that best fits the scatter plot has a positive slope, but this slope is small.

which is a Phillips curve relationship graphed in Figure 17.9. When $Y = Y^T$, we have $i = i^e$. That is, if workers are not surprised by the current inflation rate, then output is equal to its trend value.

From Equation (17.2), the position of the Phillips curve depends on i^e, the expected inflation rate. In Figure 17.10 we show the effects of an increase in the expected inflation rate from i^e_1 to i^e_2. As a result, the Phillips curve shifts up, by the change in the expected inflation rate, $i^e_2 - i^e_1$. This provides an explanation for why the Phillips curve is difficult to find in the data over some periods of time. In Figure 17.7, the high and variable inflation rate in the 1970s should have resulted in a high and variable expected inflation rate, and the reductions in the inflation rate over the 1980s and 1990s would have reduced the expected inflation rate over time. Therefore, shifts in the Phillips curve after 1970 could have produced what we observed in Figures 17.5 and 17.6, which is no discernible Phillips curve relation. Because we can observe a Phillips curve before

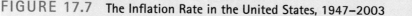

FIGURE 17.7   **The Inflation Rate in the United States, 1947–2003**

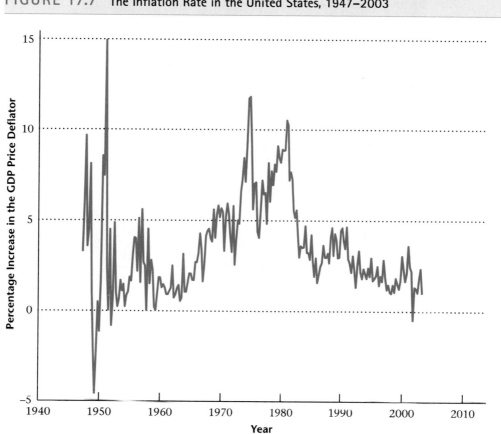

The U.S. inflation rate increased substantially during the 1970s and then decreased on trend after 1980.

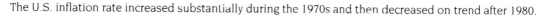

1970 in Figures 17.2 and 17.3, this data is consistent with there being more stability in expected inflation before 1970.

Understanding the Behavior of the Inflation Rate in the United States

The reduction in the inflation rate in the United States from the early 1980s through the late 1990s is viewed as an important success in the implementation of monetary policy by the Federal Reserve System. Indeed, two chairmen of the Board of Governors of the Federal Reserve System, Paul Volcker and Alan Greenspan, are often credited with this success. If it were so clear to the Fed early in the 1980s that the high inflation rate at that time was too costly and should be reduced through reduction in money growth, why was inflation not reduced earlier and why did the inflation rate increase

FIGURE 17.8   Deviations From Trend in Real GDP, 1947–2003

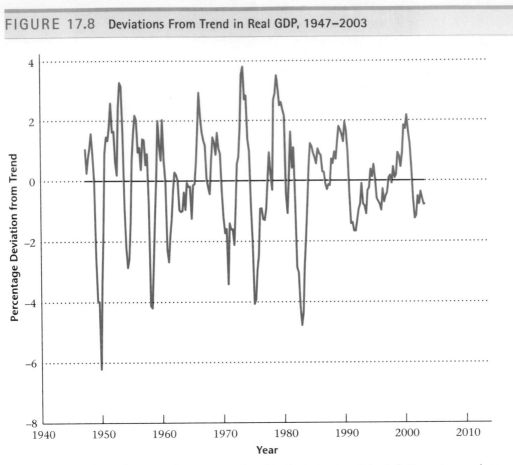

The deviations of GDP from trend appear unrelated to the behavior of the inflation rate over long periods of time (see Figure 17.7).

in the 1970s? We consider two possible answers to these questions, which we call the "central bank learning story" and the "central bank commitment story."

The Central Bank Learning Story   In the late 1950s and the 1960s, the Fed became aware of the existence of the Phillips curve through the work of A. W. Phillips and others. The Fed may have become convinced, even though a good theory was not yet available to explain the existence of the Phillips curve, that the Phillips curve represented a stable relationship between the rate of inflation and the level of real aggregate output.

Now, to determine how the Fed would behave if it operated under the belief that the Phillips curve was stable, we need a device for representing the goals of the central bank. In general, a central bank should be concerned with the welfare of private citizens, though of course there is nothing to guarantee this because central bank decision makers are guided by their own selfish motives, such as career advancement and the acquisition

FIGURE 17.9 **The Phillips curve relationship in the Friedman–Lucas money surprise model**

This is a linear Phillips curve relationship, from the version of the Friedman-Lucas money surprise model used in this chapter. When the inflation rate is equal to the expected inflation rate, then output is equal to trend output.

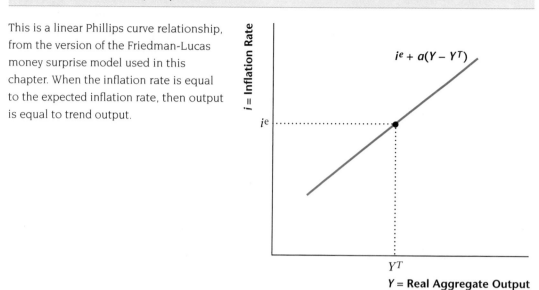

FIGURE 17.10 **The Effects of an Increase in the Expected Inflation Rate**

The increase in i^e shifts the Phillips curve up.

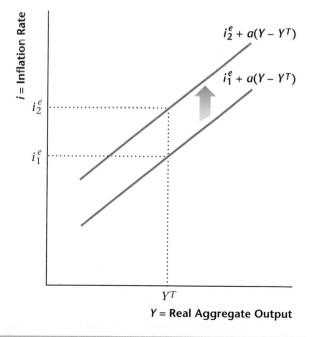

of more power. We assume, however, that the framers of the Federal Reserve Act and subsequent acts of Congress governing the Fed's behavior understood how to correctly align the selfish goals of Fed officials with the public good. Then, assuming that the Fed's goal is to maximize public welfare, it must decide how to further this goal indirectly by controlling some observable economic variables. For our purposes, we suppose that the Fed has indirect policy goals relating to inflation and aggregate output. First, there is some inflation rate i^* that is regarded as optimal by the Fed. Some economic models tell us that i^* should be the inflation rate that drives the nominal interest rate to zero (the Friedman rule; see Chapter 15), though in practice many central banks appear to behave as if $i^* = 0$ or $i^* > 0$ but small. If $i > i^*$, the Fed views more inflation as being more costly, so that less inflation is preferred to more. However, if $i < i^*$, then more inflation is preferred to less. In addition, the Fed always prefers more aggregate output to less, as higher GDP is assumed to be preferred by the public. We can then represent the Fed's preferences over inflation and aggregate output by indifference curves, as in Figure 17.11. When $i > i^*$, the Fed is happier if inflation falls and output increases, and when $i < i^*$, the Fed is happier when inflation rises and output increases. Further, the indifference curves capture a preference for diversity, in that they are concave when $i > i^*$ and convex when $i < i^*$. That is, as we move up and to the right along a particular indifference curve where $i > i^*$, output is rising and the inflation rate is rising. The slope of the indifference curve falls because the higher the inflation rate the smaller is the increase in the inflation rate that the Fed is willing to tolerate for a given increase in

FIGURE 17.11 The Fed's Preferences Over Inflation Rates and Output

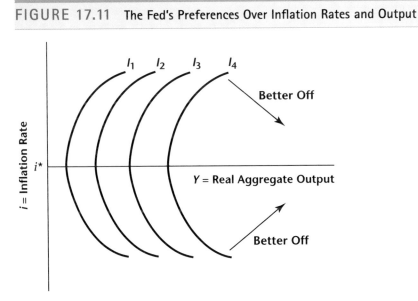

The figure shows the indifference curves for the Fed, capturing the Fed's preferences over output and inflation. The inflation rate i^* is optimal for the Fed, and the Fed always prefers more output to less. If $i < i^*$, then the Fed prefers more inflation to less, and if $i > i^*$ the Fed prefers less inflation to more.

FIGURE 17.12   The Fed Exploits the Phillips Curve

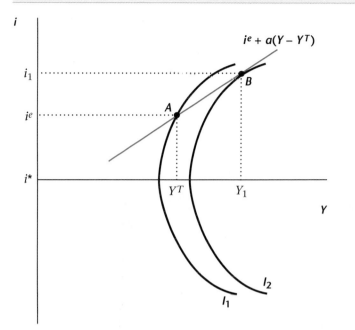

Facing a Phillips curve that it believes to be stable, the Fed optimizes by choosing point B, where an indifference curve is tangent to the Phillips curve.

aggregate output. However, when $i < i^*$, as we move down the indifference curve and the inflation rate falls, the Fed is willing to tolerate smaller decreases in the inflation rate for a given increase in output.

In Figure 17.12 we show the Phillips curve relationship, Equation (17.2), along with the Fed's indifference curves. If the Fed treats the Phillips curve as a fixed relationship, then it thinks that it can simply choose the point on the Phillips curve that best suits it. Therefore, if we suppose that the indifference curve that passes through point A, where $i = i^e$ and $Y = Y^T$, is steeper than the Phillips curve at point A, then the Fed is willing to increase the money supply growth rate so as to surprise workers with a higher than expected inflation rate and generate a level of aggregate output above trend output Y^T. That is, the optimal choice for the Fed is point B, where an indifference curve is just tangent to the Phillips curve. At B, the inflation rate is i_1 and the level of aggregate output is Y_1. Note that $i_1 > i^e$, so that the actual inflation rate is greater than what is expected by the private sector and that $Y_1 > Y^T$, so that output is above trend.

This is not the end of the story, because the public is being fooled at point B in Figure 17.12. If the Fed attempts to hold output permanently at Y_1, then the public eventually learns that the actual inflation rate is higher than what they perceived, and they revise upward their expected inflation rate. In Figure 17.13, the Fed initially chooses point A

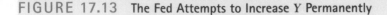

FIGURE 17.13   **The Fed Attempts to Increase Y Permanently**

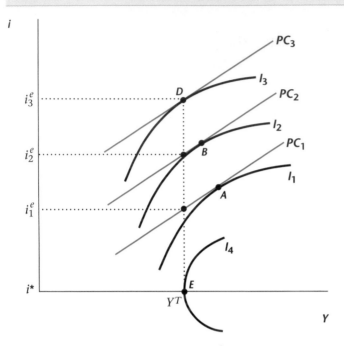

If the Fed attempts to increase Y above Y^T permanently, then initially it chooses A; but an upward revision in i^e shifts the Phillips curve up, so that the Fed chooses B on the Phillips curve PC_2. Ultimately, the economy comes to rest at D, where $i = i^e$ and $Y = Y^T$.

on Phillips curve PC_1, but as the public observes that the actual inflation rate is higher than the expected inflation rate i_1^e, the expected inflation rate is revised upward, say to i_2^e. This then implies that the Phillips curve shifts up to PC_2, and the Fed now chooses point B, where again the public sector is fooled, because the actual inflation rate is still higher than the expected inflation rate i_2^e. Again, the public eventually catches on and revises upward the expected rate of inflation. Ultimately, the economy comes to rest at point D, where $i = i^e = i_3^e$, so that public expectations about inflation prove to be correct, and the Fed has no incentive at point D to change money growth so as to change the inflation rate.

After experiencing the movement from point A to point D in Figure 17.13 and after reading Friedman and Lucas's work,[3] the Fed now realizes that the Phillips curve is not a stable relationship and that it shifts with changes in expected inflation. This implies that there is no long-run trade-off between inflation and aggregate output; in

[3]See M. Friedman, 1968. "The Role of Monetary Policy," *American Economic Review* 58, 1–17; and R. Lucas, 1972. "Expectations and the Neutrality of Money," *Journal of Economic Theory* 4, 103–124.

the long run when the public is not fooled, output always settles down to its trend level, Y^T. Once the Fed realizes this, it does not optimize by choosing a point along the upward-sloping short-run Phillips curve, but it chooses the optimal inflation rate given that the long-run level of output is Y^T. Therefore, once the Fed understands the theory correctly, it wants to set the money growth rate so that $i = i^*$, and the economy is in the long run at point E, after expected inflation adjusts downward again.

This story fits the data on inflation in Figure 17.7, in that the period 1947–1969 could be thought of as a series of short-run changes in the inflation rate, with movements about trend in aggregate output along a more-or-less stable Phillips curve. The data for 1947–1969 are consistent with the view that the Fed was unaware of the existence of a potentially exploitable Phillips curve. Then in the 1970s, there is an increase in the inflation rate as the Fed attempts to exploit the Phillips curve and achieve greater output at the expense of higher inflation. During the 1970s, the Phillips curve shifts up in a manner related to the movement from point A to point D in Figure 17.13. By the early 1980s, the Fed has understood the problem, and it begins the move from point D to E in Figure 17.13.

This is a sanguine view of central banking in the United States, because it reflects the attitude that the Fed learns from its mistakes and acts fairly quickly to correct them. In this view, the inflation of the 1970s was an experiment gone wrong and an event that is not likely to be repeated. In the central bank learning story, the Federal Reserve System is fundamentally sound in that it has the ability to absorb new economic thinking, to efficiently make sense of the new data it is constantly receiving, and to use all of this information to make better decisions.

MACROECONOMICS IN ACTION

Learning to Control Inflation in New Zealand: Inflation Targeting

Before reductions in the inflation rate occurred in New Zealand in the late 1970s, this country experienced inflation that was relatively high among developed countries. The average inflation rate in New Zealand between 1977 and 1986 was 13% per year—much higher than in the United States, for example (see Figure 17.7). However, the inflation rate was reduced in New Zealand to 3.3% per year in the 1990–92 period and to 2.3% in the 1993–96 period. In part, this reduction in inflation was brought about through changes in the legal structure within which the Reserve Bank of New Zealand (RBNZ)—the central bank of New Zealand—was constrained to operate, as discussed in a working paper by Michael Hutchison and Carl Walsh.[1]

The changes in the rules governing the operation of the RBNZ were enacted in the RBNZ Act in December 1989, which went into effect in February 1990. Under the Act, "the primary function of the Bank [the RBNZ] is to formulate and implement monetary policy directed to the economic objective of achieving and maintaining stability in the general level of prices." This

(*continued*)

statement of the goals of the central bank is quite restrictive, because left out are any Keynesian-type objectives, such as "full employment" or "sustained growth," which are goals that often find their way into the language of central bankers. Given that the objective of the RBNZ as defined by the RBNZ Act is to achieve price stability, how should this be done? The Act also specifies that the finance minister (a cabinet member in the government of New Zealand) negotiate a Policy Target Agreement (PTA) with the governor of the RBNZ (the counterpart of the chairman of the Fed) at the beginning of the governor's term of office. This PTA specifies explicitly what price stability means, in terms of numerical objectives, for the governor's term. These objectives are then publicly announced. Should the governor be judged by the prime minister of New Zealand to have failed to meet the goals set out in the PTA, he or she can be removed from office.

In practice, the PTAs that have been negotiated consist of explicit inflation targets. For example, the first PTA agreed to under the RBNZ Act specified a target range for the inflation rate of 0–2% per annum to be achieved by December 1992. As mentioned

above, the RBNZ Act appears to have been very successful in meeting its intended goal of reducing inflation in New Zealand. Inflation targeting in this instance seems to have been much more successful than was the targeting of monetary aggregates in some countries in the 1970s and 1980s.

The rules in the RBNZ Act governing the operation of New Zealand's central bank put an unusual amount of structure on monetary policy relative to what governs most central banks in the world. For example, in the United States, the Federal Reserve Act is quite vague about the policy objectives of the Federal Reserve System, and the chairman of the Fed can certainly not be fired by the President during his or her term of office because of monetary policy errors. New Zealand was highly innovative in central banking by setting up explicit objectives and penalties for its central bank. Other central banks, including the Bank of Canada and the Bank of England, have since introduced inflation targeting, though in a less restrictive structure than in New Zealand.

[1]See M. Hutchison and C. Walsh, 1998. "Disinflation in New Zealand," working paper, University of California, Santa Cruz.

The Central Bank Commitment Story   The second possible explanation for the reduction in inflation that occurred over the 1980s and 1990s in the United States is the central bank commitment story. The theory behind central bank commitment and inflation was first exposited by Kydland and Prescott,[4] who did the first work on the **time consistency problem** in macroeconomics. The fundamentals of the time consistency problem can be explained through a simple example. A teacher is giving a one-semester course in macroeconomics, and his or her goal is to make sure that the students in the class learn as much as possible. The students wish to get high grades but with as little effort as possible, because they have other things to do with their time than learning

[4]See F. Kydland and E. Prescott, 1977. "Rules Rather than Discretion: The Inconsistency of Optimal Plans," *Journal of Political Economy* 87, 473–492.

macroeconomics. If there is a final exam in the course, the students work hard to get good grades, they learn, and their teacher is happy. However, a problem is that the teacher does not like to grade exams. He or she can promise at the beginning of the semester to give a final exam, but by the end of the semester the students will have learned the course material anyway, in expectation of having to write an exam. Therefore, the teacher need not give the exam, as his or her goal has been accomplished, and he or she can avoid the work of grading exams. The plan made at the beginning of the semester to give a final exam is not time consistent. That is, when the time comes to have the exam, the teacher has no incentive to give it. However, the students are not stupid. They understand the teacher's motives and recognize that he or she has no incentive to give a final exam, even if he or she has promised to do so. They, therefore, do not learn anything. Thus, the outcome is that the students do not learn and the teacher does not give the final exam. The teacher would prefer to have to grade the exam and have the students learn than to not grade the exam and have no learning, and so the outcome is clearly bad.

Essentially, there is a commitment problem here. A better outcome would be achieved if the teacher could tie his or her hands at the beginning of the semester by somehow committing to giving the final exam. Of course, in practice such commitment is achieved through university rules that bind the teacher to carrying out the promises made in the course outline distributed at the beginning of the semester.

An analogous problem exists for the Fed if we make some modifications to our model. Suppose that each period there is a game being played between the private sector and the Fed. At the beginning of the period, the private sector chooses the expected rate of inflation, i^e. Then, the Fed chooses the rate of money growth, which effectively involves determining i. Thus, given i^e, the Fed chooses i satisfying the Phillips curve relationship

$$i - i^e = a(Y - Y^T),$$

so as to be as well off as possible. However, because the public sector is forward-looking and understands the motivation of the Fed, it must be true in equilibrium that the public cannot be fooled—that is, $i = i^e$. The assumption that $i = i^e$ is a version of the **rational expectations hypothesis,** which states that economic agents cannot make systematic errors; that is, they use all information efficiently. In this case, using information efficiently means that the public sector understands the Fed's preferences over output and inflation and uses this information efficiently to predict how the Fed will behave.

In Figure 17.14, because $i = i^e$ in equilibrium, this implies that $Y = Y^T$ in equilibrium. Therefore, if the Fed could commit in advance to an inflation rate, it would choose $i = i^*$, and the equilibrium would be at point A. However, if $i^e = i^*$, then the Phillips curve running through point A is PC_1, and the Fed then chooses point D, where $i > i^e = i^*$, and so point A is not an equilibrium. In equilibrium, the Fed's indifference curve must be tangent to the Phillips curve where $i = i_1^e$. That is, the equilibrium point is at B on Phillips curve PC_2. Point A is strictly preferred by the Fed to B, but A cannot be achieved because of the Fed's inability to commit.

FIGURE 17.14 **The Commitment Problem**

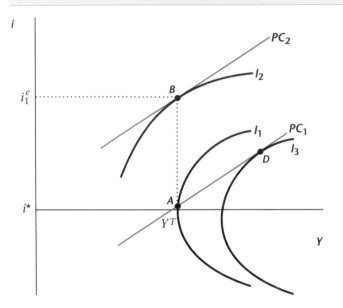

If the Fed could commit to an inflation rate, it would choose i^*, and the equilibrium would be at A. However, without commitment, the equilibrium is at B, where inflation is too high, and where an indifference curve is tangent to the Phillips curve at $i = i^e$ (rational expectations holds).

Kydland and Prescott interpreted this exercise as indicating that central bank discretion is dangerous and that there is something inherently wrong with letting central banks make decisions on an ad hoc basis. The solution to the lack of commitment problem, in their view, is to tie the Fed's hands, for example, by imposing a rule that the Fed target the growth rate of the money supply. However, there may be problems in committing a central bank to some particular policy rule, as any rule could later be shown to be inappropriate. For example, many central banks, including the Fed, adopted money supply targeting in the 1970s, but money supply targets currently play a minor role in Fed policymaking. This is because of increasing instability in the relationships among monetary aggregates, prices, and real activity, which occurred in the 1980s and 1990s.

A problem with the central bank commitment story is that it does not explain the run-up in inflation in the 1970s or why inflation decreased after 1980. Did the Fed suddenly lose its ability to commit in the late 1960s and then find it again in the early 1980s? This seems unlikely. Further, as Robert Barro and David Gordon have argued,[5] if the Fed is playing a repeated game with the private sector, then the Fed's

---

[5] See R. Barro and D. Gordon, 1983a. "A Positive Theory of Monetary Policy in a Natural Rate Model," *Journal of Political Economy* 91, 589–610; and R. Barro and D. Gordon, 1983b. "Rules, Discretion and Reputation in a Model of Monetary Policy," *Journal of Monetary Economics* 12, 101–121.

long-term reputation becomes important, and the long-run equilibrium can be point *A* in Figure 17.14. That is, the Fed understands that if it attempts to use surprise inflation to generate more aggregate output in the short run, then it destroys its reputation for producing low inflation. Therefore, a long-run equilibrium can exist at point *A* in Figure 17.14, because the Fed understands that if it loses its reputation, then the equilibrium will be at point *B* forever after. Of course, if we accept the importance of the Fed's concern for its reputation in determining its behavior, what was it about the 1970s that made the Fed willing to lose its reputation for low money growth and low inflation at that time?

In summary, several arguments cast doubt on the central bank commitment story as an explanation for recent U.S. inflation history. Commitment issues are probably not that important in the behavior of the Federal Reserve System. The central bank learning story seems to give a more plausible account of the run-up in inflation in the 1970s and the subsequent decline in the inflation rate after 1980.

MACROECONOMICS IN ACTION

Commitment to Low Inflation in Hong Kong

The world's central banks have resorted to several different means to show that they are committed to controlling inflation. During the 1970s and 1980s, many central banks announced explicit targets for the growth of monetary aggregates, and currently several central banks, including those of Canada, New Zealand, and Great Britain, have inflation targets. One device for tying the hands of the central bank is the introduction of a currency board. A prominent jurisdiction with a currency board is Hong Kong.

As was discussed in Chapter 14, a currency board is one way to operate a fixed exchange rate system. Under a currency board some governmental authority, which could be the central bank, stands ready to buy and sell domestic currency for some foreign currency at a fixed rate. All domestic currency is backed one-for-one by safe assets (including interest-earning assets) denominated in the foreign currency. If the currency board is run properly, there is no risk of the governmental authority running out of foreign exchange. Typically, a country adopting a currency board fixes its foreign exchange rate relative to the currency of a country with sound monetary policy. This is because, as we studied in Chapter 14, in the long run a country under a fixed exchange rate adopts the inflation rate of the country against which the currency is pegged.

In Hong Kong, the exchange rate was fixed at 7.8 Hong Kong Dollars per U.S. dollar in October 1983, and it has remained at that value since then.[1] The currency board in Hong Kong is operated by the Hong Kong Monetary Authority (HKMA), though there is a sense in which the Hong Kong system is not a pure currency board. This is because the HKMA commits to sell U.S. dollars at a fixed rate against Hong Kong dollars, but there is no commitment to buy U.S. dollars

(continued)

at a particular rate. As well, the rules by which the HKMA operates are not written into law; there is only an implicit commitment to continue the currency board into the future.

The HKMA has been quite successful in controlling inflation. While the inflation experience of Hong Kong has not been identical to that of the United States since 1983, the difference between the Hong Kong inflation rate and the U.S. inflation rate from 1983–2003 has not been great. The HKMA was able to maintain its fixed exchange rate through the Asian Crisis of 1997, with some changes made in the system in 1998. Recently, Hong Kong may have been too successful in reducing inflation, in that there was a deflation from 1998–2002, with the consumer price index falling by 12% over that period.[2] While this might be consistent with a Friedman rule (see Chapter 15), and thus be optimal, some would argue that deflation of this magnitude is excessive.

Hong Kong's success in controlling inflation under a currency board is not a story that was repeated in Argentina. In Argentina, the currency was pegged against the U.S. dollar in 1990 and supported by a currency board. Initially there was success, with inflation reduced from triple-digit rates in the 1980s to single-digit rates in the 1990s. However, under the pressure of out-of-control fiscal policy, the currency board was abandoned in Argentina in January 2002. Thus, a currency board is not a simple recipe for establishing the commitment to control inflation.

---

[1] See S. Gerlach, 2003. "Monetary Operations of Hong Kong's Currency Board," working paper, Hong Kong Institute for Monetary Research.

[2] See "Tony Latter: Hong Kong's Currency Board Today— The Unexpected Challenge of Deflation," available at http://www.info.gov.hk/hkma/eng/public/qb20028/fa3.pdf.

CHAPTER SUMMARY

- The Phillips curve relationship studied here is a positive relationship between the inflation rate and the deviation of real aggregate output from trend.

- Between 1947 and 1969, a Phillips curve can be observed in U.S. data, but the relationship begins to disintegrate in the 1970s and appears to disappear in the 1980s and 1990s. We used a version of the Friedman–Lucas money surprise model to explain these facts.

- In the version of the Friedman–Lucas money surprise model we use, the deviation of real aggregate output from trend is positively related to the difference between the actual and expected inflation rates. If the Fed generates a surprise increase in money growth, leading to a surprise increase in inflation, this causes an increase in labor supply, employment, and real output. The money surprise model predicts that the Phillips curve is unstable, as it shifts with changes in the expected rate of inflation.

- In the United States, the rate of inflation was moderate for most of the period 1947 to 1969, it increased substantially for the 1970s, and it then declined after 1980. We considered two possible explanations for this recent history of inflation rates in the United States.

- The first explanation for recent U.S. inflation experience was the central bank learning story, whereby the Fed discovered the existence of the Phillips curve in the 1960s and, assuming the Phillips curve was stable, attempted to exploit this relationship in the 1970s. However, the increased inflation in the 1970s did not generate permanently higher output, and it became clear to the Fed that there was no long-run trade-off between output and inflation. Higher inflation simply shifts up the Phillips curve relationship as expected inflation adjusts upward. Once the Fed discovered that there was no long-run trade-off between output and inflation, it could then, in the early 1980s, focus solely on the goal of reducing inflation.

- The second explanation for recent U.S. inflation history is the central bank commitment story. According to this story, high inflation is caused by the inability of the central bank to commit to a policy of not generating surprise inflation in an attempt to exploit the short-run Phillips curve.

- The central bank learning story provides a more plausible explanation than does the central bank commitment story for the path followed by the U.S. inflation rate, as it seems difficult to argue that the Fed found it difficult to commit in the 1970s, but easy to commit itself otherwise. However, for some countries, such as Hong Kong, a commitment mechanism appears to have been important in reducing inflation. In Hong Kong, this commitment mechanism was a fixed exchange rate enforced by a currency board.

KEY TERMS

Time consistency problem: Situation that occurs when it proves optimal to abandon a previously announced plan.

Rational expectations hypothesis: Hypothesis asserting that economic agents cannot make systematic errors; they use information efficiently.

QUESTIONS FOR REVIEW

1. Why is the Phillips curve called the Phillips curve?
2. The Phillips curve relationship examined in this chapter is a positive relationship between what two variables?
3. During what periods in the post–World War II data for the United States can a Phillips curve be observed, and when is it not observed?
4. What are two observations about empirical Phillips curve relations?
5. Explain how the Friedman–Lucas money surprise model works.
6. What is the relationship that summarizes the Friedman–Lucas money surprise model in this chapter?
7. When real aggregate output is equal to trend output, what is the inflation rate equal to?
8. What is the effect of an increase in expected inflation on the Phillips curve?
9. Describe the course of the inflation rate in the United States from 1947 until 2003.
10. What are two explanations for the U.S. inflation rate history after 1947?
11. Why can the central bank have an incentive to increase the inflation rate if it believes that the Phillips curve is stable?
12. Can the Fed permanently increase the level of aggregate output? Explain why or why not.
13. What was different about the ways in which inflation was reduced in the United States and in New Zealand?

14. Why is the inflation rate high in the long run if the central bank cannot commit itself?

15. Explain why, if the central bank is concerned with its reputation, inflation can be low in the long run.

16. Which is a more satisfactory explanation of U.S. post–World War II inflation, the central bank learning story or the central bank commitment story? Why?

17. Explain why commitment was important in reducing inflation in Hong Kong.

PROBLEMS

1. Suppose that the private sector does not have rational expectations, but instead follows an "adaptive expectations" scheme. That is, the private sector's expected inflation rate is what the inflation rate was last period. Show in a diagram how the inflation rate and output move over time if the initial inflation rate is the optimal rate i^*, and then the central bank acts to exploit the Phillips curve. Explain your results.

2. Suppose that the economy is in a long-run equilibrium where the inflation rate is greater than the optimal rate i^*, and then the central bank acts to reduce the inflation rate to i^*.
   (a) Suppose that the central bank decides to take drastic action and reduces the inflation rate within one period to i^*. Also, suppose that the private sector has adaptive expectations, so that the current expected inflation rate is last period's actual inflation rate. Show in a diagram the path that real aggregate output and the inflation rate take over time.
   (b) Now, suppose that the central bank takes the drastic strategy in part (a), but that the private sector has rational expectations, so that $i = i^e$. Again, show in a diagram the path followed by output and the inflation rate over time.
   (c) Now, suppose that the central bank takes a gradual strategy of reducing the inflation rate in a number of steps to i^*. Under a gradual strategy, show what differences there are between adaptive and rational expectations for the path of output and the inflation rate over time.
   (d) Explain your results in parts (a) to (c), and comment on what light this sheds on Figures 17.7 and 17.8 for the early 1980s period.

3. Suppose that the inflation rate is higher than i^*, that the central bank announces it will reduce the inflation rate, and that it actually proceeds to do this. Answer the following:
   (a) Suppose that the private sector believes the central bank announcement. What are the effects on the inflation rate and real output? Show this in a diagram.
   (b) Suppose that the private sector does not believe the central bank announcement. What are the effects on the inflation rate and real output now? Show this in a diagram.
   (c) Explain your results in parts (a) and (b).

4. (Warning: This is challenging.) Suppose that the central bank is in a repeated relationship with the private sector. If the inflation rate is $i = i^*$ and output is $Y = Y^T$, then suppose the reward each period to the central bank is u_1. If consumers anticipate $i^e = i^*$, then the one-period reward the central bank receives from fooling consumers and with $i > i^e$ is $u_2 > u_1$ and we will have $i > i^e = i^*$. When the central bank cannot commit and there is rational expectations, then the reward the central bank gets is $u_3 < u_1$ with $i = i^e = i_1 > i^*$ and $Y = Y^T$. Now, suppose that the government anticipates that if it deviates from $i = i^*$, then it will totally lose its reputation and consumers will anticipate $i^e = i_1$ forever after, so that the government will receive a reward of u_3 forever after. That is, suppose the central bank has two alternatives, which are (a) set $i = i^*$ forever receiving reward u_1, and (b) cheat for

this period, receiving reward u_2, implying that the reward will be u_3 in every future period. Suppose that the central bank discounts the future at the rate r.

(a) Show that it is an equilibrium for the government to choose $i = i^*$ forever if

$$u_1(1 + r) - u_3 \geq ru_2.$$

(b) Interpret the condition in part (a).

(c) Show that, as r becomes small, that the condition in part (a) must hold, and explain this.

WORKING WITH THE DATA

1. Calculate the annual percentage rate of change in the consumer price index (December to December), and graph this in scatter plots against the unemployment rate for the 1950s, 1960s, 1970s, 1980s, and 1990s. For which decades do you observe a Phillips curve relationship, and for which do you not? What reasons could there be for a shift in this Phillips curve relationship, other than shifts in inflationary expectations?

2. Use the quarterly increase in the GDP price deflator as a measure of the inflation rate and the inflation rate in the previous quarter as a measure of the current expected inflation rate. Construct a scatter plot of the inflation rate minus the expected inflation rate vs. detrended GDP.

(a) What do you observe in the scatter plot?

(b) Is there a Phillips curve relationship evident in this data? Discuss.

APPENDIX

Mathematical Appendix

This appendix provides more formal treatments of some of the models in the book, and it is intended for students with a knowledge of calculus and more advanced algebraic techniques who wish to study some of the topics of this book in more depth. The appendix assumes an understanding of mathematical methods in economics at the level of Alpha C. Chiang's *Fundamental Methods of Mathematical Economics*, Third Edition, McGraw Hill, New York, 1984. We proceed by working through results for selected models from selected chapters.

CHAPTER 4: CONSUMER AND FIRM BEHAVIOR

Chapter 4 dealt with the representative consumer's and representative firm's optimization problems in the closed-economy one-period model. We set up the consumer's and firm's problems and derive the main results of Chapter 4 formally.

The Representative Consumer

The representative consumer's preferences are defined by the utility function $U(C, l)$, where C is consumption and l is leisure, with $U(\cdot, \cdot)$ a function that is increasing in both arguments, strictly quasiconcave, and twice differentiable. These properties of the utility function imply that indifference curves are downward-sloping and convex and that the consumer strictly prefers more to less. The consumer's optimization problem is to choose C and l so as to maximize $U(C, l)$ subject to his or her budget constraint—that is,

$$\max_{C, l} U(C, l)$$

subject to

$$C = w(h - l) + \pi - T,$$

and $C \geq 0$, $0 \leq l \leq h$, where w is the real wage, h is the quantity of time the consumer has available, π is dividend income, and T is the lump-sum tax. This problem is a constrained optimization problem, with the associated Lagrangian

$$L = U(C, l) + \lambda[w(h - l) + p - T - C],$$

where λ is the Lagrange multiplier.

We assume that there is an interior solution to the consumer's problem where $C > 0$ and $0 < l < h$. This can be guaranteed by assuming that $U_1(0, l) = \infty$ (i.e., the derivative of the utility function with respect to the first argument goes to infinity in the limit as consumption goes to zero) and $U_2(C, 0) = \infty$. These assumptions imply that $C > 0$ and $l > 0$ at the optimum. In a competitive equilibrium we cannot have $l = h$, as this would imply that nothing would be produced and $C = 0$. Given an interior solution to the consumer's problem, we can characterize the solution by the first-order conditions from the problem of choosing C, l, and λ to maximize L. These first-order conditions are (differentiating L with respect to C, l, and λ, respectively, and setting each of these first derivatives equal to zero)

$$U_1(C, l) - \lambda = 0, \tag{A.1}$$

$$U_2(C, l) - \lambda w = 0, \tag{A.2}$$

$$w(h - l) + \pi - T - C = 0. \tag{A.3}$$

In Equations (A.1) and (A.2), $U_i(C, l)$ denotes the first derivative with respect to the ith argument of $U(\cdot, \cdot)$, evaluated at (C, l). From Equations (A.1) and (A.2), we can obtain the condition

$$\frac{U_2(C, l)}{U_1(C, l)} = w, \tag{A.4}$$

which is the optimization condition for the consumer that we showed graphically in Chapter 4, Figure 4.5. Equation (A.4) states that the marginal rate of substitution of leisure for consumption (on the left-hand side of the equation) is equal to the real wage (on the right-hand side) at the optimum. For our purposes, we can rewrite Equation (A.4) as

$$U_2(C, l) - wU_1(C, l) = 0, \tag{A.5}$$

and then (A.3) and (A.5) are two equations determining the optimal choices of C and l given w, π, and T.

In general, we cannot obtain explicit closed-form solutions for C and l from Equations (A.3) and (A.5) without assuming an explicit form for the utility function $U(\cdot, \cdot)$, but we can use comparative statics techniques to determine how C and l change when any of w, π, or T change. To do this, we totally differentiate (A.3) and (A.5), obtaining

$$-dC - wdl + (h - l)dw + d\pi - dT = 0, \tag{A.6}$$

$$[U_{12} - wU_{11}]dC + [U_{22} - wU_{12}]dl - U_1dw = 0. \tag{A.7}$$

In Equation (A.7), U_{ij} denotes the second derivative with respect to the ith and j^{th} arguments of $U(\cdot, \cdot)$. Now, it is useful to write (A.6) and (A.7) in matrix form, as

$$\begin{bmatrix} -1 & -w \\ U_{12} - wU_{11} & U_{22} - wU_{12} \end{bmatrix} \begin{bmatrix} dC \\ dl \end{bmatrix} = \begin{bmatrix} -(h - l)dw - d\pi + dT \\ U_1dw \end{bmatrix} \tag{A.8}$$

Then, we can solve for the derivatives of interest by using Cramer's rule.

First, consider the effects of a change in dividend income π. Using Cramer's rule, from Equation (A.8) we get

$$\frac{dC}{d\pi} = \frac{-U_{22} + wU_{12}}{\nabla}, \tag{A.9}$$

$$\frac{dl}{d\pi} = \frac{U_{12} - wU_{11}}{\nabla}, \tag{A.10}$$

where

$$\nabla = -U_{22} + 2wU_{12} - w^2 U_{11}.$$

Now, ∇ is the determinant of the bordered Hessian associated with the constrained optimization problem for the consumer, and the quasiconcavity of the utility function implies that $\nabla > 0$. This, however, does not allow us to sign the derivatives in (A.9) and (A.10). Our assumption from Chapter 4 that consumption and leisure are normal goods is equivalent to the conditions $-U_{22} + wU_{12} > 0$ and $U_{12} - wU_{11} > 0$. Thus, given normal goods, we have $\frac{dC}{d\pi} > 0$ and $\frac{dl}{d\pi} > 0$, so that the quantities of consumption and leisure chosen by the consumer increase when dividend income increases. It is straightforward to show that $\frac{dC}{dT} = -\frac{dC}{d\pi}$ and $\frac{dl}{dT} = -\frac{dl}{d\pi}$, so that the effects of a decrease in taxes are equivalent to the effects of an increase in dividend income.

Next, we can derive the effects of a change in the real wage, again using Cramer's rule to obtain, from Equation (A.8),

$$\frac{dC}{dw} = \frac{wU_1 + (h - l)(-U_{22} + wU_{12})}{\nabla}, \tag{A.11}$$

$$\frac{dl}{dw} = \frac{-U_1 + (h - l)(U_{12} - wU_{11})}{\nabla}. \tag{A.12}$$

Now, assuming that consumption is a normal good, we have $-U_{22} + wU_{12} > 0$, and because $\nabla > 0$ and $U_1 > 0$ (utility increases as consumption increases), we know from (A.11) that $\frac{dC}{dw} > 0$, so that consumption increases when the real wage increases. However, we cannot determine the sign of $\frac{dl}{dw}$ from (A.12) because of the opposing income and substitution effects of a change in the real wage on leisure. It is possible to separate algebraically the income and substitution effects in Equation (A.12) by determining the response of leisure to a change in the real wage, holding utility constant. This gives a substitution effect, which can be expressed as

$$\frac{dl}{dw}(subst) = \frac{-U_1}{\nabla} < 0,$$

so that the substitution effect is for leisure to fall and hours worked to rise when the real wage increases. This implies that, from (A.12), the income effect is

$$\frac{dl}{dw}(inc) = \frac{dl}{dw} - \frac{dl}{dw}(subst) = \frac{(h - l)(U_{12} - wU_{11})}{\nabla} > 0,$$

assuming that leisure is a normal good, which implies that $U_{12} - wU_{11} > 0$. Therefore, the income effect is for leisure to increase when the real wage increases. In general, without putting additional restrictions on the utility function, we do not know the sign of $\frac{dl}{dw}$.

The Representative Firm

We assumed in Chapter 4 that the production function for the representative firm is described by

$$Y = zF(K, N^d),$$

where Y is output, z is total factor productivity, $F(\cdot, \cdot)$ is a function, K is the capital stock, and N^d is the firm's labor input. The function $F(\cdot, \cdot)$ is assumed to be quasiconcave, strictly increasing in both arguments, homogeneous of degree one or constant-returns-to-scale, and twice differentiable. We also assume that $F_2(K, 0) = \infty$ and $F_2(K, \infty) = 0$ to guarantee that there is always an interior solution to the firm's profit maximization problem, where $F_2(K, N^d)$ is the first derivative with respect to the second argument of the function $F(\cdot, \cdot)$. The firm's profit maximization problem is to choose the labor input N^d so as to maximize

$$\pi = zF(K, N^d) - wN^d,$$

subject to $N^d \geq 0$, where π is the difference between revenue and labor costs in terms of consumption goods. That is, the firm solves

$$\max_{N^d}(zF(K, N^d) - wN^d). \tag{A.13}$$

The restrictions on the function $F(\cdot, \cdot)$ imply that there is a unique interior solution to problem (A.13), characterized by the first-order condition

$$zF_2(K, N^d) = w, \tag{A.14}$$

which states that the firm hires labor until the marginal product of labor $zF_2(K, N^d)$ equals the real wage w.

We can determine the effects of changes in w, z, and K on labor demand N^d through comparative statics techniques. Totally differentiating Equation (A.14), which determines N^d implicitly as a function of w, z, and K, we obtain

$$zF_{22}dN^d - dw + F_2 dz + zF_{12}dK = 0.$$

Then, solving for the appropriate derivatives, we have

$$\frac{dN^d}{dw} = \frac{1}{zF_{22}} < 0,$$

$$\frac{dN^d}{dz} = \frac{-F_2}{zF_{22}} > 0,$$

$$\frac{dN^d}{dK} = \frac{-zF_{12}}{zF_{22}} > 0.$$

We can sign the above derivatives because $F_{22} < 0$ (the marginal product of labor decreases as the quantity of labor increases), $F_2 > 0$ (the marginal product of labor is positive), and $F_{12} > 0$ (the marginal product of labor increases as the capital input increases). These are restrictions on the production function discussed in Chapter 4.

Because $\frac{dN^d}{dw} < 0$, the labor demand curve is downward sloping. Further, $\frac{dN^d}{dz} > 0$ and $\frac{dN^d}{dK} > 0$ imply that the labor demand curve shifts to the right when z or K increases.

Problems

1. Suppose that the consumer's preferences are given by the utility function $U(C, l) = \ln C + \alpha \ln l$, where $\alpha > 0$. Determine the consumer's choice of consumption and leisure and interpret your solutions.

2. In the consumer's choice problem, show that at least one good must be normal.

3. Suppose that the firm's production technology is given by $Y = zF(K, N) = zK^{\alpha}N^{1-\alpha}$, where $0 < \alpha < 1$. Determine the firm's demand for labor as a function of z, K, α, and w, and interpret.

4. Suppose that the firm's production technology is given by $Y = z\min(K, \alpha N)$, where $\alpha > 0$. As in problem 3, determine the firm's demand for labor as a function of z, K, α, and w, and interpret.

CHAPTER 5: A CLOSED-ECONOMY ONE-PERIOD MACROECONOMIC MODEL

Here, we show formally the equivalence between the competitive equilibrium and the Pareto optimum in the one-period model and then determine, using comparative statics, the equilibrium effects of a change in government spending and in total factor productivity.

Competitive Equilibrium

In a competitive equilibrium, the representative consumer maximizes utility subject to his or her budget constraint, the representative firm maximizes profits, the government budget constraint holds, and the market on which labor is exchanged for consumption goods clears. From the previous section, the two equations describing consumer optimization are the budget constraint, Equation (A.3), or

$$w(h - l) + \pi - T - C = 0, \tag{A.15}$$

and Equation (A.5), or

$$U_2(C, l) - wU_1(C, l) = 0. \tag{A.16}$$

Optimization by the representative firm implies Equation (A.14), or

$$zF_2(K, N^d) = w, \tag{A.17}$$

and profits for the firm are

$$\pi = zF(K, N^d) - wN^d. \tag{A.18}$$

The government budget constraint states that government spending is equal to taxes; that is,

$$G = T. \tag{A.19}$$

Finally, the market-clearing condition is

$$h - l = N^d, \tag{A.20}$$

or the supply of labor is equal to the demand for labor. Equations (A.15) to (A.20) are six equations that solve for the six endogenous variables C, l, N^d, T, π, and w, given the exogenous variables z and G. To make this system of equations more manageable, we can simplify as follows. First, using Equations (A.18) to (A.20) to substitute for π, T, and N^d in Equation (A.15), we obtain

$$C = zF(K, h - l) - G. \tag{A.21}$$

Then, substituting in Equation (A.18) for N^d using Equation (A.20), and then in turn for w in (A.16) using Equation (A.18), we obtain

$$U_2(C, l) - zF_2(K, h - l)U_1(C, l) = 0. \tag{A.22}$$

Equations (A.21) and (A.22) then solve for equilibrium C and l. Then, the real wage w can be determined from (A.17), after substituting for N^d from (A.20), to get

$$w = zF_2(K, h - l). \tag{A.23}$$

Finally, aggregate output is given from the production function by

$$Y = zF(K, h - l).$$

Pareto Optimum

To determine the Pareto optimum, we need to ask how a fictitious social planner would choose consumption and leisure so as to maximize welfare for the representative consumer, given the production technology. The social planner solves

$$\max_{C, l} U(C, l)$$

subject to

$$C = zF(K, h - l) - G.$$

To solve the social planner's problem, set up the Lagrangian associated with the constrained optimization problem above, which is

$$L = U(C, l) + \lambda[zF(K, h - l) - G - C].$$

The first-order conditions for an optimum are then

$$U_1(C, l) - \lambda = 0, \tag{A.24}$$

$$U_2(C, l) - \lambda z F_2(K, h - l) = 0, \tag{A.25}$$

$$z F(K, h - l) - G - C = 0. \tag{A.26}$$

From Equations (A.24) and (A.25), we obtain

$$U_2(C, l) - z F_2(K, h - l) U_1(C, l) = 0. \tag{A.27}$$

Now, Equations (A.26) and (A.27), which solve for the Pareto optimal quantities of leisure l and consumption C, are identical to Equations (A.21) and (A.22), so that the Pareto optimal quantities of leisure and consumption are identical to the competitive equilibrium quantities of leisure and consumption. As a result, the competitive equilibrium and the Pareto optimum are the same thing in this model, so the first and second welfare theorems hold.

Equation (A.27) can be written (suppressing arguments for convenience) as

$$\frac{U_2}{U_1} = z F_2,$$

which states that the marginal rate of substitution of leisure for consumption is equal to the marginal product of labor (the marginal rate of transformation) at the optimum.

Comparative Statics

We would like to determine the effects of changes in G and z on equilibrium C, l, Y, and w. To do this, we totally differentiate Equations (A.26) and (A.27), obtaining

$$-dC - z F_2 dl + F dz - dG = 0,$$

$$(U_{12} - z F_2 U_{11}) dC + (U_{22} + z F_{22} U_1 - z F_2 U_{12}) dl - F_2 U_1 dz = 0.$$

Then, putting these two equations in matrix form, we get

$$\begin{bmatrix} -1 & -z F_2 \\ U_{12} - z F_2 U_{11} & U_{22} + z F_{22} U_1 - z F_2 U_{12} \end{bmatrix} \begin{bmatrix} dC \\ dl \end{bmatrix} = \begin{bmatrix} -F dz + dG \\ F_2 U_1 dz \end{bmatrix} \tag{A.28}$$

Using Cramer's rule to determine the effects of a change in government spending G, from (A.28) we then get

$$\frac{dC}{dG} = \frac{U_{22} + z F_{22} U_1 - z F_2 U_{12}}{\nabla},$$

$$\frac{dl}{dG} = \frac{-U_{12} + z F_2 U_{11}}{\nabla},$$

where

$$\nabla = -z^2 F_2^2 U_{11} + 2 z F_2 U_{12} - U_{22} - z F_{22} U_1.$$

Here, ∇ is the determinant of the bordered Hessian associated with the social planner's constrained optimization problem, and the quasiconcavity of the utility function and the production function guarantees that $\nabla > 0$. To sign the derivatives above, in equilibrium $zF_2 = w$, from Equation (A.17). This then implies, given our assumption that consumption and leisure are normal goods, that $U_{22} - zF_2U_{12} < 0$ and $-U_{12} + zF_2U_{11} < 0$ (recall our discussion from the previous section); because $F_{22} < 0$ (the marginal product of labor declines as the labor input increases), we have $\frac{dC}{dG} < 0$ and $\frac{dl}{dG} < 0$, so that consumption and leisure decline when government purchases increase because of negative income effects. For the effect on the real wage w, because $w = zF_2(K, h - l)$, we have

$$\frac{dw}{dG} = -zF_{22}\frac{dl}{dG} < 0,$$

and so the real wage decreases. For the effect on aggregate output, because $Y = C + G$, we have

$$\frac{dY}{dG} = \frac{dC}{dG} + 1 = \frac{-z^2F_2^2U_{11} + zF_2U_{12}}{\nabla} > 0,$$

as leisure is assumed to be normal, implying $zF_2U_{11} - U_{12} < 0$.

Now, to determine the effects of a change in z, again we use Cramer's rule in conjunction with Equation (A.28), obtaining

$$\frac{dC}{dz} = \frac{-F(U_{22} + zF_{22}U_1 - zF_2U_{12}) + F_2^2zU_1}{\nabla},$$

$$\frac{dl}{dz} = \frac{-F_2U_1 + F(U_{12} - zF_2U_{11})}{\nabla}.$$

Here, because consumption is a normal good, $U_{22} - zF_2U_{12} < 0$, and given $F_{22} < 0$, $F > 0$, and $U_1 > 0$, we have $\frac{dC}{dz} > 0$ and consumption increases with an increase in total factor productivity, as we showed diagrammatically in Chapter 5, Figure 5.9. However, we cannot sign $\frac{dl}{dz}$ as there are opposing income and substitution effects. We can separate out the income and substitution effects on leisure by determining the response of leisure to a change in z holding utility constant. This gives a substitution effect, which is

$$\frac{dl}{dz}(subst) = \frac{-F_2U_1}{\nabla},$$

so that the substitution effect is for leisure to decrease and employment ($= h - l$) to increase. The income effect of the change in z is then

$$\frac{dl}{dz}(inc) = \frac{dl}{dz} - \frac{dl}{dz}(subst) = \frac{F(U_{12} - zF_2U_{11})}{\nabla} > 0,$$

because leisure is a normal good. Therefore, an increase in z has a positive income effect on leisure.

Problems

1. For the closed-economy, one-period model, suppose that $U(C,l) = \ln C + \beta l$, and $F(K,N) = zK^\alpha N^{1-\alpha}$, where $\beta > 0$ and $0 < \alpha < 1$. Determine consumption, employment, output, leisure, and the real wage in a competitive equilibrium, and explain your solutions.

2. For the closed-economy, one-period model, suppose that $U(C,l) = \min(C, \beta l)$, and $F(K,N) = \alpha K + \delta N$, where $\beta > 0$, $\alpha > 0$, and $\delta > 0$. Determine consumption, employment, output, leisure, and the real wage in a competitive equilibrium, and explain your solutions. Also draw a diagram with the consumer's preferences and the production possibilities frontier, and show the competitive equilibrium in this diagram.

CHAPTERS 6 AND 7: ECONOMIC GROWTH

In this section we work out explicitly the effects of changes in the savings rate, the labor force growth rate, and total factor productivity on the steady state quantity of capital per worker and output per worker in the Solow growth model. We omit an algebraic analysis of the Malthusian growth model, as this is very straightforward. We determine the golden rule for capital accumulation in the Solow model. Finally, we develop a growth model where consumption–savings decisions are made endogenously. In solving this model, we introduce dynamic programming techniques, which are useful later in this appendix.

Explicit Results for the Solow Growth Model

Recall from Chapter 6 that the aggregate quantity of capital in the Solow growth model evolves according to

$$K' = (1-d)K + I, \tag{A.29}$$

where K' is future period capital, d is the depreciation rate, K is current period capital, and I is current period investment. In equilibrium, saving is equal to investment, and so $sY = I$, where s is the savings rate and Y is aggregate income. Further, the production function is given by $Y = zF(K,N)$, where z is total factor productivity and N is the labor force, so that substituting in Equation (A.29), we have

$$K' = (1-d)K + szF(K,N). \tag{A.30}$$

Then, dividing the right-hand and left-hand sides of Equation (A.30) by N, using the relationship $N' = (1+n)N$, which describes labor force growth, with N' denoting the future labor force and n the population growth rate, and rewriting in the form of lowercase variables that denote per-worker quantities, we have

$$k' = \frac{szf(k)}{1+n} + \frac{(1-d)k}{1+n}. \tag{A.31}$$

Equation (A.31) then determines the evolution of the per-worker capital stock from the current period to the future period, where k is the current stock of capital per worker, k' is the stock of future capital per worker, and $f(k)$ is the per-worker production function.

In the steady state, $k' = k = k^*$, where k^* is the steady state quantity of capital per worker, which, from (A.31), satisfies

$$szf(k^*) - (n + d)k^* = 0. \qquad (A.32)$$

Now, to determine the effects of changes in s, n, and z on the steady state quantity of capital per worker, we totally differentiate Equation (A.32) getting

$$[szf'(k^*) - n - d]dk^* + zf(k^*)ds - k^*dn + sf(k^*)dz = 0 \qquad (A.33)$$

Then, solving for the appropriate derivatives, we obtain

$$\frac{dk^*}{ds} = \frac{-zf(k^*)}{szf'(k^*) - n - d} > 0,$$

$$\frac{dk^*}{dn} = \frac{k^*}{szf'(k^*) - n - d} < 0,$$

$$\frac{dk^*}{dz} = \frac{-sf(k^*)}{szf'(k^*) - n - d} > 0.$$

Here, capital per worker increases with increases in s and z, and decreases with an increase in n. We get these results because $szf'(k^*) - n - d < 0$ in the steady state. Because output per worker in the steady state is $y^* = zf(k^*)$, for each of these experiments, steady state output per worker moves in the same direction as steady state capital per worker.

In the steady state, the quantity of consumption per worker is

$$c^* = zf(k^*) - (n + d)k^*.$$

Now, when the savings rate changes, the response of consumption per worker in the steady state is given by

$$\frac{dc^*}{ds} = [zf'(k^*) - n - d]\frac{dk^*}{ds}.$$

Though $\frac{dk^*}{ds} > 0$, the sign of $zf'(k^*) - n - d$ is ambiguous, so that capital per worker could increase or decrease with an increase in the savings rate. The golden rule savings rate is the savings rate s_{gr} that maximizes consumption per worker in the steady state. The golden rule steady state quantity of capital per worker solves the problem

$$\max_{k^*}[zf(k^*) - (n + d)k^*];$$

letting k^*_{gr} denote this quantity of capital per worker, k^*_{gr} solves

$$zf'\left(k^*_{gr}\right) - n - d = 0,$$

and then s_{gr} is determined from Equation (A.32) by

$$s_{gr} = \frac{(n + d)k^*_{gr}}{zf\left(k^*_{gr}\right)}.$$

For example, if $F(K, N) = K^\alpha N^{1-\alpha}$, where $0 < \alpha < 1$ (a Cobb–Douglas production function), then $f(k) = k^\alpha$, and we get

$$k_{gr}^* = \left(\frac{z\alpha}{n+d}\right)^{\frac{1}{1-\alpha}},$$

$$s_{gr} = \alpha.$$

Problem

1. Suppose in the Solow growth model that there is government spending financed by lump-sum taxes, with total government spending $G = gY$, where $0 < g < 1$. Solve for steady state capital per worker, consumption per worker, and output per worker, and determine how each depends on g. Can g be set so as to maximize steady state consumption per worker? If so, determine the optimal fraction of output purchased by the government, g^*, and explain your results.

Optimal Growth: Endogenous Consumption–Savings Decisions

In this model, we relax the assumption made in the Solow growth model that the savings rate is exogenous and allow consumption to be determined optimally over time. The model we develop here is a version of the optimal growth theory originally developed by David Cass and Tjalling Koopmans.[1] In this model, the second welfare theorem holds, and so we can solve the social planner's problem to determine the competitive equilibrium. We set the model up as simply as possible, leaving out population growth and changes in total factor productivity; but, these features are easy to add.

There is a representative infinitely lived consumer with preferences given by

$$\sum_{t=0}^{\infty} \beta^t U(C_t) \tag{A.34}$$

where β is the subjective discount factor of the representative consumer, with $0 < \beta < 1$, and C_t is consumption in period t. Throughout, t subscripts denote the time period. The period utility function $U(\cdot)$ is continuously differentiable, strictly increasing, strictly concave, and bounded. Assume that $\lim_{C \to 0} U'(C) = \infty$. Each period, the consumer is endowed with one unit of time, which can be supplied as labor.

The production function is given by

$$Y_t = F(K_t, N_t),$$

where Y_t is output, K_t is the capital input, and N_t is the labor input. The production function $F(\cdot, \cdot)$ is continuously differentiable, strictly increasing in both arguments, homogeneous of degree one, and strictly quasiconcave. Assume that $F(0, N) = 0$, $\lim_{K \to 0} F_1(K, 1) = \infty$, and $\lim_{K \to \infty} F_1(K, 1) = 0$.

---

[1] See D. Cass, 1965. "Optimum Growth in an Aggregative Model of Capital Accumulation," *Review of Economic Studies* 32, 233–240; and T. Koopmans, 1965. "On the Concept of Optimal Growth," in *The Econometric Approach to Development Planning*, North Holland, Amsterdam.

The capital stock obeys the law of motion

$$K_{t+1} = (1 - d)K_t + I_t, \tag{A.35}$$

where I_t is investment and d is the depreciation rate, with $0 \le d \le 1$, and K_0 is the initial capital stock, which is given. In equilibrium, we have $N_t = 1$ for all t, and so it is convenient to define the function $H(K_t)$ by $H(K_t) = F(K_t, 1)$. The resource constraint for the economy is

$$C_t + I_t = H(K_t), \tag{A.36}$$

or consumption plus investment is equal to the total quantity of output produced. It is convenient to substitute for I_t in Equation (A.36) using (A.35) and to rearrange, obtaining a single constraint

$$C_t + K_{t+1} = H(K_t) + (1 - d)K_t; \tag{A.37}$$

we can think of the resources available in period t to the social planner on the right-hand side of Equation (A.37) as being period t output plus the undepreciated portion of the capital stock, which is then split up (on the left-hand side of the equation) between period t consumption and the capital stock for period $t + 1$.

The social planner's problem for this economy is to determine consumption and the capital stock in each period so as to maximize Equation (A.34) subject to the constraint Equation (A.37). Again, the solution to this problem is equivalent to the competitive equilibrium solution. The social planner solves

$$\max_{\{C_t, K_{t+1}\}_{t=0}^{\infty}} \sum_{t=0}^{\infty} U(C_t), \tag{A.38}$$

given K_0 and (A.37) for $t = 0, 1, 2, \dots \infty$.

Now, the problem of solving Equation (A.38) subject to (A.37) may appear quite formidable, as we need to solve for an infinite sequence of choice variables. However, dynamic programming techniques essentially allow us to turn this infinite-dimensional problem into a two-dimensional problem.[2] To see how this works, note from the right-hand side of (A.37) that the current capital stock K_t determines the resources that are available to the social planner at the beginning of period t. Thus, K_t determines how much utility the social planner can give to the consumer from period t on. Suppose that the social planner knows $v(K_t)$, which is the maximum utility that the social planner could provide for the representative consumer from period t on. Then, the problem that the social planner would solve in any period t would be

$$\max_{C_t, K_{t+1}} [U(C_t) + \beta v(K_{t+1})]$$

subject to

$$C_t + K_{t+1} = H(K_t) + (1 - d)K_t.$$

---

[2] For more detail on dynamic programming methods in economics, see N. Stokey, R. Lucas, and E. Prescott, 1989. *Recursive Methods in Economic Dynamics*, Harvard University Press, Cambridge. MA.

That is, the social planner chooses current period consumption and the capital stock for the following period so as to maximize the sum of current period utility and the discounted value of utility from the next period on, subject to the resource constraint. Now, because the problem of the social planner looks the same in every period, it is true that

$$v(K_t) = \max_{C_t, K_{t+1}} [U(C_t) + \beta v(K_{t+1})] \tag{A.39}$$

subject to

$$C_t + K_{t+1} = H(K_t) + (1 - d)K_t. \tag{A.40}$$

Then, Equation (A.39) is called a Bellman equation, or functional equation, and it determines what $v(\cdot)$ is. We call $v(K_t)$ the value function as this tells us the value of the problem at time t to the social planner as a function of the state variable K_t. Given the assumptions we have made, there is a unique function $v(\cdot)$ that solves the Bellman equation. There are some circumstances where we can obtain an explicit solution for $v(\cdot)$ (see the problem at the end of this section), but in any case the dynamic programming formulation of the social planner's problem, Equation (A.39) subject to (A.40), can be convenient for characterizing solutions, if we assume that $v(\cdot)$ is differentiable and strictly concave (which it is here, given our assumptions).

We can simplify the problem above by substituting for C_t in the objective function (A.39) using the constraint (A.40), getting

$$v(K_t) = \max_{K_{t+1}} \{U[H(K_t) + (1 - d)K_t - K_{t+1}] + \beta v(K_{t+1})\} \tag{A.41}$$

Then, given that the value function $v(\cdot)$ is concave and differentiable, we can differentiate on the right-hand side of (A.41) to get the first-order condition for an optimum, which is

$$U'[H(K_t) + (1 - d)K_t - K_{t+1}] + \beta v'(K_{t+1}) = 0. \tag{A.42}$$

Now, to determine $v'(K_{t+1})$, we apply the envelope theorem in differentiating Equation (A.41), obtaining

$$v'(K_t) = [H'(K_t) + 1 - d]U'[H(K_t) + (1 - d)K_t - K_{t+1}];$$

then, we update one period, and substitute for $v'(K_{t+1})$ in (A.42), getting

$$-U'[H(K_t) + (1 - d)K_t - K_{t+1}] + \beta[H'(K_{t+1}) + 1 - d]$$
$$\times U'[H(K_{t+1}) + (1 - d)K_{t+1} - K_{t+2}] = 0. \tag{A.43}$$

Now, we know that, in this the model, the quantity of capital converges to a constant steady state value, K^*. Equation (A.43) can be used to solve for K^* by substituting $K_{t+1} = K_t = K^*$ in (A.43), which gives, after simplifying,

$$-1 + \beta[H'(K^*) + 1 - d] = 0, \tag{A.44}$$

or

$$H'(K^*) - d = \frac{1}{\beta} - 1$$

in the optimal steady state. That is, in the optimal steady state, the net marginal product of capital is equal to the subjective discount rate of the representative consumer.

In the model, the savings rate is given by

$$s_t = \frac{I_t}{Y_t} = \frac{K_{t+1} - (1-d)K_t}{H(K_t)},$$

and so in the steady state the savings rate is

$$s^* = \frac{dK^*}{H(K^*)}.$$

In this model, because the savings rate is optimally chosen over time, choosing a "golden rule savings rate" makes no sense. Indeed, the steady state optimal savings rate in this model does not maximize steady state consumption. Steady state consumption would be maximized for a value of the steady state capital stock K^* such that $H'(K^*) = d$, but this is different from the optimal steady state capital stock determined by Equation (A.44).

Problem

1. In the optimal growth model, suppose that $U(C_t) = \ln C_t$ and $F(K_t, N_t) = K_t^\alpha N_t^{1-\alpha}$, with $d = 1$ (100% depreciation).
    (a) Guess that the value function takes the form $v(K_t) = A + B \ln K_t$, where A and B are undetermined constants.
    (b) Substitute your guess for the value function on the right-hand side of Equation (A.41), solve the optimization problem, and verify that your guess was correct.
    (c) Solve for A and B by substituting your optimal solution from part (b) on the right-hand side of Equation (A.41) and equating coefficients on the left and right-hand sides of the equation.
    (d) Determine the solutions for K_{t+1} and C_t as functions of K_t, and interpret these solutions.

CHAPTER 8: TWO–PERIOD MODEL

In this section we formally derive the results for individual consumer behavior, showing how a consumer optimizes by choosing consumption and savings over two periods and how the consumer responds to changes in income and the market real interest rate.

The Consumer's Optimization Problem

The consumer has preferences defined by a utility function $U(c, c')$, where c is current period consumption, c' is future consumption, and $U(\cdot, \cdot)$ is strictly quasiconcave, increasing in both arguments, and twice differentiable. To guarantee an interior solution to the consumer's problem, we assume that the marginal utilities of current and future consumption each go to infinity in the limit as current and future consumption go to zero, respectively. The consumer chooses c and c' to maximize $U(c, c')$ subject to the consumer's lifetime budget constraint, that is,

$$\max_{c, c'} U(c, c')$$

subject to

$$c + \frac{c'}{1+r} = y + \frac{y'}{1+r} - t - \frac{t'}{1+r},$$

where y is current income, y' is future income, t is the current tax, and t' is the future tax. The Lagrangian associated with this constrained optimization problem is

$$L = U(c, c') + \lambda\left(y + \frac{y'}{1+r} - t - \frac{t'}{1+r} - c - \frac{c'}{1+r}\right),$$

where λ is the Lagrange multiplier. Therefore, the first-order conditions for an optimum are

$$U_1(c, c') - \lambda = 0, \tag{A.45}$$

$$U_2(c, c') - \frac{\lambda}{1+r} = 0, \tag{A.46}$$

$$y + \frac{y'}{1+r} - t - \frac{t'}{1+r} - c - \frac{c'}{1+r} = 0. \tag{A.47}$$

Then, in Equations (A.45) and (A.46), we can eliminate λ to obtain

$$U_1(c, c') - (1+r)U_2(c, c') = 0, \tag{A.48}$$

or rewriting (A.48),

$$\frac{U_1(c, c')}{U_2(c, c')} = 1 + r,$$

which states that the intertemporal marginal rate of substitution (the marginal rate of substitution of current consumption for future consumption) is equal to one plus the real interest rate at the optimum.

For convenience, we can rewrite (A.47) as

$$y(1+r) + y' - t(1+r) - t' - c(1+r) - c' = 0. \tag{A.49}$$

Then, Equations (A.48) and (A.49) determine the quantities of c and c' the consumer chooses given current and future incomes y and y', current and future taxes t and t', and the real interest rate r.

Comparative Statics

To determine the effects of changes in current and future income and the real interest rate on current and future consumption and savings, we totally differentiate Equations (A.48) and (A.49), obtaining

$$[U_{11} - (1+r)U_{12}]dc + [U_{12} - (1+r)U_{22}]dc' - U_2 dr = 0,$$

$$-(1+r)dc - dc' + (y - t - c)dr + (1+r)dy + dy' - (1+r)dt - dt' = 0;$$

these two equations can be written in matrix form as

$$
\begin{bmatrix} U_{11} - (1+r)U_{12} & U_{12} - (1+r)U_{22} \\ -(1+r) & -1 \end{bmatrix} \begin{bmatrix} dc \\ dc' \end{bmatrix}
$$
$$
= \begin{bmatrix} U_2 dr \\ -(y - t - c)dr - (1+r)dy - dy' - (1+r)dt - dt' \end{bmatrix} \qquad \text{(A.50)}
$$

First, we determine the effects of a change in current income y. Applying Cramer's rule to (A.50), we obtain

$$
\frac{dc}{dy} = \frac{(1+r)[U_{12} - (1+r)U_{22}]}{\nabla},
$$
$$
\frac{dc'}{dy} = \frac{(1+r)[-U_{11} + (1+r)U_{12}]}{\nabla},
$$

where

$$
\nabla = -U_{11} + 2(1+r)U_{12} - (1+r)^2 U_{22}.
$$

Given our restrictions on the utility function, ∇, which is the determinant of the bordered Hessian associated with the consumer's constrained optimization problem, is strictly positive. Further, assuming current and future consumption are normal goods, we have $U_{12} - (1+r)U_{22} > 0$ and $-U_{11} + (1+r)U_{12} > 0$, and so $\frac{dc}{dy} > 0$ and $\frac{dc'}{dy} > 0$. Thus, an increase in current income causes increases in both current and future consumption. Saving in the current period is given by $s = y - c - t$, so that

$$
\frac{ds}{dy} = 1 - \frac{dc}{dy} = \frac{-U_{11} + (1+r)U_{12}}{\nabla} > 0,
$$

because the assumption that goods are normal gives $-U_{11} + (1+r)U_{12} > 0$. Therefore, saving increases in the current period when y increases.

To determine the effects of a change in future income y', we again apply Cramer's rule to (A.50), getting

$$
\frac{dc}{dy'} = \frac{1}{1+r} \frac{dc}{dy} > 0,
$$
$$
\frac{dc'}{dy'} = \frac{1}{1+r} \frac{dc'}{dy} > 0,
$$

so that the effects of a change in y' are identical qualitatively to the effects of a change in y, except that the derivatives are discounted, using the one-period discount factor $\frac{1}{1+r}$. The effect on saving is given by

$$
\frac{ds}{dy'} = -\frac{dc}{dy'} < 0,
$$

and so saving decreases when future income increases.

Finally, to determine the effects of a change in the real interest rate r on current and future consumption, we again apply Cramer's rule to (A.50), getting

$$\frac{dc}{dr} = \frac{-U_2 + [U_{12} - (1+r)U_{22}](y - t - c)}{\nabla},$$

$$\frac{dc'}{dr} = \frac{(1+r)U_2 - [U_{11} - (1+r)U_{12}](y - t - c)}{\nabla}.$$

The signs of both of these derivatives are indeterminate, because the income and substitution effects may be opposing. As above, we can separate the income and substitution effects by determining the responses of c and c' to a change in r holding utility constant. The substitution effects are

$$\frac{dc}{dr}(subst) = \frac{-U_2}{\nabla} < 0,$$

$$\frac{dc'}{dr}(subst) = \frac{(1+r)U_2}{\nabla} > 0,$$

so that the substitution effect is for current consumption to decrease and future consumption to increase when the real interest rate increases. The income effects are

$$\frac{dc}{dr}(inc) = \frac{dc}{dr} - \frac{dc}{dr}(subst) = \frac{[U_{12} - (1+r)U_{22}](y - t - c)}{\nabla},$$

$$\frac{dc'}{dr}(inc) = \frac{dc'}{dr} - \frac{dc'}{dr}(subst) = \frac{[U_{11} - (1+r)U_{12}](y - t - c)}{\nabla}.$$

Here, the assumption that goods are normal gives $U_{12} - (1+r)U_{22} > 0$ and $U_{11} - (1+r)U_{12} < 0$, and so given this assumption the signs of the income effects are determined by whether the consumer is a lender or a borrower, that is, by the sign of $y - t - c$. If the consumer is a lender, so that $y - t - c > 0$, then the income effects are for current consumption to increase and future consumption to decrease. However, if $y - t - c < 0$, so that consumer is a borrower, then the income effect is for current consumption to decrease and future consumption to increase.

Because savings is $s = y - c - t$, the effect on savings of a change in the real interest rate is determined by the effect on current consumption, namely,

$$\frac{ds}{dr} = -\frac{dc}{dr}.$$

Problems

1. Suppose that $U(c, c') = \ln c + \beta \ln c$, where $\beta > 0$. Determine consumption in the current and future periods for the consumer, and interpret your solutions in terms of income and substitution effects.

2. Suppose that $U(c, c') = \ln c + \beta \ln c$, where $\beta > 0$, and assume that the consumer lends at the real interest rate r_1 and borrows at the interest rate r_2, where $r_1 < r_2$. Under what conditions is the consumer (a) a borrower, (b) a lender, and (c) neither a borrower nor a lender? Explain your results.

CHAPTER 9: A REAL INTERTEMPORAL MODEL WITH INVESTMENT

There is not much to be gained from analyzing the model developed in this chapter algebraically. It is possible to linearize the model so as to make it amenable to an explicit solution, but to do analysis with this linearized model requires a good deal of tedious algebra. For this chapter, we confine attention to a formal treatment of the representative firm's investment problem.

The current and future production functions for the firm are given, respectively, by

$$Y = zF(K, N) \tag{A.51}$$

and

$$Y' = z'F(K', N'), \tag{A.52}$$

where Y and Y' are current and future outputs, respectively, z and z' are current and future total factor productivities, K and K' are current and future capital stocks, and N and N' are current and future labor inputs. The capital stock evolves according to

$$K' = (1 - d)K + I, \tag{A.53}$$

where d is the depreciation rate and I is investment in capital in period 1. The present value of profits for the firm is

$$V = Y - I - wN + \frac{Y' - w'N' + (1 - d)K}{1 + r} \tag{A.54}$$

where w is the current real wage, w' is the future real wage, and r is the real interest rate. We can substitute in Equation (A.54) for Y, Y', and K' using (A.51) to (A.53) to obtain

$$V = zF(K, N) - I - wN + \frac{z'F[(1 - d)K + I', N'] - w'N' + (1 - d)[(1 - d)K + I]}{1 + r} \tag{A.55}$$

The objective of the firm is to choose N, N', and I to maximize V. The first-order conditions for an optimum, obtained by differentiating Equation (A.55) with respect to N, N', and I are

$$\frac{\partial V}{\partial N} = zF_2(K, N) - w = 0, \tag{A.56}$$

$$\frac{\partial V}{\partial N'} = \frac{z'F_2[(1 - d)K + I, N'] - w'}{1 + r} = 0, \tag{A.57}$$

$$\frac{dV}{dI} = -1 + \frac{z'F_1[(1 - d)K + I, N'] + 1 - d}{1 + r} = 0. \tag{A.58}$$

Equations (A.56) and (A.57) state, respectively, that the firm optimizes by setting the marginal product of labor equal to the real wage in the current period and in the future period. We can simplify Equation (A.58) by writing it as

$$z'F_1[(1-d)K + I, N'] - d = r, \tag{A.59}$$

or the firm chooses investment optimally by setting the future net marginal product of capital equal to the real interest rate, given N'. To determine how changes in z', K, d, and r affect the investment decision, given future employment N', we totally differentiate Equation (A.59), getting

$$z'\Gamma_{11}dI + z'(1-d)\Gamma_{11}dK + \Gamma_1 dz - (z'K\Gamma_{11} + 1)dd - dr = 0.$$

Then, we have

$$\frac{dI}{dr} = \frac{1}{z'F_{11}} < 0,$$

so that investment declines when the real interest rate increases;

$$\frac{dI}{dK} = d - 1 < 0$$

so that investment is lower the higher is the initial capital stock K;

$$\frac{dI}{dz'} = \frac{-F_1}{z'F_{11}} > 0,$$

so that investment increases when future total factor productivity increases; and

$$\frac{dI}{dd} = \frac{z'K\Gamma_{11} + 1}{z'F_{11}},$$

which has an indeterminate sign, so that the effect of a change in the depreciation rate on investment is ambiguous.

Problem

1. Suppose that the firm produces output only from capital. Current output is given by $Y = zK^\alpha$, and future output is given by $Y' = z'(K')^\alpha$, where $0 < \alpha < 1$. Determine investment for the firm, and show how investment depends on the real interest rate, future total factor productivity, the depreciation rate, and α. Explain your results.

CHAPTER 10: A MONETARY INTERTEMPORAL MODEL

Here, we develop an explicit cash-in-advance model and show some of the implications of this model that we derived more informally in Chapters 10 and 15. The model is in some ways simplified relative to the monetary intertemporal model of Chapter 9, but this allows a clearer derivation of the results.

In the cash-in-advance model there is a representative consumer, who lives forever and has preferences given by the utility function

$$\sum_{t=0}^{\infty} \beta^t [U(C_t) - V(N_t)], \tag{A.60}$$

where β is the subjective discount factor, with $0 < \beta < 1$, C_t is consumption in period t, N_t is labor supply in period t, $U(\cdot)$ is a strictly increasing and strictly concave function with $U'(0) = \infty$, and $V(\cdot)$ is a strictly increasing and strictly convex function with $V'(0) = 0$. Assume that $U(\cdot)$ and $V(\cdot)$ are twice continuously differentiable.

For simplicity we do not have capital or investment in the model, to focus on the key results, and the production function is given by

$$Y_t = zN_t, \tag{A.61}$$

where Y_t is output in period t and z is the marginal product of labor. The linear production function has the constant-returns-to-scale property.

Within any period t, timing works as follows. At the beginning of the period, the representative consumer has M_t units of money carried over from the previous period, B_t nominal bonds, and X_t real bonds. Each nominal bond issued in period t is a promise to pay one unit of money in period $t + 1$, and each real bond issued in period t is a promise to pay one unit of the consumption good in period $t + 1$. With nominal and real bonds in the model, we can determine explicitly the nominal and real interest rates. A nominal bond issued in period t sells for q_t units of money, while a real bond sells for s_t units of period t consumption goods.

At the beginning of the period, the asset market opens, the consumer receives the payoffs on the bonds held over from the previous period, and the consumer can exchange money for nominal and real bonds that come due in period $t + 1$. The consumer must also pay a real lump-sum tax of T_t at this time. After the asset market closes, the consumer supplies N_t units of labor to the firm and buys consumption goods on the goods market, but he or she must purchase these consumption goods with money held over after the asset market closes. Consumption goods are sold at the money price P_t in period t. Therefore, the representative consumer must abide by the cash-in-advance constraint

$$P_t C_t + q_t B_{t+1} + P_t s_t X_{t+1} + P_t T_t = M_t + B_t + P_t X_t. \tag{A.62}$$

When the goods market closes, the consumer receives his or her labor earnings from the representative firm in cash. The consumer then faces the budget constraint

$$P_t C_t + q_t B_{t+1} + P_t s_t X_{t+1} + P_t T_t + M_{t+1} = M_t + B_t + P_t X_t + P_t z N_t, \tag{A.63}$$

where M_{t+1} is the quantity of money held by the consumer at the end of the period and z is the real wage in period t, which must be equal to the constant marginal product of labor in equilibrium.

Letting $\overline{M}_t$ denote the supply of money at the beginning of period t, the government budget constraint is given by

$$\overline{M}_{t+1} - \overline{M}_t = -P_t T_t, \tag{A.64}$$

and the government sets taxes so that the money supply grows at a constant rate α. That is, we have $\overline{M}_{t+1} = (1 + \alpha)\overline{M}_t$ for all t. This then implies, from Equation (A.64), that

$$\alpha \overline{M}_t = -P_t T_t. \tag{A.65}$$

Now, it is convenient to scale the constraints (A.62) and (A.63) by multiplying through by $\frac{1}{M_t}$ and letting lowercase letters denote scaled nominal variables, for example, $p_t = \frac{P_t}{M_t}$. Then, we can rewrite (A.62) and (A.63) as

$$p_t C_t + q_t b_{t+1}(1+\alpha) + p_t s_t X_{t+1} + p_t T_t = m_t + b_t + p_t X_t \qquad \text{(A.66)}$$

and

$$p_t C_t + q_t b_{t+1}(1+\alpha) + p_t s_t X_{t+1} + p_t T_t + m_{t+1}(1+\alpha) = m_t + b_t + p_t X_t + p_t z N_t. \quad \text{(A.67)}$$

The representative consumer's problem is to choose C_t, N_t, b_{t+1}, X_{t+1}, and m_{t+1} in each period $t = 0, 1, 2, \ldots, \infty$, to maximize (A.60) subject to the constraints (A.66) and (A.67). We can simplify the problem by formulating it as a dynamic program. Letting $v(m_t, b_t, X_t; p_t, q_t, s_t)$ denote the value function, the Bellman equation associated with the consumer's problem is

$$v(m_t, b_t, X_t; p_t, q_t, s_t)$$
$$= \max_{C_t, N_t, b_{t+1}, X_{t+1}, m_{t+1}} [U(C_t) - V(N_t) + \beta v(m_{t+1}, b_{t+1}, X_{t+1}; p_{t+1}, q_{t+1}, s_{t+1})],$$

subject to (A.66) and (A.67). Letting λ_t and μ_t denote the Lagrange multipliers associated with the constraints (A.66) and (A.67), the first-order conditions for an optimum are

$$U'(C_t) - (\lambda_t + \mu_t) p_t = 0, \qquad \text{(A.68)}$$

$$-V'(N_t) + \mu_t p_t z = 0, \qquad \text{(A.69)}$$

$$-q_{t+1}(1+\alpha)(\lambda_t + \mu_t) + \beta \frac{\partial v}{\partial b_{t+1}} = 0, \qquad \text{(A.70)}$$

$$-p_t s_t(\lambda_t + \mu_t) + \beta \frac{\partial v}{\partial X_{t+1}} = 0, \qquad \text{(A.71)}$$

$$-(1+\alpha)\mu_t + \beta \frac{\partial v}{\partial m_{t+1}} = 0. \qquad \text{(A.72)}$$

We can also derive the following envelope conditions by differentiating the Bellman equation and applying the envelope theorem:

$$\frac{\partial v}{\partial b_t} = \lambda_t + \mu_t; \qquad \text{(A.73)}$$

$$\frac{\partial v}{\partial X_t} = p_t(\lambda_t + \mu_t); \qquad \text{(A.74)}$$

$$\frac{\partial v}{\partial m_t} = \lambda_t + \mu_t. \qquad \text{(A.75)}$$

Now, we can use the envelope conditions, Equations (A.73) to (A.75), updated one period, to substitute for the derivatives of the value function in (A.70) to (A.72), and then use (A.68) and (A.69) to substitute for the Lagrange multipliers in (A.70) to (A.72), obtaining

$$\frac{-q_t(1+\alpha)U'(C_t)}{p_t} + \beta\frac{U'(C_{t+1})}{p_{t+1}} = 0, \tag{A.76}$$

$$-s_t U'(C_t) + \beta U'(Ct+1) = 0, \tag{A.77}$$

$$\frac{-(1+\alpha)V'(N_t)}{p_t z} + \beta\frac{U'(C_{t+1})}{p_{t+1}} = 0. \tag{A.78}$$

Next, the market-clearing conditions are

$$m_t = 1, \quad b_t = 0, \quad X_t = 0,$$

for all t; that is, money demand equals money supply, the demand for nominal bonds equals the zero net supply of nominal bonds, and the demand for real bonds equals the zero net supply of these bonds as well, in each period. Substituting the market-clearing conditions in Equations (A.66) and (A.67) and using Equation (A.65) to substitute for T_t, we obtain

$$p_t C_t = 1 + \alpha, \tag{A.79}$$

$$C_t = z N_t. \tag{A.80}$$

Equations (A.79) and (A.80) state, respectively, that all money is held in equilibrium at the beginning of the period by the representative consumer and is used to purchase consumption goods and that in equilibrium all output produced is consumed.

Now, there is an equilibrium where $C_t = C$, $N_t = N$, $p_t = p$, $q_t = q$, and $s_t = s$, for all t, and we can use Equations (A.76) to (A.80) to solve for C, N, p, q, and s. We obtain

$$q = \frac{\beta}{1+\alpha}, \tag{A.81}$$

$$s = \beta, \tag{A.82}$$

$$(1+\alpha)V'(N) - \beta z U'(zN) = 0, \tag{A.83}$$

$$C = zN, \tag{A.84}$$

$$p = \frac{1+\alpha}{C} \tag{A.85}$$

Here, Equations (A.81) and (A.82) give solutions for q and s, respectively, while Equation (A.83) solves implicitly for N. Then, given the solution for N, we can solve recursively for C and p from (A.84) and (A.85). We can solve for the Lagrange multiplier λ using Equations (A.68), (A.69), (A.79), (A.80), and (A.83), to get

$$\lambda = \frac{CU'(C)}{1+\alpha}\left(1 - \frac{\beta}{1+\alpha}\right) = \frac{CU'(C)}{1+\alpha}(1-q) \tag{A.86}$$

Now, note that the nominal interest rate is determined by the price of the nominal bond q, as $R = \frac{1}{q} - 1$, so that the nominal interest rate is positive as long as $q < 1$.

From (A.81), the nominal interest rate is positive when $\alpha > \beta - 1$, that is, as long as the money growth rate is sufficiently large. The Lagrange multiplier associated with the cash-in-advance constraint is positive, that is, $\lambda > 0$ if and only if $q < 1$. Thus, a positive nominal interest rate is associated with a binding cash-in-advance constraint.

From Equation (A.81), the nominal interest rate is

$$R = \frac{1 + \alpha}{\beta} - 1.$$

The real interest rate is $\frac{1}{s} - 1$; from Equation (A.82) this is

$$r = \frac{1}{\beta} - 1,$$

which is the representative consumer's subjective rate of time preference. Further, the inflation rate is

$$i = \frac{P_{t+1}}{P_t} - 1 = \frac{p_{t+1}\overline{M}_{t+1}}{P_t\overline{M}_t} - 1 = \alpha,$$

so that the inflation rate is equal to the money growth rate. Now, from the above, it is clear that the Fisher relation holds, as

$$1 + r = \frac{1 + R}{1 + i}$$

The effects of money growth on real variables can be obtained by totally differentiating Equation (A.83) with respect to N and α and solving to obtain

$$\frac{dN}{d\alpha} = \frac{-V'}{(1 + \alpha)V'' - \beta z^2 U''} < 0;$$

thus, employment declines with an increase in the money growth rate, and because $Y = C = zN$ in equilibrium, output and consumption also decline. This effect arises because inflation distorts intertemporal decisions. Period t labor income is held as cash and not spent on consumption until period $t + 1$, and it is, therefore, eroded by inflation. Higher inflation then reduces labor supply, output, and consumption.

What is the optimal rate of inflation? To determine a Pareto optimum, we solve the social planner's problem, which is to solve

$$\max_{\{C_t, N_t\}_{t=0}^{\infty}} \sum_{t=0}^{\infty} \beta^t [U(C_t) - V(N_t)]$$

subject to $C_t = zN_t$ for all t. The solution to this problem is characterized by the first-order condition

$$zU'(zN^*) - V'(N^*) = 0,$$

where N^* is optimal employment in each period t. In equilibrium, employment N is determined by Equation (A.83), and equilibrium employment is equal to N^* for the case where $\alpha = \beta - 1$. The optimal money growth rate $\beta - 1$ characterizes a Friedman rule, as this implies from (A.81) that the nominal interest rate is zero and that the inflation rate is $\beta - 1$, so that the rate of return on money is $\frac{1}{\beta} - 1$, which is identical to the real interest rate r. From (A.86), the cash-in-advance constraint does not bind when $\alpha = \beta - 1$, because $\lambda = 0$. Thus, a Friedman rule relaxes the cash-in-advance constraint and causes the rates of return on all assets to be equated in equilibrium.

Problem

1. Suppose in the monetary intertemporal model that $U(C) = 2C^{\frac{1}{2}}$ and $V(N) = (\frac{1}{2})N^2$. Determine closed-form solutions for consumption, employment, output, the nominal interest rate, and the real interest rate. What are the effects of changes in z and α in equilibrium? Explain your results.

CHAPTER 15: MONEY, INFLATION, AND BANKING

We work through formal results for two models here, which are a Kiyotaki–Wright monetary search model, and the Diamond–Dybvig banking model. The results on money growth using the monetary intertemporal model are derived in the previous section.

A Kiyotaki–Wright Monetary Search Model

Here, we develop a version of the Kiyotaki–Wright random matching model to show how fiat money can overcome an absence-of-double-coincidence-of-wants problem. This model is closely related to the one constructed by Alberto Trejos and Randall Wright in an article in the *Journal of Political Economy*,[3] and it generalizes the model of Chapter 15 to a case where there are n different goods rather than three. To work through this model requires an elementary knowledge of probability.

In the model, there are n different types of consumers and n different goods, where $n \geq 3$. Each consumer is infinite-lived and maximizes

$$E_0 \sum_{t=0}^{\infty} \left(\frac{1}{1+r} \right)^t U_t,$$

where E_0 is the expectations operator conditional on information at $t = 0$, r is the consumer's subjective discount rate, and U_t is the utility from consuming in period t, where $U_t = 0$ if nothing is consumed. Given that the consumer faces uncertainty, we have assumed that he or she is an expected-utility maximizer. A consumer of type i produces good i and consumes good $i + 1$, for $i = 1, 2, 3, \ldots, n - 1$, and a type n consumer produces good n and consumes good 1. If $n = 3$, then this is the same setup we considered in Chapter 15. In this n-good model, there is an absence-of-double-coincidence problem, as no two consumers produce what each other wants.

Goods are indivisible, so that when a good is produced, the consumer produces only one unit. At $t = 0$, a fraction M of the population is endowed with one unit of fiat money each, and fiat money is also indivisible. Further, a consumer can hold at most one unit of some object at a time, so that at the end of any period a consumer is

---

[3]See A. Trejos and R. Wright, 1995. "Search, Bargaining, Money, and Prices," *Journal of Political Economy* 103, 118–141.

holding one unit of a good, one unit of money, or nothing. It is costless to produce a good and costless to hold one unit of a good or money as inventory.

At the end of period 0, each consumer not holding money produces a good, and then he or she holds this in inventory until period 1. In period 1, consumers are matched two-by-two and at random, so that a given consumer meets only one other consumer during period 1. Two consumers who meet inspect each other's goods and announce whether they are willing to trade. If both are willing, they trade, and any consumer receiving his or her consumption good in a trade consumes it (this is optimal), receives utility $u > 0$ from consumption, and produces another good. Then consumers move on to period 2, and so on. No two consumers meet more than once, because there are infinitely many consumers in the population. We assume that there are equal numbers of each type of consumer, so that the fraction of the population who are of a given type is $\frac{1}{n}$. Then, in any period, the probability that a consumer meets another consumer of a particular type is $\frac{1}{n}$.

What can be an equilibrium in this model? One equilibrium is where money is not valued. That is, if no one accepts money, then no one wants to hold it and, because of the absence-of-double-coincidence problem, there is no exchange and everyone's utility is zero. If no one has faith that money has value in exchange, then this expectation is self-fulfilling. A more interesting equilibrium is one where everyone accepts money. Here, we let μ denote the fraction of the population that holds money in equilibrium, V_g denotes the value of holding a good in equilibrium, and V_m is the value of holding money. Though there are n different goods, the optimization problems of all consumers are identical in equilibrium, and so the value of holding any good is the same for each consumer. The Bellman equations associated with a consumer's optimization problem are

$$V_g = \frac{1}{1+r}\left[(1-\mu)V_g + \mu\left(1-\frac{1}{n}\right)V_g + \mu\frac{1}{n}(Vm - Vg)\right], \qquad \text{(A.87)}$$

$$V_m = \frac{1}{1+r}\left[(1-\mu)\left(1-\frac{1}{n}\right)V_m + (1-\mu)\frac{1}{n}(u + V_g) + \mu Vm\right]. \qquad \text{(A.88)}$$

In Equation (A.87), the value of holding a good at the end of the current period is equal to the discounted sum of the expected payoff in the following period. In the following period, the consumer meets another agent with a good with probability $1 - \mu$, in which case trade does not take place, and the consumer is holding a good at the end of the next period and receives value V_g. With probability $\mu(1 - \frac{1}{n})$, the consumer meets another consumer with money who does not wish to purchase the consumer's good, and again trade does not take place. With probability $\mu\frac{1}{n}$, the consumer meets a consumer with money who wants his or her good, trade takes place, and the consumer is holding money at the end of the next period. In Equation (A.88), a consumer with money does not trade with another consumer who has money or with another consumer who has a good that he or she does not consume. However, with probability $(1 - \mu)\frac{1}{n}$ the consumer meets another consumer with his or her consumption good, in which case trade takes place, the consumer gets utility u from consuming the good, and then he or she produces another good.

We can solve for V_g and V_m from Equations (A.87) and (A.88), which give

$$V_g = \frac{\mu(1-\mu)u}{rn(1+rn)},$$

$$V_m = \frac{(rn+\mu)(1-\mu)u}{rn(1+rn)},$$

so that

$$V_m - V_g = \frac{(1-\mu)u}{1+rn} > 0.$$

Therefore, the value of holding money is greater than the value of holding a good, so that everyone accepts money (as conjectured) in equilibrium. Further, consumers who have money in any period prefer to hold it rather than producing a good, and so we have $\mu = M$ in equilibrium.

The values of V_g and V_m are the utilities that consumers receive from holding goods and money, respectively. As $V_g > 0$ and $V_m > 0$, everyone is better off in an economy where money is used than in one where it is not used.

Problem

1. Suppose a search economy with the possibility of double coincidences; that is, assume that when an agent produces a good, that he or she cannot consume it herself. In a random match where two agents meet and each has the good that they produced, the first agent has what the second consumes with probability x, the second has what the first consumes with probability x, and each has what the other consumes with probability x^2.

   (a) In this economy, show that there are three equilibria; a barter equilibrium where money is not accepted, an equilibrium where an agent with a good is indifferent between accepting and not accepting money, and an equilibrium where agents with goods always accept money.

   (b) Show that x needs to be sufficiently small before having money in this economy actually increases welfare over having barter, and explain this result.

The Diamond–Dybvig Banking Model

There are three periods, 0, 1, and 2, and an intertemporal technology that allows one unit of the period 0 good to be converted into $1+r$ units of the period 2 good. The intertemporal technology can be interrupted in period 1, with a yield of one unit in period 1 for each unit of input in period 0. If production is interrupted in period 1, there is no return in period 2. Goods can be stored from period 1 to period 2 with no depreciation. There is a continuum of consumers with unit mass, and each consumer maximizes expected utility

$$W = tU(c_1) + (1-t)U(c_2),$$

where c_i is the consumer's consumption if he or she consumes in period i, for $i = 1, 2$, and t is the probability that the consumer consumes early. Here, t is also the fraction of agents who are early consumers. We assume that t is known in period 0, but consumers do not know their type (early or late consumer) until period 1. Each consumer is endowed with one unit of goods in period 0.

Suppose that there are no banks, but consumers can trade investment projects in period 1, with one project selling for the price p in terms of consumption goods. Then, each consumer chooses to invest all of their goods in the technology in period 0, and in period 1 a consumer must decide how much of the investment to interrupt and how many investment projects to buy and sell. In period 1 an early consumer wants to sell the investment project if $p > 1$ and will want to interrupt the investment project and consume the proceeds if $p < 1$. The early consumer is indifferent if $p = 1$. A late consumer in period 1 wants to interrupt the investment project and purchase invest-ment projects if $p < 1$, chooses to hold the investment project if $p > 1$, and is indif-ferent if $p = 1$. The equilibrium price is, therefore, $p = 1$, and in equilibrium fraction t of all projects is interrupted in period 1, early consumers each consume $c_1 = 1$, and late consumers consume $c_2 = 1 + r$. Expected utility for each consumer in period 0 is

$$W_1 = tU(1) + (1 - t)U(1 + r).$$

Now, suppose that there is a bank that takes deposits from consumers in period 0, serves depositors sequentially in period 1 (places in line are drawn at random), and offers a deposit contract (d_1, d_2), where d_1 is the amount that can be withdrawn in period 1 for each unit deposited, and d_2 is the amount that can be withdrawn in period 2 for each unit deposited. Assume that all consumers deposit in the bank in period 0. Then, the bank chooses d_1, d_2, and x, the quantity of production to interrupt, to solve:

$$\max[tU(d_1) + (1 - t)U(d_2)] \tag{A.89}$$

subject to

$$td_1 = x, \tag{A.90}$$

$$(1 - t)d_2 = (1 - x)(1 + r), \tag{A.91}$$

$$d_1 \leq d_2 \tag{A.92}$$

Here, Equation (A.90) is the bank's resource constraint in period 1, (A.91) is the resource constraint in period 2, and (A.92) is an incentive constraint, which states that it must be in the interest of late consumers to withdraw late rather than posing as early consumers and withdrawing early.

Ignoring the constraint (A.92), substituting for d_1 and d_2 using the constraints (A.90) and (A.91) in the objective function (A.89), the first-order condition for an optimum is

$$U'\left(\frac{x}{t}\right) = (1 + r)U'\left(\frac{(1 - x)(1 + r)}{1 - t}\right) \tag{A.93}$$

with $d_1 = \frac{x}{t}$ and $d_2 = \frac{(1-x)(1+r)}{1-t}$. Equation (A.93) then implies that $d_1 < d_2$ so that (A.92) is satisfied. Further, if we assume that $\frac{-cU''(c)}{U'(c)} > 1$, then (A.93) implies that $d_1 > 1$ and $d_2 < 1 + r$. Thus, under this condition, the bank provides consumers with insurance against the need for liquid assets in period 1, and the bank gives consumers higher expected utility than when there was no bank ($d_1 = 1$ and $d_2 = 1 + r$ if the bank chooses $x = t$).

However, there also exists a bank-run equilibrium. That is, if a late consumer expects all other consumers to run to the bank in period 1, he or she will want to do it as well.

Problems

1. Suppose that consumers can meet and trade in period 1 instead of going to the bank in sequence. Show that, given the banking contract (d_1, d_2), there could be Pareto-improving trades that early and late consumers could make in period 1 that would undo the banking contract, so that this would not constitute an equilibrium. Discuss your results.

2. Show that, if $U(c) = \ln c$, then there is no need for a bank in the Diamond–Dybvig economy, and explain this result.

CHAPTER 16: UNEMPLOYMENT: SEARCH AND EFFICIENCY WAGES

In this section we formally set up the search model of unemployment from Chapter 16, derive some of the results for that model, and construct an illustrative example. For this model, an elementary knowledge of probability is useful.

In the search model, the infinite-lived worker has preferences given by

$$E_0 \sum_{t=0}^{\infty} \left(\frac{1}{1+r} \right)^t U(C_t),$$

where E_0 is the expectation operator conditional on information known in period 0, r is the subjective discount rate, C_t is consumption, and $U(\cdot)$ is the period utility function, which is strictly increasing, continuous, and strictly concave. Here, because the worker faces uncertainty, we have assumed that he or she is an expected-utility maximizer.

A worker who is employed at a job paying the real wage w supplies one unit of labor during the period and consumes his or her labor earnings (we assume no savings). There is a probability s, where $0 < s < 1$, that the worker will be separated from his or her job and become unemployed at the end of the period. We let $V_e(w)$ denote the value of being employed at the real wage w, and V_u the value of being unemployed, where both values are calculated as of the end of the current period. Then, the Bellman equation for an employed worker is

$$V_e(w) = \frac{1}{1+r} [U(w) + s V_u + (1-s) V_e(w)]; \tag{A.94}$$

that is, the value of being employed at the end of the current period is the present discounted value of the utility from employment next period plus the expected value at the end of the period, given the separation rate s.

Next, a worker who is unemployed receives the unemployment insurance benefit b at the beginning of the period, and then with probability p receives a wage offer, which is a random draw from the probability distribution $F(w)$, which has the associated probability density function $f(w)$. Assume that $w \in [0, \overline{w}]$, where $\overline{w} > 0$. The unemployed worker must decide whether to accept a given wage offer or turn it down. Thus, the value of unemployment is given by

$$V_u = \frac{1}{1+r} \left\{ U(b) + (1-p)V_u + p \int_0^{\overline{w}} \max[V_u, V_e(w)] f(w)dw \right\}, \qquad (A.95)$$

so that the value of being unemployed at the end of the current period is equal to the discounted value of the utility from consuming the unemployment benefit plus the probability of remaining unemployed times the value of remaining unemployed plus the probability of receiving a job offer times the expected value of the job offer.

Equations (A.94) and (A.95) can be simplified, respectively, as follows:

$$r V_e(w) = U(w) + s [V_u - V_e(w)]; \qquad (A.96)$$

$$r V_u = U(b) + p \int_0^{\overline{w}} \max[0, V_e(w) - Vu] f(w)dw. \qquad (A.97)$$

From Equation (A.96), we can solve for $V_e(w)$ to get

$$V_e(w) = \frac{U(w) + s V_u}{r + s},$$

so that $V_e(w)$ inherits the properties of $U(w)$—that is, it is strictly increasing, continuous, and strictly concave. This implies that the worker accepts any wage offer greater than or equal to w^* and rejects any offer less than w^*, where w^* solves

$$V_e(w^*) = V_u.$$

That is, w^* is the reservation wage, at which the worker is just indifferent between accepting the job offer and remaining unemployed.

To determine the unemployment rate, the flow of workers from employment to unemployment must be equal to the flow from unemployment to employment in the steady state, or

$$s(1 - U) = p[1 - F(w^*)]U;$$

solving for the unemployment rate U, we obtain

$$U = \frac{s}{p[1 - F(w^*)] + s}.$$

An example shows how the model works. Suppose that, conditional on receiving a wage offer, an unemployed worker receives a wage offer w_1 with probability π and a wage offer of zero with probability $1 - \pi$, where $0 < \pi < 1$. Then, conjecturing that a wage offer of w_1 is always accepted and a wage offer of zero is always turned down, Equations (A.96) and (A.97) in this case give

$$r V_e = U(w_1) + s(V_u - V_e),$$

$$r V_u = U(b) + p\pi(V_e - V_u),$$

where V_e is the value of being employed at the real wage w_1. Then, solving the above two equations for V_e and V_u, we get

$$V_e = \frac{(p\pi + r)U(w_1) + sU(b)}{r(s + p\pi + r)},$$

$$V_u = \frac{(s + r)U(b) + p\pi U(w_1)}{r(s + p\pi + r)},$$

with

$$Ve - Vu = \frac{U(w_1) - U(b)}{s + p\pi + r}.$$

Therefore, we have $V_u > 0$, so that a wage offer of zero will be turned down as conjectured, even if the unemployment insurance benefit b is zero. Further, the wage offer of w_1 will be accepted if and only if $w_1 \geq b$, that is, if the wage on the job is higher than the unemployment insurance benefit. The unemployment rate is

$$U = \frac{s}{p\pi + s},$$

but if $b > w_1$, then no one would accept jobs, and we would have $U = 1$ and everyone would be unemployed. This is an extreme example of how an increase in the unemployment insurance benefit can increase the unemployment rate.

Problem

1. Suppose in the search model that an unemployed worker receives a wage offer with probability π. Then, conditional on receiving a wage offer, the offer is w_1 with probability α_1, w_2 with probability α_2, and zero with probability $1 - \alpha_1 - \alpha_2$, where $0 < w_1 < w_2$. Determine under what conditions an unemployed worker would turn down a wage offer of w_1, accepting a wage offer of w_2, and under what conditions an unemployed worker would accept any wage offer greater than zero. Interpret these conditions.

CHAPTER 17: INFLATION, THE PHILLIPS CURVE, AND CENTRAL BANK COMMITMENT

In this section we construct a somewhat more explicit version of the model we worked with in Chapter 17 to show some of the results of that chapter more formally.

The first component of the model is the Phillips curve relationship, which captures the key idea in the Friedman–Lucas money surprise model of Chapter 11. That is,

$$i - i^e = a(Y - Y^T), \tag{A.98}$$

where i is the inflation rate, i^e is the private sector's anticipated inflation rate, $a > 0$, Y is aggregate output, and Y^T is trend output. The second component of the model is the preferences of the central bank, which we represent by supposing that the central bank maximizes $f(Y, i)$, where $f(\cdot, \cdot)$ is a function. That is, the central bank cares about the level of output and the inflation rate. It is convenient to express $f(Y, i)$ as a quadratic function, that is,

$$f(Y, i) = a(i - i^*)^2 + b(Y - Y^*)^2, \tag{A.99}$$

where a and b are positive constants, i^* is the target inflation rate for the central bank, and Y^* is the target level of aggregate output for the central bank.

Now, suppose, according to the central bank learning story, that the central bank treats the anticipated inflation rate i^e as being given and chooses i and Y to maximize Equation (A.99) given (A.98). Solving this optimization problem, the central bank then chooses

$$i = \frac{\alpha a^2 i^* + \beta i^e - \beta a(Y^T - Y^*)}{\alpha a^2 + \beta}. \tag{A.100}$$

We then have

$$i - i^e = \frac{\alpha a^2(i^* - i^e) - \beta a(Y^T - Y^*)}{\alpha a^2 + \beta}.$$

In this circumstance, if the central bank had a target level of output that was higher than trend output—that is, $Y^T - Y^* < 0$—then even if $i^e > i^*$, in which case anticipated inflation is higher than the target inflation rate, the central bank may want to have $i > i^e$ so that the private sector is fooled by positive surprise inflation. Ultimately, though, the private sector is not fooled in the long run, so that $i = i^e$, and if the central bank learns this, then it realizes that, from (A.98), it cannot engineer a level of output other than Y^T, and the best strategy for the central bank is to set $i = i^*$.

Under the central bank commitment story, the central bank cannot commit to an inflation rate, and it is playing a game with the private sector. The private sector first chooses i^e, then the central bank chooses i, and in equilibrium $i = i^e$. In this case Equation (A.100) is the central bank's reaction function, and we can solve for the equilibrium inflation rate by substituting $i = i^e$ in (A.100) getting

$$i = i^* + \frac{\beta}{\alpha a}(Y^* - Y^T);$$

hence, if $Y^* > Y^T$, in equilibrium the inflation rate is higher than i^*, which is the inflation rate the central bank would choose if it could tie its hands and commit itself to an inflation policy.

Problem

1. Suppose that, instead of expectations being rational, expectations are adaptive. That is, each period the private sector expects that the inflation rate will be what it was the previous period. That is, $i^e = i_{-1}$, where i_{-1} is the actual inflation rate last period. Under these circumstances, determine what the actual inflation rate and the level of output will be, given i_{-1}. How will the inflation rate and output evolve over time? What will the inflation rate and the level of output be in the long run? Explain your results.

INDEX

Page numbers followed by *f* and *t* refer to figures and tables, respectively.